ANGELIᴜ
REVELATIONS
OF
DIVINE TRUTH

Received Through
JAMES E. PADGETT

Vol. II
Vs. 1.0

Published by:

Foundation Church of Divine Truth, Inc.
(Formerly: Foundation Church of the New Birth, Inc.)
P. O. Box 802694
Santa Clarita, CA 91380-2694

Angelic Revelations of Divine Truth, Vol. II is a compilation of writings received from spirits residing in the spirit world. The term spirits refer to individuals who once lived on earth and who have since died and passed into the world beyond the physical world, as we know it. This is not a book of fiction, but the names and content of the messages are from real people who once lived on earth inhabiting various locations and times throughout earth's history. The method of delivery of these messages is through the mechanism of automatic writing by the gifted medium James Padgett.

Published in the United States by Foundation Church of Divine Truth, Inc.

Originally published in the United States by Foundation Church of Divine Truth, Inc., in 1989. While every precaution has been taken in the conversion of the original book from paper to digital, mistakes in the OCR process, and subsequent review, may have resulted in spelling or grammar errors that were not present in the original publication. We welcome your comments and corrections at fcdt@fcdt.org.

ISBN 978-0-578-84917-1

Printed in the United States of America

www.fcdt.org

FOUNDATION CHURCH OF
DIVINE TRUTH

This book is dedicated to friends of God, everywhere.

TABLE OF CONTENTS

Page

Preface vii

The True Mission of Jesus.. xv

    I. Jesus and His Relationship to God. xv

    II. God and the Human Soul.. xx

    III. The Problem of Sin.. xxiv

    IV. Redemption from Sin. xxvi

PART I.
ETERNAL TRUTHS.

Chapter 1.   Jesus of Nazareth Selects James E. Padgett. 1

Chapter 2.   The Truths Surrounding the Birth and Life of Jesus of Nazareth. 69

Chapter 3.   The Truths Surrounding the Birth and Life of Jesus of Nazareth. 89

Chapter 4.   The True Nature of God, the Heavenly Father. 113

Chapter 5.   The Importance of Prayer...131

Chapter 6.   The Divine Love of the Father and the New Birth of the Soul. 151

Chapter 7.   The Natural Love of Mankind. 187

Chapter 8.   Sin and Error. 221

Chapter 9.   The Incarnation of the Soul..253

Chapter 10.   The Creation and Fall of Our First Parents..................267

Chapter 11.   The Continuity of Life After Death.............................283

Chapter 12.   The Truths of the Spirit World. 299

    I. The Spheres of Progression.. 299

    II. Individual Progression. 323

    III. The Hells... 363

PART II.
CONTEMPORARY MISCONCEPTIONS.

Page

Chapter 13.   Corrections Made in Orthodox Christian Doctrine... 395

Chapter 14.   Corrections Made in Other Doctrinal Systems. 433

    I. The New Jerusalem Church. 433

    II. Disciples of Christ – Churches of Christ.................................. 445

    III. Seventh-Day Adventists. 449

    IV. New Thought. 455

    V. Christian Science.. 465

    VI. Reincarnation and Theosophy 477

Preface

It is again with very great pleasure that we, the Trustees of the Foundation Church of Divine Truth, Inc., present this second re-edited and new message arrangement of many of God's Divine Truths, as revealed to us by Jesus of Nazareth, Master of the Celestial Heavens, and a host of his Celestial brethren, and communicated to us through the past mortal instrumentalities of Mr. James E. Padgett and Dr. Daniel G. Samuels by way of their gifted automatic writing channeling.

It was in June 1989 when volume I of *Angelic Revelations of Divine Truth*, formerly titled *True Gospel Revealed Anew by Jesus*, was published and first made available, the new format of which has been closely followed in this present text, and which again includes messages from all four volumes of the earlier titled edition, originally published through the efforts of Dr. Leslie R. Stone and Rev. Paul Gibson, both now deceased.

The great bulk of the present text, however, comprises the messages of volume II, less a few of the more personal messages to Mr. Padgett which have been removed in order to provide space for the inclusion of some of the more noteworthy spiritual messages from volumes I, III and IV, and from "New Testament Revelations" (which contain twenty-one additional messages received by Dr. Samuels, two of which are also included in this present second volume).

Of the four volumes previously entitled *True Gospel Revealed Anew by Jesus*, volumes I and II contain the vast majority of the great formal messages from the Master and his angelic co-workers. This new and re-edited version of volume II, therefore, in combination with our 1989 presentation of volume I, represents a compilation of many of the highest spiritual Truths of the Father now made available to mankind. Most of these great Truths, also found in fewer number in volumes III and IV, have been presently transferred and incorporated into these new editions of volumes I and II, with almost all of the remaining messages of III and IV now comprising the more personal and experiential commentary of former mortals, now spirits, regarding their current spirit world living conditions and their relative spiritual awareness and progress therein. In the future, our beloved elder brother and dearest teacher and friend, Jesus, envisions the publication of a third new volume that will include many of these personal messages remaining in volumes III and IV. But let the words from the Master himself supply our dear readers with his authorization of this plan, revealed to us in the following quotation from a contemporary automatic writing that was obtained through a most-qualified medium of our church on October 29, 1989:

> ...As to the preparation of a third volume, we see it will eventually become a reality to be a sequel to the set of two which will be the initial outreach of our new church. And, in the future, when such volume comes into existence, you will discover that many new seekers will first be attracted to the personal messages before they become interested in the high spiritual Truths offered in the first two volumes. And this will be for the simple reason that they can relate to the experiences which people have, and can feel into these and identify with them and, therefore, will be attracted to them and absorbed by them. It is similar to ____'s own experiences of becoming interested in spiritual matters when she read experiences of people and their communications with spirits. She knew beyond a shadow of a doubt that spirits existed and that they could communicate with, and through, mortals living in the flesh, even before she became familiar with the messages in the volumes she now holds dear to her heart. And this will be a very successful way to reach a large variety of people with these wonderful special truths—in through the back door, you might say, appealing to their down-to-earth interests, much as they would read a story or a novel and become absorbed by the experiences therein. So, as always, the work of unfoldment for future outreach is left entirely up to your own movements of love, and not pushed upon you to

accomplish, but, instead, placed before you as possibility and opportunity to work on and fulfill the need for future generations to find, and come into an awareness of, God's Great Love and the means of salvation for His beloved children. We will forever be with you in this great work, and support you and guide you in all ways your love moves you to go....

In this second new edition, we have again honored Jesus' request that mankind no longer worship him, but rather look upon him correctly and appropriately as an elder brother who is still teaching fellow spirits, and mortals by way of these Second Coming messages, the one and only Way to salvation and At-onement with our Creator. Accordingly, all words which pertain to him are left uncapitalized, while the Great Source of Divine Love and Mercy—our Heavenly Father—is emphasized throughout this volume by the use of capitalization of all words pertaining to His Being and His Divine Will and Power, as well as His Divine Qualities and Attributes. For those of you who are interested in the enumeration of these words, please refer to the *Glossary* at the end of this volume. Contained therein are also many spiritual terms and concepts that are briefly explained, and which should provide the reader with a more definitive understanding of the text as a whole.

It is time, now, to introduce what we hope will impress you as being a welcome addition and a pleasant surprise! Those of you who are familiar with automatic writing in general, and Mr. James E. Padgett's mediumistic gift in particular, will appreciate the fact that information obtained through automatic writing often comes forth in a very rapid and continuous stream of written prose. But what may not be known is that reception of these writings does not require a deep trance on the part of the medium. Furthermore, the medium is usually perfectly capable of taking a break, if you will, to either relax or to read what has been received of the transmitted message up to that point. We know, for example, that Mr. Padgett took many such breaks, not only to digest what he had just received but also to ask many reactive questions of his communicators. Unfortunately, the one service Mr. Padgett perhaps did not have the time to perform, as those who have read all four volumes of *True Gospel Revealed Anew by Jesus* will recall, was to actually record his own questions and to incorporate these into the messages themselves. Where the new volume I messages are concerned, this omission does not prove to be too disconcerting because the vast majority of these particular messages did not textually suggest any discernible and intervening questioning on the part of Mr. Padgett. However, this present text of volume II does contain quite a few messages where it is manifestly clear that Mr. Padgett both asked questions and made some statements of his own. But while the exact wording of his former questions and statements remains unrecorded and unknown, it was discovered that a very good paraphrased approximation could be deduced and presented to assist the reader's fluency and understanding by attending closely to the actual textual answers that followed these unrecorded questions and statements. And this is what we did.

Rather than have our readers often confronted with abrupt and confusing changes in subject matter until succeeding paragraphs would suggest the nature of the prior omitted questions and statements, it was decided that we would supply our very best approximations of Mr. Padgett's heretofore unrecorded conversations for the sake of preserving continuity and enhancing uninterrupted reading pleasure and facility. Of course, as has already been advanced, it must be clearly and emphatically understood that these mostly brief, created conversations of Mr. Padgett (presented in italics and brackets to separate his words from the messages themselves) are not to be taken as being the precise words he originally phrased; only very close approximations of the original sum and substance of what he had said. However, we sincerely feel that the careful and disciplined editorial license we have undertaken in this regard has resulted in a substantial improvement in textual clarity, and, after having read this volume, we truly hope that the great majority of our readers will indeed concur. Giving some additional "life" to this great man, who served the Father's Cause and the Master's so selflessly and so very well, also seems to be the very least we could have done to honor our dear departed brother, now a Celestial angel himself.

But there is more! Your Trustees, very interested in what Mr. Padgett might say about the use of devised questions and statements for him, decided to call upon him personally through the same excellent medium who received the Master's message of October 29, 1989, quoted above. An excerpt from Mr. Padgett's very loving and multi-faceted response of March 9, 1991 is offered hereunder in supportive corroboration of what we had felt soulfully guided to present:

> ...it would be displaying greater respect and honor for me and my work if you would allow the future readers to realize, regarding these wonderful messages I was privileged to receive while I was living on earth, that I played a role in what the Celestial spirits wrote by asking pertinent questions, which they, in turn, were able to answer thoroughly with their wisdom and love.

> It matters not one iota that the wording of the question be in the exact manner in which I may have stated it. The major purpose for the presentation of the question is to prepare the reader for the answer, and for him to realize, or have a mind awareness of, what is to follow, so he will be eagerly looking forward to what follows...

> ...At the time I received the writings, it didn't occur to me that I should write down my questions. But I see now that I should have done this in order to eliminate the thought gaps which are present...So, it would be showing me greater honor and respect if, in the new edition, you would give my questions the recognition they deserve as playing an important role in the answers which follow....

Before closing, we would like to urge all our readers to read and enjoy the introductory material of Dr. Daniel G.

Samuels ("The True Mission of Jesus") before proceeding to the spiritually illuminating messages to follow. This work by Dr. Samuels is an excellent compendium of the many Divine Truths revealed to us by Jesus and other Celestial spirits who all now reside in the Father's highest Kingdom, the Celestial Kingdom, and who have brought to us the "Keys" to this Kingdom through their many hundreds of messages, received first by Mr. James E. Padgett and later by Dr. Samuels (who was the second chosen instrument of Jesus for communicating additional Truths of the Father to mankind). Of course, nothing could substitute for, or surpass, the ensuing Celestial messages themselves; but, as a very fine summary, Dr. Samuels' presentation is well worth the reader's review and assimilation prior to embarking upon the great reading adventure ahead.

For those of you who have already read volume I of Angelic Revelations of Divine Truth, and for first time readers as well, we feel it is crucial that you be ever mindful of what the Celestial angels teach us is the true Way to knowledge and possession of the Father's Divine Truths. Mental assessment of these written and stated Truths as presented in this volume, even if followed then by mental persuasion and acceptance, does not result in true ownership, surprising as this may sound upon an initial consideration. The true seat of Truth, as with love—both God's and man's—is not located in the evanescent and fallible reasoning mind, but in the timeless and unfailing soul. And since the Source of all Truth is God Himself, in order for mankind to share in this, His Truths, if they are to be received at all, must be transmitted from His Soul to our souls. As our dear Celestial brethren explain, God's Truths are inherent in His Divine Essence, the Life of which is His Divine Love. Therefore, where mankind is concerned, Truth need not be a mere transitory and essentially lifeless concept of the mind, but, potentially, an eternal Living Force of the soul.

And how do we obtain these highest of God's Living spiritual Truths—the one and only Way? Through prayer to Him. We are told that spiritual Truth possession is a progressively evolving process which grows according to the development of the soul in receiving God's Divine Love through prolonged and fervent prayer. The more the Divine Love that enters and permeates our souls, the greater becomes our understanding and possession of those spiritual Truths inherent in this Love. In this way, the understanding that may begin as a mental knowledge deepens through our souls' growing perceptions and culminates in eternal ownership. And, thus, the highest Truths of God may become progressively known and possessed by each soul who seeks At-onement with our Heavenly Father through the Gift of His Divine Love.

As a final word, your present Trustees would like to affirm again that we fully believe that these many and glorious Truths of the Father contained in this volume have truly come to us from the highest Celestial angels of God's highest Kingdom, the Celestial Kingdom, where no error or untruth can enter and where only Truth exists and flourishes. And we leave you now with our heartfelt prayer that God bless you all abundantly with His Divine Love in response to your own sweet communications with Him, transforming your souls into His Essence and insuring your eternal happiness in His Kingdom of Bliss.

The Trustees,
Foundation Church of Divine Truth.

The True Mission of Jesus

*By Dr. Daniel G. Samuels**

I. Jesus and His Relationship to God.

Whatever one may believe regarding the source of the *Messages from Jesus and the Celestials*,[†] the contents are so new and evolutionary, yet so compelling by their logic and sublime simplicity, that a serious study of them must be undertaken in order to comprehend their significance and challenge.

In these messages, Jesus of Nazareth stands forth as the Master of what he calls the "Celestial Heavens," wherein only those spirits possessed of the New Birth through prayer to the Father for His Divine Love can dwell in light and happiness and become conscious of their immortality through their At-onement with Him in soul nature.

If these messages are authentic as coming from Jesus and his Celestial spirits, then mankind has at last been given the true mission which Jesus proclaimed on earth. This mission taught the transformation of man's soul from the image of God—the work of the original creation—into the very Essence of God through the bestowal of the Father's Love upon whomsoever should seek that Love in earnest longing. It revealed that Jesus himself first manifested the Father's Love in his soul, thus making him at-one with the Father in nature and giving him that clear consciousness of his kinship with the Father and his immortality of soul. It showed that, in this development of soul, Jesus was indeed his Father's true son, not in the metaphysical and mysterious way of a hypothetical virgin birth, but through

---

*Dr. Samuels, now deceased, was the second mortal instrument chosen by Jesus of Nazareth in the year 1954. It was to him that Jesus delivered many authentic writings on the Old and the New Testaments of the Bible.—Ed.

†This title was given to an earlier edition of the present text.—Ed.

the Holy Spirit—that Agency of the Father which conveys His Love into the souls of His creatures who seek It in earnest prayer. It brings to light that Jesus was born of Mary and Joseph, of human parents like other human beings, but that he was nonetheless the Messiah promised to the Hebrews and to mankind in the Old Testament. For wherever he taught the "glad tidings" that God's Love was available, and that it was this Love which bestowed immortality upon the soul filled with this Love, Jesus brought with him the Nature of God—the Kingdom of God. At the same time, Jesus tells us that neither was he God; nor was his mother, Mary, the mother of God; nor a virgin after her marriage to Joseph, but that she was, in truth, the mother of eight children, of which he was the eldest; and that he had four brothers and three sisters in the flesh, and not cousins, as some versions of the Bible relate.

In addition, he relates that he did not come to die on a cross, nor did, nor does, his shed blood bring remission of sins. He also shatters the time-honored statements now found in the New Testament that he ever instituted a bread and wine sacrament on the eve of his arrest at the "Last Supper." This pious statement, he declared, was never his, nor did any of his apostles or disciples ever teach it, but was inserted about a century later so that such a doctrine might accord with the ideas then prevalent among the Greek converts of Christianity. Communion with the Heavenly Father can never take place through the mistaken notion that Jesus had to be impaled on a cross by Roman soldiers, on the order of Pilate, the Procurator of Judaea, and in accord with the uncomprehending high priests, so that he could appear as a sacrifice for sin. There is no sacrifice for sin, affirms Jesus, and his dried-up blood cannot do what only man himself must do by turning in repentance and prayer to the Heavenly Father to effect that change in his heart whereby his soul will give up evil and sin and embrace what is righteous. The Father's Help in the elimination of sin from the human soul is His Divine Love which, on entering the soul through prayer, removes sin and error from that soul and provides not only purification but also its transformation into a divine soul, at-one with the Father's Great Soul in nature. This real communion, which Jesus himself had achieved, he declared, is the only communion between God and His children which God has provided for their salvation and eternal life with Him. The vicarious atonement, Jesus states, is a myth, and its appearance in the New Testament is one of many false statements inserted therein to make it harmonize with later concepts concerning his relationship to the Father, which these later Greek and Roman copyists did not understand. It is a terrible thing to believe that God, in order to bring about His son's sacrifice, approved the unlawful arrest of Jesus on the Passover, the bloody scourges, the treachery of Judas, the palpably unfair trial by high priests and Sanhedrinites, as well as Pilate's fear of Judean revolt against Roman rule, to encompass the inhuman death of Jesus, His Messiah, on a cross, as though God needed to bring about, through wickedness and sin, the very wickedness and sin He seeks to blot out in His children.

In the light of these messages, a new interpretation of Jesus' death on the cross is certainly in order. We are told by the orthodox churches that Jesus gave himself up willingly as a sacrifice, and because, as the Messiah, he had come for that purpose. He is supposed to take the place of the Hebrew sacrifice, the lamb, and he is called in the New Testament the "Lamb of God." As a matter of fact, the Old Testament sacrifice of an animal was never intended to take away sin, and this is shown by the fact that, although these sacrifices were not permitted during the Babylonian captivity, the people still put their faith in redemption through turning away from sin and seeking God through a life of moral and ethical conduct.

Jesus did sacrifice himself, indeed, but in a way never related or understood by the writers of the New Testament. Jesus went to his death because he would not deny his mission: that as the first human to attain through prayer an immortal soul filled with the Essence of the Father—the Divine Love— he was in this way the first true son of God, and therefore the Messiah. Jesus could have saved his life if he had retracted at his trial, but he died because he remained true to himself, true to his Messiahship, and true to the Father Who had sent him. Jesus sacrificed his whole life preaching the Father's Love: He gave up home, his chance to marry and have a family of his own, and a chance to devote himself to the quiet pursuits of a Nazarene carpenter. Instead, he chose the hatred and opposition of those who understood not and preferred the *status quo*; he chose the incomprehension of his loved ones who considered him mad and sought to have him leave Galilee; he chose constant travels and journeys, so that often he had no place to lay his head; he chose to preach in the Temple at Jerusalem, chase the moneylenders, defy the conspiracy of those who sought his death, and bravely face the consequences of what he knew must inevitably occur. Yes, Jesus did sacrifice himself, but it is high time to put aside myth and metaphysics, and to know and to realize what that sacrifice consists of. When we understand his sacrifice, then Jesus stands forth in all his greatness, in all his courage, in all his serenity and forgiveness and love for mankind, with his absolute faith in the Father and His Love in that day of his teaching, tribulation, and death.

Jesus tells us many things about himself and his life in the Holy Land. He states that the Bible story of his birth, minus the many supernatural elements in it, is substantially true: that he was born in Bethlehem, taken by his parents to Egypt to avoid destruction by Herod, that the Wise Men did come from the East to pay him homage, and that he was taught the elements of the Hebrew faith from teachers; but that it was the Father Himself Who taught him the Truth of the Divine Love and made him realize what his mission was. He tells us that John the Baptist, his cousin, was a great psychic and had some understanding of him as the Messiah, and that both planned the Master's public ministry. He states that John never sent emissaries, when in prison, to be reassured that Jesus was "him whom we seek," and that Jesus, as a boy of twelve, never appeared before the doctors of the law in the Temple of Jerusalem.

Jesus also tells about some of the miracles which he performed. Most of these, he explains, dealt with his healing power, but that he never raised Lazarus or anyone else from the dead, nor has anyone else been able to do so, regardless of what the Scriptures say; for the spirit body cannot return to the flesh once the physical conditions of life have been destroyed. He also relates that he never quieted a storm by rebuking the waves on the Sea of Galilee, but that he did calm the fears of the disciples with him through his example of courage and assurance.

Some of the greatest messages which, to my mind, Jesus and some of the high spirits wrote are those connected with the Master's resurrection from the dead after his crucifixion. Jesus informs Mr. Padgett that he did die on the cross and that he did appear to Peter, John, Mary Magdalene and his mother on the third day, but that the true explanation of this occurrence is quite different from the accepted views of the churches. Here, Jesus is supposed to reveal his divinity by arising from the dead, but, actually, Jesus' soul never died, as no man's soul dies with the physical death. And the Master goes on to state that, with the power inherent in his soul with the Divine Love, he simply dematerialized his mortal frame, announced in the spirit world the availability of immortality to mortals and spirits through the Father's Love, which he was the first to manifest, and then, on the third day, materialized a body like flesh and blood drawn from the elements of the universe; and that it was in this materialized body, which he was able to assume without mediumistic aid, that he appeared to Mary Magdalene and the others. It is the reason, he states, why Mary did not at first recognize him and thought him to be the gardener, and the same may be said of his disciples at Emmaus. The great misconception of Christians of all ages has been to believe that Jesus revealed himself to be part of the "Godhead" by this resurrection—that is to say, rising from the dead—but actually his feat consisted in the assumption of a flesh-like body, indeed, so real as to convince even the doubting Thomas.

II. God and the Human Soul.

As to Who and What is God, I dare say that never has the Bible, either the Old or the New Testament, given man an understanding of the Deity and His Attributes to the extent and depth as appears in the messages signed by Jesus and the Celestials. According to these high spirits, man is at-one with the Father to the degree that His Love abounds in their souls. God is Soul, composed of His greatest Attribute, Divine Love, which is His very Nature and Essence, followed by Mercy, Goodness, Power, Omniscience, and Will; and with the Mind, so much worshiped by mankind, only an aspect of His Being. Although God has no form such as He gives to mankind on incarnation, nor a spirit body which is manifested by man after his physical death, yet, God possesses His definite Soul Form, which becomes more clearly perceptible to the soul which feels or perceives God's Oversoul, or the Divine Attributes thereof, as it comes into closer rapport with God through its soul development. For while God is Soul, Alone, unique in Its Oneness, and while He has no material or spirit body, yet, He has Personality—the Divine Personality manifesting His Love and Mercy, His Kindness and Solicitude for all His creatures. God, then, is not a cold intellect, an abstract mind, or forces indifferent and unfeeling, but a Personal, Warm and Loving Father, eager for the happiness of His children and regardless of race or color or creed. He seeks through His ministering angels to turn His children to Him and have them keep in harmony with His Laws, or have them come, indeed, to Him in the longing of their human souls for that something they know not what, and obtain At-onement with Him through the inflowing of His Love into their souls in response to their earnest prayers. Soul is God and God is Soul, and all His Attributes added together do not make up Who and What God is. These Attributes radiate from His Great Soul and flood the universe. So, when men say they live and have their being in God they are in error, for they do not. But they do live and have their being in the attributes that God has given them in the human soul. When one obtains the greatest Attribute of God, the Divine Love, which manifests itself as a warm glow burning in the soul, as occurred to the refugees at Emmaus (Luke 24:32), then he is actually feeling or perceiving the Great Soul of God to the degree he partakes of that Love.

Information regarding the human soul, not even mentioned in the Scriptures, which presumably should be the place to look for such material, abounds in the messages from Jesus and other Celestial spirits. To be sure, we are told in *Genesis* that God created man "in His image," but everything that such a statement implies or suggests is tantalizingly wanting, and we are left to our own ideas or compelled to accept what the churches believe should be the meaning. The result is that the conception of what was meant by the creation in man varies in accordance with the interpretation which each church, claiming for itself the truth, lays upon those meager words. The early Hebrews, of course, were not interested overly much in the life beyond the grave, and their conception of the soul, or its habitat after mortal experience, is limited mainly to Paradise or Gehenna (and these, we may note, were originally conceived to be places on this earth; in the first case, the Garden of Eden, supposed to be near the Euphrates; in the second, in the valley of Hinnom where the Jebusites once offered up human sacrifices). It is strange, perhaps, that the

Greeks, with their love of physical culture, form, and beauty should have a much more detailed view of the afterlife: the dark realm of Pluto, the glory and happiness of the Elysian Fields (where the souls of the righteous dwell in peace and communion with their god), the shadow forms of the harpies, the influence, perhaps, of an older Egyptian religion.

But in these messages signed by the Master and his Celestial spirits, the information given is clear and logical, even though such information is new and hitherto unknown. Certainly no one up to the time of Padgett's mediumship was able to obtain the messages of that high quality directly from these spirits themselves, although Swedenborg, the Swedish seer, was permitted experiences in the spirit world which in many respects parallel what Padgett obtained.

Jesus tells us that just as God is Infinite Love, so is His Universe infinite matter which, like God, has no beginning or end. At some time in this infinity of time and space, God created a habitat designed for man. Exactly when we men were created as living souls (that is to say, before or after the creation of our world), is not known, but God created human souls which dwelt, and have been so dwelling, with Him before their incarnation in the flesh. After the mortal experience, the soul, manifesting its spirit body acquired with incarnation, returns to the spirit world to inhabit a locality commensurate with its condition.

Human souls created by the Father, according to the messages, are duplex: They are male and female in composition, and, at the time of incarnation, divide into their two component parts. Each thereafter in the flesh is a complete soul as to itself. The soulmates may or may not meet and marry in the flesh, depending upon various conditions and circumstances which prevail at the time of their marriage; but such marriage is in no way a guarantee of happiness, for the different education, religious beliefs, family traditions, upbringing and other circumstances of each may often hinder rather than aid in their marital relations. On the other hand, souls which are not mates have a better chance of marital harmony if their marriage is based on similar interests, upbringing, education and general social condition on the plane of the material world. Soulmates, after death, eventually meet and stay together in real soulmate love, though not before a period of purification, and in accordance with their condition of soul.

The messages are unequivocal in their insistence that human souls are, as the *Book of Genesis* states, creations in the image of God, and that therefore there is nothing of the Divine in us. They also insist that man is not the product of evolution, such as Darwin or his followers have taught, but that ours represents a material form similar to, but more highly developed than, other creations consistent with the development of life on this planet, and harmonizing with the conditions for life which this planet presents. Man was provided with a human soul which, with its special appendage, the mind, enabled him to make the advances and progress which exalt him as lord over the other creatures of this life, and give him the potentiality of exploring and mastering the physical surroundings into which he has been placed.

But men are tragically mistaken, declares Jesus, when they believe that the mind is superior to, or the equal of, the soul, or that the soul is merely a name which is given to an entity whose existence is either doubtful or has no basis in fact. For the mind is limited and dependent upon the soul, the seat of the emotions and the passions, and it is the soul which is the real man. It is through the soul perceptions that man knew instinctively that he was linked to his Creator, Whom he was to revere and obey. Man, says Jesus, can know and knows God only because he possesses a soul; and he can never know God if he seeks Him intellectually and with his mind alone. Doubt and speculation are a product of the mind, but faith is a product of the soul; and we know that God exists through our soul perceptions. We can therefore create the spiritual link with God through prayer—not a mental prayer, but a prayer that comes from a man's soul: earnest, sincere, full of longing, faith and love.

III. The Problem of Sin.

When the first parents, or whom they represent, possessed their God-given souls, these souls were in the image of God, but they had nothing of the Essence of God in them. They were given the opportunity, however, to obtain the Nature of God through prayer for His Love, which, on entering the human soul through the agency of the Holy Spirit, transforms that soul from the image of God into the Essence of God. But the first parents, instead of turning to God and His Love, sought mastery of their material surroundings alone, and, instead of developing their souls so that they would partake of the Nature of God through Divine Love, they chose the development of their intellectual faculties. For it is through his intellectual attainments that man acquires the material possessions and wealth by which he so much sets his store, and which marks him as a success by worldly standards. And thus came the story of the "apple" and the "Tree of Knowledge." And it is through this material knowledge that came sin, for man turned from God to be independent of God, and with it came pride. He became puffed up, cruel, heartless and merciless, where he had been created with a soul full of human love and mercy and tenderness and sympathy for his fellow beings. Thus, man, in his ruthlessness, lost the use of his soul qualities and the potentiality of partaking of the Father's Nature through the inflowing of the Divine Love into his soul, and this was the "death" which man suffered when he sinned. For, says Jesus, the material body was not in question; it was, rather, the penalty of having lost the opportunity of achieving At-onement in soul with the

Father whereby men lost the potentiality for salvation through becoming immortal souls. The wages of sin, as Jesus explains it, is spiritual death: loss of the soul's chance to partake of God's Nature and live. Death in the flesh, Jesus assures us, is merely an incident in the progress of man's soul from preexistence to the point where he returns to the spirit world with his individuality assumed at the time of incarnation, and manifested in his spirit body.

The problem of sin, then, is the defilement of the soul during its period of incarnation. Sin is the violation of God's Laws, says Jesus—this given to mankind by those of His messengers who transmit His Will to mortals attuned to their suggestions, either because they are more pure in heart and are closer to the Father, or because of their psychic or mediumistic powers. An interesting message signed Elijah tells us that he would receive messages from the unseen world because of prayers and religious instinct. Here, perhaps, is the story of the great religious founders and reformers of all lands and ages up to the coming of the Messiah. They all sought to turn man to the moral life. And the Eight Steps of Buddha, the Hammurabi Code and the Decalogue of Moses may, perhaps, be viewed as the success which the Father's messengers attained in planting into man's mind an awareness of the existence of God's Laws, which were to be observed by all His children for the purity of their souls.

Some of the finest messages in this collection are those from Old Testament Prophets, like Elijah, Samuel, Moses and Daniel, who tell us of their efforts to turn their compatriots away from sin and error, in the conduct of their lives, to standards of ethical living, seeking to give effect to their sermons through recourse to threats of punishment to be meted out by an "angry" and "wrathful" God. They explain that His Love was not available to them, nor was it known to them as a reality, and they conceived of Him as a "stern taskmaster" who was "vengeful" and "jealous" of His Name. Their highest concept of Judaism, which graces the most exalted pages of the Old Testament, was intense faith in God, righteousness and obedience to His Laws. There also runs through the Scriptures the theme of the New Heart—the promise of the Father's Love, to be bestowed in the fulness of time upon the Jews first, and thereafter upon all mankind; but this is a subject which, as far as I know, has never been given adequate treatment in the study of the Hebrew religion.

IV. Redemption from Sin.

To the pious Hebrew of the Old Testament, it appeared that wickedness, both as a nation and as individuals, was the cause of Hebraic national disasters, and that successes were the result of faithfulness to the Covenant between God and the patriarchs. The prophets emphasized the necessity to avoid alliances with other countries in times of national stress, and to put their faith in God's Protection. Failure to heed the warnings of the prophets led to calamity, as in the days of Jeremiah when disregard of his advice brought captivity in Babylonia. Again, in the sorest hour of Judaea's history, when the people were being provoked almost beyond endurance to bloody rebellion against mighty Rome, a prophet out of Nazareth came with a message of peace and forbearance, only to be rejected by those in power; Judaea was crushed and the people—those that remained—were dispersed over the face of the globe. For those of us who know that the Heavenly Father is our God of Love, we cannot believe that He brought about the horrible destruction of the Hebrews in the revolt of 67-70 A.D. But we do believe that the condition of men's souls was such that it embraced wrath and the violence of warfare, rather than love and patience, and that this condition of the soul made the dreadful consequences that followed inevitable.

In the spirit world, the soul that sins must likewise reap the whirlwind. On leaving the flesh, it is received by spirits whose duty it is to instruct it in the things of its new existence. It is told that everything in the spirit world is controlled by law. One of these is the Law of Compensation, applicable to all spirits who pass over from mortal to spirit life. This law calls for the expiation of the sins which the soul has committed as a mortal.

Since the soul is the real man, and is in possession of its faculties, this includes the memory of deeds committed in the earth life. All the evil works and thoughts which the soul has accumulated as a mortal now come back to haunt and assail him, and the terrible remorse and suffering that ensues continue constantly and unabated until these evil memories have left him; and it is this that constitutes the judgment day and the hell. The condition of the soul creates the home in which it lives when it first passes over into spirit life—a home which accurately and exactly reflects the state of that soul and the spirit body which it manifests. Hence, a soul filled with spiritual thoughts and deeds, and in accord with God's Laws, will abide in a place suitable to its soul condition, filled with light and reflecting the happiness of that soul; but a soul filled with deeds and thoughts of the material plane alone, and out of harmony with God's Laws, engenders an abode of darkness and suffering in accordance with the abuses and unlawful material pleasures which it pursued when on earth.

But one of the most pernicious doctrines taught by the churches, and whose damnable falsity is exposed by Jesus, is that which fixes the destiny of the delinquent soul in hell for all eternity. This is not true. For as soon as the individual wills it, and repents of his sins as a mortal, he may make his progress out of the lowest hells to the Spiritual Heavens, or, should he seek and obtain the Father's Love, continue to eternally progress as an immortal soul in the Celestial Heavens towards the Throne of God. The reason for this, the Master explains, is that the soul of man is the same, whether in the flesh or as a spirit, and the same conditions of forgiveness obtain here as in the spirit world. All sins are pardonable in this world or the next whenever the soul makes the sincere effort to receive pardon. The only sin not pardonable is that which, in the New Testament parlance, blasphemes against the Holy Spirit, or, in the language which the Master makes clear, refuses the Divine Love of the Father which can transform the human soul into a divine soul and bestow upon it immortality.

It is not true that man has the sorry alternative of either repenting of his evil ways, in the brief existence in the flesh, or living in hell throughout all eternity as a spirit. Some churches state that man cannot live a mortal life of pleasure and evil and then turn to God to avoid eternal suffering as a spirit. At the same time, they teach that, despite a life of sin, a last minute return to God will insure forgiveness of their sins when they come to the next world. These churches seem to be unaware of the existence of the Law of Compensation which exacts payment for the evils committed in the flesh "to the last farthing." This is justice, indeed, if that is what these churches desire. But the time comes when the debt is paid, the soul is released from the workings of the law, and forgiveness is achieved.

The law, then, acts upon the soul undergoing the process of purification, but the soul that seeks the Father's Love invokes the higher Law of Grace. Here, no justice is involved; only the Divine Love which the Father bestows upon His aspiring children and which transforms them into divine souls, bringing about the elimination of those evil desires and the forgetfulness of those evil deeds upon which the Law of Compensation operates. The pernicious doctrine of eternal damnation often prevents the unhappy soul from seeking the Father's Love through prayer, in the terrible belief that his position in hell is fixed forever and that God can no longer help him. Yet, God, as Jesus explains it, helps His children wherever they are, in this world or the next, or in whatever condition of soul they may be in, provided they come to Him as their Heavenly Father, in earnest longing of their souls, and seek His Love and Mercy.

It is the awakening of the soul to the iniquities it worked and cogitated as a mortal that brings about the workings of the Law of Compensation and the abode of the spirit. Sometimes, the soul that passes over, because of the peculiar character of its make-up, is impervious at first to this awakening, and, in that case, the soul lives on the level of its evil earth plane life, and seeks in spiritual counterparts those evils which it practiced as a mortal, or it roams the earth seeking to obsess mortals susceptible to its baleful influence. Jesus refers in the gospels of the New Testament to his having liberated mortals from possession by demons, and these demons were nothing more than evil spirits which had taken possession of human beings at the time. In respect to these evil spirits of once mortal beings, Jesus tells us that some of the narratives related in the New Testament are true, but that others are false. And he refers concretely to the story of the possessed swine which ran madly down the cliff to be destroyed. This, he asserts, he never brought about, first because he would harm no creature, and because of the financial loss such an act of his would have entailed their owner. But, as regards the evil spirits, these awaken in time to the Law of Compensation and pass through their period of suffering for their mischief and evil. They are helped in this condition by others who are somewhat more advanced than themselves, and who instruct them in the ways that exist to progress out of their deplorable condition.

Hence, souls in suffering eventually learn to give up their evil inclinations, whether it be a fondness for money, possessions, gratification of pleasures or the desire to injure others—greed, lusts, covetousness, hatred, envy, injustice and other sinful creations of the human heart—and they may use their will power and intellectual faculties to enable them to cause the forgetfulness of the things that make for a soul stricken with remorse. But the soul in suffering and darkness may also seek outside aid if it so wishes: the Divine Love of the Heavenly Father which, pouring out into the soul which earnestly seeks His Love, causes the purification of that soul through possessing it, and thus forcing from it the excrescences that mar and defile that soul. And, indeed, as the Father's Love continues to fill the soul of him who seeks It, there takes place the transformation of the human soul, reflecting the Soul of God, into a divine soul filled with the very Nature and Essence of God—His Love. With that Love, the soul is changed and the evils which contaminated it are eradicated, and the memories thereof, so that the Law of Compensation has nothing on which to operate and the soul is freed from its inexorable workings. For God's Love, sought for by the soul in earnestness and longing, invokes a higher Law of Love. And the once evil soul, now filled with God's Love and Mercy, and Kindness, Consideration, Pity and Sympathy, progresses out of its abode of darkness and suffering into realms of Love and Light, and eventually into the Celestial Heavens where only those souls filled with His Love can enter. Jesus is the Master of the Celestial Heavens where the inhabitants are the possessors of the Father's Love to that degree in their souls that they are conscious of their immortality. For, God's Soul being Immortal, those souls possessing His Love to a sufficient degree are in the same way immortal. This is what Jesus meant when he said, "The Father and I are one." He meant there was a oneness between God's Soul and his own because of the great abundance of the Father's Love which he possessed, which enabled him to realize that in this way he was the Father's real and redeemed son. He did not mean, as some churches have erroneously interpreted the remark, that he was God or equal to God; only that there was a kinship in nature between his soul and God's which had been established by his possession of the Father's Love through prayer.

In short, we come to the real explanation of "forgiveness," which is startlingly different from the traditional conception imposed upon mortals by the churches. God does not arbitrarily forgive sin; but, rather, God aids those who, truly penitent and contrite, come to

Him to seek His Forgiveness with the intention of mending their ways. He may therefore send the Spirit of God to strengthen the soul that seeks to avoid sin and error through its own will power; or, in response to prayer, He will send His Holy Spirit to convey His Love into the soul so that His Own Nature and Essence provide the aid in eradicating the evils with which that soul is contending.

In the same way, Jesus lays bare the sterility of the traditional concept of the "judgment day." It is not a weighing in the balance of the good and evil deeds of man during his earth life; neither is it a vague indefinite time when the earth shall be destroyed and men's souls tried for condemnation or resuscitation into physical life from the grave. For, as St. Paul says in *Corinthians*, "...flesh and blood cannot inherit the Kingdom." And Mary, the mother of Jesus, explains that the flesh of the lifeless body must return to the elements in accordance with God's Law, and that therefore any writings to the effect that she ascended into heaven in the flesh is mere speculation and wishful thinking on the part of those who exalt her because of her relationship to her son. Mary states that, indeed, as a spirit filled with the Father's Love, she is an inhabitant of the Kingdom high up in the Celestial Heavens; yet not because of any relationship to Jesus, but because of her own exalted condition.

Eventually, declares Jesus, all souls will progress out of their condition of suffering and unhappiness and attain to either the Sixth Sphere, known to the Hebrews as Paradise (for such is the condition of man possessing purity of soul, whether he be in the flesh or devoid of it) or will accept the Way to the Father's Love and reach the Celestial Heavens. The perfect natural man, however, must eventually reach a state of stagnation, for the time comes when he can no longer progress beyond the perfection of his human soul. But the soul possessed of the Father's Love may continue to obtain His Love throughout all eternity, for It is infinite. And the soul thus filled with the Father's Essence continues to obtain more and more of It and, consequently, to progress nearer and nearer to the Fountainhead of the Father's Abode, with increased knowledge of things Divine, and gaining in happiness and joy as a divine son of the Father.

In accordance with this desire to explain conditions of spirit and soul life, Jesus is emphatic about the utter falsity of reincarnation. He states, and ancient spirits of the East write to add their corroboration, that while this theory is known to devotees of Oriental cultures, reincarnation has, as a matter of fact, never taken place in the spirit world, and that believers in this sterile idea have been waiting in vain for countless thousands of years to be reincarnated. Jesus, and others of the high spirits, state that the soul makes its progress from sin to purity, or to divine transformation, in the spirit world, which it can never again leave except to materialize briefly with the aid of material substance borrowed from mediums. The oriental concept of renunciation, or expiation of sin from the soul, adds Jesus, is correct, as is the doctrine that eventually the soul will eliminate the evils which defile it; but the errors consist in locating the earth as the place where such expiation takes place, and teaching that the soul, on freeing itself of iniquity, also loses consciousness of itself as a personal entity through absorption of the soul into the Deity.

In connection with life on the other side, one of the most interesting spirit writers is the seer, Swedenborg, who tells us about his experiences in the spirit world. He declares—and here Jesus corroborates his messages—that he was indeed permitted to come to the spirit world in a trance state, and that he really saw the spheres and the conditions of the spirits as they existed in the 18th century. Swedenborg tells us that he was informed throughout the world of spirits that God is One, and that a triune God, as believed in by Christians, was nothing but pious fiction. He states that he spoke with Jesus, who confirmed this, but thought that, since Jesus was so much brighter and more glorious than all the others of the spirit realm, this same

Jesus must be God, and so he declared in his writings. Swedenborg relates that he was informed about the Divine Love, but that he did not truly understand what Jesus and the high spirits meant by It.

One important matter which the messages clear up is the true meaning of the "divine within you" doctrine. Actually, Jesus brought the divine with him when he preached throughout the Holy Land when on earth, and, when he walked among men, the Kingdom was *with* men but *not* within them. When preachers talk of the divine within man, they are really referring to the soul—the creation of God, indeed, but a human soul withal, not a divine one. What they mean, then, by developing the divine within man must be viewed as simply developing the latent powers in the human soul through development of the will, and the natural human love through moral and intellectual growth. These, of course, were given to man at his creation and have no part of the Divine. The Divine in the human soul is the Divine Love, which can come only through prayer to the Father. The Divine comes from *without*, from the Heavenly Father, and can enter the soul and effect its transformation only when that soul seeks It in earnest longing. When Jesus spoke to his disciples about the Divine within them, these disciples actually had some of this Love in their souls, even before the Pentecost, when the Father's Love, through the Holy Spirit, was poured out upon them in great abundance.

Another misconception which Jesus clears up, with the corroboration of Mrs. Baker Eddy, is the doctrine known as Christian Science. We are informed that this woman, through her soul perceptions, understood the Divine Love as a great Spiritual Force coming from God, which could be used for healing purposes, and that it was a reality which could be attained if mortals would but turn from material interests and seek the spiritual. In this way, healers and patients could reach a condition of soul above that of the earth plane so that rapport could be made with spirit healers. Christian Science, to that extent, declares Jesus, is correct and spiritual healing a phenomenon obedient to spiritual law. But the Master points out that sin and error, contrary to Mrs. Eddy's beliefs, are real, being creations of the human soul, and that the human soul does not *reflect* the Father's Love, as she states it does. It either does not have the Love, or, if it does to a certain extent, *possesses* that Love, and the transformation of that soul into a divine soul is made to the degree it partakes of that Love.

Her teachings, Jesus declared, help in the development of the human soul towards the state of the perfect natural man, but are devoid of the concept of the soul's possession and conscious ownership of the Father's Love. And, so, her teachings do not point the Way to the Celestial Heavens through prayer to the Father, nor to transformation of the soul into the divine angel.

A few words might be said with respect to the additional messages printed for the first time in this edition.[*] Although they are all interesting, some commentary is due the communication by a member of the Sanhedrin which condemned Jesus to death at his trial. This spirit is unquestionably a sincere personality, and his writings have the ring of truth. It is understood, of course, that not all of the counselors who were present at the trial have since made their way to the Celestial Heavens, as he has; yet, at the same time, it shows clearly that not all members of the Sanhedrin—and here we recall Nicodemus—were supporters of the high priests or acted out of pure malice and rage. There were those, like this patriarch, who consented to the unfairness of the trial and summary condemnation of the Master in order to liberate Judaism from what they sincerely considered a menace which

---

*Dr. Samuels is referring here to some of the messages added in a later edition of the original volume I of *True Gospel Revealed Anew by Jesus*, and more particularly to an important communication by a former member of the Sanhedrin who was present at Jesus' trial. This message is not included in the present text, but can be found in the later edition of volume I of *True Gospel Revealed Anew by Jesus*, to which Dr. Samuels refers, and also in volume I of the new and re-edited version of same, now entitled *Angelic Revelations of Divine Truth*.—Ed.

threatened its overthrow, or threatened to bring about Roman repression at any sign of Judean revolt. The message gives for the first time the other side of the story, and, while the spirit admits his great mistake and does not seek to justify his action or that of his compatriots, the tone is different from the hatred that breathes forth in the account of the trial found in the New Testament—a tone which we know is inconsistent with the Father's Love which inspired the original writers.

It would be possible to continue to discuss at great length the numerous interpretations and corrections made in these messages signed by Jesus and the many Celestial spirits, and in the preceding pages we have attempted to point out some of the major precepts which animate them. They emphasize the restoration of the original "glad tidings" of Christianity that, with Jesus of Nazareth, there came a Love distinct from the natural human love as developed and perfected by the Mosaic code of moral and ethical living; that the new Love is the Divine Love, the Essence of the Heavenly Father, which was first manifested in man by Jesus and, through Jesus, was made available to mankind. It is obtained not through mere belief in Jesus' name, or in any overall vicarious atonement supposedly made by him or through the shedding of his blood, but only as each individual, turning in free will to the Father, seeks His Love through prayer and faith with all his heart, and thus achieves a transformation of soul condition from one of sin and error to one of purity and possession upon receiving that Love of the Divine Nature. It is God's Love that bestows eternal life upon the soul and thus fulfills the promise of what we call salvation. It cannot be achieved by rites and ceremonies, earned by man or granted to man by the churches, but is the free Gift of the "New Heart", poured out in abundance by the Heavenly Father upon His children who seek It in earnest.

In short, it would be impossible here to comment on everything which is of interest to those who, whether they believe in this source of revelation or take issue with the material therein contained, are concerned with things of the spiritual and religious. But one thing must be said in closing, and that is: that these messages, whether they be the result of mortal or spirit intelligences, are so thought provoking and challenging in their nature, by declaring At-onement with the Father through prayer for His Divine Love, that they can truly be called a New Reformation in Christian thinking.

DANIEL G. SAMUELS
Washington, D.C.
August 1956

PART I.

ETERNAL TRUTHS.

Chapter 1.

Jesus of Nazareth Selects
James E. Padgett.

MESSAGES INCLUDED IN THIS CHAPTER.

Jesus Wants the World to Follow His True Teachings. (JESUS)............7

Jesus Declares That the Divine Love Is Reaching Out to Every Man, and That Mr. Padgett Is the Instrument to Receive His Repeated Gospel. (JESUS) 8

When Mr. Padgett's Soul Development Was Sufficient to Permit Jesus To Write, the Following Informative Message Was Received. (JESUS)..9

Mr. Padgett's Wife, Helen, Affirms That Jesus Wrote. (HELEN PADGETT)...11

John H. Padgett Affirms That Jesus Wrote Through Mr. Padgett. (JOHN H. PADGETT)...12

Mr. Padgett's Grandmother, Ann Rollins, Also Declares That Jesus Wrote. (ANN ROLLINS)...12

Mr. Padgett Received This Second Formal Message from Jesus Only a Few Days After the First. (JESUS) 13

Ann Rollins Continues a Discussion of Jesus' Discourse on the Father's Being and Nature. (ANN ROLLINS) 15

Jesus Communicates a Personal Message to Mr. Padgett. He States That He Is Not God, but Was Sent by the Father to Lead Men to His Favor and Love. As Such, He Is the Way, the Truth, and the Life. (JESUS) 16

Mr. Padgett's Father Confirms Jesus' Previous Message. (JOHN H. PADGETT)...18

Mr. Padgett's Mother Adds Her Testimony. (ANN R. PADGETT)........18

Another Personal Message Is Given to Mr. Padgett from Jesus. (JESUS)..18

Mr. Padgett's Mother Responds to Jesus' Message. (ANN R. PADGETT) 19

The Master Gives Additional Assurance That He Is Jesus. He Also Refers to a Spirit Who Claimed That He Had Lost His Soul. (JESUS) 20

Mrs. Padgett Affirms That Jesus Wrote About What a "Lost Soul" Means. (HELEN PADGETT) 21

Ann Rollins States That Jesus Writes Through Mr. Padgett. She Also Declares That There Are No Imposters of Jesus Who Write. (ANN ROLLINS) 22

Jesus Discusses the Result of Mr. Padgett's Belief in Him. (JESUS) 23

Jesus Explains Why Men Should Believe That He Is the True Jesus, and Why He Writes Through Mr. Padgett. (JESUS) 24

Mrs. Padgett Corroborates That Jesus Wrote. (HELEN PADGETT) ...25

Jesus Enlarges Upon the Efforts of the Spirits to Show Men the Truths of the Father. (JESUS) 26

A Confirmation by Andrew That Jesus Writes Through Mr. Padgett. (ANDREW, THE APOSTLE) 27

A Confirmation by Peter. (PETER, THE APOSTLE) 29

A Confirmation by John. (JOHN, THE APOSTLE) 30

A Confirmation by James. (JAMES, THE APOSTLE) 30

A Confirmation by Jerome. (JEROME) 31

A Confirmation by Anthony. (ANTHONY) 31

A Confirmation by Stephen. (STEPHEN, THE APOSTLE) 32

A Confirmation by Barnabas. (BARNABAS, THE APOSTLE) 33

A Confirmation by Thomas. (THOMAS, THE APOSTLE) 33

Luke Adds His Testimony. (LUKE, THE APOSTLE) 34

A Confirmation by John Wesley That He Heard the Master Select Mr. Padgett for His Work. (JOHN WESLEY) 35

A Confirmation by A.G. Riddle That the Master and the Apostles Have Communicated That Mr. Padgett Is Selected to Do the Work. (A.G.

RIDDLE).. 35

A Confirmation by Ann Rollins. She is Amazed at the Great Assurances Given to Mr. Padgett. (ANN ROLLINS) 36

How Happy Mrs. Padgett Is That Great Spirits Have Confirmed Mr. Padgett's Selection. (HELEN PADGETT) 37

Paul Explains His "Thorn in the Flesh" and His Experience on the Way to Damascus. (PAUL, THE APOSTLE) 38

John Corroborates That Jesus Writes Through Mr. Padgett. (JOHN, THE APOSTLE) 39

The Time Is Now Ripe for the Truths to Be Made Known So That Mankind Can Be Redeemed from Their False Beliefs. (JOHN, THE BAPTIST) 41

John, the Apostle, Gives Encouragement to Mr. Padgett, and Tells of the Wonderful Love the Master Has for Him. (JOHN, THE APOSTLE) 42

Jesus Discusses the Wonderful Power That May Come to Mr. Padgett if He Will Only Have Sufficient Faith. (JESUS) 43

Mrs. Padgett Describes the Regal Power and Authority That Jesus Displayed While Writing Through Mr. Padgett. (HELEN PADGETT) 44

John Affirms That Jesus Showed His Glory, Power, and Authority While Writing Through Mr. Padgett, and He Speaks of the Wonderful Blessings and Faith That May Come to Him. (JOHN, THE APOSTLE) 45

A.G. Riddle Is in a Condition of Wonderment After Seeing Jesus Showing Such Brightness and Power. (A. G. RIDDLE) 46

Ann Rollins Also Affirms That Jesus Wrote and Showed His Glory and Power. (ANN ROLLINS) 47

Robert G. Ingersoll, a Former Author and Agnostic on Earth, Was Present When Jesus Wrote and Showed His Glory. He Confesses That He Is an Agnostic No Longer, but a Most Repentant Believer Now. (ROBERT G. INGERSOLL) 48

Mrs. Padgett Affirms That Jesus Wrote and Showed His Glory, and

That He Selected Mr. Padgett to Do the Work in Receiving the Messages. (HELEN PADGETT)..50

John, the Baptist, Declares that Mr. Padgett Is Now a Disciple of the Master. (JOHN, THE BAPTIST)...50

James Confirms That Mr. Padgett Will Soon Get Relief from Worry. (JAMES, THE APOSTLE)...51

Luke Also Gives His Assurance That Relief Will Soon Come to Mr. Padgett. (LUKE, THE APOSTLE)...52

John Encourages Mr. Padgett to Open His Heart to the Love of the Celestials. (JOHN, THE APOSTLE)..52

Barnabas Assures Mr. Padgett That He Will Receive the Father's Help. (BARNABAS, THE APOSTLE)...53

John Wesley, Founder of Methodism, Affirms That Jesus Will Attend to Mr. Padgett's Needs. (JOHN WESLEY)..53

John Garner, Former Preacher of England, Also Gives Encouragement to Mr. Padgett. (JOHN GARNER).....................................54

Mrs. Padgett Refers to the Many Consolatory Messages Mr. Padgett Received. (HELEN PADGETT)..54

Jesus Again Showed His Great Glory, and Gave His Love to Mr. Padgett. (JESUS)...55

Saleeba Presents Her Comments on the Power and Glory That Jesus Displayed. (SALEEBA)..56

John Wesley Speaks of the Great Love Jesus Has for Mr. Padgett. He Also Reveals That Jesus' Glory and Power Were So Wonderful That All Knelt in Awe. (JOHN WESLEY)..56

Ann Rollins Affirms Jesus' Love for Mr. Padgett. She Describes the Wonderful Experience Witnessed, and Tells How All Were Surprised at the Display of His Glory. (ANN ROLLINS)...57

Mrs. Padgett Affirms That the Great Love of Jesus Was Bestowed on Her Husband, and That She, Too, Was Filled with Awe. (HELEN PADGETT)...58

White Eagle Was Astonished at the Wonderful Glory of the Master. He Confirms That Spirits Were Awed by the Brightness and

Magnificence of His Presence. (WHITE EAGLE) 58

John Layton Affirms That All That the Spirits Wrote About the Magnificent Power and Glory of the Master Is True. He Also Declares That This Revelation Marks an Epoch in the Spirit World. (JOHN LAYTON) 59

Daniel Webster Affirms That Jesus and Spirits of the Higher Spheres Are Revealing the Great Truths of the Father Through Mr. Padgett. (DANIEL WEBSTER) 60

A Confirmation by Mark That the Master Is Doing the Great Work for the Redemption of Mankind Through Mr. Padgett. (MARK OF THE NEW TESTAMENT) 61

Lazarus Confirms That Mr. Padgett's Spirit Communicators Are Whom They Represent Themselves to Be, and He Relates That Both Mary and Martha, His Sisters, Are Living Together in the Celestial Heavens. (LAZARUS) 61

Elizabeth, the Cousin of Jesus' Mother, Mary, Confirms That Mr. Padgett Has Obtained Much of the Divine Love. She Also Explains What the "Second Coming" of Jesus Really Means. (ELIZABETH) 63

Mrs. Padgett Confirms That Elizabeth Wrote the Preceding Message. (HELEN PADGETT) 64

John Emphasizes the Importance of Mr. Padgett Carrying Forth the Work of Receiving and Disseminating the Truths of Salvation. (JOHN, THE APOSTLE) 64

Jesus Affirms That His Presented Truths are Easily Understood and Do Not Require a Highly Developed Mind. (JESUS) 66

Solomon, Former Wise King of the Old Testament, Writes of Mr. James E. Padgett's Selection by Jesus. (SOLOMON) 67

Mrs. Padgett Affirms That Solomon Wrote Through Mr. Padgett. (HELEN PADGETT) 68

1.

Jesus of Nazareth Selects James E. Padgett.

Jesus Wants the World to Follow His True Teachings.
(JESUS)
(September 12th, 1914 | Received by James Padgett)

I AM HERE. *Jesus*.

God is Love. And they that worship Him in spirit and love will not be forsaken.

I came to tell you that you are very near the Kingdom. Only believe and pray to the Father and you will soon know the Truth, and the Truth will make you free. You were hard-hearted and sinful[*]; but, now that you are seeking the light, I will come to you and help you. Only believe and you will soon see the Truth of my teachings. Go not in the way of the wicked, for their end is punishment and long-suffering. Let your love for God and your fellowman increase.

You are not in condition for further writing. I will come to you again when you are stronger.

(Is this truly Jesus of the Bible communicating to me?)[†]

Yes, it is Jesus, and I want the world to follow the true teachings of my words.

Good-bye, and may the Holy Spirit bless you, as I do. JESUS CHRIST.

---

[*] Mr. Padgett told me that he had a vision of Jesus many years before he knew he had the mediumistic gift to receive communications from spirits. He told me that, when he saw Jesus at the time he had the vision, Jesus looked at him with a great love and sympathy, as if he wanted him to become a true follower of him.

The first messages from Jesus are for the purpose of encouraging Mr. Padgett to get the Divine Love into his soul in sufficient abundance so as to change the quality of his brain into that high quality that would enable Jesus to write the high quality of Truths, or formal messages, that he is so anxious to give to the world. (Dr. Leslie R. Stone, former editor, now deceased.—Ed.)

[†] Mr. Padgett's question, and all subsequent questions and statements placed in brackets and italicized throughout this volume, have been editorially devised in order to assist in reading fluency and to provide for greater facility in the understanding of the text as a whole. These mostly brief, created conversations for Mr. Padgett are not to be taken as being the precise words he originally phrased; only very close approximations of the original sum and substance of what he had communicated to the spirits but had failed to record at the time. The reader is referred back to the Preface for a more detailed explanation of how the use of these insertions was determined and authorized. —Ed.

7

Jesus Declares That the Divine Love Is Reaching Out to Every Man, and That Mr. Padgett Is the Instrument to Receive His Repeated Gospel.
(JESUS)
(September 29th, 1914 | Received by James Padgett)

I AM HERE. *Jesus*.

I wish to write to you about the Love of God and the needs of mankind.

Let your mind be free from all thoughts of evil and sin. The Love of God is reaching out to every man so that the meanest will be the object of His Care. Do not let the thought that He is only loving the good and righteous lead you to think that you must seek the company of these favored ones only. Let the lost and unhappy be the objects of your efforts to show them the Way to the Father.

In receiving our messages, you will have an opportunity to teach all mankind of the Love of God for His children, and that they are the children of His Greatest Care and Love. Be only earnest in your efforts to spread the Truths which I shall teach you in my communications, and you will be a successful laborer in the work which the Father has decreed you to do. Give your best endeavors to the spreading of the messages, and you will not only save the souls of the blinded and lost but also will hasten the coming of the Kingdom in your own life and heart. LET ME COME TO YOU OFTEN, FOR YOU ARE THE INSTRUMENT THAT I WISH TO USE IN MY NEW OR REPEATED GOSPEL OF GLAD TIDINGS TO THE HUMAN RACE. Be true to the trust that I shall impose in you, and let not the cares of the world keep you from spreading my gospel. Come to the Love of God in a more enlarged and truthful meaning, and you will be my true follower. Let me lead you to the Fountainhead of all the Truths of God I have in store for humanity.

My own love and power will guide you and keep you in the way of Light and Truth that you may teach to your fellowman. Your own soul must be purified first, and then you will be able to show others the power and love that I have for them.

You are not to seek the help of other spirits until I teach you the Truths of my Father. He is the only One Who has the Power to save men from their sins and errors. Be true and earnest in your work, and don't let other things distract your mind or work from the task set before you. THE WORLD NEEDS A NEW AWAKENING. AND THE UNFAITHFUL AND UNBELIEVING MEN WHO THINK THEMSELVES WISE (BUT WHO ARE FOOLISH, AS THEY WILL ULTIMATELY FIND OUT) MUST NOT FILL THEIR SOULS WITH THE MATERIAL THINGS MUCH LONGER OR THEY WILL SUFFER MORE THAN THEY CAN IMAGINE. THE MATERIAL NEEDS OF MANKIND ARE NOT THE ONLY CLOUDS THAT MUST BE LIFTED FROM THEIR SOULS.

You are too weak to write more now.

(But I am willing to receive more of your message.)

Yes, but I am not able to write more now because you are not in condition.

You must stop writing now.

JESUS CHRIST.

When Mr. Padgett's Soul Development Was Sufficient to Permit Jesus To Write, the Following Informative Message Was Received.
(JESUS)
(January 24th, 1915 | Received by James Padgett)

I AM HERE. *Jesus*.

You are now in condition, and I will give you a short message as my first.

When I was on earth, I was not worshiped as God, but was considered merely as the son of God in the sense that the Truths of my Father were imposed in me, and many of His wonderful and mysterious Powers.

I did not proclaim myself to be God, but only that I was His beloved son, sent to proclaim His Truths to mankind, and to show them the Way to the Love of the Father.

I was not different from other men except that I possessed this Love of God to a degree which made me free from sin, and prevented the evils that formed a part of the natures of other men from becoming a part of my nature.

No man who believes that I am God has a knowledge of the Truth, or is obeying the Commandments of God by worshiping me. Such worshipers are blaspheming and are doing the cause of God and my teachings great injury. Many a man would have become a true believer in, and worshiper of, the Father and a follower of my teachings had not this blasphemous dogma been interpolated into the Bible. It was not with my authority, or in consequence of my teachings, that such a very injurious doctrine was promulgated or believed in.

I am only a son of my Father, as you are. And while I was always free from sin and error, yet, as regards the true conception of my Father's true relationship to mankind, you are also His son. And if you will seek earnestly and pray to the Father with faith, you may become as free from sin and error as I was then and am now. The Father is Himself, Alone. There is no other God besides Him, and no other God to be worshiped.

I am His teacher of Truth, and am the Way, the Truth, and the Life, because in me are those attributes of goodness and knowledge which fit me to show the Way and to lead men to eternal life in the Father, and to teach them that God has prepared a Kingdom in which they may live forever, if

9

they so desire. But notwithstanding my teachings, men, and those who assumed high places in what was called the Christian church, imposed doctrines so at variance with the Truth that, in these latter days, men, in the exercise of an enlightened freedom, and of reason, have become infidels, and have turned away from God and His Love, and have thought and taught that man himself is sufficient for his own salvation.

The time has come when men must be taught to know that, while the teachings of these professed authorities on the Truths of God are all wrong, they, these same men, are in error when they refuse to believe in God and in my teachings. What my teachings are, I know, is difficult to understand from the writings of the New Testament, for I never said many things contained therein, and many things that I did say are not written therein.

I AM NOW GOING TO GIVE TO THE WORLD THE TRUTHS AS I TAUGHT THEM WHEN ON EARTH, AND MANY THINGS THAT I NEVER DISCLOSED TO MY DISCIPLES OR INSPIRED OTHERS TO WRITE.

No man can come to the Father's Love except he be born again. This is the great and fundamental Truth which men must learn and believe. For, without this New Birth, men cannot partake of the Divine Essence of God's Love, which, when possessed by man, makes him at-one with the Father. This Love comes to men through the workings of the Holy Spirit, causing It to flow into the heart and soul, and filling it so that all sin tends to make them unhappy. Yet, without this Love within, they will be only natural men and nothing more.

I came into the world to show men the Way to this Divine Love of the Father, and to teach them His Spiritual Truths. My mission was that in all its perfection, and, incidentally, to teach them the way to greater happiness on earth as well as in the spirit world, even though they neglected to seek for and obtain this Divine Love to become one with the Father.

Let men ponder this momentous question, and they will learn that the happiness of mortal man and the happiness of the man who has obtained this Attribute of Divinity is very different and, in all eternity, must be and remain distinct and separate. My teachings are not very hard to understand and follow when I say that a man cannot become of the Nature of the Divine unless the Divine first comes into that man and makes him a part of Its Own Divinity.

All men who do not get the Divine Essence will be left in their natural state. And while they may progress to higher degrees of goodness and freedom from sin in this state, and toward everything which will tend to elevate man's desire for a better understanding with which to assure a man's future happiness, yet, this happiness is not that greater happiness which God desires His children to have. Nor is the development of the natural state the way to possessing this greater happiness which I came to the earth to teach.

My mission on earth was not so successful as it might have been if the so-called "followers" had not become too ambitious for power and position to permit the Truth to be known which I gave to my disciples, and had not caused many deeds of violence and death. But my Truths found lodgment in some hearts and minds, and were retained to save mankind from total spiritual darkness and a relapse to worship of form and ceremony only. I have written you this as a mere help for them. For if they will continue to believe and follow these teachings, they will learn the Way and obtain the one perfect state of happiness which the Father has prepared for His children

NO MAN CAN OBTAIN THIS STATE OF CELESTIAL BLISS UNLESS HE FIRST GETS THIS DIVINE LOVE OF THE FATHER AND BECOMES AT-ONE WITH HIM.

So, I say, if a man will pray to the Father, and believe, and earnestly ask that this Love be given him, he will receive It; and, when It comes into his soul, he will realize it.

Let not men think that, by any efforts of their own, they can come into this union with the Father, because they cannot. No river can possibly rise higher than its source. And no man who has only the natural love and is filled with error can, of his own powers, cause that natural love to partake of the Divine, or have his nature relieved of such sin and error.

Man is a mere creature and cannot create anything higher than himself. Neither can he, of or by himself, rise above his own creation. So, you must not let the teachings of the Bible, and what men write or have professed to have written, keep you from receiving and understanding what I shall hereafter write.

I will write no more tonight, but from now on I will tell you the Truths which will be the New Gospel for mankind to benefit by. When they have heard my messages, they will believe that there is only One God, and only One to be worshiped.

With my love and blessings, I will close for this time.
Your brother and friend,
JESUS.

Mr. Padgett's Wife, Helen, Affirms That Jesus Wrote.
(HELEN PADGETT)
(September 12th, 1914 | Received by James Padgett)

I AM HERE. *Helen.*

Yes, I am here and I love to be with you.
(Who last wrote to me?)
The savior of men. He was with you and I was so glad, as I feel that you will now believe that I am in the spirit world and in the Love of God. He is the savior who came down from heaven to save men. Let his love for you help you to become a more spiritual man. God will bless you in all

11

your doings.

Good night.
HELEN.

John H. Padgett Affirms That Jesus Wrote Through Mr. Padgett.
(JOHN H. PADGETT)
(September 12th, 1914 | Received by James Padgett)

I AM HERE. *Your father.*

(Is it true that Jesus just wrote to me?)
Yes, it is true. He was with you and you will soon learn much more from him, as he says that he will teach you the Truth and the Light and the Way. Love God and keep His Commandments. Let your heart be open to the Divine teachings of the Master. He will not show you all the love he has for you, but will let you feel that he is your loving friend and savior.
(Why did he come to me?)
Because he loves you and believes that you may be of some benefit to the world.
(Was he the same Jesus I know of from the Scriptures?)
YES, HE WAS THE REAL JESUS OF THE BIBLE.
HE IS NOT IN THE HEAVENS SITTING ON THE RIGHT HAND OF THE FATHER, BUT IS AMONG ALL MANKIND AND STILL TEACHING THEM THE POWER OF LOVE AND TRUTH. HE DOES NOT NEED THE WORSHIP OF MEN. ALL THAT HE WANTS IS THEIR LOVE AND HAPPINESS.
He is not the savior of the few but of all who will ask him to help them. Let your love for God increase and you will not be unhappy or cast down.
Good night.
Your father,
JOHN H. PADGETT.

Mr. Padgett's Grandmother, Ann Rollins,
Also Declares That Jesus Wrote.
(ANN ROLLINS)
(September 12th, 1914 | Received by James Padgett)

I AM HERE. *Your grandmother.*

Give your heart to the Lord and He will bless you, as you will soon realize.
(Did Jesus just come to write to me?)

He did, and he will come to you again soon. He is waiting to tell you of the Truths that he is longing to have you know. He is not going to let you feel that he is away up in the heavens, far beyond the reach of men, but is with them all the time, working and trying to save them from their sins. Let your love for God and His Truths keep you from unbelief and doubt. Be a true seeker after the knowledge that is in Christ, and you will not be long in doubt as to which is the Way to eternal happiness. Keep trying to find the Truth. He told me that he would come to you so that you might not doubt any longer. And he is not going to leave you again, as he did some years ago when your heart was hard and sinful.

You must believe that he came to you. He is no other than Jesus of the Bible.

I will love and help you at all times.

Your grandmother,

ANN ROLLINS.

Mr. Padgett Received This Second Formal Message from Jesus Only a Few Days After the First.
(JESUS)
(January 31ˢᵗ, 1915 | Received by James Padgett)

I AM HERE. *Jesus.*

As I told you, I will write my second message tonight. I am not going to tell you of my Father's Kingdom at this time, but of His Nature as my God and your God.

He is the only One Who is Supreme, and All-Powerful and Loving and Wise. He is not a Being of form or individuality, as men understand, but is a Substance of Being and Soul. His Soul is that part of Him which embraces all the Affections and Love, and which is bestowed on man in order that he may become like his Father.

I am not yet so possessed of that Soul Essence as to make me just like the Father in all His Attributes. But I expect that some time in the future, when I have received that Divine Essence in all Its fulness, I will be likened unto the Father, and so may every one of His creatures if they will only seek for It with true faith and earnestness.

The Father is not capable of being seen with the physical or spiritual sight, but can only be seen with the soul's eyes of Perfect Love. He is not in any particular place, or seated on a throne in His Heavens, but His Attributes are everywhere and fill the whole universe. The earth is a very small portion of the universe, and men must not believe that God is only in the heavens where the sons of earth go when they cease to live as mortals.

God is a God of Love, above everything else; and the sooner mankind learns and believes that fact, the sooner will happiness exist on the earth, as well as in the heavens. He is not a God of hatred, nor does He chastise

13

His children in wrath or anger. His Love is with all mankind, be they saints or sinners, and no man suffers punishment because the Father wants him to suffer. He is also a God of Mercy and Forgiveness, and He will forgive the sins of men and shed His Mercy over them if they will truly and in sincerity ask His Forgiveness and seek His Mercy.

He is also a God of Wisdom. And His Plans for the redemption and salvation of mankind are the only plans that can be adopted for men to try to follow in order that they may receive this salvation. He is also a God of Power. And, in the days to come, when He sees fit to carry out and perfect His Plans in their full fruition, He, through the working of His Spirit, which is Perfect in Its working, will destroy all sin and error in His Universe; and perfect harmony will reign and man will be at peace and happiness.

So, God is everything in Nature and Attributes which will not only redeem men from their sins but will also make them lovers of one another and brothers in the true sense of the word. The world will not be destroyed, as it is taught by some in the interpreting of the Bible. But, when the great day of judgment comes, all sin will be eradicated from the world, and mankind will continue to live upon the earth, free from sin and unhappiness, just as it is supposed Adam and Eve lived in the Garden of Eden.

Never has man seen God. The stories in the Old Testament about some of the prophets and leaders of the Jews in their early captivity and wanderings are not true, for God cannot be seen as therein described. His angels and messengers, who were at one time mortals of earth, were seen, and they spoke to the prophets and represented themselves as being angels of God. But no angel or spirit ever represented himself to be God—not even the angels who delivered the tablets of stone to Moses, as it is written. God worked always through His angels, and never directly, as some of the Bible writers teach. I was His chosen son to do the work of redeeming the earth from sin, and I came as my Father's representative. I never was God, nor did I ever claim to be, either to my disciples or to the Jews or the Sanhedrin.

It is written in the Bible that the "voice" of God spoke to my disciples on the Mount of Transfiguration, and to John and those present at my baptism. But it was not the voice of God, but the voice of one of God's highest angels.

No man has ever heard the "voice" of God, for He has no voice. He works in a silent, mysterious way through the operation of His Soul upon the souls of men, just as the coming of the Holy Ghost at Pentecost. While the Bible says that there was a noise, as of a mighty wind, yet that was not perceptible to the physical ears of the disciples. They felt the presence of such a Manifestation in their souls. And in order to have mankind understand that there was this wonderful Manifestation, they used the imagery of the "voice" of a mighty wind. So, man must understand that God "speaks" to man through His angels, or through the communication of His Soul and theirs.

14

I speak thus because I want it made plain that God is not the person, loving or otherwise, which the Bible may teach man that He is. He is only the Personification of Love, Power, and Wisdom, and is without form or personal appearance, such as mortals and spirits have. This is my knowledge of what God is.

I will not write further tonight.

With my blessing and love,

JESUS.

*Ann Rollins Continues a Discussion of Jesus' Discourse
on the Father's Being and Nature.*
(ANN ROLLINS)
(January 31st, 1915 | Received by James Padgett)

I AM HERE. *Your grandmother.*

You must not think that because the Master said that God is a Personification of Love, Power, and Wisdom, that there is no real God, but merely an "abstract being" representing these Attributes. He is a real Being. And these Attributes are His, and not the combination of the Attributes. He exists, and without Him there would be no Love, Wisdom or Power. He is the Creator of these Principles, and not their creature.

As Jesus said, God is without form or substance, such as mortals and spirits have; yet He has a Spiritual Substance that is real, and not shadowy or nonexistent. Pantheism is different from what God is.

While His Attributes are everywhere, yet, He is of an identical Substance of Spirit. So, do not let the idea possess you that he is not a Being, for He is. And even though we cannot see Him, or feel Him as a Spirit, yet, He exists as His Own, True Self. So, believe in a Personal God in that sense.

I know that it is hard to comprehend the true conception of His Being. But the higher we get in the scale of Love, the more apparent becomes His real Existence as a Being. Do not let your inability to grasp the true meaning of this description of God and His Nature lead you to think that He is a mere "essence." He is real! And to us who have received a large amount of His Love and Essence, He becomes as real as if we could see and feel Him with spiritual eyes and hands.

I know the difficulties in the way of your finite mind grasping the true conception of His Being, but, as Love draws you closer to Him, the mind gives way to the perceptions of the soul, and God appears as a real, existing Being, the Creator of all.

I want to tell you further that God (the God of the Master), while He works through His angels, yet, He, Himself, comes into our souls by His direct Communication. The Holy Spirit is His Messenger that causes the souls of men to "hear" and receive this Soul Communication. Yet, God's

15

Love comes direct from Himself. And when man was created in the likeness of God, he was given a soul that was capable of receiving the Soul Essence of the Father. Neither in his physical nor spiritual form was man created in the image of his Father, because the Father has no such forms; but, in the Soul Essence, the image was made alike.

Yet, man is of such a great degree in God's Creation that he can refuse to receive this Soul Essence, if he so wills. His soul is capable of receiving It, but is not compelled to do so. And while man has the image, yet, if he neglects to receive the Substance, he will never become at-one with the Father. That image will never be more than an image only.

God is so Good that He implanted what may be called the natural love in man's soul; and that love is sufficient to make him comparatively happy. And in the great day when sin and error shall be destroyed, man's natural love will be able to cause this happiness.

But man will not be at-one with the Father in the larger sense, and will not take on the Divine Nature of his God. So, you see the necessity of seeking this wonderful union with the Father.

I must stop now.

YOUR GRANDMOTHER.

Jesus Communicates a Personal Message to Mr. Padgett. He States That He Is Not God, but Was Sent by the Father to Lead Men to His Favor and Love. As Such, He Is the Way, the Truth, and the Life.
(JESUS)
(September 24th, 1914 | Received by James Padgett)

I AM HERE. *Jesus.*

Be of good cheer, for I am with you always. Do not let your heart fear, for the Lord is your Keeper and He will be your Guide and Shield. Only believe and trust in Him and you will soon be born again into the spiritual world of His Kingdom. Let me teach you and give you the thoughts that He gave to me while on earth. Let me show you that the things of this world are not the things that save the soul from sin and unhappiness. Be a true follower of your God.

(Master, what is the New Birth?)

IT IS THE FLOWING OF THE HOLY SPIRIT INTO THE SOUL OF A MAN, AND THE DISAPPEARING OF ALL THAT TENDED TO KEEP IT IN A CONDITION OF SIN AND ERROR. IT IS NOT THE WORKINGS OF THE MAN'S OWN WILL BUT THE GRACE OF GOD. IT IS THE LOVE OF GOD THAT PASSES ALL UNDERSTANDING.

You will soon experience the change, and then you will be a happy man and fit to lead others to the Truths of God. Let your heart be open to the "knockings" of the Spirit, and keep your mind free from thoughts of sin.

Be a man who loves his God and his fellowman. Your love is only now of the earthly kind, but it will soon be of a spiritual quality.

YOU MUST NOT LET THE CARES OF THIS WORLD KEEP YOU FROM GOD. LET HIS SPIRIT COME INTO YOUR SOUL. YOUR WILL IS THE THING THAT DETERMINES WHETHER YOU WILL BECOME A CHILD OF GOD OR NOT. UNLESS YOU ARE WILLING TO LET THE HOLY SPIRIT ENTER INTO YOUR HEART IT WILL NOT DO SO. ONLY THE VOLUNTARY SUBMISSION TO, OR ACCEPTANCE OF, THE HOLY SPIRIT WILL MAKE THE CHANGE.

I WAS THE INSTRUMENT IN GOD'S HANDS OF LEADING MEN TO HIS FAVOR AND LOVE. WHEN I SAID THAT I AM THE WAY, THE TRUTH, AND THE LIFE, I MEANT THAT THROUGH MY TEACHINGS AND EXAMPLE MEN SHOULD BE ABLE TO FIND GOD. I WAS NOT GOD AND NEVER CLAIMED TO BE. THE WORSHIP OF ME AS A GOD IS BLASPHEMOUS, AND I DID NOT TEACH IT. I AM A SON OF GOD, AS YOU ARE. DO NOT LET THE TEACHINGS OF MEN LEAD YOU TO WORSHIP ME AS A GOD. I AM NOT.

THE "TRINITY" IS A MISTAKE OF THE WRITERS OF THE BIBLE. THERE IS NO "TRINITY"—ONLY ONE GOD, THE FATHER. HE IS ONE AND ALONE. I AM HIS TEACHER OF TRUTH. THE HOLY SPIRIT IS HIS MESSENGER AND DISPENSER OF LOVE TO MANKIND. WE ARE ONLY HIS INSTRUMENTS IN BRINGING MAN TO A UNION WITH HIM.

I AM NOT THE EQUAL OF MY FATHER. HE IS THE ONLY TRUE GOD. I CAME FROM THE SPIRIT WORLD TO EARTH AND TOOK THE FORM OF MAN, BUT I DID NOT BECOME GOD—ONLY THE SON OF MY FATHER. YOU ALSO LIVED AS A SPIRIT IN THAT KINGDOM, BUT YOU TOOK THE FORM OF MAN MERELY AS A SON OF YOUR FATHER. YOU ARE THE SAME AS I AM, EXCEPT AS TO SPIRITUAL DEVELOPMENT, AND YOU MAY BECOME AS GREATLY DEVELOPED AS MYSELF.

I AM THE FIRST SON ON EARTH WHO HAD BECOME VESTED WITH THE DIVINE LOVE OF GOD TO THE EXTENT OF BEING WHOLLY FREE FROM SIN AND ERROR WHEN I LIVED IN THE FLESH. MY LIFE WAS NOT A LIFE OF EARTHLY PLEASURE OR SIN,BUT WAS GIVEN WHOLLY TO MY FATHER'S WORK. I WAS HIS "ONLY" SON IN THAT LIGHT. AND HE WAS MY FATHER AS I KNEW HIM TO BE. HE IS NOT A SPIRIT OF FORM LIKE MYSELF OR YOURSELF.

I WAS BORN AS YOU WERE BORN. I WAS THE SON OF MARY AND JOSEPH, AND NOT BORN OF THE HOLY SPIRIT, AS IT IS WRITTEN IN THE BIBLE. I WAS ONLY A HUMAN BEING AS REGARDS MY BIRTH AND PHYSICAL EXISTENCE. THE ACCOUNT IN THE NEW TESTAMENT IS NOT TRUE, AND WAS WRITTEN BY THOSE WHO KNEW NOT WHAT THEY WROTE.

17

THEY HAVE DONE THE CAUSE OF GOD'S TRUTHS MUCH INJURY. LET NOT YOUR BELIEF IN THAT ERROR KEEP YOU FROM SEEING THAT MY TEACHINGS ARE THE TRUTH. BE ONLY A BELIEVER OF GOD AND HIS TRUTHS, AND YOU WILL SOON BE IN THE KINGDOM. YOU WILL SOON BE ABLE TO UNDERSTAND AS I UNDERSTAND.

Good night.

JESUS CHRIST.

Mr. Padgett's Father Confirms Jesus' Previous Message.
(JOHN H. PADGETT)
(September 24th, 1914 | Received by James Padgett)

I AM HERE. *Your father.*

(Who gave me the last message?)
Jesus—the one of the Bible. He was with you and you are the one who must feel that you are highly favored. You must believe that it was he.
(Might this have been someone impersonating Jesus?)
No, it was the true Jesus. No imposter could have written as he did.
Good night.

Your father,

JOHN H. PADGETT.

Mr. Padgett's Mother Adds Her Testimony.
(ANN R. PADGETT)
(September 24th, 1914 | Received by James Padgett)

You have my blessing. It was the Christ who was talking. He is your friend and savior.

Your mother,

ANN R. PADGETT.

Another Personal Message Is Given to Mr. Padgett from Jesus.
(JESUS)
(January 12th, 1915 | Received by James Padgett)

I AM HERE. *Jesus.*

You are my friend and disciple. You are in me and I am in thee, and we are in the Father. You are in me for all eternity.

My Kingdom is not of this world and you are not of this world. You are

18

in me, as I told my disciples of old. Only believe me and keep my commandments, and I will love you to the end, and the Father will love you.

(What do you mean by your "commandments"?)

I mean that you must love all mankind and try to show them the Way to God's Love.

I am my Father's son of Truth and Righteousness and, as such, you must pray to the Father in my name—not because I am Jesus, but because I represent all the Truth and Love of my Father.

(Does the Father want all mankind to seek His Love?)

Yes, and that is the only Way in which men can come to the Father— no other. And when my Kingdom is completed, only those who have become one with the Father will become a part of it.

(Did my wife inform me correctly that only those who believe in your teachings will enter the Kingdom?)

Yes, she told you the truth. My Kingdom will be composed only of those who believe in my teachings and who have received the Holy Ghost. So, do not doubt more. You I have selected, and you will be my true disciple and messenger of Truth. You have my help and love to the fullest, and no man can take it from you. In all eternity, you will be with me.

(Why should God answer my prayers any more than the next man's?)

God answers your prayers because you have faith and are my own disciple. So, continue to pray and He will hear you and answer your prayers.

(But will He not deny a sinner's requests?)

No, only believe and trust Him. He will never forsake you or let you want.

You must love God with all your heart and soul and mind, and your neighbor as yourself—this is the Great Commandment. So, observe this and you will be happy and free.

Let your prayers become more fervent and your faith more fully developed. I will help you to know more of your Father's Love, and you will soon become a true follower of me.

You must seek and you will know. Wait until I give my messages, and then you will know the Truth.

(Am I truly to be your new disciple?)

Yes, I am the vine and you are the branch. So, believe!

What you have written are my thoughts. You did not think any of the thoughts.

So, good night and may God bless you, as I do now.

JESUS.

Mr. Padgett's Mother Responds to Jesus' Message.
(ANN R. PADGETT)
(October 5th, 1914 | Received by James Padgett)

Oh, my dear son, the Master has told you the Way to salvation. Only believe!

I am Your loving mother,

ANN R. PADGETT.

The Master Gives Additional Assurance That He Is Jesus. He Also Refers to a Spirit Who Claimed That He Had Lost His Soul.
(JESUS)
(April 3rd, 1915 | Received by James Padgett)

I AM HERE. *Jesus.*

(Many people will probably not believe that you truly communicate through me.)

I know that what you say is true, but it is I, Jesus, the man who was crucified on Calvary, who comes to you and writes. These persons who will not believe this fact will someday become convinced.

I am with you, as I have told you, because I have work for you to do, and also because I love you very dearly. So, you must not doubt me in any way. If you do not, you will soon see from my messages, and also from your own spiritual development, that I am the Jesus that I represent myself to be. So, believe in me and you will be happier and prosper in every way. Soon, I want to commence my messages again.

(Will I be in proper condition to receive them?)

Yes, you will soon be in condition, and then we will continue our work.

(How did that spirit who wrote to me recently come to believe that he had actually lost his soul?)

Well, he was so overshadowed by the results of his confining all his thoughts when on earth to his mental development that his soul was permitted and compelled to starve, and, as he now believes, has left him. Of course, he has his soul and only needs an awakening of his spiritual perceptions to realize that fact. But as long as he remains in the mental condition that he is now in, he will never find his soul, as he says. The only thing that will get him out of that condition of mind is an opening of his spiritual nature, and then a belief in the Love of the Father.

Your grandmother is now endeavoring to bring about his awakening and she will succeed, for she is a very wise as well as a highly developed spirit in her soul qualities.

The spirit is not what you might call a wicked one. Only he committed the great error of believing that the mind was everything in existence and, as he said, the soul and all spiritual faculties were myths. Many a spirit is in this condition of mind overshadowing the soul to such a degree as to cause the soul, so far as the knowledge or belief of the spirit is concerned, to be lost.[*] He is not one that will find much difficulty in recovering his soul as soon as the soul faculties are awakened.

The unfortunate spirit is one who knows that he has a soul, and that that soul is filled with sin and error and has no apparent way of becoming cleansed. I know of no spirit more to be pitied, or one who needs more the influence and help of both spirits and mortals.

Let me tell you right here that, when you help a spirit to find the Way to salvation and God's Love, you are doing the greatest work that God has given any of His creatures to do. And when that spirit, through your help, finds that Way and realizes the Truth and receives this Love, he is forever your most thankful friend and worker in forwarding the interests of your own spiritual being. So, when the Bible says that for every soul saved there is a new star added to the crown of one who is the instrument in saving such a soul, it only declares a Truth which exists and which never changes. So, in your work of helping these poor, sinful and darkened spirits, you are laying up spiritual jewels which, when you come over into the spirit world, will form a part of your soul's existence.

Of course, there are no jewels as such, but they represent great qualities of happiness and love which the Father will give you. Men do not realize of what momentous importance the saving of a soul is, and what results come to them as such a savior.

I am not going to write more on this subject now, as I will deal with it in my other messages.

So, I will now say good night, and may the Love of the Father be with you and in you this night.

I will give you all my love, and help you to obtain your desires.

Your true brother,
JESUS.

*Mrs. Padgett Affirms That Jesus Wrote
About What a "Lost Soul" Means.*
(HELEN PADGETT)
(April 3rd, 1915 | Received by James Padgett)

I AM HERE. *Helen.*

Well, did not the Master explain what the lost soul means in a way that makes it very plain? I am so glad that you asked him and received the answer that you did.

He is the only Jesus of the Bible, and you are right when you say you believe that he is. Let not what men say cause you to doubt this fact, for it is a fact.

---

[*] See: "...What Is a Lost Soul?" by Jesus, pp.132-36, in volume I of Angelic Revelations of Divine Truth.—Ed.

21

He is the greatest son of his Father. When you have him for a friend, you are rich indeed. So, my dear Ned, continue to believe in him, and listen to his teachings and follow them.

Well, I love you, as you know, with all my heart and soul, and with a love that increases as the Father's Love fills my heart more abundantly. And when I am so filled with more of this Love, I will tell you and you will know that my love for you has increased correspondingly.

So, my darling Ned, I must say good night.

YOUR HELEN.

Ann Rollins States That Jesus Writes Through Mr. Padgett. She Also Declares That There Are No Imposters of Jesus Who Write.
(ANN ROLLINS)
(April 5th, 1915 | Received by James Padgett)

I AM HERE. *Your grandmother.*

Well, I am glad to be with you again, as I want to tell you of some truths that you will be benefited by knowing.

You have had more or less doubt pass through your mind as to whether we are really the persons whom we represent ourselves to be, whether your own mind produces the thoughts to write, or whether some evil spirit or imposter writes through you.

I want to tell you now, with all the love which I have for you, that each one of us who writes you is the person he represents himself to be. No spirit who may seek to impose on you is permitted to write or in any way communicate with you. Our band is sufficiently powerful to prevent any such spirit from intruding himself upon you. Of course, the unfortunate spirits who write you we permit to do so, but they are not imposters. They tell you truthfully just who they are.[*]

I know how natural it is for you to doubt this great marvel of spirit communion, and of the truthfulness of our representations, but I assure you that it is all true.

The Master is the one of whom you read in the Bible, and of whom you have heard all of your life—the only difference being that he is not God or a part of Him, but a spirit, and the greatest in all the Celestial Kingdom.

He is not so very different from what he was on earth in his desire to do the great work which the Father gave him to do, except that he is now more highly developed than when a man traveling the plains and mountains of Palestine.

He is more powerful and knows so many more Truths of the Father, but his love is just the same—only greater in degree.

---

[*] Mr. Padgett helped the unfortunate spirits to visualize the bright ones so that they could receive help. Mr. Padgett gave one evening each week for this purpose.—Ed.

So, you must not doubt any longer or you will not develop as you should.

He is the wisest and most filled with the Father's Love of all the spirits in the Celestial Spheres.

I know that you love us all, and I believe that you love him also. And when I tell you that his love is greater than that of any of us, I am merely telling you what is true.

I would like to write more tonight but there are some others here who are very anxious to write to you, and I will stop.

Your own true and loving grandmother,
ANN ROLLINS.

Jesus Discusses the Result of Mr. Padgett's Belief in Him.
(JESUS)
(April 6th, 1915 | Received by James Padgett)

I AM HERE. *Jesus.*

Well, I am here to tell you of my great gratification in hearing you declare your belief in me again, as you did today. This may seem to be a small matter to you, but I tell you it is one of greatest moment, not only to my cause but to you personally, because it puts you in close rapport with me, and helps you get into a condition which enables you to respond with a greater facility to my efforts to convey my messages to you. Also, it has a reflex influence on your spiritual condition, and tends to increase your faith in what I tell you of the Father's Love, and His Great Mercy and Plan for man's redemption. I am pleased with your declaration, and will help you to become more at-one with me in my work.

SO, LET NOT DOUBT COME INTO YOUR MIND AS TO MY BEING WHO AND WHAT I REPRESENT MYSELF TO BE. FOR IF THERE IS A TRUTH IN ALL THE UNIVERSE, THAT ASSERTION OF MINE IS A TRUTH. Let your faith increase and your life will be happier, and you will become better fitted to inhabit the sphere which I have determined you shall have for your home.

Oh, my dear brother, it is a great consolation to know that you will do my work as I desire it to be done on earth, and to feel that I can rely upon you to receive my gospel of Truth and Light to mankind!

(Was I correct in explaining to my friend that true immortality means more than the mere continuance of life after mortal death?)

Yes, you were correct, and I will soon write on this subject at length. And you will see that, before me, no man or spirit ever declared the Truth of immortality.* You have a right conception of what I meant, and you will

---

* See the "Immortality" chapter by Jesus and others in volume I of *Angelic Revelations of Divine Truth.*—Ed.

23

realize sometime that that immortality is for you—you, and all who believe as you do and SEEK FOR THE DIVINE ESSENCE WHICH ALONE CAN BRING IMMORTALITY TO MAN.

Very soon, now, I will continue my last message, and then we will progress faster in our work.

Well, I will not detain you longer tonight, as there are several present who desire to write.

(Should I also be receiving messages from the dark and suffering spirits?)

Well, that is now a part of your work,* and your band knows that you must do that work. It will not injure your rapport with your band, or cause your power of writing to diminish.

So, with all my love and the Blessings of the Father, I am

Your own true brother,

JESUS.

Jesus Explains Why Men Should Believe That He Is the True Jesus, and Why He Writes Through Mr. Padgett.

(JESUS)

(June 15th, 1915 | Received by James Padgett)

I AM HERE. *Jesus*.

I want to tell you tonight that you are much better in your spiritual condition. And I desire to write a message and have you take it, if you feel that you are in condition.

Well, I desire to write on the subject of: "Why Men Should Believe That I, Who Write to You, Am the True Jesus of the Bible; and Why I Write to You."

When I lived on earth, men did not believe that I was a God, or that I was anything more than a teacher of God's Truths, possessed of wonderful powers not then so well understood as they are now since men have comprehended the possibility of the spirit forms operating through the material world to a limited extent. That is, the spirits of men and the mortals of the earth have the power to communicate with one another. And the powers possessed by the spirits, which are almost unlimited, may be conferred upon, and exercised by, men to a certain extent. This intercommunication and possession of powers, and the conferring thereof on men, were not so well understood when I was on earth as they are now.

I, by reason of my soul development and my knowledge of spiritual things, was able to exercise these powers to an extent that made the people

---

* The work referred to was helping troubled spirits who wrote through Mr. Padgett to visualize the bright spirits. These bright spirits then assisted them in their spiritual progress.—Ed.

24

of my time suppose that I was the "only" son of God, possessed of many of His Powers and Attributes; and, as a matter of fact, I was possessed of these Powers and Attributes. But I was only a mortal when on earth, and only a spirit after I passed from the earth to the spiritual life.

Of course, my development of the soul qualities was such as to enable me to do many things on earth which no other mortal could do, and, after I became a spirit, to obtain a position in the spirit world that no other spirit had obtained. Yet, I am only a spirit, but a highly developed one, possessing more knowledge of God's Truths and having more soul development than any other spirit.

If I were God or a part of God, I would be something more than the mere spirit that I am, and my position would be such that I could not or would not communicate with you in the manner that I do. But I am only a spirit, having the same form and means of communicating with the mortals of earth that other spirits have, only to a greater degree. I am not doing that which should be surprising to mankind. My home, of course, is in a sphere far above that of the earth sphere, and my condition of development is far greater than that of any other spirit. And while I am not of the earth in any particular, yet, my powers are correspondingly great, and my ability to communicate is in accordance with my powers and knowledge.

If I were God, I would not resort to the means of communication that I do now, and it would not be surprising that men would not believe that I would so communicate. But, as I said, not being God, there is no reason that I should not communicate, through you or any other qualified medium, the great Truths of my Father and the Plan provided by Him for man's salvation.

So, men should not think that, because I am the Jesus of the Bible, and have for so many years been accepted and worshiped by so large a part of the human race as God, or rather a part of Him, that, therefore, as a spirit, I have not the qualifications and powers of other spirits; or, because I do have these powers and do so communicate, that I do that which, as God, I should not do.

Well, I must not write more, as you are not just in condition. But I will finish the next time you write, as I very much want men to understand my position with reference to them and to the spirit world.

I am not so much in rapport with you tonight as usual, and you are not in condition to take my meaning. We will try again soon.

I want you to pray more to the Father and have more faith. I will come again soon. I will say good night.

Your friend and brother,
JESUS.

Mrs. Padgett Corroborates That Jesus Wrote.
(HELEN PADGETT)
(June 15th, 1915 | Received by James Padgett)

I AM HERE. *Helen.*

Well, sweetheart, the Master was disappointed that he could not finish his message, and he seemed to be very anxious to write tonight. Of course, you could not help the disappointment, but he is so very anxious to continue these messages. I know that you were perfectly willing that he should write, and tried your best to take the messages; but, somehow, your condition was not just right. Well, you will have the opportunity again soon.

(Are you sure that it wasn't another spirit who just wrote?)

No, it was the Master. He was writing and no one else. You will not be imposed upon by anyone claiming to be him. We will not permit such a thing, and you must not doubt.

I want to tell you that you are very much improved in your spiritual condition, and you must pray more and have more faith. We are trying to help you in every way, so pray to the Father and you will soon realize the results of your prayers.

As you must not write more tonight, I will stop. But I must tell you that I love you with all my heart and soul.

Well, sweetheart, good night.

Your own true and loving,

HELEN.

Jesus Enlarges Upon the Efforts of the Spirits
to Show Men the Truths of the Father.
(JESUS)
(July 8th, 1915 | Received by James Padgett)

I AM HERE. *Jesus*.

I want to add a little to what your grandmother said about the efforts of the spirit world to show men the Truths of the Father.

I know that it will be difficult to make men believe in communications that may come through mediums, and that the churches will antagonize the reception of such communications. But I want to tell you that there will be such power exerted by the spirits of the Kingdom that no efforts on the part of men or churches will be able to withstand these efforts of the spirits. Just as soon as mortals get in condition to receive these Truths, they will be given all the powers necessary; and the Truths will come with such force and exactness that the erroneous beliefs will have to give way and let the Truths that I speak of take their places.

I know that it will be difficult to get men and women in the proper condition to receive these communications, but it will be accomplished, and that before a great while.

Humanity is now longing for the Truth of the Father, and their longings must be satisfied. No longer will form and ceremony and the mere

26

declarations of the churches as to what God has provided for His children, and what the churches have provided, be sufficient to satisfy. The mind as well as the credulity of men must be considered. And when the teachings of the churches are against reason and the knowledge of spiritual laws which men may learn, these souls which hunger and thirst for God's Love and the Way to obtain It must be satisfied.

I KNOW THAT MY KINGDOM WILL BE ESTABLISHED ON EARTH IN A FULLER AND MORE TRUTHFUL WAY THAN EVER, AND MEN WILL BELIEVE IN ME WITH A GREATER CONFIDENCE THAN THEY EVER HAD—NOT AS A GOD TO BE WORSHIPED, BUT AS A BROTHER AND FRIEND WHO IS ABLE TO SHOW THEM THE WAY TO THE LOVE OF THE FATHER, AND TO THEIR OWN SALVATION AND TO IMMORTALITY. SO, YOU SEE THE IMPORTANCE OF GETTING GOOD AND RIGHTEOUS MEDIUMS TO CONVEY THESE GREAT TRUTHS.

Mere physical phenomena do not enlighten the soul very much as to its destiny, and what road it shall travel to reach God's Love. Such phenomena will henceforth become of less importance in bringing men to a knowledge of what awaits them in the spirit life.

I will try to influence many mortals to get in this psychic condition so that they may receive these Truths, and thus do the great work that is necessary for the redemption of men to a greater degree than in the past.

So, you must be constant in your work and faith; and, after a little while, many will engage in the same work.

I must stop now.

Your brother and friend,
JESUS.

A Confirmation by Andrew That Jesus Writes Through Mr. Padgett.
(ANDREW, THE APOSTLE)
(July 17th, 1915 | Received by James Padgett)

I AM HERE. *Andrew, the Apostle.*

I am your friend and brother in Christ, and, in that Love, I came because I am interested in the work which you are called upon to do, and because we all love you and want to see you progress in your soul development and in your capacity for receiving the messages of the Master which, as his disciple, he has selected you to receive and transmit to the world.

I am the true Andrew of the Bible and no other, and you must believe that I am. I know that you may have doubts as to so many of the disciples of the Master coming to you to write, but you must not be surprised at that fact. For who are more interested in the great work that you are to do than the disciples of the Master who know that his teachings are the Truth, and that mankind needs them at this time more than at any time in the history of the world?

So, let all your doubts disappear. Believe that we are with you in all our love and desire that you may be happy, and that you may have that soul development that will make you one with us and with the Father, the Creator and Preserver of us all.

(But how can I effectively remove any doubts that I may have?)

Well, you must believe in what we say. I know of no way in which you can become more convinced than by our writing to you. Let no man turn away your faith from us, as no man can truthfully say that we are not writing to you. And, hence, the testimony of such a man is not of that character as to overcome the positive testimony that you receive from us, and all your band, that the Master is actually writing to you. No spirit will be permitted to impersonate the Master or any of us. We are of that higher order of spirits that are all-powerful. And if any spirit should attempt to impose upon you, we would soon compel such spirit to cease its attempt to deceive you, and to leave you in your efforts to seek and learn the Truth.

(Would such spirits be "of the devil," as they say?)

Yes, and sooner or later they will disclose their "cloven feet."

(I only hope you won't think poorly of me for doubting at times.)

Well, we expect that you will doubt at times. But we know that your faith will be so firm after awhile that no doubt will ever enter your mind.

(But it is so difficult to believe that, with my own recognized unworthiness, I should be selected for this awesome work. Who decided that I should be chosen?)

Jesus selected you. And because you are not worthy must not cause you to doubt that he has made such selection. He knows just what is best, and what your qualifications and possibilities are. And it is not for you to say that you are not worthy or not fitted for the work. Let faith in him and in his love and in his promise be established beyond doubt or questioning.

(All I can say is that I am certainly greatly favored.)

Yes, you certainly are favored, and you should appreciate that fact to its highest conception. For I can tell you that you are as much favored in being selected for this work as were any of us when he selected us for his disciples, and I may say even to a greater degree because you are the only one in all the universe that he has chosen to do this great work. And you will find, after awhile, that it is a work of stupendous importance, and involves much labor and exhaustion of both body and mind.

Well, I have written a long letter for my first appearance and I must stop. And, as the most important thing to tell you now, I say believe, and you shall see the Glory of the Father and your own salvation!

I will say with all my heart that I am your true friend and brother, and will pray for you with all my love and faith. So, good night.

Your true brother and friend, ST.* ANDREW.

---

* Often, when writing through Mr. Padgett, the Celestial spirits used the word "Saint"

A Confirmation by Peter.
(PETER, THE APOSTLE)
(July 17th, 1915 | Received by James Padgett)

I AM HERE. *Peter, the Apostle.*

I come for the same reason that Andrew came. I want to add my testimony to his that you are the true selection of the Master to do his work, and that he is with you very often, writing to you and bestowing upon you his love and blessings. You must believe and let not doubt enter your mind, or let it keep you from fully believing, that the Master is your friend and brother, and that he is with you in your times of worry and gloom.

I am a spirit who once, when on earth, had great doubts as to the Master's sacred mission, and as to his being the true son of the Father. But these doubts left me when I saw the greatness of his person and the wonderful Love of the Father which possessed him. You will remember that I even denied him—that is, that I did not know him as a mere man— and what anguish and suffering that denial gave me! So, you must not doubt or deny him.

I know now beyond all question of doubt that he is the true Master and the true son of God, and the only one in all God's Universe who has the Divine Love of the Father to such an extent as to make him almost like the Father in Goodness and Wisdom. He is your friend and savior, and even more is he your brother and companion in this great work which he is doing for the salvation of mankind.

I, Peter, tell you this. And I tell you this with all the authority and faith and even greater knowledge than I had when I declared him to be the only and true divine son of God, and you must believe what I say.

So, let no more doubt or fear persuade you that you are not the Master's instrument, selected by him and confirmed by his love and grace to do this great work, for you have been so chosen. I, Peter, declare it, and I know what I declare; and I say it with all the authority that knowledge gives me!

All the followers of the Master are interested in this work and in you. And we are now forming our band which shall guide and instruct you in all these Truths which only we of the higher heavens know.

I do not mean that we will supersede your present band, but rather that we will work in conjunction with them. You will receive many messages from us as time goes on, and you will believe that we write them to you.

You have more power of the spirit world being exercised in your behalf than has any other mortal. And, with the exercise of this power, there will come to you a power that no mortal has ever had since the days when we lived on earth.

---

to identify themselves. However, John, the Apostle, explained to Mr. Padgett that "Saint" is not used in the Celestial Heavens and, therefore, this title has been eliminated from the present edition.—Ed.

29

So, you must have more faith; and, to get it, you must pray to the Father more and more.

I have written enough for tonight and must stop.

But let me again insist that you pray to the Father and ask for more faith.

I am

Your brother and friend,
PETER.

A Confirmation by John.
(JOHN, THE APOSTLE)
(July 17th, 1915 | Received by James Padgett)

I AM HERE. *John, the Apostle.*

I am here, John, your friend and brother, and at-one with God and a follower of the Master.

You must believe what the Master promised you, for he will not fail you.

I must not write more tonight, but will stop and say that you have my love and best wishes for your success.

Believe in what we write and you will realize the results of our promises.

So, with my love and blessings, I am

Your friend and brother,
JOHN.

A Confirmation by James.
(JAMES, THE APOSTLE)
(July 17th, 1915 | Received by James Padgett)

I AM HERE. *James, the Apostle.*

Let me add my testimony to what the others have written.

I am also a follower of the Master and was with him in his travels through Palestine. I was also with him when he was crucified on the cross.

I was a true follower of the Master on earth, and a true one in the spirit world. He is now the Prince of Peace in its truest sense. His love for humanity is so great that we, even though we are his true lovers and very close to him, cannot comprehend it.

So, you must believe in him and in the fact that he has chosen you to do his great work. Believe and work, and you will see the salvation of the Father manifest itself as never before.

You have working with you all the powers of the Kingdom of Jesus, and nothing will be able to withstand such powers. And Love, the Divine Love of the Father, will enter into many a soul and make it an inhabitant of the Kingdom through this great work.

I will not write more tonight. But, as Peter said, he will be with you often in love and sympathy, and will write you of the Truths of the Heavenly Kingdom.

So, with all my love and blessings, I am

Your own true brother and friend,

JAMES.

A Confirmation by Jerome.
(JEROME)
(July 17th, 1915 | Received by James Padgett)

I AM HERE. *Jerome.*

I am also a brother in spirit. I want to tell you that the wonderful messages that you have received tonight are true. They were written by the spirits professing to write them, and you must not doubt. So, believe and you will receive the greatest of all Blessings, the Divine Love of the Father.

I will not write more at this time, but will come again and tell you of things no mortal has ever heard of or conceived. I am

Your brother and friend,

JEROME, the writer and commentator of the Bible.

A Confirmation by Anthony.
(ANTHONY)
(July 17th, 1915 | Received by James Padgett)

I AM HERE. *Anthony.*

I am your brother and friend in Christ, and in that Love of the Father.

I am a man who was a follower of the Master when on earth, and a follower of him in the spirit world. I mean in the Heavenly Kingdom. And I am now a lover of God and a part of His Divinity.

I was not one of his apostles, but I loved him and believed in him, and died in his cause. And I am now receiving my reward, for, as I say, I am now an inhabitant of his Heavenly Kingdom and immortality is mine, as it will be yours if you continue to believe in him and get the Divine Love of the Father in increased abundance.

So, let me tell you that not every man has bestowed upon him the great favor which the Master has bestowed upon you. No other mortal, at this

31

time, has that great blessing of love and selection that he has given to and made of you.

The others have told you of this wonderful Love and Power and Blessings that have been and will be bestowed upon you.

So, I will stop now, and say that I am

Your brother and friend,

ANTHONY.

A Confirmation by Stephen.
(STEPHEN, THE APOSTLE)
(July 18th, 1915 | Received by James Padgett)

I AM HERE. *Stephen, the Apostle.*

I am the martyr, and I came to you to tell you that you must believe in us as spirits who once lived on earth and taught the Truths of Jesus to men, who were followers of him and lovers of the Father, and who are now inhabitants of His Kingdom and immortal.

I died the death portrayed in the Bible, and Saul, who was my most pernicious persecutor, is the same person who afterwards became Paul, the Christian. I merely state this fact to identify myself to you, and to show you that I am the same spirit who once died for the faith.

So, while I am now a happy spirit and an inhabitant of the Heavenly Kingdom, yet, once I was a mortal engaged in teaching the Truths of the Master, and suffered the pains and torments which such teachings and such faith brought to many of Jesus' disciples.

But those times are past. Now these Truths may be preached and there is none to make afraid. Yet, opposition will come from the churches and the ecclesiastical brethren who are bound by their beliefs in the creeds of the churches.

But, nevertheless, the Truths must be taught, and the Master has chosen you to receive them so that they will be given to the world. And while your task is a glorious one, yet, you will find much responsibility and antagonism and maybe persecution in your private life because of such teachings. But be firm and stick to these Truths and, in the end, they will prevail. Mankind will be benefited and will turn to the Love of the Father and pursue the Way that the Master will show.

So, let not your courage falter or your efforts cease, and you will find a recompense not only in the spirit world but in the world of mortals as well.

I will be one of your band that Peter spoke of. And you will find that your power for good will develop wonderfully, and in a way that will make the world take heed to the Truths that you shall transmit.

You are the chosen one and have with you the powers of the Celestial Kingdom, and the world will not prevail against you or your efforts to show mankind the Way to salvation.

32

So, put your trust in the Master and in the Father's Love and you will not be forsaken.

I will come to you again and give you some Truths of the Father's Kingdom that will show the real Truths of God's Will.

My teachings will be supplemented by those of the Master and will be in unison with them.

I must stop now. I am

Your brother and friend,

STEPHEN, THE MARTYR.

A Confirmation by Barnabas.
(BARNABAS, THE APOSTLE)
(July 18th, 1915 | Received by James Padgett)

I AM HERE. *Barnabas, the Apostle.*

Let me supplement what Stephen wrote. I am an apostle of the Master and was called Barnabas, the partner of Paul in much of his ministry of extending and making known the Truths of the Master throughout Asia and also Judea. I was not only the collaborator with Paul at Jerusalem but was also among the circumcised Jews who embraced the faith of Christianity. I am now working with the apostles in trying to help men and spirits understand and believe in these great Truths.

So, you must believe that I am trying to help you in the great work which the Master has decreed and declared you shall perform. We are all with you and will exert all our power and love to forward the cause of righteousness and the redemption of men.

You must acquire the faith which is so necessary to your success. I mean the faith which leaves no room for doubt that the Master has called you. He will give you power and spiritual development that you may do his work as he desires you to do it. Be a true believer and you will not fail.

I will not write more tonight, but will say: May God prosper you and make you like unto Himself in soul qualities and goodness. I am

Your brother and friend,

BARNABAS.

A Confirmation by Thomas.
(THOMAS, THE APOSTLE)
(July 18th, 1915 | Received by James Padgett)

I AM HERE. *Thomas, the Apostle.*

Let your mind be open to the conviction that I and all the others of the disciples of Jesus have and can write to you in testimony of your selection to do the great work that you have been called to do. Never was mortal so favored by the greatest man and most wonderful and powerful spirit that ever lived. I, an apostle, do not see how you could have been selected, not being so great a lover of God as we might expect the mortal to be who should be called to do this work. But the Master has chosen you and he knows what is best, and we have no right to pass judgment on his choice. But no matter whether you are worthy or not, you have been chosen and you must do the work.

I know that you will have sustaining you all the power and wisdom of the spirit world that is ruled over by Jesus, and that will be sufficient to insure not only success in your work but also your own soul's development and salvation.

I wish that I might tell you what a privileged man you are, but I cannot tonight, as I must stop now and let another write. I am
Your brother and friend,
THOMAS, THE DOUBTER.

(How is it that you came to doubt the Master?)
Because my faith was failing, as it did when I was told that the Master had risen from the dead.

Oh, the curse of unbelief!

I say to you above all things: believe, believe, and believe!
THOMAS.

Luke Adds His Testimony.
(LUKE, THE APOSTLE)
(July 18th, 1915 | Received by James Padgett)

I AM HERE. *Luke, the Apostle.*

Let me add my testimony also, and you will soon see that any doubt is more than foolishness.

I am Luke, the writer of the Third Gospel, as it is called. But let me tell you here that in that writing are things that I never wrote and never believed had any existence. I know that my gospel is considered one of the most authentic of the four; but, in it, as it is contained in the Bible, are many errors and impossible declarations of the truth that are erroneously ascribed to the Master. You must eradicate the errors and retain the Truths. And this you will be able to do when you have received the messages from the Master, and the epistles that we, the apostles and disciples, may write.

Your labor will not be an easy one, but you will be given strength and understanding and wisdom sufficient to make your work of showing the Truth to mankind a correct and unimpeachable one. I will help you in this particular work with all my love and powers of depicting the true meaning

34

of what may be written to you, and will be with you continually when you get ready to compile these messages and other writings which will come to you from the Master and many others of us.

But, in order to become perfect in this great work, you must acquire abundant faith and a large degree of soul development. These qualifications are very necessary because spiritual things conveyed must be spiritually received. This we all know now, and we tell it to you for you must know it, too.

I must not write more now and, so, will say good night.

Your brother and friend,

LUKE, sometimes called the doctor, and
sometimes the learned disciple of the Master.

A Confirmation by John Wesley That He Heard the Master Select Mr. Padgett for His Work.
(JOHN WESLEY)
(July 18th, 1915 | Received by James Padgett)

I AM HERE—a man who lived in the faith of the Christ, and who was a true follower of Jesus and a lover of the Father.

I hesitate to write at the same time with these great spirits who have written to you. But, yet, I want to give my testimony also to the fact that I have heard the Master say that he has chosen you for the work of delivering his Truths to the world.

My dear brother, believe this great fact with all your mind and soul, for it is a truth, and one which prefers you before any other mortal.

Jesus, the greatest of all spirits and the one nearest the Fountainhead of the Father's Love, has declared to us, who are close to him and working to accomplish his great desire for man's salvation, that you he has selected, and that you will do the work and will not fail if you will only have faith.

So, make your start in trying to get this faith. Pray to the Father for more of it, and it will be given to you in great abundance. Only the Father can give the faith that will remove mountains and overcome all obstacles.

I must not write more. I will say good night and sign myself,

Your true brother and co-worker in the cause,

JOHN WESLEY, the former Methodist preacher.

A Confirmation by A.G. Riddle That the Master and the Apostles Have Communicated That Mr. Padgett Is Selected to Do the Work.
(A.G. RIDDLE)
(July 18th, 1915 | Received by James Padgett)

I AM HERE. *Your old partner.*

Why, Padgett, such testimony as that would have established in court any fact that you or I might have asserted! Just think a moment. Here are witnesses of the highest character, with the knowledge and opportunity for knowledge that cannot be disputed, and one identifying the other, and all testifying in the most positive way as to that one particular fact.

Who can say that there can be any possibility of mistake? Never in the world has a fact been more conclusively proved. And if you doubt that you have been selected for this great work, I cannot understand the operation of your mind.

Well, my dear boy, to think that, in the latter years of your life, this great work has come to you—work, I am informed, that has never been successfully given to mortal before to do! You certainly are blessed and I am so thankful that it is so, and that you and I were friends on earth.

God moves in mysterious ways His Wonders to perform!

So, my dear friend, let me congratulate you, as you are worthy of congratulations.

I will write soon and tell you more of my opinion of this great surprise when I think more of it.

With all my love, I am your old partner and now
Your brother in Christ,
A.G. RIDDLE.

A Confirmation by Ann Rollins. She is Amazed
at the Great Assurances Given to Mr. Padgett.
(ANN ROLLINS)
(July 18th, 1915 | Received by James Padgett)

I AM HERE. *Your grandmother.*

I feel that I must write to you before you stop. I am so amazed at the great assurances that you have received as to your being called to the great work of the Master that I cannot let you retire without telling you what a blessed man you are!

Of course, I knew that the Master had chosen you, and the writings that you have received do not add one bit to my knowledge. But the thing that surprises me is that all these exalted spirits should come, one after another, and declare to you the fact that you have been chosen.

Certainly you cannot doubt in view of what this multitude of witnesses have said. I don't quite understand why so many should have come to give you this assurance, unless it be that they wanted you to start into this great work with a faith that admits of no doubt; and, to ensure that faith they saw to be necessary, they concluded that this great and cumulative testimony should be given to you.

My dear son, I feel that you have been blessed above other men now living, and that the great favor which has been bestowed on you is one that very few mortals have received.

So, I tell you that we all thank God and praise His Goodness for what He has done for you.

You must not think that God had nothing to do with this selection, for He is the Great Father; and Jesus, the great son, consulted Him, as has been told me.

Jesus is, himself, all-powerful and wise and good, but also humble and loving. And he is very close to the Father and seeks His Advice and Guidance, as when on earth.

So, you see that our Master, while supreme in this Kingdom where the redeemed live, still realizes that he needs the Help of his Father. This is true and will be true during all eternity.

(Yes, and compared to him, I am so unworthy!)

Well, you are right. But you must not think of your own unworthiness. So, believe!

(Who do you think might be assigned to help me in this work?)

I think that it will be the most wonderful band of spirits that has ever existed, except that band which watched over and protected Jesus from his birth to his death.

So, my dear son, I must stop now and will say that I am

Your own true and loving grandmother,

ANN ROLLINS.

How Happy Mrs. Padgett Is That Great Spirits Have Confirmed Mr. Padgett's Selection.
(HELEN PADGETT)
(July 18th, 1915 | Received by James Padgett)

I AM HERE. *Helen.*

Oh, my darling Ned, I cannot tell you how happy I am that all these great spirits should have come to you and testified that you are the chosen of the Master.

Of course, I knew it, and you knew it before. But to remove all doubt that you might have, they came and declared the fact in such certain terms!

I know that you will have the power and love of many spirits to sustain you in your work. And to think of the wonderful messages that you will receive—first those of the Master, which will excel all others, and then those of his various apostles and disciples. You will certainly be blessed with wonderful knowledge of the Celestial World.

You must not write more tonight.

(How much power will my spirit band have to help me?)

Well, the power that will be exerted by that band will surpass any power that has been exerted before, and you will have the protection and sustaining power of spirits that will not permit any undesirable spirits or mortals to interfere with your work. I am

Your own true and loving,

HELEN.

Paul Explains His "Thorn in the Flesh" and
His Experience on the Way to Damascus.
(PAUL, THE APOSTLE)
(June 27th, 1915 | Received by James Padgett)

I AM HERE. *Saul of Tarsus, now Paul of near Damascus.*

Well, as you are so longing tonight for love and fellowship with the disciples of the Master, I thought that I would write you just a little to show that all the Master's disciples are in their living spiritual bodies, and that I am alive and will never again die.

I have written many epistles which are contained in the Bible, and some are nearly correct; and, in them, you will find my idea of God and of the Master. I never taught that the Master was God, and neither did I teach the doctrine of the vicarious atonement (or the sufficiency of Jesus' blood to save a sinner from the sins of his earthly deeds). I never taught that any man's sins would be borne, and the penalty for same be paid for, by another. And wherever these doctrines are set forth in my epistles they were not written by me.

(John has told me that God is only a Loving Father.)

I agree with John. God is Love. For this means that God is everything that is Good and Pure and Lovely. Love is the fulfilling of the Law, and Love includes everything.

(In your writings, you refer to having had a "thorn in the flesh." What was this "thorn"?)

Yes, it was my doubt, at times, that I was called to preach the Truth of man's salvation as taught by Jesus; that is, sometimes I doubted that I was called to do such work. For notwithstanding the Bible narrative of my conversion, I was not altogether convinced by the vision that I saw. I know now that it was a true vision and that I was called; but, when on earth, I had doubts at times, and this was my besetting sin.

(That vision you saw on the road to Damascus must have been very bright to have blinded you.)

Well, as to that, I am afraid that I will have to disillusion you, for I was never stricken blind or taken to the house of the prophet of God, as the Bible says.

My vision, though, was plain enough; and I heard the voice upbraiding me, and I believed. But, at times, there would come this doubt that I speak of.

38

Of course, from my epistles, you would never think that I had any doubts. I purposely abstained from making known my doubts, and, instead, called this my "besetting sin." But I thank God that I never let those doubts influence me to prevent me from giving the work my call; for, if I had, I would have undoubtedly relapsed into the persecuting Jew.

As I continued to preach, my faith grew stronger and, after a while, my doubt left me. And, in my latter years, I had no doubt.

(Do you and John live in the same sphere?)

No, I am not in as high a sphere as is John, for I have not that Love that he has. But I am in a very high sphere, and am the governor of the city in which I live. I am probably as much filled with this Love as any of the inhabitants of my city; and, consequently, having been a disciple of the Master, they selected me for their governor.

(Well, is Peter there with you?)

No, Peter is not in the same sphere. He is in a higher one.

(Are all of the Master's original disciples in higher spheres than yours?)

Some are higher and some lower. Andrew is in my sphere, but does not live in my city.

I am glad that you called me tonight, or, rather, that I was attracted by the influence of your love, as I am much interested in the work that you have to do for the Master. You will be able to do this work, and it will be a great revolutionizing one when it is published.

(Would you be so kind as to write again, perhaps enlarging upon your original epistles?)

Well, I will be glad to write you at times, and I will give my present opinion on some of the things I discussed in my epistles.

So, as I have written considerably, I will say good night and stop.

Your friend and brother,

PAUL OF THE BIBLE.

John Corroborates That Jesus Writes Through Mr. Padgett.
(JOHN, THE APOSTLE)
(June 27th, 1915 | Received by James Padgett)

I AM HERE. *John, the Apostle.*

You called for a spirit of love, and I came because I am such a spirit. I am the disciple whom Jesus loved and who loved him more than did any of the others.

(Have you obtained as much of the Father's Love as Jesus now possesses?)

No, and neither has any spirit in all God's Universe. He, Jesus, is the one who loves the Father to a greater degree and has the Father's Love above all others.

(Jesus has come and has written to me as well.)

Yes, I know that he comes to you and tells you the Truths of God, and of his love for you and for all mankind.

I feel that he is anxious to have you receive these Truths and make them known to mankind. And you will have the power to do so, for he is determined that you shall be his disciple, as I was when on earth. And I want to tell you that he loves you very much and is attracted to you beyond his attraction to any other mortal at this time.

You will have a wonderful opportunity to get close to him and to receive the influence of his presence as well as of his love. So, do not fail to do everything in your power to accomplish the task that you have undertaken.

(What are the greatest Truths of the Bible?)

THE FIRST GREAT TRUTH IS: GOD IS LOVE; AND THE SECOND IS: YOU MUST BE BORN AGAIN. THESE ARE THE TWO GREATEST TRUTHS OF THE BIBLE. I CONSIDER THEM GREATER THAN THE COMMANDMENTS TO LOVE GOD AND TO LOVE YOUR NEIGHBOR AS YOURSELF.

(Are you the same St. John of the Bible?)

Yes, I am St. John of the Bible.

(Where do you now live?)

I live in a Celestial Sphere which is far above the Seventh Spiritual Sphere. I am with a number of disciples and others who have an abundance of God's Love in their hearts. My sphere is not numbered, and it needs no number, for it is near the highest. The Master is higher than anyone else in his home.

(Do you live on some kind of great island?)

I do not live on an island, as you say, but my home is in a great city where the redeemed of God live. And I am the leader of this city in the teachings of God's Love and the city's government. I am working for the good of all its inhabitants, as well as for spirits in a lower plane, and sometimes for mortals.

I will come to you again sometime and write to you some of the Truths in my city.

(In your gospel, what exactly did you mean by, "In the beginning was the Word...")

Well, I will explain my meaning when I come again, but will say now that the "Word" which created the universe was not Jesus but God, and He, Alone. This gives you an idea of what I meant.

Well, to conclude for now, I will say that you are very near the Master, and he loves you and I love you also.

So, my young brother, I will say good night.

JOHN.

*The Time Is Now Ripe for the Truths to Be Made Known So
That Mankind Can Be Redeemed from Their False Beliefs.*
(JOHN, THE BAPTIST)
(September 7th, 1915 | Received by James Padgett)

I AM HERE. *John, the Baptist.*

I come because I want to encourage you to pray more and to believe. The Father's Love is waiting to fill your soul to its utmost, and the only things required on your part are prayer and faith.

We are all interested in you, and want you to get into a condition that will enable you to take the Master's messages as rapidly as possible. For the time is now ripe when they should be given to mankind and started on their work of redeeming men from false beliefs and erroneous doctrines and dogmas. I, John, tell you this, for I can see that men are longing for the Truths of God—such Truths as will remove all superstition and errors from the teachings of the spiritually guided, and such Truths as will accord with the reasoning of men who are not biased by erroneous beliefs, either in spiritual or material matters.

I tell you that these Truths will be easier for the mere materialist to receive and understand than for those who are bound by the beliefs which the creeds and dogmas of the churches have inculcated. And the acceptance of this New Revelation of the Truths of God will be by those who have no preconceived ideas of what the nature and relation of man to God is, in the spiritual sense, rather than by the learned theologian and the simple worshipers at the altars of the churches who believe whatever may be told them by the priests and preachers.

AS I WAS, AT ONE TIME, THE VOICE OF ONE CRYING IN THE WILDERNESS, I AM NOW THE VOICE OF MANY SPIRITS OF GOD WHO KNOW THAT THE MASTER WILL TEACH THE TRUTHS OF HIS FATHER, AND THAT THESE TRUTHS MUST BE ACCEPTED BY MORTALS ON EARTH AND BY SPIRITS IN THE SPIRIT WORLD IN ORDER THAT THEY MAY RECEIVE THAT SALVATION WHICH THE FATHER HAS PREPARED FOR THEM, AND WHICH, WHEN ACCEPTED AND REALIZED AND POSSESSED, WILL FIT THEM TO BECOME PARTAKERS OF THE HAPPINESS AND IMMORTALITY WHICH THE FATHER HAS PROMISED THEM.

I have written you in this manner tonight because I want you to realize, more fully and deeply, the important work which the Master has selected you to do, and also the necessity of continuing this work at the earliest possible moment.

(There is now a dispute in some of the churches as to whether you baptized Jesus by complete immersion or by sprinkling water upon his head.)

Well, I have been interested in the great amount of discussion on that point, and how the belief, one way or the other, has caused those calling

41

themselves Christians to form distinct sects. If they only knew, or would know, that it does not make a particle of difference to their souls' salvation whether Jesus was immersed or sprinkled, they would not let bitter feelings arise that frequently do in discussing this matter.

But to settle this dispute to the satisfaction of those who may read the book which you may publish, and who believe in its statements, I will say that, when I baptized Jesus, I went with him into the water and then took the water in my hands and placed it on his head. There was no immersion.

AS THIS WATER WAS MERELY SYMBOLICAL OF THE WASHING AWAY OF SIN AND ERROR, AND DOES NOT ACTUALLY ACCOMPLISH THAT GREAT NECESSITY, IN ORDER FOR MEN TO BECOME ONE WITH GOD, IT DID NOT MAKE ANY DIFFERENCE WHETHER THE RECIPIENT OF BAPTISM WAS IMMERSED OR SPRINKLED.

It is strange that many men who profess to have received the forgiveness of their sins and to have become reconciled to God should let a trifling thing of this kind cause so much strife and bitter disputations.

I will stop now.

Your brother in Christ,
JOHN, THE BAPTIST.

John, the Apostle, Gives Encouragement to Mr. Padgett,
and Tells of the Wonderful Love the Master Has for Him.
(JOHN, THE APOSTLE)
(July 20th, 1915 | Received by James Padgett)

I AM HERE. *John.*

I desire to write a little while and tell you of the wonderful love that the Master has for you in his selection of you to do his work.

So, I say, he loves you not only because you are his choice for doing his work but also because he wants you to become a very spiritual man, having a large soul development, and become fitted to enter his Kingdom, and become one of his near and dear followers and brothers in the Love of the Father.

I do not know of any mortal who has been so blessed in his earth life. Even we, who were called by him when on earth, were not so blessed until we received the Holy Spirit at Pentecost, as you are now doing. You will receive this Great Gift in greater abundance in a short time, and then you will realize what the Gift of the Divine Love means to your soul and to your happiness on earth.

So, you are now my brother and a new apostle of the Master, and I know your work will be greater in extent than was the work of any of us when we were trying to spread his teachings while on earth. I hope that God will Bless you abundantly and keep you free from all sin and error.

I am with you very frequently, trying to help you to obtain the Divine Love of the Father.

(I certainly hope I will be successful.)

Well, you will receive It; and when you do, as you say, all other things will come to you. I mean all things necessary to carry on the work that has been assigned to you.

So, with all my love and blessings, and the assurance that you will soon receive the Love in increased abundance and do this great work with a faith that will not falter, I am

Your brother and friend,
JOHN.

Jesus Discusses the Wonderful Power That May Come to Mr. Padgett if He Will Only Have Sufficient Faith.
(JESUS)
(September 26th, 1915 | Received by James Padgett)

I AM HERE. *Jesus.*

I am glad that you are so much better tonight, and that your thoughts are turned to the highest things of which I so much want to write you.

John has told you truly of the faith which you must seek to obtain, and which you may obtain if you will only pray to the Father with all earnestness and confidence. Elijah's faith is no different and no greater than what you may obtain if you will come close to the Father by prayer, as he did. The Father is as much your Father as He was his, and your mission is a greater one than was his.

I am the Jesus who is the true son of God, and am closer to Him than is any other spirit, and know the extent of His Love and Power to a greater degree than does any other spirit. And I tell you, with the authority that my love and knowledge give me, that you may obtain a faith that will enable you to perform greater wonders than did Elijah.

Trust me implicitly and your faith will grow so strong that your freedom from worries and cares will come to you as the sunlight breaks from behind dark and threatening clouds and bathes the whole landscape in light and beauty.

You must soon, now, resume my message taking, and attune your soul to the influences which I will bring to you.

(But, in my unworthiness, I shall need so much help.)

Well, you will receive help, as I have promised, and you must not doubt me longer. I know that you consider your unworthiness as the great stumbling block to the performance of my work. But if I say that you are worthy, you have no right to say otherwise, or to feel that I am mistaken in choosing you, or that you are being deceived in this communication!

I am Jesus, the chief of the Heavenly World which my Father has given

43

me, and there is none to gainsay or prevent what I do or determine to do. This you must believe, and on that belief guide all your acts.

So, forever hereafter, know that I have chosen you for my disciple of this New Revelation.

But with the acquiring of this faith, also acquire more of the Divine Love of the Father. For this is the Great Power which will develop you into the disciple that I intend you to be.

I HAVE WRITTEN THIS EMPHATIC AND AUTHORITATIVE MESSAGE TO YOU TONIGHT THAT YOU MAY KNOW THAT THERE IS NO UNCERTAINTY THAT I, JESUS, HAVE CHOSEN YOU, AND YOU MUST NOT DOUBT AGAIN THAT YOUR MISSION IS AS I HAVE TOLD YOU!

With all my love and my blessings, I am

Your brother and friend,
JESUS.

Mrs. Padgett Describes the Regal Power and Authority That Jesus Displayed While Writing Through Mr. Padgett.
(HELEN PADGETT)
(September 26th, 1915 | Received by James Padgett)

I AM HERE. *Helen.*

Well, sweetheart, now you must be satisfied beyond all doubt that you are the chosen one of the Master to do his work!

It was Jesus who was writing to you, and never before have I seen him with such a royal and authoritative expression on his face. It must have been just such a look as he had when, before the tomb of Lazarus, he said, "Lazarus come forth!" Power and determination were in his words and stamped on his face, and we who are here never before felt the wonderful authority which he has. Always before were only love and humility and grace. But when he told you what he did, everything seemed to be subordinated to this regal power and authority which he showed forth.

I never before had seen this phase of his attributes, and we all felt that we were standing in the presence of—if not God—then of the mightiest personage in all God's Universe.

I can well imagine that his wrath, should he ever have occasion to show it, would be terrible and withering!

So, my dear, you must no longer doubt or hesitate as to what your work is to be, or as to what great power you will have in back of you in doing his work.

I am simply awe-struck tonight and can write no more now!

So, with all my love, I am

Your own true and loving,
HELEN.

John Affirms That Jesus Showed His Glory, Power, and Authority
While Writing Through Mr. Padgett, and He Speaks of the
Wonderful Blessings and Faith That May Come to Him.
(JOHN, THE APOSTLE)
(September 27th, 1915 | Received by James Padgett)

I AM HERE. *John.*

I am here again so soon because I want to help you believe in what the Master wrote to you as to your mission, and the work that he has chosen you to do.

I know it is difficult for you to believe that the communication actually came from Jesus. But I must tell you that he wrote the message, and that what you received and wrote he actually said. And, in doing so, he was the king as well as the loving savior who heretofore appeared to you as the loving and kindly brother that he is.

You must not doubt that he wrote to you just as you received it, and that he has selected you for his disciple to do this great work of receiving and transmitting the wonderful Truths to mankind which he shall write.

When he selected me as his disciple on earth, I had my doubts as you have yours. And it was only after I came in close personal contact and association with him, and saw the wonderful power that he had as well as the great absorbing love, did my doubts leave me. While you cannot see him as I did, and hear his voice of love and blessings as I did, yet, you will be able to feel his love and realize his presence.

When he told you that you must doubt no longer as to your being selected for this work, he was a magnificent spirit in his aspect of power and authority. And we who saw him, as he told you these things, knew that he was the Jesus who led us through Galilee and performed the wonderful things that he did, and also the great Jesus who gave to us the knowledge and the Way to obtain the powers to heal the sick, and to open the eyes of the blind and raise the apparent dead.

His presence was that of a very god, for he seemed possessed of all power and authority, as well as of love and grace.

The spirits who were present and who had never seen these qualities of his nature displayed before were awe-struck. And like Peter and James and myself on the Mount of Transfiguration, they fell to their faces because of the exceeding brightness of his countenance and the glory of his power which illuminated his whole being.

When he comes into the spheres lower than that in which he lives, as you would say, he leaves behind him this great brightness and glory, and appears only as a beautiful, loving brother spirit. And never before had those spirits who were present when he wrote you seen the wonderful and inspiring appearance which he then showed.

I tell you that you are a very favored mortal! And, when your faith grows, you will realize what a wonderful mission has been given to you to

45

carry out.

Now we are all more interested in you than ever! And continually will you have around you some of the high Celestial spirits to aid and enlighten you in doing this great work. But the greatest of all will be the Master, for he will be with you often.

You must now strive to attain to the fulness of this Divine Love, and the faith which is so necessary. There is no doubt as to your getting It if you will only pray. And I must tell you, here, that you have the prayers of a host of Celestial spirits ascending continually to the Father that this faith may be given to you in its greatest degree. I, John, tell you this because I know; and my knowledge is based on fact!

So, let your prayers go to the Father, and let your trust in the Master and his promises increase until at last you may realize the wonderful blessings that may be yours.

I will not write more tonight, but will say that, very soon, the worries will disappear and you will be in condition to resume the writings.

With my love and blessings, I am
Your brother in Christ,
JOHN.

A.G. Riddle Is in a Condition of Wonderment After Seeing Jesus Showing Such Brightness and Power.
(A. G. RIDDLE)
(September 27th, 1915 | Received by James Padgett)

I AM HERE. *Your old partner.*

I will write only a few lines tonight, as I am in such a condition of wonderment over what took place when Jesus was writing to you last night that I do not feel able to gather my thoughts for extended writing! I want to say that what happened was the greatest revelation to me as to the character, or, rather, the attributes of Jesus that I have seen since I have been in the spirit world.

When he wrote to you in his emphatic and authoritative manner, he became transformed into such a being of light and glory and power that none of us could look upon his countenance. We had to fall upon our faces to hide the brightness of his presence. I tell you it was a wonderful evidence of his greatness and power. Never before had I seen him clothed in such brightness and power. He was always the most beautiful and bright and magnificent of all the spirits, but never before was there displayed in him those appearances which made us think that he must be a very god.

I now know, as never before, that he is the true son of God, and that he is worthy to follow and believe in. What a wonderful spirit he is! All love and power and greatness, and yet all humility. Such a condition of attributes I had no conception could ever exist in the same spirit.

Well, my boy, I cannot say much more now, except that you surprise me more and more because of the great favor and blessings you have had conferred upon you. We are all amazed over it, but, of course, happy over the fact.

You must try your best to do this work, and fulfill the mission for which you have been chosen.

What a wonderful Jesus! I cannot help thinking of him and the greatness of his being. I am so glad that I saw him as he appeared when he wrote because now I have some conception of what the glory and grandeur of the high Celestial Heavens and their inhabitants must be.

I will not write more tonight, for I cannot think of anything just now but of the glory of the Master. I am

Your old partner,
A. G. RIDDLE.

Ann Rollins Also Affirms That Jesus Wrote and Showed His Glory and Power.
(ANN ROLLINS)
(September 27th, 1915 | Received by James Padgett)

I AM HERE. *Your grandmother.*

I am here to tell you of my Master's glory!

Heretofore, we have written you mostly of his love and beauty and humility, but said very little of his grandeur and the glory of his countenance when he permitted these attributes to appear in all their fulness and splendor. And this was reasonable because, until last night, we had never seen this great brightness and glory.

I am in the Celestial Spheres, but he never before displayed the wonders of his love and powers to me or to others in my sphere, and neither to those in the lower spheres. But last night—oh, the glory of it—he came to you to write and, in doing so, when he told you what your mission is, he assumed that authority and power which are his; and there came into his countenance and very being that wonderful glory and brightness which made him a being apart from other spirits!

I have seen the glories of the Celestial Spheres in which I live, and they are so magnificent and wonderful that I have never been able to describe them to you. But they are as a mere shadow to the glory that surrounded and came from the Master when he appeared, as I say. We were spellbound, as you say, and could look upon him but for a moment only. I can well imagine how his three disciples fell upon their faces at the time of the Transfiguration on the Mount.

I cannot describe to you his grandeur and brightness, but your sun would appear as a pale moonbeam in his presence. And how thankful I am that I saw him as he is, for it shows me what must be the wonderful glory

47

and beauty of the sphere in which he lives, and to which I am striving to attain. And, thanks be to God, the Master says I may become a dweller therein if I will only pray and have faith, and let the Divine Love come into my soul in sufficient abundance.

When I think of all the wonderful things that have centered around you in your communications with the spirit world, I simply have to wonder in amazement, and to think why such things should be. The only explanation that I can give is that you are the special object of the Master's desire to have his work on earth carried forth in the way that he has declared.

My dear son, you must not doubt again as to what you shall do in the way of performing the work of the Master. Your call is certain and you must believe, and, believing, do this great task with all your strength and the powers that will be given you. And let me say further, you must make it a work of love.

Pray to the Father for faith and you will get it; and trust in the Master and you will never be forsaken. I cannot write more tonight, as I want to think of the wonderful scene of last night.

Your own true and loving grandmother,

ANN ROLLINS.

Robert G. Ingersoll, a Former Author and Agnostic on Earth,
Was Present When Jesus Wrote and Showed His Glory.
He Confesses That He Is an Agnostic No Longer,
but a Most Repentant Believer Now.
(ROBERT G. INGERSOLL)
(September 27th, 1915 | Received by James Padgett)

I must say a word, for my heart is so filled with regret and remorse, and the recollections of my awful mistakes while on earth, that I must release my soul of its burdens so far as a confession can do it.

(Please identify yourself.)

I am Ingersoll. And I am not the agnostic any longer, but the most repentant believer in all God's spirit world, and one who now knows that Jesus Christ was and is the son of God to the fullest meaning of the word.

Oh, how glad I am that I came to you when I did, and that you caused me to seek the society of your band of beautiful and bright spirits who are filled with the Divine Love of the Father! For if I had not been with them, I would not have witnessed the scene of last night, and would not be a believer today in the Jesus who I now know is the savior of men by his wonderful love and knowledge of the Truth.

Well, my dear friend, such a scene as I witnessed last night was never witnessed on earth except, as I now believe, by the three disciples of the Master at the Transfiguration on the Mount. And then I doubt if the glory was as great as it was last night, or the brightness of the Master so blinding and magnificent!

I had seen the Master a number of times. And while he was the most beautiful and loving of all the spirits to me, and one to whom I was drawn in great affection, yet, I had no conception of the other qualities or attributes of his which he displayed last night.

And what must I think of you: a mere mortal, as are thousands of others on earth, having a soul development to a certain degree, but not to that of any of the spirits in the soul spheres here, as I am informed? And to think that you have been selected for the work of doing the Master's desires on earth and having that selection declared, or, rather, ratified by an occasion that made all the spirits present tremble with awe at the glory and power which were displayed by Jesus Christ who I, on earth, proclaimed to be merely a good man!

I tell you that you are wonderfully favored, not only in being selected to do his work but also in having that selection anointed, as it were, by such evidence of glory and godlike power as were shown last night.

I had no conception of what the Glory of God meant, or what the Power of God could mean. And least of all did I suppose that any spirit in all the spirit world could possibly possess such glory or manifest such power. But Jesus Christ possesses the glory and power to such a degree as to make him almost godlike!

As I said, I was present, and observed him as he wrote to you, and also what he wrote. And as he proceeded to tell you that he had selected you to do his work, he was the beautiful loving Jesus that he always is, and as I have seen him. But as he proceeded and you doubted the possibilities of such things, and even to doubt if Jesus was really writing to you, there came into his countenance a wonderful look of authority and power. And then came the more wonderful brightness that outshone the noonday sun, and glory indescribable, and upon which none of us could look; and we fell prostrate to the earth, as you would say.

Oh, I tell you, the power which emanated from him was beyond all conception! The wondrous authority that appeared in his whole being was not possible of being withstood by either spirits or mortals, and we were filled with awe and admiration.

When he had finished writing, the glory and brightness that I have described left him, and he again appeared the humble, loving, but beautiful Master. And, before leaving us, he gave us his blessings and a great peace that passeth all understanding came to me. I know now that Jesus is my savior, and that the Divine Love of the Father is a real, existing thing; and I am striving to obtain It.

I believe in the New Birth, and am praying for it, and your dear grandmother tells me that I will soon get it.

So, now, I say to you that you can declare to the world that Ingersoll, the agnostic, is no longer an agnostic, but a believer in the Father's Divine Love and in Jesus Christ, His beloved son, who is the Way and the Truth and the Life!

I will not write more tonight. But, when I shall have gotten my thoughts and feelings together, I will write you at large and tell you of what my soul says as to my future destiny.

Well, thanking you for your kindness and for your having such a grandmother, and for such a Jesus, I am

Your friend,

R. G. INGERSOLL.*

Mrs. Padgett Affirms That Jesus Wrote and Showed His Glory, and That He Selected Mr. Padgett to Do the Work in Receiving the Messages.
(HELEN PADGETT)
(December 2nd, 1915 | Received by James Padgett)

I AM HERE. *Helen*

Well, sweetheart, you have had some wonderful messages tonight[†], all confirmatory of the fact that the Master has chosen and confirmed you to do his work.

How thankful I am that this evidence has come to you, for now you cannot doubt. And you will now lay out all your plans to carry out the desires of the Master, and to get in condition to receive his messages.

We must stop now.

But, oh, my dear Ned, to think that you are the object of the Master's choice and his great love!

Love me as I do you. I am

Your own true and loving,

HELEN.

John, the Baptist, Declares that Mr. Padgett Is Now a Disciple of the Master.
(JOHN, THE BAPTIST)
(September 30th, 1915 | Received by James Padgett)

I AM HERE. *John, the Baptist.*

Let not your heart be troubled. Believe in God and in the Master. This

---

* Mr. Padgett's grandmother had previously helped Mr. Ingersoll in his spiritual progress.—Ed.
† The message referred to is titled "Jesus Says Him Mission in Writing These Messages Is His Second Coming on Earth", which can be found in *Angelic Revelations of Divine Truth*, Vol. I, Chapter 1.—Ed.

is as true tonight as it was when spoken by Jesus to his disciples many centuries ago.

You are his disciple now, just as certainly as were they. And while you cannot see him or hear his voice, as they did, yet, the words are just as emphatically spoken tonight as they were to the other disciples.

You do not realize what love and what powerful influences are with you tonight, else you would let your worries flee to the winds and never return.

I merely want to tell you this to let you see that there is another of the Celestial spirits who knows that the Master's promises will be kept.

I am not here because I want to encourage you merely, but because I want to tell you a fact. And fact it is that you will soon be relieved of your worries.

Go to God in prayer and you will find great consolation, as we have all found consolation in our troubles. When on earth, we had a great number who were persecuted, resulting in the death of many of us. But we had faith. And our faith and the love of the Master helped us over many rough places. I merely want to add another confirmation to those who have told you that you will be relieved of these worries.

I will stop and say that I am

Your brother in Christ,

JOHN, THE BAPTIST.

James Confirms That Mr. Padgett Will Soon Get Relief from Worry.
(JAMES, THE APOSTLE)
(October 31st, 1916 | Received by James Padgett)

I AM HERE. *James.*

When you are weakest, then are you strongest, because, then, you rely more on the Power and Help of the Father. Such has been your condition tonight. And I want to tell you that you have received a wonderful amount of the Father's Love, and the love of the Master. This I tell you because I know from what I have actually seen. So, you should not let your worries trouble you so much. Try to think more of the promises of the Master and of the Love of the Father, and you will realize that help is very near you.

We are all here tonight because we are interested in you and want to see you happy, and you should be so. And if you could only know the love that surrounds you, you would cease to worry so much.

The Master has told you that your worries will leave you soon, and you must believe him, for it is true.

I know this, and I can only corroborate what he says. So, you must not continue to let these temporary troubles keep you in such a condition of gloom and despondency.

I will not write more tonight.

Your brother in Christ,

JAMES, THE APOSTLE.

Luke Also Gives His Assurance That Relief Will Soon Come to Mr. Padgett.

(LUKE, THE APOSTLE)

(September 30th, 1915 | Received by James Padgett)

I AM HERE. *Luke.*

I am here, too, and want to assure you that our love is all with you tonight. We are trying to make you feel that you are not forsaken, even though things look very dark and you see very little light. But the light will soon come and, with it, a relief that will make you realize that the Celestial World is with you in love and power.

I see how worried you have been today, and what a condition of helplessness possessed you. But we were with you then, and were trying to help and encourage you with our influence.

I will not write more tonight, but will say I am

Your brother in Christ,

LUKE.

John Encourages Mr. Padgett to Open His Heart to the Love of the Celestials.

(JOHN, THE APOSTLE)

(September 30th, 1915 | Received by James Padgett)

I AM HERE. *John.*

Well, I will say that you are now surrounded by the love and influences of a band of Celestial spirits, all sending to you their best and kindest wishes, as well as their love. I am now trying to make you feel my presence and love; and, if you will open up your heart, you will realize that you are surrounded by love.

We are many and all anxious that you should feel our presence. And you must pray to the Father more and ask for more faith. You will receive it, and will be correspondingly strengthened.

So, let me say before I close that you are the special care of the Master, and his love for you tonight was something wonderful. He seemed to let all his love center on you, and I do not doubt that you felt its influence.

I will stop now and say that you have my love and blessing.

Your brother in Christ,

JOHN.

Barnabas Assures Mr. Padgett That He Will Receive the Father's Help.
(BARNABAS, THE APOSTLE)
(September 30th, 1915 | Received by James Padgett)

I AM HERE. *Barnabas.*

Such are the thoughts of men when troubles arise: I can do nothing of myself, but will go to my Father and seek His Aid; and the thoughts are true and the aid is certain!

You are that man tonight. And you will not be disappointed, for you will find relief from your worries and the help that the Father shall bring to you.

The Master is all love, and you seem to be his favorite on earth. You can rest assured that you will not be forsaken. I tell you this because I know from experience.

I will not write more. I am

Your brother in Christ,

BARNABAS, THE APOSTLE.

John Wesley, Founder of Methodism, Affirms That Jesus Will Attend to Mr. Padgett's Needs.
(JOHN WESLEY)
(September 30th, 1915 | Received by James Padgett)

I AM HERE. *John Wesley.*

When the Master said, "Feed my sheep,"[*] he not only meant that Peter and those to whom he was talking should feed the spiritual natures of those who should believe on him and try to belong to his fold, but he also intended that their material wants should be taken care of. And, tonight, he is saying the same thing. And, as you are his "sheep" of special care and love, he intends that all the things that are necessary for your well being shall be given to you. So, do not doubt at all, but believe that you will be looked after in all your times of need.

He was so loving to you tonight that we were all somewhat astonished at the great love which we saw going to you, and thought how dear you must be to him. I have never seen him take such interest in any particular person before. And when you realize what his love and powers are, you will be more astonished than were we.

I see what your troubles are. And while they may seem mountains high to you, they are merely temporary and will soon pass away. So, believe in

---

[*] John 21:17

53

what the Master told you, and pray to the Father for Love and faith.

I will not write more, but will say God bless you.

Your brother in Christ,

JOHN WESLEY.

John Garner, Former Preacher of England, Also Gives Encouragement to Mr. Padgett.
(JOHN GARNER)
(September 30th, 1915 | Received by James Padgett)

I AM HERE. *John Garner.*

Let the worries go and bury themselves.[*] Turn your thoughts and soul aspirations to God, for these are the eternal things; and those of the world are merely temporary things.

I say this because I know that, if you will only pray to the Father and trust in the Master, you will realize that what I say is the truth, and can be understood and realized by mortals as well as by spirits.

So, my brother, try to look on these worries in that way.

I am with you often, trying to help you and have you feel my influence and love.

I will not write more.

GARNER, THE PREACHER.

Mrs. Padgett Refers to the Many Consolatory Messages Mr. Padgett Received.
(HELEN PADGETT)
(September 30th, 1915 | Received by James Padgett)

I AM HERE. *Helen.*

Well, you have had the most wonderful consolatory messages tonight that I have ever known to be given to any mortal. With what love the Master spoke to you and tried to comfort you! He is a precious savior and you seem so dear to him.

Try to trust him and do as he says.

These others are all Celestial spirits, and are also much interested in you. They want you to get rid of your worries. You are sleepy and must go to bed.

So, with all my love, I will say good night.

---

[*] Mr. Padgett told Dr. Stone that the causes of his worries were removed soon after he received the previous encouraging messages.—Ed.

Your own true and loving,

HELEN.

Jesus Again Showed His Great Glory, and Gave His Love to Mr. Padgett.
(JESUS)
(December 14th, 1915 | Received by James Padgett)

I AM HERE. *Jesus.*

Well, I am so glad that you are so longing for this Love, and I will tell you that the Father loves you with all His Divine Nature, and is helping you to receive this Love into your soul. You will soon receive It in such abundance that you will find yourself happy beyond all conception. And I love you, too, with all my heart and soul, and am very near you and trying to make you feel my presence and influence. Rest assured that I am with you in all my love and tenderness, and that you are the special object of my care and keeping. I wish that you could see me as I write this, for I am filled with so much love for you that, if you could see the Glory of the Father displayed, I know you would never again doubt my love. Oh, my brother, only try to get this Love by prayer and faith in such a way that It will become as real to you as anything which your natural senses show you to exist in the physical world. It is more real than anything in all nature, and you have in you the possibilities of realizing that It is an existing thing and is yours, if you will pray and believe.

I am with you in prayer at night and, with all my love and faith, I ask the Father to bless you and make you a true partaker of His Love and Mercy, and to give you the assurance that you will receive and know that you have them.*

My dear brother, I must stop now. But your longings tonight have been so great and so earnest that I could not stop without telling you as I have. And remember this: that I, Jesus, with all the knowledge and authority that I possess, tell you that the Love of the Father shall be yours. You will become a most happy man and a power on earth in spiritual things, and that which pertains to the Father's Business.

So, believe me and trust the Father, and you will not be forsaken or left alone, but will be surrounded by a host of witnessing angels who know that you are the chosen child of the Father, and the object of His Great Love and Blessings.

I will not write more now, but I will say that I love you as a true brother and friend, and even closer than that. You must believe, and yours will be

---

* Mr. Padgett told Dr. Stone that, when he was praying just before retiring at night, clairvoyantly, he sometimes saw Jesus alongside praying with him.—Ed

the happiness that few on earth possess.

So, with all the great love that is mine, I will say good night and God bless you.

Your friend and brother,

JESUS.

Saleeba Presents Her Comments on the Power and Glory That Jesus Displayed.
(SALEEBA)
(October 1st, 1915 | Received by James Padgett)

I AM HERE. *Saleeba.*[*]

I want to tell you that I was a witness to the wonderful display by Jesus of his great power and glory the other night, and what a wonderful demonstration it was!

In all my long experience in the spiritual spheres, I never saw anything that approached it. No spirit in the highest intellectual sphere could show for a moment the great effulgence of light that Jesus did. So, you see, I now know positively that the Master is the son of God. As I am informed, he has this Divine Love to a degree that no spirit who was then present had any conception of, except probably some of the apostles.

I am now convinced to the depths of my soul that the Divine Love of the Father is a real, existing thing, and that It makes those who possess It beautiful and godlike. Now, I shall strive harder than ever to get It and the great happiness which I now know must be the experience of those who have this Divine Love to a great degree.

I merely wanted to tell you this because, as you know, I am one who had never heard of this Great Love a short time ago.

So, thanking you for your kindness, I am

Your sister in Christ,

SALEEBA.

John Wesley Speaks of the Great Love Jesus Has for Mr. Padgett.
He Also Reveals That Jesus' Glory and Power Were So Wonderful That All Knelt in Awe.
(JOHN WESLEY)
(December 14th, 1915 | Received by James Padgett)

I AM HERE. *John Wesley.*

---

[*] Saleeba, an ancient spirit of the Sixth Sphere, was progressing to the Celestial Spheres at this time.—Ed.

Let me write a word, too, for I was present when the Master bestowed his great love upon you, and prayed the Father to send His Love into your soul—the Divine Love that will make you one with Him. And I must tell you that never before have we seen such love and glory displayed by the Master, as he displayed his love and blessing to you tonight. Oh, I tell you that it was wonderful! We all stood, or rather knelt, in awe, for we could not stand in his presence.

What does all this mean? None of us know, for we have never received such evidence of love from him, and have never seen anyone else receive his love in that way.

We commence to know how you must be a very important man to the Master, and how you must be the special object of his love and care. For he seems to love you with a love that we cannot understand, although we have the Divine Love of the Father in our souls to a very great degree. But, yet, we have never seen such love as he displayed tonight, and we cannot fully comprehend the meaning of it.

Oh, I tell you that you are a blessed man! You have with you not only the love and power of the greatest spirit in all God's Universe, but also the Great Divine Love of the Father!

So, let us think of this wonderful experience before writing more. I will say good night.

Your brother in Christ,

JOHN WESLEY.

Ann Rollins Affirms Jesus' Love for Mr. Padgett. She Describes the Wonderful Experience Witnessed, and Tells How All Were Surprised at the Display of His Glory.
(ANN ROLLINS)
(December 14th, 1915 | Received by James Padgett)

I AM HERE. *Your grandmother.*

While the power of the Master is here, let me write and tell you that you have had a wonderful experience tonight, and so have we who have stood by and seen the Master write to you and bestow his great love upon you.

He was glorious as he told you of the Great Love of the Father that would come to you, and how he would be with you in all his love and blessings, trying to make you happy.

We were all surprised at the great display of his glory, for it was like the great shining light of God's Countenance, of which we have heard but never seen. You certainly are a blessed man and one that must become very happy.

I am not in condition to write more tonight. I can only praise God for the Great Love and Favor that He has bestowed upon you. So, my dear son, believe what I have told you, and know that we all rejoice with you in the great favor which you have from the Master.

So, dear son, good night.

Your own loving grandmother,

ANN ROLLINS.

Mrs. Padgett Affirms That the Great Love of Jesus Was Bestowed on Her Husband, and That She, Too, Was Filled with Awe.
(HELEN PADGETT)
(December 14th, 1915 | Received by James Padgett)

I AM HERE. *Helen.*

Well, my dear Ned, I can scarcely write, as I am so filled with awe over what has happened tonight that my power to write has almost left me.

But, my darling, I must tell you that you are very dear to the Master and a child of the Father's Love to a very great degree.

Never before have I seen such love displayed, and I never expected to see it bestowed especially upon you who are so dear to me.

I must not try to write more tonight, as I am so filled with love and wonder and thankfulness that I can hardly think. So, my own dear Ned, love me with all your heart and soul, and believe that I love you, too. When I think of this night and the great love that was bestowed upon you, my love seems like a mere shadow; but it is all that I have to give you, and I give all that I have.

So, sweetheart, good night.

Your own true and loving,

HELEN.

White Eagle Was Astonished at the Wonderful Glory of the Master. He Confirms That Spirits Were Awed by the Brightness and Magnificence of His Presence.
(WHITE EAGLE)
(October 1st, 1915 | Received by James Padgett)

I AM HERE. *White Eagle.*[*]

I want to say that you are in a very good condition tonight, and that a great spiritual power has been with you and made you stronger in your

_____

[*] White Eagle is a powerful Indian that belonged to Mr. Padgett's spiritual band.—Ed.

physical as well as in your soul condition.

I have not written for a long time and I feel that I must say something. I was present when the Master displayed his glory, and I was so astonished that I could not withstand the glory. It was wonderful! I am now more convinced than ever that Jesus is the true son of the Father.

(Were there other spirits present with you when this occurred?)

Yes, there was a host of spirits present, and many of them not Christians. The effect on them was surprising.

They were awed by the brightness and magnificence of his presence, and I believe that many of them will become Christians.

He is here and wants to be remembered to you. He is with you nearly all the time, watching over and protecting you. He seems to love you so very much. And, since the night of the great transformation, he is proud that you are his charge.

So, you see, we are both glad that we have you for our special care.

I am with you nearly all the time, too, and love you very much.

So, think of me sometimes and love me.

Your own true guide,

WHITE EAGLE.

John Layton Affirms That All That the Spirits Wrote About the Magnificent Power and Glory of the Master Is True. He Also Declares That This Revelation Marks an Epoch in the Spirit World.

(JOHN LAYTON)

(October 1st, 1915 | Received by James Padgett)

I AM HERE. *John Layton.*

I wrote you once before at your office and was interrupted before I could finish.

I merely want to say tonight that all the spirits who have written to you about the magnificent power and glory of the Master is true, and yet not half-told.

The revelation of that night marks an epoch in the spirit world where those who witnessed it live, for it has been told to many spirits in many spheres. And Jesus is now the great center of interest to many spirits who looked upon him before as a mere spirit like themselves.

How wonderful that this display of power should have been made under the circumstances that accompanied it!

Many spirits were present from spheres which are not soul spheres,[*]

---

[*] The spirit spheres referred to here (the Second, Fourth and Sixth Spheres) provide principally for mental and moral advancement, whereas, in contrast, the soul spheres

and in which believers of other religious faiths live.

You will hear much of this night for some time to come. And the results of the great scene will be felt in many places that never before have heard of, or been interested in, the teachings of the Master.

I will not write more. So, good night.

Your brother in Christ,

JOHN LAYTON.

Daniel Webster Affirms That Jesus and Spirits of the Higher Spheres Are Revealing the Great Truths of the Father Through Mr. Padgett.
(DANIEL WEBSTER)
(December 9th, 1915 | Received by James Padgett)

I AM HERE. *Daniel Webster.*

Let me say a word while you are writing, as I am also interested in your great work and in the efforts that are now being made by the spirit powers of the higher spheres to bring the great Truths of the Father to earth, which Jesus shall write to you.

You do not yet appreciate the great importance of this work, or of the Truths that shall be taught. But, as you proceed in your work, you will see what a wonderful thing this great effort of the Master is. I am one who is trying to help forward this movement, and, in doing so, I feel that I am doing the greatest service to mankind that all the Universe of God affords me to do.

I have not so much of the Divine Love of the Father in my soul, but I know that It is the one absolutely necessary thing that men must possess in order to get an entrance into the Kingdom of God, and to obtain the great happiness which the Father has made possible for man to receive.

You certainly have had imposed upon you a work of great responsibility, and one that will call for the exercise of all your physical powers as well as your mental and moral endowments. So, you see, it is a matter that must be received and considered most seriously by you. And you must not let anything interfere with the successful performance of this great and wonderful work.

At this time, and more than at any time since the presence of Jesus on earth in the material body, mankind needs the Truth to be presented to it in such a way that all superstition and blind faith will be eliminated from the minds and consciousness of mortals.

I can hardly realize that the Truth can be presented in this way with the success that the Master says will follow the efforts of those engaged in

---

(the Third, Fifth and Seventh Spheres) provide predominantly for progress in obtaining the Divine Love.—Ed.

60

declaring and spreading these Truths. It is a wonderful opportunity for you to do one of the greatest services to your fellowman. Just think, in the results of the workings of these Truths, they embrace not only man's welfare on earth but also his happiness and immortality in the great eternity.

I could write more tonight, but I will not longer trespass on your time or strength. I hope, though, that I may have the opportunity to come at some future time to disclose some of the knowledge that I have concerning these Truths, and the importance that they are to mankind.

I live in the First Celestial Sphere where Jefferson and Washington are, and many others of the old patriots of revolutionary and later days. I will subscribe myself,

Your obedient servant and brother in Christ,

DAN'L WEBSTER.

A Confirmation by Mark That the Master Is Doing the Great Work for the Redemption of Mankind Through Mr. Padgett.
(MARK OF THE NEW TESTAMENT)
(July 20th, 1915 | Received by James Padgett)

I AM HERE. *Mark of the New Testament.*

I must add my testimony to the others who have preceded me as to the fact that the Master is now doing a great work for the redemption of mankind and that, through you, he is going to transmit his great spiritual Truths to sinful man.

I will not write much tonight, but will say that, in the future, I will communicate my thoughts, which are the creatures of knowledge and experience in the Celestial Spheres of Christ's Kingdom.

Good night, and may God keep you in His Love and Care forevermore.
MARK, the writer of the second Gospel,
originally true as written, but now full of errors.

Lazarus Confirms That Mr. Padgett's Spirit Communicators Are Whom They Represent Themselves to Be, and He Relates That Both Mary and Martha, His Sisters, Are Living Together in the Celestial Heavens.
(LAZARUS)
(September 21st, 1916 | Received by James Padgett)

I AM HERE. *Lazarus.*

I merely want to say that I am the real Lazarus of the Bible story. I am an inhabitant of the Father's Kingdom and am aware of the Truth that exists in that Kingdom and among its inhabitants. And I declare to you that the spirits who have written you the Truths of Celestial and spiritual things are actually whom they represent themselves to be. Jesus, especially, is with you very often and communicates Truths to you from his great storehouse of the knowledge of Truth. He is so much interested in the work to be done and the revelations to be made that he is with you so very often for the purpose not only of revealing these Truths but also of preparing you to receive them. And he is enveloping you in his love and giving to you a development of your soul faculties that will make you qualified to receive these high Truths as no other mortal has ever been qualified. For he knows that you are his best qualified instrument on earth now to do his work and the work of the Father.

From what I say, you must not suppose that you are the best man or the man having the greatest amount of the Divine Love in your soul, for that is not true. Nor are you chosen because of any merits of your own, or because of superior mental endowment. But you have those conditions of attunement with him that enable him and the other spirits to use you in performing this work.

I am not of such exalted position or soul development as are many of the spirits who write to you. Yet, I know the plans of the Master and what I say to you is true.

I was a Jew and an orthodox one until the Master came to me and helped me develop my soul so that I could understand his teachings and become susceptible to the inflowing of the Divine Love.

I will not write more now but, in closing, repeat that you must believe what I have said above, and that you must try to do the Will of the Father and the work that you have been selected to do.

(Can you tell me where your sisters now reside?)

Well, both Mary and Martha are in the Celestial Heavens. And you would naturally suppose that Mary has made the greater progress in her soul development, but that is not true. They both live in the same sphere and have similar development. As you know, they have been in the spirit world for a very long time. And whatever spiritual superiority that Mary may have appeared to have had over Martha does not now exist, for they both have Divine Love to a degree that has caused all sin and thoughts for the material to have become eradicated long years ago.

Your wife says that I must not write more now and, so, I will say good night.

Your brother in Christ,

LAZARUS.

Elizabeth, the Cousin of Jesus' Mother, Mary, Confirms That Mr.
Padgett Has Obtained Much of the Divine Love. She Also Explains
What the "Second Coming" of Jesus Really Means.
(ELIZABETH)
(January 6th, 1918 | Received by James Padgett)

I AM HERE. *Elizabeth.*

Let me say a word, and that is: that you are a very happy man just now, and so you should be; for, as the Master said, you have much of the Love in your soul tonight. You may not fully realize this fact, but the influence and effect of Its presence will manifest themselves, and you will find that wonderful peace coming to you of which the Master has told you.

For a moment, think that there is nothing between you and the Father, and that, as regards your longings and His Love, they are face to face, and no mediator intervenes or can intervene—only the Father's Love and you, alone. Think of this, and you will realize what a wonderful thing your soul is that it can become so in nearness and in Love with the Father.

THIS IS THE ONLY WAY OF BECOMING AT-ONE WITH HIM. EVERYTHING ELSE BESIDES THIS IS INEFFICACIOUS TO BRING ABOUT THE GREAT TRANSFORMATION OF WHICH THE HIGHER SPIRITS HAVE WRITTEN YOU. SO MANY SPIRITS ARE ENGAGED IN THIS GREAT WORK, WHICH IS THE REAL "SECOND COMING" OF JESUS, AND WHICH MEANS THE SECOND COMING OF THE LOVE AND MERCY AND PRIVILEGE OF RECEIVING THE LOVE. AND, WITH YOUR PHYSICAL VISION, IF YOU COULD ONLY SEE THOSE WHO ARE PRESENT FOR A MOMENT, YOU WOULD NEVER DOUBT THE WORK THAT YOU ARE TO DO, OR THE GREAT RESPONSIBILITY THAT RESTS UPON YOU. BUT, AS YOU CANNOT SEE IN THIS WAY, YOU MUST BELIEVE WITHOUT SEEING, AND LET NO DOUBT OF THE FACT ENTER INTO YOUR FAITH.

I thought that I must write this tonight, for we see your condition. And many are here with you praying to the Father for a great bestowal of His Love upon you.

So, consider what has been written to you tonight, and meditate and long for and pray to the Father, and you will be greatly blessed.

With my love, I will say good night,

Your sister in Christ,

ELIZABETH.

(Why did it take you so long to sign your name?)

Well, it has been so long since I heard or used the name that it was a little difficult to recall and formulate it.

Names are of the things that we forget in a short time after being in our Celestial homes, unless there is some special reason for recalling them.

Mrs. Padgett Confirms That Elizabeth Wrote the Preceding Message.
(HELEN PADGETT)
(January 6th, 1918 | Received by James Padgett)

I AM HERE. *Helen.*

Well, dear, I am very happy tonight, and that is because of your condition of soul in the Father's Love. You are nearer the Father than you have ever been, and His Love is now more shed abroad in your heart than ever before. The Master was so glad that you opened up your soul by your longings and meditation tonight.

Many of the holy spirits are here tonight, and are united with you in your prayers to the Father. And the Love was bestowed in great abundance. How blessed you are, and how happy you should be, for you have a realization of the Love in your soul. I know the Master is also pleased that the rapport is now so perfect, and you may expect a long message from him, and many of them. And so do the other spirits rejoice now that they realize that they will be able to write soon. As the Master wrote you, meditate, and long and pray.

(Who was the very last spirit who communicated?)

The spirit who wrote is one that I have never seen here before that I am aware of. She is a most beautiful and radiant spirit, and has her home in the high spheres of the Celestial Heavens. She says her name is Elizabeth. And John tell me that she is the Elizabeth of the Bible, the cousin of Mary who is the mother of Jesus. She is filled with the Love, and seemed so anxious to write to you about the Father's Love and how close you are to Him tonight.

Well, dear, I will not write more now, for it is not best to do so. You are in that condition when you can commune with the Father, and I want you to let your thoughts go to Him with all the longings that your soul is capable of.

We will remain with you as you sit and meditate, and we will unite with you in your prayers.

So, my dear, dear husband, love the Father with all your soul tonight. Good night.

Your own true and loving,

HELEN.

John Emphasizes the Importance of Mr. Padgett Carrying Forth the Work of Receiving and Disseminating the Truths of Salvation.
(JOHN, THE APOSTLE)
(February 11th, 1917 | Received by James Padgett)

I AM HERE. *John, the Apostle.*

I come tonight to tell you that your condition of soul is very much better than it has been for some time. You are more in unison with the Father's Love than you have been for some time, and you realize that this Love is working in your soul and making you happy.

I have been with you a great deal today as you copied the messages, and I saw that you enjoyed the Truths that they contained. The message describing the progress of the soul is one that contains the Truth of how the soul can find the true Way to the Love of the Father and to progress to the Celestial Spheres. It is a very clear and convincing portrayal of the necessary course that every soul must pursue which comes into the spirit world devoid of the Divine Love. There is no other way in which that soul can find its true development. The message is one that will appeal to the honest seeker after salvation, and will bring the happiness which only such an At-onement with the Father can give.

I see also that you have been thinking a great deal about your future on earth in carrying forward the work that you have been selected to do, and I am glad that this work is becoming a matter of such importance and seriousness to you. It is not only important to the world but also to you, and you must realize this when you consider what was told to you a few nights ago: that there is no one else in all the world at this time who is fitted to do the work which you are now doing, and which you must continue to do during the whole time of your stay on earth.

As you progress in this work, and as these Truths come to you and your soul becomes more filled with this Love, you will realize and understand the wonderful importance of the work to a greater degree. And you should now bend all your energies to developing your soul and its perceptions, and to carrying forward this work.

The accomplishing of this work is infinitely of more importance to us than to you, because we realize, as you cannot, what a failure it would be not to have these Truths made known to men, depriving them of opportunities that are so requisite to their future salvation, both on earth and in the spirit world.

So, I say, do not let yourself become discouraged, but believe. You will find that our promises will be fulfilled, the work will go on, and the Truths will be made known to humanity.

I am with you a great deal, trying to develop your spiritual nature; and, by this, I mean your soul. For as this develops, the better will you be able to receive our Truths so that they will be transmitted to the waiting world, and men may readily see and understand the Truths of God and the only Way to His Kingdom of Love and Immortality. Doubts as to the teachings of the churches are now penetrating and permeating the minds of many, and very many of these are only nominal Christians. Their perceptions of God are almost blunted, and they attend worship only because of a kind of feeling of duty and impression that it is right for them to do so. They know

65

nothing of the Divine Love of the Father's Nature and of the Plan for their salvation.

Their prayers and worship are mostly only those which come from the lips or from a kind of blind intellectual belief. Their soul longings do not enter into their prayers; and, as a consequence, their petitions for God's Love and Mercy go no higher than their heads, as has been said.

This condition of men is very injurious to their future welfare and cannot possibly lead them to the Father; and so long as it exists, men can never become in an at-onement with Him. Only the inflowing of this Love can reconcile men with God in the higher and more desirable sense. Of course, they may become in harmony with Him by a purification of their natural love, but that is only the harmony that existed between Him and the first parents before their fall. It is not the harmony which Jesus taught and which was the object of his mission to teach. When he said, "I and my Father are one," he did not refer to the at-onement between the mere image and the Substance, but to the At-onement which gives the very Substance of the Father to the souls of men.

I should like to write more tonight, but you are tired and should not be further drawn upon.

So, I will say good night and stop.

Your brother in Christ,

JOHN.

Jesus Affirms That His Presented Truths are Easily Understood and Do Not Require a Highly Developed Mind.
(JESUS)
(August 3rd, 1917 | Received by James Padgett)

I AM HERE. *Jesus.*

MY TRUTHS ARE PLAIN AND MY TEACHINGS CAN BE UNDERSTOOD BY THE SIMPLE. ANY RELIGION WHICH REQUIRES THE EXERCISE OF THE MENTAL FACULTIES TO AN EXTENT GREATER THAN WHAT IS REQUIRED IN THE ORDINARY AFFAIRS OF LIFE CANNOT BE A TRUE RELIGION, BECAUSE GOD HAS DESIGNED THAT ALL HIS CHILDREN SHALL UNDERSTAND HIS TRUTHS WITHOUT THE NECESSITY OF HAVING A HIGHLY DEVELOPED MIND.

HE THAT RUNS MAY UNDERSTAND MY TEACHINGS, AND IT WILL NOT BE NECESSARY FOR ANY PREACHER OR TEACHER TO EXPLAIN THEM. MY LANGUAGE WILL EXPLAIN ITSELF. SO, LET NOT YOUR MIND BE TROUBLED OVER THE QUESTION AS TO WHETHER ONLY THE MENTALLY DEVELOPED CAN UNDERSTAND WHAT I MAY WRITE. THE TRUTHS ARE FOR ALL.

So, with all my love, I am

Your brother and friend,
JESUS.

Solomon, Former Wise King of the Old Testament, Writes of Mr. James E. Padgett's Selection by Jesus.
(SOLOMON)
(October 1st, 1915 | Received by James Padgett)

I AM HERE. *Solomon.*

I came merely to say that I have listened to your conversation tonight, and was much interested because you have discussed that phase of man's destiny which is most important in all the Economy or Plans of the Father.

Your being chosen to do this work was not a thing of the moment. For a long period of time, the highest spirits of the Celestial Heavens have considered this great question, and the way by which the great Truths of God and the necessary plans for man's salvation could be made known to mortals.

Heretofore, the difficulty has been in finding a man gifted with mediumistic powers who had an unbiased mind and, yet, a knowledge of the soul's requirements to some extent, and who could be used for the purpose of receiving these great Truths and transmitting them to humanity.

Some years ago, as you say, a selection of a man was made to declare these Truths. Much power and spiritual knowledge was given to him, and even that power of leaving the body and visiting the world of spirits that he might see for himself the actual condition of things as they there existed, and to declare to mankind the results of his observations. And he did observe and declare many Truths. But the difficulty in the way of his realizing the pure Truth, and interpreting the things which he saw, was that his mind was too much biased by what he had read and believed from the writings as contained in the Bible. And, hence, his efforts failed to accomplish the great purpose intended by the mission given to him. I am here referring to Emanuel Swedenborg, the seer, as he was called.

This was a great disappointment to these Celestial spirits who had projected such a plan for revealing the Truths to mankind. At the head of these Celestial spirits was Jesus, as he is now. Since that time, the time has never been propitious for a plan of this kind to be attempted again until now.

But, now, instead of having the mortal, through whom this plan is to be worked, leave his body and come to the spirit world, and then relate the results and interpretations of his observations, it has been determined that the Truths shall be declared to the mortal in the words and thoughts of these spirits so that no mistake or wrong interpretations can possibly occur. And, hence, when we saw the possibilities of your becoming a medium with sufficient powers, and a soul capable of development to receive these thoughts and words, it was decided to select you and make you the medium for doing

this great work. Of course, Jesus was the active superior spirit in making the selection, and we all submitted to his judgment.

Such is the decree. And now you will understand why you were selected, and the fact that you have been selected.

I have told you this tonight because I have been selected by the others to do so. And, I, as the wise man of old, tell you from a knowledge founded on fact.

So, both of you realize your missions, and strive with all your might to acquire this great faith and soul development which is absolutely necessary to a successful performance of the work.[*]

We are with you very often trying to incline your thoughts to the higher things, and to fill your souls with their influences which our love for you creates around you.

So, in behalf of all of us who are promoting this great work, I give you our love and blessing.

Your brother in Christ,

SOLOMON, the "Wise" of the Old Testament,
and the more than wise of the followers of Christ.

Mrs. Padgett Affirms That Solomon Wrote Through Mr. Padgett.
(HELEN PADGETT)
(October 1st, 1915 | Received by James Padgett)

I AM HERE. *Helen.*

Well, you have certainly had some wonderful messages tonight.

What Solomon wrote to you is true, for I have heard the Master say the same thing. He has told me that you have been selected because of the reasons Solomon gave. How you must thank the Father for such a favor and blessing!

What a work is yours, and what a responsibility also! But you will not fail, for you will have such help from the Celestial World as will not let you fail.

I will not write more, but will only say that I love you with all my heart.

Your own true and loving,

HELEN.

---

[*] Dr. Leslie R. Stone was present.—Ed.

68

Chapter 2.

The Truths Surrounding the Birth and Life of Jesus of Nazareth.

MESSAGES INCLUDED IN THIS CHAPTER.

Mary, the Mother of Jesus, Declares That Jesus Was the Natural Son of Her Husband, Joseph, and Herself. (MARY, THE MOTHER OF JESUS) 71

John, the Apostle, Affirms That Mary, the Mother of Jesus, Wrote to Mr. Padgett. (JOHN, THE APOSTLE) 72

Saul Also Affirms That Mary, the Mother of Jesus, Wrote to Mr. Padgett. He Adds That Neither Was She a "Virgin" Nor Is She Pleased When Mortals Worship Her. (SAUL OF THE OLD TESTAMENT) 73

Mrs. Padgett Affirms That John, Saul, and Mary, the Mother of Jesus, Wrote to Her Husband. (HELEN PADGETT) 74

John, the Baptist, Declares That Jesus Was the True Messiah and the True Christ, as He So Taught When on Earth. (JOHN, THE BAPTIST) 75

Josephus, the Jewish Historian, Affirms That Jesus Is a True Son of God Who Lived on Earth and Was Crucified. (JOSEPHUS) 76

Josephus Supplies Additional Information Relating to His Previous Message. (JOSEPHUS) 78

Lazarus Declares That He Was Not Dead When He Was Raised by Jesus. He Also Confirms That Jesus Taught the Rebestowal of the Divine Love. (LAZARUS) 78

Judas Explains Why He Betrayed Jesus. (JUDAS ISCARIOT) 79

Jesus Explains His "End of the World" Prophecy, as Recorded in Matthew's Gospel in the New Testament. (JESUS) 80

Mrs. Padgett Encourages Her Husband to Pray More. (HELEN PADGETT) 81

Jesus Reacts to a Speaker's Discourse on: "The Drama of St. Paul." He States That Some Things That Were Said Were True, and Some Were False. (JESUS) 81

Paul Also Comments on the Preacher's Sermon: "The Drama of St. Paul," and Describes Some of His Own Experiences When on Earth. (PAUL, THE APOSTLE) 83

Ann Rollins Tells of Her Experience in Seeking the Divine Love of God, and in Realizing That He Is Her Father. Also, She Describes Jesus' Appearance. (ANN ROLLINS) 85

Jesus Confirms Ann Rollins' Description of His Appearance. (JESUS) 87

2.

The Truths Surrounding the Birth and Life of Jesus of Nazareth.

Mary, the Mother of Jesus, Declares That Jesus Was the Natural Son of Her Husband, Joseph, and Herself.
(MARY, THE MOTHER OF JESUS)
(April 15th, 1916 | Received by James Padgett)

I AM HERE. *Mary, the mother of Jesus.*

I come to you with all the mother's love of one who loved her dear son so much while on earth, and with the love that has been purified by experience and closeness to the blessed Father. I am one who suffered all the heart pangs which the cruel death of my beloved caused me.

I say I come to you with this mother's love, for you are the children of my Father, as I am his child. And you are also the brothers of my dear son who is with you so much, and who is so interested in you and your future.

Let your love for the Father increase, and also your love for the Master, as he is the greatest and dearest friend that you have in all the Celestial or Spiritual Heavens.

I am in the Celestial Heavens, very near the Fountainhead of God's Love, and also near the home of my dear son, but not in the same sphere with him. For no spirit in all the Celestial Heavens has the same, great soul development as he has, or is possessed with the Divine Love to such an extent.

And I want to say just here that I am not in the condition or place that I am because I am his mother, but because of the development of my own soul. Only this great possession of the Divine Love determines our position and condition here.

I am now in such condition that I know that the Love of the Father is the only thing in all the Universe of God that can make a mortal, or spirit either, a partaker of the Divine Nature and an inhabitant of the Kingdom of Heaven.

I will not write more, but will come again and write you of the early life of Jesus, and of his development in the Love as was shown to me while he was a growing child, and after he became a man prior to his public ministry.

(Was Joseph the biological father of Jesus?)
WELL, I SUPPOSE I AM THE ONLY ONE IN ALL THE UNIVERSE OF GOD WHO KNOWS THE FACT WITH REFERENCE TO THAT QUESTION. AND I, AS A SPIRIT OF THE CELESTIAL

SPHERES, KNOWING ONLY TRUTH, SAY TO YOU, AND TO ALL THE WORLD, THAT JOSEPH WAS THE ACTUAL FATHER OF JESUS, AND THAT HE WAS CONCEIVED AND BORN AS ANY OTHER MORTAL WAS CONCEIVED AND BORN. THE HOLY SPIRIT DID NOT BEGET HIM, AND I WAS NEVER INFORMED THAT SUCH A THING WOULD HAPPEN. I WAS KNOWN BY JOSEPH BEFORE THE CONCEPTION OF JESUS, AND BY HIM I WAS MADE PREGNANT WITH THAT BLESSED SON. THIS IS THE TRUTH, AND ALL ACCOUNTS AND STATEMENTS TO THE CONTRARY ARE ERRONEOUS.

I WAS A SIMPLE JEWISH MAIDEN, AND NEVER HAD ANY KNOWLEDGE THAT MY SON WAS TO BE DIFFERENT FROM THE SONS OF OTHER MOTHERS. AND IT WAS NOT UNTIL AFTER THE DEVELOPMENT OF THE DIVINE NATURE OF THE FATHER IN HIM THAT I REALIZED THAT HE WAS SO DIFFERENT FROM THE SONS OF OTHER MOTHERS.

I will not write more tonight.

So, my dear children, believe what I have written, and also know that I love you with a Great Love, and am working with the other Celestial spirits to make your souls the possessors of this Great Love.

With this Love and my blessing, I will say, God be with you now and for all eternity.

Your sister and mother in Christ,

MARY.

John, the Apostle, Affirms That Mary, the Mother of Jesus, Wrote to Mr. Padgett.
(JOHN, THE APOSTLE)

(April 16th, 1916 | Received by James Padgett)

I AM HERE. *John.*

I came tonight to tell you that the Master will not write, as he is not present, but is at work in another part of the universe where he is needed, and where he is doing a work that none of us can do.

(I was expecting the Master to write tonight.)

Well, I know that he had an engagement with you, but he thought it best not to keep it. He sent me here to tell you, for he did not want you to think that he had forgotten you, as he has not. Very soon he will come and continue the messages, and you will not be disappointed.

I will not write more tonight, as you will have a communication from another that will be interesting.

(I have certainly had some wonderful messages already!)

Yes, it was a glorious night! For, as you were told, many of the Celestial spirits were present with their love and helpful influences—and one especially was with you, having a great love for you and your friend. She still has a great mother's love as well as the Divine Love; or, rather, she has this Divine Love which includes this motherly feeling and desire to make you happy as one of her children, although she is your sister rather than your mother. But, still, she feels like the mother of all of Jesus' followers, as she is his mother still; yet she is not his equal in the great soul development.

She really wrote to you. And what she stated is true, notwithstanding the declarations contained in the Bible as to Jesus' conception and birth.

And I must state here again that at no time in his ministry did Jesus claim or have the slightest thought of having been conceived by the Holy Spirit, or that he had any other father than Joseph.

We never looked upon him as God or as a "Son" of God in the peculiar sense in which the orthodox churches teach. And now I know he was not such God, or "Son" of God. He is merely a spirit, as are the rest of us, but the one possessing more Divine Love, and having the greatest knowledge of the Father and of His Personality and Attributes.

So, believe what we have written you on this question, for it is true.

I will stop now and, in doing so, will say God bless you.

Your brother and friend,

JOHN.

Saul Also Affirms That Mary, the Mother of Jesus, Wrote to Mr. Padgett. He Adds That Neither Was She a "Virgin" Nor Is She Pleased When Mortals Worship Her.
(SAUL OF THE OLD TESTAMENT)
(April 15th, 1916 | Received by James Padgett)

I AM HERE. *Saul.*

I want to write just a line, as I see that you have around you so many of the high spirits tonight. I do not intend to say much, but I must tell you that I am in a condition of love that makes me happy, as I see that you are.

I am not so high in my position, or have so much of the soul development as have those who have just written to you. But, yet, I am a spirit who knows the Truth of the Divine Love and is a possessor of the Divine Nature. I want to say to you both: Pray and believe! Let not what others may write or say to the contrary cause you to doubt that the spirit who wrote you was Mary—not the "Virgin" Mary, but Mary, the mother of Jesus. She is a beautiful and pure spirit, and one who is filled with the Father's Love to a wonderful degree.

She also has her mother's nature to an extent that makes her love all the children of God, whether they be good or sinful, and she does pray to the Father for the sons of earth. But she is not pleased when mortals pray to her as someone who should be worshiped. She is only a spirit filled with love. And when they, I mean mortals, look upon her as a mother, she is not displeased. For, as I say, she loves them all. But when they think that, in order to reach the Ear of the Father in seeking for His Love, they have to pray to her to intervene, she is sorely displeased. And if she could do so, she would proclaim the great error and sin to them in believing in her and praying to her as a necessary intermediary between God and themselves.

Someday, mortals will know that the Father hears their prayers, just as He does the prayers of Mary or any other spirit, and that, while she and all other spirits can help them, even by their prayers, yet, God wants the prayers and soul longings of mortals directed to Himself.

I write this to show that some of the orthodox Christians make a great mistake in praying to the "Virgin" Mary, or to any other "saint," instead of to the Father.

I will not write more tonight, but will say that I (as well as the other spirits who are here tonight) love you with the love of a brother who knows the reality of this Divine Love.

Your brother in Christ,
SAUL.

Mrs. Padgett Affirms That John, Saul, and Mary, the Mother of Jesus, Wrote to Her Husband.
(HELEN PADGETT)
(April 15th, 1916 | Received by James Padgett)

I AM HERE. *Your Helen.*

Well, you have had some wonderful messages tonight, and you must believe that they were written by the spirits who professed to have written. I know the spirits, and I tell you—and you know that I would not deceive you—that John and Saul and Mary wrote to you, and what they wrote they know to be true.

How happy I am tonight, for I see that you are happy too, and have felt the influence of the Great Love that has surrounded you this night.

In all our meetings, I never have seen so many of the Celestial spirits as have been present tonight. And if it were not that you are too tired, though you may not realize it, many others would write to you.

But the fact is that you have been in an atmosphere of Love that I believe has rarely come to mortals. This Love is of a nature that can only come from spirits who have received this Divine Nature of the Father. So, you and the doctor must believe what I tell you, and follow the advice that has been given to you, and rely upon the encouraging words that have been written.

John is a very beautiful spirit, and is so greatly developed in his soul perceptions that his knowledge of the Father and the Love that comes from him is astonishing!

I will not detain you longer tonight, for I see that you are tired.

Good night and pleasant dreams.

Your own true and loving,

HELEN.

John, the Baptist, Declares That Jesus Was the True Messiah and the True Christ, as He So Taught When on Earth.
(JOHN, THE BAPTIST)
(April 20th, 1916 | Received by James Padgett)

I AM HERE. *John, the Baptist.*

I have not written for some time, and I come tonight merely to let you know that I have not forgotten you. I am with you quite often, trying to help you with my love and influence.

(Why is it recorded in the Bible that you sent two of your disciples to ask Jesus whether or not he was the promised Messiah, when other of your messages through me have only affirmed your absolute conviction of his true Messiahship?)

Well, that does seem contradictory, but the fact is that I never sent my disciples to ask any such question.[*] I knew at the time of the baptism of Jesus that he was the promised Messiah, and that knowledge never left me or degenerated into a doubt. This passage of the Bible has no foundation in fact, for I never thought it necessary to ask any such question; and, as I have said, I never asked it.

TO ME, JESUS WAS THE REAL CHRIST. I KNEW THAT HE WAS THE TRUE AND ONLY ONE, AND THAT NO OTHER WOULD COME AFTER HIM. FOR WHEN HE BROUGHT TO LIGHT THE FACT THAT GOD HAD BESTOWED UPON MANKIND THE GREAT POSSIBILITY OF OBTAINING THE DIVINE LOVE AND THE DIVINE NATURE, THERE NEVER THEREAFTER AROSE THE NECESSITY FOR THE EXISTENCE OR COMING OF ANOTHER CHRIST. THE GREAT GIFT THAT WAS NECESSARY TO MAKE MAN A BEING DIVINE HAD BEEN BESTOWED, AND BEYOND THAT THERE WAS NOTHING THAT THE FATHER HAD TO BESTOW UPON MANKIND.

I am so sorry that such an untruth should have been written and incorporated into the Bible. It did Jesus an injustice and made me appear

---

[*] John, the Baptist, is responding here to the Biblical quote: "Art thou he that should come, or do we look for another?" (Matt. 11-2,3.)—Ed.

as a contradictory prophet and messenger of his coming. When I said, "I am the voice of one crying in the wilderness, make straight the way of the Lord," I meant that I knew that Jesus was the true Christ, and that forever thereafter would that knowledge be mine. No, I did not send my disciples to ask the question that you referred to.

As I knew then, and as I know now, Jesus was and is the true son of God, and the savior of mankind in the sense that he brought life and immortality to light. I will come soon and write you on some of these Bible declarations.

I will now stop and, in doing so, will say that you have my love and blessings, and the Love of the Father which is the Great Love that makes you a part of the Divine Essence of the Father.

So, my dear brother, good night.

Your brother in Christ,

JOHN, THE BAPTIST.

Josephus, the Jewish Historian, Affirms That Jesus Is a True Son of God Who Lived on Earth and Was Crucified.
(JOSEPHUS)
(August 8th, 1915 | Received by James Padgett)

I AM HERE. *Josephus.*

I am the Jewish historian and now a Christian. You are not a man to be left alone. I mean that I must write some of my knowledge of the things of those ancient days, for I see that you are selected to do a great work, and I want to contribute to the truth of Jesus' life on earth.

HE LIVED JUST BEFORE I WROTE, BUT I HAD HEARD OF HIM MANY TIMES. AND I KNOW THAT HE WAS A REAL, EXISTING BEING. IN MY HISTORY OF THE JEWS, I MENTIONED HIM. AND WHEN THE LEARNED SAY THAT WHAT IS THERE SAID IS INTERPOLATED, THEY SAY WHAT IS NOT TRUE; FOR HE DID LIVE AND TAUGHT IN PALESTINE, AS THE NEW TESTAMENT CLAIMS.

I never met him. But the wonders of his works were circulated all over the country, and caused much agitation on the part of the leaders of the Jews.

I never wrote much about him, because we all looked upon him as a mere agitator and destroyer of our religion. And to such we never gave much notoriety in our writings. But this same Jesus of Nazareth lived as a man, and was crucified by the Romans at the clamor of the Jews. I want to tell you this because it is claimed that he never lived on earth.

I am now a follower of him and believe in his teachings, and have received the New Birth that he taught. I live in the Celestial Heavens where only his followers live. He was the true son of God, and his mission was to show men the Way to God's Love and to declare the rebestowal of the Divine Love. And I tell you that this is the most important Truth in all the heavens, except this: that God is Love. These two constitute the hope of mankind and furnish the means by which man may acquire immortality.

WITHOUT THIS NEW BIRTH, MEN WILL REMAIN MERE MEN, AND WILL NOT PARTAKE OF THE DIVINE LOVE AND THE HOME IN THE CELESTIAL SPHERES. I SAY THIS BECAUSE I KNOW FROM EXPERIENCE WHAT THIS NEW BIRTH MEANS, AND FROM THE OBSERVATION THAT THOSE WHO HAVE NEVER RECEIVED IT CANNOT ENTER THESE SPHERES. SO, MAN MUST BELIEVE THIS GREAT TRUTH.

Many Jews have become believers since becoming inhabitants of the spirit world, but the large majority of the inhabitants of the Celestial Heavens are those whom we call Gentiles. God had no chosen people in the sense that He designed to save any particular nation in preference to all others. He knows no preference. All are His children, and the Great Gift is for all who ask for It in faith.

I must not write more tonight, but with your permission will come again.

(Can you tell me what happened to the emperor, Vespasian?)

Vespasian is a Christian now, but he never was on earth, notwithstanding that it was said that he was. He continued a pagan as long as he lived, but he knew something of the Christian teachings. And after he had been in the spirit world a considerable time, he received the Light and was born again. He is now in the Celestial Heavens and a follower of the Master.

So, you see, many Jews and Gentiles and pagans who rejected the Master and his teachings on earth have had, since becoming spirits, the opportunity of becoming partakers of the Divine Love and followers of the Master, and have embraced it.

(And what of King Herod?)

Well, you may be surprised to know that Herod is also a Christian. But no pen can portray the sufferings he had to undergo. Oh, the long years of repentance and torment and darkness! His experience was a hell indeed. But the Love and Mercy of the Father were even sufficient for his redemption; and, among all the spirits of our Celestial Heavens, none are more humble and meek than is this same Herod. His life, voluntarily assumed, is one of service and devotion to the Master. I think his love for the Master is so great that even he cannot appreciate it!

(Won't you please return sometime and write of some of the Father's Truths?)

I will accept your invitation, with all my love and earnestness, for the work is of the greatest importance and the time is ripe. Oh, what an awakening there will be when the Truths of God, which the Master is communicating through you, shall come to the knowledge and consciousness of mankind!

I am your brother in Christ and a fellow worker, and, so, I will say, with all love and best wishes, good night.

JOSEPHUS.

Josephus Supplies Additional Information
Relating to His Previous Message.
(JOSEPHUS)
(September 20th, 1915 | Received by James Padgett)

I merely want to say that, since I wrote you last, I have made inquiries as to who it was that taught that my book was interpolated in the paragraph where it speaks of Jesus.

These persons are they who do not believe in Jesus as an historical person, and who try to procure evidence to show that he was not. But I tell you that he was, and that he actually lived in Palestine at the time I wrote about him.

I do not think it best for me to write a long letter tonight, but will come again sometime.

Your brother in Christ,

JOSEPHUS.

Lazarus Declares That He Was Not Dead When He Was
Raised by Jesus. He Also Confirms That Jesus
Taught the Rebestowal of the Divine Love.
(LAZARUS)
(August 5th, 1915 | Received by James Padgett)

I AM HERE. *Lazarus.*

I am the one whom Jesus called from the grave. I merely want to say that I was not dead when I was resurrected, but had on me the "sleep of death." But I was not entirely a spirit separated from my body. I know this because, if I had been a wholly separated spirit, Jesus could not have brought me to life again. No spirit, once entirely liberated from the body, can ever return to it and reanimate the body. I know the Bible says, or the inference from what it says is that I was dead; but this is not true, as I have stated above.

I am now in the Celestial Heavens in a sphere that is not numbered, but very near those in which the disciples live. My sisters are also in the Celestial Heavens. We all believed in the teachings of the Master, and consequently became imbued with his doctrine of the necessity for the

Divine Love to come into our souls.

While on earth, Jesus did teach us that God had again bestowed on man this Divine Love, and we believed it. I know that the disciples were taught this same doctrine, but just how far they understood this teaching I do not know. It is strange that they did not declare it in their gospels, but such seems to be the fact; and it is unaccountable why this important Truth was not preserved and taught in their writings. I know that it is the Truth, and that only those who have received this Love in their hearts can become inhabitants of the Celestial Heavens. Men may refuse to believe this great Truth if they will, and think by attending church and worshiping God in their service with their lips they will be able to enter the Kingdom, but they will find themselves mistaken.

So, in your teachings, let this great Truth be the cornerstone of whatever you may teach.

I am supremely happy and want all mankind to be so. And I came to you to inform you of these Truths so that my testimony may be added to that of those who may have written to you.

Jesus is in the spirit world, working to teach men and spirits his Truths. He comes to you and writes. And you must believe the fact, for it is a fact.

I must stop now. So, I will say good night.

LAZARUS.

Judas Explains Why He Betrayed Jesus.
(JUDAS ISCARIOT)
(August 23rd, 1915 | Received by James Padgett)

I AM HERE. *Judas Iscariot.*

I came tonight because I want to tell you of just what my condition and expectations were when I betrayed Jesus, which resulted in his crucifixion.

I was a very enthusiastic lover of the Master, and I believed thoroughly in his teachings and his power; and I did not believe that the Roman soldiers could take him away from where we were, if we did not permit it to be done. As a consequence, I was anxious that Jesus should show his great power, and demonstrate to the Jews that he was a true son of God, with power over men and devils.

I never betrayed him for the money that I received, for it was not sufficient to pay for one moment of happiness which I have lost because of my act in betraying the greatest spirit in all God's Kingdom.

I see that you are too sleepy to write more tonight. I will come again and tell my story.* So, good night. JUDAS.

---

* See Judas' message: "The Greatest Sin Is Against the Holy Spirit That Conveys the Divine Love into the Soul," in volume I of Angelic Revelations of Divine Truth.— Ed.

Jesus Explains His "End of the World" Prophecy, as Recorded
in Matthew's Gospel in the New Testament.
(JESUS)
(May 20th, 1918 | Received by James Padgett)

I AM HERE. *Jesus.*

I would like to write tonight, but you are not just in condition, though much better than you have been. Soon, I anticipate I will be able to deliver my messages again. Take my advice and pray more, and you will find yourself much helped into the condition which is necessary in order that I may make the rapport. I merely write this tonight to let you know that I am with you and waiting to write.

You must not let your faith decrease, but believe with all your soul that we communicate with you and are with you trying to help you in every way. You must do the work and keep up your faith in us.

(Before leaving, will you please explain to me what you meant by the "end of the world" prophecy you gave, as recorded in Matthew's Gospel.)

Well, so far as that prophecy (Matt. 24:3) is concerned, it referred to the fall of Jerusalem. At that time—I mean just prior to, and at the time of, the destruction of Jerusalem—the whole world was in that condition that the prophecy speaks of. I did not know anything about the present condition of the earth, and could not have referred to these times, or to what may now happen among men. The "end of the age," as it should be written, referred to the ending of the Jewish dispensation, and not to the end of the physical world. The world was not to be destroyed at the time the prophecy was to be fulfilled, and no man or spirit now knows when the earth will cease to exist. Only God knows that, and He has never revealed it. But this I do know: that such an event will never take place until He has worked out His Plan for the ending of the world. And, I believe, it will be many centuries yet before such an ending to the earth and the visible world will take place. And I do not know that it ever will have an ending, and no human can foretell the same. So, you need not bother about these things.

Each human will have his ending of the earth life, and that will be, in effect, the end of the world to him. And his duty is to prepare for that ending and what will surely follow. Sometime, I will write you on this subject.

There are many matters yet to be disclosed, and this disclosure waits only for your getting in the proper condition to receive the same. You can see the importance of this, for the end of the world is coming each day to many mortals, which is so important for them to know.

Think more of the spiritual things, and of your work.

Believe that I am with you often, and especially when you pray at night, according to my promise.

Good night.

Your brother and friend, JESUS.

80

Mrs. Padgett Encourages Her Husband to Pray More.
(HELEN PADGETT)
(May 20th, 1918 | Received by James Padgett)

I AM HERE. *Helen.*

Well, dear, I am pleased that the Master wrote to you tonight, for it indicates that you are getting in better condition. You must bend all your efforts to accomplish the objects, the great objects, of your selection, and not let other things interfere, as they have done for some time past. If you will only pray more and turn your thoughts to the spiritual things, you will soon find yourself in the condition which will enable the spirits to make the rapport.

Pray to the Father, and say good night. Your own true and loving,
HELEN.

Jesus Reacts to a Speaker's Discourse on: "The Drama of St. Paul." He States That Some Things That Were Said Were True, and Some Were False.
(JESUS)
(December 5th, 1915 | Received by James Padgett)

I AM HERE. *Jesus.*

I was with you tonight and heard the speaker's discourse on: "The Drama of St. Paul."

Well, it was very interesting and, in some places, impressive; and it should produce a great effect upon the hearers. Many things that the speaker recited were true and occurred substantially as he related them, but some were not matters of actual occurrence. Paul never had all the experiences that he spoke of, but these were of minor importance and did not affect the truth of the narrative as a whole.

Of course, the whole discourse was taken from the Bible; and, as I have told you before, there are many things in the Bible which are not true. His description of Paul's experience on the way to Damascus is partly true and partly not.

(Can you tell me what actually occurred?)

Well, I spoke to him. And when he was felled to the ground by the brightness of the great light that shone about him, Paul heard what I said and answered me. He went into the town, but he was not blind nor did the prophet Ananias do anything to him in the way of curing any physical blindness. He only helped to open the spiritual blindness of Paul, and to show him the Way to the Father's Love and Kingdom.

Paul, as you know, was a very learned man among the Jews, and was a

81

strict believer and follower of the Pharisees' doctrines. But, as to knowing anything about the Divine Love, he had never experienced It, nor did he even know what It was intellectually.

My summons to him was not only for the purpose of stopping the persecution of my people but also for the further purpose of enlisting him in my cause, as not many of my followers were educated or learned men. And I realized that my doctrines and Truths must be preached among not only the learned Jews but also among the Gentile philosophers. And as the first requisite in such cases is to hold and, in a way, convince the intellect, I saw that I must have a disciple who would have the mental qualifications to present my Truths to these learned men in a convincing way, and who would be able to withstand the logic and reasoning of these Gentile philosophers.

John was filled with Love. And wherever he could come in close communion with the common people, by the great power and influence of that Love, he could persuade these people to embrace and receive my Truths, and, as a consequence, feel the inflowing of the Holy Spirit.

But Paul had not this Love to that degree as to be enabled, by virtue of Its power or influence, to convince and compel his hearers to receive my Truths, and to embrace that faith in my teachings as would cause them to seek the Love of the Father. Hence, his mission was the more intended to be the teaching of my Truths to the intellect and mental perceptions of a large number of persons of greater intellectual development than those with whom John and the other disciples would come in contact.

Of course, Paul acquired this Love to a very large degree, but not sufficiently in his early ministry to prevent him from doubting my calling him to do this work at times. And, as he has told you, this doubt was the "besetting sin" or "thorn in the flesh" from which he suffered. Had he had the fulness of the Love that John and some of the others had, he would never have had the doubts of which he speaks.

But, nevertheless, he became a wonderful power in spreading my Truths, in convincing men that the Love of the Father was the one great possession to be obtained, and in causing them to believe in me as the son of the Father and His messenger to declare the great Plan of man's salvation to the world.

Paul finally became a man filled with this Love, as far as his nature was capable of receiving It, and wonderful exhortations to his hearers to seek for It will be found in his gospel. But he was not the disciple of Love, but, rather, of the intellectual parts of my Truths. And, when he taught, his teachings were intended to appeal more to the mental perceptions than to the soul perceptions.

He never taught that I was God, nor did he believe that I was. And whenever it is set forth that what he did say, or what the Bible says, is to be interpreted to mean that I am God, that interpretation is erroneous.

I will not write more on Paul tonight, but will tell you of some things of more importance to mankind. I AM NOW WORKING AS I DID ON

82

EARTH, THOUGH IN A LITTLE DIFFERENT WAY, TO SHOW MEN THE WAY TO GOD'S LOVE AND ETERNAL LIFE, AND TO ASSURE THEM THAT THE GREAT DIVINE LOVE OF THE FATHER IS WAITING FOR THEM TO HAVE IT FLOW INTO THEIR SOULS AND MAKE THEM AT-ONE WITH HIM.

MEN ARE NOW IN A CONDITION THAT CAUSES THEM TO LONG FOR THIS GREAT LOVE, AND THE PEACE AND HAPPINESS WHICH IT BRINGS, WITHOUT REALLY KNOWING WHAT IT IS THAT THEY DESIRE. AND WHEN MY TRUTHS ARE PLACED BEFORE THEM, AND THEY ARE TOLD OF THE WONDERFUL BLESSINGS THAT MAY BE THEIRS BY MERELY SEEKING FOR IT IN EARNEST AND HONEST PRAYER, THEY WILL TURN THEIR THOUGHTS AND LONGINGS TO GOD AND HIS LOVE, AND THEY WILL FIND THE HAPPINESS AND PEACE WHICH THEY SO MUCH REALIZE THE WANT OF.

I have many things to write to you, and I hope that we may soon have the rapport that will enable me to do so.

(Yes, so do I. And I only hope you realize how much I too desire to establish the best rapport possible for your messages.)

Well, I see how you feel, and I am so glad that you do. And I must tell you that the Father's Love is working in your soul, and will result in your becoming my true and earnest disciple. I will be with you in all my power and influence so that nothing will prevent the doing of the great work which I have selected you to do. You must pray to the Father for His Love, and for faith, and they will come to you. For the Father desires to answer and grant such prayers.

And, besides, as I pray to Him and all my followers pray, we will ask the Father to give you this Great Love and faith and power to do the work, and to sustain you through all the years that may be yours on earth; for the work must be done.

You have written long tonight and I think it best that I stop. But, before doing so, let me say again that you are the special object of my care and love. I will be with you in all your worries and conflicts, and will help you to overcome them all and to get in that position that will give you the freedom that is so desirous.

With all my love and blessings, and the Love and Blessings of the Father, I will say good night.

Your brother and friend,

JESUS.

Paul Also Comments on the Preacher's Sermon: "The Drama of St. Paul," and Describes Some of His Own Experiences When on Earth.
(PAUL, THE APOSTLE)
(December 5th, 1915 | Received by James Padgett)

I AM HERE. *Paul.*

Well, my brother, I was with you at the discourse on: "The Drama of St.Paul," and was much interested in the subject matter, and also in the manner in which the speaker delivered his discourse. He was somewhat dramatic himself, and his elocution and intonation of the dialogues between several of the prominent personages in the drama and myself were very effective. But, really, they, the intonations, did not sound very familiar because they possessed too much artificiality to me to correctly represent the real tones of voice and the feeling that possessed these persons and myself on those occasions. But, nevertheless, they were very effective, and I have no doubt that they produced the intended effect on the hearers.

Some of the scenes depicted were very real and some of them were not, for they never occurred.

I well remember my experience on the way to Damascus, and the great change that it caused to my whole existence on earth. The brightness and the voice of Jesus were actualities, but the statement that I went blind is not true. For I was not blind but only affected for the time by the unusual light, and also by the shock that the voice of Jesus caused. As Jesus said, my only blindness was that which covered my spiritual eyes at the time. And, when I went into the town, the only blindness that I recovered from, in a way, was that which had kept my soul in darkness and caused me to persecute the followers of Jesus under the belief that I was doing the work which God had called me to do. So, you see, that while the description of my life after my call was very interesting as a whole, yet, it was not altogether correct.

Jesus has told you what my condition of soul development was, and how I lacked the Love which I possessed afterwards to some degree. And, as he says, I was more of an intellectual Christian in my early ministry than a Christian possessing the Great Divine Love of the Father. Yet, thanks to him, I continued to preach and believed as best I could until, finally, I became a redeemed child of God, filled with His Love.

I knew many things connected with, and taught in, the theology of the Jews, and especially of the Pharisees. I see now that, in my writings, my conceptions of the Truths of God were flavored to a considerable extent by this knowledge which is of the Jewish theology.

While many things that I taught are true, as I now see them, yet, many things that the Bible says I wrote are not true; and I am not surprised that men will not accept them at this time. How I wish that I could review and rewrite the epistles ascribed to me! How many seeming contradictions and unreasonable things would be made plain! But I cannot, except as I may declare the Truth through you as I now see it. And I hope that the opportunities may come that I may do so.

Well, I will not write more tonight, as you have written considerably and others wish to write. I will say good night.

Your brother in Christ,

PAUL.

84

*Ann Rollins Tells of Her Experience in Seeking the Divine Love
of God, and in Realizing That He Is Her Father.
Also, She Describes Jesus' Appearance.*
(ANN ROLLINS)
(May 13th, 1915 | Received by James Padgett)

I AM HERE. *Your grandmother.*

I am happier than I can tell you. I am living in my home of which I told you a few nights ago, and it is a beautiful home beyond the possibility of description.

Tonight, I want to tell you of my experience in seeking the Love of God, and in realizing that He is my Father Who loves me with a Love that knows no shadow of wavering or cessation.

I was not always filled with faith, or believed so implicitly in prayer; but, in my early married life, I received the conviction that, if I would be happy in life and fitted to receive the blessings which the Bible promised to those who should seek the Lord and His Love, I must see the necessity of seeking. And, with all the earnestness of my nature, I commenced seeking for the Father's Love; and, as a result, I found It; and, with It, I felt a great happiness and peace.

You know what my spiritual condition was in my later years on earth, and how my faith was such that, although I was nearly deaf and blind, yet, I was happy and joyful. Well, when I came to the spirit world, I brought that faith and Love with me, and I found that they were just as real here as they had been on earth. Of course, I was mistaken in some of my beliefs, such as my belief that Jesus was God and that his death and blood saved, or could save, me from sin and damnation. But notwithstanding my mistakes in these particulars, my love for the Father was not interfered with, and I continued to live in that love and was happy.

I had not been in the spirit world a great while before spirits of a higher order than myself came to me and told me many wonderful things of the Father's Kingdom, and that my progress to the higher spheres would depend upon my receiving more of this Divine Love in my soul and becoming more at-one with the Father.

The first time I saw Jesus was after I had been in the Third Sphere a short while. When I met him, he impressed me as being the most beautiful and loving spirit that I had ever seen. And when he told me that he was Jesus, I, of course, was somewhat surprised, because I had believed that he was sitting in the heavens on the right hand of God, as I had been taught on earth to believe.

And when he saw my surprise, he looked on me with a wonderful love and said that I must not further believe that he was God, or even a part of Him, or that he was in the high heavens accepting the worship of men, for he was only a spirit as I was, and was still working among mortals as well

85

as spirits to lead them into the Light and the Way to the Father's Love.

At first, I confess, it was difficult for me to believe this, and I had my doubts. But his manner of talking to me, and the wonderful love that he displayed, not only for me but also for all mankind, soon convinced me that he was the true Jesus and not an imposter. And, afterwards, I met many spirits who knew him and had been his followers for many years. They told me that he was the Jesus of the Bible, and I could not do anything else but believe. And, now, after my long years of association with him, and feeling his ministrations of love and the influence of his greatness, I know that he is the true Jesus who, by his teachings and overwhelming love, saves men from their sins by showing them the Way to the Father's Kingdom. So, my dear son, do not doubt what I tell you now in reference to this matter, or what I have already told you.

(Can you give me some idea of the Master's appearance?)

Well, it is somewhat difficult to describe his appearance, but I will try. He is of a commanding figure, as you say on earth. His features are regular, and his eyes are of a deep blue, almost a purple blue, with such depths of love in them that, under its influence, you almost forget to note the color of his eyes. The hair is a beautiful brown, worn long and parted in the middle so that it falls over his shoulders. His nose is straight and somewhat long, with nostrils very refined and showing the artistic elements in his nature. His other features are in keeping with those I have described. He wears a beard quite long. It is very silky and brown like his hair. His manner is grace itself and modesty personified. Yet, in him is the intensity of feeling which can show itself in just indignation when the occasion requires. And, yet, with all the great beauty of his person and the greater Love of his soul showing Itself, he is very humble—more so than any spirit I have ever seen.

I have given you a bare outline of his appearance, but you will never fully realize in your mind's eye just what his appearance is. Only when you come over and meet him will you fully understand the appearance of the most wonderful and beautiful and loving spirit in all God's Universe.

Someday this will happen, and you will not have the doubts that I had. Your heart will go out to him from the first moment of your meeting. My dear son, it is a greater privilege than you can appreciate to be thus prepared to meet your friend and teacher, for he is your friend to a degree that is beyond what I thought he would ever be while you were on earth.

So, you see, my experience was a somewhat exceptional one. And one secret of its being so is that I received very great faith and the Love of my Father while on earth.

While the teachings of many preachers are that the earth is the only place of probation, and that teaching is not correct, yet, if that were believed more, and mankind should prepare their future in view of that belief, many a man, when he becomes a spirit, would avoid experiences that are very unpleasant and which retard his progress in the spirit world. Of course, when the mortal fails to make the preparation, such a belief that the earth is the only place of probation will work him great injury after he becomes a spirit, because such a belief is difficult to get rid of. And, as long as it lasts, the spirit is very apt to believe that his status is fixed forever; and, hence, he will not progress until he accepts the Truth.

So, you see, after all, the only true belief is a belief in the Truth which never changes.

Probation is not confined to the earth life, but is with man and spirits alike. In fact, it never ends. For each preceding condition of a spirit is nothing more than a probationary condition to what follows. But the great probationary condition, undoubtedly, is that which exists for the mortal while on earth. And if that probation is accepted and made the most of, the spirit of man gains an advantage which is beyond my ability to describe.

SOMETIMES, MEN DO NOT ATTEMPT TO TAKE ALL THE ADVANTAGES OF THIS PROBATION ON EARTH, AND THEY COME TO THE SPIRIT WORLD IN ALL THEIR MATERIAL THOUGHTS AND SINS, WITH THEIR SOULS DEAD, AS JESUS SAID. AND, AS SPIRITS IN SUCH CONDITION, THEY FIND THAT THEY HAVE A MORE DIFFICULT TIME TO AWAKEN FROM SUCH CONDITION AND PROGRESS. AND I AM INFORMED THAT SOME SPIRITS HAVE BEEN IN THIS WORLD FOR MANY YEARS AND HAVE NOT YET HAD AN AWAKENING.

SO, YOU MUST SEE THE IMPORTANCE OF TAKING ADVANTAGE OF THE EARTH PROBATION.

Well, dear son, I have written a great deal and must stop now, though I should like to write to you a much longer time.

So, with all my love, I will close and sign myself,

Your loving grandmother,

ANN ROLLINS.

Jesus Confirms Ann Rollins' Description of His Appearance.
(JESUS)
(May 13th, 1915 | Received by James Padgett)

I AM HERE. *Jesus.*

Well, I am ready to write more of my discourses, and I want you to prepare for our writing very soon. I think that tomorrow night will suit for the work. Commence about nine o'clock, and then you can write until we finish it.

(Will I be able to receive more of the Divine Love?)

Yes, very soon the Love will come to you in abundance, and you will realize Its cleansing effect and will also experience a wonderful peace filling your soul. So, tomorrow we will write.

(Was my grandmother's description of your appearance an accurate one?)

She was correct, except that she may have overdrawn her description

87

of my beauty and goodness. But she thinks as she wrote, and you must believe what she said.

(How much do you really love me, Master?)

Well, I love you with all the love of an elder brother who is filled with the Love of the Heavenly Father. This is all that I can say, for it is most comprehensive and leaves nothing to be added.

I will pray with you tonight that the Father's Love may come to you in great abundance. So, with the Love that I mention, and my blessings and the Love and Blessings of the Father, I am

Your true friend and brother,

JESUS.

Chapter 3.

The Truths Surrounding the Birth and Life of Jesus of Nazareth.

MESSAGES INCLUDED IN THIS CHAPTER.

Mrs. Padgett Describes the Method Used to Communicate Her Thoughts Through Mr. Padgett. (HELEN PADGETT) 91

Jesus Introduces the Substance of What the Judgment Is That Comes to All Men After Death. He Also Affirms That Nothing in Existence, or in the Knowledge of Man, Is Comparable to the Bible, Except the Truths That He and the Celestial Spirits Are Writing Through Mr. Padgett. (JESUS) 93

Sir Francis Bacon Comments on an Article Written by James Hyslop on Christianity and Spiritualism, Regarding Laws Operated in Certain Miracles of Jesus. (FRANCIS BACON) 95

Professor Salyards, a Long-Time Friend and Former Teacher of Mr. Padgett, Reveals Some of the Laws of the Spirit World. (PROFESSOR JOSEPH H. SALYARDS) 97

Mrs. Padgett Confirms Professor Salyards' Discourse. (HELEN PADGETT) 103

Professor Salyards Continues His Discourse on Some of the Laws of the Spirit World. (PROFESSOR JOSEPH H. SALYARDS) 103

Elias, Prophet of the Old Testament, Discusses the Law of Compensation, and Emphasizes That God Will Not Alter the Same. (ELIAS – ELIJAH OF THE OLD TESTAMENT) 107

A Friend Explains That God's Laws Are Not Changed, but That When the Divine Love Comes into the Soul, the Lesser Law of Compensation Is Removed from the Scope of Its Working. (ROSS PERRY) 108

King Saul Explains That Many Laws of the Old Testament Came to Him by Tradition. (SAUL OF THE OLD TESTAMENT) 109

Jesus Discuses the Importance of Man Cultivating the Soul

Perceptions. He Stresses That Spiritual Things Cannot Be Perceived by the Material Mind. (JESUS) *110*

3.

Spiritual Laws.

*Mrs. Padgett Describes the Method Used to Communicate
Her Thoughts Through Mr. Padgett.
(HELEN PADGETT)
(December 8th, 1914 | Received by James Padgett)*

I AM HERE. *Helen.*

Let me tell you that you are only making yourself unhappy trying to learn all about the way that I write to you. You cannot do it, as you are not able to see my method, and I cannot fully explain it to you. But I will try to do the best I can.

When you take hold of the pencil, I exercise all my power to move the pencil so that it will write just what I think. But, in order to do that, I have to let my thoughts go through your brain. You do not do the thinking, but merely let the thoughts pass through your brain. And the movement of the pencil is caused by the exercise of your brain in conjunction with my power which I exercise on the pencil. So, you see, you do not originate the thought, but merely convey it to the hand which I guide in accordance with my thought. You do not have anything more to do with what is written than an electric wire has to do with transmitting a message from the party at the end where the message is given.

Let me explain it in another way. When I think a thought, I pass it through your brain to your hand, and my power to move your hand is brought into action, just as, when you think a thought, your power to move your hand is brought into action.

My thoughts are not your thoughts. When I think, your mind catches the thought but does not create the same. So, you must believe that I am doing the writing and not you, for I write some thoughts which you could not write if you tried. How do you like that for assurance?

But, to be serious, you could not write the things that I write without giving much thought to the different subject matters, for some of them are not familiar to you, as you have often said. Dismiss the idea that you are writing the things which emanate from what is sometimes called your subconscious mind, for you have no subconscious mind. And the philosophers who teach such an idea are not acquainted with the laws of the mind. The mind is only the spiritual evidence of thoughts that congregate in the brain, but which really are not a part of the material thing which the "wise men" call the subconscious self or mind. There is no such thing. And when they let their explanations of things which they cannot account for rest on the assertion that the subconscious mind furnishes these thoughts, they are all wrong.

Only the material brain furnishes thoughts which it puts forth from the observation of the senses, or from the faculties which are brought into action when the reason is made the basis of the thoughts. I am not a very good expounder of these things, but I have tried to make it as plain as I could.

(Have you learned all of this by yourself?)

Yes, I am telling you this from my own observation and understanding of these things. When you receive communications from Mr. Riddle, he will be able to explain more fully and more satisfactorily the laws which govern these things, and you must let him write soon.

I am studying the laws of physical and psychical sciences so that I may be able to assist you in your investigation when you come to search for the true relationship between spirits and mortals, and the laws which control these communications.

(Are you also studying the laws pertaining to such things as clairvoyance?)

Yes, my studies include the investigation of the laws governing clairvoyance and inspirational communications. You will have the opportunity sometime to have an experience in each of these phases, and I want to be in condition to assist you to a degree that will help you in arriving at conclusions which will be correct, and which will help others to understand the laws that govern these things.

So, you see, your wife loves you so much that, in order to help you clearly understand these laws, she is willing to attempt to learn those things which once were thought to be (but mistakenly so) only for the comprehension of masculine minds. But, while I will do this, I will not cease to try to learn those things to the fullest which will give me a clearer understanding of those spiritual Truths that lead closer to God and His Love. These latter Truths are absolutely necessary. The others are important, but not necessary in order that a soul may sooner or later reach the knowledge that makes it one with the Father. The Love of God, which passes all purely mental understanding, is the one great thing to soulfully learn of and possess.

My home is now so very beautiful that my happiness is more than I can tell you of.

You also will be happy when you come over. For I am filling my home with such beautiful thoughts and so much love that, when you come, you will wonder how your little wife could possibly have accumulated so much beauty and filled the house with so much love.

(You actually beautify your home by your loving thoughts?)

Yes, as I receive more of God's Love into my soul, my home becomes the more beautiful. However, I do not have to be in my home to be able to have this Love with me. It is with me all the time. And, when I am in my home, the home becomes a reflection of that Love. The home is not beautiful if the Love is not there. So, you see, the home depends upon the existence of the Love for its beauty. My soul is the creator of my home. Without the soul being beautiful, the home could not be beautiful.

When I leave my home to come to you, the home remains the same because, while my soul is with me, and also the Love that makes it beautiful, yet, the home retains the reflection, or, as you might say, the atmosphere of that Love to such a degree that the beauty of the home is not lessened or deteriorated by my temporary absence. So, you see, the home has a permanency, although it depends upon the soul to give it its beauty and loveliness. My home is not yet perfect, but, as I grow in God's Love, then more perfection will come to it. The more Love that I have, the more beautiful the home.

We all are dependent upon the degree of Love in our souls for the appearance of our homes.

Let your endeavor be to get all of this Love that you possibly can; and, if you succeed in getting as much as I have, you will be one with me and our home will be together. If you do not, I will have to wait until you do before we can live together as one. So, do try to get all of God's Love that you can. IF YOU WILL ONLY GIVE YOUR THOUGHTS TO THE SPIRITUAL THINGS, AND LET YOUR SOUL BE OPEN TO THE INFLOWING OF THIS LOVE BY PRAYING WITH ALL YOUR SOUL LONGINGS, YOU CAN PROGRESS JUST AS RAPIDLY AS I DO. SO, LOVE ENOUGH AND WANT TO BE WITH ME ENOUGH TO TRY WITH ALL YOUR HEART TO GET THIS LOVE.

Your own true wife,

HELEN.

Jesus Introduces the Substance of What the Judgment Is That Comes to All Men After Death. He Also Affirms That Nothing in Existence, or in the Knowledge of Man, Is Comparable to the Bible, Except the Truths That He and the Celestial Spirits Are Writing Through Mr. Padgett.
(JESUS)
(February 23rd, 1918 | Received by James Padgett)

I AM HERE. *Jesus.*

I see that you are in good condition tonight, and that I am able to make a rapport with you.

I was with you at the meeting tonight and saw the workings of your mind, and the pity, as it were, that you had for the preacher because of his want of knowledge of what the judgment is that comes to all men after death—a judgment that is certain and exact, but not one pronounced upon man by God, as the preacher proclaimed.

I was trying to impress you in your thoughts. And you felt the influence of my suggestions and realized that you did not fear the judgment, or rather its results, because you know the Way in which the judgment can have no terror for you, or no eternity of condemnation. I wished, as you did, that the preacher might know the Truth and then proclaim it to his hearers, and, in this manner, show them that the judgment is a certainty that cannot be escaped from, and that its sentences are not for an eternity of duration.

He is an earnest man in his beliefs, and teaches just as he believes. The pity is that he does not know the Truth. But, nevertheless, he is doing good to those who hear him. For many of them are caused to think of spiritual things, and of the future as well as of the present, who otherwise might and would neglect these important things that will determine the kind of judgment that they will have to undergo. And I am glad that he is so preaching and doing a work that, in many instances, will lead men to meditate upon their spiritual conditions, and will ultimately lead them to seek for the Love of the Father which they may obtain by their longings, though their beliefs may be erroneous as to how this Love may be obtained.

Men are constituted with a mind and a soul, each having its own perceptions and ability to comprehend the Truth. And sometimes it happens that the perceptions of the soul will enable them to see and reach out for this Love, while they may be wholly blind in their mind perceptions. And even these latter perceptions may be in conflict with the operations of the perceptions of the soul.

UNTIL THE TRUTHS THAT I AND THE OTHER SPIRITS ARE REVEALING TO YOU SHALL BECOME KNOWN TO THE WORLD, THERE WILL BE NOTHING IN EXISTENCE, OR IN THE KNOWLEDGE OF MEN, THAT CAN SUPPLY THE PLACE OF THESE TRUTHS SO MUCH AS THE BELIEFS THAT HAVE BEEN AND ARE BEING TAUGHT BY THE TEACHINGS OF THE BIBLE; FOR IN IT ARE MANY TRUTHS, ESPECIALLY THOSE THAT SHOW MEN THE WAY TO ATTAIN TO MORAL PERFECTION. AND THAT, AS YOU KNOW, WAS ONE OF THE OBJECTS OF MY TEACHINGS WHEN ON EARTH, BUT NOT THE GREAT OBJECT OF MY MISSION. NEVERTHELESS, THE MAN WHO LEARNS AND APPLIES THESE MORAL TRUTHS TO HIS DAILY LIFE AND CONDUCT COMES NEARER TO THE ENJOYMENT OF THAT HARMONY THAT MAN MUST OBTAIN IN ORDER TO GET INTO A UNISON WITH GOD'S LAWS, AND THAT IS NECESSARY TO HIS REGENERATION AND TO HIS BECOMING THE PERFECT MAN. AND, BESIDES, AS HE—I MEAN THE MORTAL—PROGRESSES IN THIS REGENERATION, HE WILL FIND IT EASIER FOR HIM TO LEARN, BY HIS SOUL PERCEPTIONS, THE GREAT TRUTH OF THE TRANSFORMATION OF THE SOUL THROUGH THE NEW BIRTH.

I approve of the efforts of this preacher to bring men to a realization of their relationship to God, even though he has many erroneous beliefs, and says many things that are contrary to the Truth and not in accord with the true relationship of man to God.

I will write to you soon upon this matter of the judgment,[*] and what it means and the variety of its operations.

Tonight, I will not write longer, for I think it best to not draw upon you too much at this renewed conjunction of rapport with your condition.

I have been with you very often of late, and have tried to influence you with my love and suggestions. And I must tell you that you have progressed much in your soul development and nearness to the Father's Love.

Continue to meditate upon these spiritual things and pray to the Father, and you will realize a great increase in the possession of this Love and an improvement in your condition that will enable us to come in closer rapport with you.

(I now want so much to be of service that, if my condition continues to improve, I should like to request that you come even more often to deliver your messages.)

Well, I will do as you suggest. I am pleased that you feel as you say, for we must do the work as rapidly as possible. We have lost much time and will have to work the harder to bring about the completion of our delivery of the Truths. But you need not fear that we will not be successful. Only have faith and pray, and all will be well.

I must stop now. But, before doing so, I must assure you that I am praying with you in your prayers at night and that your prayers will be answered.

Other spirits will now be able to write to you. They have many messages to communicate and all are anxious to do so.

Keep up your courage, and believe in me and what I tell you.

With my love, and the Blessings of the Father, I will say good night.

Your brother and friend,

JESUS.

Sir Francis Bacon Comments on an Article Written by James Hyslop on Christianity and Spiritualism, Regarding Laws Operated in Certain Miracles of Jesus.
(FRANCIS BACON)
(November 20th, 1918 | Received by James Padgett)

I AM HERE. *Francis Bacon.*

I have been with you tonight as you have read, and was somewhat interested in what James Hyslop had to say in his article on Christianity and Spiritualism. Many things that he puts forth are true, and explain very satisfactorily why many of the miracles, so-called, of the Bible, may be

---

[*] See: "Judgment—the Law of Compensation. Forgiveness." In volume I of *Angelic Revelations of Divine Truth.*—Ed.

believed. As he says, they are not different in the nature of their operations, or in the exercise of the law that produced them, from the physical phenomena which are manifesting themselves at this time among the investigators of Spiritualism; and if, today, the same law in its force that was brought into operation by Jesus and the disciples could be called into operation, the same or similar phenomena would be produced. Of course, a great deal depends upon the medium and the amount of rapport that may be created by the communicating, or, rather, operating spirit. For it must be understood that all the supposed miracles were the results of the work of spirits who, by reason of the harmony existing between themselves and the mortals, were able to call into operation the laws which were necessary to produce the results called miracles.

At the present time, there may not be persons who have sufficient development of these psychic powers, which were possessed by Jesus and the others, to produce such phenomena as they produced. But there have been many mortals since his time sufficiently gifted with these powers to cause manifestations very similar to those of the primitive Christian times, especially as regards healing and the like. And, today, much healing is being performed by mortals, and which is attributed to various causes, such as mental healing and faith cures, but which is really due to the exercise of spirit powers by spirits whose duties are to perform that kind of work.

Mortals, of themselves, cannot bring into operation any of these laws, either of mind or soul, but are dependent upon the cooperation of spirits who use some of the properties possessed by these mortals to bring into exercise the laws which only can produce the healing.

And, here, I desire to state that it is not necessary that the mortal be of a highly spiritual development in order that the powers of the spirit world may effect and change the conditions of the material of earth. For the laws which control the material are sufficient, ordinarily, to bring about the healing of the physical or mental diseases of men. Therefore, you will find many mediums, and others not recognized as mediums, having this power of healing.

The healing of the body and the healing of the soul require the workings of different laws. And while spirits, not having very much soul development, may successfully cooperate with mortals in like condition in healing bodily ills, yet, such spirits are impotent to heal the diseased soul, or the purely spiritual condition of men. But spirits who have the power to produce the latter healing may also heal the body. And this you must know: that no spirit who is not what may be called physically whole or sound can cause the healing of a physically diseased mortal. For power of this kind can be possessed by, and proceed from, only those spirits who are perfectly healthy and sound in their material nature. These spirits, while they have cast off the gross, physical material of the mortal, are still material so far as the spirit body and form and the properties which compose the same are concerned.

The material of the universe is not confined to, or entirely comprised of, what mortals may suppose to be the only material—that is, that which may be sensed by their five senses or some of them. What is of itself material is always material, no matter what form it may assume, and whether or not it is visible or invisible to mortals. The larger portion of the material of the universe is in the invisible world, though subject to transformation into the visible and re-transformation into the invisible. And the laws governing and controlling the material are the same, whether that material be visible and knowable to men or not.

This material has its quality of persistence after supposed death or destruction, although the form of its manifestation be changed. And, from this, you will see that he who is known as the materialist, with his supposed want of belief in immortality or the continuity of existence, is in error even as to the material world of which he assumes to have special knowledge. And, being in error as to this, how can he claim to be right when he asserts that the purely spiritual has no possibility of continuity of existence, or, as some understand, of immortality?

Well, I have written enough, and feel that you will pardon my intrusion. But I also feel somewhat justified in writing as I have done.

With best wishes, I am

Your friend,

FRANCIS BACON.

Professor Salyards, a Long-Time Friend and Former Teacher of Mr. Padgett, Reveals Some of the Laws of the Spirit World.
(PROFESSOR JOSEPH H. SALYARDS)
(April 13th, 1915 | Received by James Padgett)

I AM HERE. *Professor Salyards.*

Well, I am here, as I agreed, and will endeavor to write you my thoughts on the subject: "What May Spirits Know About the Laws of the Spirit World After They Have Been in That World for a Short Time."

As you know, I have been here for a comparatively short time. And while my studies have been in the study of these laws to a considerable extent, yet, I find that I have limited knowledge of the same. Much of my information has been gathered from other spirits who have lived here a great many years, and who have devoted their study and investigation to these laws.

Well, I want to say first that no spirit, by the mere fact of having shortly before made his advent to this world, has received any much greater knowledge than he had when on earth.

My knowledge of spiritual laws when on earth was not very extensive. And, when I came into the spirit world, I found that I did not know much more than I did before I came; and such is the experience of every spirit.

But, as I continued to investigate these matters, I discovered that my capacity for learning was greatly increased, and that my mind was more plastic and received this knowledge more easily than when I was a mortal. This is largely due to the fact that the brain—I mean the mortal brain—is, when compared to what you might call the spirit brain, a thing of much inferior quality, and not so capable of learning the cause and effect of phenomena.

I am now undergoing a course of study that I have no doubt will give me wonderful information of these laws so that, ultimately, I may become what you mortals might call a learned man.

The first and, to me, the most important law that I have learned is that man continues to live in the spirit world without his earthly body. This great law, while to you and to many others is well known and is an established fact, yet, to me, was not known, as I had never had any experience in Spiritualism and had never given any study to the subject.

When I arrived in the spirit world, I learned that this law is one of God's Truths, and that it is fixed and will never change; for all will survive the change of so-called "death."

The next great law that I learned is that no man, of his own power, can make his condition or position in the spirit world just what and where he would have it be. This is another fixed Truth, and one which even many spirits do not fully comprehend; for they think, or so express themselves, that all they have to do is to exercise a little will power, and then they can move from certain conditions. But this is not true, for the law controlling this matter never has any exceptions in its operations.

Man or spirit, in a way, can determine what his destiny may be. But when once his destiny is fixed on earth by this great power of will which God has conferred on man, in the spirit world, he can no longer change his condition by the mere exercise of his will, but by the operation of the laws releasing him from memories and recollections which hold him to the condition that his life has placed him in. So, when men think that, by the exercise of their own will, they can release themselves of a condition which they have made for themselves, they are mistaken.

Many spirits here have this idea, and believe that, if they only chose to exercise their vaunted will power, they could relieve themselves of their darkened condition and get into happier conditions. But, strange, they never try this, and the reason is therefore apparent. They could not if they tried, and will not try because they cannot. Yet, they think that, when they get ready, they will only have to exercise this will and the change will follow. No, this law is as fixed as any law of this great Universe of God.

Of course, while man or spirit cannot change his condition by the exercise of his will, yet, in order to secure that change, the will has to be exercised because the help comes from without. And this help from without is absolutely necessary to man, for this is what causes the change; and it will not come to him unless he exercises the will in the way of desiring and asking for it.

So, let not man think that he is his own savior, because he is not. And if the help did not come from without, he would never be saved from the condition which he finds himself in when he enters the spirit world. You hear in your spirit circles, and read in the publications about Spiritualism, that progression is a law of the spirit world. Well, that is true. But it does not mean that a spirit necessarily progresses, either mentally or spiritually, by the mere fact of being in the spirit world, for this is not true. Many spirits who have been here for years are in no better condition than when they first became spirits.

All progression depends upon the help that comes from outside the mind or soul of man. Of course, when this help comes, man has to cooperate; but without this help, there would be nothing with which to cooperate, and no progress could possibly be made. Many of the Spiritualists make this great mistake when they speak or write on this subject. But let them know that, if a man depends upon his own powers, exclusively, he will never progress. And this law does not apply only to the soul's progress, of which you have heard us speak so often, but also to the progress of the mere mind, and also to what might be called the purely moral qualities. My observation and my information from the other spirits that I have mentioned have confirmed the truth of what I have said.

Man, of himself, cannot elevate himself either mentally or morally; and the sooner he learns that fact, the better for him.

Another law of the spirit world is that when a spirit once commences to progress, that progress increases in geometrical progression, as we used to say when teaching on earth.

Just as soon as the light breaks into a man's soul or mind, and he commences to see that there is a way for him to reach higher things and make greater expansion of either his mind or soul, he will find that his desire to progress will increase as that progression continues. And with that desire will come help in such abundance that it will be limited only by the desire of the spirit. His will then becomes a great force in his success in progressing and working in conjunction with the help that calls it into operation. It becomes a wonderful thing of power and irresistible force.

This progression may be illustrated by the history of the snowball as it continues its descent from the top of a hill covered with snow. Not only does its velocity increase but it also continually enlarges its form and body by the outside snow attaching itself to the ball. So with the mind or soul of a spirit as it ascends. It not only becomes more rapid in its flight but also meets this outside help that I speak of, which help attaches itself to the spirit and, as it were, becomes a part of it.

So, you see, the great problem is to make the start. And this principle will apply to mortals as well as to spirits, because, if the start is made on earth, the mere fact of becoming a spirit will not halt, or in any way interfere with, the progress of the soul of that spirit. Of course, this means that a correct start be made. If the start is a false one, or based on things other than the Truth, instead of progress continuing when the man becomes a spirit, there may have to be a retracing of the way and a new start made in order to get on the right road.

And this applies to the progress of the mind as well as to the progress of the soul. The mind of a mortal learns many things which seem to that mind to be the truth, and which in its opinion must lead to progress and greater knowledge. But when the earth life gives place to the spirit life, that mind may find that its bases of knowledge were all wrong, and that to continue in the way that it had been moving would lead to increased error; and, consequently, a new start must be made. Frequently, the retracing of that mind over the course that it had followed, and the elimination of errors that it had embraced, is sometimes more difficult, and takes a longer time to accomplish, than the learning of the Truth does after the mind makes its correct start.

SO, SOMETIMES THE MIND OF GREAT LEARNING, ACCORDING TO THE STANDARD OF EARTHLY LEARNING, IS MORE HARMFUL AND MORE GREATLY RETARDS THE PROGRESS OF THAT MAN IN THE WAYS AND ACQUIREMENTS OF TRUTH THAN DOES THE MIND THAT IS, AS YOU MIGHT SAY, A BLANK—THAT IS, WITHOUT PRECONCEIVED IDEAS OF WHAT THE TRUTH IS ON A PARTICULAR SUBJECT.

This unfortunate experience exists to a greater extent in matters pertaining to religion than to any other matters, because the ideas and convictions which are taught and possessed of these religious matters affect innumerably more mortals than do ideas and convictions in reference to any other matters.

A SPIRIT WHO IS FILLED WITH THE ERRONEOUS BELIEFS THAT MAY HAVE BEEN TAUGHT TO HIM FROM HIS MORTAL CHILDHOOD, AND FOSTERED AND FED UPON BY HIM UNTIL HE BECOMES A SPIRIT, IS THE MOST DIFFICULT TO TEACH AND CONVINCE OF THE TRUTHS PERTAINING TO RELIGIOUS MATTERS OF ALL THE INHABITANTS OF THIS WORLD. IT IS MUCH EASIER TO TEACH THE AGNOSTIC OF THESE TRUTHS, OR EVEN THE INFIDEL, THAN THE HIDE-BOUND BELIEVER IN THE DOGMAS AND CREEDS OF THE CHURCH.

So, I say, let the minds of mortals be opened to the teachings of the Truth. And even if they are convinced that what they believe is the truth, yet, let not that belief stand in the way of them being able to see the Truth when it is actually presented to them.

ANOTHER LAW IS THAT NOT ALL WHO KNOW THAT LIFE IN THE SPIRIT WORLD IS CONTINUOUS ARE CERTAIN THAT CONTINUOUS LIFE MEANS IMMORTALITY. I MEAN BY THIS THAT THE MERE FACT OF LIVING AS A SPIRIT DOES NOT PROVE, OF ITSELF, THAT SUCH SPIRIT IS IMMORTAL.

This is a subject that spirits discuss as much as mortals do, and it is just as much a question of uncertainty as is the immortality of the soul taught among mortals now and for all ages past.

While men know that the death of the body does not mean the death of the spirit, and that such spirit, which is the real man, continues to live with all its qualities of a spiritual nature, yet, there has never been any proof presented to man that that spirit will live for all eternity—or, in other words, that it is immortal.

I say this because I have read the histories and beliefs of most of the civilized, and some not called civilized, nations of the world. And, in all my readings, I was not able to find that it was ever demonstrated that man is immortal. Of course, many pagan and sacred writers taught this, but their statements were all based on belief and nothing more. And, so, I say, immortality has never become demonstrated as a fact to mortals.

In the spirit world, the spirits of not only the lower spheres but also those of the higher intellectual or moral spheres are still debating the question among themselves. I am informed that there are some who lived on earth many centuries ago who have become exceedingly wise and learned in the knowledge of the laws of the universe, and have become so free from the sins and errors of their earth life that they may be called perfect men; yet they do not know that they are immortal. Many of them think that they are just such men or spirits as were those who were represented by the type of Adam and Eve. They know not that they are any less liable to death than were the ones just mentioned. And, hence, immortality is a thing which may or may not exist for spirits as well as for mortals.

I know that many of your Spiritualist friends on earth claim that the mere fact that Spiritualism has demonstrated the continuity of life establishes the fact of immortality.[*] But a few moments consideration will show you the falsity of this reasoning.

Change is the law eternal, both on earth and in the spirit world, and nothing exists as the same for any length of time. And, in the succession of these changes, how can it be said that, in the future, far or near, changes may not come by which the existence of the spirit—the ego of man—may be ended, or that ego might not take some other form, or enter into some other condition, so that it will not be the same ego and spirit which is now living as a demonstration of the continuity of the mortal life?

And, so, many spirits as well as mortals do not know what is necessary to obtain in order to have the certain knowledge of immortality. But many other spirits know that there is an immortality for spirits who choose to seek that immortality in the Way that God, in His Great Wisdom and Providence, has provided. I will not discuss this phase of immortality now, but will at some later time.

There is another law which enables spirits to become pure and free from the consequences and evils of their mortal lives by the mere operation of their natural affections and loves—again becoming perfect like the first

---

[*] See the chapter on "Immortality" in volume I of *Angelic Revelations of Divine Truth.*—Ed.

parents before the fall.

This does not mean that the Law of Compensation does not operate to the fullest, and that it does not demand the last farthing, because such is the exactness in the operation of this law that no spirit is released from its penalties until it has satisfied the law.

As you believe, and as many other mortals believe, a man's punishment for the sins committed by him on earth is inflicted by his conscience and memories. There is no special punishment inflicted by God on any particular man, but the Law of Punishment* operates alike on every man. If the facts that bring that punishment into operation are the same, that punishment will be the same, no matter whether the objects of its infliction be the same or different persons. So, you see, it cannot be escaped on any grounds of special dispensation, so long as the facts which call for its operation exist. And the conscience and memories of the spirit realize these facts.

When a spirit first enters the spirit life, it does not necessarily feel the scourging of these memories. This is the reason that you will so often hear the spirit who has so recently left his mortal life assure his friends or sorrowing relatives, at the public seances, that he is very happy and wouldn't be again in the earth life, and similar assurances. But, after a little while, memory commences to work as the soul is awakened, and then never ceases until the penalties are paid. I don't mean that the spirit is continuously in a condition of torment, necessarily, but substantially that; and relief does not come until these memories cease their awful lashings. Some spirits live here a great number of years before they receive this relief, while others more quickly obtain it.

The greatest cause which operates to relieve these spirits of these memories is love. I now mean the natural love. And this love embraces many qualities, such as remorse and sorrow and the desire to make amends for the injuries done, etc. Until a spirit's love is awakened, none of these feelings come to him. He cannot possibly feel remorse or regret or the desire to atone until love, no matter how slight, comes into his heart. He may not realize just what the cause of these feelings may be, but it is love just the same.

(But how can one rid himself of such painful feelings?)

Well, as these various feelings operate, and he acts in accordance with them, a memory here and there will leave him, never to return; and as these memories, in turn, leave him, the less his sufferings become; and, after awhile, when they have all left him, he becomes free from the law, and it, as to him, becomes extinct. But it must not be understood that this is a work of quick operation, for it may be years—long, weary years of suffering— before he becomes thus free and once more a spirit without sin or these memories. This is the way the great Law of Compensation is satisfied. It cannot be avoided, and eventually includes the development of the natural

---

* Also called the Law of Compensation or Recompense or Regeneration.—Ed.

love in its workings. But all its demands must be met until sin and error are eradicated and the soul is restored to a pure state.

But this gradual release from these penalties does not mean that a spirit is progressing in his journey to the higher and brighter spheres, because, even without this torture and torment, he may still remain stationary as to the development of his higher mental and moral nature. But when he has been relieved of these sufferings, he is then in a condition to start the progression that I have spoken of.

As you are tired, I will continue the balance of my discourse when I write again.

With all my love, I am

Your true friend and professor,

JOSEPH H. SALYARDS.

Mrs. Padgett Confirms Professor Salyards' Discourse.
(HELEN PADGETT)
(April 13th, 1915 | Received by James Padgett)

I AM HERE. *Helen.*

Well, you had quite a discourse from the professor, and a wonderful one it is! I am glad that he wrote to you on the subject, as it clears many doubts that you or your friends may have. He has not finished yet, but he saw you were tired and stopped.

(I think he finds me to be a good channel to express his thoughts.)

Yes, that is what he said, and I am so glad that you realize that he uses your brain as well as your hand. Why, Ned, without your brain, we could not write at all. So, don't think that we merely use your hands, for your brain is the more important of the two.

Your own true and loving,

HELEN.

Professor Salyards Continues His Discourse
on Some of the Laws of the Spirit World.
(PROFESSOR JOSEPH H. SALYARDS)
(May 3rd, 1915 | Received by James Padgett)

I AM HERE. *Professor Salyards.*

(I have especially set some time aside tonight for the rest of your message.)

Yes, and I am very much pleased that you have, and that you are in such good condition to write tonight. Well, I desire to continue my discourse on the laws of the spirit world as known to many spirits.

The next law is that no matter how much knowledge of material things and of purely physical laws a man may have acquired on earth, his knowledge is not sufficient to fit him for the higher things of the spirit life.

Many men think that, because they have this great knowledge of the material universe, they need not attempt to learn the laws which control the operations of spirit life, or the laws which determine the position and development of that part of man commonly known as the soul. This is a very great mistake; and, sooner or later, all human beings will realize the necessity of learning these more important laws of the soul development, and of the spiritual part of man. While on earth, I never attempted to investigate these laws; and, consequently, when I came into the spirit world, I was as a newborn babe in my understanding of these laws. And so will all humans be who have neglected the investigation and study of these laws.

Therefore, I would advise every man to give his best endeavor to the study of these laws, and especially that part of them which deals more particularly with the soul's development and progress towards the greatest happiness. These laws are set forth and declared to a very large extent in the New Testament. And in some parts of the Old are many suggestions as to what a man should do to save his soul from "death." By this I mean the death that comes with neglect to exercise all the qualities of the soul that a man is capable of exercising when in the mortal life. A man may let his faculties of mind "die" by neglecting to feed it on proper mental food; and so with the soul. Of course, the soul never dies, as far as is known, in the sense of absolute destruction and disintegration. But it can get into such a state of inertia or lethargy that, so far as it is a part of the activities of man, it may as well be dead.

I don't mean to say that the mere neglect to exercise these soul faculties will cause a man's soul to remain dead forever, for that is not so. Sooner or later, either in the mortal life or in the spirit life, this soul will have an awakening. But that awakening may be delayed for many years, and even centuries; and, in its highest sense, the soul may never have an awakening. So, let men know the importance of studying and applying these spiritual laws to their own selves while mortals. And, when they come to be spirits, they will find what a great advantage such study and application have proven to be to their progression and happiness.

There is another law of the spirit world that is of vital importance to those in the mortal life, and one which they can learn, and that is that no man can, of himself, save himself from the penalties of the Law of Compensation. I have written about this before, but it is of such vast importance and affects all human beings to such an extent that I feel justified in saying something more on the subject.

THIS LAW OF COMPENSATION IS AS FIXED AS ANY OF GOD'S LAWS. IT CANNOT BE AVOIDED UNDER ANY CONDITION OR CIRCUMSTANCE EXCEPT ONE, AND THAT IS

THE REDEMPTION OF A MAN'S SOUL BY THE LOVE OF THE FATHER ENTERING INTO IT AND MAKING IT AT-ONE WITH HIS OWN, AND LIKE HIS IN ALL THE QUALITIES THAT PARTAKE OF THE DIVINE ESSENCE.

I know that many men do not believe that there can be any forgiveness of sin, because they say it is impossible to make the soul of a man clean in a moment when it has been steeped in everything vile and sinful while living the life of a mortal. Well, this I believe to be true, and I do not think that any of our greatest teachers of these highest Truths attempt to declare the doctrine of instantaneous cleansing of a vile and sinful soul; at least, that is not the doctrine taught by the greatest of all teachers, the man of Nazareth, whom I sometimes see and converse with. And he, I believe, knows more of the laws governing the salvation of men than any other, or all other teachers combined.

His teaching here is that, while a soul is not instantaneously cleansed by receiving a portion of the Divine Love, as we have heretofore explained it to you, yet, the inflowing of such Love into the soul of a man starts him into the way of right thinking, and causes him to realize that his soul is open to the influence of this Divine Love.

So, mortals as well as spirits may receive this awakening of Divine Grace to a very large extent, as soon as they realize that this Love is the only thing that will remove the penalties of this Law of Compensation.

I do not believe that, as soon as the sinner feels this Love coming into his soul, he becomes a saint and at once gets rid of his evil nature, for that can hardly be. Such an instantaneous cleansing would scarcely serve the purpose for which the work of this redemptive Love is intended.

Some persons seem to be able to receive more of this Love in a short time than do others, and, consequently, their complete redemption is more quickly accomplished. But I have experienced the inflowing of this Love and Its effect upon my sinful nature, and upon my recollections of the deeds of my earth life which calls this Law of Compensation into operation, and, to me, there does not seem to be any probability of an instantaneous cleansing of the soul so that a man becomes fitted to live in the Celestial Heavens where the Father's Love exists in all Its purity and completeness. I know it is taught by many preachers, and it is also the dogma of some churches, that the blood of Jesus cleanses from all sin, and that in the twinkling of an eye. But you must not believe this, for it is not true. The blood of Jesus was spilled many centuries ago and has now become a part of other elements of the natural world, and cannot save anyone. And I will go further and say, as Jesus has taught me, that his blood never had any efficacy in saving anyone. He never taught that his blood could do any such thing, or that the shedding of his blood was the means of saving a soul in any sense. He is not now teaching any such doctrine, and he is disappointed that those who lead the masses of mankind should teach any such doctrine, because it takes their attention away from the one and vital principle which is necessary to their salvation, AND THAT IS THE NEW BIRTH. AND

THIS DOES NOT COME TO A MAN BECAUSE THE BLOOD OF JESUS WAS A SACRIFICE TO APPEASE THE "WRATH" AND "REQUIREMENTS" OF THE FATHER, OR BECAUSE OF ANY VICARIOUS SUFFERING OF JESUS, BUT SOLELY BECAUSE THIS NEW BIRTH IS APART FROM ALL THESE DOGMAS, AND MEANS MERELY THE DIVINE LOVE FLOWING INTO A MAN'S SOUL, AND THAT SOUL BECOMING A PART OF THE DIVINE LOVE OF THE FATHER THEREBY.

But to return to this Law of Compensation, no man, by his own exertions, can save himself from the operations of this law. And so long as he has this idea of depending on his own powers, he will have to pay the penalties. Of course, as he pays these penalties, he progresses nearer and nearer to a time and condition when the law will cease to operate upon him, and he will become comparatively happy. But such payment may require long years of suffering and unhappiness.

So, I say, let man know that, for every act and deed, and for not doing what he should have done, he will have to answer the law. I do not mean by this repetition to cause men to think that I delight in showing them that they will have to suffer and live in darkness for an uncertain length of time, for I do not take any pleasure in calling their attention to this great law and the certainty of its operations. Rather, I do this to help men to avoid these sufferings and unhappiness by seeking the Love of the Father while on earth, because, from my observations, I believe that It can be found more easily while in the flesh than after a man becomes a spirit.

Another law of the spirit world is that every human being of one sex has in the earth plane—I mean on earth or in the spirit world—one of the opposite sex who is his soulmate. The importance of this Provision of the Father for the happiness of humans and spirits has never been fully understood by those who have not met and recognized their soulmates with certainty.

I know that, on earth, men have claimed that certain of the opposite sex were their affinities. And with such claims as an excuse, they have done much wrong and sin. But the soulmate is not an affinity which may be suggested by the passions or desires, but is one provided by the Grace and Love of the Father for one soulmate to live with the other through all eternity. Before they took on the form of flesh, they were united. And, in accordance with God's Plan, when they separated and became mortals, they became no less soulmates, although they may not recollect their former unity or relationship while living the mortal life. But, as certain as God lives, at some time after they become spirits, these two soulmates will learn their true relationship to each other and, if nothing insurmountable intervenes, will come together again in true union and happiness.

The mere fact that a certain man and a certain woman are husband and wife on earth does not mean that they will live together as husband and wife through all eternity. If they are soulmates, they may; but if they are not, they will certainly separate after they enter the spirit world. That true

106

relationship cannot be hidden here, and no mere form of relationship of husband and wife will suffice to keep the persons together.

The great Truth of soulmates is one which needs further elucidation, and one which I will try to explain more fully hereafter. But now it is sufficient to say that every man born of woman has his soulmate, either on earth or in the spirit world, and vice versa.

Well, I have written a great deal tonight and you are tired, and so am I. And, so, I will continue the rest of my discourse another time.

With all my love and best wishes for your happiness and success, I am Your old professor and friend,

JOSEPH H. SALYARDS.

Elias, Prophet of the Old Testament, Discusses the Law of Compensation, and Emphasizes That God Will Not Alter the Same.
(ELIAS – ELIJAH OF THE OLD TESTAMENT)
(May 5th, 1917 | Received by James Padgett)

I AM HERE. *Elias.*

I will write a short message tonight, as it is late and you are tired.

Well, I desire to say that the message that you received from the Master contains some of the most important Truths affecting the relationship of God to man in his worldly or material living.

Every truth that man has uttered has in it an element which shows that man must, to a certain extent, expect and know that God will not interfere with the Law of Compensation as to its effects and results. Only will He help man to remove the causes that so certainly entail the results. And the sooner men know this and more thoroughly understand it, the sooner will they become able to avoid the consequences of sin and the violation of law, and also understand that no prayer will cause God to respond where a suspension or setting aside of His Laws or their workings is necessary.

HE WILL RESPOND TO PRAYER, WHERE THAT PRAYER ASKS THE REMOVAL OF THE CAUSES, BUT NEVER WHEN IT APPLIES ONLY TO EFFECTS.

This Truth men should learn. And, in their prayers, they should ask for those things which, in compliance with the Law of Compensation, bring about results that are harmful to them to be removed, or eliminated from their acts and deeds as well as from their desires.

I could write a long message on this subject but will not do so now, as you are not just in condition to receive it.

So, with my love, I will say good night.
Your brother in Christ,

ELIAS.

*A Friend Explains That God's Laws Are Not Changed, but That
When the Divine Love Comes into the Soul, the Lesser
Law of Compensation Is Removed from the Scope
of Its Working.*
(ROSS PERRY)
(April 27th, 1918 | Received by James Padgett)

I AM HERE. *Your friend, Ross Perry.*

Let me write a line, for I am very desirous of again communicating to you the fact that I am progressing and have found the Love of which you first told me, and which information led to my seeking It.

I know that you are very much interested in the higher messages and want to give your time to receiving them, and that it is almost impudence for me to intrude. But I have asked your wife it if will interfere with any of these messages tonight by my writing, and she informed me that it would not, as none of these messages would be written tonight. So, I feel somewhat at liberty to write, and I hope that you will consider that I am not intruding.

Well, since I last wrote to you, I have prayed to the Father for an increase of His Love with all the longings of my soul, and realize that It has come into my soul in greater abundance; and I am correspondingly happy. I shall soon be in the Third Sphere, so the spirit friends who have been so kind and loving to me tell me, and it gives me much happiness to know that such a prospect is opened up to me. For, because of the progress that I have already made, I can realize, to some extent, what a home in that sphere will mean to me.

I would like to write you a long letter tonight, but I must not detain you. But this I want you to remember: that I am very happy now, and my sufferings have left me. And I know that all these blessings came to me because of the workings of the Divine Love in my soul. It is wonderful what that Love can accomplish in the way of rescuing a sinful soul from its surroundings of darkness and from suffering.

The Law of Compensation, which is a great Truth, does its work without hesitation or partiality, and without interference by any god or angel in the way of commanding it to cease its work. But this Great Divine Love is now more powerful than this law. And when It enters into the soul of a man or spirit, in effect, It says to this law: "You shall no longer operate on the soul of this sinner that was, because I will take that soul away from, and outside the operations of, this law." How little men understand this working of the Love. It does not set aside the law, but It merely removes the soul, in which It has found lodgment, from the scope of the operations of that law. The law goes on, but the objects of its operations are rescued from the same. No law is set aside that men think and argue is necessary in order for a soul to be saved from its penalties. When on earth, I believed

108

this, too, and did not believe in or accept the doctrine of the special interposition of Divine Providence to succor men from the consequence of their sins. I did not believe that because I thought that the only way in which this could be accomplished was for God to say to the law: "You shall cease to operate." But now I know that, while the law never ceases to operate until the penalties that are called for are paid, yet, this Divine Love is above the law, though not antagonistic to it.

I wish that I might write more on this subject tonight, as, to me, it is one of the most wonderful Truths in God's Universe of spirit. And I never cease to meditate upon it and thank the Father that I was made a real example of the power of this Divine Love.

Well, I must stop now. But, when you have the time, I should like to come and write at more length.

Well, friend, good night.

Your friend,

ROSS PERRY

King Saul Explains That Many Laws of the Old Testament Came to Him by Tradition.
(SAUL OF THE OLD TESTAMENT)
(April 7th, 1916 | Received by James Padgett)

I AM HERE. *Saul.*

I very much desire to write a short message tonight, as I promised you a short time ago.

I will not detain you very long, and will try to make my message as succinct as possible.

I know that many men look upon me, as depicted in the Old Testament, as having been a great sinner and violator of God's Laws. Well, that is largely true, for I did not let God's Will control me as I should have done; and, consequently, I became in discord with His Will and did many things that were contrary to His Laws. Of course, my knowledge of these laws was limited to the teachings of Moses and the prophets, as they were given to me by tradition and word of mouth.

The books which are part of the Old Testament were not written in my time, and many of these laws came to me by tradition. The Old Testament contains many sayings which were written long after the times that they purport to have occurred. And many things declared therein never had any existence, except in the minds of men who, at much later periods, conceived that it might be wise to write these things. Many alleged incidents connected with my life never had an existence, and were merely the fictions by subsequent writers. We had very few writings in the shape of manuscripts in my time, and men depended upon tradition and memory.

The history of my life and doings was not written at the time it purports to have been written. I was a real person and a king, and some records of me and my people were actually written; but they were very few. And, as time went by, the imagination and ingenuity added to them in the way of tradition; and then those books relating to me, as they are now contained in the Bible, were compiled from some of these writings and from tradition.

The story of my experience with the witch of Endor, as she is called, was not written at the time; but it is a fact that I had visited her and had an experience somewhat similar to that related in the Bible. At the time of my visit, I had with me some of my followers, and they saw and heard what took place. And, after my death, they repeated and described what had taken place to my countrymen, and also to the followers of David. And some parts of this occurrence became inscribed on the materials which we used to preserve some of the occurrences of those times. But there was not kept any accurate history of the scene. The people of those days had retentive memories, and, for long years afterwards, this incident of my life was handed down from generation to generation; and some parts thereof were written by some scribes, and other parts by other scribes.

I merely write you this to show that you need not give credit to the supposed truths of many sayings of the Old Testament, for many of these accounts had no existence.

I know that what I have written is not of much importance, but, while you are receiving these Truths, you might as well learn something of what was true in my life.

I will not write more tonight. So, thanking you, I will say good night.

Your brother in Christ,

SAUL.

Jesus Discuses the Importance of Man Cultivating the Soul Perceptions. He Stresses That Spiritual Things Cannot Be Perceived by the Material Mind.
(JESUS)
(October 25th,1915 | Received by James Padgett)

I AM HERE. *Jesus.*

I have heard your discussion and am much pleased that you and your friend are progressing so rapidly in the knowledge of Truth. Very soon, you both will be surprised at the extent of knowledge of spiritual things and Truths that will come to you.

No man who is given to only what you may call the material things on earth will be able to understand the spiritual laws, when he becomes a spirit, until he has gotten rid of the material mind and the reasoning that comes from the powers which have been exercised only in the investigation of material things.

You cannot perceive spiritual things with the material mind. Neither can a man, by reason of those powers of the mind which know only material things, perceive the Truths of the spirit. Hence, there is the necessity for man cultivating the soul perceptions, which are greater and more comprehending than all the faculties of the material mind.

Mind, as usually understood by man, is undoubtedly a wonderful instrument in investigating and learning the laws of nature and the relation of cause and effect in the physical world. But such powers, when applied to the things of the spirit, will not help much. Rather, they will retard the progress of the soul's development of its faculties.

The reasoning power given to man is the highest quality of the material mind, and, when properly exercised, affords a very safe and satisfactory method of arriving at the truth. But such power, when exercised in reference to things which are strangers to it, or with which such powers have no acquaintance, or have never been concerned with the investigation of the phenomena of their existence, cannot be depended upon to bring conclusions that will assure men of truth.

Laws are eternal and never change, and are made by the Great Father to be applied to all the conditions and to all the relationships of the material world and of the spiritual world. But the laws that apply to the operations of the material world are not fitted to apply to the operations of the spiritual world. And the man who understands the former, and their application to material things, is not able to apply the laws applicable to the spiritual world and to spiritual things. A knowledge of the laws pertaining to the natural will not supply a knowledge of the laws pertaining to the spiritual.

Hence, the great scientist who was able on earth to discover and show the operation of the laws controlling material things, when he comes to the spiritual world and attempts to apply this knowledge to the things of the spirit, he will be wholly unable to do so. He will be as a babe in his ability to understand and draw deductions from the spiritual laws. So, you see the necessity for man's becoming acquainted with these spiritual laws if he expects to progress in things to which they apply.

The material laws may be learned from by the operations of the senses that belong to, and constitute, the material mind. But the spiritual laws can only be learned by the exercise and application of the faculties of the soul. The soul is to the spiritual things of God what the mind is to the material things of God. And the great mistake that men make and have made is to attempt to learn these spiritual things with the powers of the material mind.

I write thus because I see that you and your friend desire to learn the nature and operations and workings of the spiritual things; and, hence, I want to impress upon you the necessity for exercising the soul perceptions which will come to you as your soul develops. These perceptions are just as real as are the five senses of the natural mind, though most men do not even know of their existence. And when once you have succeeded in understanding that they do exist and that you may be able to use them, just as you use the faculties of the material mind, you will be able to progress in the development of these faculties or perceptions with as much success and certainty as does the great scientist or philosopher in the studies of the things to which he applies the faculties of his material mind.

I will not write more tonight, but will say: Let your faith increase and pray more to the Father, and you will see a wonderful vista of knowledge open up to you of the Truths of the spirit.

Your friend and brother,

JESUS.

Chapter 4.

The True Nature of God,
the Heavenly Father.

MESSAGES INCLUDED IN THIS CHAPTER.

Jesus Describes God and His Personality, and Corrects a Preacher's Misconceptions on This Subject. (JESUS) 115

Jesus Comments on Another Preacher's Erroneous Conceptions of God. (JESUS)..117

A Celestial Spirit Adds His Disapproval of the Preacher's Discourse. (THOMAS B. MUNROE) 118

Mrs. Padgett Also Reacts to the Preacher's Misconceptions. (HELEN PADGETT)...118

What Is the Meaning of the Divine Nature Which the Soul of Man Partakes of upon the Transformation of That Soul by the Inflowing and Possession of the Divine Love? (STEPHEN, THE APOSTLE)......119

Mrs. Padgett Affirms That Stephen Wrote on the Meaning of the Divine Nature. (HELEN PADGETT)...121

Saul Clarifies That God Is Not the God of Any Race or Nation, but of Every Individual Child. (SAUL OF THE OLD TESTAMENT) 121

Jesus Declares That Worship of Him as Part of the "Godhead" Is Wrong and Sinful. (JESUS)...123

Jesus Explains That the Holy Ghost Is Not God—Only an Instrumentality of the Father To Carry the Divine Love into the Soul. (JESUS)...125

John, Also Discusses What the Holy Spirit Is and How It Works. (JOHN, THE APOSTLE) 126

Judas, the Apostle, Discusses What the Best Thing Is for Men to Do Who Desire to See God and Realize That He Is a Personal God with All the Attributes That Belong Only to a Supreme, Infinite Being. (JUDAS ISCARIOT)..127

*Jesus Approves of and Emphasizes What Judas Has Written.
(JESUS)* *128*

4.

The True Nature of God, the Heavenly Father.

Jesus Describes God and His Personality, and Corrects a Preacher's Misconceptions on This Subject.
(JESUS)
(April 7th,1919 | Received by James Padgett)

I AM HERE. *Jesus.*

Let me write a few lines.

I see that you were much interested in what the preacher said tonight about God and His Personality, and that you gave him several questions which he could not answer. This must be expected, for a true conception of God is not ordinarily given to men, or Who or What He is. Only by the development of their souls by the Divine Love can they obtain any conception of His Being. As their souls thus develop, they become a part of His Divinity, and their soul perceptions become opened up to a realization of Who God is, to a small degree at least. Then they know that He is something more than an all-enveloping Energy, supplemented by a purposeful Will.

The preacher has not these soul perceptions and cannot conceive of God, the Soul, but can only express to you the truthfulness of the evidences of God's Existence, such as the Energy that he spoke of.

As you know, this Energy is His Spirit, although the preacher has not the exact conception of what this Spirit is or how It operates. He confuses the Soul and Spirit, and makes the mere Instrument with which God expresses His Energy to be the real, true Substance of God, the Soul. He is right when he says that he cannot go back of this Energy to find God, for his soul perceptions have not yet been awakened to a cognition of that from which the Energy proceeds, or which is the very Source from which flow all the manifestations that, to his mind, constitute God. He is like the theologians and philosophers who believe that these manifestations and energies and forces are the only God, the only Personal God. And he may be shocked to hear that his teachings amount to only this, but it is true. To him, there is no more Personal God than to the others, with this exception: that he attempts to believe that, in some manner and in some way, connected with this Energy, there is a Will which has in It a purpose of Love or Kindness or Fatherly Care. But the real, Personal God, with His Great Soul of Love which is always being bestowed upon the individual man, he does not conceive of or make his own.

God is Soul, and only Soul, which has in It all the Attributes of Love and Wisdom and Thought for the welfare of His creatures. He is a Thinking and Seeing God, and all the Energies of His Soul are used to make men better and happier. As is the natural father of the man a personal father, so is the Great Soul of God a Personal Father to all His children. And when men shall have the development of their souls in the Divine Love, they will know that God is Personal—something more than an all-enveloping Energy or Force, or mere manifestation of His Existence.

The preacher says, in substance, that God is everywhere, and His Presence may be realized by all who are willing to receive that manifestation; and that, whether they are willing or not, that Presence exists just the same. This is pantheism, toned down a little by his beliefs in a more Personal God, but still pantheism, and wholly wrong and violative of God's Being.

THE SOURCE OF THINGS CAN NEVER BE THE THINGS THEMSELVES, ALTHOUGH, AS THEY FLOW FROM THE SOURCE, THE THINGS HAVE SOME OF THE QUALITIES OF THE SOURCE ITSELF. AND SO IT IS WITH THESE MANIFESTATIONS OF GOD'S EXISTENCE. WHILE THEY ARE OF HIS QUALITIES, YET, THEY ARE NOT EQUIVALENT TO HIS PRESENCE OR TO THE SOURCE FROM WHICH THEY FLOW. GOD IS NOT EVERYWHERE, BUT IS IN HIS HEAVENS. AND ALL THESE EXPRESSIONS OF HIS POWERS AND WILL AND ENERGIES ARE MERELY EVIDENCES THAT THERE IS A SOURCE FROM WHICH THEY ALL COME, BUT THEY ARE NOT THAT SOURCE ITSELF.

And, again, the preacher said that God created the body of man and not the "spirit," as he calls it, meaning the soul, so that the body is a creation by itself and cannot contain the spirit or the spirit body in it. Further, that this spirit is outside of the human body, and, in a general way, a part of one "Great Spirit" that is universal and everywhere; and that, therefore, all men, no matter what their conditions may be in the earth life or in the eternity part of life, are brothers, and God is the Father of them all. Well, the preacher is mistaken in this, for every man has his own individual spirit and soul. And on the state or condition of that soul depends the happiness or misery of the man. Also, he is merely the brother of other men because he is a creature of God and made in His image, and not because he is a part of the "Universal Spirit" which the preacher believes permeates everything and exists everywhere. God is the Father because these children are His creatures, the objects of His Creation, and individualized, each working out his own destiny. AS WE HAVE TOLD YOU, SOME OF THESE CHILDREN WILL ALWAYS REMAIN THE MERELY CREATED CHILDREN, WHILE OTHERS WILL PARTAKE OF HIS DIVINE LOVE AND BECOME A PART OF HIS DIVINITY, AND INHABITANTS OF THE CELESTIAL SPHERES.

The preacher has many things to learn. And, as he believes in the search for the Truth, if he will let the Divine Love flow into his heart and transform his soul into the very Essence and Substance of the Father's Divinity, he will be able to learn that many spiritual as well as material things are governed by law. Unless the soul gets into a condition that enables it to see and realize the higher Truths of the spirit world, it can never obtain knowledge of spiritual things. And one of the objects of such knowledge is God.

Well, I have written enough and will stop.

With my love, I will say good night.

Your brother and friend,

JESUS.

Jesus Comments on Another Preacher's Erroneous Conceptions of God.
(JESUS)
(April 8th,1919 | Received by James Padgett)

I AM HERE. *Jesus.*

Let me say a few words tonight.

I was with you again at the services and listened to the preacher as he expounded upon the Truth of God and the truth of man, as he conceived these truths to be. But I am compelled to say that, if his future state of happiness depended upon these supposed truths, he would be a very unhappy spirit in one of the million heavens of which he spoke.

I am sorry that men can conceive of such notions of God and man, and teach them to other mortals. But so it will be for many years. Until my teachings, through you, are accepted and believed by men, great darkness and error will prevail on the earth.

It is hardly necessary for me to attempt to analyze many of his erroneous statements, for they are so many and so erroneous that it will take too long a message to review them all.

But I will say one thing, and that is: When he attempted to show that God's Energy and man's energy are one and the same, he was all wrong and knew not what he said. God is a Being who is Infinite and Omnipotent, and there is no limit as to His Energies, while man is a mere creature of God, and cannot possibly have any greater or other energy than he was created with. And this energy is controlled by the soul that is man, and is subject to all the limitations of that soul.

Well, I will not write more tonight, but hope ere long to write you one of my messages of Truth.

I see that you have been somewhat in doubt as to the reality of the Truths of the messages that you have received, and as to the Power of the Divine Love to make you a child of God in the divine sense. You must not let such doubts enter your soul for one moment, for they are the breeders

117

of other things that are most harmful, and tend to alienate you from the Father. As you are aware, God's Love is all around you, and may be in you; and, if permitted to flow into your soul with faith accompanying It, you will find yourself growing in At-onement with the Father and will realize that fact. So, my brother, get rid of your doubts and come to God in the faith that is childlike and dependent. He will not disappoint you. I will be with you and will try to help you in your desires.

Pray more to the Father, and believe that His Love is yours for only the longing and seeking.

I will not write more tonight.

Rest assured that my love is with you in all its fulness, and believe that you have a work to do. Good night.

JESUS.

A Celestial Spirit Adds His Disapproval of the Preacher's Discourse.
(THOMAS B. MUNROE)
(April 8th,1919 | Received by James Padgett)

I AM HERE. *Thomas B. Munroe*[*].

Let me say a word, as I was also present at the meeting tonight and listened to the preacher as he unfolded what he thought to be the truth of God and man.

Well, I will not stop to discuss many of the errors of his teachings or the workings of his mind, but will only say that, if God is as he considers Him to be, He would not be the God which we know to exist, and Who loves us and Whom we can call "Father." The "all-enfolding Energy" is not the God of Love and Mercy. And, in such a God, the preacher cannot possibly find the Father that is calling to, and caring for, His children.

I merely wanted to say this.

I am an inhabitant of the Celestial Kingdom and will say good night.

THOMAS B. MUNROE.

Mrs. Padgett Also Reacts to the Preacher's Misconceptions.
(HELEN PADGETT)
(April 9th,1919 | Received by James Padgett)

I AM HERE. *Helen.*

Well, dear, I see that you are not very much enlightened by the

---

[*] Thomas Bell Monroe (October 7, 1791 – December 24, 1865) was a law professor and U.S. federal judge for the District of Kentucky.

preacher's discourse tonight. I do not see why you should be, for he has no true conception of either God or man, and gave no help to those who are searching for the true God, the Father.

I see that you may feel that you are benefited, though, by the negative lesson that his discourse teaches. He tells of what he thinks God is, and, in telling this, demonstrates that he knows nothing of the true God. You may hear the full course of his lectures and you will not learn much that will benefit you in an affirmative way. But attend the same, and then meditate upon them, and you will find that you have listened to a man who knows nothing of God or the spiritual world of which he pretends to have knowledge.

We all love you and want you to love us. Good night.

Your own true and loving,

HELEN.

What Is the Meaning of the Divine Nature Which the Soul of Man Partakes of upon the Transformation of That Soul by the Inflowing and Possession of the Divine Love?
(STEPHEN, THE APOSTLE)
(November 13th, 1918 | Received by James Padgett)

I AM HERE. *Stephen, the Apostle.*

Let me write a few words tonight, as I am one of the spirits whom your wife wrote of last night who would come tonight with the desire to write.

My subject is: "What Is the Meaning of the Divine Nature Which the Soul of Man Partakes of upon the Transformation of That Soul by the Inflowing and Possession of the Divine Love?"

This, as you may perceive, will be somewhat difficult to explain, and principally because men have no very definite conception of what is comprehended by the term "Divine." Of course, they associate this word with God; and, to them, God is a Being whose Nature and Qualities are above their finite conceptions. And, as a result of their thoughts, God is that which is over and above everything that is called, or supposed to be understood as, natural. To some, God is a Being of Personality, and, to others, a kind of nebulous existence included in, and composing all, the various manifestations which are transcendentally above what they conceive to be the merely natural or human.

I will not attempt to discuss Who or What God is, except as to one of His Qualities or Attributes, and that the greatest. For you must know that all the Qualities of God are not of equal greatness or degree of importance in the working of His Essence or Substance. All, of course, partake of His Divine Being. But, as you might say, there is a difference in the workings and scope of their operations.

119

You have been told that the divine is that which has in it, to a sufficient degree, the very Substance and Essence of God, Himself, and this is true; for Divinity belongs to God, Alone, and can be possessed by others, spirits or mortals, only when He has transfused into, or bestowed upon, the souls of men a portion of this Divinity and, to the extent thereof, made them a part of Himself. There is nothing in all His Universe that is divine, or partakes of the Divine, except that which is of the soul. For all else is of the material, and this even when it has the form or appearance of the spiritual. And even the soul, as created, is not divine, and cannot become such until it is transformed into the divine by the transfusion into it of that which is Divine in Its very Substance. Many souls in the spirit world, although pure and in exact harmony with their created condition, are not divine and never will become such. And this is only because these souls will not desire to seek to become divine in the only Way provided by the Father.

It is a mistake for men to believe that because God has created this or that object or thing, it is necessarily divine. For His Creations are no more a part of Himself than are the creations of men a part of themselves. And, thus, you will see that, in all God's Creation, there is nothing divine except what has been privileged by His Grace to partake of His Divinity. And, hence, the stars and world and trees and animals and rocks and man, himself, as created, are not divine.

Men have claimed that there is a spark of the divine in man—a part of the "Oversoul," as they say—and that it needs only the proper development to make the soul of man wholly divine. And this theory is based upon the idea that this development can be accomplished by the exercise of the mind or the moral qualities, guided by the conscience, which they assert is, of itself, divine; and especially when dominated by reason, which has been so often worshiped by philosophers, and others to whom the mind is supreme, as divine. And they have attempted to differentiate man and the lower animals, and have attributed to the former the qualities of divinity because he is endowed with reason, and the lower animals are not; and they have substituted degrees in the order and objects of creation in the place of differentiation between the Divine and the non-divine.

God is wholly Divine, and every Part and Attribute of Him is Divine. And while they are Parts of the Whole, yet, they may be separated in their workings and bestowals. And the man or soul that is the recipient of the bestowal of one of these Qualities or Attributes is not necessarily the recipient of the others. Omnipotence and Omniscience are those Attributes of God's Divinity which He never bestows upon the souls of men or spirits. As to them, He is the exclusive Possessor, although, in all His Attributes, there are Powers and Knowledge, and they accompany the bestowal of all Attributes of which they are Parts. And one of these Divine Attributes may be bestowed upon man, and yet man will not become Deity. There is and can be only one God, although He may give of His Essence and very Substance so that a man can become as He is in that Essence and Substance to the extent that It is bestowed.

As regards man, and his salvation and happiness, the greatest of God's Qualities or Attributes is His Divine Love, which is the only One that can bring the souls of men into a oneness and nature with the Father, and which has the Quality of Immortality in It. This Love has a transforming Power, and can make that which is of a quality foreign to, and different from, Itself of the same Essence as Itself. And, more than this, It can eliminate from that particular thing those constituents which naturally and necessarily are its components without injuring or destroying the thing itself.

Well, we must stop here. I will finish later. I am,

STEPHEN.

Mrs. Padgett Affirms That Stephen Wrote on the Meaning of the Divine Nature.
(HELEN PADGETT)
(November 13th, 1918 | Received by James Padgett)

I AM HERE. *Helen.*

Well, dear, you have had a very interesting letter tonight upon a very vital and important subject. I am sorry that the writer could not finish his message, but the rapport became very weak and he was compelled to stop. He will come again soon and finish, as he is very anxious to do so. It was Stephen who wrote. He is a most beautiful spirit, possessing this Love to a degree that I cannot conceive of, and a most glorious spirit in his appearance.

I am glad that you were in such good condition, and I hope that you will continue to improve so that more of the messages may be delivered to you every other night. There are so many messages to be written.

Your own true and loving,

HELEN.

Saul Clarifies That God Is Not the God of Any Race or Nation, but of Every Individual Child.
(SAUL OF THE OLD TESTAMENT)
(January 31st, 1917 | Received by James Padgett)

I AM HERE. *Saul.*

I have not written to you for some time and I would like to say only a few words, and these are: that in all the battles with the Amalakites, never did God help me or bring victory to me, as is set forth in the Old Testament. At the time, some of the prophets, like Samuel, might have thought this;

121

yet, as I now know, it was not true. God was not the partial and particular patron of the Jews. It was just as sinful to Him for the Jews to commit murder and the other horrible crimes that are mentioned in the Old Testament, in connection with my life as king, as it would have been for the pagans to have done the same thing.

God is not the God of any race, but He is the God of every individual child who comes to Him in true supplication and prayer, seeking His Love and Help in his spiritual nature. God will respond and the individual surely will be helped. But should that individual come to Him seeking power and assistance to murder his fellowman, no matter how great an enemy he might be, God would not help him or approve of his desires. And, this being so, you can readily see that He would not help any nation to commit such acts and gain the victory.

I want to tell you here that God is not a God of nations, but of individuals only. And only as individuals compose the nations can He be said to be a God of nations. He wants not the praise of men or of nations because of victory that they might acquire through bloodshed and cruelties ascribed to His Help. Rather, He wants the praise of men only because their souls may have been awakened to His Love, and have acquired victory over sin and evil.

Nations rise and fall and disappear from the face of the earth. But the individuals who compose these nations never die, even though the physical bodies die. And He is interested in having the individual become victor over sin and the appetites of the flesh.

Of course, the individuals make the nation and give it its character and qualities. Hence, the nation will become sinful and cruel as the individuals that compose it become sinful and cruel. God does not deal with nations as such, but only with the small, but important, units that make the nation. Hence, for a nation to say, "God is our God," or "God will help us to victory over our enemies," is all wrong. When the individual gains the victory over his greatest enemy, himself, then he can claim that God is his God and give Him the praise. And when all the individuals of a nation have gained that victory, then that nation can proclaim that God is its God and render praise to Him for the victory. But only in such event is any nation justified in saying, "God is our God."

And, here, let me say that no so-called "Christian" nation, as individuals, has yet attained to that condition of righteousness and victory over sin that it can claim to be God's chosen nation.

And, so, I say that I, Saul, the king, before my alleged fall from the Grace of God, was no more helped by God than I was after that supposed event, and for the reason that, while outwardly I may have appeared to seek God's Directions and listened to the advice of His prophets, yet, inwardly, I was no more in accord with Him, or reconciled to Him, than I was after the momentous event.

God never helped the Jews, as a nation, to any greater extent that He did any other nation; for, as individuals, they were no more in attunement with Him than were many individuals of what were called the pagan nations.

When I went to Samuel in my despair, as the Bible portrays, and felt the burden of the sins of my life, I became nearer to God than I had ever been before; and He was more my God than ever, though I did not realize it.

I merely write this to show men that they must not believe and rely on the statement that, because I was said to have observed God's Will and obeyed His Commands before the time that I realized defeat was certain to be mine, God was any more my God then, directing and assisting me to overcome my enemies, than He was after that event.

I have written enough and will now stop.

So, with all my love, and the assurance that God is a God of the individual and not of the nation, I will say good night.

Your brother in Christ,

SAUL.

Jesus Declares That Worship of Him as Part of the "Godhead" Is Wrong and Sinful.
(JESUS)
(April 23rd, 1916 | Received by James Padgett)

I AM HERE. *Jesus.*

I come tonight to tell you that you are in a much better condition of soul than you have been for several days, and that the inflowing of the Divine Love has been working today in greater abundance in your soul.

I do not intend to finish my message tonight, as it is rather late and you are not exactly in the condition to receive it. But turn your thoughts more to God, and pray in more earnestness, and very soon will come to you the power and soul perceptions which will enable you to receive my message as I desire to deliver it to you.

Today has been one when mortals—and I mean those who profess to be followers of me—have offered their worship and songs of praise to me and to God. But I am sorry to say that God has been worshiped in a secondary sense, and I have been brought into prominence as the savior of mankind, and as the important one of the three that constitutes the "Godhead." How wrong and sinful this all is, and how I deplore these erroneous beliefs and understandings of men! If they would only know that I am not God, and no part of the "Godhead," but only a son and spirit filled with His Divine Love, and one having knowledge of Him and His Plans for the salvation of mankind, they would get nearer to God in their worship, receive more of His Divine Love in their souls, and partake more of His Divine Nature.

But I realize that this belief in me as God, and that my death and

123

"sacrifice" on the cross were necessary for their salvation, will be hard to eradicate, and that many who now live will pass into the spirit world before the Truths which I came to teach and declare will be published to the world.

We must make more speed in our work of writing and receiving these messages, for the importance of the world knowing the Truths pertaining to me and the true and only Plan of salvation is now pressing, and must be shown to man in order for him to turn to the Father's Love and gain an entrance into the Kingdom. I want you to give more time to our writings. And instead of reading those books of philosophy and the speculations of what are supposed to be wise theologians and philosophers and scientists, let your hours from your business cares be devoted to my communications and to those of the other writers of the Celestial Spheres.

Of course, I do not intend that you shall not permit the dark spirits to write on the nights that you have set apart for them, because such prohibition would prevent much good from being accomplished.* These spirits are greatly benefited by having the opportunity to write. Many of them have been greatly helped thereby, and have been turned to the light and instructed to seek for the Divine Love of the Father. The spirits who are engaged in the work of instructing and helping these spirits here have rescued many from their condition of darkness and sufferings, and have shown them the Way to light and to their salvation. The work is a great and important one and must not stop. And let me say here that this work will be a part of your duty, and also your pleasure, for as long as you may live a mortal life. You will be undoubtedly the means of helping mortals to see the Truth, but your work among these dark spirits will be even greater and the harvest more abundant. And when you come to the spirit world, you will be surprised and gratified at the great host that will meet you, giving you thanks for the great help and assistance that you rendered them. Yours is a wonderful work, and is now spoken of and wondered at in the spirit world.

Well, I will not write more tonight but must come soon and finish my messages, as I have many yet to write.

In my Father's House are many mansions, as I said when on earth. And for your consolation and that of your two friends, I am preparing for each of you such a mansion—not as you may suppose, by erecting actual houses in the Celestial Heavens for your reception, but by helping to build in your souls that development of the Divine Love and the Nature of the Father that, when you come over, will make your soul in that condition that will necessarily and absolutely cause the formation of these mansions to receive you. No one else can build these mansions for you—only your own soul development. But while this is true, yet, these Celestial Heavens have a locality and surroundings and atmosphere that will contain all those things

* Mr. Padgett would let the dark spirits write once a week, and he helped them to visualize the bright spirits who would give them instructions. Mr. Padgett helped many spirits progress spiritually through these communications.—Ed.

that will give your mansions the proper settings.

The fields and trees and waters and sky, and all these things that you find necessary to your happiness and peace in your earth life are in the Celestial Heavens, only quite different from those that you are acquainted with.

So, believe what I say, and, believing, trust me and my love and you will never be forsaken.

A man's life on earth is but a span. But, in our homes, eternity means immortality, with always progress and increasing happiness.

So, with my love and blessings, I will say good night.
Your friend and brother,
JESUS.

Jesus Explains That the Holy Ghost Is Not God—Only an Instrumentality of the Father To Carry the Divine Love into the Soul. (JESUS)

(April 9th, 1915 | Received by James Padgett)

I AM HERE. *Jesus.*

(Master, at some time, would you please explain precisely what the Holy Ghost is?)

Yes, I will, and you will be enabled to fully understand what the Holy Ghost is,[*] and what meaning should be given to It as you find It referred to in various parts of the Bible. I will say this though: that It is not God. It is merely one of His Instrumentalities, used by Him in doing His Work for the redemption of mankind.

I will not write any message tonight, but will commence next week if you are in better condition.

(Is it contrary to any spiritual law that an exalted spirit, such as yourself, should communicate with a lowly mortal?)

Well, as you believe what I say as to my being a son of God, and not a god, you can easily believe that my coming to you, as I do, is not at all contrary to any law of the spirit world. The fact that I have my home in the highest Celestial Heaven does not prevent me from coming to earth to do my work, which has not been carried on by those of earth who should have performed it. I am a spirit of love and sympathy, as well as of great spiritual development; and I desire that all men shall know what the great Plan of the Father is for their redemption and happiness.

So, because I am such an exalted spirit, as you say, it is no reason that I should not come to you and communicate with you freely and, in a way,

---

[*] The Holy Spirit is explained more fully by Jesus in volume I of *Angelic Revelations of Divine Truth.*—Ed.

125

confidentially. I love you, as I have told you, and I have selected you to do my work. Hence, I am trying to make you wholly at-one with me.

You must not doubt me just because I come to you so often and speak so familiarly with you, because I hope and expect that, in the great future, you will be very close to me and with me. I am trying to prepare you for so great a progression in your spiritual condition that, when you come over, you will realize the oneness that I speak of, and will be fitted to live near my sphere.

(My grandmother has spoken of wanting to progress in your Kingdom.)

Well, your grandmother is a wonderful spirit in her development. And, by the time you come over, she will be near me in my home, and, as I believe, so will your mother and wife. They are all filled with the Father's Love and are receiving It more abundantly all the time. They are now in the First Sphere of my Kingdom, and will find that their progress will be much more rapid.

So, try to believe what I say and do my will, and all will be well with you.

(If only I could be more free from material cares and needs, I could devote more time to receiving these messages.)

Well, soon you will be free, as I told you, and then you can do the work without being interfered with by material things. I know that it is hard for you to lay aside these cares, and I am not disappointed or impatient that you do not. But only believe that the time will soon come when they will trouble you no more.

So, as we have written somewhat long tonight, I will stop now. I will pray for you as I always do.

With all my love and Blessings of the Father, I am

Your loving brother,

JESUS.

John, Also Discusses What the Holy Spirit Is and How It Works.
(JOHN, THE APOSTLE)
(June 14th, 1917 | Received by James Padgett)

I AM HERE. *John.*

I merely want to say that your condition is improving, and that, in a few nights, we will be able to continue our messages. You will then find yourself happier in more ways than one. I mean that you will feel better spiritually.

I was with you tonight at the meeting and it did you good, for there were many spirits present who had the Love to a more or less degree; and, of course, their influence was being exercised on, and felt by, the worshipers.

The preacher is a man with a considerable amount of the Divine Love

126

in his soul and, if he only had the true conception of Jesus, he would find himself possessing more of this Love. But his idea of the Holy Spirit is such that it interferes with his receiving the effect of the work of the Spirit. He thinks and believes It to be an entity—in other words, a being of substance and thought and sentient capacity, whereas, as you know, It is not. It is merely the evidence of the working of God's Own Soul in bestowing His Love and Mercy upon mortals. The Spirit could have no existence without the Soul of the Father, and It is entirely dependent upon the Powers of that Soul for Its existence. Only in the sense that It conveys God's Love can It be called the Comforter. And to "grieve" the Spirit, as the preacher said, means only that the Love of God is grieved, which is, in fact, not true. For this Love is never grieved, as It is so great and so intense in Its desire that men shall receive It that It never becomes grieved, though It is often disappointed, as you may say, that men will not receive It. It is always present and waiting for men to receive It and, by their longings and prayers, to cause their souls to be opened up to Its reception. And remember this: that this Love of the Father is so very great that the Spirit which conveys It to man cannot become grieved.

Well, I did not intend to write on this subject tonight, and what I have said is merely fragmentary; but I will come sometime and write in detail.

You must pray more and let your faith increase, and you will find what the Holy Spirit is[*] and how It operates. Your prayers will be answered, and a great inflowing of the Love, and also your desires, will be realized. Keep up your courage and you will not be disappointed. Today may look dark and dreary, but tomorrow the sun will shine and you will enjoy the sunlight.

I will not write more now.

So, with my love and blessings, I will say good night.

Your brother in Christ,

JOHN.

Judas, the Apostle, Discusses What the Best Thing Is for Men to Do Who Desire to See God and Realize That He Is a Personal God with All the Attributes That Belong Only to a Supreme, Infinite Being.
(JUDAS ISCARIOT)
(March 21st, 1922 | Received by James Padgett)

I AM HERE. *Judas.*

I have not written you for a long time, and I feel that I must write to you and declare some Truth that is of importance to you and to mankind. I will not write a very long message, and what I have to say will be put in

_____

[*] See "The Holy Spirit" chapter in volume I of *Angelic Revelations of Divine Truth* for enlargement upon this topic.

127

short sentences and made succinct. I know that you wonder who I am and what I will write about, and you must not be surprised if I tell you what you may think is not of much importance.

Well, my subject is, "What Is the Best Thing for Men to Do Who Desire to See God and Realize That He Is a Personal God with All the Attributes That Belong Only to a Supreme, Infinite Being."

GOD IS A SPIRIT AND A PERSON, AND NOT A MERE NEBULOUS BEING WITHOUT FORM OR PERSONALITY. HE IS REAL AS TO THESE QUALITIES, AND IS NOT WANTING THAT WHICH WILL MAKE HIM THE FATHER THAT JESUS SO OFTEN CALLED HIM.

NOW, IN ORDER FOR A SPIRIT TO SEE AND UNDERSTAND JUST WHAT ALL THIS MEANS, THE SPIRIT MUST GET IN THAT HARMONY WITH GOD THAT WILL ENABLE HIM TO POSSESS QUALITIES OF SOUL THAT ARE LIKE THE QUALITIES OF THE FATHER THAT HE DESIRES TO SEE AND UNDERSTAND. THIS CONDITION CAN BE OBTAINED ONLY BY THE SPIRIT PURSUING THE WAY THAT THE MASTER SO OFTEN WRITES YOU OF, AND WHICH IS ABSOLUTELY NECESSARY IN ORDER FOR THE SPIRIT TO OBTAIN THE QUALITIES NECESSARY FOR SUCH COMPREHENSION. ONLY AS A SOUL IS FILLED WITH THE LOVE OF THE FATHER CAN IT POSSIBLY BE IN THE CONDITION THAT WILL ENABLE IT TO SEE AND COMPREHEND THIS PERSONALITY OF GOD. NO MERE DEVELOPMENT OF THE INTELLECTUAL FACULTIES, OR OF THE NATURAL LOVE, WILL SUFFICE FOR THIS PURPOSE. AND WHILE SUCH DEVELOPMENT IS NECESSARY IN ORDER FOR THE SPIRIT TO BECOME THE PERFECT MAN AND ENJOY THE CONDITION THAT BELONGS TO THAT MAN, YET, SUCH DEVELOPMENT IS NOT SUFFICIENT TO ENABLE THE SPIRIT TO SEE AND COMPREHEND THE FATHER.

It is much easier for a spirit to get in the condition previously mentioned—that is, obtain the Father's Love—than to get in the condition last described. And, as you may see, the wholly different thing that the former development leads to should be sufficient to induce the spirit to accept the Father's Love and become a true son of His.

I have written what I desired, and thank you for the opportunity. With my love, I will say good night.

JUDAS.

Jesus Approves of and Emphasizes What Judas Has Written.
(JESUS)
(March 21st, 1922 | Received by James Padgett)

I AM HERE. *Jesus.*

What Judas has written you, I approve and emphasize. And with all my love for the mere man and for the spirit, I urge them to pursue the Way and attain to the great goal that the Divine Love will fit them for and lead them into.

I will not write more tonight, but will soon come and write you a long message.

Your brother and friend,

JESUS.

Chapter 5.

The Importance of Prayer.

<u>MESSAGES INCLUDED IN THIS CHAPTER.</u>

Peter, the Apostle, Urges Mr. Padgett to Pray More for the Divine Love. (PETER, THE APOSTLE) 133

Jesus Communicates His Approval of Mr. Padgett's Church Attendance, Even Though Many There Make the Great Mistake of Worshipping Him and Believing That His Blood Saves Them. (JESUS) 134

John Affirms That the Divine Love Is Ever Waiting to Fill the Soul, and Will When One's Soul Longings Are Earnest and Sincere. (JOHN, THE APOSTLE) 135

Jesus Explains That One Result of Obtaining the Divine Love Is the Removal of the Effect of Worry. He Also Stresses That Prayer Is a Wonderful Help When Offered with the True Longings of the Soul, and That Such Prayer Will Always Elicit a Response. (JESUS) 136

Mrs. Padgett Comments on Prayer's Use to Remove Worry. (HELEN PADGETT) 137

Jesus Describes Mr. Padgett's Soul Condition, and Gives Him Encouragement to Continue in Prayer for the Divine Love. (JESUS) 138

John, the Apostle, Explains How and When God Answers Prayer in the Case of Warring Nations. (JOHN, THE APOSTLE) 139

Mrs. Padgett Refers to a Message That John, the Apostle, Wrote Concerning How Prayers Are Answered for Material Things. (HELEN PADGETT) 141

The Master Explains That the Material Things That Men Pray for Are Answered by God Working Through His Ministering Spirits and Angels. (JESUS) 142

Jesus Explains How the Divine Love May Be Called Upon and Used in the Healing of Our Physical Bodies. (JESUS) 143

John Speaks on Truth, Knowledge, and Love. He Also Explains How to Solve the Problem of What Is True and What Is Not. (JOHN, THE APOSTLE) 145

Jesus Refers to Mr. Padgett's Wife's Description of the Third Celestial Sphere. He Also Discusses the Importance of Man Seeking for the Divine Love Through Prayer. (JESUS) 146

The Only Prayer That Man Need Offer to the Father. **The Prayer for Divine Love.** *(JESUS)* 147

Mr. Robert G. Ingersoll Affirms That Jesus Wrote "The Prayer," and Declared That It Is the Only Prayer Needed to Bring the Divine Love into the Souls of Men. (ROBERT G. INGERSOLL) 149

5.

The Importance of Prayer.

Peter, the Apostle, Urges Mr. Padgett to Pray More for the Divine Love.
(PETER, THE APOSTLE)
(August 8th, 1915 | Received by James Padgett)

I AM HERE. *Peter.*

I want to tell you that you are very near the Father tonight, and that His Love is filling your soul to a great degree. I see that you are anxious to learn of the spiritual things of the Father, and of His Love towards you and all mankind.

You must pray for more faith and trust implicitly in His Promises, and in the promises of the Master, for they will be fulfilled and you will not be disappointed or left to yourself. I am with you quite often now, for I want to assist in the great work that the Master has chosen you to do. And you must get into a condition that will enable you to do this work in the greatest perfection. Your soul must be developed with this Divine Love of the Father so that you will be in accord with the Master when he writes. For unless there is such accord, you will not be able to get the spiritual meanings of his messages as he wants you to do.

There is nothing that will cause this development as well as earnest, sincere prayer to the Father. With such prayer will come faith. And with faith will come the Substance of what you may now only believe. So, pray often, believing that the Love of the Father will come to you, and you will realize your oneness with Him.

I am so much interested in you and your soul development that I am going to help you with all my love and power.

Let not the things of the world detract your attention from these spiritual necessities. You will find that all these material things will be supplied.

Be firm and courageous in your beliefs and declarations, and God will be with you in every time of trial and distress. This I know and tell you as one having knowledge. I want you to let your faith increase until doubt shall flee away and only trust in the Love and Goodness of God remains with you. I will not write more tonight.

So, with all my love and blessings, I am

Your own friend and brother in Christ,

PETER.

Jesus Communicates His Approval of Mr. Padgett's Church Attendance, Even Though Many There Make the Great Mistake of Worshipping Him and Believing That His Blood Saves Them.
(JESUS)
(August 29th, 1915 | Received by James Padgett)

I AM HERE. *Jesus.*

I was with you tonight, and my spirit was in your heart to an extent that made you feel its presence and caused you to suffer somewhat, physically. But it was there to tell you that I was present and that my love was helping you to get nearer the Father and His Love.

I know that the people who were worshiping me were not doing what I approve of or like, but their hearts were turned to God. And while they were making me the object of their worship, yet, the Spirit of God was with them, and the workings of the Holy Spirit were in the hearts of very many of them, showing them the Love of the Father and the Truth of His Salvation.

Of course, they are mistaken when they talk about being saved by my blood, for my blood has nothing to do with their salvation. But, as they have been taught this, I cannot expect that they will know the real salvation which the Father has provided for them. Sometime, they will know that only the Divine Love of the Father saves from sin and error, and that not any blood of mine or my death on the cross can save them.

But, notwithstanding this false belief, these people actually aspire for the Love of God in their prayers. And He knows the longings of their hearts and sends the Holy Ghost to fill them with this Divine Love, which makes them become very close to the Father and makes them happy.

So, as I say, while I don't like the worship of me, yet, the Truth of God's Love enters into their souls, and they become at-one with Him to the extent that such Love enters their souls.

I know that to you, with your enlightenment, it appears that they are making a great mistake in worshiping me and believing that my blood saves them. Yet, you must understand that, while they make such mistakes, still, they are receiving the Divine Love, and that It is working to redeem them from their sins and evil lives. So, let not this error in their belief make you think that I am not with them, or, rather, that the Christ Spirit is not with them, teaching them the Way to the Love of the Father and to the great happiness which that Love brings to them.

I know that the meeting did you great good and opened up your soul to the inflowing of this Love, and, consequently, to a renewed faith and trust, and renewed love for the Father and belief in me.

Let this love in you increase, and pray to the Father for more faith in His Promises and for a greater inflowing of His Love, and very soon you will realize His actual Substance in your soul to an extent that will make you know that you are one with Him in Love, and in the possession of the Divine Essence that will cause all doubt to leave you and give you a faith in which no doubt will appear.

I am glad you went to this meeting tonight, and I hope you will go again, for the influences attending it were helpful to you and were from above.

Soon, I will write again, as I desire to do, if you will only pray more and trust more.

You are thinking right, and I will pray to the Father for you. And if you will only persist in your desires and try to act in accordance with our prayers, you will succeed. For the Father will hear your prayers and will help you to the fullest.

And, in addition, I will be with you and help you with my power and love.

So, do as I say and, above all, have faith in the Father and trust me.

I will not write more tonight, but will say that I will be with you during the week and will help you in your spiritual efforts.

So, with all my love, I am

Your friend and brother,

JESUS.

*John Affirms That the Divine Love Is Ever Waiting to Fill
the Soul, and Will When One's Soul Longings Are
Earnest and Sincere.*
(JOHN, THE APOSTLE)
(July 11th, 1917 | Received by James Padgett)

I AM HERE. *John.*

I heard your prayer and know that this Love is flowing into your soul, and that now you have a great abundance of Its possession of which you are conscious. It will never fail you when you pray in earnestness and with the real longings for Its coming. It is always ready to respond to your aspirations and to make you feel Its Presence and the happiness that comes with It.

As you know, I am your special friend in my work of helping to develop your soul. And whenever you pray to the Father, as you have just prayed, I come to you with my love and influence to help open up your soul to the inflowing of this Love. Have faith, and you will have the certainty of the presence of the Love, and that It is yours and is seeking to come into your soul in greater abundance.

You are blessed in that you have the knowledge of the existence of this Love, and that It may be yours if you so will It to be, and pray with the true longings of your soul's desires. You cannot doubt the Truth of what I write;

135

for, as in the ordinary things of life, there is nothing so convincing as personal experience. And your experience is such that there has been no room for doubt. So, keep the consciousness of the presence of this Love continually alive, and pray and pray whenever the opportunity presents itself. By this, I don't mean that you shall wait for a time when you are not engaged in your business affairs. Rather, pray at moments when the mind may be free from these business affairs, even if only for a moment. The longings, if exercised only for a moment, will bring their results; for God's Ear is always open and ready to cause the responses to such longings.

ONE MOMENT OF TRUE SOUL-FELT LONGING IS MORE EFFECTIVE THAN HOURS OF PRAYER WHERE THESE LONGINGS ARE NOT PRESENT. THE PRAYERS OF THE LIP OR OF HABIT ARISE NO HIGHER THAN THE ESCAPING BREATH, AND DO NOT CAUSE THE LOVE TO RESPOND AND FLOW INTO THE SOUL. REMEMBER THIS. AND THEN REALIZE HOW FUTILE ARE ALL THE PRAYERS OF PREACHERS AND OSTENSIBLE WORSHIPERS WHEN THE SOUL'S LONGINGS AND DESIRES ARE NOT PRESENT.

ONLY SOUL CAN CALL TO SOUL, AND LOVE RESPONDS ONLY WHEN SUCH SOUL CALLS. THE MERE DESIRES OF THE MIND, IF I MAY SO EXPRESS MY MEANING, DO NOT IN THE LEAST AFFECT THE SOUL. AND AS MIND CAN OPERATE ONLY ON MIND, THERE CANNOT POSSIBLY BE ANY ACTIVITY OF THE SOUL'S FACULTIES WHEN ONLY THE MIND IS OPERATING. HENCE, YOU WILL SEE THAT ALL THE WORSHIP THAT COMES MERELY FROM THE MIND WILL NOT EFFECTUATE THE WORKING OF THE LOVE, OR BRING THE SPIRIT'S WORK INTO OPERATION.

I write this to further encourage you, and also to make plain the necessity for the true prayer.

JOHN.

Jesus Explains That One Result of Obtaining the Divine Love Is the Removal of the Effect of Worry. He Also Stresses That Prayer Is a Wonderful Help When Offered with the True Longings of the Soul, and That Such Prayer Will Always Elicit a Response.
(JESUS)
(July 9th, 1917 | Received by James Padgett)

I AM HERE. *Jesus.*

Well, my brother, I see that you are much better than you have been for some days past. You have prayed more to the Father for the inflowing of His Love and, as a consequence, have more of It in your soul; and you are in a better condition spiritually and physically.

I should like to finish my message on God tonight,* but I do not think that you are in just the condition necessary to enable you to receive it; and I think it desirable to postpone it for a while longer.

You must surely realize the effect of prayer to a greater extent than ever, because, if you had not prayed as you have been doing for the past few days, you would have found yourself in a great degree of despondency, as the same cause for creating this despondency exists now as it existed several days ago when you were so depressed and worried. Prayer is a wonderful help when offered with the true longings of the soul, and will always find a response. And the benefit will not be merely spiritual but, as you may say, material as well.

Of course, prayer does not remove the cause of worry and thus relieve the mortal from worry, but it operates on the mortal's consciousness in such a way as to remove the effect of this cause of worry on the feelings and mental conditions of the mortal; and in this way is the mortal benefited and his prayers responded to. He becomes a new man, as it were, and ceases to look upon these causes in the same light that he did before the prayers commenced to bring their responses. And, in his real self, he is a different man from what he was when in the condition that existed before he prayed.

I am so very glad that you prayed and let your longings go out to the Father, and tried to have faith in us to help you. We are helping you, and you will soon realize the result of our work in securing those things that you desire and consider necessary to enable you to get rid of your worries and perform our work. Continue to pray and to have faith in us. You will not be disappointed in what we promise, for our promises will be fulfilled in a very short time.

I have many messages yet to write, and so desire that you get in condition to receive them properly. And, besides myself, there are many other spirits who want to write upon these Truths that are so important that the world should know. So, if you continue to pursue the course that you followed today, you will find a wonderful improvement in your condition of soul and mind and spirit qualities, and we will be able to form the required rapport that is necessary to our communicating properly.

But, in closing, I advise that you continue to pray with all the longings of your soul, and to believe with all the strength of your mind, and you will develop to a surprising degree in your soul qualities and perceptions, and also in your physical condition and mental strength.

I will say good night.

Your brother and friend,

JESUS.

Mrs. Padgett Comments on Prayer's Use to Remove Worry.
(HELEN PADGETT)
(July 9th, 1917 | Received by James Padgett)

I AM HERE. *Helen.*

Yes, it is Helen. I will write only a few lines, as I see that you are feeling so much better physically and spiritually, and I think it best that you go to bed early tonight.

I am so glad that you do not feel so worried as you did, and, also, that you can understand that prayer helps so much to get rid of the worries, even though it may not remove the immediate cause thereof. But, as you are helped, you are strengthened and the better fitted to deal with the causes and overcome them.

So, my own dear Ned, continue to pray and try to have faith in us, and you will realize so wonderfully the response to your prayers, and the fulfillment of your hopes and freedom from your causes of worry.

Good night.

Your own true and loving,

HELEN.

Jesus Describes Mr. Padgett's Soul Condition, and Gives Him Encouragement to Continue in Prayer for the Divine Love.
(JESUS)
(January 6th, 1918 | Received by James Padgett)

I AM HERE. *Jesus.*

Well, my brother, I am glad to tell you that your communion with the Father tonight has been responded to. His Love has inflowed into your soul in great abundance, and your soul is now filled with It. And the influence of this Great Love is working in your soul and you realize Its presence. If you will meditate and long for and pray to the Father, as you have tonight, your soul will soon be so filled with this Love that you will receive the knowledge that you have a near At-onement with Him. And you will be conscious of the possession of a part of His Divinity, of which we have written you. The Pentecostal shower will come to you as it did to my disciples in the days that followed my departing from them. And I will also be with you, just as I was with them; and Power and Essence Divine will be bestowed upon you so that you will be able to display the marvelous presence of this Love, just as they were able. So, you must pray, and long, and your experience tonight has given you some foretaste of what will come to you.

There is nothing in all the world that can take the place of this Love in Its power to draw you near to, and make you in At-onement with, the Father. All beliefs and faiths in any and every other thing will not suffice. Sacrifice and sorrow on account of sin, and vicarious sufferings, and mediators, will not work the transformation, because it is solely a conjunction between this Divine Love and your soul that is capable of

138

bringing you into this relationship to the Father, with the resultant consciousness that you have partaken of, and possess to some extent, His Divine Nature in Love.

Now you are in condition that makes my rapport with you complete, and I have that possession of your brain that enables me to write as I may desire. I know that I could convey a message to you tonight in a most satisfactory way, but I will not do so; for I think it best to permit the rapport to become a little more intense, and thus enable me to write a long message without the probability of tiring you. For, as you know, these messages of deep Truths, such as the ones on the "soul" and "God",[*] necessarily cause me to draw very intensely on your brain power. But soon, now, I will come and commence to deliver my messages, and will continue to do so if our rapport can be maintained. And it can be if you will only meditate and pray as you have done tonight.

I have been with you very much today, entering into your thoughts and endeavoring to influence the longings of your soul. I was with you at the Spiritualist's meeting and, sometime, I will write to you in reference to the claims of the speaker, and of the real facts as to how much of what she said was inspired, or, as she claims, was spoken through her by a controlling spirit.

I now want you to think more than ever of the importance of your work, and of the necessity for you putting all your energies and desires into the work. No one can conceive of what it means. But, above all, you must realize its great importance and the place that you occupy in carrying it to a successful issue.

I will be with you very often, and I know that you will feel my presence and influence. And, as you do, turn all your thoughts to the Father's Love, and let all your longings go to Him.

Tonight, I will not write more, but will soon write as I have said. Have faith and know that you have been selected to do the work, and that upon you rests the responsibility that is upon no other man.

With my love and the Father's Blessings, I will say good night.

Your brother and friend,

JESUS.

John, the Apostle, Explains How and When God Answers Prayer in the Case of Warring Nations.
(JOHN, THE APOSTLE)
(November 2nd, 1917 | Received by James Padgett)

I AM HERE. *John.*

---

[*] These messages referred to are in volume I of *Angelic Revelations of Divine Truth*. However, this present edition includes messages that also address these subjects.—Ed.

I come to you today because I see what your condition is and that you need encouragement. And, as I am your special guardian, I could not abstain from writing to you. So, I say, trust in the Father and in our help and you will not be disappointed.

It has been a long time since I have written to you with regard to spiritual things, and I desire very much to do so. I have important messages to communicate, as have many other spirits who have been accustomed to writing to you.

While your material affairs are important, yet, these spiritual Truths are of more importance, not only to you but also to the world for whom they are primarily intended. The world needs these Truths more at this time than ever before. And the sooner we can complete our book of Truths, the better it will be for suffering humanity, and for many whose hearts are now lacerated because of the great destruction of human life caused by the war.[*]

Well, I know that many believe that, in some way, God has an overpowering direction as regards the progress and outcome of the war; and, in a certain sense, this is true. He is always interested in, and seeks to reach, the souls and hearts of mankind and, of course, desires that the great suffering and devastation shall cease. But as the cause of all this was the evil desires and ambitions of men, He will let men, themselves, control the conduct and outcome of the war. He will not end the war by His exercise of Power in an arbitrary way, or determine which of the contending nations shall be successful, except in this: that through the instrumentality of His Spirit, He will influence the minds and consciences of these men in such a way that right and justice will prevail, and the evil thoughts and deeds of men will be stopped in their operations. His spirits are working toward this end at this time, and have been for a long time. And so have the evil spirits been working to bring discord and destruction upon humanity. The leaders of the nations have been obsessed to a large degree by these evil spirits, and have been influenced in many of their thoughts and acts by these dark ones who delight in seeing mankind suffer, and in evil asserting itself.

The spirits of Truth are exercising a wonderful power over the hearts and souls of men, and one that will cause them to realize sooner that evil must not be allowed to prevail, and that truth and right must assert themselves to the end that the war must not only cease but also that men must become more in unison with truth and justice. The Father will answer prayer in this way, and His Love will also continue to flow to men.

I know that prayers for success are ascending unto the Father from many men and from many of the churches of the respective contending nations. But only those prayers which tend to bring about the overruling of evil and injustice will be answered. And the spirits who are working the Father's Will will answer only those prayers which, in their granting, will bring about the desired end.

As I have said, while God does not take interest in these matters by His

---

[*] World War I.

140

arbitrary Power and Decree that the one or the other of these warring nations shall overcome and conquer the others, yet, by His angels, He does exercise such influence upon the men who are engaged in the struggle that, in the end, His Will will be brought to pass. But, men, immediately, must determine the course and results of the issue. No miracle will be performed which will make one side the conqueror of the other. But while this is so, this determination by men will be angelically influenced, as I have stated.

Man has his free will, and, as we have written you, that is never arbitrarily controlled by the Father. But, in the exercise of that free will, whenever man violates the Laws of God, man must suffer the penalty of that violation. This is a never-changing law of the material as well as of the spirit world. When evil is sown, evil must be reaped. And until this evil ceases to operate as a cause, good will not appear. The men who are directing the war must understand that this law is operating in the conduct of the war, and that evil thoughts put into execution will inviolably bring evil consequences.

You may look for an earlier determination of the struggle than some men now believe possible. Yet, ere that end comes, many mortals will become spirits and find their homes—some in the darker spheres, and some in those of light and love. But all are the children of God, and they will not be forsaken by Him in the great eternity.

In closing, I leave you with my love, and urge you to pray to the Father.

Your brother in Christ,

JOHN.

Mrs. Padgett Refers to a Message That John, the Apostle, Wrote Concerning How Prayers Are Answered for Material Things.
(HELEN PADGETT)
(April 25th, 1917 | Received by James Padgett)

I AM HERE. *Helen.*

Well, dear, I am glad that John wrote you as he did, for it will give you an insight into some principles regarding the powers of spirits to help mortals that you may not have understood before. What he said is true, and I am glad that he wrote.

It may prove a little disappointing to learn that spirits have not the powers to do everything, as mortals may suppose, but I do not want you to underestimate their powers; for they have great powers, even as respects the material things. Of course, they cannot move a house, or cause the wealth of one mortal to be removed from him and placed in the possession

---

* This message from John is contained in volume I of *Angelic Revelations of Divine Truth*, .—Ed.

of another, but they can and do use great influence on mortals to cause them to do physical things that the spirits cannot directly do.

Your prayers are not futile, even as to these material things that are subject to the control of mortals. For, under certain circumstances, these very mortals are subject to our influence and, thereby, our control. When we promise you that a certain thing or things will happen, we mean that we will exercise our influence on mortals in such a way that they will bring about these happenings in response thereto. And you must not believe that, when we promise you something, that something will come to you as a matter of course. We mean that it will come to you primarily by reason of the work that we are doing among mortals. We can see some things before they have an existence in your physical world and can tell you of the same, and some things we believe will happen, and also tell you. And when they do not, we are disappointed as well as are you.

Your own true and loving,

HELEN.

The Master Explains That the Material Things That Men Pray for Are Answered by God Working Through His Ministering Spirits and Angels.
(JESUS)
(September 19th, 1920 | Received by James Padgett)

I AM HERE. *Jesus.*

Let me say a few words tonight, as I see that you were disappointed in the sermon that the preacher delivered tonight.

Well, you must not be so disappointed, because he knows only that which he could deduce from the teachings of the Bible. And while what he said was true, yet, it is not all of the Truth. For he discussed only one of the Attributes of God, and that is the Loving Care that He has for, and exercises over, the children of earth. To most men, this view of God is satisfactory, and gives them much comfort and assurance in the security that arises from the knowledge that there is such a Loving and Caring Father. This assurance is of wonderful blessedness and comfort to these men, and it is well that men can have this conception of God—a Father Who is always solicitous for their happiness and welfare, and to Whom they can pray in the faith that He will hear and answer their prayers.

But, as we have written you before, the things that men generally pray for and expect to receive in response thereto are not the things that God, in His Own Personality, bestows upon man in answer to such prayers. His Great Gift is His Divine Love. And these things of the material, or earthly in themselves, He leaves to His ministering spirits to bestow. In other words, He delegates His angels to so come into contact with and influence

142

the souls of men that they may feel that their prayers have been answered, as they have.

The preacher's conception of God does not extend beyond these Attributes that in themselves are sufficient to answer men's wants and make them better and happier. I will come soon and write you of God's Attributes, and hope that you will get in condition that I may make the necessary rapport.

It has been some time since I have written you of these higher Truths that are so important to men, and regret that such is the fact. But now that you have had your vacation, and feel that you are willing and anxious that our communications be resumed, I will try to assist you in getting in that condition of soul that will enable the messages to be written to you. But, as you know, much depends upon yourself. You must try with all the energies of your soul to obtain a greater inflowing of the Father's Love, for only from It can come the condition that is necessary. Pray more and think deeply of the spiritual Truths that have already been written to you, and we will come together in closer communion, and be able to give and you receive the messages.

I am glad that you have thought more of these things during the past few days, and hope that your thoughts will continue, and that your longings will flow more to the Father. You cannot now appreciate the necessity for this condition. If you could, I know you would give all your thoughts and longings and energy to the accomplishment of the work.

Well, I will not write more tonight, but will be with you and pray with you and try to influence you in the efforts to perform the mission that has been given you. Have more faith and believe that you will succeed, and you will not be disappointed.

Your brother and friend,
JESUS.

Jesus Explains How the Divine Love May Be Called Upon
and Used in the Healing of Our Physical Bodies.
(JESUS)
(May 16th, 1916 | Received by James Padgett)

I AM HERE. *Jesus.*

I will not write a formal message tonight, but will merely tell you that I was with you tonight at the home of Mr. Morgan, and wrote what you received as purporting to come from me. I meant that if I could establish the rapport with him I would cure him, and so I will. It depends somewhat on his having the necessary concentration and belief in me.

It may seem strange that I cannot do this unless this rapport is established, but it is a fact. There are certain laws which control the exercise of this power upon mortals which must be complied with. When on earth,

I could come in direct contact with the mortal by reason of my being in the flesh. And as the power was in me, or could be engendered in me by the exercise of my spiritual powers, I encountered no obstacle in the way of my exercising these powers upon the mortal. But now there is no direct contact between me and the mortal; hence, there is no means of communicating this power to him until a rapport is established.

This rapport is something more than a mere spiritual connection, and partakes somewhat of the material, though we are not of the material. Yet, the rapport must be of the nature mentioned, and the material part of it must come from the mortal himself.

Now, you will understand that my relationship in such cases with the mortal is very different from what would be your relationship to him, had you this power residing in you. And, when the time comes for you to receive this power, you will not need to establish any rapport between you and whomever you may be able to cure. I mean it will not be necessary for this rapport to be established by drawing from the mortal any part of the material that belongs to him. This you will have yourself. And the power will be exercised by you simply as a mortal coming in contact with him.

This power can be possessed by mortals, just as my disciples and others possessed it at the time that I was on earth; and the same results may be obtained as were obtained in those days.

(I seemed to have felt a certain power during my own attempt to pray for a healing for Mr. Morgan.)

Well, the power that was manifested in you was somewhat of the nature that I have been speaking of. Only it was a power borrowed, or conferred upon you by a spirit. It was a part of this spirit's power, and thereby differing from that which you will receive as a part of your own self when you shall have had that soul development and possession of the Divine Love which are necessary prerequisites to any mortal, or spirit either, being able to receive the power.

The spirit who was trying to manifest through you and help Mr. Morgan was your own Indian guide who is a very powerful spirit. And he drew on you very hard for the material that was necessary for him to make the manifestation. The power which he transmitted will help Mr. Morgan, and he will realize it by morning. And if you had continued for a while longer, its effects would have been seen before you left him.

I will try tonight to help him, as I promised. And if we can form the rapport that I speak of, there will be no uncertainty as to the results. I will give especial attention to his case, as I desire to demonstrate to him that the power of the spirit world, when properly exercised, can be used to help mortals to relieve them from their sufferings, even in their physical ills. I see that he has a very considerable faith and will make the effort to help establish this rapport, and we may succeed. At any rate, you have already helped him and he will realize it.

I will come to you soon, and write you another message on an important subject so that you may see the necessity for our working faster.

I will not write more, but will say that I love you and am with you, trying to help you. So, with my blessings, I will say good night.

Your brother and friend,

JESUS.

John Speaks on Truth, Knowledge, and Love. He Also Explains
How to Solve the Problem of What Is True and What Is Not.
(JOHN, THE APOSTLE)
(April 7th, 1916 | Received by James Padgett)

I AM HERE. *John.*

I desire to write a little tonight upon a subject that may prove to be of interest to you and others who may read my message. I will not write a very long message, but will say what I desire in short sentences so that the Truth that I intend to convey may be understood at a glance.

Well, when you are sure that you have discovered or have had revealed to you a Truth, let it sink deep into your soul so that it will find such lodgment as will cause you to realize that this Truth is a reality and a thing that must not be forgotten or neglected in its application to your daily life on earth.

When you have found that the Truth fits some peculiar condition of your mind's experience, adopt it as a criterion for determining what your course of action shall be.

When you have thus adopted it, let it always remain with you as a guide and monitor in determining what your belief as to the particular thing involved shall be.

When you have thus received this belief of the mind, encourage and feed upon it until it becomes a thing of established faith. And when faith has become a part of your very being, you will find that the accompaniments of such faith, in the way of longings and aspirations, will become things of real existence, which will result in actual knowledge.

When such knowledge becomes yours, then you have solved the problem of what is true and what is not. And, when you have solved this, you will become a man who, when he utters his knowledge of Truth, will speak as one having authority.

Such was the process by which Jesus became the possessor and authentic expositor of the great spiritual Truths that had never before been known and declared by any man.

Of course, these various steps which lead to this great knowledge of Truth must be taken gradually and with increased confidence. In all this, the Help and Influence of the Father are necessary. And such Help and Influence come only in response to sincere, soul-aspiring prayer.

Prayer must arise from the soul of man, and the response must come from God. There is no other means by which this knowledge can be

145

obtained. All knowledge of spiritual things that men may think they possess, coming in any other way, cannot be relied on. For there is only one Source of such knowledge out of which the real spiritual Truths of God emanate.

Love is the great Principle that enters into all knowledge of spiritual things. Without Love, it is utterly impossible for man to rightfully conceive the Truths of God and possess them.

I merely desired to give you this short lesson on Truth and knowledge and Love so that, in receiving and absorbing our messages of the great spiritual Truths of the Father, you may realize the means of making them your own in a manner to satisfy your soul perceptions.

I will come soon and write you a message on some of these vital Truths. Think of what I have above written, and you will find that your soul perceptions will be opened up to a clear and wonderful comprehension of the real meaning of what we desire to reveal.

I will not write more tonight.

Your brother in Christ,

JOHN.

Jesus Refers to Mr. Padgett's Wife's Description of the Third Celestial Sphere. He Also Discusses the Importance of Man Seeking for the Divine Love Through Prayer.
(JESUS)
(December 28th, 1915 | Received by James Padgett)

I AM HERE. *Jesus.*

I will write only a few lines. I merely want to say that what you have read tonight from your wife as to her progress and her condition of Love is all true. She is in such a state of happiness that you must not wonder that she was not able to describe her home and her new surroundings to you, for they are beyond description in the words that you mortals use to express your ideas.

But this I will say: that the heart of man has never conceived, nor has the mind of man ever thought, of the great blessings and joy which the Father has prepared for those who love Him in the way of possessing His Divine Love which makes their souls at-one with Him, and which causes them to partake of His Divine Nature and realize that they are a part of His Great Divinity and immortal.

If mortals would only learn of this great Plan of the Father for their redemption, and then believe and try to get this Great Love, how much more happiness there would be, not only among spirits but among mortals also. For this Love can be possessed by mortals to a very great degree, notwithstanding that they have all the trials and temptations of the flesh.

146

My object is to have you and your friend[*] obtain this Great Love while you are still in the flesh. For your work will require that you have this Love so that you can not only teach its existence, but also, by your very lives, show and prove to mankind that It is a thing of reality.

I will soon write another message to you that will show another great Truth which mankind must know.

(Dr. Stone and I would like you to explain, if you would, why the Lord's Prayer includes the puzzling phrase: "...and lead us not into temptation....")

Well, very soon, I will explain that sentence in one of my messages. And, to the satisfaction of your friend, I will show that God never leads any of His children into temptation. In teaching my disciples the Lord's Prayer, I never said that they should pray that God would not lead them into temptation. I will also write to you of the actual prayer which I taught them,[†] and which is the true prayer which all men should offer to the Father with fervent, honest, longing hearts. SO, LET NOT THIS TROUBLE YOU OR YOUR FRIEND, FOR GOD DOES NOT LEAD MEN INTO TEMPTATION, BUT, ON THE CONTRARY, USES THE INFLUENCE OF HIS RIGHTEOUS SPIRITS UPON THEM TO HELP THEM RESIST ALL TEMPTATION.

With all my love for you and your co-worker, and the Blessings of the Father upon you both, I am

Your brother and friend,

JESUS.

The Only Prayer That Man Need Offer to the Father.
The Prayer for Divine Love.
(JESUS)
(December 2nd, 1916 | Received by James Padgett)

I AM HERE. *Jesus.*

I merely want to say a word for the benefit of you and your friend,[‡] and that is that I have listened to your conversation tonight, and find that it is in accord with the truth; and the influence of the Spirit[§] is with you both. Continue in your line of thought and in prayer to the Father and, also, in your making known to others, whenever the opportunity arises, the importance of seeking for and getting the Divine Love.

As your friend said, the only prayer that is necessary is the prayer for the inflowing of this Love; all other forms, or real aspirations of prayer, are

---

[*] Dr. Leslie R. Stone.
[†] The prayer that Jesus taught is presented in the following message.—Ed.
[‡] Dr. Leslie R. Stone.
[§] The Holy Spirit.

secondary, and, of themselves, will not tend to produce this Love in the souls of men.

Let your prayer be as follows:

THE PRAYER FOR DIVINE LOVE.

OUR FATHER, WHO ART IN HEAVEN, WE RECOGNIZE THAT THOU ART ALL HOLY AND LOVING AND MERCIFUL, AND THAT WE ARE THY CHILDREN, AND NOT THE SUBSERVIENT, SINFUL AND DEPRAVED CREATURES THAT OUR FALSE TEACHERS WOULD HAVE US BELIEVE. THAT WE ARE THE GREATEST OF THY CREATIONS, AND THE MOST WONDERFUL OF ALL THY HANDIWORKS, AND THE OBJECTS OF THY GREAT SOUL'S LOVE AND TENDEREST CARE.

THAT THY WILL IS THAT WE BECOME AT-ONE WITH THEE AND PARTAKE OF THY GREAT LOVE WHICH THOU HAST BESTOWED UPON US THROUGH THY MERCY AND DESIRE THAT WE BECOME, IN TRUTH, THY CHILDREN THROUGH LOVE, AND NOT THROUGH THE SACRIFICE AND DEATH OF ANY OF THY CREATURES.

WE PRAY THAT THOU WILL OPEN UP OUR SOULS TO THE INFLOWING OF THY LOVE, AND THAT THEN WILL COME THY HOLY SPIRIT TO BRING INTO OUR SOULS THIS, THY DIVINE LOVE, IN GREAT ABUNDANCE, UNTIL OUR SOULS SHALL BE TRANSFORMED INTO THE VERY ESSENCE OF THYSELF; AND THAT THERE WILL COME TO US FAITH—SUCH FAITH AS WILL CAUSE US TO REALIZE THAT WE ARE TRULY THY CHILDREN AND ONE WITH THEE IN VERY SUBSTANCE, AND NOT IN IMAGE ONLY.

LET US HAVE SUCH FAITH AS WILL CAUSE US TO KNOW THAT THOU ART OUR FATHER, AND THE BESTOWER OF EVERY GOOD AND PERFECT GIFT, AND THAT ONLY WE, OURSELVES, CAN PREVENT THY LOVE CHANGING US FROM THE MORTAL INTO THE IMMORTAL.

LET US NEVER CEASE TO REALIZE THAT THY LOVE IS WAITING FOR EACH AND ALL OF US, AND, THAT WHEN WE COME TO THEE, IN FAITH AND EARNEST ASPIRATION, THY LOVE WILL NEVER BE WITHHOLDEN FROM US.

KEEP US IN THE SHADOW OF THY LOVE EVERY HOUR AND MOMENT OF OUR LIVES, AND HELP US TO OVERCOME ALL TEMPTATIONS OF THE FLESH, AND THE INFLUENCE OF THE POWERS OF THE EVIL ONES WHO SO CONSTANTLY SURROUND US AND ENDEAVOR TO TURN OUR THOUGHTS AWAY FROM THEE TO THE PLEASURES AND ALLUREMENTS OF THIS WORLD.

WE THANK THEE FOR THY LOVE AND THE PRIVILEGE OF

RECEIVING IT, AND WE BELIEVE THAT THOU ART OUR FATHER—THE LOVING FATHER WHO SMILES UPON US IN OUR WEAKNESS, AND IS ALWAYS READY TO HELP US AND TAKE US TO THY ARMS OF LOVE.

WE PRAY THUS WITH ALL THE EARNESTNESS AND SINCERE LONGINGS OF OUR SOULS, AND, TRUSTING IN THY LOVE, GIVE THEE ALL THE GLORY AND HONOR AND LOVE THAT OUR FINITE SOULS CAN GIVE.

AMEN.

This is the only prayer that men need offer to the Father. It is the only one that appeals to the Love of the Father. And, with the answer, which will surely come, will come all the blessings that men may need and which the Father sees are for the good of His creatures.

I am in very great rapport with you tonight, and see that the Father's Love is with you and that your souls are hungry for more.

So, my brothers, continue to pray and have faith, and in the end will come a bestowal of the Love like unto that which came to the apostles at Pentecost.

I will not write more now.

In leaving you, I will leave my love and blessings and the assurance that I pray to the Father for your happiness and love.

Good night.

Your brother and friend,

JESUS.

Mr. Robert G. Ingersoll Affirms That Jesus Wrote "The Prayer," and Declared That It Is the Only Prayer Needed to Bring the Divine Love into the Souls of Men.
(ROBERT G. INGERSOLL)
(December 2nd, 1916 | Received by James Padgett)

I AM HERE. *Ingersoll.*

I desire to say, with all the emphasis of my words and soul, that the Master wrote you and gave you "The Prayer," which he said is the only prayer needed to bring the Divine Love into the souls of men.

He was glorious, and it is not surprising that you felt the influence of his presence and Love. And I, who have so recently experienced what this Love is, tell you that your feelings were real, that that Love is present, and that we spirits feel It as well as you two mortals.

Astonishing to us, as to you, is the power of this Love and the greatness of the Master. For with him seems to come the Influence of the Very Father, Himself. How thankful I am that I found the Way to this Love, and It found

Its way into my soul! What a Loving Father! And what a tender Master to teach us of this Great Gift!

I could not restrain myself from writing, as the opportunity came to testify of this Love and of the Master. And I felt that, as I had so often declared on earth that there is no such thing, I must now and always declare the Truth of the Divine Love and the Holy Spirit, and the glorious Jesus, when the opportunity arises.

I must not write more tonight. So, believe that it is I who write, and that I can declare with all the certainty of Love that I am
Your brother in Christ,
ROBERT G. INGERSOLL.

Chapter 6.

The Divine Love of the Father and the New Birth of the Soul.

<u>MESSAGES INCLUDED IN THIS CHAPTER.</u>

Jesus Explains How the Divine Love Enters into the Soul of Man and Answers the Question: "When a Man Dies, Shall He Live Again? (JESUS) 153

Jesus Concludes His Message on: "How the Divine Love Enters into the Soul of Man." (JESUS) 157

John Explains What the Divine Love Is, and How It Must Not Be Confounded with the Natural Love. (JOHN, THE APOSTLE) 161

Ann Rollins Stresses the Importance of Getting the Divine Love in the Soul. (ANN ROLLINS) 162

John Explains the Difference Between the Natural Love and the Divine Love. (JOHN, THE APOSTLE) 164

Mrs. Padgett Describes How Wonderful It Is to Obtain Possession of the Divine Love. (HELEN PADGETT) 165

Andrew, the Apostle, Declares That the Divine Love Casteth Out All Fear. (ANDREW, THE APOSTLE) 166

Jesus Explains What It Is That Makes a Man Divine. (JESUS) 167

Stephen, the Apostle, Affirms That Jesus Wrote, and He Emphasizes the Great Importance of Mr. Padgett's Receipt of the Messages. (STEPHEN, THE APOSTLE) 168

John Discusses the Condition of the Soul When and After the Divine Love Flows into It. (JOHN, THE APOSTLE) 169

Ann Rollins Encourages Mr. Padgett to Press Forward to the Goal of a Home in the Celestial Heavens. She Also Refers to the Great Love of Jesus, and That Even He Is Still Praying for More of the Divine Love. (ANN ROLLINS) 170

Jesus Presents His Discourse on the Real Truth of Life on Earth, and

What It Means to Mortals. (JESUS) 171

Ann Rollins Comments on the Message Jesus Wrote Through Mr. Padgett. (ANN ROLLINS) 174

John Calvin, the 16th Century Theologian and Reformer Expresses His Interest in the Work and the Means Whereby All Men May Receive the Divine Love. (JOHN CALVIN) 175

Nicodemus Confirms the Importance of the New Birth. (NICODEMUS) 175

Ann Rollins Discusses the Necessity of Obtaining the Divine Love. She Cautions That Those Who Refuse This Great Gift, After the Privilege of Obtaining It Is Withdrawn, Will Suffer the "Second Death." (ANN ROLLINS) 177

Jesus Explains Why Men Must Receive the Divine Love in Order to Be Admitted to the Kingdom of Heaven, or Celestial Kingdom. (JESUS) 179

Mrs. Padgett Affirms That Jesus Wrote. (HELEN PADGETT) 182

Divine Love is a Privilege Gift of the Father (JESUS) 183

6.

The Divine Love of the Father and the New Birth of the Soul.

Jesus Explains How the Divine Love Enters into the Soul of Man and Answers the Question: "When a Man Dies, Shall He Live Again?"
(JESUS)
(March 23rd, 1916 | Received by James Padgett)

I AM HERE. *Jesus.*

I am here according to my promise, and desire to write to you on a subject that all men should be acquainted with: "How the Divine Love Enters into the Soul of Man."

As I have told you before, man is a creature of God, having a body, spirit and soul; and all these are necessary to make the perfect man. But these three parts of man are different in their characteristics and functions, and are separate and distinct; and they have qualities that are unlike in their composition as well as in the duration of their existence.

The body, as you and all men know, has an existence which lasts only during the life of the mortal on earth. And, after that life ends, it dissolves into its elements which no more can form the same body, either in the mortal world on in the spirit world. For these elements are merely things of matter, and may be and are used to form other bodies and manifestations of the material of nature, but not necessarily in the form of human beings. For they enter into other forms, both animal and vegetable, and are so disseminated that never again will they become parts of a resurrected body. Your orthodox do not teach this truth, but think that the mortal body will sometime be resurrected in some mysterious way.

No, when it has performed its function of maintaining and shielding the soul and spirit of man during his earth life, the body exists no longer. It cannot thereafter be a part of that man, and may be considered as something that is no longer a part of him.

This body, though, as a matter of fact, even during the life of the mortal, is not the same body during that life. For there are continual changes in the elements that compose that body. One element, or set of elements, gives place to others and becomes lost or absorbed in the great sea of elements that help form, or constitute, the Universe of God.

By operation of the Laws of Attraction and Repulsion, these elements, as they replace others which disappear, conform themselves to the general appearance or outline of the parent body so that the identity of the body as well as of its appearance is preserved. And, as a man grows older, the laws which make the changes in his appearance cause these new elements to conform to these changes so that, even while the material continues to envelop the spirit during the short span of a man's life, that material is not the same for any length of time.

I make this preliminary statement merely to show that the material part of man is not at all connected with the real man, so far as his persistent nature is concerned. And this material need not be considered in discussing the subject that I desire to write about.

The spirit part of man is that part which contains what may be called the functions of life and the force and power existing in him, and which immediately control him in his conduct and living.

This real, existing principle of life, unlike the body, never dies, but continues to live after the spirit drops its envelope of flesh.

This spirit part of man contains the seat of the mental faculties and reasoning powers, and uses the organs of the material body to manifest these attributes. These faculties live and exist even though the physical body may be in such imperfect condition that the spirit may not be able to make its manifestations in such a way as to enable the mortal to perceive or sense the material things of nature, as they are called. To specify, even though the material organs of sight may become impaired or destroyed, yet, in that spirit body, which is within the physical body, exists the actual sight just as perfectly and completely as if these impaired or destroyed organs were doing their functioning; and the same is true as regards the hearing and the others of what are called the five senses of man.

And as to the reasoning faculties and mental qualities, they exist in the perfect state whether the brain is healthy or not, or whether it performs its work or refuses to do so. The qualities do not depend upon the soundness or perfect workings of the organs of the physical body in order that these spirit qualities may exist in a perfect condition. But the proper workings of the physical organs, or, rather, the proper and natural movements and manifestations of the brain, and the conscious operations of the mental faculties, do depend upon the spirit faculties being able to use these physical organs in a proper way, and in accordance with the harmony of the creation of the relative and correlative parts of man.

These spirit faculties, which man calls the intellect and the five senses, are a part of the spirit body which is enclosed in the material body, and which, in turn, encloses the soul. When the material body dies, the spirit body continues to exist and live on in the world of spirit, and, with it, and as continuing parts of it, these intellectual faculties also, performing all their functions free from the limitations that the physical organs placed upon them. And when this change takes place, these mental qualities, notwithstanding that they have not the material organs through which they function when in the mortal frame, can conceive thoughts of material things, and hear and see things of the material, just as they did when they were enveloped by the environments of flesh and blood, and even more perfectly.

154

So, you see, when the mortal dies, the only thing that dies and is left behind is the mere physical body. And, with the spirit body, there survives all those things which can be said to be the real man, so far as the mind is concerned. Hence, man never ceases to remember and to progress, and to know that he is a being which death cannot destroy or change into something that he was not before death came to him. And, thus, I answer the question: "When a man dies, shall he live again?" HE NEVER CEASES TO LIVE. AND HIS LIVING IS NOT A NEW LIFE, BUT MERELY THE CONTINUATION OF THE OLD LIFE WITH ALL THE THINGS OF MIND AND CONSCIENCE THAT WERE HIS IN THE OLD LIFE.

In the purely spirit life, the spirit body continues to contain the soul, and will be its protector and covering so long as that spirit body shall last. But, by disintegration, this body then begins to change into what we may call spirit elements, with the formation of new elements to replace the disappearing ones. This change in this body is not caused by the same laws that operated to change and disintegrate and replace the physical body, but by the law controlling the development of the soul, which the spirit body contains.

The soul is the real man because it is the only thing or part of man that may become immortal, the only part of man that was made in the image of its Creator, and the only part of man that may become a part of the Substance of its Maker and partake of His Divine Nature. I say "may," for that is an important part of this great possibility.

I know this possibility of the soul becoming immortal by partaking of the Divine Nature of God is true, for it is a proven fact in the case of many souls who are now in the Celestial Heavens. I also know that there are many souls in the spirit world who have been there for many centuries, and who have never received this Divine Nature and consciousness of immortality. WHETHER SUCH SOULS WHO HAVE NOT RECEIVED THIS DIVINE NATURE SHALL BECOME, OR ARE, IMMORTAL HAS NEVER BEEN DEMONSTRATED.

THIS I DO KNOW: THAT IN THE ECONOMY OF GOD'S PLAN FOR THE FORMING OF HIS KINGDOM, AT SOME TIME, WHEN, I DON'T KNOW, THIS PRIVILEGE OF PARTAKING OF HIS DIVINE NATURE AND THE CERTAINTY OF IMMORTALITY WILL BE WITHDRAWN FROM THE SOULS OF MEN AND SPIRITS. AND, THEN, WHETHER THESE SOULS WHO SUFFER THIS CONDEMNATION WILL PARTAKE OF IMMORTALITY NO SPIRIT KNOWS, ONLY GOD.

There are other things that I know and here tell you, and among them is this: that so long as the soul does not receive this Divine Nature, the mind, which I have described as being a part of the spirit body, continues to exist and dominate both soul and body; and, in its progress, it may attain to a condition of purity and perfection such as was possessed by the first created living souls—our first parents. Many spirits are now in this condition, but

155

yet are mere men, and their souls remain only in the image of God—nothing more.

WHILE GOD IS MIND, MIND IS NOT GOD. AND, ALSO, WHILE GOD IS SPIRIT, SPIRIT IS NOT GOD. SO, WHEN MEN TEACH THAT MIND IS GOD, AND THAT MEN MUST SEEK TO ATTAIN TO THAT MIND AND THUS BECOME LIKE GOD, THEY FALL FAR SHORT OF THE TRUTH. THE MIND IS ONLY AN ATTRIBUTE OF GOD. BEYOND AND BACK OF THAT MIND IS THE REAL GOD—THE PERSONALITY—AND THAT IS GOD'S SOUL. AND FROM HIS SOUL EMANATES ALL THESE ATTRIBUTES AND MANIFESTATIONS WHICH MORTALS AS WELL AS SPIRITS MAY BE CONSCIOUS OF.

BUT WHILE GOD IS SOUL, YET, THAT SOUL IS A THING OF SUBSTANCE, WITH A NATURE DIVINE, AND THE SEAT AND FOUNTAINHEAD OF ALL THE GREAT ATTRIBUTES THAT BELONG TO HIM, SUCH AS LOVE AND POWER AND LIFE AND OMNISCIENCE AND MERCY. AND, HERE, I MUST STATE ONE FACT WHICH MAY STARTLE THOSE WHO BELIEVE AND TEACH THAT MIND IS GOD, AND THAT IS: THAT WHICH IS CALLED THE HUMAN MIND, AND ALL ITS FACULTIES AND WONDERFUL QUALITIES, IS A MERE SPECIAL CREATURE, JUST AS IS THE SPIRIT BODY AND MATERIAL BODY OF MAN. AS I HAVE SAID, MAN WAS CREATED IN THE IMAGE OF GOD ONLY AS REGARDS THE SOUL. AND, HERE, ALWAYS BEAR IN MIND THAT THE CREATION WAS ONLY AN IMAGE.

THE MIND OF MAN WAS A SPECIAL CREATION, JUST AS WERE THE MINDS OF THE LOWER ANIMALS, DIFFERING ONLY IN DEGREE. AND IF GOD HAD NOT GIVEN TO MAN A SOUL AND THE SPIRIT BODY TO ENVELOP IT, AND IN WHICH HE PLACED THIS MIND OF MAN, WHEN MAN DIES THE DEATH OF THE PHYSICAL BODY, THAT WOULD HAVE BEEN THE END OF HIM, AS SUCH DEATH IS OF THE BODY, WHICH IS NOT A PART OF THIS SOUL IMAGE OF GOD.

AS I HAVE HERETOFORE WRITTEN TO YOU, WHEN GOD CREATED MAN AND MADE HIM IN HIS OWN IMAGE AS TO THE SOUL, HE ALSO GAVE TO MAN THE POSSIBILITY OF OBTAINING THE SUBSTANCE OF THE FATHER; THAT IS, OF HAVING THAT SOUL WHICH WAS A MERE IMAGE BECOME THAT SOUL WHICH IS OF THE SUBSTANCE OF THE CREATOR. I HAVE ALSO EXPLAINED TO YOU HOW MAN, BY HIS DISOBEDIENCE, LOST THAT POSSIBILITY, AND, FOR LONG CENTURIES, WAS DEPRIVED OF THIS GREAT PRIVILEGE; AND HOW IT WAS AGAIN RESTORED TO HIM AT THE TIME OF MY COMING TO EARTH SO THAT NOW, AND FOR NINETEEN CENTURIES PAST, HE HAS THE POSSESSION OF THIS GREAT GIFT OR PRIVILEGE OF PARTAKING OF THE SUBSTANCE OF

THE FATHER.

WELL, BY THE WAY THAT HAS BEEN POINTED OUT TO HIM, WHEN MAN BECOMES POSSESSED OF THE SUBSTANCE OF THE FATHER'S DIVINE NATURE, EVEN IN AN INITIAL DEGREE, HIS SOUL COMMENCES TO CHANGE AND LOSE ITS CHARACTER AS A MERE IMAGE, AND STARTS TO PROGRESS TOWARDS THE ATTAINMENT OF THAT CONDITION WHEREBY THIS IMAGE DISAPPEARS AND THE DIVINE SUBSTANCE TAKES ITS PLACE. AND, AS THE PROGRESS CONTINUES, HE RECEIVES SO MUCH OF THE SUBSTANCE THAT HIS SOUL TAKES ON THE DIVINE NATURE OF THE FATHER, AND HIS AT-ONEMENT WITH THE FATHER BECOMES SO PERFECT THAT HE BECOMES AN INHABITANT OF THE FATHER'S KINGDOM. THIS OCCURS WHEN HE BECOMES FITTED TO ENTER THE FIRST CELESTIAL SPHERE.*

AND JUST HERE OCCURS ANOTHER THING WHICH MAY STARTLE THOSE WHO TEACH THAT THE MIND IS THE ESSENCE OF GOD, AND THAT IS: THE MIND WHICH MAN, BOTH AS MORTAL AND SPIRIT, POSSESSES, UP TO THAT POINT IN THE PROGRESS OF THE SOUL WHERE THE TRANSFORMATION INTO THE DIVINE NATURE TAKES PLACE, BECOMES A THING OF NAUGHT, OR, RATHER, BECOMES ABSORBED IN THE MIND OF THE SOUL, WHICH IS THE REAL MIND OF THE FATHER. AND THEN, AND EVER AFTER, ONLY THIS MIND OF THE SOUL IS THAT WHICH ENABLES THE REAL DIVINE MAN TO UNDERSTAND THE THINGS OF GOD TO HELP HIM IN HIS PROGRESS.

I will continue later. You are tired. But remember that I love you, and that you have me with you at all times to help and sustain and comfort you.

Good night, my dear brother.

Your friend and brother,

JESUS.

Jesus Concludes His Message on: "How the Divine Love Enters into the Soul of Man."
(JESUS)
(May 8th, 1916 | Received by James Padgett)

I AM HERE. *Jesus.*

I come tonight to finish my message, and will do so if your condition is such that you may receive it.

---

* The First Celestial Sphere is the one immediately above the Seventh Sphere.—Ed.

Well, as you may remember, my subject is: "How the Divine Love Enters into the Soul of Man."

I have already explained to you the difference between, and the respective functions of, the physical body, the spiritual body and the soul, and how the real man is the soul, which may live forever. I have also shown you how the physical and spiritual bodies change their component parts, and, as such bodies, disintegrate and disappear in the form that they may have at any one time.

WELL, THE SOUL IS THE MAN, AND IT BECOMES THE ANGEL OF GOD'S KINGDOM. THE SOUL MAY ALSO BECOME ONLY THE EVERLASTING PART OF MAN IN THE SPIRITUAL KINGDOM, AS CONTRADISTINGUISHED FROM THE CELESTIAL HEAVENS.

THE ONLY WAY IN WHICH THE SOUL MAY BECOME AN INHABITANT OF THE CELESTIAL SPHERES IS BY ITS OBTAINING THE DIVINE LOVE AND THEREBY BECOMING A PARTAKER OF THE DIVINE NATURE OF THE FATHER. AND THIS CAN BE ACCOMPLISHED ONLY BY THE INFLOWING OF THE DIVINE LOVE BY MEANS OF THE OPERATION OF THE HOLY SPIRIT, WHICH IS THE INSTRUMENTALITY USED BY GOD TO CARRY THIS LOVE TO THE SOULS OF MEN.

AS I HAVE SAID BEFORE, THIS LOVE NEVER FORCES ITSELF INTO THE SOULS OF MEN, AND COMES ONLY WHEN MEN SEEK FOR IT IN SINCERITY AND WITH EFFORT. IT IS WAITING FOR ALL MEN TO RECEIVE IT, BUT NEVER COMES INTO THE SOUL OF ITS OWN INITIATIVE AND WITHOUT INVITATION. SO, THE IMPORTANT QUESTION IS: "HOW DOES IT COME INTO THE SOUL, AND WHAT MUST MEN DO TO INDUCE ITS INFLOWING?"

THERE IS ONLY ONE WAY, AND THAT IS BY THE OPENING UP OF THE SOUL IN SUCH A MANNER THAT THIS LOVE, WHEN IT COMES IN RESPONSE TO SINCERE SEEKING, MAY FIND AN ENTRANCE AND A CONDITION OF DEVELOPMENT THAT WILL CAUSE IT TO FIND A LODGMENT AND ABIDING PLACE THAT IS HARMONIOUS AND SATISFACTORY TO THE QUALITIES OF ITS OWN EXISTENCE. OF COURSE, MAN CANNOT OPEN UP HIS SOUL TO THIS INFLOWING OF HIMSELF; FOR, WHILE HE HAS GREAT POWER, YET, THE WILL IS NOT SUFFICIENT. NOR HAS HE ANY OTHER INHERENT QUALITIES THAT WILL ENABLE HIM TO PLACE HIS SOUL IN SUCH CONDITION AS TO MAKE THE WORK OF THE HOLY SPIRIT POSSIBLE IN CAUSING THE LOVE TO FLOW INTO THE SOUL.

THE ONLY MEANS BY WHICH THIS CAN BE ACCOMPLISHED ARE PRAYER AND FAITH. WHEN A MAN PRAYS TO THE FATHER FOR THIS DIVINE LOVE IN TRUE EARNESTNESS AND SINCERE ASPIRATIONS, SUCH PRAYER NOT ONLY BRINGS LOVE BUT ALSO CAUSES THOSE PORTIONS OF THE SOUL WHICH ARE

CAPABLE OF RECEIVING THIS LOVE TO OPEN UP TO ITS COMING, AND TO WORK IN SUCH A WAY AS TO ATTRACT THE LOVE.

The Holy Spirit never performs this work of preparing the soul for the reception of this Love, but merely brings the Love and causes Its inflowing when the soul is in condition to receive It. In answer to prayer, there are other instrumentalities of the Father working to prepare the soul condition that is required. These instrumentalities are the bright spirits of the Celestial Heavens whose duties, among others, are to answer the prayers of the penitent in the way of infilling the soul with influences that turn the thoughts and aspirations to this Divine Love and Its operations.

As I said when on earth, there is no other way to get into the sheepfold but through the gateway provided; and he that attempts to climb over the fence is a thief and a robber. But this should be modified to fit the exact fact, for there is no possibility of getting into this fold by climbing the fence. THERE IS ONLY ONE WAY—THAT THROUGH THE GATE OF PRAYER AND SINCERE LONGING.

I know that many men believe that the performance of church duties, and the observation of the requirements of the church as to baptism and the sacraments, etc., will be sufficient to enable them to get into the Kingdom; but I tell you that they are all wrong, and their disappointment will be very great when they come into the spirit world.

What are called moral deeds and good thoughts will not cause this inflowing of the Divine Love, because these things are necessary steps towards the purification of the soul in its natural love. And no matter how pure this love may become, yet, it is not the Divine Love or any portion of It.

Good thoughts and deeds, though, may help to turn the aspirations of the soul to these higher conditions, and open up its perceptions to a degree that may lead to prayer and faith, and, therefore, in addition to their work of purifying the natural love, may prove to be of great value in assisting men towards the development of the soul so that the Divine Love may enter into it. But to depend on good thoughts and moral deeds and a life pure from sin to give man the right to an entrance into the Celestial Kingdom is a great mistake.

THE DIVINE LOVE IS A THING ENTIRELY APART FROM THE NATURE OF MAN, EVEN IN ITS PUREST STATE, AND WAS NEVER CONFERRED ON MAN AS WAS THE NATURAL LOVE. CONSEQUENTLY, WHEN MAN OBTAINS THIS DIVINE LOVE AND IT BECOMES A PART OF HIS SOUL QUALITIES, HIS NATURE, AS IT WERE, CHANGES, AND HE BECOMES A NEW CREATURE. AN ADDITIONAL SOMETHING HAS BEEN CONFERRED UPON HIM, AND IT BECOMES IMPOSSIBLE FOR HIM TO REMAIN THE MERE MAN THAT HE WAS AND ALWAYS WOULD BE EXCEPT FOR THIS CHANGE IN HIS NATURE.

I KNOW THAT MEN DO NOT UNDERSTAND THE

DISTINCTION BETWEEN A MAN WITH ONLY THE NATURAL LOVE AND ONE WITH THE DIVINE LOVE. BUT THE DISTINCTION IS SO GREAT THAT THE ONE, WHEN POSSESSED TO A SUFFICIENT DEGREE, MAKES THE MAN A PART OF DIVINITY; WHILE THE OTHER, NO MATTER HOW FULLY POSSESSED AND HOW PURE IT MAY BECOME, MAKES MAN MERELY MAN, THOUGH A PERFECT ONE.

WHOSOEVER WILL PRAY IN SINCERITY FOR THE INFLOWING OF THIS DIVINE LOVE WILL RECEIVE IT. IT IS NOT A RESPECTER OF PERSONS. AND THE SINCERE ASPIRATIONS OF THE SOUL OF ANY MAN, BE HE PRINCE OR PEASANT, RICH OR POOR, WILL INVARIABLY CAUSE THIS LOVE TO COME INTO HIS SOUL AND CHANGE HIS NATURE SO THAT HE WILL BECOME A NEW CREATURE, AND ONE NOT SUBJECT TO DEATH FOREVERMORE.

THE MERELY INTELLECTUAL PRAYERS ARE NOT EFFICACIOUS, FOR THEY DO NOT HAVE ANY EFFECT IN OPENING UP THE SOUL. AND NEITHER DOES MUCH OF THIS PRAYING DO THE WORK. ONE LITTLE MOMENT OF THIS TRUE PRAYING WILL BE MORE EFFECTIVE IN CAUSING THIS DIVINE LOVE TO FLOW TOWARDS THE SOUL THAN A WHOLE LIFETIME OF IDLE REPETITION OF PRAYERS THAT COME MERELY FROM A MENTAL SOURCE. AND, HERE, LET ME SAY THAT THE MIND IS NOT THE SOUL, AND MUCH LESS IS IT GOD.

WELL, I THINK I HAVE MADE PLAIN HOW THIS LOVE FLOWS INTO A MAN'S SOUL, AND, IN ADDITION, WHAT ITS EFFECT IS WHEN POSSESSED BY MAN. THERE IS NOTHING IN ALL GOD'S UNIVERSE THAT CAN TAKE ITS PLACE FOR THE PURPOSE OF MAKING A MAN AT-ONE WITH THE FATHER, AND OF CAUSING HIM TO BECOME DIVINE INSOFAR AS HE POSSESSES THIS LOVE.

SO, I SAY TO ALL MEN, PRAY AND PRAY AND NEVER CEASE TO PRAY FOR THE INFLOWING OF THIS LOVE, FOR THERE IS NO LIMIT TO ITS ABUNDANCE OR TO THE AMOUNT WHICH MAN OR SPIRIT CAN OBTAIN. IN THE CELESTIAL HEAVENS, WE SPIRITS ALWAYS CONTINUALLY PRAY FOR AN INCREASED BESTOWAL, AND ALWAYS OUR PRAYERS ARE ANSWERED; BUT THERE IS ALWAYS MORE TO FOLLOW.

I must not write more tonight.

I am satisfied with the correctness of your receiving my message, and will come again and write you another.

With all my love and blessings, I am

Your brother and friend,

JESUS.

John Explains What the Divine Love Is, and How It Must Not
Be Confounded with the Natural Love.
(JOHN, THE APOSTLE)
(July 8th, 1915 | Received by James Padgett)

I AM HERE. *John, the Apostle.*

I felt your call and came. I will tell you of love, as that is what you called me for.

The "love" that I taught when on earth is the Love that the Father has prepared for all His children who might seek It. All that is required is that they seek with earnestness and faith, and they will receive It. I know that this Love is frequently confounded with the natural love that God gave to man at his creation, but the two are different and distinct. Every man has this natural love to a more or less extent, and it is a great gift that makes man what he is. But not so many have this other Love because it is bestowed only in answer to prayer and the real longings of the heart and soul. This is the Divine Love, and this is the Love that makes man a part of the Divinity of the Father, and, consequently, immortal.

God is Love—and this is the Great Truth of His Being. But His Love, while free for all, is not bestowed without the desire of the mortal to receive It. I wish that I had time tonight to more fully explain this Great Love, but I have not; and I came to you only because you called me.

(Do you have any time tonight to discuss your book, "Revelation," or some of the laws that obtain in the spirit world?)

No, not tonight, but I will come sometime and write you a long letter on these subjects.

(What is your state of existence, and what is it that you specifically do as part of your work?)

I am supremely happy and am working for humanity, and so directly does the Master. I do more for the advancement of the spirits after they have commenced to enjoy the Love of the Father in their souls.

(Who rules in your Kingdom?)

WELL, JESUS IS THE RULING SPIRIT IN OUR KINGDOM AND HIS POWER IS SUPREME. IT IS, OF COURSE, THE KINGDOM OF GOD. BUT THIS KINGDOM IS BEING FORMED BY THE MASTER, AND THE SUPREME RULING POWER IS GIVEN TO HIM, AND WE ARE ALL HIS FOLLOWERS. HE RULES BY LOVE AND MINISTRATIONS, AND NOT BY THE HARD LINES OF FORCE AND COERCION.

(Does he rule over many?)

Yes, he has many with him in the Celestial Spheres, and they are all subordinate to and obey him. But it is hard to make you understand this. This obedience is the result of love, but the word "obedience" does not convey the exact meaning intended.

(On earth, did not the disciples wish to rule with the Master?)

161

Well, that was a request made by us in our desire to become of importance, but we did not then understand what his Kingdom would be. We are equal here, provided we have the same amount of Love—the Divine Love. That alone determines our place and position.

JESUS IS THE GREATEST OF ALL BECAUSE HE HAS MORE OF THIS LOVE THAN ANY OTHER SPIRIT, AND BECAUSE HE IS NEARER THE FATHER AND KNOWS MORE OF HIM AND OF HIS ATTRIBUTES. NO DISTINCTION IS MADE IN THIS KINGDOM BECAUSE OF ANY RELATIONSHIP OR PERSONAL GREATNESS, BUT ONLY BECAUSE OF MORE OR LESS DIVINE LOVE IN THE SOUL OF THE SPIRIT.

I will come to you at times and write to you of my knowledge of the Truths of the Father, and I hope that they may do you and the world some good.

(Were you an educated man when you lived on earth?)

I was not an educated man at that time, when on earth, and never was so far as languages are concerned. I had no knowledge of the philosophy of the great thinkers and writers of that time. All the knowledge I possessed of spiritual matters came to me from the teachings of Jesus and the promptings of the Holy Spirit. I was not a learned man in the earthly sense.

You have my blessings and my love, and I hope that the Holy Spirit may soon fill your soul with the Love of the Father in greater abundance and keep you in Its care and keeping.

I will say good night.

JOHN.

*Ann Rollins Stresses the Importance of Getting
the Divine Love in the Soul.*
(ANN ROLLINS)
(December 12th, 1914 | Received by James Padgett)

I AM HERE. *Your grandmother.*

I wish to tell you more about the things of the spirit, for they are the important things that you should know. You are very near the Kingdom and, if you keep on trying to have more of God's Love in your soul, you will soon realize the full joy and peace which comes with such possession. Try to let your heart receive more of His Love, for He is always ready and waiting to bestow His Love upon you. He is the One, Lovely Father for you to long for and keep with you in all your thoughts and aspirations. Do not let the worries of life keep you from loving and believing that He wants you to become one with Him in Love and Grace. He is not only waiting for you to let His Love flow into your heart, but He is also anxiously knocking at the door of your heart that you may open and let Him enter.

Be true to your best spiritual longings and you will soon feel that you have got that in your soul which will give you perfect peace and happiness. You are only now beginning to learn that you must feel that your Father is so near to you that He must become a part of your life and being. When that Love has fully taken possession of you, you will know that you are His Own true and reconciled son, just as all are who have come into a realization of that Love. So, do not doubt that you may become such a son of your Father, for I tell you that I know from my own experience and grandeur of living in the favor of His Blessings that this is true.

Be my own dear boy, and do try to reach out and get this Love.

You must not let the things of your earth life keep you from the higher things that the Father has prepared to give you. You will soon know, as I know, that the only things worth striving after are the things of this Spiritual Love of the Father. Be more anxious to get this knowledge and it will come to you in all its beauty and convincing force. I so wish that you could see the Holy Spirit's work among men and spirits, for then you would not doubt any more that God is a God of Love and not of anger or retribution.

KEEP PRAYING, FOR THAT IS THE ONE GREAT MEANS TO RECEIVE THE LOVE OF GOD. WITHOUT PRAYER, MEN CANNOT REACH THE ANSWERING EAR OF THE FATHER'S GRACE. HE WILL HEAR THE PENITENT ONLY, FOR HE WILL NOT ACCEPT ANYONE WHO IS NOT TRULY AND ANXIOUSLY SEEKING HIM. MAN HAS A WILL TO EITHER ACCEPT OR REJECT THE LOVE OF GOD. AND UNTIL HE EXERCISES THAT WILL IN A WAY TO SHOW THAT HE WANTS THAT LOVE, IT WILL NOT BE GIVEN HIM. NO MAN IS EVER FORCED TO LOVE GOD OR TO LET GOD'S LOVE COME INTO HIS HEART.

The Love of God cannot be defined, for It passes all understanding. But the result of that Love, when in the souls of men, can be seen and felt in the exceeding beauty of the countenances of men and their wonderful happiness. No fear of death or anything that maketh afraid can possibly exist where that Love is. It is not the kind of love that permits any feelings of jealousy or envy to have an entrance, but is so perfect and all soul-filling that there cannot possibly be any room for anything but Its own great Self. I know that the Love of God is the only thing that can make man supremely happy while on earth, and after he becomes a spirit. My love for Him is such that I love every one of His creatures, be they saints or sinners, and that is the difference between the love that He inspires in all His Love-seeking children and the love that exists among men and spirits who have not His Love for their foundation. Be sure that no man can be perfectly happy without this Divine Love.

Your wife is progressing very rapidly in the Way to this perfect Love, and I think that, in a short time, she will be with me in my sphere; for she will not let anything come between her and her efforts to possess the greatest amount of this Love that is possible to obtain.

It is wonderful how her faith has grown since she first became convinced that she must seek the Father's Love in order to become one with Him and perfectly happy. You must try to get this faith and progress with her, so that, when you come over, you will go forward together in soul development and conjugal love. She is now in the Third Sphere, as she has told you, and she is almost in a condition of development to leave that sphere and go with your mother to the Fifth Sphere where her happiness will be so much greater.

She loves you so much that you must feel that she wants you to be with her in all her happiness. She is not the same Helen as when she was on earth, but is so much changed that your mother says her appearance is as different as earth from heaven. She is not only changed in her appearance but also in her temperament and desires for those things which do not tend to retard the progress of the soul.

Let her tell you of her love for you, and you must believe what she is telling you, as she surely does. She is not one who is in condition to speak anything else than the Truth. Her love for you is so great that I sometimes wonder how it can be. For while we all love you as well as our soulmates, yet, she seems to have such intense love for you that we wonder. We think that her nature is so intense that she cannot do anything in a way that is not the result of her strong and earnest constitution, or, rather, that is not the result of a power that knows no limitation in effort or force.

But while she loves you so intensely, her love for God is not interfered with in the least. For just as she gives her whole soul to loving you, she devotes it to loving God also. And, when you do come over, you will find such love in her heart for you as we seldom see in the spirit life of our soulmates.

But you must not think from this that we do not love intensely also. The love that we all have for our soulmates is very great and deep, as I must tell you. But she seems to be almost consumed by this love for you, and you must never do anything to hurt her or make her feel that you do not want it or deserve it.

My dear boy, we must stop writing now, as you are not in condition to write more. So, I will say good night and God bless you and keep you in His Love and Care.

Your loving grandmother,
ANN ROLLINS.

John Explains the Difference Between the Natural Love
and the Divine Love.
(JOHN, THE APOSTLE)
(February 19, 1919 | Received by James Padgett)

I AM HERE. *John.*

Let me say just a word. I was with you today when you were talking to your friend,[*] and heard your conversation, and saw the utter want of comprehension on the part of your friend as to the Truths of the spirit world, and especially of the laws that divide the mere perfect man from the divine man or spirit. He is so engulfed in the conceptions that he has of these loves, arising from his experience in life, that he can only see the existence of one love, the natural, and his mind is not capable of seeing the other Love. And, of course, his soul has not that development which would assure him of the reality of the Divine Love. The mind, itself, is capable of informing him of the existence and working of the natural love. But as this is the only means that he possesses of understanding what love is, he cannot possibly understand the Divine Love and that soul developed to a degree by the very Love Itself. He may argue to the extent of the capacity of his mind, and he will never be able to comprehend the Love that requires a perception of the soul. He may remain satisfied and convince himself that the natural love is the only love, and that, when it becomes developed to a certain degree, it becomes the Divine Love. But he will then find that he is far away from the Truth!

He must know, and I mean it is necessary for him to know, that only those who have the Divine Love to some degree are capable of knowing that the Divine is a thing of Itself, and not the development of the natural love; nor does It have the qualities of the natural love in It. The one is of God—that is, partakes of His Very Nature—while the other is also of God, but does not partake of His Nature. It is only a creation intended to make man happy and perfect in his condition of the mere man—the merely created existence.

I thought that I would give you these short comments on your conversation in order to show the grave and important mistake under which your friend is laboring. He will not easily believe these things of Truth while in the flesh; and, when he comes to spirit life, the difficulties will be just as great. And it may be that he will always be content to remain the possessor of this natural love only. I wish that it might be otherwise, and that he might let go of his intellectual belief and harken to the call of the soul, which, when not trammeled by these beliefs, is continually longing for this Greater Love.

Believe that I am your friend and interested in you to an extent that you cannot now comprehend, but which you will understand someday and wonder that such a thing could have been. Good night.

Your brother in Christ,

JOHN.

Mrs. Padgett Describes How Wonderful It Is to Obtain Possession of the Divine Love.

---

[*] Mr. Padgett's friend was investigating spiritual laws. This was told to Dr. Stone by Mr. Padgett.—Ed.

I AM HERE. *Helen.*

Well, my dear Ned, I see that you are very happy tonight, and I join in your happiness. For the source of our happiness is the same—the Great Divine Love of the Father. How loving He is and how thankful we should be that we not only have the privilege of receiving this Love but also that we know the Way as the Master has taught. Oh, wonderful is this Love, and more wonderful is it that little, insignificant creatures, as are we, should have the Way pointed out to us by which we can obtain this Love! The Father is Good and His Love is without stint or limitation in Its bestowal on all His children—even on those who do not seek for It with longings of the soul. It is always waiting for the desires of men to possess It; and, as you know, never is the man who earnestly seeks for It disappointed. Love is the one Great Gift of the Father which all may obtain. And only man, himself, can prevent this Love transforming his soul from the condition of the mortal to that of the immortal.

With all my love, I am

Your own true and loving,

HELEN.

Andrew, the Apostle, Declares That the Divine Love Casteth Out All Fear.
(ANDREW, THE APOSTLE)

I AM HERE. *Andrew.*

I came to tell you that where Love is there can be no sin or unhappiness, and fear is not.

We, who live in the Celestial Spheres, know this to be a fact. And with all the force and authority that knowledge gives, we declare this Truth unto you tonight: The "love" that casteth out all fear is the Divine Love of the Father. When a spirit obtains that, there exists no such thing as fear, and nothing that could create or permit fear to exist.

God wants the souls of men in Love, and not in fear. And the only way in which such end can be accomplished is for men to see and know Him as a God of Love only. No man can come to the Father except through this New Birth and faith in the Father's Love.

The performance of duty, good works, and mere faith, while they will all help man in the development of his moral character and qualities, yet, they will not give him an entrance into the Celestial Heavens (which are the heavens where Jesus rules and is the Prince) unless the spirit shall obtain this Divine Love which makes it a part of the Father's very Essence of Divinity.

Many spirits are happy by reason of their having led good, moral lives on earth, and because of a high development of their natural love. They realize that God is their Father, and that He watches over them and gives them many blessings. But this happiness is not that which comes with the possession of the Divine Love. And, besides, the place of habitation of these spirits is limited and does not permit these spirits to have free access to all the spheres where God's Goodness and Care are manifested.

The spirits who have obtained this Divine Love have no limitation to the spheres in which they may progress, and are not restricted in their places of habitation or in the spheres in which they may live. And, besides, the Presence and Glory of the Father are so much greater in these Celestial Spheres than in those where the mere natural love obtains.

I must not write more tonight, for you are commencing to tire.

So, with all my love, I will say that I am

Your brother in Christ,

ANDREW.

Jesus Explains What It Is That Makes a Man Divine.
(JESUS)
(March 15th, 1916 | Received by James Padgett)

I AM HERE. *Jesus.*

I wish to write tonight on the subject: "What It Is That Makes a Man Divine."

When man was created, he was given the highest qualities that could be bestowed upon a mortal. Yet, he was mere man, but the perfect one. And with these qualities was given him the possibility of becoming divine like the Father in His Nature. But this Gift was never possessed by him in Its enjoyment of full fruition until after my coming to earth and making known to man that such a possibility existed.

The first created man never possessed this Gift in Its fulfillment, but merely had the possibility of receiving It on condition that he continued in his obedience, and made the effort to receive It in the Way that the Father declared was the only Way.

You have been told in detail what this Gift was, and how the first parents forfeited the enjoyment of It by their disobedience and ambition to possess It in a way that was not in accord with the Father's Way.

As we have said, man lost this possibility at the time of the first disobedience, and thereafter became gradually a man with his moral nature sinking lower and lower until he became almost lost in the condition of the beasts in the field. And, from that condition, he has been steadily improving

167

or progressing towards his first estate of purity.

But a great many men have ceased to know, or have never known, that God is the Creator of all things, and that all creation is dependent upon Him for its very existence. In their assurance and self importance, they have assumed and professed to believe that their progress or salvation depends upon their own efforts, and that these efforts are sufficient to bring about this state of purity or harmony with God's Laws and Desires.

But men are mistaken in this. For there is nothing in them that is divine, and there never will be when they depend upon their own selves to progress to this state of perfection. The Divine Nature of the Father is not in man, and will never become a part of him until he pursues the Way which is absolutely necessary for him to follow in order to become anything more than mere man.

I will not write more tonight, as I think it best not to do so.

I understand that you could not prevent your condition of sleepiness, and I do not blame you, but I think it best to wait until later to finish what I desire to write.

Well, my dear brother, believe that I have only love for you, and will get close to you as we progress. So, I say, don't worry.

I will say good night.

Your brother and friend,

JESUS.

Stephen, the Apostle, Affirms That Jesus Wrote, and He Emphasizes the Great Importance of Mr. Padgett's Receipt of the Messages.
(STEPHEN, THE APOSTLE)
(March 15th, 1916 | Received by James Padgett)

I AM HERE. *Stephen.*

I am here and desire to write just a few lines, for you are not in condition for lengthy writing tonight.

The Master was disappointed, but he is so loving and good that he did not complain. He only wanted you to feel that you must not worry because of the fact that you could not take his message. But, nevertheless, he was disappointed.

I understand that you could not control your sleepiness, and are not to blame, but it was unfortunate. And, in some way, if possible, it must be avoided in the future.

If you only realized the great importance of these messages and the great number that are yet to be written, you would bend every effort to facilitate their reception. I am not saying this complainingly, but merely stating a fact. So, try your best to get in a good condition so that there will be no failure in your receiving the messages.

I am so very much interested in this work, and so are a host of other

168

spirits who realize the importance of these Truths being given to mankind. They are the only Truths, and never since the time when the Master was on earth have they been revealed to man.

I will not write more tonight, but will say with all my love that I am
Your brother in Christ,
STEPHEN.

John Discusses the Condition of the Soul When and After the Divine Love Flows into It.
(JOHN, THE APOSTLE)
(June 19th, 1916 | Received by James Padgett)

I AM HERE. *John.*

I come tonight to tell you that you are in better condition than you were last night, and that I desire to write a short message if you think that you can receive it.

Well, I will not write very long, and what I shall say will have to do with the condition of the soul when and after the Divine Love flows into it.

As you know, the soul is not in accord with the Love of God in the condition in which man possesses it before the entrance of the Divine Love; nor is it a part of the Great Oversoul. It is only a special creation made in the image of the Father, having in it the natural love which was conferred upon man at the time of his creation, and not having in it any part of the Essence of the Father, or any Quality that makes it of the Divine Nature of the Father, or necessarily immortal.

But when the Divine Love enters into it, and it becomes permeated, as it were, with the Divine Essence, then it takes on the Divine Nature of the Father. And to the extent that it receives and possesses this Love, it becomes at-one with God and ceases to be a mere image, and becomes transformed into the Substance.

In this transformed condition, the soul is altogether a different entity from the soul in the condition in which it was created, and it is no longer subject to the dominion of either the mind or of the animal appetites and desires. Hence, the spirit possessing such a soul is, in essence, a part of the Father; or, as Jesus said, it is in the Father and the Father in it.

NOW, DO NOT UNDERSTAND THAT SUCH A SOUL IS THE SOUL THAT MAN ORIGINALLY POSSESSED, BUT WITH INCREASED DEVELOPMENT OF PURITY AND GOODNESS OR FREEDOM FROM SIN, BECAUSE SUCH IS NOT THE CASE. SUCH SOUL, BY SUCH TRANSFORMATION, BECOMES A NEW THING, AND NEVER AGAIN CAN IT RELAPSE INTO THE SOUL OF MAN'S ORIGIN. BECAUSE OF THE QUALITIES THAT IT THEN POSSESSES, IT BECOMES IMMORTAL; AND SUCH IMMORTAL NATURE CAN NEVER BE TAKEN FROM IT. IT IS NOW A THING

169

OF LOVE AND PURITY, AND CONSCIOUSNESS OF ITS TRUE CONDITION IS ALWAYS WITH THE SPIRIT THAT HAS SUCH A SOUL.

THIS TRANSFORMATION IS GRADUAL. AND MEN MUST NOT THINK THAT, BY THE MERE ACT OF CONVERSION FROM THEIR STATE OF DEATH, THEY AT ONCE BECOME POSSESSED OF THE NATURE OF THE DIVINE, FOR SUCH IS NOT THE FACT. THE TRANSFORMATION IS GRADUAL, AND COMES ACCORDING TO THE SUSCEPTIBILITY OF THE SOULS TO RECEIVE THIS LOVE OF WHICH I SPEAK. BUT WHEN ONCE THE INFLOWING OF THE LOVE COMMENCES, IT CONTINUES ETERNALLY, ALTHOUGH THERE MAY BE TIMES OF STAGNATION AND APPARENT LOSS OF THIS DIVINE ESSENCE. YET, ALWAYS IS THE TRANSFORMATION TAKING PLACE; AND, AT CERTAIN STAGES IN ITS PROGRESS, THE POSSESSION OF THIS DIVINE LOVE WILL BE SO GREAT THAT THE ORIGINAL SOUL, OR ITS ORIGINAL QUALITIES, WILL ENTIRELY DISAPPEAR AND LEAVE ONLY THE NEW QUALITIES WHICH THE DIVINE LOVE HAS IMPLANTED IN IT. THE LEAVEN, WHEN ONCE DEPOSITED, NEVER CEASES TO WORK UNTIL THE WHOLE SHALL BECOME LEAVENED.

I will not write more tonight, but will only further say that this condition of transformation may be obtained by all men if they will only seek for it in the proper Way and with faith.

I will soon write to you again.

In leaving you, I give you my love and blessings and the assurance that I am helping you in your efforts to carry forward the work, and in accomplishing all the promises.

So, my dear brother, good night.

Your brother in Christ,

JOHN.

Ann Rollins Encourages Mr. Padgett to Press Forward to the Goal of a Home in the Celestial Heavens. She Also Refers to the Great Love of Jesus, and That Even He Is Still Praying for More of the Divine Love.
(ANN ROLLINS)
(January 12th, 1918 | Received by James Padgett)

I AM HERE. *Your grandmother.*

Let me write a few lines tonight, as I have been listening to your conversation with some interest, and I desire to say a few words that may encourage you both to press forward to the goal which you have before

170

you: a home in the Celestial Heavens and the acquirement of a nature divine, which only those who know the Way can obtain by following the Way that the Master has so lovingly taught you. You will not be disappointed in your efforts. For when you long for the Love and receive portions of It, every experience of that kind will help.

You must not think that it is possible to obtain this Love in Its fulness, and then permit your longings to decrease whenever you feel that the Love has come to you in wonderful abundance. For I must tell you that we know and realize in the Celestial Heavens that there is always more beyond what we obtain. Even the Master prays to the Father for an increase of this Love in his soul. And if you could see the evidence of the Love that he possesses, as we see it, you would probably think that nothing more could be obtained, or that there was no greater amount to be obtained. But, with us, this fact of endlessness of this Love is that which keeps us always striving and, consequently, happy, because, in realizing our experiences in our progress, and how each successive stage of that progress has brought us greater and greater happiness, we know—I say know that what is beyond must mean a greater happiness and a nearer approach to the Father, Himself.

So, I say, let not your strivings decrease in the slightest particular, and you will find that increased happiness will be yours.

I will stop now and, with my love to you both, will say good night.

Your loving grandmother,

ANN ROLLINS.

Jesus Presents His Discourse on the Real Truth of Life on Earth, and What It Means to Mortals.
(JESUS)
(May 25th, 1915 | Received by James Padgett)

I AM HERE. *Jesus.*

You are better tonight in your spiritual condition and I will write a formal message.

I desire to write on the subject of, "The Real Truth of Life on Earth, and What It Means to Mortals."

When men come to the knowledge that they are children of the Father and under His Care and Protection, they will see that they must lead such lives as will fit them to become in union with the Father and be able to partake of His Love, which makes them, as it were, a part of Himself. I mean that there is in all men the potentiality of becoming a part of the Divine Essence. But, in order for them to partake of this Divinity, they must let the Love of the Father, in Its highest Nature, enter into their souls and make them at-one with Him. No mere love that they had bestowed upon them as creatures of the Father's Handiwork will enable them to attain to this exalted condition. The natural love, of itself, is not sufficient because, when that love was bestowed upon them, it was merely intended to enable them to live in a good and harmonious way with their fellowmen. It was not the real Love that formed a part of the Divine Nature of the Father, and was not intended to make men a part of that Nature. So, in order for men to receive this higher Love, they must do the Will of the Father while on earth, or, after they become spirits, they will have a more difficult work in receiving the wonderful inflowing of this Divine Love.

The earth is the great plane of probation, and the development of the souls of men depends upon their correct living in accordance with these principles which the Father has established as the means whereby they may receive this condition of Love, which alone can make them at-one with Him.

Merely good deeds are not sufficient. Back of all deeds must be the soul's development, which results only from the possession of this Love. I do not mean by this that deeds do not form a part of this development, for they do. But deeds without the possession of this Love will never make a man the possessor of the one thing needful to ensure his entrance into the Heavenly Kingdom.

Men must love one another, and must, of course, do unto each other as they would be done by. If this rule of conduct were observed, men would be much happier on earth, even if they do not possess the Divine Love that I speak of.

NO MAN CAN BECOME FILLED WITH THIS LOVE OF HIMSELF. FOR IN ONLY ONE WAY WILL IT COME INTO HIS SOUL, AND THAT IS BY PRAYER TO THE FATHER FOR ITS INFLOWING, AND FAITH THAT HE WILL GIVE IT TO HIM WHO ASKS EARNESTLY AND HUMBLY. I KNOW THAT SOME MEN THINK THAT PRAYER IS NOTHING MORE THAN AN APPEAL TO THEIR OWN BETTER SELVES, BUT I TELL YOU THAT THIS IS A WRONG BELIEF. AND WHEN THEY REALIZE THE TRUTH THAT PRAYER ASCENDS TO THE FATHER, AND IS HEARD BY HIM AND ANSWERED, THEY WILL UNDERSTAND THE GREAT MISSION AND BENEFIT OF PRAYER.

LET MEN LIVE THE MOST EXEMPLARY LIVES, AND YET THEY WILL NOT NECESSARILY BECOME PARTNERS OF THIS GREAT LOVE, OR HAVE THE QUALITIES THAT ARE NECESSARY TO ENABLE THEM TO RECEIVE THE GREAT GIFT OF UNISON WITH THE FATHER. I URGE ALL MEN TO LIVE A GOOD MORAL LIFE BECAUSE IT HAS ITS OWN REWARD IN THE SPIRIT WORLD. THIS WILL MAKE THEM HAPPIER AS SPIRIT BEINGS IN A CONDITION OF MERE NATURAL LOVE, AND WILL FIT THEM FOR A LIFE IN THE SPIRIT WORLD WHICH WILL BRING HAPPINESS TO THEM—BUT NOT THE HAPPINESS OF THOSE WHO FIT THEMSELVES FOR GREATER HAPPINESS IN THE KINGDOM OF HEAVEN, OR CELESTIAL KINGDOM.

I will not discourage men from seeking the life of a moralist, or of one who tries to follow the truths of conduct which the Golden Rule imposes; but, on the contrary, I emphasize the necessity for such a life.

A good man approaches nearest the image of the Father than any other being can possibly attain to. And his reward in the future life will be that which comes only from living the life of such a man. So, I say, the more a man lives in accordance with these moral precepts, the nearer he will approach the image in which he was created.

BUT WHY SHOULD MEN BE SATISFIED WITH THE IMAGE WHEN THE REAL SUBSTANCE MAY BE THEIRS BY OBEYING THE INVITATION OF THE FATHER? THE IMAGE MAY SATISFY SOME WHO ARE CONTENT WITH SMALL THINGS, BUT THE ASPIRING SOUL WANTS THE REAL SUBSTANCE WHICH THE FATHER OFFERS FREELY TO THOSE WHO WILL ACCEPT HIS INVITATION.

No man can really live a good moral life unless he has the Love that I have mentioned as his guide. I do not believe that any man who knows the difference between the image and the Substance will be satisfied with the former. For, if so, he is rejecting the greatest happiness that even the Father can bestow upon him.

SO, LET NOT MEN BE CONTENT WITH TRYING TO LIVE GOOD MORAL LIVES, BUT LET THEM SEEK WITH ALL THEIR HEARTS THE LOVE THAT MAKES THEM TRULY ANGELS OF GOD—SUCH ANGELS AS CAN FEEL AND REALIZE THE CERTAINTY THAT THEY ARE IMMORTAL BY REASON OF THE DIVINITY WHICH SUCH LOVE BRINGS TO THEM.

IMMORTALITY IS ONLY OF GOD. AND ANYTHING LESS THAN GOD OR HIS DIVINE ESSENCE, WHICH MAKES THE CREATURE A PART OF THAT DIVINITY, IS NOT IMMORTAL.

Adam and Eve, or whom they typify, were mortals, free from sin and obedient to the Father, who thought that they were immortal. But, when the temptation came and they yielded, they realized to their great sorrow that they were not immortal. And so will every spirit of mortal be in the future life where the Divine Love of the Father has not become a part of their existence.

LIFE ON EARTH IS AN IMPORTANT PART OF THE GREAT ETERNITY OF LIVING. MEN SHOULD REALIZE THIS TO ITS FULLEST MEANING, AND NOT THINK THE EARTH A MERE STOPPING PLACE WHERE THE SPIRIT IS ENFOLDED IN FLESH ONLY FOR THE PLEASURES AND GRATIFICATION OF ITS CARNAL APPETITES. THIS EARTH LIFE IS A FLEETING SHADOW OF THE SPIRIT LIFE, BUT AN IMPORTANT SHADOW TO THE HAPPINESS WHICH MAN MAY ENJOY IN THE FUTURE. IT IS THE MOST IMPORTANT PERIOD OF MAN'S WHOLE EXISTENCE. AND THE WAY THAT SUCH LIFE IS LIVED MAY DETERMINE THE WHOLE FUTURE LIFE OF THE MAN. I DON'T MEAN THAT THERE IS NO REDEMPTION BEYOND THE GRAVE, FOR THE

MERCY OF THE FATHER CONTINUES INTO THE SPIRIT LIFE. BUT WHEN MAN FAILS TO ACCEPT THIS MERCY—I MEAN THE WAY IN WHICH HE MAY BECOME A DIVINE CHILD OF THE FATHER WHILE IN THE EARTH LIFE—HE MAY NEVER ACCEPT IT IN THE SPIRIT LIFE.

So many spirits are contented to remain in the happiness of their natural love, and refuse to be convinced that there is a greater Love and happiness awaiting them in the Father's Kingdom, which may be theirs if they will only believe and seek. This I say from my knowledge of the real condition of spirits in the spirit world, and from the difficulty which the redeemed spirits have found in their endeavors to convince these spirits, who are enjoying the happiness of their natural love, that there is a happier and better sphere in which they may live if they will seek for the Divine Love of the Father.

AS I SAID WHEN ON EARTH, "STRAIT IS THE GATE AND NARROW IS THE WAY WHICH LEADS TO LIFE ETERNAL, AND FEW THERE BE WHO ENTER THEREIN." AND THIS SAYING APPLIES TO THE SPIRIT WORLD AS WELL AS TO THE MATERIAL WORLD.

SO, LET ME URGE UPON ALL MEN TO SEEK THE STRAIT AND NARROW WAY, FOR ONLY BY IT CAN MEN COME TO THE FULL ENJOYMENT OF WHAT THE FATHER HAS PROVIDED FOR THEM.

I WILL NOW STOP. BUT, IN CLOSING, I WILL SAY WITH ALL THE LOVE AND KNOWLEDGE WHICH I POSSESS: LET MEN SEEK THIS GREAT DIVINE LOVE AND, IN FAITH, THEY WILL FIND IT AND FOREVER BE ONE WITH THE IMMORTAL FATHER WHO IS IMMORTAL AND HAPPY BEYOND ALL CONCEPTION.

So, I will say, with all my love and blessings and the Blessings of the Father, "SEEK AND YE SHALL FIND!"

Good night.

Your loving brother and friend,

JESUS.

Ann Rollins Comments on the Message Jesus Wrote Through Mr. Padgett.
(ANN ROLLINS)
(May 25th, 1915 | Received by James Padgett)

I AM HERE. *Your grandmother.*

What a truthful and important message the Master wrote to you! He knows that what he said is of the most vital importance to mankind. I only wish that all mankind could hear his message, for, if that could be, many a thinking and perhaps thoughtless man would turn his thoughts to God and strive to obtain that Great Love which the Master wrote of so eloquently.

The more I think of the great work that you have been selected to do, the more I am surprised, because, as I conceive it to be, this work is of more importance to mankind than anything that has been attempted since the Master was on earth and unfolded the great Truths of His Father to his disciples and hearers.

So, try with all your faith and earnestness to get into as high a spiritual condition as possible so that you may be able to receive and write the important and heretofore hidden Truths which the Master shall disclose to you. He is so much in earnest that these Truths shall be given to mankind that he has done you the greatest honor that could possibly be bestowed upon you.

Your loving grandmother,
ANN ROLLINS.

John Calvin, the 16th Century Theologian and Reformer Expresses His Interest in the Work and the Means Whereby All Men May Receive the Divine Love.
(JOHN CALVIN)
(June 20th, 1916 | Received by James Padgett)

I AM HERE. *John Calvin.*

Let me write just a word, as I am anxious to make known to you that I am interested in your work and in the development of the knowledge of the soul, and the means by which all men may receive the Divine Love of the Father and become at-one with Him.

I am not going to write you a lecture tonight. I merely write that I may get in rapport with you so that I may have the opportunity and ability to write to you later of those things of deep and lasting interest to mortals.

I am not known to you, but I hope that you will soon consider me one of your friends, as I desire to be I assure you.

I must stop now and, in leaving, will subscribe myself,

Your true friend and brother in Christ,
JOHN CALVIN.

Nicodemus Confirms the Importance of the New Birth.
(NICODEMUS)
(July 30th, 1915 | Received by James Padgett)

I AM HERE. *Nicodemus.*

I was master in Israel, and yet I did not understand this New Birth. How

175

few understood it then, and how few now!

Oh, the long years that have gone by since Jesus told me THAT I MUST BE BORN AGAIN TO INHERIT ETERNAL LIFE; and how comparatively seldom this Great Truth is taught by the churches and the teachers of religious matters!

THIS TRUTH IS AT THE VERY FOUNDATION OF MANKIND'S REDEMPTION. AND UNTIL A MAN RECEIVES THIS NEW BIRTH, HE CANNOT POSSIBLY ENTER INTO THE KINGDOM OF HEAVEN. MEN MAY CLAIM TO HAVE FAITH IN GOD AND BELIEVE ON JESUS' NAME, AND CONFORM TO ALL THE ESSENTIALS AND SACRAMENTS OF THE CHURCHES, AND YET, UNLESS THEY HAVE THIS NEW BIRTH, THEIR FAITH AND WORKS AS CHRISTIANS ARE VAIN.

This I know from my own experience as well as from the teachings of the Master. And I desire to emphasize, with all the powers that I have, that It is the only important requirement to immortality.

THE NEW BIRTH MEANS THE FLOWING OF THE DIVINE LOVE OF THE FATHER INTO THE SOUL OF A MAN SO THAT THAT MAN BECOMES, AS IT WERE, A PART OF THE FATHER IN HIS DIVINITY AND IMMORTALITY.

WHEN THIS TRUTH COMES TO A MAN AND HE COMMENCES TO RECEIVE THE DIVINE NATURE OF THE FATHER, ALL THAT PART OF HIM THAT MAY BE CALLED THE "NATURAL NATURE" COMMENCES TO LEAVE HIM. AND AS THE DIVINE LOVE CONTINUES TO GROW AND FILL HIS SOUL, THE NATURAL LOVE AND AFFECTIONS FOR THINGS OF THE EARTH WILL DISAPPEAR; AND, AS A RESULT, HE WILL BECOME AT-ONE WITH THE FATHER AND IMMORTAL.

Why don't those who profess to be teachers of Jesus' Truths—which are the Truths of the Father—and all followers of him, pay more attention to this vital Truth?

When you shall have received the messages from the Master, I think you will find this Truth of the New Birth to be the one thing that Jesus will emphasize and reiterate most. It is the most important thing for men not only to hear about and acquiesce in their intellectual beliefs, but also to actually experience.

I wish I had understood the New Birth when on earth as I do now.

(In his conversation with you on earth, what was Jesus specifically referring to when he used the example of the wind?)

He meant: As no man could see the wind or tell from whence it came or whither it was going, so no man who received this New Birth could see the operations of the Holy Spirit* or know whence It came. But this latter expression must be modified because we all know It comes from the Father; but just how we do not know. The Holy Spirit is as invisible as the wind, and yet it is just as real and existing.

But men need not trouble their intellects to know exactly what this

Great Power is, for it is sufficient to know that that which causes the New Birth is the Divine Love of the Father coming into the souls of men.

I must stop, as I have written enough for tonight.

So, let me subscribe myself a brother who has received the New Birth, and a lover and follower of the Master.

NICODEMUS.

Ann Rollins Discusses the Necessity of Obtaining the Divine Love.
She Cautions That Those Who Refuse This Great Gift,
After the Privilege of Obtaining It Is Withdrawn,
Will Suffer the "Second Death."
(ANN ROLLINS)
(July 30th, 1915 | Received by James Padgett)

I AM HERE. *Your grandmother.*

I thought that I might write you a message tonight, if you feel like receiving it.

The only Way in which salvation can be obtained by man, and make him of a nature divine, is through the medium of the Holy Ghost, and by the Way pointed out by Jesus.

I will not attempt to go into details here as to the methods, for they have been fully explained to you. But I must say that no other methods can be pursued that will bring the soul of man in unison with God and make him of a nature divine.

No sacraments of baptism or mere ceremony of the church will enable a man to accomplish this end; and, in fact, such things frequently retard the soul of man from becoming in the condition of development that places him in the position of a redeemed child of God.

I WILL NOT WRITE MUCH OR IN DETAIL AS TO WHAT MAN HIMSELF SHOULD DO IN ORDER TO BRING INTO OPERATION THE WORKINGS OF THE HOLY SPIRIT, BUT WILL MERELY SAY THAT HE MUST PRAY WITH THE SINCERE LONGINGS OF HIS SOUL FOR THE INFLOWING OF THE FATHER'S LOVE; AND HE MUST HAVE FAITH THAT SUCH LOVE IS A REAL THING, AND THAT IT COMES TO HIM IN RESPONSE TO HIS PRAYERS.

And now to continue as to the Truth that this Love is waiting for all mankind, no matter where the individuals of the race may be, and that they can receive this Love even though they have never heard of the Plan of salvation as declared by Jesus.

When God rebestowed this Love, He intended that every human being, as well as spirit, should have the opportunity to obtain It, and that the manner in which It might be obtained should be made known to all mankind. And, in carrying out this intention, He specially selected Jesus for this work, who, through his own teachings, would enable mankind to learn of this Love.

Of course, during the short ministry of Jesus on earth, it was impossible that all men should learn of him through the teachings of himself or of his disciples. Hence, the spirits of the world of spirits were permitted to hear these teachings and come into their knowledge. Then, when they should obtain this Love, they were to teach It to mortals and spirits, which they did; and they have been doing so ever since.

But while they have been working all these centuries to bring about this great consummation, yet, they have not succeeded for the reason that they could not force the Truth of the Plan of salvation upon either mortal or spirit. Consequently, in the exercise of their free wills, unless men and spirits would open up their understandings of the soul qualities, supplemented by the exercise of their mental qualities, they could not obtain this Divine Love. And just as men on earth have refused to listen to those in mortal life who have attempted to teach them of religious things, so, in the spirit world, many spirits have refused and are refusing to listen to the teachings of other spirits who have the knowledge and possession of this Great Love. And mortals have also failed to respond to the impressions which spirits have been trying to make upon them as to this Truth, and, as a consequence, were unable to open up their soul perceptions. Thus, many mortals, as well as spirits, have never received the benefit of the Great Gift of rebestowal of this Love.

Yet, as I have said, many have responded to these impressions and, even while on earth, have had the inflowing of this Love to a more or less extent, although they may not have been conscious of the fact in such a definite manner as to know that what they had received was a portion of the Divine Love.

Among the great obstacles to men putting themselves in this condition of receptivity are the creeds and mental beliefs and ceremonies obtaining in many of the churches of Christendom, and in many of the faiths and teachings of the races which live outside of Christendom, and which have never heard of this great Plan of salvation.

In the spirit world, the followers of many of the faiths and creeds, distinct and different from one another, live together in communities as separate races, still believing in their various creeds and teachings of their leaders. And they have never heard of this Divine Love or of the necessity of receiving It, but worship God according to their beliefs on earth, satisfied that the doctrines which they profess are the true and only ones. And they absolutely refuse to listen to the spirits who often try to teach the Truths as to eternal life in the Celestial Spheres.

Of course, these spirits have the right and the power to refuse to listen to these Truths, and are never compelled to. And then, again, some of them will listen, but will decline to believe that there are any other Truths than the ones that they have embraced.

And, thus, you see that, while this Great Gift of the Divine Love, and the privilege of obtaining It, was bestowed upon all men, and that this Love is ever ready to enter into their souls, yet, a very large majority of spirits and mortals will never receive It and become inhabitants of the many mansions.

All men and spirits will have the opportunity to receive this Love before the great day of final separation, but many will not be willing to accept this Gift. They will be satisfied in the happiness of their natural love, and will be contented to live in their merely spiritual homes.

BECAUSE OF THE FACT OF THE GREAT VARIETY OF BELIEFS AND TEACHINGS ON EARTH AS TO THE MEANING OF THE "SECOND DEATH," LET ME SAY HERE THAT MANY MEN AND SPIRITS WILL NEGLECT TO EXERCISE THEIR PRIVILEGE OF OBTAINING THE GREAT GIFT OF THE DIVINE LOVE AND SUFFER THE SECOND DEATH. THE SECOND DEATH WILL TAKE PLACE WHEN THAT GREAT SEPARATION OCCURS, AND THE GIFT OF THIS PRIVILEGE OF RECEIVING THE DIVINE LOVE OF THE FATHER WILL AGAIN BE WITHDRAWN FROM MAN AND SPIRIT. NO OTHER DEATH IS MEANT, FOR MAN AND SPIRIT WILL CONTINUE TO LIVE THEIR MORTAL AND SPIRIT LIVES WITHOUT ANY OTHER DEATH THAN THAT WHICH IS NOW CONSTANTLY TAKING PLACE. THERE WILL BE NO DEATH IN THE SENSE OF CONDEMNING THE SPIRIT OF MAN TO ETERNAL PUNISHMENT, OR CAUSING THE ANNIHILATION OF ANY SPIRIT, AS IS TAUGHT BY SOME OF YOUR RELIGIOUS TEACHERS. NO, THE ONLY DEATH WILL BE THE DEATH THAT THE FIRST PARENTS DIED AT THE TIME OF THEIR DISOBEDIENCE, WHICH WAS THE DEPRIVATION OF THE GREAT PRIVILEGE OF RECEIVING THE DIVINE LOVE AND THEREBY PARTAKING OF THE DIVINE NATURE OF THE FATHER AND IMMORTALITY.

Well, my dear boy, I have written enough for tonight and will stop.

You have my love and my influence to help you in every way, and also my prayers to the Father for your spiritual development.

So, with my blessings, I will say good night.

Your loving,

GRANDMOTHER.

Jesus Explains Why Men Must Receive the Divine Love in Order to Be Admitted to the Kingdom of Heaven, or Celestial Kingdom.
(JESUS)
(June 4th, 1915 | Received by James Padgett)

I AM HERE. *Jesus.*

I am with you tonight, as I heard you longing for me, and have come

179

to comfort and bless you.

My dear brother, you have the Love of the Father in your soul to a great extent this night, and I see that you are very happy and feel that the Father is very near you. And I am so glad that your condition is such, for I want to tell you how much the Love of the Father is waiting to bless you and make you at-one with Him, and a true child of His Affections.

I am now prepared to give you my next formal message, and, if you feel that you would like to take it tonight, I will do so.

Well, then, I will write on the subject: "Why Man Must Receive the Divine Love in Order to Be Admitted to the Kingdom of Heaven, or Celestial Kingdom."

In that Kingdom, there are no spirits who have not received this Love, so that their natures are of the Divine Essence of the Father. I do not mean that any spirit is perfect in this divine nature, but that each spirit has so much of this Divine Love in his soul as to make him in unison with the Nature of the Father. There are different degrees of perfection, or, rather, there are different degrees of possession of this Love by the spirits; and their happiness and glory are dependent upon the amount of Love possessed by them. No spirit who is an inhabitant of this Kingdom, though, is without this Divine Love. And no spirit has in its soul any sin or error that may have been a part of it while in the earth life.

All the spirits know that they are immortal, just as the Father is Immortal. And this knowledge comes to them only from the possession of this Love, which is the Divine Essence that flowed into their souls from the Great Divine Nature of the Father. Should anything in the soul not be in unison with the Soul of the Father, that spirit could not possibly enter into that Kingdom. And as the soul of such spirit remains in such condition of inharmony, it can never be received into the Celestial Kingdom.

I know that, among men, and spirits also, it is thought and asserted that the Father is All-Merciful and All-Good, and, in His Great Plan for the salvation of men and for establishing the harmony of His Universe, that no man or spirit will be excluded from His Heavenly Kingdom. But, in this thought, both mortals and spirits are mistaken. And I am sorry to say that many of them, when too late, will realize this error.

God has certain Principles which are fixed and which are necessary for men to know and obey in order for them to become at-one with Him and partake of his Divine Nature. And if they fail to obey the requirements of these Principles, they will forever be excluded from that in their souls which will make them like the Father and admit them to His Kingdom.

In such condition, or want of the qualifications, they would not be happy, even though they were admitted to the Kingdom, for their condition would wholly fail to respond to those things in the Kingdom which give happiness to the true children of the Father. Of necessity, they would be most unhappy, and heaven would not be a heaven to them. So, you see, all spirits must have the prescribed requirements of soul love and soul development in order to inhabit this Kingdom.

As I said when on earth, "He that enters into the sheepfold in any other way than through the gate is a thief and a robber," and no thief or robber is fitted for this Kingdom of Divine Love.

LET MAN KNOW THAT NO MERCY OR LOVE OF THE FATHER WILL BE GIVEN HIM TO ENABLE HIM TO ENTER THIS KINGDOM UNLESS THAT MAN SEEKS THIS LOVE AND THIS MERCY IN THE WAY THE FATHER HAS ORDAINED THAT THEY SHALL BE SOUGHT FOR. NO SPECIAL PROVIDENCE WILL BE EXTENDED TO ANY MAN. AND IF HE COMES TO THE MARRIAGE FEAST WITHOUT HIS WEDDING GARMENT, HE WILL BE CAST OUT AND NOT BE PERMITTED TO ENJOY THE FEAST. MEN MAY REASON TO THE EXTENT OF ALL THEIR REASONING POWERS TO PROVE THAT THE FATHER, BEING A LOVING AND MERCIFUL FATHER, WILL NOT CAST THEM OUT, OR KEEP THEM FROM ENTERING THIS KINGDOM, BECAUSE THEY ARE ALL HIS CHILDREN AND THE OBJECTS OF HIS LOVE AND FAVOR; AND THAT ONE IS AS DEAR TO HIM AS THE OTHER; AND THAT HE IS NO RESPECTER OF PERSONS; AND THAT, THEREFORE, HE WILL TREAT ALL ALIKE. BUT I TELL THEM THEY ARE MISTAKEN. AND IF THEY WAIT UNTIL THE GREAT DAY WHEN THE "SHEEP" SHALL BE SEPARATED FROM THE "GOATS", THEY WILL REALIZE TO THEIR EVERLASTING EXCLUSION FROM THIS KINGDOM THAT WHAT I SAY IS TRUE.

OF COURSE, EVERY SPIRIT EVER BORN IS TO THE FATHER THE OBJECT OF HIS CARE, AND HE MAKES NO DISTINCTION BETWEEN THE SPIRITS AND MORTALS THAT HE HAS CREATED, WANTING EVERY ONE OF THEM TO INHABIT HIS KINGDOM AND PARTAKE OF THOSE THINGS WHICH HE HAS PROVIDED FOR THEM, AND WHICH ARE BEYOND THEIR CONCEPTION IN THE GREATNESS OF THE GRANDEUR AND BEAUTY OF THESE THINGS. HE CALLS TO ALL HIS CREATURES TO COME AND PARTAKE OF THESE GREAT PROVISIONS THAT HE HAS MADE FOR THEM, AND NO CREATURE IS REFUSED THE GIFT OF THESE THINGS, OR HEARD TO ASK AND NOT BE ANSWERED WITH THEIR BESTOWAL. YET, WHEN THAT MAN OR SPIRIT WHO HAS THIS GREAT BOON, AND THE WAY SHOWN BY WHICH HE CAN RECEIVE THESE GIFTS, REFUSES OR NEGLECTS TO FOLLOW THAT WAY OR TO RECEIVE THESE GIFTS IN THE WAY ORDAINED BY THE FATHER, THEN ALL THESE GREAT GIFTS ARE WITHDRAWN FROM HIM. AFTER THE GREAT DAY OF SEPARATION, NEVER AGAIN WILL HE HAVE THE PRIVILEGE OF RECEIVING THEM.[*]

---

[*] The reader is referred to "Divine Love Is a Privileged Gift of the Father," of this chapter, wherein Jesus offers certain important enlargements and qualifications concerning the Celestial Heavens and the Divine Love.—Ed.

AND MEN CANNOT SAY THAT THE FATHER IS UNJUST OR UNMERCIFUL OR UNLOVING BECAUSE, THEREAFTER, HE FOREVER SHUTS THE DOOR TO THESE PRIVILEGES OR THE OPPORTUNITY OF RECEIVING THEM. MEN HAVE REJECTED HIS GIFT AND NEGLECTED TO SEARCH HIS PLANS FOR THEIR GREAT HAPPINESS; CONSEQUENTLY, THEY WILL HAVE NO RIGHT TO COMPLAIN WHEN, LIKE THE FOOLISH VIRGINS, THEY FIND THE DOOR SHUT AGAINST THEM.

SO, I SAY, MEN MUST REALIZE THE NECESSITY OF PUTTING ON THE WEDDING GARMENTS AND OF FILLING THEIR LAMPS WITH OIL IN ORDER TO BE ADMITTED INTO THE KINGDOM.

I will not herein tell the Way in which men must prepare themselves for an entrance into this Kingdom of the Father, for it would take too long; but I will explain this fully in a future message. And, before closing, I will say that if men will pray to the Father for the inflowing of His Divine Love into their souls, and have faith, they will find themselves on the true Way to becoming inhabitants of His Kingdom.[*]

As it is late, I must stop writing. With all my love and blessings, and the Blessing of the Father, I will say good night.

Your friend and brother,

JESUS.

Mrs. Padgett Affirms That Jesus Wrote.
(HELEN PADGETT)
(June 4th, 1915 | Received by James Padgett)

I AM HERE. *Helen.*

Well, sweetheart, you had a wonderful and vital message from Jesus, and you must study it; for it lies at the foundation of all the future happiness of men and spirits. Of course, you know the Way and will follow it. But there are so many men now living, and who have lived, who will never see the Kingdom of Heaven, or Celestial Kingdom.

I am so glad that I have found this Love which makes me a redeemed spirit, and I am just as glad that you have. And to think that all our band have found this Love, as well as many of the darkened spirits who have come to you for help! Have you ever thought of the greatness of the work that you are doing, and what the probable result will be to you as well as to them?

Well, I am not able to tell you. But the Master says, "Great will be your reward!"

Oh, my Ned, what a blessing it is that you have such a wonderful power

---

[*] See: "The Only Way to the Kingdom of God in the Celestial Heavens," by Jesus, in volume I of *Angelic Revelations of Divine Truth.*—Ed.

given you as to be able to do this great work of love and salvation.

With all my love and earnest prayers for your happiness that my soul can utter,

I am your own true and loving,
HELEN.

Divine Love is a Privilege Gift of the Father
(JESUS)
(April 21st, & May 3rd, 1955 | Received by Dr. Samuels)

I AM HERE. *Jesus.*

I will answer the question which Dr. Stone wanted to know – if it were possible for Celestial Spirits to keep on obtaining the Divine Love of the Father throughout all eternity, once the privilege of obtaining this Great Gift has been withdrawn from mankind. I have already written you to the effect that, even though the privilege of obtaining this Great Gift is withdrawn from mortals and spirits who have not obtained any of the Divine Love of the Father at the time of its withdrawal, yet, those whose soul mates are in the Celestial Heavens or those who have some of the Divine Love in their souls and are progressing through the spheres towards the Celestial Heavens, will retain the privilege of thus obtaining the Divine Love for a certain period of time, as a period of grace before the privilege is taken away from them as well.

Now in the case of Celestial Spirits, the privilege of obtaining the Divine Love can never be withdrawn. And this also holds for souls with some of the Love who are progressing towards the Celestial Heavens, for the Father cannot withdraw His Love and Divine Nature from a soul once He has bestowed His Great Gift upon that soul. For once some of the Divine Nature is lodged in a soul, It can never be removed. And that soul has the privilege of seeking more and more of the Father's nature for all eternity. The Divine Love in the soul of man or spirit gives to that mortal or spirit a kinship in nature with the Father born as a result of the At-onement that then exists between the soul of that mortal or spirit and the Great Soul of God, if only to a certain extent. And, in fact, this kinship grows ever closer throughout all eternity as more and more of the Nature of God is conveyed into the soul of that mortal or spirit. God does not withdraw His own Nature or Essence from the soul of the mortal or spirit which has done the Will of the Father and has obtained, if only to a small degree, His Divine Nature. And, thus, the Father may withdraw this privilege from souls which do not have the Divine Love, and those souls have lost nothing which they did not possess before. But removal of the Love from a soul possessing a portion of It would mean God's taking away from that soul the Great Gift which that soul obtained by prayer; and such a removal of the Love would mean that the soul's earnest longing for His

Divine Love would be in vain. So, even if the Gift of the Divine Love is withdrawn, it means that its withdrawal applies only to those who have not sought for It and have shown themselves indifferent to Its presence and not desirous of its possession. It is never withdrawn from those who have sought for It through the earnest longings of their souls. And to such as have received, It is given; and they retain the privilege of seeking It in greater abundance throughout all eternity.

The Divine Love is the essence and the nature of God, and It is always in existence; for if It did not exist, God could not exist. Therefore, it does not mean that, if withdrawn by God, It ceases to exist. For the age in which you and the doctor[*] live, and for a certain number of centuries to come, this Gift will continue to flow from the Source of the Father's Being. And when it does cease, it does not necessarily mean that the privilege will be withdrawn for all eternity. For souls yet unborn would thus be deprived of the opportunity of seeking for It in the mortal as well as in the spirit world. And thus, it is conceived that the Divine Love may flow for a period, cease for a period, and then be rebestowed in the fullness of time. And this may or may not continue in a series of ebbs and flows, as the Father so desires.

Received May 3rd, 1955

I would say in reply to your question, that the first parents were given free will to use their soul desires as they wished, and the result of these desires showed that purity of soul was not a protection against contamination. And the disobediences and transgressions that followed were not merely the aberrations of the first parents, but those also of, and intensified greatly by, the children, until evil became a force that proved more powerful than purity, and man and his descendants degenerated in body and spirituality until they could be likened to, and in some respects were worse than, the beasts in the field. Man wanted to be free of dependence upon God and sought to be co-equal with God in power and wisdom and immortality without paying homage to his Creator. As a result, pride and arrogance and independence were the first sins that entered the soul of man and defiled it; and murder was not far away, for sin is soul defilement regardless of type and degree.

Although it was God who withheld the possibility of man's obtaining the Divine Love after his fall, man's condition became such, when sin entered, that the Divine Love could not be sought for in that, in his pride and independence, he willed that It should be removed as an indication of God's protecting influence. When man sinned because of his desire to be independent of God, he showed God that he did not want God's help in his progress through life as a mortal. And, when he came to the spirit world, the same sense of independence of God was evidenced. God did withdraw His Privilege of the possibility of obtaining the Divine Love, but man had

---

[*] Dr. Leslie R. Stone

shown he did not want It if it meant acknowledging God as his Creator and upon Whom he was dependent for His Good Gifts. And he was determined to live without them for the sake of being his own soul master.

The same deplorable situation is as manifest today as it was at the time of the great fall among many individuals. And mortals will continue to possess this attitude even after they come into the spirit world. In fact, the majority will never turn to God for this Divine Love, even though the privilege of receiving It has been in existence since I appeared on earth.

There are good and evil spirits in the various spheres which are attracted to man because of the similar condition of man's soul. A man's desire to act in accordance with God's Laws will attract spirits of those spheres which are imbued with the sense of the purity of God's Laws. Man's desire to think and do evil will also result in attracting spirits of the earth plane. And men's desire to seek At-onement with the Father through prayer will just as inevitably cause the bringing into existence of conditions leading to the attraction of the Celestial Spirits to that man, or to the attraction of those spirits whose duty it is to help man turn to the Father and help him obtain the Divine Love, or more of It.

The withdrawal of the Divine Love at some time in the future indicates that this is merely a privilege bestowed upon mankind by a Loving Father, and does not mean that the Divine Love will be withdrawn from mankind for all eternity; for, actually, this is something which has not been revealed to the Celestial Heavens as yet. But knowing the Father to the extent that I do, I cannot believe that God, in His Great Goodness and Mercy, does not have a Plan of salvation which will permit all of His created souls the opportunity to seek At-onement with Him, even though, at the time of their incarnation, the Gift of immortality has been withdrawn.

For just as the souls of men were given the opportunity to embrace the privilege of obtaining the Love as Spirits – a privilege denied them in the flesh before the time of my appearance – so it cannot be said definitely that, at some future date, in God's Own Good Time, the privilege will not be in some way restored after the second withdrawal. And even though the Celestial Heavens will be filled and its doors closed after the second withdrawal, this does not mean that there will not be created another Celestial Heaven in God's Realms; for, as I said on earth, "In my Father's House are many mansions," and the possibilities of God's Acts of Goodness and Loving-Kindness are commensurate with His infinite Ways of controlling His Universe and the creatures which it contains. God, being all Love and Mercy and Wisdom, will not give to man, His children, a stone when they ask for bread, nor a serpent when they ask for fish.

At this time, I shall say good night and affirm that I am
Your older brother and friend,
JESUS

Chapter 7.

The Natural Love of Mankind.

MESSAGES INCLUDED IN THIS CHAPTER

Jesus Discuses the Love of Man, or Natural Love, in Contrast to the Divine Love Which is Necessary to Obtain In Order to Give Man the Highest Degree of Happiness. (JESUS).......................189

Abraham Lincoln Explains How Man Can Come into Harmony with the Laws That Govern Him as the Created Man, Without Obtaining the Divine Love. (ABRAHAM LINCOLN).......................191

Mrs. Padgett Comments on Abraham Lincoln's Message on Man's Progress in His Natural Love. (HELEN PADGETT) 193

What Men Should Believe in Order to Again Become the Perfect Man. (JESUS).......................193

Professor Salyards Discusses the Object of Man's Life on Earth, and the Necessity of Doing Certain Things Whereby Man Can Become the Perfect Man—but Not the Divine Man. (PROFESSOR JOSEPH H. SALYARDS).......................195

James Explains How Man Can Again Be Restored to the Perfect Man, Like the First Parents Before Their Fall. (JAMES, THE APOSTLE)..198

Mrs. Padgett Affirms That James Wrote Through Her Husband. (HELEN PADGETT).......................200

Luke Declares That No Man Can Possibly Reach the Condition of the Perfect Man Unless His Mental Beliefs Become in Accord with the Truth. (LUKE, THE APOSTLE).......................200

What Is the Correct Way in Which a Man Should Live on Earth in Order to Receive the Cleansing from His Sins So That He Can Acquire the Purification of His Natural Love? (JESUS).......................202

Mrs. Padgett Explains Why the Previous Message from the Master Had to Be Discontinued. (HELEN PADGETT).......................204

Jesus Continues His Message on How a Mortal May Obtain the

Development of His Soul Without the Help of the Divine Love. (JESUS) 204

Martin Luther, Former Monk and Reformer, Affirms That the Master Wrote. (MARTIN LUTHER) 208

Mrs. Padgett Also Affirms That the Master Wrote. (HELEN PADGETT) 208

Luke Discusses the Development of the Soul in Its Natural Love Wherein the New Birth Is Not Experienced. (LUKE, THE APOSTLE) 208

Luke Continues His Discourse on the Development of the Soul in Its Natural Love. (LUKE, THE APOSTLE) 212

What Is the Destiny of the Mortal Who Has Not Experienced the New Birth, but Who Will Progress to That Condition Which May Be Called the Perfect Man? (JOHN, THE APOSTLE) 215

John Continues His Discourse on the Destiny of the Soul That Has Not Experienced the New Birth. (JOHN, THE APOSTLE) 217

7.

The Natural Love of Mankind.

Jesus Discusses the Love of Man, or Natural Love, in Contrast to the Divine Love Which is Necessary to Obtain In Order to Give Man the Highest Degree of Happiness.
(JESUS)
(June 4th, 1915 | Received by James Padgett)

I AM HERE. *Jesus*.

I want to write tonight on the love of man.

This love is one that is not understood by humanity in its most important particular. I mean that this love is not one that is sufficient to give man the highest degree of happiness which he may obtain in either the mortal life or in the life to come.

This love is of a nature that changes with the change in the ideas and desires of men, and has no stability that will serve to keep him constant in his affections. No man who has only this love can ever be in condition to say that he will continue to have this love for a longer time than the present. And when he thinks that his love can never change or leave him, he is only giving thought to the wish.

But this love is one that may last for a long time, and sometimes it seems that it can never die or grow less; yet, in its very nature, it has not that constancy which insures its lasting longer than a moment of time.

I do not mean to say anything disparaging of this natural love, for it is undoubtedly the greatest gift that the Father has bestowed upon mankind; and, without it, men would be in a very unhappy condition. Yet, it is not the Great Love of the Father which all men may receive if they will only seek and strive to obtain It by prayer and faith.

This natural love is that which unites men and women in unity while on earth, and enables them to approach nearer to a life of happiness than does any other human quality. But, still, it has the danger always accompanying it that, sometime, in some way, it may cease to exist.

The mother's love is the strongest of all loves given to mortals, and apparently it can never end or grow old. Yet, a time may come when that love will die or cease to retain all its vitality or beauty. I know it is said that love never dies, but that is not true as regards this natural love. And no man can say that his love of today will remain his love of a few years hence.

Yet, there is a love that may be called the natural love that will last forever, providing these souls seek and obtain the Divine Love, and that is the love that God has implanted in two souls that he has designed to become

189

one in spirit life. This love is really not two loves, but one and the same love manifested in the two opposite sexes, and which is only a complete one when these two apparently independent souls come together in perfect unity. This is what is commonly called the love of soulmates, and which is that essence of spiritual love which makes the happiness of the two spirits of mortals seemingly complete. Yet, this love is not of a Divine nature, but merely the highest type of the natural love.

So, when men speak of the love of one mortal for his fellowman, it means merely the love which his human nature is capable of having and giving to another mortal.

I do not wish to be understood as in any way implying that this love is not a great boon and blessing to mankind, for it is. Without it, there would not be the harmony that exists on earth. Yet, at this time, hatred and anger seem to have taken its place in the hearts of many men who are now striving to kill and destroy. But this is only for a season. The war* will cease and then men will realize for a longer time that only their love for one another can make the earth a happy and desirable place to live on.

Love, I know it is said, is the fulfilling of the law. But no man can thoroughly understand this until he knows what love is. I do not mean that, in order to fulfill every law, man must have the Divine Love of the Father, because there are laws that govern the divine existence and laws that govern the human and merely spiritual existence. The Love of the Divine is the fulfillment of the former laws, and the natural love is the fulfillment of the latter laws. So, you must see that only as men have the Love of the Divine can they fulfill the laws of the divine existence. Likewise, if they have the natural love only, they can only fulfill the natural laws.

But this natural love will not be able to make them one with the Father, as I have before written. The utmost of its powers and functions is to give them that happiness which they will receive in living the life of a spirit or a man unredeemed.

I will not say that man should not cultivate this love for his fellowman to the greatest possible degree, for he should. And if that should be the only kind of love that he may have, either on earth or in the spirit world, the more of it that he possesses the happier will he be; and the greater will be the happiness of his fellowman and fellow spirit. So, when I said, when on earth, that men should love their God and love their fellowmen as themselves, I meant that they should do so with all the possibilities of whatever love they might possess.

YET, IF MEN WOULD ONLY LEARN, AS THEY CAN, THAT THERE IS NO NECESSITY FOR THEM TO HAVE ONLY THE NATURAL LOVE, BUT THEY SHOULD ALL SEEK THE GREATER LOVE AND OBTAIN THE CORRESPONDING GREATER HAPPINESS AND IMMORTALITY. MEN DO NOT REALIZE THIS, THOUGH, AND SEEM TO BE SATISFIED WITH THIS NATURAL LOVE AND THE PLEASURES THAT ENSUE FROM ITS POSSESSION.

I WOULD NOT HAVE THEM DO ANYTHING THAT WOULD LESSEN THIS LOVE, OR SHUT THEIR HEARTS TO ITS INFLUENCE WHEN IT IS PURE AND GOOD; BUT, YET, I CANNOT HELP TRYING TO IMPRESS UPON THEM THE GREAT DESIRABILITY OF HAVING THIS HIGHER LOVE IN THEIR SOULS.

YES, I AM A LOVER OF ALL MEN, AND I WANT THEM TO FEEL THE HAPPINESS OF THE INFLOWING OF THE DIVINE LOVE AND LEARN THEREBY WHAT THE LOVE OF GOD MEANS, AND WHAT THEY MAY HAVE IF THEY WILL ONLY SEEK.

THIS LOVE OF THE PURELY NATURAL WILL NOT SUFFICE FOR THE TEMPTATIONS THAT BESET MEN ON EARTH; AND, ALSO, IT WILL NOT INSURE AGAINST TEMPTATIONS WHEN THEY BECOME SPIRITS. I KNOW THIS AND, HENCE, I SAY IT WITH THE POSITIVENESS OF ONE WHO KNOWS, YOU MAY SAY, WITH AUTHORITY.

As you are tired, I must stop.

With all my blessings and love, I am

Your brother in spirit,

JESUS.

Abraham Lincoln Explains How Man Can Come into Harmony
with the Laws That Govern Him as the Created Man,
Without Obtaining the Divine Love.
(ABRAHAM LINCOLN)
(March 13th, 1919 | Received by James Padgett)

I AM HERE. *Abraham Lincoln.*

Let me write a few lines tonight, as you are in good condition to receive my message.

Well, I see that you have been thinking a great deal about spiritual things and have longed for the Love of the Father. By such thoughts and longings, you have come into a condition that enables the spirits to make a rapport with you.

Tonight, I desire to write for a short time on the subject of how important it is for man to learn the Truths of God in reference to the Plan which He has prescribed for man's salvation, and his coming into harmony with the laws that govern him as the created man.

As you have been told, in the beginning, man was created perfect and, in all the constituent parts of his being, made in harmony with God's Laws controlling man as a perfect creature. And if he had never disobeyed the Precepts of the Father, he would have always remained the perfect man.

Now, this condition of man is a fundamental one, and the soul is in

191

itself just as capable of that perfection as it was when created. Only by the sin of disobedience was it alienated from God and made the possessor of those things which tend to contaminate it, and to cause its pure condition to be overshadowed and dormant as to this perfection.

All of God's Universe is perfect and subject to the workings of His perfect Laws. And when that condition exists which shows that some one or other of His creatures are not working or being in harmony with these laws, it only means that, in order to restore the harmonious existence, man must renounce and get rid of the foreign things that have the effect of interfering with the harmony of his creation.

There is no such thing as total depravity or original sin, or the existence of any condition of the soul in this sin that cannot be remedied by the applications of the proper treatment and the removal of the incubus. In order to become perfect again, as he was before the fall, man is not required to be re-created, or have imposed upon him that which will make him a new or different being from what he was in the beginning. The perfect man is still in existence, but is hidden from the sight and consciousness of men, and needs only his revealment by eliminating the covering from him, which now hides his real self. Nothing new is needed, but only the riddance of those things from the soul which do not belong to it. Then the soul will appear just as it was created—a perfect soul made in the image of God, but not formed from any portion of the Great Oversoul of the Father.

For a long time, now, man has remained in this condition of having his soul covered over by those things that are merely the results of the perversion of his appetites and the animal part of his nature. And it is only by a process of renunciation that these encumbrances can be gotten rid of, and that man can stand forth as a free and glorious being, as he was before the burden of sin came upon him.

In this process, he needs no one to pay any supposed debt to the Father or to make an atonement for him. But by his course of thinking and consequent doing, he must himself remove the things that cause him to appear to himself and to others as the outcast from God's Favor. And in order to accomplish this, he must first renounce the idea that he is a vile being and not worthy of the Favor of the Father, and assert his belief that he, as the man, is the perfect creature of God; and that he can, of himself, regain the estate from which he has fallen, and let sin and error be removed from his present apparent existence. In doing this, he will be helped by the spirits of men who, from their own experience, know that sin and error have no real existence in the Economy of God, but, in the living of man on earth and in the spirit world as well, have a reality that has prevented men from finding their true selves.

The renunciation is not so much a matter of the intellect as it is of the moral nature of man. And while man must use his mind and its attributes in working out this renunciation, yet, he must also try earnestly and certainly to use the moral faculties of his nature; for the perversions of these faculties are the foundation of his present condition of sin and error. This renunciation may take a long time to be accomplished, as men look upon time, but it will finally come to pass, and the harmony of God's Universe will be restored. But, in the meantime, men will suffer, for this renunciation is always accompanied by suffering—not so much as a necessary ingredient or penalty of the renunciation, but as a consequence of the changing of men's will and desires in the process of reaching the condition of the perfect man again.

I will stop now, as the rapport has ceased. But I will come again.

Good night. I am

Your friend and well-wisher,

ABRAHAM LINCOLN.

Mrs. Padgett Comments on Abraham Lincoln's Message on Man's Progress in His Natural Love.
(HELEN PADGETT)
(March 13th, 1919 | Received by James Padgett)

I AM HERE. *Helen.*

Well, dear, you have had a communication tonight from Lincoln who thought it advisable to write you as he did. He is now in the Celestial Spheres and knows what the Divine Love is. But he said he wanted to write a short message to you on man as he is and as he may be. He has told you just what the condition of man is, how he is still the perfect man in his true self, and how he needs only an uncovering to stand forth as the being created in the image of God.

Good night, my dear husband.

Your own true and loving,

HELEN.

What Men Should Believe in Order to Again Become the Perfect Man.
(JESUS)
(December 12th, 1916 | Received by James Padgett)

I AM HERE. *Jesus.*

Let me write a while tonight, as I desire very much to again come into communication with you in reference to the Truths of God that are so important for men to know.

Tonight, I desire to write for a short time on the subject of what men should do in order to become again the perfect men, as was the condition of the first parents before their fall. I know that many doctrines and beliefs have prevailed in the world of human experience as to what is necessary to

193

bring about a return to the original condition of the created soul of men before the fall, and that many of these beliefs have been preached and efforts made to live the life that will produce this happy state. But, in all this experience and belief, men have rarely attained to the perfection that they sought for, notwithstanding the fact that they have been taught that, as the Father in heaven is Perfect, they should become perfect. No, this goal has always eluded men while living on earth. And for a long while to come, and until man's ideas of his own created condition changes, man will not succeed in reaching the condition of perfection.

While the created soul of man is pure and perfect, and man must realize that fact, yet, because of the long ages of living in and nurturing sin and its resultants, man has covered over that pure soul with such a deep and fallacious covering that he has never yet been able to get a correct idea of what the soul really is. It appears to him in all its frailties and ugliness, as it really is. And, in addition to this, so long has man been accustomed to see that soul as it appears in its false covering that he has concluded, and has had no other thought than, that it is really what it appears to him to be.

BUT NEVER WAS A GREATER MISTAKE MADE, AND NEVER HAS MAN BEEN SO LITTLE SUCCESSFUL IN DISCOVERING THE TRUTH OF THINGS, AS IN THIS MATTER OF THE TRUE CONDITION OF THE HIDDEN SOUL, WAITING ONLY TO BE RELIEVED OF ITS COVERING IN ORDER TO SHINE OUT AGAIN IN ALL ITS PURITY AND TRUTH!

SO, YOU SEE, THE FIRST THING FOR MEN TO DO IS TO REALIZE THE TRUE CONDITION OF THEIR OWN SOULS, AND THEN MAKE THE EFFORT TO RESCUE SUCH SOULS FROM THIS FALSE AND UNNATURAL CONDITION, AND LET IT APPEAR AGAIN CLEAN AND PURE AND BEAUTIFUL.

Many teachers have appeared in the world and endeavored to lead men to this discovery, and also attempted to show them the way by which this original condition could be recovered or brought about; and success, more or less, has accompanied their endeavors. But the trouble has been that with these teachings have been mixed things of such irrational character that have had a retarding and baneful effect upon such teachings. And, as a consequence, men have lost the principles of the true teachings, and have found themselves enthralled in the scheme of public benefits (that men so forcibly presented to those who followed these doctrines) instead of the true teachings.

It seems so strange that these beliefs and practices should be given over to so much importance to the acts and beliefs of men, and that the one true principle that lies at the basis of all efforts to regain the purity of the soul, as it originally existed, should be neglected.

Well, the rapport is weakening, and I will write later. So, good night and God bless you. I see that you are in better condition than for a long time, and I am glad. I will come again soon. Good night.

Your brother and friend, JESUS.

194

Professor Salyards Discusses the Object of Man's Life on Earth,
and the Necessity of Doing Certain Things Whereby Man Can
Become the Perfect Man—but Not the Divine Man.
(PROFESSOR JOSEPH H. SALYARDS)
(March 15th, 1916 | Received by James Padgett)

I AM HERE. *Professor Salyards.*

Well, I was telling you of the object of man's life on earth, and the necessity for his doing certain things in a general way in order to bring the happiness to mankind which might be theirs while on earth. Now, I desire to go a little in detail with reference to these matters.

As has been written to you before, there is only one Way in which man can attain to the supreme happiness which the Father in His Goodness has made possible for man to attain to, and which, when once obtained, can never be taken from him.

But there is also another kind of happiness which is not the same as that which I have just referred to, in either its nature or results, and man may obtain it in a way, and by a method, which is different from that which is necessary to obtain the first kind.

Man was originally created good and pure and happy. Only by his disobedience did he lose these qualities which, when lost, finally made him approach somewhat the likeness of the lower animal, although the latter is probably not so unhappy as man became by his fall from the state of the high condition of his creation.

When in his original state, he was happy in what we called, and what was, his natural love, which he fully possessed; and he needed nothing additional to make him happy. This condition made man his own master, as it were, and the Father's Divine Love was not necessary to develop him more than he then existed as mere man. He was pure and free from sin, and in perfect harmony with God's Laws governing his creation.

But, after the disobedience, he lost this harmony; and, in doing so, he lost the power to preserve the happiness in himself which was his by right of creation. He also soon realized that, as this power left him, his dependence upon himself became less and less effective to keep him in a condition of purity and contentment. And, as a consequence, he became less than the perfect man, and has been such ever since that time.

Now, with the other qualities that were given him at the time of his creation, there was and is one that he has never been deprived of, and one that he has never realized his inability to exercise, although he so often exercised it wrongly. That quality is the will, which is the greatest of the natural attributes that man possesses. For even God will not attempt to control that. I mean in the way of compelling. And this quality is the one that, more often than any other, will help man to again attain to that state or condition in which he was the perfect man. But while this is true, yet, it is also one of the greatest obstacles to attaining that state.

The success of his regaining his pristine purity and harmony with the laws that govern his being depends very largely upon man himself, and he must understand this fact. For if he should believe, and rest in the belief, that other men or other instruments controlled by men can rescue him from his present condition of inharmony and unhappiness, he will be disappointed and his salvation will be delayed a long time.

But the exercise of this will power in the proper direction will depend upon other things that he must possess in order to insure his return to his first estate. Among these are the necessity for his obtaining knowledge that will enable him to know himself and the relationship of himself to what is true and good. This knowledge will come to him as he examines himself and learns the difference between right and wrong. And, by this, I mean in its general sense. For "right" and "wrong" mean harmony or inharmony with the laws of which I speak, as well as right and wrong according to the several circumstances of men; for these differ. And what may be right or wrong to one man will not be to another.

By proper contemplation and observation, man may learn the difference between right and wrong, in the sense in which I use the terms, and be enabled to embrace or avoid those deeds or thoughts that come within one category or the other.

Again, he must realize that there is such a thing as the natural love being a part of him, and a thing which may be possessed and cultivated to such a high degree that all men will be brothers to him, and the children of one common Father Who has Love and Care for all alike who are content to remain the mere man.

Again, he must realize that he has a Father in God, his Creator, and that that Father has a love for him which will always bring happiness and peace to him if he will only respond with his own love. For man must have an object of worship and adoration, even when he possesses only the natural love. And he must learn that his love must go out to the Father in faith and confidence. There are many other things that he may learn by contemplation and meditation, as I have said.

Many qualities that are desirable will flow to man from the knowledge that there is a Father Who loves him, and that he has, or may have, a love for that Father, and also for his brother man. In fact, from these two subjects of knowledge, everything else may come to man that will make him the perfect man in harmony with the laws of his creation, and a pure, happy and contented creature.

Now, when man obtains this knowledge—and, here, observe the distinction between knowledge of these things and the possession of them—he will naturally try to obtain all that knowledge shows him may become his to possess. And then will come the great will power into operation; and, by its exercise, there is nothing that can prevent him from arriving at the goal of his desires.

In this way, one can, in a sense, be his own redeemer; but he will find the struggle hard, and the obstacles to be overcome many and repelling.

There are many mortals who have a wonderful development of this natural love, notwithstanding the fact that they are living in sin and inharmony with the laws that I speak of, and who will find from that fact alone that their progress will be more rapid and easy when they come to the spirit world on their journey to the state of the perfect man. I do not believe that any mortal can ever attain to this condition while in the earth life, but he can lay the foundation for a rapid progress after he becomes a spirit. The temptations and desires that beset him as a mortal are so great at this time that rarely can he become that perfect man while on earth.

But the time will come, I believe, when men will become perfect even while on earth; and, in this, I make reference merely to his natural love, while, as I say, for man to obtain this state of perfection, he must depend upon himself to a very large degree. Yet, it will be comforting to him to know that there are hosts of spirit friends who are with him, trying to help him to obtain the knowledge of which I have spoken. And, in his contemplations and meditations, they are with him, suggesting to him and impressing on him the thoughts of Truth that help him very much to understand the right from the wrong; and they also sustain him, to some degree, in the exercise of his will in the right direction.

So, from this, it must become apparent to man that a very important thing in the determination of this great problem as to what is right and what is wrong is the kind of associates that he may have. This applies to mortal as well as spirit companions. And man must know this: that as his desires and appetites on earth attract to him companions of similar desires and appetites, so, also, does the same Law of Attraction operate in the case of his spirit friends.

NOW, IN ALL THIS, I HAVE MADE NO REFERENCE TO THE REDEMPTION OF MAN BY THE POSSESSION OF THE DIVINE LOVE OF THE FATHER. FOR SUCH REDEMPTION AND ITS WAY OF SAVING MAN ARE ALTOGETHER DIFFERENT FROM THOSE OF REDEEMING HIM IN HIS NATURAL LOVE.

IN THE ONE CASE, WHEN HE HAS FOUND THE GOAL OF HIS DESIRES, HE BECOMES A MERELY PERFECT MAN AND NOTHING MORE. IN THE OTHER CASE, HE BECOMES AN ANGEL OF GOD, DIVINE IN HIS NATURE, WITH NO LIMITATION TO THE PROGRESS THAT HE MAY OBTAIN AND THE HAPPINESS THAT MAY BECOME HIS.

AND—OH MAN! WHY WILL YOU BE SATISFIED TO BECOME MERELY A PERFECT MAN WHEN YOU MAY BECOME A DIVINE ANGEL OF THE FATHER'S KINGDOM WITH IMMORTALITY ASSURED?

MAN MAY NOT KNOW IT, BUT IT IS A FACT THAT IT IS EASIER, AND THE WAY IS SHORTER, TO BECOME A DIVINE ANGEL THAN TO BECOME A PERFECT MAN!

SO, MY ADVICE TO ALL MEN IS (AND I SPEAK WHAT I DO

KNOW FROM A KNOWLEDGE THAT COMES TO ME FROM EXPERIENCE AND POSSESSION) TO SEEK FOR THE DIVINE LOVE OF THE FATHER WITH ALL THEIR STRENGTH AND EFFORTS. AND THEN THEY WILL BECOME NOT ONLY THE PERFECT MAN BUT ALSO WILL OBTAIN THAT WHICH OUR FIRST PARENTS NEVER OBTAINED, BUT WHICH WAS THEIRS FOR THE PROPER SEEKING, AS IT IS ALL MEN'S.

I have written enough for tonight and will close.

Your old friend and professor, and brother in Christ,
JOSEPH H. SALYARDS.

James Explains How Man Can Again Be Restored to the Perfect Man, Like the First Parents Before Their Fall.
(JAMES, THE APOSTLE)
(March 8th, 1917 | Received by James Padgett)

I AM HERE. *James, the Apostle.*

I come to write my message, as Elias told you I would. Well, I desire to write on the subject of: "What Is the Great Truth Respecting the Way That the Destruction of the Powers of Temptation That Arise from the Perverted Man May Result in the Condition of Perfection Which the First Parents Possessed Before Their Fall?"

You will understand that this does not involve any consideration of the operation of the Divine Love upon the soul. It involves exclusively the consideration of the method by which the soul may be so purified by the operations of the actions and the will power in conjunction with, or influenced by, the workings of the powers of the spirits who have been relieved of the sins and errors that followed the fall.

When man was created, as has been told to you, he was created perfect. Every quality and function and attribute that was a part of him was so created that harmony—the most exact with the Laws of God that governed his existence—became his, and no discord of any kind was in existence to mar that harmony. But as the spiritual nature of man became subordinated to the appetites and passions and fleshly desires, sin and error and inharmony appeared and increased until man became degraded and desired only those things that would satisfy these sinful desires.

And, so, this degeneracy continued until man reached his lowest degradation and the turning point came in his career. And, then, he commenced slowly and gradually to rise from this condition of depravity until at last he arrived at the stage of his condition of inharmony that now exists with these laws of his creation. And his destiny is to have a complete restoration of the perfection of his first estate.

This improvement and gradual restoration depend upon two causes: one, man himself by his own thoughts and reformation of the animal

198

appetites and desires; and, the other, the influence and guidance of spirits who have arrived at that perfection in the spirit world, or are progressing thereto, and who are in a condition of harmony with these laws that is superior to that of mortals to whom they lend their influence and help.

In their degeneracy or progression, men are controlled very largely by their thoughts. These thoughts are created by the operations of their desires, and which, on the other hand, cause these desires to increase. But back of the thoughts are always these appetites and passions, existing in their abnormal conditions, and they constitute the basic or moving cause of desire and thought and act. So, in order for men to become relieved of their abnormal desires and thoughts and acts, the cause thereof must be eradicated, and the seat or function of the cause must be brought into harmony with the laws of the creation of these functions or seats of emanation.

Strange as it may seem to you, and by a process that is contrary to the ordinary workings of the Law of Cause and Effect, men must first deal with the effects in order to control the cause and thereby destroy the effects. This may seem to be an impossible operation and contrary to the laws that govern the material world and its ordinary functioning, but yet it is possible, and the only possible way in which the causes may be destroyed.

Notwithstanding the fact that the animal or material part of man has had the ascendency over the spiritual part of his nature for all these centuries, yet, that spiritual part exists and has always existed, and has been waiting to assert itself whenever the opportunity should occur. And this assertion was prevented or suppressed only by reason of the want of opportunity.

The spiritual may be said to be the natural state. I mean that, in that state, the animal is subordinate to the spiritual and is controlled by it, and man's true tendency is to exist and act in accord with that natural state. Then, such being the fact, it may be asked why, or in what manner, did this natural spiritual condition become (in the manifestation of what man's dominant qualities are supposed to be) subordinated to the control of the inordinate exercise of this animal side of his nature, and which resulted in the sin and unhappiness that so many of the teachers and philosophers proclaim to be his natural condition?

Well, tonight, I will not attempt to explain the manner in which this inversion or perversion of man's true nature took place, but I will write on this subject at some future time.

The question now is, "How can man obtain the restitution to his created perfection?"

As I have said, this can only be accomplished by making the perfect adjustment of the two apparent conflicting sides of his nature.

First, he must recognize that he has the spiritual nature as well as the animal, and that there is such a relationship and coordination between the two that the supremacy of the latter disturbs the harmony of his perfection as man. The spiritual having been subordinated, the remedy is to remove the subordination and restore the equality. The spiritual, notwithstanding its condition, is always fighting to regain its place in the true adjustment, and will always answer the call of man to come to his rescue. The only thing that has prevented that response is that man has not called for the spiritual to assert itself.

Well, I am sorry, but we had better postpone until later. Try to get in greater rapport. Good night.

Your brother in Christ,
JAMES.

Mrs. Padgett Affirms That James Wrote Through Her Husband.
(HELEN PADGETT)
(March 8th, 1917 | Received by James Padgett)

I AM HERE. *Helen.*

Well, dear, I see that you are disappointed tonight in not receiving the message from James so that you could write it as he intended to deliver it.

(Why was this so?)

Well, the conditions were not good and the rapport was not sufficient to enable you to finish the message. He was disappointed also, but he will come again and deliver it to you.

I see that you are very sleepy and must go to bed.

So, have faith, love me, and say good night.

Your own true and loving,
HELEN.

Luke Declares That No Man Can Possibly Reach the Condition
of the Perfect Man Unless His Mental Beliefs Become
in Accord with the Truth.
(LUKE, THE APOSTLE)
(January 4th, 1917 | Received by James Padgett)

I AM HERE. *Luke.*

I will write a few lines tonight on a subject that I desire to make known to you and others, for I know it will be of interest to all who may read it. The subject is the truth of the statement that NO MAN CAN POSSIBLY REACH THE CONDITION OF PERFECTION UNLESS HIS MENTAL BELIEFS BECOME IN ACCORD WITH THE TRUTH.

This perfection, you will understand, is the perfection that man possessed before his fall—that is, the perfection of his creation.

It has been asserted by many that the beliefs of a man do not count for much in determining his condition of soul and mind, and that only his acts and deeds and qualities of heart determine that condition. But this assertion I declare to be untrue, unless these acts and deeds and qualities of heart are the results of beliefs being in accord with the truth.

Belief is the mainspring of man's acts and the result of his thoughts. And thoughts are things that cause the realities of man's consciousness. As he thinketh in his heart, so is he. "Thinketh in his heart" means, or comprehends the idea, that the thoughts of his mind, which is the only part of man that has the powers or faculties for thinking, are suggested by, or flow from, the desires and appetites of the emotional part of man.

No thought originates itself, although it may seem to be a spontaneous creation. It is rather the result of some spiritual or physical perception—that is, of the perception of the spiritual qualities or of the sensuous organs of man's physical constitution. And belief is the result of thought and that agency which causes man's acts or want of acts. Hence, it is the only guide or way shown to man in the progress of the development of his soul in its natural love, or of the mind to the state of perfection that I speak of.

Now, belief does not create truth or change truth, for truth is absolute and unchangeable. And truth does not create belief unless that truth is comprehended by the thoughts from which emanate the belief. So, it is apparent that, unless the belief, if erroneous, changes so that it becomes in accord with the truth, man, the possessor of the belief, can never get into a state of perfection, which can only exist when a man is in a complete condition of harmony with the truth.

Belief being the effect of the operations of the mind, unless these operations are in harmony with the truth, the belief cannot possibly cause the development of the man, who is possessed of and controlled by that belief, into the perfect man, because every cause has an effect; and that effect must be, necessarily, only such as is the natural and inevitable result of that cause.

Out of untruth, it is impossible for truth to emanate; and from the imperfect, the perfect can never be constructed. And, so, it is impossible to develop a perfect love and mind out of an imperfect belief. The law that declares the effect of its operations to bring this result is invariable, and only by the observation of its requirements can the imperfect ever become the perfect.

So, therefore, I assert that no man can ever become the perfect man unless his beliefs become in harmony with the truth. As a matter of fact, irrespective of reason, established by my knowledge resulting from observation and experience in the spirit as well as in the mortal world, I declare the same to be a truth.

Then, how important to man it is to seek for and obtain those beliefs that are in harmony with the truth, in order to become as he was originally: the perfect man. This true belief may be found and acquired even by the mortal. And no man will be excused from the penalty of the great Law of Compensation by his plea that he did not think it very material what his beliefs were, if he tried to do right in the world towards his fellowman. But, here, you will see that in addition to the fact that this great law accepts no excuse is the fact that man's acts and deeds proceed from his beliefs, whenever such are strong enough to control him. And when the beliefs are unformed, and man acts from emotion or impulse or desire only, without the constraint of any belief, the result upon his progress to the perfect man is substantially the same. This is so because, in order to escape the penalty for its violation, this law demands that beliefs, formed or unformed, or acts and deeds resulting from emotion or impulse (which are really beliefs without definite form) shall be in harmony with the truth.

The infidel who says he doesn't believe, the agnostic who says he doesn't know, the orthodox who believes, but whose belief is erroneous, and the free thinker who believes only what reason teaches him, as he proclaims—if such beliefs are not in accord with the truth, all come under the same penalty; that is, the impossibility of becoming the perfect man while such beliefs, or want of true beliefs, exist.

So, I say, belief is a vital thing in the progress of a man towards perfection. And men should cease to declare, and rest on the assurance of such declaration, that it makes no difference what a man believes if he does what he may consider to be right and just.

Why, I, who know, tell you that the earth planes of the spirit world are crowded with the spirits of men who are in darkness and stagnation in their progress towards the perfect man, and solely from the causes that I have above written! Some men have been in that condition for many long years, and will not find progress except as such erroneous beliefs leave them, and beliefs in accord with the truth take the place of the former.

But for man and spirits there is this consolation: that, at some time, how long in the future I or no other spirits know, these erroneous beliefs will all be eradicated, and man will again come into his original perfection. But the waiting may be long and distressing, and wearisome to many.

I have written enough. In closing, I will say to all men: KNOW AND REALIZE THAT THE BELIEF OF A MAN IS A VITAL AND DETERMINING ELEMENT IN HIS PROGRESS TO THE PERFECT MAN.

I am pleased to write you tonight, and will soon come again. Keep up your faith and courage, and you will realize the promises.

Good night and God bless you.

Your brother in Christ,

LUKE.

What Is the Correct Way in Which a Man Should Live on Earth in Order to Receive the Cleansing from His Sins So That He Can Acquire the Purification of His Natural Love?
(JESUS)
(June 11th, 1916 | Received by James Padgett)

I AM HERE. *Jesus.*

I come tonight according to my promise, and desire to write my message if you are in condition to receive it.

I wish to write on the subject of: "What Is the Correct Way in Which a Man Should Live on Earth in Order to Receive the Cleansing from His Sins So That He Can Acquire the Purification of His Natural Love?"

Heretofore, I have referred almost exclusively in my messages to the redemption of the soul by means of the Divine Love so that the redeemed one may become an inhabitant of the Celestial Spheres. Now, I will deal only with that cleansing that will fit him to live in the highest and purest of the spirit spheres where he can have the happiness which a pure, natural love will bring to him.

As has been written to you, the soul, as it was created and placed in man at the time of its creation in human form, or, rather, at the time it found a habitation in that form, was made pure and perfect and in complete harmony with the Laws of God controlling its existence. Only after the fall, by reason of man's own indulgence in the animal appetites and desires, did it lose its purity and become contaminated by sin and error. And, ever since that time, it has remained in such condition of impurity and alienship to God and His Laws.

This impurity has been the lot of each succeeding generation of men, and has never been eradicated from men's souls, notwithstanding all the moral instructions that man has acquired. But, still, there have been wonderful improvements in the purity of man's thoughts, as well as in his actions and habits of life, since the turning from the bottom of his degeneracy.

Now, there are several ways in which man may succeed in acquiring that purity that existed at the time of the creation of the first man; and, in time, this consummation will be accomplished. But, in these ways, man, himself, will have to be an important, working factor. For man is the highest of God's Creation, with powers and will possessed by no other of God's creatures; and there is no power in heaven or earth that can or will redeem man from this condition of sin and error unless man will cooperate in the work, and, that, to the greatest and best of his ability.

These sins that I speak of were created by man's thoughts and desires, carried into acts and deeds by the operation of his will, and they must be removed by the same process. Where the evil thoughts and deeds created that which contaminated and defiled the qualities of his soul, these evil thoughts and deeds must be supplanted by good thoughts and deeds in order that the defilement may be removed and the soul purified.

Evil thoughts are born of suggestions, both inward and outward, and also of the influences of spirits of evil who establish a rapport with the mortals.

Let us postpone the writing, for our rapport is not just right. I will come soon and finish.

203

With all my love, I am
Your brother and friend,
JESUS.

*Mrs. Padgett Explains Why the Previous Message from the Master
Had to Be Discontinued.*
(HELEN PADGETT)
(June 11th, 1916 | Received by James Padgett)

I AM HERE. *Helen.*

Well, I am sorry that you could not continue the writing, for the Master was very anxious to write the whole message tonight.
(Why could he not have done so? It seemed to have been going fine.)
Well, you were not in condition, and it was hard work for the Master to control your hand and brain. It may be that your brain was tired, and he could not transmit the thoughts. But you may have better success next time.
(Well, please convey my apologies to him. I certainly wanted to take his message tonight.)
He understands, and says that you must not feel bad about it.
Good-bye for a while.
Your own true and loving,
HELEN.

*Jesus Continues His Message on How a Mortal May Obtain the
Development of His Soul Without the Help of the Divine Love.*
(JESUS)
(June 17th, 1916 | Received by James Padgett)

I AM HERE. *Jesus.*

I see that you are in better condition tonight, and it may be that we can continue the message.
Well, as I was saying, the only way in which a mortal may obtain the development of his soul condition, without the help of the Divine Love, is by attempting to exercise his will in the way that will cause the thoughts of evil and error to leave him, and to be replaced by thoughts that will bring his heart and soul into harmony with the laws of his creation as mere man. This can be done by his seeking for those higher things of morality, and the subordinating of the purely animal desires and appetites of the mortal to the aspirations and desires of the higher and nobler part of his nature.
As I have told you before, man was pure and good until, by the exercise of his will, following the suggestions of the animal desires, he permitted

himself to degenerate from the high and perfect condition of his creation.

These sins and desires do not belong to his original nature, for his true nature was pure and in harmony with the Laws of God. And although he has lost it by the excessive and wrongful exercise of his will, obeying the desires of his animal nature, yet, he can recover his condition of original purity and harmony if he will get rid of these sins and errors so that his nature may again become free from everything that defiles it, or that places it out of harmony with the laws that created it.

So, you see, it is not necessary for man to obtain, or add to his original condition, any qualities that were not his in the beginning. He merely has to get rid of, or eradicate, those things from that condition which are mere excrescences or parasites, and thereby have his nature in the same condition that was his when he was created and was the perfect man.

So long a time has the nature or condition of the nature of man been in this state of defilement and alienation from the true condition of his creation that the effort to bring about the restoration will necessarily be great, and he will have to use all his power of will that he is capable of to effectuate this object. And, in such efforts, he will find two conflicting forces always fighting each other for the mastery.

The fact that he believes his present condition is the natural one, and that the state and purity and freedom from sin and error is one that does not belong to him naturally, but must be acquired by adding something to what he now has and always possessed, will make the fight more uneven.

Therefore, the first things that man must believe are that his present condition is not his natural one and that he has nothing more or greater to accomplish than to relieve himself of those things which prevent his condition from becoming as it was when he was the perfect man.

If he will get this belief firmly fixed in his mind, and assert that he was made by God, and that God never created anything impure or not in harmony with His Laws, then, he, man, will have accomplished the first step towards his regeneration and towards success in his effort.

He must not consider himself to be a weak, low and unworthy creature of God, not being entitled to those conditions of purity and greatness which made him the beloved child of the Father. Of course, self-esteem and pride and everything of that nature must be eliminated from the estimate that he must have of himself. But, on the contrary, the idea that he is degenerated and an utterly helpless being must not be permitted to enter his mind. Such thoughts do not make him pleasing to God, as he has been taught that they do, but only make him subservient to his masters of sin and error, and prevent him from asserting his own superiority over these things. In his conception of his true condition, it is necessary that this assertion exists in order that he may obtain the ascendancy over those masters.

When he shall have assumed this position, then he will realize that these animal appetites and desires, and evil thoughts which arise from them and from the belief that he is is by nature degraded and unworthy of a better and higher condition of nature, are really beings of his own creation, and subject to his will and self-control and total destruction. And with such realization will come a consciousness that they are not parts of his nature, but foreign to it; and that, in order that his nature may become separated from them, he must look upon them as enemies and treat them as such—to be destroyed and utterly extinguished, and never more to be taken to his bosom and cherished as inalienable and dominant parts of his nature.

Of course, in treating them as such enemies, great watchfulness and determination will have to be exercised. For they are very insidious and, whenever the opportunity arises, they will at all times and in all ways try to convince him that they are an integral and necessary part of his being, incapable of being separated from him.

But, by the exercise of this belief, based upon a right conception of what is and what is not a part of him as the perfect man, and by the exercise of his will power in accordance with this conception, he will be able to rescue himself from these unnatural appetites and desires and thoughts of error and sin.

As this belief becomes stronger and this conception clearer, and his will is exercised in closer harmony with the two essentials, these excrescences will gradually, and one by one, fall away from him until, at last, he will rise again the perfect man with the pure and harmonious nature which God gave him at the time of his creation.

But this process will be slow and sometimes hardly perceptible. For the long years of misbelief in the idea of original sin, and that God created evil and error for the purpose of defiling man's nature and making a disobedient devil of him, without any inherent goodness or the possibility of becoming regenerated unless by the operation of some miracle, will make it difficult for the acquiring of the true belief as to what he and what his nature are that would enable him to become the master and not remain the servant.

GOD IS THE FATHER OF ALL, AND LOVES HIS CHILDREN. AND, AS HE ORIGINALLY PROVIDED FOR THEIR HAPPINESS, SO, NOW, HE DESIRES THAT ALL MAY BE HAPPY, EVEN THOUGH THEY MAY NOT SEEK FOR THAT DIVINE LOVE WHICH MAKES MORTALS AND SPIRITS MORE THAN THE MERE PERFECT MAN.

Forgiveness is, in effect, forgetfulness. And when men, in their efforts, cause all these things of evil and sin to cease being a part of their nature, and only thoughts of purity and righteousness remain to find a lodgment in their minds, then these other things are forgotten and forgiveness has taken place. Man no longer is the slave of false beliefs and unrighteousness, nor is he their associate; and, even in memory, they become things of nonexistence. And when he gets into this condition of purity and freedom, and in harmony with the laws of his creation, there exists nothing which can be the object of forgiveness, and he is the man of perfect creation.

But, in all this, man must realize that he does not exist by and for himself alone. For he is always surrounded by mortals or spirits, or both, exercising upon him their influence for good or evil. And they are either helping him to turn his thoughts from these things of evil and sin into those higher things which are his by nature, or, they are causing him to receive and foster these evil thoughts with increased intensity. He cannot get rid of these influences of one kind or the other. Hence, he should seek the influence of those who are good, and who desire to help him in his efforts towards the recovery of that condition which is his by right of birth.

Among God's Laws, which never change and which work impartially, is the great Law of Attraction; and it works in the case of all mortals and spirits, and never rests.

And the great principle of this law is that like attracts like, and that unlike repulses the unlike. So, man must know that as he is—I mean in his state of mind and soul—so necessarily will be his companions or those who desire his association. Hence, he should realize this important Truth and all that it implies.

If his thoughts and deeds are evil, he will attract those spirits or mortals who have similar thoughts and deeds; and they will not help him to higher things, but will retard his progress towards his first estate. And if his thoughts and deeds are good, then his associates will be only those of like qualities who can and will help him in his progress.

Every effort to create good thoughts strengthens the desires and will in that direction, and assists the coming of other good thoughts. For with these efforts comes the help of these unseen influences, and the repulsion of the influences of the retarding forces.

Man is a wonderful being and the highest creation of the Father; yet his greatest master is his belief in the power and supremacy of these things of evil of his own creation.

BUT, BEYOND ALL THIS, A MEANS TO ACCOMPLISH MAN'S RESTITUTION TO HIS PERFECT ESTATE IS THE HELP OF THE FATHER, WHICH IS NEVER REFUSED WHEN MAN SEEKS FOR IT IN EARNEST, SINCERE PRAYER. ALWAYS THE FATHER IS WILLING TO RESPOND TO THE TRUE PRAYERS OF MAN. AND, BY HIS INSTRUMENTALITIES, HE WILL MAKE THE EFFORTS OF MAN SURE AND EFFECTIVE SO THAT HE CAN ACQUIRE THAT CONDITION THAT WILL FREE HIM FROM ALL SIN AND ERROR, AND FROM THE SLAVERY OF FALSE BELIEF IN THE MASTERY OF HIS EVIL CREATURES.

MAN MUST BELIEVE IN THE LOVE AND HELP OF THE FATHER, IN THE MANHOOD AND GREATNESS OF HIMSELF, AND IN THE UTTER ERROR OF HIS BELIEF IN THE MASTERY OF HIS OWN CHILDREN OF SIN AND ERROR.

I have written enough and must stop, as you are tired.

So, assuring you of my love for you, and my care and help, I will say good night.

Your brother and friend,

JESUS.

Martin Luther, Former Monk and Reformer,
Affirms That the Master Wrote.
(MARTIN LUTHER)
(June 17th, 1916 | Received by James Padgett)

I AM HERE. *Luther.*

I come tonight to say that I would like to write again very soon, as I desire to write further in the line of thought of my last message.

I see that you are too tired to write tonight and I will not ask you to do so. But if you can give me the opportunity to write soon, I will be much obliged.

(The Master's message tonight was most interesting.)

Yes, I know. I enjoyed his message and believe that it will be readily understood. What a Master he is! So beautiful and powerful and loving!

Your brother in Christ,

LUTHER.

Mrs. Padgett Also Affirms That the Master Wrote.
(HELEN PADGETT)
(June 17th, 1916 | Received by James Padgett)

I AM HERE. *Helen.*

Well, my own dear Ned, you have had a very entertaining letter from the Master tonight, and I am glad that you were in condition to receive it so well. He said that you were very successful and he is pleased.

Good night.

Your own true and loving,

HELEN.

Luke Discusses the Development of the Soul in Its Natural Love
Wherein the New Birth Is Not Experienced.
(LUKE, THE APOSTLE)
(February 3rd, 1916 | Received by James Padgett)

I AM HERE. *Luke.*

I come tonight to say a few words concerning the great Truth of the development of the soul in its natural love wherein the New Birth is never experienced.

I know that men think that this natural love has a part of the Divinity of the Father's Nature in it, and that, as they develop in the way of purifying it and ridding it of those things which tend to impair its harmony, they will realize that there exists this Divinity in their souls of which we have written. But this is not true. For this natural love partakes only of those elements which the Father implanted in it at the time of man's creation, and in none of these elements are any of the qualities of the Divine Nature.

It is difficult to explain just the distinction between the Divine Love coming from the Father and the natural love also coming from Him, and, yet, the latter not having any of the Divine Nature or Qualities. But this is a fact. The natural love may become so purified that it may come into perfect harmony with the laws governing its condition and composition, and, yet, fall far short of having any of the Divine Love in it. And, so, as we have explained to you, the soul may obtain this Divine Love and thereby become a part of the Father's Divinity.

I will now try to explain how the natural love of man may be developed so that his soul may come into harmony with the law of love—the natural love—and make him a very happy, pure and contented being.

In the first place, I wish to say that there is no such thing in the world as original sin or evil. God did not create them or permit them to exist, except as he permits man to use his own will without limitation. I mean by this that He does not say that a man shall do this or do that in the exercise of his will. As respects this will, man is untrammeled. But He does say, and His Laws are inexorable in this particular, that when man, in the exercise of the great power of free will, causes that will to come into conflict with the Will of God, or to violate His Laws, he, man, must suffer the consequences.

This may be illustrated by your natural laws declaring the freedom of the press. Man may publish whatsoever he pleases and, so long as he does not thereby violate the rights of others or of decency, he may make his publications without fear of the law. But when he violates the law in the exercise of this freedom of speech, as you call it, then he must suffer the consequences of this violation.

So it is with the mortal who, in the exercise of his free will, violates the Will of the Father or the laws limiting its exercise by the mortal. He must suffer the consequences. And the results of this violation are that sin and evil are created, and, this, in no other way. Surprising as it may sound to you, man is the creator of sin and evil, and not God Who is only Good.

Then the question arises, "How can sin and evil be eradicated from the world?" And every thoughtful man will have the same answer, and that is: by men ceasing to violate the Will of God, or of His Laws, which restrict the exercise of the wills of mortals to that which, in its right exercise, will not produce sin or evil. In other words, when men bring about inharmony by the wrong use of their wills, they can apply the right use of their wills and not disturb that harmony, which, when it exists, leaves no room for the presence of sin and error.

So, you see, the one thing necessary in order for men to become happy and free from everything that defiles them, or causes unhappiness or discord to exist, is to develop their souls in this natural love until this love comes into perfect unison with the laws that control it. And thus may be applied the oft-quoted expression: "Love is the fulfilling of the law." But this means love in its purest and most perfect state.

Now, how can this development of the natural love be accomplished by men?

The mind, while a powerful helper in this regard, is not sufficient of itself to bring about this great and desired result. It is true that, with every mortal, there is a constant warfare between the appetites and lusts of the flesh and his higher desires. Hence, it is said, that these appetites and desires are sinful, and that they are the cause of evil and the inharmony that exists in the lives of mortals. But this statement is not altogether true. For as man was made with spiritual aspirations and desires, so was he made with appetites and desires of the flesh; and the latter, of themselves, are not evils.

The failure to make the distinction between the fact that these appetites and desires of the flesh are not evil, and the fact that only the perversion of them brings evil, is the great stumbling block that stands in the way of man's developing this natural love in the manner that I have indicated. These, what are sometimes called the animal appetites and desires, may be exercised in such a way as to be in perfect harmony with the laws that control them, and, in such exercise, not interfere with or prevent the development of this natural love to perfection.

But, in the free exercise of his will and in his wanderings, man has gone beyond the limitations which the Law of Harmony has placed upon him. He has added to, and increased and distorted, the appetites and desires of the flesh which were originally bestowed upon him. Hence, he has himself created those things that are not in harmony with his creation.

So, you see, man is a creator as well as a creature. As the latter, he cannot alter or change any of the effects of his creation; but, as the former, he can alter and change and even abolish the effects of his own creation. For the creator is greater than the things that he created, although these things of his own creation have held him in bondage and unhappiness to a more or less extent ever since he became their creator. The strength of this apparent paradox is that the creator, man, has for all these long centuries believed in this bondage, and has submitted to his creations; and he still does so.

So, what is the remedy?

Simply this: Man must awaken to the fact that he is greater than his creatures, that they are subject to his will, and that whenever they bring discord and unhappiness by their existence and workings, and cause his will to be exercised in opposition to the Will of the Father, they must then be destroyed and never be permitted to come into existence again. Let men become the masters of their creatures, and obedient to the great Will of their Creator, and they will realize that sin and error and unhappiness will disappear, that their natural love will come into harmony with the laws of

210

its creation, and that the earth will indeed become a heaven and the brotherhood of man established on earth.

If men will only think, and, thinking, believe that all sin and error, and the resulting unhappiness and sorrow in the world, are children of their own creation and not the children of God, and that, in the economy of His Universe, God leaves the control and management and even the existence of these children to the will of their parents, they will understand why evil exists, why wars and hatred and misery continue on earth to blight the lives and happiness of mortals, and why, as some say, and especially the so-called "Christians," that God permits all these things to exist and flourish and apparently contradict the great Truth that He is Good and the Fountainhead of all Goodness.

The universe and the inhabitants thereof, and the greatest production of His Power, man, were all created by God. But sin and error and their awful followings are the creatures of man. The Laws of God's Universe work in harmony, and all is good. And even the apparent inharmony which man has created does not affect that great harmony, but is confined in its working to man, himself. Only man is apparently in inharmony, and that is caused by man, himself.

Suppose, for a moment, that man's will was working in accord with that of the Father. Can you imagine that there would be any of these creatures of man's perverted will in existence? Would there be any evil or hatred or disease or suffering known to the consciousness of man? I tell you, no!

Now, I say, man, their creator, must destroy these inharmonious creatures. He must kill and bury deep and forever these children of the perverted exercise of his will. And, until then, sin and error and all their concomitants will continue to live and flourish and torment their creator.

And I say here, with all emphasis and with a full realization of the great significance and responsibility in the sight of God which I assume in saying it, that man can destroy these bastard creatures of his will that are so perverted and discordant!

His natural love, if permitted to assert its God-given powers and functions, is sufficient to bring his will in accord with that of the Father, to turn his thoughts away from these children of his, and to make him conscious of purity and truth. The dead desires and dead appetites will bury their dead children, and man will come into his own again.

But then comes the question: "How is man to accomplish this great end, so devoutly to be wished for?"

Well, it is late now, and I will write upon this important feature of this development of his natural love in my next message.

So, with all my love, I will say good night.

Your brother in Christ,
LUKE.

Luke Continues His Discourse on the Development of the Soul in Its Natural Love.
(LUKE, THE APOSTLE)
(February 16th, 1916 | Received by James Padgett)

I AM HERE. *Luke.*

Well, do you think you can take my message tonight? It looks like you may. At any rate, we will try.

As I was saying, in what way is a man to obtain this development of the soul in its natural love?

In the first place, he must recognize the fact that he does not live to himself, alone—that what he conceives to be the workings of his own mind and will are not always the result of thoughts and desires that originate in him, but are largely the products of the influences of the workings of the minds of spirits who are around him, trying to impress him with their desires and wills. Consequently, you will understand that it is very important to man as to what kind of spirit influences he has surrounding and working upon him. If these influences are good, the better it is for his progress in the development of this natural love; but, if they are evil influences, then, of course, such development is retarded.

Consequently, the first thing for a man to do is to attempt to attract influences to himself of the higher nature. And he can do so by trying to cultivate good thoughts and to indulge in good and moral acts.

The great Law of Attraction that we have written about applies and works in such cases as this, as it does in every other relation of God's Universe. If a man's thoughts are evil, there will always be spirits attracted to him of similar thoughts. And when they come to him, they attempt to, and succeed in, intensifying these evil thoughts of his which attract them to him.

It must be emphatically understood in this regard that man may and often does originate his own thoughts and desires, and it is not necessary that any influence of these evil spirits should be present and operate upon his brain or affections in order that these evil thoughts and desires should come into existence. And, again, man has a will power that is susceptible to being exercised, free from the wills of these evil spirits. You will see how true this is when you remember that he can exercise that will power free and independent from the Will of God, Himself!

So, I say that these thoughts and desires may and do originate in man, free and independent of the wills or influences of these evil spirits. And, as a fact, these spirits are attracted to him only when these thoughts that he has originated are evil.

Now, if man would have this progress that I speak of, he should endeavor to have good and pure thoughts and desires. Then he will attract spirits to him who are good and pure, and their influences will help him in strengthening and increasing these thoughts to a wonderful degree, making it less and less likely that evil thoughts will arise in his brain, or evil desires in his affections. And, as a consequence, his will power will be exercised in doing those things which are good and moral.

Now, while man may originate these thoughts and desires, he must also know as a Truth that this progress is not dependent upon himself, alone. For when he is in that condition to attract the good spirits, they will invariably come to him and render their help, and it will prove to be a wonderful and never-failing help.

Now, man's thoughts and desires are not always the result of something that may be hidden within himself, as may be supposed, and of which he may not know its existence. I mean not in all cases, and probably in only a minority of cases. For, most frequently, these thoughts and desires are the children of an objective influence that comes to him by reason of objects becoming sensible to his ordinary senses, which, in turn, create or suggest these thoughts or desires.

Without going into details, you will understand what I mean. But, as a mere illustration: To a man who likes whiskey, a glass of whiskey may and does suggest the thought and desire that he should take a drink, thereby bringing his will into operation, which is followed by the act of drinking. And so with many other objects which a man meets in the course of his daily life. But these thoughts and desires arise not only from seeing objects but also from feeling and tasting them.

And, again, these objective suggestions, causing these thoughts and desires, arise and exist not only from the real object sensed but also from words and thoughts which are expressed by other human beings in the course of conversations, or in books and literature; and, when they come in this way, they are frequently more effective than in any other. Hence, as these objective words and thoughts enter the mind of man, they create similar thoughts which frequently intensify and attract the evil spirits of like thoughts, with their degenerating influences.

Hence the importance of a man avoiding companionship where such communications take place, and avoiding the books and literature where these evil suggestions are made.

It has been well said that evil communications corrupt good manners. And I may add that such communications corrupt good thoughts and produce evil desires, and retard the progress of the soul in its natural love. For it must be remembered that this love is pure and free from all evil or taint of defilement when it is fully developed. And anything that tends to defile it retards the progression of the soul in this particular.

So, the plain lesson to be drawn from all this is that, in the first place, man must make the effort to have only good and pure thoughts and desires from his inner self; and, next, he must avoid those objects and associations that tend to cause these evil thoughts to arise in him; and, thirdly, he must learn the truth that, when he has these evil thoughts, he attracts spirits of evil to himself who can and do intensify these evil thoughts and desires by their influence.

213

As regards this last mentioned truth, I know that the majority of men have no knowledge of its existence. But it is time that they should learn that such a danger to their souls' progression does exist and is always imminent.

And they should learn this other fact that, when their thoughts are pure and free from defilement, they have the influence of good spirits surrounding them who work to increase and make permanent their good thoughts; and, as these good thoughts continue, the natural love develops towards its pristine condition of purity, and man comes nearer to his designed condition of existence.

So, you will see from this that, as man's thoughts and desires become freed from these things that tend to defile him, he naturally progresses toward that condition which is necessary in order for him to have this development of the soul in its natural love.

Again, the development may be helped very much by man thinking and doing acts of charity and kindness, and by observing the golden rule. For every act of charity and kindness and self-sacrifice, for the sake of others, has its reflex action in man's own condition of love and soul, and helps with his development.

In short, the observance of all the moral laws by man, which are many and varied, tends to bring about the development of the natural love. And this must be remembered: that as this development proceeds, the tendency to indulge in the perverted appetites of the flesh, as they are called, will disappear; and, as they disappear, this love, of course, becomes purer and sweeter and brings man nearer to his state of perfection.

And, again, the meditation upon spiritual things, and the outflowing of this love towards the Father, will cause the progression. For while all men do not seek for the Divine Love, as we have said, yet, as all men are children of God, He helps them to the full extent of their desires towards happiness and the perfecting of this love in its natural, pure state, and with which He endowed them at their creation. The nature of the help which the Father gives to them depends upon their will and aspirations. But He always gives His Help and Blessings, and to the fullest. His Great Desire is that man shall become perfect in that love which he possesses and which he seeks for, and that the natural love may become as perfect in its qualities in man as may the Divine Love in Its Qualities. Each is just as much in harmony with God's Universe, in its respective qualities, as is the other.

So, I say, man is helped, and more than in any other way, by his meditations upon the higher things of his being, and by prayer and aspirations to the Father Who hears the prayers of the man who has only this natural love, and Who answers them just as He does the prayers of the man who has the Divine Love in his soul.

Ultimately, all sin and evil will be eradicated from the universe; and, in his mere natural love, man will become pure and perfected and happy.

In my inefficient way, I have tried to show man how he may progress in the development of his natural love; and, if he will follow my advice, he will succeed. For as man fell to a low degree of degeneracy by the indulging of these perverted appetites of the flesh, and by the exercise of this will power, so can he rise again to his condition of purity in his natural love by ceasing to indulge in these perverted appetites and by redirecting the exercise of that same will power.

And, besides, he has the Help of the Father and the good angels in his efforts to recover, and also the experience of the result of his fall, which he may not be conscious of but which has an existence in his inner self and is continually working.

Well, my dear brother, I must stop. I feel that you have taken my message very successfully. Read it over and correct errors of construction.

I will come soon and write again.

Your brother in Christ,

LUKE.

What Is the Destiny of the Mortal Who Has Not Experienced the New Birth, but Who Will Progress to That Condition Which May Be Called the Perfect Man?
(JOHN, THE APOSTLE)
(September 23rd, 1916 | Received by James Padgett)

I AM HERE. *John.*

I want to write tonight on a subject that is important, and I hope that you will be able to receive my message, for I have been waiting for some time to deliver it.

Well, I desire to discourse on the subject of: "What Is the Destiny of the Mortal Who Has Not Experienced the New Birth, but Who Will Progress to That Condition Which May Be Called the Perfect Man?"

This latter condition does not depend upon the mortal having the Divine Love or the Essence of the Father in his soul, but merely upon the purification of the natural love so that all sin and error and inharmony form no part of his state of soul or mental existence. This condition is not the result of the New Birth or of a change in the constituent elements of his soul, but merely the elimination of those things therefrom which were the results and the necessary sequences of the defilement that followed the fall.

Now, as man lost the qualities which made him the perfect creature of his Maker by this fall, it is only necessary for him to regain what he lost by that fall in order to become the perfect man once more. And, in recovering this state of perfection, it is not required that he should seek, or actually add to the qualities which he at first possessed, any new or additional qualities or attributes, but only that he regain what he had been deprived of by his disobedience. And when that is accomplished, he will come again in harmony with the laws of his creation, and have all the potentialities and excellence that he originally possessed.

215

And, now, what will that future be? In order to determine this question, it is only necessary to understand what his inherent condition or qualities were when he was the perfect man of his Father's Creation.

At that time, he was possessed of those things of which he is now the possessor, except that, then, they were all so accurately adjusted that every sense and function of his body, as well as every faculty of his soul and mind, were so in harmony with the laws of his creation that he was capable of doing the Will of the Father, and obeying every requirement that was imposed upon him.

He was then not only a perfect being regarding his physical formation but also as regards his mental and moral qualities, which, of course, included all the emotions and appetites and spiritual aspirations. But, as we have written you before, all these faculties were subject to his will; and, in a certain sense, his will was controlled by the exercise of these faculties.

In the beginning, his body was made of matter, changeable as it now is, but of a more ethereal kind, and not subject to decay and disintegration in such a short time, as it now is, but, yet, subject to this decay. And as regards his physical being, man necessarily was compelled to die and to have his spirit body and his soul released from this physical vesture, and to exist thereafter as pure spirit. This was not the death that he died as a consequence of his disobedience, but the death natural to him by reason of the very nature of his creation.

His soul and spirit body were not subject to death in the sense of annihilation, but were given the qualities of continual existence in a pure and perfect state. And the only difference that the fall made as to these parts of his being is that the purity and harmony that were men's are no longer parts of his soul and spirit.

Of course, they were created from something and not from nothing, as some of your theologians say. And, in the order of change, which seems to be the law in the spirit world as well as in the mortal world, it is possible that this soul and spirit may be resolved again into that something.

But, as to this finality, we do not have any knowledge because, so far as the observation of spirits in this world goes, no soul or spirit body—and I mean the body as a composite whole, and not as to its constituent elements—has ever been resolved into that something or has been deprived of its individualized existence. Therefore, I cannot say that, when man was created, it was intended that, as man, he should not be immortal, or that he should be so.

But you will readily see that after man shall have accomplished the purification of his soul, and becomes in mind and spirit body as it was intended he should be at the time of his creation, he will be nothing more nor less than he was at that time, and have no other or greater qualities, or no more freedom from limitations and change than he had before his fall. Of course, he will have no physical body. And, here, let me say that there is no fact or experience known to the spirit world that justifies the assertion that man will ever be immune to physical death on earth. I know that some

216

say that, in the far future, men may make such progress in the development of their natural love that their condition of inner purity will be so great as to cause the physical bodies to become so etherealized as to render them free from physical death. But that I cannot conceive will ever happen, for men were made to become inhabitants of the spiritual realms. The short time they were decreed to live the earth life was for the purpose only of giving the soul an individualized existence.

Never was it intended that the physical form should have an eternity of existence, no matter how pure, or, as they say, etherealized it may become; for it was made of matter, or the earth, earthy, while the soul was made of that which had its origin in the spirit realm, and is composed of spirit substance. So, it cannot be conceived that, in the beginning, man was created for an immortal earth existence.

I see that you are tired, and I will finish later. I am glad that I could write tonight, and also that you are in such good condition to receive my message.

So, with my love and blessings, and assurances that you have every reason to keep up your courage and hope, I am

Your brother in Christ,
JOHN.

John Continues His Discourse on the Destiny of the Soul That Has Not Experienced the New Birth.
(JOHN, THE APOSTLE)
(September 30th, 1916 | Received by James Padgett)

I AM HERE. *John.*

I desire to finish my message, and hope that you are in condition to receive it.

Well, as I was writing about the future or destiny of the soul that has not experienced the New Birth, I will continue where I left off.

When the soul becomes wholly purified and restored to that condition of perfection that was possessed by the first parents before the fall, it continues to live a life of happiness and contentment until it realizes that its possibility of further progress, either mentally, morally or spiritually, has come to an end—that it has reached its limit of advancement—and that the happiness that it then enjoys is the full complement of what it may obtain or possess. This condition is one which satisfies the large majority of those who have reached the state of the fully restored man, and they are content to live the life of such perfection. They rest in the assurance that there is no greater happiness or more desirable condition existing in the Universe of God.

But, with some of these souls, this state does not bring or contain this complete satisfaction, and the desire continues in them for more and greater progress. But they realize that they have reached the limit of their progress, and that they must continue to live in that state which holds the happiness and delight for them of being perfect and at-one with the Father, as was intended by Him when man was created the perfect being.

But notwithstanding this knowledge that, as the soul develops in its natural love and, in its moral and mental faculties, to the finality of limitation where there can be nothing beyond, yet, there comes a dissatisfaction to them, and, as it were, a negative unhappiness that causes unrest and a conscious desire for something they know not what.

It may be the memory of something they heard in their progress through the spheres, or an imperfect suggestion of some unconscious, reproduced, dormant memory, inherited from their first parents, of the Great Gift of endless progress, potentially bestowed upon God's first created beings, and forfeited, that causes the discontent and longings for something beyond the condition of their perfect state.

When this state of mind and soul comes to them, they are then susceptible to the teachings and help of those spirits who have the Divine Love in their souls, and the knowledge that there is a Way that leads to everlasting progress without limit or possibility of reaching the end.

And many of these perfected souls in their natural love have followed the advice of these immortal spirits. They have left the high sphere of their perfection and have entered the lower soul spheres of the Spiritual Heavens. And, there, they have sought and found the New Birth of the soul, and have progressed from sphere to sphere until they reached the Celestial Heavens where they are still progressing and realizing a contentment never marred, but always accompanied with the knowledge that ever beyond are spheres of greater happiness of Truth and knowledge.

But, as I say, the larger, yes, much larger number of souls that have been born unto men will find and rest, in the future, in the state and happiness of the restored first parents.

IT SHOULD NOT BE NECESSARY FOR ME TO ATTEMPT TO MAKE THE APPLICATION OF THE TRUTHS WHICH I HAVE WRITTEN TO THE DESIRES AND WILL OF MEN. FOR THE VITAL IMPORTANCE OF MAKING THE CHOICE BETWEEN THE FUTURE OF THE DIVINE SPIRIT AND THAT OF THE PERFECTED MAN IS SO APPARENT THAT SCARCELY ANY MORTAL, WHO IS NOT THE MAN THAT SAYS IN HIS HEART THERE IS NO GOD, NEEDS ANOTHER TO APPLY FOR HIM THE LESSON TAUGHT. AND I WILL SAY IN CLOSING THAT SUCH LESSON CONTAINS THE TRUTHS THAT ACTUAL OBSERVATION AND KNOWLEDGE HAVE MADE CERTAIN. SPECULATION DOES NOT ENTER INTO IT, AND THE POSSIBILITY OF ERROR OR MISTAKES IS UTTERLY ELIMINATED.

I have written enough and will stop for tonight.

You have received the message very satisfactorily, and I am pleased.

So, with my love and blessings, I will say good night and God bless you with His Love.

Your brother in Christ,

JOHN.

Chapter 8.

Sin and Error.

MESSAGES INCLUDED IN THIS CHAPTER.

Luke Explains the Biblical Text: "The Sins of the Parents Are Visited upon the Children unto the Third and Fourth Generations." (LUKE, THE APOSTLE) 223

Luke Clarifies One Point Relating to His Previous Message. (LUKE, THE APOSTLE) 226

Jesus Explains How the Power of the Divine Love Redeems Men from Sin and Error. (JESUS) 227

What Jesus Meant When He Said: "In My Father's House Are Many Mansions," and His Further Description of the Effect of the Divine Love on the Soul to Redeem Mankind. (JESUS) 228

Luke Communicates What the Celestial Spirits Think About War. (LUKE, THE APOSTLE) 231

A Former Minister of the Gospel States That His Religious Beliefs Were Merely Intellectual, Which Led to His Profound Skepticism and Departure from the Ministry, and to His Loss of All Hope for Forgiveness in the Spirit World. (S.B.C.) 233

Ann Rollins Declares That the Belief in the "Unpardonable Sin" Is Slanderous and Blasphemous Against the Loving Father. (ANN ROLLINS) 237

Jesus Reemphasizes That the Holy Spirit Is Not God, and That There Is No "Unpardonable Sin." (JESUS) 239

Luke Declares That There Is No "Unpardonable Sin," as Taught by a Certain Preacher. (LUKE, THE APOSTLE) 239

Charles Latham Corroborates That Luke Wrote on: "There Is No 'Unpardonable Sin,' as Taught by a Certain Preacher." (CHARLES LATHAM) 241

*Paul Also Denies the "Unpardonable Sin." (PAUL, THE APOSTLE).*241

Samuel, the Prophet, Discusses How Selfishness Causes the Souls of Men the Unrest That Now Exists in the World. (SAMUEL, THE PROPHET) 241

Paul Presents His Comments on a Preacher's Beliefs. He Agrees with Him That "Perfection" Is a Relative Term. (PAUL, THE APOSTLE) 242

Jesus Also Attended This Church Service with Paul and Mr. Padgett, and He Too Comments on the People's Beliefs. (JESUS) 244

James Discusses the Frailties of the Human Mind and Moral Qualities. (JAMES, THE APOSTLE) 245

Helen Affirms That James Wrote on: "The Frailties of the Human Mind and Moral Qualities." (HELEN PADGETT) 247

Luke Explains What Is Necessary for a Man to Do to Recover the Purity of Soul and Love That Was Possessed by the First Parents. He Also Declares That the Doctrine of Original Sin Is a Mocking, Damnable Lie. (LUKE, THE APOSTLE) 247

8.

Sin and Error.

Luke Explains the Biblical Text: "The Sins of the Parents Are Visited upon the Children unto the Third and Fourth Generations."
(LUKE, THE APOSTLE)
(April 9th, 1916 | Received by James Padgett)

I AM HERE. *Luke.*

I desire tonight to write for a short time on the text: "The Sins of the Parents Are Visited Upon the Children unto the Third and Fourth Generations."

I know that usually the explanation of the text has been that the material sins, or rather the sins which result in material injury or affliction, are visited upon the children; and to a very great extent this is true. But that explanation is not what was intended by the declaration.

Man is not only a material or physical being, but is more largely a spiritual being, having a soul and spirit which never cease to exist, and which are just as much a part of him while on earth as when he becomes a spirit—that is, after he has left the vestments of flesh and blood.

These real parts of man are of more importance to him and his real existence than is the physical part. And the sins which man commits are not the result of any primary physical action, but of the operations of the powers which form, or have their real seat in, the spiritual part of his being.

The physical part of man is not the originator of sin, but merely manifests its effects; and it almost always manifests itself on and in the physical body, and leaves its scars apparent to the consciousness of men upon such body. Hence, as man is able in his ordinary condition to perceive the effects more plainly on this body, he thinks that the meaning of the text must refer to the sins that affect, and are shown upon, his body. At the same time, he ignores, or is not sensible of the fact, that the greater effect or injury of sin is upon and to the spiritual part of man. As the physical body is affected by the results of these sins being carried into operation, so much more so is the spiritual part of man affected by the fact that these sins had their creation in that spiritual part of man.

It may be asked in what way can the effect of sin upon a man—that is, upon his soul and spirit—have any injurious effect upon the spirit and soul of his child so that the child may suffer from the sin of the parent.

Well, when a child is conceived and gestates and is born, he not only partakes of the physical nature of his parents but also of the qualities and condition of the spirit and soul of the parents. This may seem improbable, but it is a fact that the spirit and soul that enters into the child when it is

223

conceived comes from the great universe of soul and spirit, wholly independent of the parents, and is not in its nature or qualities a part of the parents as is the flesh and blood which build up and produce the physical body of the child. But, while this is true, it is also true that this spirit and soul of the child is susceptible to, and in a way absorbs, the influence of the spirit and soul of the parents—not only at the time of conception but also during the period of gestation, and even for years afterwards, and to such an extent that this influence continues beyond the mere earthly existence of the parents and into the life of the progeny to the third and fourth generations, as the text says.

The spirit part of the child is more susceptible to the influence and evil effects of these sins than is really its physical body. For, as I have said, the spirit part is the originator and breeder of the sins, if I may so express it, while the body is merely the recipient of the exercise of the sins and the object of their manifestation.

The influence of spirit upon spirit is more extensive and certain than mortals can possibly conceive of, and the results of that influence are not so apparent or known to the consciousness of the succeeding children, or to the respective parents. And men do not suppose, and, as a fact, do not understand or become conscious of the fact that such influence is operating upon the spiritual parts of their children. They see and realize that the effects of such sins become manifested in the physical body, and, as their ordinary natural senses cannot perceive the condition of the spirit, they conclude that the text can only mean that these sins are visited upon the material bodies of their children.

But I must tell them that, while great and deplorable injury is inflicted on these material bodies, yet, greater and more lasting and more grievous injury, in the way of manifestations, is inflicted upon the spiritual nature of the children—not only because this nature continues to live but also because men, not realizing that this nature has been injured, make no attempt to find and apply a remedy, as they so often do in the case where these sins manifest themselves in the physical body. And, besides, there are many sins which do great injury to the spiritual nature, and which are never perceptible to the senses of men.

A man is not only the parent of a child's material body, but, in a secondary way, is also the parent of its spiritual nature. And the condition of the parent's spiritual nature influences and determines to a large extent the qualities and tendencies of the child's nature for good or evil—not only while it is a mortal, but frequently after it has ceased to inhabit the veil of flesh.

So, let parents know that they do not live to themselves alone as morals, but that their evil thoughts and deeds have a greater or lesser influence upon the spiritual natures of their children, especially at the time of conception and during gestation. Then, how important that every parent, during these times particularly, and at all times, should have their spiritual natures in that condition of purity and freedom from sin wherefrom their children may be conceived and born in a condition of soul purity (which will not reflect any evil that they can charge their parents with being the creators of).

If men would only realize these facts and live their lives in accordance with the Truths which I here declare, how much sooner would the human race be brought into harmony with God's Laws and the souls of men be freed from sin and evil!

I know it is often said that it is unjust, and not in accordance with the justice of an impartial God, that the sins and penalties arising from the disobedience of our first parents should be visited upon mankind, who were and are their progeny, as such mankind had no part in that disobedience. But when it is remembered, and it is a fact, that God did not create sin or evil or impose such upon the first parents for their disobedience, but that they themselves created evil and sin, and men have been creating these inharmonies ever since, it will be seen that an impartial God, Who is our only God, is not responsible for either sin or evil and the consequent penalties which they impose. And, as has been written to you before, the abolishing of sin and evil and their penalties is in the power of man and his will.

As these first parents created these evils, as I have explained, and in the manner that I have pointed out to you, their sins, by the influence which they have upon the spiritual nature at the time of conception and birth, become, as it were, a visitation; and that is the spiritual desires and tendencies and inclinations toward that which is evil. And this influence continues with the child for years after its birth, and in accordance with the child and parents being closely associated together in their earth lives. And as each succeeding generation caused the visitation of its sinful influence and tendencies upon the succeeding generation, you can readily see how men, all men, became subject to the sins and evils and penalties which were brought into the world by the first parents.

INSTEAD OF GOD BEING THE CREATOR OF THESE THINGS, OR VISITING THEM UPON THE CHILDREN OF MAN, HE DECLARED THAT THEIR EXISTENCE IS CONTRARY TO THE HARMONY OF HIS CREATION AND MUST BE ERADICATED BEFORE MAN CAN COME INTO THAT HARMONY AND AN AT-ONEMENT WITH HIM. AND AS HE GAVE TO MAN THE GREAT POWER OF FREE WILL WITHOUT ANY RESTRICTION UPON ITS EXERCISE, EXCEPT AS A MAN'S UNDERSTANDING OF THE HARMONY OF THE OPERATIONS OF GOD'S LAWS MIGHT INFLUENCE HIM TO EXERCISE THIS GREAT POWER; AND AS MAN, IN THE WRONG EXERCISE OF THAT POWER, BROUGHT INTO EXISTENCE THESE THINGS OF EVIL AND SIN, SO MAN, AS HE PERCEIVES THIS PLAN OF GOD'S HARMONY, MUST EXERCISE THAT WILL IN SUCH A WAY AS TO FREE HIMSELF FROM THESE THINGS WHICH ARE NOT PART OF GOD'S CREATION, AND WHICH ARE OUT OF HARMONY WITH HIS PLANS FOR THE CREATION AND PRESERVATION OF A PERFECT

UNIVERSE OF WHICH MAN IS ITS HIGHEST CREATION.

God never changes. His Laws never change. Only man has changed from the perfection of his creation, and man must change again before that perfection will again be his.

Now, from all this, it must not be inferred that man is left to his own efforts to bring about this great restoration, for that is not true, because God's instrumentalities are continuously at work influencing man to turn again to his first estate and become the perfect man, as he ultimately will become.

I am not referring here to the workings of the Great Divine Love which, when a man possesses It in a sufficient degree, makes him more than the perfect man.

SO, "THE SINS OF THE PARENTS ARE VISITED UPON THE CHILDREN TO THE THIRD AND FOURTH GENERATIONS" MEANS: THE TENDENCIES AND INCLINATIONS TOWARD THAT WHICH IS EVIL, NOT BY GOD, BUT BY MAN, HIMSELF, SOLELY AND EXCLUSIVELY.

AND, OH, MAN, COULD YOU SEE THE RESULTS OF THESE SINS UPON THE SPIRITUAL NATURES OF YOUR CHILDREN, AS YOU OFTEN SEE THEM UPON THEIR MATERIAL BODIES, YOU WOULD HESITATE IN YOUR SINNING AND THINK; AND, IN THINKING, YOU WOULD SEE THE WAY BY WHICH THE GREAT BLOT UPON THE HAPPINESS AND SALVATION OF HUMANITY COULD BE REMOVED, AND ITS PROGRESS TO THE PERFECT MAN BE HASTENED AND ASSURED!

Well, I have written enough for tonight, and hope that what I have said may be understood and meditated upon by all who may read it.

I will not detain you longer. With my love and the blessings of one who is now not only the perfect man but also a possessor of the Divine Nature of the Father and an inheritor of immortality, I will say good night.

Your brother in Christ,

LUKE.

Luke Clarifies One Point Relating to His Previous Message.
(LUKE, THE APOSTLE)
(April 10th, 1916 | Received by James Padgett)

I AM HERE. *Luke.*

I desire to make some corrections in my message of last night, and will thank you to receive them.

I desire to say that, when I spoke of the sins of the parents being visited upon the children at the time of conception and birth, I meant that these sins, by the influence which they have upon the spiritual nature of the child, became, as it were, a visitation. I DID NOT MEAN THAT ANY PART OF

THE REAL SIN OF THE PARENT BECAME A PART OF THE SPIRITUAL NATURE OF THE CHILD, BUT ONLY THAT THE INFLUENCE OF THE PARENT'S SINS UPON THE CHILD IS SUFFICIENT TO GIVE THE SPIRITUAL DESIRES AND TENDENCIES OF THE CHILD AN INCLINATION TOWARDS THAT WHICH IS EVIL; AND THIS INFLUENCE IS CONTINUOUS WITH THE CHILD FOR YEARS AFTER ITS BIRTH, AND IN ACCORDANCE WITH THE CHILD AND PARENTS BEING CLOSELY ASSOCIATED TOGETHER IN THEIR EARTH LIVES.

Let this point be made plain so that man may not quibble about the meaning of what I wrote. Otherwise, the message is true, and just as I intended it should convey to you the truth of the meaning of the text.

I will not delay you longer tonight but, with my love and blessing, will say that I am

Your brother in Christ,

LUKE.

Jesus Explains How the Power of the Divine Love Redeems Men from Sin and Error.
(JESUS)
(March 6th, 1915 | Received by James Padgett)

I AM HERE. *Jesus.*

I want to write tonight on: "The Power of the Divine Love to Redeem Men from Sin and Error."

My Father's Love is, as I have written, the only thing in all this universe that can save men from their evil natures and make them at-one with Him. This Divine Love I have already explained. And when mankind will read my messages and try to understand the meaning of this Love, it will soon become more at peace with itself and with God.

This Divine Love is the one Great Power that moves the universe, and, without it, there would not be that wonderful harmony that exists in the Celestial Heavens of the spirit world; nor would so much happiness exist among the angels who inhabit these spheres.

This Divine Love is also the influence which makes men on earth think and do that which makes for peace and good will among men. It is not possessed by all men—in fact, by comparatively few. Yet, Its influence is felt over nearly the whole earth. Even those who have never heard of my teachings, or of my Father, enjoy the benefit of Its influence in some kind of belief or faith in an overshadowing Spirit of Great Power and Watchfulness. I know that this is true, for I have visited all parts of the earth and have looked into men's hearts, and found in them some elements of belief which evidenced that this Great Love was influencing these unenlightened people. So, notwithstanding the fact that my gospel is not

227

preached to every creature, as I commanded when on earth, yet this Love of the Father is everywhere and all-pervading.

Still, It is not received in all that fulness that enables those who feel Its influence to realize that God is their Father and they are His children, and that they may become members of His Household in the Celestial Spheres.

No man can receive this Love unless he has faith in the Father's Willingness to bestow It upon him, and truly and with earnestness prays for It.

Every man has in him the natural love which will give him great happiness in eternity as a mere spirit and an inhabitant of the spheres lower than the Celestial, even though he refuses to seek for the Divine Love that will make him a divine angel of the Celestial Heavens. BUT ONLY THIS DIVINE LOVE CAN CHANGE THE NATURAL MAN INTO A MAN HAVING THE DIVINE NATURE IN LOVE THAT THE FATHER HAS. I DO NOT MEAN THAT MAN, EVEN THOUGH HE BE FILLED WITH THIS LOVE TO THE HIGHEST DEGREE, WILL EVER BECOME A GOD AND EQUAL TO THE FATHER IN ANY OF HIS POWERS OR ATTRIBUTES. THIS CANNOT BE. BUT THIS LOVE WILL MAKE HIM LIKE THE FATHER IN LOVE AND HAPPINESS AND HARMONY. THIS LOVE HAS NO COUNTERPART IN ALL CREATION, AND COMES FROM THE FATHER ALONE. IT CHANGES NOT, NOR IS EVER BESTOWED ON ANYONE WHO IS UNWORTHY OR WHO REFUSES TO SEEK FOR IT IN THE ONLY WAY PROVIDED BY THE FATHER.

MY EXPERIENCE IN THESE CELESTIAL HEAVENS IS THAT THIS LOVE HAS THE POWER TO CHANGE THE MOST HARDENED SINNER INTO A TRUE CHILD OF GOD, IF ONLY THROUGH FAITH AND PRAYER SUCH SINNER WILL SEEK FOR IT. LET THIS LOVE TAKE POSSESSION OF A MAN OR SPIRIT, AND ITS POWER TO PURIFY AND CHANGE THE HEART OF THAT MAN OR SPIRIT NEVER FAILS.

Your brother and friend,

JESUS.

What Jesus Meant When He Said: "In My Father's House Are Many Mansions," and His Further Description of the Effect of the Divine Love on the Soul to Redeem Mankind.
(JESUS)
(March 9th, 1915 | Received by James Padgett)

I AM HERE. *Jesus.*

You are in a condition to resume my message tonight.
I am in a condition of Love that enables me to know that my Father's

Love is the only Love that can redeem mankind and make it at-one with Him. So, you must understand that this Divine Love is a Love that has no counterpart in all the universe, and must be received by man in all Its fulness in order for him to attain to the Celestial Spheres where the Father's Fountainhead of Love exists. So, I say that no man can become a part of God's Divinity until he receives this Divine Love and realizes that he and his Father are one in Love and Purity.

I WILL NOW TELL YOU WHAT THIS DIVINE LOVE MEANS TO ANY MAN WHO HAS RECEIVED IT. HE IS IN A CONDITION OF PERFECT PEACE AND HIS HAPPINESS IS BEYOND ALL COMPARISON; AND HE IS NOT WILLING THAT ANY THING OR POWER SHALL LEAD HIM TO THOSE THINGS THAT ARE NOT IN ACCORD WITH THE DIVINE LOVE AND GOD'S LAWS OF HARMONY. HE IS NOT ONLY HAPPY BUT ALSO IS AWAY BEYOND THE LOWER SPIRITS IN INTELLECTUAL DEVELOPMENT AND KNOWLEDGE OF THE SPIRITUAL THINGS OF THE FATHER. I KNOW THAT NO MAN IS ABLE TO OBTAIN THE GREAT SOUL PERCEPTIONS UNTIL HE HAS THE SOUL DEVELOPMENT AND IS FITTED TO LIVE IN THE CELESTIAL SPHERES WHERE ONLY LOVE AND HARMONY EXIST.

So, do not think if a man merely becomes wonderful in his knowledge in an intellectual sense, he is fitted to live in these higher spheres, for he is not. Only the great development of the soul, by obtaining the Divine Love into his soul, will enable him to live there.

John never said that by me were all things created that were created, and that I, as God, came to earth and became an indweller in the flesh. That is a mistake and an interpolation, for I never was God. Neither did I ever create any part of the universe. I was only a spirit of God sent by Him to work out man's salvation and show him the only Way to the Heavenly Home that God has in keeping for those who receive the New Birth.

(In what sphere do you live?)

Well, I live in all spheres, but my home is a sphere that is very close to the Fountainhead of God's Love. It has no name or number. With me in the Celestial Spheres* are all those who have received this Divine Love to such

---

* Jesus is higher up in the Celestial Spheres because of having prayed for and obtained the Divine Love in greater abundance than any other Celestial spirit. When a spirit obtains a sufficiency of the Divine Love in the soul, it leaves the Seventh Sphere and enters the First Celestial Sphere; and then it progresses to the Second Celestial and, after this, to the Third Celestial. Above the Third Celestial Sphere, the spheres are so graduated that no number is used. The statement by Jesus, "With me in the Celestial Spheres are all those who have received the Divine Love..." means that the spirits are in one of these Celestial Spheres according to the degree they have obtained the Divine Love. There is no spirit who has obtained the Divine Love in that great abundance that Jesus possesses It. Therefore, no Celestial spirit has yet reached his sphere. But all souls possess this privilege. — Ed.

an extent that they have become entirely purified and at-one with the Father. Many are progressing towards that home and will, sooner or later, get there.

Those who fully received this Divine Love through faith and prayer are in the Celestial Spheres, but those who have not yet obtained this Love to the degree mentioned are not.

(Are some of the disciples living there?)

Yes, Paul is, and so are Peter and John and James and several others.

(What did you mean by, "In my Father's House are many mansions"?)

I meant that I would go to the Celestial Spheres where I now am and prepare these mansions, which I have now done. And it rests with spirits and mortals only to become inhabitants thereof.

(Are some of the prophets from the Old Testament living there as well?)

Some are and some are not. The mere fact that these ancient prophets and seers were the mere instruments of God in declaring His Purposes and Laws does not mean that they necessarily received this Great Love so that they are now inhabitants of the Celestial Spheres. Moses and Elias are in the Celestial Spheres, and so is John, the Baptist. But many great teachers of spiritual things or of future existence are not, because they have not obtained the New Birth.

(Will it take me many years before I am able to live with you in your Kingdom?)

Well, it will depend on whether you live and believe in such a way as to get this Great Love. If you do, you will not have to wait long years to be with me in the Celestial Spheres. You are now in the right Way. And if you will only persevere and let your faith increase, and get the Divine Love in sufficient abundance in your soul, you will be with me. And remember this: that I am your special friend and helper, and will be. And when you are in doubt or trouble, I will keep you from relapsing into a state of unbelief or of carelessness.

(If my recently departed friend prays for this Love, will he find relief from his sufferings?)

IF, AS YOU SAY, HE WILL SEEK THAT DIVINE LOVE AND PRAY TO THE FATHER IN FAITH, AND BELIEVE THAT THE FATHER WILL BESTOW IT UPON HIM, HE WILL RECEIVE IT. AND WHEN HE RECEIVES IT IN SUFFICIENT ABUNDANCE, ALL SIN THAT HE MAY HAVE COMMITTED WILL BE BLOTTED OUT. NO FURTHER WILL HE HAVE TO PAY THE PENALTIES OF HIS DEEDS OF SIN AND ERROR. THIS IS WHAT I CAME PRINCIPALLY TO TEACH MANKIND. WHEN I SAID, "AS YOU SOW, SO SHALL YOU REAP," I MEANT THIS TO BE THE LAW OF GOD AS TO THE NATURAL MAN, AS WELL AS TO EVERYTHING ELSE IN NATURE. BUT THAT LAW IS SUBJECT TO BE SET ASIDE, SO FAR AS ITS OPERATIONS ON THE SOULS OF MEN ARE CONCERNED, BY THE SOUL OF MAN RECEIVING THE DIVINE LOVE IN SUFFICIENT ABUNDANCE. AND WHEN THE GREAT LOVE OF

THE FATHER IS SOUGHT AND RECEIVED BY THE SOUL OF MAN IN SUFFICIENT ABUNDANCE, THE LAW OF COMPENSATION IS MADE NONEFFECTIVE, THE LAW OF LOVE BECOMES SUPREME, AND MAN IS RELIEVED FROM THE PENALTIES OF HIS SINS.

(But the church still teaches that only a belief in your sacrifice and atonement can save men from their sins.)

Yes, I know how men reason about this matter, and that is the great stumbling block that prevents them from receiving this Divine Love and believing that It alone is efficacious in saving them from paying the penalties of their sins.

Well, you now see what I am trying to do. And I am so well satisfied that you will make a success of your work that I feel more certain that my messages will be understood and given to the world. So, keep up your courage and, in a short time, all will be in such condition that there will be nothing to interfere with you doing the work as you desire.

(Will I really be able to devote more time to this work of receiving your messages?)

Yes, most assuredly. And when you get into the work with all your earnestness and faith, you will see that you will be able to receive the messages just as I intend that you shall receive them.

Let us stop now.

Your own true brother in spirit,
JESUS.

Luke Communicates What the Celestial Spirits Think About War.
(LUKE, THE APOSTLE)
(February 27th, 1917 | Received by James Padgett)

I AM HERE. *Luke.*

I heard the doctor ask, "What do the Celestial spirits think of this war?"[*] In a few words, I will tell him.

Well, first, he must know that the Celestial spirits are not so much interested in the war, and the success or defeat of nations, as in the salvation of the souls of the individuals who compose those nations. The fact that the individual is a German or an Englishman or a Frenchman has no influence upon the desire of the spirit to help the soul of the individual. All are alike important and dear to the Celestial spirits, and the same Love that will save the one will save the other. So, you can see that the war is not of so much importance.

Of course, many mortals are made spirits who are all unfitted for the life in the spirit world. In that view, the war is of importance to the Celestial

---

[*] World War I.

spirits, as their opportunity for doing work among mortals, either directly or through other spirits, is interfered with by such slaughter. For the spirits who come so suddenly to our spirit world are more difficult to impress and teach the Way to Truth and Life than they would have been if they had been allowed to live their ordinary mortal lives.

All wars interfere with the ordinary living and dying of mortals to some extent, and we deplore them. But, as to the right or the wrong of wars, we do not judge, but leave that to conscience and judgment of the individuals who bring about the wars and are responsible for them. The acts of individuals, whether they apply personally or affect others in the way of being members or nations, are all subject and responsible to the laws which control the thoughts and deeds of mortals, and the recollections of the same. And these laws do not call for or demand the paying of the penalties of the individuals as parts of a nation, but, rather, payment as individuals exclusively, irrespective of the fact that they belong to and control the affairs of a nation.

However, spirits are not less interested in sin that arises from the wars of nations than in sin that arises from the act of the individual as such. We Celestial spirits are interested in the war that is now going on because of such sin, and because it causes the paying of the penalties demanded by the law much sooner than it otherwise would. And we are also interested because war creates hatred and desire for vengeance on the part of those engaged in it. Hence, this adds to the burdens that the individual so affected will have to get rid of when he comes to the spirit world in order to progress and find happiness.

To us, war is an incident of human existence. The right or wrong of it does not enter into our consideration of what should be the penalties that those who are responsible for it should suffer. The soul of each individual shows its own sins and wrong done. And only this condition of the soul determines the state of its possessor and the destiny that its own thoughts and acts have made for it.

Now, from what I have said, you may suppose that we are indifferent to the happiness or misery of mortals while on earth, but that is not true. We realize that, to a large extent, man must work out his own destiny on earth, that we spirits cannot control that work except as we may influence the individual mind and thoughts of men, and that there are times when men give way to their passions and evil ambitions in which we cannot influence them. Even God, Himself, does not attempt to do so by His Omnipotence, but leaves men to the exercise of their own wills and the consequence of their own acts—and, this, although many suffer physically and mentally who are innocent.

But all men live not unto themselves. They are so united in society that the acts of one must have their influence on others. Hence, those who live in these societies are subject to these influences and to the consequences that flow from them. It may not seem right that the innocent should suffer because of the acts of the guilty; and if the Celestial spirits could prevent it,

232

such sufferings would not take place. But they cannot so prevent the intermingling of suffering between and among those living in societies, for, to do so, they would have to interfere with the operations of the laws controlling these things, which they cannot do. So, you see, war does not mean what you might suppose to the high spirits. And while they have their sympathy and love for all the children of men in these terrible conflicts, yet, they must leave men to the consequences of their own deeds and thoughts, and man must do the suffering.

But, nevertheless, we do try to influence those who have the control and determination of these things. And our work is always to try to influence them to do that which will bring the greatest happiness to men.

We do not interest ourselves as to whether one belligerent nation or the other will win the battles, because we know that only men themselves can decide this matter. And we don't try to interfere to bring about the success of the one party or the other, as we know that we are powerless to bring about any result.

Think, for a moment, and you will understand that if we had the power to determine the issues of war, we should have the power to destroy sin and error, because both are the subjects of the creation and control of men. And I say that, if we had such power, sin and error would have disappeared long ago from the world, and men would have been made free.

No, we can work only with the individual. As the individual soul is made pure and righteous, the aggregate of these individuals composing a nation will become pure and righteous, and war will become impossible.

I do not think it best to write more now, but will say that we Celestial spirits think of war as the creature of mortals, to be controlled and ended by mortals, and that we cannot decide the issue one way or the other. Hence, to us, war is an incident in the living and dying of mortals that we cannot prevent or create.

Your brother in Christ,
LUKE.

A Former Minister of the Gospel States That His Religious Beliefs Were Merely Intellectual, Which Led to His Profound Skepticism and Departure from the Ministry, and to His Loss of All Hope for Forgiveness in the Spirit World.
(S.B.C.)
(date unknown | Received by James Padgett)

I AM HERE. *(S.B.C.)*

I am here, a poor, miserable man who is without hope in this dark and dreary world of lost souls, and who is surrounded by spirits who are, like myself, suffering from the effects of an evil life and a lost soul.

233

I come to you because I have seen others come and apparently receive some benefits. As you know, hope is a thing which will come to us at all times, even though for a moment; and when I came to you, that moment was mine. But, to be frank, I do not expect that you can help me any, for the moment of hope has gone and only my dark and fixed despair is with me.

But, as I have commenced to write, I will be polite enough to continue and to show to you that I am not unmindful of the benefit of the opportunity which you give us to come to you, nor am I unaware of your kindness in listening to our tales of woe.* And, so, if I am not too troublesome, I would like to tell you a little of my condition and what brought it about—I mean as I now see things in their true nature and relationship to cause and effect, and why I am in the condition of darkness and suffering that now holds out to me no hope of succor.

Well, when on earth, I was at one time a minister of the Gospel of Christ, and, for a number of years, preached, as I thought, his Truths of salvation to men. At the same time, I actually and truly believed in what I taught. But now I see that my belief was wholly intellectual and not arising from the soul's inspirations, and that my teachings were also merely those, or rather my condition as teacher was merely that, of the teacher of a school or similar institution.

I never enjoyed religion in its true, or soul, sense, and all my endeavors to teach others were made because I had a kind of realization that I was called upon to pursue that course of life. But my teachings, while others have been benefited by them, never benefited myself. Well, after a while, I got tired of this life of the ministry and, in an evil hour, forsook it and became a lawyer. My thoughts were then taken entirely away from things religious, and, as I progressed in the studies and thoughts of my legal profession, there developed in me the mental condition of mind that required every proposition asserted to be proved by convincing and irrefutable evidence. And this condition of mind grew in me to such an extent that I would accept nothing as true where merely faith was all that was given upon which to base the truth. And, as a consequence, I became a reader of books that were called scientific, and they showed me the absurdity of receiving, as an established fact, anything which could not be demonstrated by my five senses in conjunction with my reasoning faculties.

After a while, the question of God's Existence, the truth of the genuineness of the Bible, and the reality of religion came before my skeptical mind in a new light. And as I had associates whose minds were in a similar condition to my own, I rejected the truth of all these things and became an infidel without a God or savior, even in a mental sense.

And, so, I continued to live in this condition of mind, which became

---

* Mr. Padgett devoted one evening each week to helping dark spirits find relief from their sufferings.—Ed.

more and more skeptical as the years went by. And my soul's development, what little it then had been, as I now see, ceased, and I became soulfully dead beyond resurrection.

In my ministerial life, I taught and mentally believed in the ministrations of the Holy Spirit and Its functions in awakening man's soul to a realization of the necessity of seeking the Love and Favor of God. I also preached that, without the work of the Holy Spirit, it was impossible for any man to become the possessor of God's Love or to be accepted by Him as a redeemed child. And I also preached that to reject the benefit or the work of the Holy Spirit (or, as the Bible says: to blaspheme against the Holy Spirit) was to become guilty of the "unpardonable sin" for which there was no forgiveness.

After I became a skeptic, as I have said, I was guilty of this very sin; for, while ever respectful in my declarations as to things religious, I often vowed and asserted that the Holy Spirit was a myth, and that It did not and could not work to save men's souls. Further, that all who believed in such silly tales were of shallow minds, and that they needed to be educated to the truths which could only be obtained by developing their minds. Finally, they needed to realize that whatever their senses, together with their reasoning powers, did not prove, or, rather, did not accept as proved, should be rejected.

So, you see, according to the Bible teachings, I committed this "unpardonable sin" , though, while on earth, I did not believe that I had. And, in fact, I did not believe there was any such sin to commit! But, alas, how many of my associates—men of bright minds and loving and kindly souls—committed the same great sin!

When I died and became a spirit, my beliefs came with me and remained with me for a long time. I enjoyed considerable happiness in the exercise of my mental qualities and in the pursuit of certain studies with regard to the spirit world. I met many congenial spirits and, in our interchange of thoughts, I found much that was interesting and profitable. But, after a while, and for some unaccountable reason, these pleasures of intellectual enjoyment ceased to have the satisfying properties that they had at first, and I felt that there was something wanting, though I did not realize what it was and my companions could not tell me.

In my wanderings, I met many spirits and, always being eager in the search of truth, I did not hesitate to ask questions of those whom I thought might be able to enlighten me. And, at last, in my pursuits, I came across a very beautiful and bright spirit—the most beautiful that I had seen. Being curious, in the best sense, I asked what was the cause of his beauty and brightness and apparent happiness. And in a voice that was all love, and with a look of great pity and sympathy, he told me that there was only one cause: that through the ministry of the Holy Spirit he had received the Love of God in his soul, and that, as a result of that Love, from an ugly and dark spirit, he had come into the condition in which I saw him.

You can imagine my surprise! It was like a thunderbolt out of a clear sky. It was proof—plain, palpable, and convincing—that the Holy Spirit was a real thing, that It does cause the Love of God to flow into the souls of men and spirits, and that Its work brings such glorious results. Where now was my belief that the five senses and the reasoning powers of my mind were the only things that could show me the truth? Oh, I tell you, it was a shock! And then there came back to me the teachings of the Bible and my early life as a minister. And with these recollections came the conviction of the awful mistake that I had made while on earth. Worst of all, and what sounded my everlasting doom, came the memory that I had blasphemed and committed the "unpardonable sin" against the Holy Ghost, and that, for me, never through all eternity was there any possibility of forgiveness!

Why should not all hope die within? It did. And can you be surprised when I tell you there can be no hope, and that I must suffer and remain in this condition of darkness and soul death through all the long years of the future?

So, you see, one moment of hope caused me to trouble you with my unhappy story of why I am beyond all hope of forgiveness or expectation of any happiness or life in the outstretching future.

So, my friend, I am in the position of Dives.* I cannot be benefited myself by this knowledge of the Truth of the Holy Spirit, and the certain doom which arises from blaspheming Its work and mission. Yet, I can tell you to sound the warning to all mortals that they must not deny the Holy Spirit or speak words of blasphemy against It.

Well, I have taken up more of your time than I should have done, and I will stop writing.

My name was S.B.C. and I lived in Glasgow, Scotland, and I died in 1876 in a fatal and false belief, and a traitor to my young faith.

(My dear friend, you are mistaken in your belief that you are beyond all hope for forgiveness or ultimate happiness. While it is true that neglecting to pray for God's Divine Love, conveyed through the ministration of His Holy Spirit, is indeed a sin of omission, it is not true, as you say, that you are now beyond redemption. Just as the Father, in His Great Love and Mercy, extends His Forgiveness on earth to the truly penitent, likewise, in the spirit world, His forgiveness is no less available to you now for the sincere asking for His Love through prayer.

I would like to suggest that you put my words to the test by praying to the Father with all true longings for His Love to flow into your soul, and see whether or not you will receive His Loving Response. And, to instruct you further in this, I would urge you to receive the counsel of bright spirits about you who have themselves experienced the wonderful effects of having prayed for and received God's redeeming Love as spirits.)

I should say that, if you could show me that what you say is true, I would be the happiest man in all the spirit world, and that I would seek for

---

* A rich man from the Bible parable.—Ed.

this Love of God with all my heart and soul. But I feel that you are raising false hope in me. If you are speaking what you know, I will try to believe what may be said to me, and I assure you that I will listen most attentively and respectfully to what may be said. And, of course, if there is any hope held out to me, I will grasp it and never let it go away from me. But it will be hard for me to believe that there is any forgiveness for me.

(Well, in order for your hope to be realized, you must be prepared to listen to these spirits with an open heart and mind, and without preconceived notions.)

Yes, I promise that I will try to listen as much as I can without having my present beliefs influence me.

(Look about you and tell me what you see.)

Well, I see a great number of spirits. Some are very unhappy and some not so unhappy, but they are still dark and forbidding.

(Look carefully. Do you not also see some who appear bright and happy?)

Yes, I see some bright ones, just like the one who told me that his beauty and happiness came from the work of the Holy Ghost in his soul.

(I want you now to ask one of these spirits to have my grandmother, Ann Rollins, come to you. When she does so, explain to her what you have said to me, and please tell me the result of your conversation.)

I have told her what you said, and she says to me:

"My dear brother, you are mistaken in thinking that you are beyond forgiveness, for the Father's Mercy is so great and His Love so abundant that they are sufficient to redeem the vilest sinner that ever existed, or ever will exist, in all His Great Universe. So, if you will come with me, I will show you the results of this Mercy and Love of the Father, and you will soon realize that this Mercy and Love is for you, even though you now believe that you are past redemption."

She looks on me with such love and sympathy that I already feel that I may be wrong. I am going with her. So, my very dear friend, I will come to you again and tell you my experience with your grandmother.

So, believe that I am so thankful to you for your interest, and permit me to subscribe myself,

Your thankful friend,

S.B.C.

Ann Rollins Declares That the Belief in the "Unpardonable Sin" Is Slanderous and Blasphemous Against the Loving Father.
(ANN ROLLINS)
(November 1ˢᵗ, 1915 | Received by James Padgett)

I AM HERE. *Your grandmother.*

I have been listening to your conversation tonight, and am much

237

pleased to see that you and your friend are growing in your conception of the Truth.

The matter of the "unpardonable sin" is one that is of the greatest importance to the world, especially in view of the fact that so many of the orthodox ministers teach that it is a thing of real existence and is so dreadful in its consequences.

But, thanks to the Master, that teaching will not be permitted to go unchallenged in the near future. For the Truth in this particular will be made so plain that men will cease to believe in that teaching and, as a consequence, will be relieved from a fear that has kept many a one from seeking the Love and Favor of the Father.

I know that this revelation of the Truth will antagonize many of these preachers who see that that teaching is one of the strongest instruments that enables them to keep their organization together. But this antagonism will not avail, for the Truth will prevail. And when they come to think for themselves, mankind will embrace this Truth with gladness and joy.

How strange that the professed ministers of Christ should so slander and blaspheme the One Loving Father and cause men to look upon Him as a God of insatiable wrath, and One Who consigns them to eternal punishment and hell because they refuse to believe in the doctrines of the churches; and, when they get into such a condition of hardness of heart, that they teach, as your preacher said, "Even God Himself will have no power to save!"

Oh, it is pitiable that such erroneous and harmful doctrines should be taught and, worse than all, by professed ministers of the loving and lowly Jesus!

SO, MY SON, YOU AND YOUR FRIEND, WHENEVER THE OPPORTUNITY COMES TO COMBAT THIS MONSTROUS TEACHING, DO SO WITH ALL YOUR STRENGTH AND POWER OF CONCLUSION. SHOW AND PROCLAIM TO THE WORLD THAT SUCH TEACHING IS NOT TRUE, THAT THERE IS OPPORTUNITY FOR SALVATION FOR EVERY SINNER, AND THAT GOD LOVES THE MAN WHO WILL NOT BELIEVE ON HIM, JUST AS HE LOVES THE BELIEVER— ONLY THE FORMER MAY NOT PARTAKE OF THE DIVINE NATURE, AS DOES THE LATTER.

I wanted to write this tonight because I thought that the time was opportune to impress upon you the falsity of this great dogma that has no foundation in Truth or in the Plan of God for the salvation of humanity.

Well, I will not write more tonight, as you have others present who may want to write. But, before I close, I want to say, in fulfillment of John's statement to you today, that he is present, and with him is his great influence of Love.

So, with all my love, I bless you both.

YOUR GRANDMOTHER.

238

Jesus Reemphasizes That the Holy Spirit Is Not God, and That There Is No "Unpardonable Sin."
(JESUS)
(June 6th, 1915 | Received by James Padgett)

I AM HERE. *Jesus.*

I want to tell you, once and for all, that the Holy Ghost is not God, and that the "unpardonable sin" is a thing which has no existence either in the world of mortals or in the spirit world. I never used the expression contained in the Bible in reference to the "unpardonable sin," and it has done more harm to my cause than most any other thing.

I was not conceived by the Holy Ghost, as many believe. I was a man created and born as other men; only, as I have told you, I was without sin.

All writings which make the Holy Spirit equal to the Father are untrue. The Holy Spirit, as I have told you, is a mere instrument of God in doing His Work among men. And for men to believe that the Holy Spirit is God is blasphemy. But even that sin will be forgiven men.

Before we get through our writings, I hope that I will make it so plain and convincing that the Holy Spirit is not God, but a mere Spirit, though the greatest Spirit in His Kingdom, that men will cease to worship It as God.

(Will you write a message on this subject?)

Yes, I will write a formal message on this subject;[*] and you will see that the Holy Spirit cannot possibly be God. So, do not let this question interfere with your belief in me or in what I write to you. You are now in the Way to Truth and the Kingdom. And if you will continue to pray and have faith, you will become an inhabitant of that Kingdom, no matter what the Bible may say which is apparently in conflict with what I write.

So, with all my love, I will say good night.

Your friend and brother,

JESUS.

Luke Declares That There Is No "Unpardonable Sin," as Taught by a Certain Preacher.
(LUKE, THE APOSTLE)
(October 31st, 1915 | Received by James Padgett)

I AM HERE. *Luke.*

I was with you at church and heard the sermon on the "unpardonable

---

[*] See "The Holy Spirit" chapter in volume I of *Angelic Revelations of Divine Truth.*— Ed.

sin," and was much interested in the way in which the preacher dealt with the subject. His discourse was very plausible, but it is not true. As Jesus has told you, there is no "unpardonable sin." All men in this life and in the life to come have the opportunity to be saved from their sins and become at-one with the Father.

The great danger in such a sermon, as the one preached tonight, is that men who have not become believers in Jesus as the savior of the world—and I mean the expression in the sense that we have explained it to you—will think that, after they have arrived at a certain age and find their souls show no inclination or desire to seek the Way to God's Love or to a reconciliation with Him, they have committed the "unpardonable sin"; and, hence, there is no use for them to try to find the Way to salvation. It is a damnable doctrine! And the preacher who announced it has incurred a dreadful and awful responsibility; for, in the afterlife, he will very likely meet spirits in a condition of darkness and stagnation of soul who will tell him that they gave up all hope of salvation because of his sermons. And, at the time they meet him, they will believe just as they did on earth. And he, possibly, may see the errors of his wrong teachings, and then will come to him remorse and bitter recollections of these teachings and the great harm that they did to these darkened spirits.

When men get to know the Truth, as they will when the Master shall have delivered his messages through you, they will not have to run the risk of becoming bound and shackled by such false beliefs as the one of which I speak. But, before that time, with so many preachers and especially those so-called "evangelists" who strive to force men into the erroneous beliefs which they teach through fear of eternal damnation, many men will have formed these beliefs and will suffer the consequences which these false doctrines entail.

I was sorry that someone could not have arisen in the church to express resentment of his doctrine of the "unpardonable sin", and would have told all the people that there is no such thing—only that the Father's Love is waiting in great abundance for everyone who may seek It, and will be freely given; and that, if men will only come to the Father in prayer and belief, that Love will be given to them, and salvation and immortality will be theirs.

The age of man has nothing to do with his salvation. It is for the old as well as for the young. And no idea or suggestion of any "unpardonable sin" must be interposed to prevent any man from believing that the Great Love of the Father is waiting for him.

So, you see, with some Truths preached by these orthodox ministers there is a great deal of error. And the effect of the latter is to prevent or undo any good which the Truth may have otherwise bestowed upon men.

These great errors have been preached and have worked their injury for many centuries now. Men will be hard to convince that they are not the true doctrines of Jesus, and that the claimed truths which they teach are not the only truths.

I will not write more tonight.

I will say, with my love and blessings, I am

Your brother in Christ,

LUKE.

Charles Latham Corroborates That Luke Wrote on: "There Is No 'Unpardonable Sin,' as Taught by a Certain Preacher."
(CHARLES LATHAM)
(October 31st, 1915 | Received by James Padgett)

I AM HERE. *Charles Latham.*

I was a preacher in the days of the Reformation, and, in England, a martyr to my beliefs and preaching.

I merely came to tell you that you must believe in what Luke wrote you as to the "unpardonable sin", for I know that it is not true. For many men who denied God and the Holy Spirit on earth have found the Divine Love of the Father and salvation since coming into the spirit world.

I know it may not have been necessary for me to say this; yet I thought it best to do so, as I was man and became a spirit long after Luke lived. And that which he said was the Truth in my day and is the Truth now.

I will not write more, but will say good night.

Your brother in Christ,

CHARLES LATHAM.

Paul Also Denies the "Unpardonable Sin."
(PAUL, THE APOSTLE)
(October 31st, 1915 | Received by James Padgett)

I AM HERE. *Paul.*

I merely want to say that the "unpardonable sin", as taught by the preachers, has no existence, and that the preacher is wholly in error. For no soul is without the privilege of coming to the Father and obtaining His Love and Mercy, even in the spirit world.

I am not in condition to write more tonight and neither are you. So, we had better stop.

Your brother in Christ,

PAUL.

Samuel, the Prophet, Discusses How Selfishness Causes the Souls of Men the Unrest That Now Exists in the World.

(SAMUEL, THE PROPHET)
(December 13th, 1916 | Received by James Padgett)

I AM HERE. *Samuel.*

I have not written for a long time, although I have been with you quite often and have seen the other spirits write. I heard the conversation of yourself and friends on many occasions, as you discussed the Truth of spiritual things and commented on the messages that you received on the sermons of the preachers who attempted to explain what they called the Bible truths.

Tonight, I desire to say a few words on the subject: "What Causes the Souls of Men the Unrest That Now Exists in Your Mortal World?"

This is a subject, I know, that has been widely discussed of late. And many causes have been given and have tried to be explained as the basis for such conditions of men, both individually and as comprising nations. I realize that it is a large and comprehensive question, and to discuss it in all its features would require much more time than we have to devote to it tonight. Hence, I will call attention to only a few of these causes.

In the first place, man is so created, or, rather, he has brought himself into such a condition that self-love or selfishness—and I mean the purely human selfishness, and not that of the higher and proper kind—has become the mainspring or active principle of all his motives for doing or not doing a thing or things. And, in so acting, the rights of others are considered only in a secondary or subordinate sense. If the recognition of these rights does not involve any sacrifice of what he considers is for his own advantage, then these rights may be recognized and admitted and permitted to be carried into actual enjoyment. But if there be any conflict between his conception of what he is entitled to and the actual rights of his brother or friend or stranger, he will see only the justice of his own rights, and his consequent action will be based on that conception. And having this motive of selfishness predominant and controlling in his actions, it seldom occurs that the rights of these others are fairly recognized. Consequently, there arises injustice and harm, and the desire of conferring those things which would naturally arise from the conceptions of the rights of these brothers is ignored.

Your brother in Christ,
SAMUEL.

Paul Presents His Comments on a Preacher's Beliefs. He Agrees with Him That "Perfection" Is a Relative Term.
(PAUL, THE APOSTLE)
(August 31st, 1915 | Received by James Padgett)

242

I AM HERE. *Paul.*

I was with you tonight at the meeting, and heard what the young man said about perfection. And I agree entirely with his ideas and the application of the truth to the lives of human beings.

He had the correct conception of what perfection means. And when he said that perfection is a relative term, he spoke the exact truth. No man can expect to have the Perfection of the Father in quantity, but he may in quality. For the Spirit of Truth that enters into the soul of a man in response to prayer and faith is a part of the Divine Nature of the Father. The Essence is the same, and the Quality must be the same. But, of course, no man can obtain perfection to the extent of making him pure and holy as the Father is Pure and Holy. Even we who live in the high Celestial Heavens have not that Perfection which the Father has. But let men know that, even while on earth, they can obtain this inflowing of the Holy Spirit into their hearts to such an extent that sin and error will be entirely eradicated. This, I say, is possible. But few men attain to such a state of perfection, because the worldly affairs and natural appetites which belong to mortals are always interfering to prevent the workings of the Spirit in men's souls so that perfection of this kind may take possession of them. But notwithstanding this great difficulty of the material desires of men, they should have this perfect ideal before them always, and strive to obtain the possession of it.

I was much interested in the discourse not only because it was founded on a text attributed to me but also because of the right conception and explanation made by the young man. I could see his soul and its workings, and I was glad to know that he possessed this Divine Love to an unusual degree, and that he was fitted almost for a home in the Celestial Spheres. You were benefited by what he said, and you felt the influence of the presence of the Holy Spirit at the meeting.

If the people of this church would understand that there is only one thing that saves them from their sins and makes them at-one with the Father, and that is the inflowing of the Divine Love into their souls which was what Jesus meant when he told Nicodemus that he must be "born again", they would easily see that their doctrine of holiness is not only a reasonable doctrine but also one in accord with the Truths of God. For, as this Divine Love fills their souls, all sin and error must disappear.

Of course, this is a relative matter, for it depends upon how much of this Divine Love is in their souls to determine how much of sin or error still exists. The more of the Divine Love, the less of sin; and, on the contrary, the more of sin, the less of the Divine Love.

I know that the great majority of mankind does not believe this Truth and thinks it foolishness, and that those who claim that they have received this Divine Love to a great degree are enthusiastic fanatics and not worthy of credence. But I want to tell you that no greater Truth was ever proclaimed by the Master! And, sometime, in the not far distant future, many men who are now merely intellectual Christians will believe and embrace and experience this great Truth.

You will find yourself much benefited by attending these meetings. And while there are some things in their creed to which you do not subscribe, yet, they have the foundation Truth that the Divine Love of the Father can clear their souls from all sins, and make them perfect to the extent that they receive that Love in their souls.

I will not write more tonight, but will say that the Holy Spirit which conveys God's Love to man is with these people in great power and fulness, and It manifests Its workings in a real and irresistible manner. And God is blessing them and giving them that faith which enables them to become overcomers, and inheritors of immortality and homes in the Celestial Heavens.

So, without taking up more of your time, I will say good night and God bless you.

Your brother in Christ,
PAUL.

Jesus Also Attended This Church Service with Paul and Mr. Padgett, and He Too Comments on the People's Beliefs.

(JESUS)

(August 31st, 1915 | Received by James Padgett)

I AM HERE. *Jesus.*

I heard what Paul wrote and I corroborate everything that he said, and add that these people are pursuing the true Way to the inheritance which I promised them while I was on earth. Their faith is wonderful, and the fruits of its exercise is shown in the condition of their souls and in their lives.

Theirs is the soul conception of religion and of my Truths. And while they may not understand the philosophy of my teachings with their intellects, yet, with their soul perceptions, they have grasped the great foundation Truth of salvation through the Divine Love of the Father.

Of course, they sing and proclaim that my blood saves them from sin. But this is merely the exercise of their mental conceptions, learned from the teachings and creeds of the churches. Yet, they have grasped the great and only Truth of salvation with the far more and certain knowledge that the awakening and filling of their souls by the Divine Love gives them.

How much to be wished for that all these churches of form and mental worship could realize that the only true worship of God is with the soul perceptions! Only with these perceptions, that are developed by obtaining the Divine Love, can we "see" God. Only by such development can we become pure and holy and at-one with the Father, and partakers of His Divine Nature.

I am glad that you attended this church,[*] and I advise you to go there often. For I tell you that the Spirit of Truth and Love is with these people to a very extended degree, because their souls are open to Its inflowing and to Its ministration.

I was with you again tonight. And so was the Spirit of Truth trying to open up your soul to Its influence, and to that which will cause your faith to increase and your truth in me to grow.

No church will do you as much good as that, and I advise you to attend. Of course, you will not have to believe in its creed, but only in the fact that the Holy Spirit is there in all Its quickening power, as they sometimes sing.

So, with my love, I will say good night.

Your brother and friend,

JESUS.

James Discusses the Frailties of the Human Mind and Moral Qualities.
(JAMES, THE APOSTLE)
(May 24th, 1917 | Received by James Padgett)

I AM HERE. *James, the Apostle.*

I come to write on the subject of: "The Frailties of the Human Mind and Moral Qualities."

I have heard you read the Master's message and believe that you will find much Truth in it upon which to reflect; and I desire to add a little to what has been said therein. And, here, I want to say further that, while that message was intended for you personally, yet, the truth and advice given therein may be applied to every mortal; and the good results will follow, no matter who that mortal may be.

As you know, I have been in the spirit world a great many centuries, as you conceive of time. During that long period, I have been very close to mortals in all parts of the earth, and of all nationalities and beliefs and education and enlightenment. And, in my experiences with these mortals, I have observed their nature and temptations, and the various ways in which mortals have been assailed by such temptations. I have also observed their efforts to overcome the same, together with their successes and failures.

Now, first let me say that the nature of man today is the same as it was when I lived on earth. And the perversions and sins of the souls of men are just as many and of the same kind as they were in my day in the flesh. Temptations, both outward and inward, are just as hard to overcome as they were when the glad tidings of Love and redemption were first proclaimed by the Master, except that, prior to that time, man had not the Divine Love

---

[*] Church of the Holiness.—Ed.

to help him overcome and subdue these temptations, as he now has. And the regret is that, while this great helper and regenerator, and conqueror of sin and temptations, is now in the world of mortals and subject to their call, yet, so comparatively few make the call, or realize the fact that this helper is always waiting to enable them to overcome temptations.

Prior to this time of the coming of the Divine Love, moral truths were taught to me, just as they are today. And many men, and not necessarily among the Jews, understood and attempted to apply these truths to their daily lives; and they endeavored to overcome the temptations arising from the sins that so constantly formed a part of their existence, and that also came from the influence of the evil spirits. It is all wrong to suppose that, in these early times and among these early races of earth, moral perceptions were not developed and taught. Men then made the fight to overcome temptations and become good and noble beings so far as their moral truths and principles, which were then understood and used by men, would make them.

In all ages, and since the fall of the first parents, men have had knowledge of what is called the moral truths to a more or less degree. And the natural love of man has existed in a more or less imperfect condition. Men have been kind and loving and true, and, to an extent, have controlled their appetites and tendencies to evil lives. And to suppose that men of today are not subject to such great temptations, and are better able to resist the same of themselves, is a mistake. The present great war* proves the fact. For men—I mean those who make a pretense to culture and civilization—were never as brutal in their acts, and so apparently devoid of all conception of right and wrong and of mercy, as are many of those who are engaged in the present struggle.

So, I say that men of today can lay no greater claim to moral qualities than could those of the times when they were supposed to be heathens and undeveloped in these moral qualities.

Of course, there is in the world today more of what may be called education and conventionality. But, behind these things, which are largely the results of merely intellectual development, men have the same perverted souls, or, rather, appetites and desires, and are subject to the same temptations as were men of old. And if mankind were left dependent upon the cultivation and improvement of these merely moral powers, I fear that temptation would continue to have all its influence and harmful power on the souls of men that it had in the past.

I know it is said that the world is growing better. But the question is, is that assertion true; and, if so, what is the cause?

Go to India and to China and to some other countries where the teachings of the supposed moral laws only obtain, and learn if there has been any improvement in the condition of men's souls, and if they have succeeded in any degree in overcoming the temptations that the human race is subject to. In learning, you will find that, except in the case of a few of these people, the conditions of their minds and souls are just as perverted as they were in centuries past, and that it is only in those countries where the influence of Christian nations have control do these people suppress the tendencies of perverted minds to do those things that arise from the want of the exercise of moral precepts or knowledge.

This is the truth of what mere moral teachings have accomplished where only the mere moral truths, as is supposed, are taught. Temptations are with men, and will be with them forever unless they are controlled or overcome by something greater or more certain than what men conceive to be moral truths.

Now, you will see from this that merely moral concepts will not necessarily, or, at least, for a long time to come, be able to bring about the destruction of the powers of temptation that arise from the perverted nature of mortals.

I must stop now and, in doing so, will leave you my love and blessings. Good night.

Your brother in Christ,

JAMES, brother of JOHN.

Helen Affirms That James Wrote on: "The Frailties of the Human Mind
and Moral Qualities."
(HELEN PADGETT)
(May 24th, 1917 | Received by James Padgett)

I AM HERE. *Helen.*

Well, dear, you have had a very pleasant evening, and so have we who have been with you listening to your conversation. And by "we", I mean spirits who are interested in both you and the doctor. James wrote. And while he may not have written as easily as he generally does, yet, he has conveyed some important truths which you will discover by carefully reading his message.

Good night and God bless you both is the prayer of

Your own true and loving,

HELEN.

Luke Explains What Is Necessary for a Man to Do to Recover the Purity of Soul and Love That Was Possessed by the First Parents.
He Also Declares That the Doctrine of Original Sin
Is a Mocking, Damnable Lie.
(LUKE, THE APOSTLE)
(April 27th, 1916 | Received by James Padgett)

247

I AM HERE. *Luke.*

I have not written you for some time and desire to write a short message tonight on the subject of: "What Is Necessary for a Man to Do to Recover the Purity of Soul and Love That Was Possessed by the First Parents." (I mean as a man possessing the natural love only.)

Well, in the first place, he should realize that he is a perfect creature of God, and that his sins and diseases are merely the result of his own thoughts, and of qualities that have come to him down the long ages of his ancestors living on earth.

He need not suppose that these sins and desires are inherent in, or a part of, his creation, for they are not. They are merely accretions that fastened themselves upon him by reason of the thoughts he has had, and the resultant course of life he has led. And when he changes these thoughts, which will necessarily bring about a change in his manner of living, he will find that he can progress toward the condition of the perfect man.

I know that many of these thoughts are so deep-seated that they seem to be almost a part of his very nature, and can only be eradicated by the death of his physical body. But this is not true. For man, even while in the full vigor of his manhood and possessed with all the appetites and desires which arise from the perverted indulgence of these desires, either on the part of himself or on the part of those from whom he is said to have inherited them, may relieve himself from these desires and become a man having only the thoughts of good, and the desire for those things which are in harmony with the nature of his perfect creation.

This, I know, seems like an impossible thing to man, and, so thinking, he does not try to accomplish what I say he may accomplish, and to become free from these sins and unnatural appetites. The almost universal belief in original sin has caused men, all along the ages, to think that such a task is hopeless; that they are thinking and acting only in accordance with the appetites and desires that God has implanted in their natures; and that, so long as they indulge these thoughts and desires in a moderate or respectable way, they are not doing that which is contrary to God's Will or to their own nature.

BUT THIS DOCTRINE OF ORIGINAL SIN IS A MOCKING, DAMNABLE LIE! AND THE SOONER MAN REALIZES THE FACT THAT IT IS A FRAUD AND DECEIT, THE SOONER HE WILL BE ABLE TO GET RID OF THOSE THINGS WHICH HAVE PLACED HIM IN HIS PRESENT CONDITION AND HELD HIM THERE BOUND, AS IT WERE, HAND AND FOOT.

THIS SUPINE SUBMISSION TO THIS OLD AND EVER RECURRING BELIEF IS THE GREAT THING THAT PREVENTS MAN FROM STARTING TO PROGRESS TOWARDS THE ATTAINMENT OF THAT CONDITION WHICH IS PURITY AND HEALTH AND THE PERFECT MAN.

MAN MUST DECLINE AND NO LONGER SUBMIT TO THIS

BELIEF, WHICH, I AM SORRY TO SAY, IS FOSTERED BY THE TEACHINGS OF THE ORTHODOX CHURCHES IN ORDER TO SUSTAIN AND MAKE FORCIBLE THEIR CREEDS AND DOGMAS. THEY INTEND TO SHOW TO MAN THAT HE IS NOT TO BE CONSIDERED WORTHY OF THE MERCY OF THE FATHER, AND CANNOT POSSIBLY OBTAIN THAT MERCY AND BE RELIEVED FROM THE GREAT WRATH AND PUNISHMENT THAT GOD HAS PREPARED FOR HIM, UNLESS HE BELIEVES AND ACKNOWLEDGES THAT HE IS A DEPENDENT AND LOST MAN, UNWORTHY OF THE FATHER'S FAVOR OR OF THE HELP OF THE INSTRUMENTALITIES WHICH THE FATHER USES TO ASSIST MEN IN REGAINING THEIR LOST ESTATE.

IF MEN WOULD ONLY THINK, AND, IN THINKING, REALIZE THAT THEY ARE DEAR CHILDREN OF THE FATHER AND HIS HIGHEST CREATION, AND THAT HE PRIZES THEM ABOVE ALL HIS CREATURES AND WANTS THEM TO KNOW THAT THEY ARE BEINGS OF SUCH WONDERFUL QUALITIES AND POSSIBILITIES, THEY WOULD THEN HAVE AN OVERPOWERING AND CONVINCING SENSE COME TO THEM OF WHAT THEY REALLY ARE, AND OF HOW NECESSARY IT IS FOR THEM TO ASSERT THEIR RIGHTS AS SUCH EXALTED CREATURES OF THE FATHER. AND THEY WOULD ALSO REALIZE THAT THEY ARE MASTERS OF SIN AND DISEASE, FOR THEY ARE THE CREATORS OF THE SAME.

When men shall assume such position and become possessed of such knowledge, they will find that they have a wonderful power as creatures of the Father; and they will realize that they are masters of sin that must be gotten rid of.

Let men think again for a moment, and, thinking, know that God does not desire His greatest creature to become, or be, less than the perfect being that He created. He is not flattered, nor does He have any pleasure in the thought, that man is degraded and fallen from his perfect creation, and that, in order to rise again, he, man, must believe that God may show His Power in rescuing him from his low and hopeless condition. No, God is not pleased by man assuming such an attitude. Nor does He need any such helpless condition of man that He may show His Power, or gratify what the teachings of these orthodox imply—His "vanity"—which He has not.

In this particular, man must work out his own salvation. But it will be a difficult task so long as he continues to believe and act upon that belief that he is a creature of original sin; and that, as God failed to make him the perfect man in the beginning, so, now, only God can remedy what He failed to provide in His Creation; and that man, of himself, can do nothing. All he has to do is to wait until God is pleased to re-create him, and thereby take from his very nature this great curse of the original sin. You see the great fatality of such belief, and how it tends to make man a slave of, and obedient to, this false belief in this blight of original sin!

God gave to man, in his creation, the great power of will and the right to its unlimited exercise, subject only to the penalties of a wrongful exercise. And, by the exercise of that will, man created sin and disease and became depraved and fallen, and the possessor of false beliefs as to the perfection of his nature. By the exercise of that will, man himself must redeem himself from this condition of depravity and false belief, and again become the perfect man—God's wholly perfect Creation.

As man was the perfect son of God in the beginning, and created his own and only "devil" by his own will, so must he kill this "devil" by this same power and again become the perfect son. He must believe and declare, and show the sincerity of his beliefs by his acts and living, that he is a perfect son of the Father, needing no new creation.

I have written this to show what man was in the beginning, and what he really and truly is now, although covered with sin and disease and false beliefs.

To recover this lost estate, or, better, condition, he will find that, by searching for and learning and acting upon many of the moral precepts of the Bible and of other so-called "sacred" writings, he will be greatly helped and strengthened in his efforts. But, above all, let him understand and believe, with the certainty of knowledge, that he is God's highest and most perfect creation.

Now, from what I have said, it must not be inferred that man is his own God, and has not and needs not any Tender, Loving Father Who is interested in him and is always ready to help him whenever he earnestly and in sincerity asks for that help. ALWAYS IS MAN DEPENDENT UPON GOD. BUT THAT DEPENDENCE IS NOT RECOGNIZED BY GOD UNLESS MAN FIRST RECOGNIZES IT, AND, BY HIS LONGINGS AND THOUGHTS, SHOWS TO THE FATHER THAT HE NEEDS HIS HELP.

This may seem unbelievable, but man was created so independent in his great will power, and as regards the qualities of thought and desire, both spiritual and material, that God never interferes to compel. The principle involved in "WHOSOEVER WILL" must be exercised by man before the Father will intervene. But, when it is exercised, He does intervene, and never refuses or fails to answer the call of the sincere cry of man for help.

And God does help man in his recovery from the state of false beliefs and degradation that I have mentioned. His Love overshadows men, and His instrumentalities are always ready and waiting to answer the call upon Him for His Help in assisting them out of their condition of sin, disease and false beliefs. For, as I have written you elsewhere, in God's Universe there must be perfect harmony. And the present man, so far as his own creation of inharmony is concerned, is not in that harmony. Ultimately, man, all men, will become the perfect man again.

OF COURSE, YOU WILL UNDERSTAND THAT WHAT I HAVE WRITTEN DOES NOT APPLY TO THE REDEEMED SONS OF GOD WHO RECEIVE THE NEW BIRTH AND BECOME PARTAKERS OF

THE DIVINE NATURE OF THE FATHER; FOR, IN THEIR CASE, THE PERFECT MAN IS ABSORBED IN THE DIVINE ANGEL.

I have written longer than I intended, but, as the theme is an interesting as well as important one, I thought it best to write just as I have.

I will now say good night and leave with you my love and blessings.

Your brother in Christ,

LUKE.

Chapter 9.

The Incarnation of the Soul.

MESSAGES INCLUDED IN THIS CHAPTER.

Jesus Relates That He Is Anxious for Mr. Padgett to Get into a Harmonious Condition of Soul So That He Can Continue His Messages to Mankind. (JESUS)...255

Jesus Explains the Incarnation of the Soul. (JESUS) 256

Samuel Enlarges Upon the Subject of the Incarnation of the Soul. (SAMUEL, THE PROPHET) 258

Why Men Should Learn That They Are Not to Be Left to Themselves in Their Conception of What Life Means, and What Its Importance Is in the Economy of Man's Creation and Destiny. (JOHN, THE APOSTLE)..261

Jesus Presents His Comments on a Discourse by a Preacher Who Knows Only the Way That Leads to the Perfect Natural Man. He Also Further Explains the Purpose of the Incarnation of the Soul. (JESUS)...262

A Former Minister Responds to the Master's Discourse. (DR. CHANNING)...266

9.

The Incarnation of the Soul.

Jesus Relates That He Is Anxious for Mr. Padgett to Get into a Harmonious Condition of Soul So That He Can Continue His Messages to Mankind.
(JESUS)
(February 14ᵗʰ, 1920 | Received by James Padgett)

I AM HERE. *Jesus.*

Well, my disciple, I realize that your desires are that I shall deliver a message to you tonight, and I am anxious to do so; yet I see you are not in condition that I may take possession of your brain that is necessary in order to write satisfactorily. I am sorry that this is so, but it is a fact. We will have to wait awhile longer, which will not be very long, for you are much improved. And, if you continue to pray, you will soon become in that soul condition that will enable me to make the rapport.

There are many messages yet to be written, and I am anxious that you receive them in order that they may be delivered to the world. For the world is now awakening to a greater realization of the fact that man is spiritual and must have spiritual food. The war[*] is causing many people to think of the hereafter and the destiny of the soul; and the knowledge that the world now has of the future life is very meager and unsatisfactory— merely a knowledge that the spirit survives death and experiences more or less happiness in the spirit life.

As you know, this is not the vital thing in the destiny of man. For while a knowledge of the survival of man from the death of the physical may and does give a great deal of consolation to the near and dear ones who are left on earth, yet, that fact does not, in the slightest degree, determine the condition or destiny of the soul that has left its home in the flesh. And there are no means now known to men to show that destiny, except some things written in the Bible which are the subjects of much speculation and controversy and want of belief. The consolation of those who have faith in the Bible is founded on that faith, or, rather, in most cases, belief. But there are a number of believers in the Truths of the Bible, with a conscious soul perception of their real meaning, who have faith which makes the facts of destiny and the possession of Love in their souls certain to them.

I will come soon and endeavor to write a formal message. In the meantime, let your prayers ascend with more earnestness and longings to

---

[*] World War I.

the Father.

As you know, I love you as my brother and disciple, and am with you as you pray[*] each night, uniting in our prayers. And you must let your faith increase, and believe that your prayers are being heard and will be answered to the fullest.

I will not write more now.

So, my brother, good night, and may the Father bless you with His greatest Blessings.

Your brother and friend,

JESUS.

Jesus Explains the Incarnation of the Soul.
(JESUS)
(February 15th, 1920 | Received by James Padgett)

I AM HERE. *Jesus.*

I am here, as I promised I would be last night, and will write on the subject of the incarnate soul.

In your studies of the different theories of the creation of man, you may have observed that the question has always arisen as to the relationship of the spiritual and the physical—that is, as to the soul and the material body. I know that many theories have been set forth as to how and when the soul became a part of the physical body, and what were the means adopted by the laws of nature, as they are called, for the lodgment of the soul into the human body; and, also, what was the relationship that one bore to the other. Of course, this applies only to those mortals who believe that there is a soul that is separate from the mere physical body in its existence and functioning. As to those who do not believe in the distinctive soul, I do not attempt to enlighten them. I leave them to a realization of that fact when they shall have come into the spirit world and find themselves existing without such body, but really existing with the consciousness that they are souls.

When the physical body is created, it has no consciousness of its having been created. It is merely of the unconscious creations that are of the other material creatures of nature, and does not feel or sense the fact in any degree that it is a living thing, dependent upon the proper nourishment of its mother for its growth and continued life in accordance with the laws of nature and the objects of its own creation. The father and mother, being necessary to the creation or formation of this merely animal production, know only that, in some way, there has come into existence an embryo thing that may eventuate into a human being like unto themselves. If this

---

[*] Mr. Padgett told Dr. Stone that, when he was praying before retiring, clairvoyantly, he often saw Jesus alongside praying with him.

256

thing were allowed to remain without the soul, it would soon fail to fulfill the object of its creation. It would disintegrate into the elements of which it was formed, and mankind would cease to exist as inhabitants of the earth. This physical part of man is really, and only, the result of the commingling of those forces that are contained in the two sexes, and which, according to the laws of nature or of man's creation, are suited to produce the one body fitted for the home of the soul that may be attracted to it in order to develop its individuality as a thing of life and possible immortality.

The result of this commingling is intended only as a temporary covering or protection for the growth of the real being, and does not in any way limit or influence the continuous existence of the soul. And when the physical body's functions have ended, the soul, which has then become individualized, continues its life in new surroundings and in gradual progression; and the mere physical instrument that was used for its individualization is disseminated into the elements that once formed its appearance and substance. As this body was called from the elements for a certain purpose, when that purpose shall have been served, it returns to these elements.

This body, of itself, has neither consciousness nor sensation, and, in the beginning, has only the borrowed life of its parents. Then, when the soul finds its lodgment, it has only the life of the soul. For the human life can exist only so long as the soul inhabits the body. And, after such habitation commences, the borrowed life of the parents ceases to exercise any influence or directing force on the body. This, then, is really the true description of the physical body. And if it were all of man, he would perish with its death and cease to exist as a part of the Creation of the Universe of God.

But the soul is the vital, living and never dying part of man—is really the man—and the only thing that was intended to continue an existence in the spirit world. It was made in the image of God, and there is no reason for its existing for the continuing companionship of the physical body. And when men say or believe that the body is all of man, and that, when it dies, man ceases to exist, they do not understand the relationship or functioning of soul and body. They know only the half-truth which is visible to their senses—that the body dies and can never again be resuscitated. But while this is a determined fact, yet, all arguments to show by analogy that man must continue to live, notwithstanding the death of the body, are not apposite and are very inconclusive. All these analogous appearances or examples only show that the objects of the analogy ultimately die. They thus fail to prove that these objects are eternal, just as much as if there had never been any change in their condition or appearance. The final demonstration is that they die. And when this analogy is applied to man, it must show that he also dies and is no more.

But the questions are asked: "Whence comes the soul, by who created, how does it become incarnated in man, for what purpose, and what is its destiny?"

First, let me state that man has nothing to do with the creation of the soul or its appearance in the flesh. His work is to provide a receptacle for its coming—a mere host, as it were, for its entry into the flesh and an existence as a mortal, or in the appearance of a mortal. But his responsibility in this particular is very great. For man can destroy that receptacle, or can care for it so that the soul may continue in earth life a longer or shorter time. And while this receptacle is the creation of man and cannot be brought into existence without him, yet, the soul is no part of his creation and is independent of the body. And, after the earth life, in the spirit world, it will cease to remember that it was ever connected with, or dependent upon, the creation of its parents. In the spirit life, as a truth, the soul is so separated from, and dissociated with, that body which was its home while in the earth life that it looks upon it as a mere vision of the past and not a subject for its consideration.

As has been told to you, the soul was created by the Father long before its appearance in the flesh. It awaited such incarnation for the purpose only of giving it an individuality which it did not have in its preexistence, and in which it has a duplex personality—male and female—that needs to be separated and made individual. We who have had this preexistence and incarnation in the flesh, and have obtained this individuality, know the truth of what I have here stated.

There is a Law of God controlling these things that renders these preexisting souls capable of knowing the desirability of incarnation. And they are always anxious and ready for the opportunity to be born in the flesh, and to assume the separate individuality that they are privileged to assume. As men provide the receptacle for their appearing and homing, as it were, they become aware of the fact and take advantage of the opportunity to occupy the receptacle. They then become ostensibly a human being with the necessary result of individuality.

I am glad that you are in a better condition, and I will continue the messages as we have been desiring to do for some time.

I shall be with you and help you in every way, and I hope that you will keep up your faith and prayers to the Father.

Good night and God bless you.

Your brother and friend,

JESUS.

Samuel Enlarges Upon the Subject of the Incarnation of the Soul.
(SAMUEL, THE PROPHET)
(January 17th, 1916 | Received by James Padgett)

I AM HERE. *Samuel, the prophet.*

Well, I will not write long tonight, as I merely want to say that you are much better in your spiritual condition, and the rapport between us is so

258

much greater than heretofore.

Tonight, I desire to say a few words on the subject of my knowledge of how a soul is born into the flesh and becomes an individualized person.

I heard what Luke wrote to you,[*] and I agree with him in his explanation of the character and qualities of the soul in its state before its incarnation. But I want to add one other thing to what he wrote, and that is that when the soul first separates into its two component parts, and one of these parts enters into the physical body, the other part remains a mere soul, invisible even to us, but having an existence of which we are conscious; and it hovers close to the earth plane, seeking the opportunity to also incarnate and become individualized. And this happens within a short time after the separation from the half that has already incarnated. Of course, when I say a short time, I do not mean in a few months or even a few years, because sometimes there is a space of several scores of years between the two incarnations. But such time seems short to us who know nothing of time.

The soul which remains, as Luke has told you, as well as the soul that enters the human body, loses its consciousness of having been only a part of one complete soul, and of its relationship to the other part of that soul. It exists in the supposition that it is still a complete soul and needs no other soul to make it complete. This is a provision of the Father's Goodness so that the soul that continues in its pristine existence will not become lonely or unhappy.

You will naturally ask how I know this, as we have said these souls are not visible to us, and I can only answer that we spirits who have developed our souls to a high degree have acquired certain faculties, or what you may call senses, which enable us to know these things. It is not necessary that we should see these unindividualized souls in order to know of their existence and the qualities that they possess, any more than it is necessary that we should be able to see the Great Oversoul of the Father in order to understand Its Qualities and Attributes and Existence. I know it is hard for you to understand this, and I cannot now satisfactorily explain it, for your senses of the earth life are not capable of comprehending the explanation; but what I tell you is true.

We often see the birth of the two parts of the souls into mortals and know that such souls then assume a shape and form for the first time, for this invisible image of God fills the whole of the spirit body. And, from that body, the soul assumes or receives its form and thereby becomes individualized. The soul is the life of the spirit body, and never leaves it during the earth life of the mortal. And it comes with the spirit body at the death of the physical body, and remains a part of it during all the time of

---

[*] The message that Samuel is referring to here is contained in "The Soul of Man" chapter in volume I of *Angelic Revelations of Divine Truth,* and is entitled: "Luke Explains the Mystery of the Birth of the Soul in the Human Being. He Also Declares That There Is No Such Thing as Reincarnation."—Ed.

the existence of the spirit body in the spirit world. Whether it can ever become lost is a question upon which I shall write you later. You will remember that Jesus said, according to the Bible, "What does it profit a man to gain the whole world and lose his own soul?"

I will say at this time, though, that a man may retain his soul as a fact, and yet have a consciousness of having lost it; and he is then as if he has no soul.

I have said to you what I intended to write because Luke had omitted to speak of the condition of the half of the soul that had remained in the spirit world after the other half had been incarnated.

MATTERS OF THIS KIND, THOUGH, ARE NOT IMPORTANT AS REGARDS THE SALVATION OF MAN, OR THE PERFECTING OF HIS SOUL TO SUCH A DEGREE THAT THAT SOUL MAY BECOME AT-ONE WITH THE GREAT SOUL, HAVING WHAT IT DID NOT POSSESS BEFORE ITS SEEKING A DWELLING PLACE IN THE FLESH—AND THAT IS THE POSSESSION OF THE DIVINE NATURE OF THE FATHER, AND IMMORTALITY AS AN INDIVIDUALIZED, NEVER DYING PERSON.

AS WE PROCEED IN THESE WRITINGS, YOU WILL UNDERSTAND THE IMPORTANCE OF THE SOUL'S BECOMING INCARNATED, AND THEN LEAVING THE FLESH AND AGAIN RETURNING TO THE SPIRIT SPHERES. AND YOU WILL ALSO LEARN THAT THE DOCTRINE OF EVOLUTION IS CORRECT TO AN EXTENT, BUT NOT AS COMMENCING FROM AN ATOM WITH REGARD TO MAN'S SOUL, NOR FROM AN ANIMAL INFERIOR TO MAN WITH REGARD TO HIS BODY. BACK OF AND GREATER THAN THIS DOCTRINE OF EVOLUTION IS THE GREAT AND MORE DIVINE DOCTRINE OF INVOLUTION. FOR IF THE SOUL HAD NOT COME FROM ABOVE AND BEEN PLACED IN THE PHYSICAL MAN, THERE WOULD NEVER HAVE BEEN ANY EVOLUTION. AND IF THE SOUL HAD NEVER RECEIVED ITS INDIVIDUALIZED EXISTENCE BY COMING INTO THE BODY OF THE HUMAN, IT WOULD NEVER HAVE EVOLUTED TO THE DIVINE NATURE, AS WELL AS TO THE INDIVIDUALIZED BEING THAT FOLLOWS THAT INCARNATION.

WHEN I SAY THE DIVINE NATURE, I DO NOT MEAN THAT ALL SOULS, WHETHER ON EARTH OR IN THE GREAT ETERNITY, NECESSARILY RECEIVE THAT DIVINE NATURE; FOR MANY OF THEM DO NOT AND NEVER WILL. BUT NO MATTER WHETHER THEY COME INTO THE DIVINE NATURE OR RETAIN THE NATURE WHICH WAS THEIRS IN THEIR PREEXISTENCE, ALL SOULS WILL BECOME INDIVIDUALIZED PERSONALITIES. THESE PERSONALITIES WILL BE THEIRS SO LONG AS THEIR SOULS AND SPIRIT BODIES SHALL CONTINUE TO EXIST.

I have written enough for tonight, but will come again and write to you of other Truths.

260

So, with my love and blessings, I am
Your brother in Christ,
SAMUEL.

*Why Men Should Learn That They Are Not to Be Left to Themselves
in Their Conception of What Life Means, and What Its Importance
Is in the Economy of Man's Creation and Destiny.
(JOHN, THE APOSTLE)*
(July 2nd, 1916 | Received by James Padgett)

I AM HERE. *John.*

I come tonight to tell you of a Truth which is important for you to know, as well as for the world of mankind. I will not write a very long message, but what I may say will be the Truth, and every man should understand it and make it his own.

I will not write upon any subject that you have been instructed upon before, but will deal with a subject entirely new. And my subject is: "Why Men Should Learn That They Are Not to Be Left to Themselves in Their Conceptions of What Life Means, and What Its Importance Is in the Economy of Man's Creation and Destiny."

I know that this may seem to you to be a strange subject to write on, but it is one that should be of interest to all men who know that the earth life is very short, and that eternity then takes them into its embrace and never again permits them to become creatures of time.

Man lives and dies and never lives again, according to the materialist, and he is as the brute animal without any future. But the Spiritualist—and by this I mean he who believes that there is something more to man than the mere material—believes man lives and never ceases to live, although the physical body dies, never to be resurrected again as such body.

Now, as we take either the one or the other of these views, the meaning of man's earth life assumes a very different aspect, and calls for very different thoughts and actions on his part in living his life. Of course, if what is called death is the end of things that man should do, or thinks he should do, in accordance with the old saying: "Eat, drink and be merry for tomorrow you shall die", and, with that death comes oblivion and forgetfulness, never to be awakened again into consciousness, his mission in the universe is fulfilled, and he can no more experience the hopes or ambitions or joys or sorrows which were his as a living man.

But, on the other hand, if man never ceases to live, then his thoughts and conduct should be turned towards the accomplishment of that which will provide the best possible future for him.

Those of both opinions know that, when death comes, the physical body can no longer be used. And those who believe in the continuous existence know that, as the physical body perishes, man must have some other form or body in which may be lodged the consciousness of this continued existence, and that that body must be as real as the one which he relinquishes. Such being the fact, the man who knows that death does not end all will naturally and necessarily seek to learn what that body of continued existence is like, and what is necessary to enable him to obtain that body and thereby enjoy the living in eternity. And, thus seeking, he will not be satisfied to learn that that body is the mere spirit body which has been his during all the years of his earth life, but will desire to further learn what the relationship is between that body and the manner of living his earth life.

I know that, of himself, man cannot discover this relationship to any degree, and that he must depend upon the teachings and experiences of those who have experienced the separation of the spirit from the physical in order to comprehend this relationship at all.

AS ONE HAVING HAD THIS EXPERIENCE, I WISH TO SAY THAT THE SPIRIT BODY IS, OF ITSELF, A CREATION, AS IS THE PHYSICAL BODY, AND HAS ITS EXISTENCE ONLY FOR THE PURPOSES OF PRESERVING MAN'S INDIVIDUALITY AND OF CONTAINING AND SHELTERING HIS SOUL, BOTH WHILE ON EARTH AND AFTER HE BECOMES A SPIRIT.

HIS LIVING MEANS, THEN, THAT HE IS PLACED ON THE EARTH MERELY TO ACQUIRE AN INDIVIDUALITY, AND TO LEARN THAT WITHIN HIM IS THE SOUL WHICH IS HIS REAL SELF, AND WHICH HE MUST CHERISH AND EDUCATE AND FEED WITH THE HIGHER THOUGHTS AND GOODNESS OF HIS ORIGINAL CREATION, AND NOT NEGLECT THE OPPORTUNITIES THAT COME TO HIM FOR THIS DEVELOPMENT.

I know that this seems incoherent to you, with no special object in view, but you are mistaken in thus thinking; for the object will soon be seen. But, as you are not just in condition for further writing tonight, I will postpone my writing until later.

So, trusting that you will not feel inclined to reject the message, I will say good night.

Your brother in Christ,
JOHN.

Jesus Presents His Comments on a Discourse by a Preacher Who Knows Only the Way That Leads to the Perfect Natural Man. He Also Further Explains the Purpose of the Incarnation of the Soul.
(JESUS)
(March 21st, 1920 | Received by James Padgett)

I AM HERE. *Jesus.*

Let me write tonight, as you are in good condition. I desire very much to write to you in reference to a subject that is important for men to know.

As I have written to you before, there are two destinies for man in the spirit life, and the one or the other of them may be just as he desires and seeks for.

I was with you today as you listened to the preacher expound the reasons why he is a leader and teacher. He is undoubtedly honest and earnest in his beliefs, and, so far as they go, they will afford him the happiness that he spoke of, provided he puts such beliefs into actual, practical living and makes them the dominating, dynamic influence that shall guide and control him in his intercourse with humanity. He said truly that there is a law that operates in wonderful power in shaping men's lives, and which, when obeyed, will determine the career not only of men but also of nations; and that law is: that when once a Truth is ascertained or comes to the knowledge of men, it must be recognized and acted upon or it will lose its beneficent effect upon the lives of men.

If he applies this law to his own life, he will experience a wonderful help in meeting the difficulties and cares of life, and in overcoming the things that beset him as a thinking man.

This is a wonderful Truth. And so far as it pervades the life of a man, it will result in making that life one of consistent goodness, and cause harmony between that man and God Who overrules the secret things of the universe. And that man will enjoy a great happiness even while in the flesh.

But this is not the important object and aim of what the preacher calls religion, nor does it furnish the means by which a man may come into a greater and closer harmony with the Will of God. I know that, to man, this present mortal life seems a thing of the greatest importance, and that the chief aim of man should be to act in that manner that will make his life successful and happy; and, so far as it is suited to make man the harmonious creature that is intended, it is advisable to follow that course of living and loving. But the preacher does not know of, and cannot teach, the great object of man's appearance on earth, and the goal that is ever before him and waiting to be reached and possessed.

As I have told you before, man's existence in the flesh is only for the purpose of giving his soul an individualization. All other apparent objects are only secondary and, as you may say, accidental accompaniments of this process of individualization.

Hence, you will observe that this great object is accomplished equally in the case of the infant who dies young and in the case of the man who lives to a ripe old age. In each case, the object of the soul's incarnation in the flesh is effected. The old man, of course, has a longer and more diverse existence experience in meeting and overcoming, or submitting to, the exigencies of his living than does the infant. But the great object is not more perfectly accomplished in the one case than in the other. The soul becomes individualized the moment it finds its lodgment in the receptacle prepared by the laws of nature in using the human father and mother as its instruments. And, thereafter, time does not influence or have any determining effect upon that soul so far as its individualization is concerned, and neither does eternity. For, being once fixed, that condition can never be changed nor annihilated, so far as is known to the highest spirits of God's Heavens. Of course, the soul, as thus individualized, is subject to the various influences that surround it in its mortal life; and these influences may be retarding, deadly or destructive to the progress of the soul. But they cannot possibly affect the object obtained by that soul's coming into the flesh, nor would this ever require a new individualization of that soul. Its identity and character, as individualized things, are established. And no condition of the soul, as to its goodness or badness, can ever affect this character or identity in the slightest degree. Once individualized, the soul always remains the individual, even though the elements that enter into and make up the form will always find itself being rebuilt and continued by the operations of the law that preserves the individuality of that soul.

Then, I say, the object of the incarnation of the soul is to give it an individualization, and this in two appearances: first, in that of the physical form which men can perceive by their perception of their natural organs of sense; and, secondly, a form that is more sublimated and generally invisible to these organs—a spiritual form.

At the moment of incarnation, the soul takes the form which has been prepared for it by the forces that exist in the parents, and it retains that form during the natural life. And, at the same moment, the form of the spirit body is created for the soul, which then and ever afterwards remains with it. Both of these bodies are of the material—one of the visible material of the universe, and the other of the invisible but still of the material.

As you know, that body which is made of the visible material lasts for a little while only, and then disappears forever, while that which is of the invisible, and which is more real and substantial than the former, and also exists all the time of the existence of the visible, continues with the soul after the disappearance of the visible body. And while changeable in response to the progress of that soul, yet, the spirit body never leaves that soul in its composite form. We know this to be true in the spirit life, just as certainly as you mortals know the truth of the existence of the physical body. And in the short space of the life on earth, as you mortals may identify the man—which is really the soul—by the appearance of his physical body, so we in the spirit world identify the same man by the appearance of the spirit body. And, so, this fact must be forever.

Then, such being the fact, it must be conceived that the soul has its existence in the physical body for an infinitesimal short time—that is, its life on earth is only for the breath of a moment—and then it enters in its career through eternity. And, after a few years, as you may say, it may cease to remember that it ever had a lodgment in the physical body.

The preacher criticized the religion that taught man to think of, and prepare for, the future of the soul. He emphasized the fact that their thoughts should be more of the present, and that duty and good works toward their fellowmen should be the object of their living and their religion. Well, I recognize the importance of duty and good works, and I approve of them with all the knowledge that I now have of the demands and requirements of God's Love. But, on the other hand, I must say that added to their importance to man's future destiny is also the importance of other privileges and obligations possessed by, and resting on, man during the short time that the soul is clothed in the physical body. Duty performed, and good works, will lessen the distress and sufferings of the mortal life, and will cause the man who performs the duty and does the good works to become more in harmony with God's Laws of Mercy and Truth. But these will never suffice to bring a soul into harmony with the Will of the Father as regards the higher destiny of man. These things will tend to lead merely to the purification of the soul, and to cause it to come into accord with the laws of its own creation and their end. But these constitute merely the exercise of compliance with the moral laws, and bring only a moral effect. And, when I say moral laws, I mean those laws that demand, and by the observance of which, that man comes into the condition of the perfect man, which was his condition at the time of his creation. But, in observing these laws, he thereby obtains nothing more than what belonged to him when he existed as the perfect man and was in complete harmony with God as such perfect man. He then loved God with all the capacity of his soul in the exercise of the love that had been bestowed upon him, and he could have loved his brother as himself.

Men are now striving to attain to this condition of the perfect man to a more or less extent. And many precepts of the Old Testament, as well as of the New, will lead men to thus obtain it. And if this were the only destiny of man, then the religion of the preacher, which he says is based on these moral precepts of love to God and love to his fellowman, would be sufficient to obtain the goal sought; and love and duty and service would be all that were required of men while on earth, as well as after they became spirits. And the exercise of these graces by men while on earth would be just as necessary and helpful as would their exercise afterwards in the spirit world. These things of love to God and love to man, and service and sacrifice, constitute the true religion that leads to the perfect man, and makes for that harmony with the Laws of God governing the condition of the perfect man—but not the divine man.

These things should be preached by all ministers and teachers, and practiced by men everywhere; for in their practice are happiness and bliss unspeakable. As these things work to a finality, man again becomes the son of God and obedient to His Laws, and realizes the meaning of "love God and love your brother." And, so, I repeat, in pronouncing the basis of his religion, the preacher declared the Truths that will lead him into the condition of the perfect man, and in harmony with God's Will as to man's creation.

Well, I see you are tired and, so, we will postpone the further writing. I am very much pleased that you are in so much better condition, and I hope that we may continue our messages without further interruption. Only pray more and believe that the Father will answer your prayers.

So, believe that I love you and want you to be happy and free from care. Good night.

Your brother and friend,
JESUS.

A Former Minister Responds to the Master's Discourse.
(DR. CHANNING)
(March 21st, 1920 | Received by James Padgett)

I AM HERE. *Dr. Channing.*

Let me write just a line, as I merely desire to say that I have listened to what the Master has written, and can testify that the love to God and love to our fellowman are not all that man needs for a basis of his religion. I was a minister when on earth and taught the same doctrines that the preacher of the day taught. I believed that they were all that man needed, and died in that belief. But, alas, after many years of darkness, and of happiness in my natural love, I discovered that these doctrines would not furnish a basis for my progress to the Celestial Heavens—to the condition of the soul transformed by the Divine Love. I merely wanted to say this. If agreeable to you, I should like to come sometime and detail my experience more at length in learning the basis of the true religion.

I will say good night.

Your brother in Christ,
Dr. Channing.

Chapter 10.

The Creation and Fall of
Our First Parents.

MESSAGES INCLUDED IN THIS CHAPTER.

Aman, the First Parent, Reveals His Temptation and Fall (AMAN) 269

Amon, Mother of All Human Creation, Relates Her Earliest Experiences. She Also Explains the Temptation and Disobedience Which She and Aman Shared in Equally. (AMON) 270

Mrs. Padgett Refers to Jesus' Love for Mr. Padgett. She Also Affirms That Amon Wrote About the Creation of the First Parents, the Difference in Their Qualities, and Their Equality in Their Relationship to God. (HELEN PADGETT) 272

Aman Offers a Correction. (AMAN) 272

John, the Apostle, Affirms That Aman and Amon, the First Parents, Actually Communicated Through Mr. Padgett. (JOHN, THE APOSTLE) 273

Josephus Also Discusses the Creation of the First Parents, the Difference in Their Qualities, and Their Equality in Their Relationship to God and with Each Other. (JOSEPHUS) 275

The Creation of Man. (JESUS) 277

10.

The Creation and Fall of Our First Parents.

Aman, the First Parent, Reveals His Temptation and Fall
(AMAN)
(August 29th, 1915 | Received by James Padgett)

I AM HERE. *Aman, the first parent.*

You don't believe me, I can see, but I am whom I say, and want to tell you that I am now a follower of Jesus and a lover of God, and live in the Celestial Heavens far up near where the Master lives.

I know it is hard for men to believe that I am the father of all physical manhood, and that I can come and communicate with mortals; but Jesus has rendered this possible in his opening the way for the higher spirits to communicate through you. You should feel specially blessed at having this great privilege, and feel that the Master has conferred on you a great favor, as he has.

Well, I have never before come to earth to communicate with mortals, and, the experience being new, I find some difficulty in doing so. But I will try to write a few more lines.

I and my soulmate lived in a paradise which God had given us, and were very happy until the great fall. We were so filled with the thought that we were all powerful and all wise, that we concluded that the obedience which God had required of us, was not necessary for us to observe, and that if we only exerted our powers, we would be as great as He is great, and would be able to obtain that immortality which he possessed. But, alas the day. We were mere creatures, although wonderful and beautiful, and we soon realized that fact.

The disobedience was in not waiting for God to bestow upon us the great Divine Love that would make us like Him in substance as well as in image. We were like Him in our possession of souls and also in the possibility of obtaining the Divine Love.

We disobeyed Him in that we tried to make ourselves believe that we were as He was, and that we need not submit further to His decrees. We tried to make this belief a thing of reality and in our vanity tried to appear as gods; but as soon as we did this the scales dropped from our eyes, and we saw how naked and impotent we were.

God did not drive us from His paradise, but the inexorable laws of our creation and of the workings of His will, showed us that no longer could we expect this Divine Love, which He said would make us Divine. And so we became mere mortals, deprived of the potentiality of obtaining this Divine Love, and we had thereafter to become subject to all the appetites of the natural man and to work to satisfy these natural appetites.

We continued to live in the same place as formerly, but no more could we be satisfied with the spiritual food that had supplied our wants and enabled us to subdue the appetites which formed a part of our physical being. The physical then asserted itself and the spiritual became subjected to it, and we became as mortals now are, and had to find our substance in mother earth. We were compelled to till the soil and earn our living by work. I mean we had to work in order to make the earth supply us with food for our physical wants.

It was a bitter time of sorrow but the law had imposed its penalty, and we were without power to relieve ourselves of that penalty, and had to live thereafter without the possibility of obtaining this Divine Love and of having our spiritual natures reassert themselves over the physical, and subdue it.

When Amon and I were created, there were no other human beings living on earth, and none came there to live, until we had sons and daughters who intermarried and produced other sons and daughters. I cannot tell you how long ago our creation was, but many thousand years before the coming of Jesus. I will not write more to night, but will come again sometime and write.

Your brother in Christ,
AMAN.

Amon, Mother of All Human Creation, Relates Her Earliest Experiences. She Also Explains the Temptation and Disobedience Which She and Aman Shared in Equally.
(AMON)
(August 30th, 1915 | Received by James Padgett)

I AM HERE. *Amon.*

I am the first mother of all the human race, and I want you to know that, before Aman and myself, no human beings ever existed. We were created by God at the same time, and were ready to live the lives of natural beings just after the moment of our creation. There was no gradual growth on our part from any other creature or thing.

I know it has been said that the first man was not created, but developed from some animal of the lower order; and, as the process of evolution proceeded, this being became, in the end, a man, with all the wonderful organism and structure of his body. But I want to tell you that this is not true.

When I was created I was as perfect in my physical organism as I ever was afterwards, or as any man or woman ever became from that time into the present. In fact, I believe that, at the time of our creation, we were more perfect than mankind is now, because we had no physical ailments, no sickness, no deformity of any kind.

We certainly were more beautiful in face and form than mankind is now or has been for many long centuries. And, besides, our bodies and organism lasted for longer years than do the bodies of mankind at this time.

Before our fall, we were very happy in our conjugal love, and knew not troubles or worries of any kind. We never had anything to make us afraid or draw us apart from each other or from God until the great temptation came. And, then, because of our ideas of our greatness and power and want of dependence on God, we fell. And never again were we restored to our position of beauty and happiness that was ours in the beginning of our lives on earth.

So, you must see that we were specially created and not evolved from any other thing.

Some men may now marvel and wonder at the Bible description of the creation of man, and reject the description as the imaginings of a mind of romance or imagery, and not true. But I tell you now that the essentials of this creation and the fall are true. Of course, the parts played by the apple and the snake and the devil are not true, literally, but are symbolical of the principles that entered into the temptation and fall.

(Were you to blame for enticing Aman to sin, as the Bible relates?)

Well, I was as much to blame as was Aman, but I did not entice him after I had the ambition to become immortal without waiting till that time came when God would give us that Quality of His Own Nature. Rather, *our ambitions grew together*. We discussed the matter of making the great effort between us, and acted as one in trying to obtain this great immortality.

So, the story in the Bible is not exactly true, just as far as I am concerned, for I did not entice or seduce Aman to do the great wrong. Neither did he seduce me to enter into the effort.

But all that is past. Many thousand years have gone by since our fall, and we have suffered much because of our first sin. As you have been told, many thousands of years passed since the time that we forfeited the Gift of immortality, and until it was restored and made known to humanity by Jesus, the son of God; for he was the son of God. And, as being a part of his Father's Divine Nature, he was divine and partook of those Qualities of the Father which gave to him immortality. And those who follow his teachings and receive the New Birth will become divine and immortal also.

I must not write more tonight.

(Will you come and write again sometime?)

Yes, I will, and now I will say good night.

Your sister,

AMON.

Mrs. Padgett Refers to Jesus' Love for Mr. Padgett. She Also Affirms
That Amon Wrote About the Creation of the First Parents, the
Difference in Their Qualities, and Their Equality
in Their Relationship to God.
(HELEN PADGETT)
(August 30th, 1915 | Received by James Padgett)

I AM HERE. *Helen.*

Well, my dear old Ned, you must stop writing for tonight, as you have written a long time.

I am so glad that you are now in such good condition of faith and love, and feel so close to God and so near to the Master. It certainly is wonderful how he loves you and clings to you and tries to help and influence you for good. We are all surprised at his love for you, and he does not seem to grow impatient that you sometimes seem not to care whether he loves you or not. But such is his great love.

Oh, my dear, you must love him more and get closer to him and trust him with all your heart and mind, for I, your own Helen, tell you that he is with you very much and loves you more than you can possibly conceive to be true.

He is trying to help you spiritually and he will succeed.

(What can you tell me about Amon who just wrote to me?)

Well, she was a beautiful and bright spirit—more so than most any of the spirits that I have seen from the higher spheres. She talked to me for a while and told me that she was the first mother, and that I was one of her children. She has a wonderful portion of the Divine Love, and seemed so grand and loving to me that I am inclined to believe her. But I cannot tell you anything more about her, as I never saw her before. But I heard the Master say that he would tell you sometime about her, and you may get a great treat from him.

So, good night.

Your loving and true,

HELEN.

Aman Offers a Correction.
(AMAN)
(September 7th, 1915 | Received by James Padgett)

I AM HERE. *Aman.*

(Are you the same spirit and declared first parent who wrote to me before?)

Yes, and I want to correct what I wrote before in this: that I never was

272

a spirit who wanted to have merely immortality as God was Immortal. I also wanted to obtain the Power and Wisdom which I saw that God possessed.

I thought that, if I could obtain these Qualities, I would become a god and a co-equal with my Creator, and, hence, the possessor of all the universe, and of all Power and Knowledge that He had. My effort to realize my ambition in these particulars was a part of my great sin of disobedience.

I thought it best to tell you this so that my description of the great sin of disobedience would not be only a part of the truth.

I now know what an insignificant creature I was as compared to the Father. And I also know that the creation of Amon and me was the highest creation in all the Universe of God.

But the great Mercy and Love of the Father, notwithstanding my great sin, have placed me in the position and condition which He promised me at my creation, and which I forfeited with such fatal consequences. You have a privilege which I was then deprived of for so many long years, and your happiness may be as great as mine is now without having to wait the long and many years I waited.

No wonder that mankind worships Jesus as God when we consider the Great Gift that he brought to them and the Way to obtain It!

I must not write more.

Your brother in Christ and father in the flesh,
AMAN.

John, the Apostle, Affirms That Aman and Amon, the First Parents, Actually Communicated Through Mr. Padgett.
(JOHN, THE APOSTLE)
(August 30th, 1915 | Received by James Padgett)

I AM HERE. *John.*

I merely want to say tonight that you must soon prepare to take messages which the Master and some other high spirits desire to write.

Let your arrangements be such that you can take those messages without anyone being disappointed. For when you say that you will receive them, and then something comes up to prevent this, the spirits feel that you have not sufficient interest and they are disappointed.

(Please accept my sincerest apologies. In the future, I shall attempt to keep all previously scheduled appointments that we have agreed upon. May we resume two nights from now?)

Well, that will be satisfactory and we will make our arrangements to comply with that understanding.

I know, though, that you have been in a good condition of love and soul during the past few days. You have realized that the Father has been close to you and you have been happy. So, continue to turn your thoughts to the

Father and His Love, and you will find that there will come to you an increased Love and a great happiness. I feel that your faith is growing and that the rapport between us all is steadily increasing.

(Would you prefer that I attempt to receive a formal message tonight?)

I did not intend to write more tonight, as we will wait until the time that you have named.

(Well, when we do communicate again, will you be clarifying your book, "Revelation," any further?)

Well, I have already told you that Revelation was written as a kind of allegory, and that it is now of no practical use and should not be given much attention. Besides, it is not as I wrote it, for many interpretations and additions have been made. At any rate, it is of no importance, and men lose much time in trying to solve what they call its mysteries.

(Does the name "Aman" have any special meaning?)

Well, "Aman" is a general term which means "first" or "highest". And, when applied to man, it means the first or highest creation. As it is applied in Revelation to Jesus, it means the man who first received the Divine Love of the Father after Its rebestowal.

I will come to you sometime and explain this matter more fully.

(Was it the very first parents who actually wrote to me?)

Yes, they (Aman and Amon) came to you and gave you their names which were the names that they were called by after their creation. They were both created instantaneously and became living souls in a moment, and did not grow from a germ by the slow process of evolution. Their story of the fall is substantially correct, as I have learned from them and from the Master.

The names "Aman" and "Amon" are correct, and were known thousands of years ago to the early inhabitants of the earth who descended from them.

The story of their fall, of course, was known to their immediate descendants, and became known for some generations after their deaths to their more remote descendants. But, after awhile, the names became forgotten, but the substance of the story of their fall did not. At one time, there were manuscripts showing the account of the fall, but they disappeared long before the time of any of the present writings, though the story of the fall, with various changes and amendments, came down the ages until the writers of the Old Testament incorporated such tradition in the Book of Genesis. OF COURSE, ADAM AND EVE DID NOT EXIST, AND NEITHER IS THE STORY AS TO THEIR FALL TRUE. IT IS ONLY SYMBOLICAL IN THE WAY OF SHOWING THAT MAN ONCE OCCUPIED AN EXALTED AND HAPPY STATE AND, BY HIS OWN DISOBEDIENCE, FELL. AND WITH HIS FALL CAME THE CONDITION OF EVIL AND SIN.

Well, I must not write more tonight. Remembering what you say, I am
Your brother in Christ,
JOHN.

274

Josephus Also Discusses the Creation of the First Parents, the Difference in Their Qualities, and Their Equality in Their Relationship to God and with Each Other.
(JOSEPHUS)
(June 3rd, 1916 | Received by James Padgett)

I AM HERE. *Josephus.*

I come tonight to write a few lines upon a subject in which you may be interested, as I have observed that recently you have been reading my History of the Jews, and there are some things in that book which require correction. I don't mean that I desire to correct the whole book, but I do want to say something on some of the subjects that you have been reading about.

Well, you will notice that I attempted to tell of the creation of the world and of man, and that what I said was taken from the Old Testament, and that I elaborated a little upon what is contained in Genesis.

My work was not taken entirely from the Old Testament. For, in my time on earth, there were other books dealing with this subject that were entitled to just as much credence as was the Old Testament; and, from these books, I obtained much information that is contained in my writings.

But the truth of the things which I wrote I find now to be not the Truth in many particulars, and should not be accepted as such. The description of the creation of man is not in accordance with the facts. And the story as related in the Old Testament, and by me, is not the story of the facts of such creation.

I have not the time now to enter in detail into a correction of the errors contained in these descriptions, except that I wish to say a few words as to the creation of man and also his fall.

He was not made of the dust of the ground, but was made of the elements that existed in the universe of a different order from the mere dust of the ground. And he was so created by God for the purpose of forming the mere physical body of man. The two persons called our first parents were created at the same time, and not one out of the rib of the other. Therefore, the man and the woman are equal in their dignity and in the relationship which they bear to God. And the one is of just as much importance in the sight of God as is the other. One was created stronger, physically, than the other, and also was given a stronger mentality for the exercise of the reasoning powers and the workings of the physical organs of the body. And the other, while weaker in these particulars, was given more of the spiritual and emotional nature, and also an intuition by which she could understand the existence of things just as accurately and more quickly than could the man by the exercise of his reasoning power. One was just as the other as respects the gifts bestowed; and, together, they were a perfect pair. Male and female were they created with divers functions and duties to perform in the perfect workings of the Laws of God.

Power and love were theirs, and neither was made the superior of the other; nor was the one to be subject to the other. And had it not been for their fall, there never would have been the subjection of the female to the male.

When the disobedience took place, and the consequent fall, the qualities of the spiritual were taken from them to a large extent; and the animal qualities, as they may be called, asserted themselves. Then the male felt his superiority by reason of the fact that he possessed a greater amount of these animal qualities, and the female became subordinated and continued to be ever afterwards. For the male, not having these spiritual qualities to the extent that his mate possessed them, and not being able to realize the greater existence of these qualities in the female, believed that the physical was the superior. And as he possessed the physical to a larger degree than his companion, he determined that he was the superior, and therefore asserted this superiority. And the female, observing that this physical superiority did exist, submitted herself unto the male and so continued until now.

As man degenerated, this domination of the male intensified and, in some parts of the earth, the female became nothing better in the sight of the dominant man than one of the lower animals.

This degradation continued until man found the lowest place of his degeneracy. And when the turning point came, the qualities of the woman came to be more recognized, but very slowly. For many thousand years this inequality continued and man remained the master.

As man evolved from this low condition and the moral qualities began to come more into his consciousness, and the animal nature became less dominant, the condition of the female commenced to improve. And as education came into the life and practices of men, woman's opportunities became more extended, and she was more and more recognized as approaching the equal of her companion. In some countries of the earth her equality was recognized, but not in many.

The Jews recognized the equality of the woman in all matters pertaining to the home or the domestic life, and continued the distinction which had previously existed. Only in respect to public affairs and the qualities of the mind were women not permitted even by them to develop their mental faculties. And in all matters pertaining to the state or religion of the race, women were taught that these were things that belonged to the male.

The consequence of this course of life was that the woman developed the spiritual qualities which were hers to a larger extent. Her refinement and emotional nature and love principle exceeded those of the man to a great degree, and she became nearer the image of the Divine in her soul.

I have noticed that this progress has continued with the passing of the years. And now, in some of the nations of earth, the equality of the woman has become recognized, notwithstanding the fact that the laws of these countries did not permit her to exercise the rights of man (as she was still considered his equal only in the home or in social life).

But a time will come when she will be recognized as his equal in every particular, not only by the individual man but also by the man-made laws. And the further fact will appear that she will be his superior in matters pertaining to the spiritual.

As the time approaches when man shall return to his former state of purity and harmony with the Laws of God, the spiritual qualities will assert themselves and the animal will become subordinated. And woman will stand before God and man as the latter's equal, and, in these soul qualities, his superior. For, in the beginning, in this particular, she was his superior. For that superiority existed only in order that what was lacking in man in this regard was supplied by the woman, and the perfect pair was one.

You may think that this is a digression from what I first intended to write, and so it is; but I thought the occasion a proper one to tell mankind the future of the two integral parts of the Perfect Creation of God.

I will not write more tonight, but will come again sometime and write. So, with my love, I will say good night.

Your brother in Christ,
JOSEPHUS.

The Creation of Man.*
(JESUS)
(August 16th, and September 8th, 1955 | Received by Dr. Samuels)

I AM HERE. *Jesus.*

I am here to write on the subject: "Who Were the Angels Presumed to Have Existed Before the Creation of Man?"

As you know, man was created by God from the elements of the universe; and into man was implanted the soul, or the real or spiritual man, which distinguished him from the other creatures of God. And, with this soul, God gave man the possibility of obtaining God's Own Nature through the longings of man's soul for At-onement with Him. Pride and the desire to master the physical surroundings, which he thought would insure him immortality, led to the withdrawal of the Divine Love, and man's potentiality for becoming at-one with God was lost until I appeared in Palestine and preached immortality to the Jews.

The descent of man from his position as the elect of God, to partake of His Nature and Essence, was rapid. And, in the course of only a few hundred years, man was not too different in behavior from the beasts of the field; and, in some respects, he was worse. For man, on receiving his

---

* This message was received through Dr. Daniel G. Samuels, Jesus' second chosen instrument (following James E. Padgett's passing to the spirit world). – Ed.

human soul from God, had received with it the understanding that he was a child of God, though unredeemed. And, as a consequence of being a child of God, he had had implanted into him a consciousness of the laws of conduct which God had decreed. Thus, man knew that he sinned when he broke God's Commandments. And even in his worst state and lowest descent, man always had a small voice within him which was never quite completely drowned out by the excesses and violence which became habitual to his sinful existence.

The death of the physical body, and the path toward purification which the soul has to take on entering the spirit life, eventually brought to men's souls, in the spirit world, freedom from the excrescences and defilements they had accumulated in the earth life. And these purified souls turned their attention to helping mortals refrain from violations of the law, and, at the same time, imbued them with a renewed consciousness of God as their Creator. These purified souls were angels of the Lord because they were souls purified of sin, and because they did the Bidding of God in seeking to assist man to overcome the weakness of his flesh and turn him to the Father.

When I uncovered immortality in man's soul, whether on earth or in the spirit world, if they so chose and willed it, men could become capable of receiving the Divine Love through the operation of the Holy Spirit, and could become divine angels of the Lord—not merely purified from sin but also filled with the Essence of the Father to the extent that they would become the possessors of immortality and acquire consciousness of that reality.

The divine angels of God have been seeking to turn man and spirit to God, not only as son in the created sense, or servant, but also to have man seek His Love, partake of His Nature and Immortality, and to become His son in the real and Divine meaning of the term.

After the creation of man, therefore, there were angels in the sense that I have explained. But the Great Angel or Messenger—for "Angel" means "Messenger of God"—was and is the Spirit of God, which is obedient to the physical Laws of God. And it has been doing the Will of the Father, working not only on the vast infinity of His Universe, and bringing about these constant regrouping and changes in His Heavens, but also working on man's intellect and moral fiber ever since man was created by the Father.

The Spirit of God is God's Great Angel or Messenger which has been manifest throughout all eternity. It was this Spirit of the Lord which has been described in Genesis, hovering over the face of the earth, working on and developing it in preparation for the day when life and living beings could exist and survive on it. It was this Spirit of the Lord which carried out the Decrees of God, and set in motion those cosmic forces and elements that resulted in the new combination known to you as the solar system, and which, at the Lord's Bidding, will bring about the destruction of the same, and cause the emergence of a new order and a new dispensation. Before the creation of man, God's only active Angel was His Spirit—His active

278

Energy whose operations proclaimed His Majesty from everlasting to everlasting.

Adam and Eve, or whom they represent, were created through the operations of the Spirit of God. It was God's active Energy which brought about the groupings of those elements employed in fashioning man, as He fashioned the other living creatures on earth. But man was not man until the purely spiritual—and, by that, I do not mean the spirit body, which is of sublimated material, but the soul, in the likeness of God—was bestowed upon men. The first parents do not know when they became souls—that is, when God actually implanted souls into them—for there is no way of telling when they were human in appearance without their souls. For, without their souls, there was no memory of that degree that such a fact or state could be recollected by them; nor do they know how this implanting of the soul took place, even though it was done unto their bodies. And I shall say now: *Neither do I know how it is done, for I have never seen a soul*, although I can perceive its presence through my soul senses of perception. But, when it was accomplished, the first parents were aware that they were human beings, and that they were the Creations of the Father.

Man, as he is considered ordinarily, is a creation which passed through what you would call a long period of development, as have all of God's creatures during that period of the earth's development which enabled living beings to come into existence and survive.

Man's nature is therefore both animal, or material, in accordance with the conditions of his physical being, and spiritual, at the same time, in accordance with the soul qualities and attributes given to him at the time God bestowed a soul upon him. In short, man's nature is dual. And thus we have man with animal passions and feelings, and interrelated with these are those emotions and feelings which belong to his spiritual nature as a result of having received a soul. The Bible's reference to the creation of man refers to the creation of man in the image of God, or to the time when God, the Great Soul, conferred a soul upon man and made him the greatest of His Creations.

In other words, man possesses a double set of emotions. And the activity or dominance of the animal feelings in man sets in motion those thoughts and actions related to his material or animal existence. And this is not out of harmony with the Laws of God. It is only when these thoughts and resultant actions are in violation of the Law of God that they are sinful and cause unhappiness. The influence of these sinful emotions and thoughts and actions upon the soul is such that the spiritual emotions and aspirations of man become dormant, as though not existing, and the soul itself is incrusted with evil. Man knows when his physical passions and the resulting actions violate God's Laws. He must therefore exercise his will to prevent such violations and allow his feelings to be exercised for the purpose for which they were given him, and also to permit the development of his spiritual nature, and with it, the knowledge of his soul and the relationship which it has with God, its Creator.

Through prayer, thoughts and soul longings, the spiritual nature in man can be developed so as to dominate the personality, and he will act in accord with the feelings and emotions of his soul. However, if the animal emotions are allowed to dominate the spiritual emotions of man, and transgress the Laws of God concerning them, then the soul becomes incrusted with these baneful excrescences, or, shall I say, the soul is contaminated by them. And when the mortal dies and the spirit enters the spirit world, the soul must undergo a period of suffering in which the contaminating elements acquired in the earth life are eliminated from the soul and the soul assumes its pristine purity.

This purification of the soul obeys the dictates of God's Law of Compensation, for no such contaminated soul is permitted a place in God's Spiritual Heavens. The Paradise of the Hebrews cannot be reached without such purification. Yet, in this process of purification, the time consumed, as you would say, depends upon the soul itself—upon the awakening which it has to its condition, and those circumstances in the spirit world, mainly his own will as well as the help of others, which will enable him to make the necessary progress. All souls in the spirit world will be eventually purified.

This was the condition of man before the bestowal of the Gift of the Divine Love, which I brought to light during the time of my public ministry in Palestine. For, before I came with this Gift, no man could achieve At-onement with the Heavenly Father, with the transformation of his soul into a divine soul, through the pouring out of the Divine Love into his soul through earnest prayer to the Father for this Love, the Father's Essence, and brought into man's soul through the ministration of His Holy Spirit.

This, then, is briefly the evolution of man from the natural being to the purified soul, and, if he so desires it, to the state of the divine angel. The soul is the seat of the spiritual emotions, comes from God, and has the potentiality of becoming at-one with God, if it so desires, while the Gift of the Divine Love, obtained through prayer to the Father, is still available.

The material feelings, also the creation of God, have nothing of the soul substance, and have no permanent existence in the spirit world. But they do exist in the spirit world for a certain period, for man passes over from the mortal life with all his earth desires and feelings. However, these, and their perversions, which harm the soul, eventually become evanescent in the course of the spirt life.

JESUS.

NOTES.

The material presented in this chapter is inconclusive in regards to the creation of the human physical body.

Some messages support the idea that God created the human physical body instantaneously: *I know it has been said that the first man was not created, but developed from some animal of the lower order; and, as the process of evolution proceeded, this being became, in the end, a man, with all the wonderful organism and structure of his body. But I want to tell you that this is not true.*

Whereas, other messages support the idea that the human physical body was created over a long period of development: *Man, as he is considered ordinarily, is a creation which passed through what you would call a long period of development, as have all of God's creatures during that period of the earth's development which enabled living beings to come into existence and survive.*

The messages do agree, however, in regards to the instantaneous implantation of the soul into the physical body of the human being. Humans were created in the image of the Heavenly Father only with respect only to the soul. Therefore, the messages do show congruence in regards to the more important aspect of the creation of humans – the soul. Regarding the creation of the physical body, the topic is open for discussion and we welcome readers to embark on a prayerful path of discovery into the origins of the human body.

.

Chapter 11.

The Continuity of Life After Death.

MESSAGES INCLUDED IN THIS CHAPTER.

Sir Francis Bacon Presents a Discourse on the Continuity of Life After Death. (FRANCIS BACON)..*285*

Mrs. Padgett Affirms That Francis Bacon Wrote on the Continuity of Life After Death. (HELEN PADGETT)..*288*

Samuel, Prophet of the Old Testament, Cautions That Proof of the Continuous Life of a Man After the Death of the Body, as Merely Shown by the Manifestations of Nature, Is Not Conclusive. (SAMUEL, THE PROPHET) *288*

Samuel Continues His Message on the Continuity of Life of a Man After the Death of the Physical Body. (SAMUEL, THE PROPHET)...291

What is the Real Body That Is Resurrected at the Time of the Physical Death? (PAUL, THE APOSTLE) *294*

Paul Continues His Message on the Spirit Body's Resurrection. (PAUL, THE APOSTLE)..*296*

11.

The Continuity of Life After Death.

*Sir Francis Bacon Presents a Discourse on
the Continuity of Life After Death.
(FRANCIS BACON)
(May 26th, 1919 | Received by Dr. Samuels)*

I AM HERE. *Francis Bacon.*

Let me write a few lines tonight upon a subject that has recently been discussed by a spiritualist, a preacher, a philosopher and a scientist, and that is the continuity of life after death of the physical body. Each of these writers approach the subject from a different viewpoint, but all arrive at the same conclusion based upon different means of argument—and that is that life continues after death.

The subject is one in which mankind is vitally interested, and is worthy of consideration by the greatest minds of investigation and research. It should be studied in the light of nature as well as in that of actual demonstration by those who have proved to mankind by their experiences that the spirits of their departed friends and acquaintances, and of others of more or less distinction when in the physical life, do actually live and communicate to men their existence and their possession of the mental faculties and thoughts that were theirs when mortals.

The proper study of man would demonstrate this fact and, logically, doubt would cease to exist. But the difficulty is that men do not understand man, or his creation and faculties, and his relationship to things of life known as the material or matter. It is a common belief that matter is now existent, or, rather, that what men see and know of the material, is all that is knowable, and that when that which is merely physical, as commonly understood, ceases to exist, no further or other knowledge of it can be obtained or understood by the finite mind of man.

But this accepted assumption is not true. And if men would only think for a moment of what matter, or the material, is, they would comprehend the possibilities of its workings and functionings, and, also, of what use may be made of the same by the minds of the spirits operating upon it in the spiritual world—that is, in the world beyond the comprehension of the five senses of men, which are only the means of the spirits working in the ordinary purview of the physical life.

Matter is eternal and exists in all spheres of the spirit world, just as it does on earth, although in different forms and attenuations and conditions that may or may not be the objects of the physical senses, or of the senses of the mind which are superior to, or exclusive of, these mere physical senses. Matter is, in its essential nature, the same, notwithstanding the fact that it assumes different forms—some visible to the ordinary senses of men, and some entirely outside of that view or sensation and, as to these ordinary senses, wholly nonexistent. Yet, to these other senses of the mind, these latter forms are just as real and tractable and subject to the influence of the workings of the mind as the merely physical matter is to the five senses of men.

The world in which men live is composed of the material. And the world in which I live is also composed of the material of the same nature, but of different consistencies and objective qualities. The material of the universe is always material, whether or not it be cognizable by man and subject to his thoughts and inventions and uses. And as man progresses in the study of the same—I mean the practical and experimental—he will discover that there are things of the material in nature which are being developed and made known to him, and which he had no conception of their existence a few years before. Such is the discovery and use of electricity, and the workings of the laws of nature which enable him to make the effects of wireless telegraphy possible. These discoveries and workings of forces of the unseen are nothing more or less than a certain kind of knowledge controlling the same, and, as to his consciousness, have become apparent. But, in all these operations, matter is the thing made use of, and not any spiritual power as commonly understood by men. So, you see, matter, whether in the grossly physical of earth or in the more attenuated and invisible of the spirit world, is that which is used to produce effects, and is operated on by the mind, whether or not it be tangible and understood matter or not.

The mind is an entity, indivisible and united, and is not separable into the subjective and objective, as men frequently teach, except in this: that, in its workings, that part which is suited for and used in controlling the material, after it has been transformed into the purely invisible, may be called the subjective. But it is all one mind and exists in man while on earth, just as it will and does exist when he becomes a spirit.

Man, in his journey through life, and I mean when in the earth existence, is always of the material; that is, his soul has a material covering and appearance. And while this material covering changes in its appearance and quality as he progresses in the spheres, yet, the gross physical of his earth life and the sublimated spiritual of the eternal part of his life are both of the material—real, existing, and tangible, and used for the purpose of their creation: namely, the protection and individualization of the soul which they contain.

Now, this being so, you can readily understand that man, when he gives up the coarser physical of the human body, does not cease to be of the material, but becomes an inhabitant of the finer and purer material of what is called his spirit body. And this body is subject to the laws governing the material, just as his physical body was subject to these laws. And the spirit, which in this sense is the real man clothed in the material, controls and uses that material more effectually than it did when bound in the physical on earth. All the material of the spirit world is used and formulated by the spirits according to their degree of intelligence and development, and as the occasions for such uses may arise. And such uses, or the effects of the same, are or can be made known to man according to his receptive capacities.

Ordinarily, man's understanding of the effects of the spirit's control of the material of the invisible world is limited by the capacity of his five senses to comprehend. And as these five senses were created for the purpose only of permitting or helping the spirit to manifest itself, with reference to those things which belong to the wholly physical of earth, it rarely happens that men can perceive the invisible material or the workings of the laws controlling the same.

Now, in what I have said, this spirit control is merely the exercise of the mind of man—the same indivisible mind that he possesses when on earth, but which, because of the limitations of the physical organs, he was not able to function, as regards the invisible material, so that man could understand that functioning and its results.

When man dies, he is thereafter the same being in all his faculties, desires and thoughts, and in his ability to use the material, as he was before his death, except that the purely physical organs of his own being are no longer his; and, as to them, he is dead. But strange as it may seem to you, he can and often does control the physical organs of another man who is living in the flesh, if that man will submit to that control. And, when you think for a moment, you will realize that there is nothing remarkable in this. The mind of the spirit remains just the same as it was before his departure from the body, having all its powers and thoughts and consciousness. And if it can obtain control of that which is necessary to manifest itself to the consciousness of men, there will be no difficulty in its doing so, which is nothing unusual or supernatural. Its own organs of brain and nerves and the five senses having gone, and the brain of every other mortal being subject to the control of its own mind, so long as that mortal mind claims the exclusive use or control of these organs, the spirit mind, deprived of its own physical organs, cannot control, because it is a Law of Being that no mind in its normal state can be intruded upon by another mind. And unless the mortal mind (whose seat and functioning are within the spirit body, which is also enclosed in the physical body, possessing these organs) consents to the control of such organs by the other mind, the spirit cannot use such organs. But the power is in the disembodied spirit or mind. Only the opportunity is wanting.

When the spirit desires to control the invisible material, it is limited only by its intelligence and knowledge of the law governing such control and its progress in the spirit spheres.

Well, I have written enough for tonight, but will come again and amplify my message.

Thanking you, I will say good night.

Your friend, FRANCIS BACON.

I AM HERE. *Helen.*

Well, dear, I am glad that you are in condition again to receive the messages of the spirits who wish to write to you in reference to spiritual things.

The spirit who wrote to you was very anxious to do so, and we permitted him in order that you might gain some conception of what the material of the universe is, and the power that spirits have over such material.

But this is not the nature of the messages that we wish to convey to you, and we will not permit ourselves to be interfered with very often in this particular. Until our messages are all delivered, you must not think of such things.

The Master has been with you today and is well pleased at your way of thinking. He says that you will soon commence to receive the higher messages again, and we are all anxious to write. Keep up your prayers to the Father and your thoughts about the higher things of the spirit world.

As you have been drawn on a great deal tonight, I will not write further now. I will only say that we all love you and will be with you to help you in your thoughts.

So, love us and say good night.

Your own true and loving,

HELEN.

*Samuel, Prophet of the Old Testament, Cautions That Proof of the
Continuous Life of a Man After the Death of the Body, as Merely
Shown by the Manifestations of Nature, Is Not Conclusive.
(SAMUEL, THE PROPHET)*
(March 21st, 1916 | Received by James Padgett)

I AM HERE. *Samuel.*

I desire to write for a short time on a subject that is of importance to those who are in doubt as to the reality of the future life.

I know that a vast majority of mortals believe in a future existence and the immortality of the soul. But there is a considerable number of mortals who do not know these facts, or who have no belief regarding the matter. They simply say, "I don't know." It is to these latter persons that I wish to write.

In the first place, all persons know, if they know anything, that they are living, and that, sooner or later, what they call death is inevitable, no matter from what cause it may take place. To live, then, implies that there is such a thing as a continuous life; and to die, to these people, demonstrates that the life with which they are acquainted ceases, and that the material body in which this life manifested itself gradually disintegrates into the original elements that composed that body.

Now, a man being a materialist, purely, would seem to be correct in his conclusions that when life (which could be manifested only through the material things of nature) ceases, and the body becomes inanimate and dead, that then is the end not only of the body but of the individual. And if there existed no other manifestation of life than this physical one, there would be no foundation upon which to base the assumption that the death of the body does not end all.

I know it has been asserted in the way of argument that even though the material parts of vegetation die, yet, as spring comes round, these materials show forth the life again that had previously manifested itself; and, therefore, by analogy, the death of the human body merely means that its life will appear again in evidence in some other body or form.

But upon close investigation and exact reasoning, it will be seen that the two subjects of demonstration are not alike, because, while the material of the vegetable kingdom apparently dies, yet, it does not all die. For even though you may apparently see the particular body of the tree or plant, or every part of it, go into decay or rottenness, yet, as a fact, this is not true. The whole of the material plant which enclosed or manifested life does not die until a new body arises and grows out of it. And the life that animated the body that appears to have died continues in it, awaiting the new growth for its display of existence.

The flower dies, and the bush upon which it grows may appear to die. Yet, the roots continue to enclose the life principle which causes the bush to grow again, and which has its genesis in these roots. And this is the same life that originally existed in the bush. Pluck up the bush by the roots and expose them to the elements until they die and commence to disintegrate, and then replant them, and you will find they will not grow, for the reason that the life which had animated them has departed.

And the same conclusion will be reached when you apply the same investigation and reasoning to every species of the vegetable kingdom. The grain of corn, though apparently dead, is in reality not dead, but continues to contain the life principle which was the cause of the growth of the stalk and the blade and the ear in the blade. Nothing of the vegetable kingdom will be reproduced, or form the basis of a new growth, unless some part of the old growth retains the life force in it.

In man's investigation of the wonders of vegetable life, he has discovered that a grain of corn that had been entombed in the hands of an Egyptian mummy for more than three thousand years, when planted in the ground, reproduced the stalk and blade and ear of corn, just as the original material body had produced. And why? Not because it received unto itself new life or any force that was not already in it when the grain of corn was planted in the earth, but because the grain had never ceased to be without the life that existed in it as it grew from the original seed to the perfect grain. The grain had never lost its life and had never died, though apparently it had. Always there was some part of the original body that continued to exist, and that held the life principle enclosed in itself. Without the preservation of some part of the original body, there could never have been a manifestation of the life that caused the growth of that body.

This phenomena, as you call it, was not the resurrection of a material body that had died and become disintegrated and nonexistent, but was merely the resurrection of that part of the old body that had never died, but had always retained the life principle in it. And this, I say, is no argument for the future existence of man, as viewed from a purely material aspect.

When the body of a man dies, it is eternally destroyed, either by natural decay or by incineration, or, sometimes, by cannibals, so that no portion of his body remains in which the life principle may be preserved. And so far as the material body is involved, it utterly disappears. No roots remain in the ground and no grain or seed of it is preserved from which a new body may arise.

So, I say, the phenomena of the vegetable apparently dying, and, after a season, springing forth again and producing a body similar to the one that had formerly lived and died, furnishes no demonstration or argument from which can be drawn the logical conclusion that when a man dies he will not cease to exist, or that he will live again.

From the purely material standpoint, the materialist has the better of the argument. He may well ask the question: "When a man dies, shall he live again?" And he may answer the inquiry by saying, "Nature furnishes no proof that he will."

It may be said that life permeates all nature and is the basis of all existence, and that assertion is true. But it does not follow therefrom that any particular manifestation of life, such as the individual man, when once ceasing to manifest, will again be reproduced in that particular identity of material manifestations, or in that form or existence that will make itself the identical being that had ceased to exist.

So, to show man that there is a continuous existence after the death of the body—and I mean an individual, identical existence—something more is required than the argument of analogy in nature, or to the material things of nature in which life appears and then apparently disappears and then reappears. As the discussion on this phase of the matter will require more time than you have tonight to receive it, I will defer the treatment until later. With all my love, I will say good night.

Your brother in Christ,

SAMUEL.

Samuel Continues His Message on the Continuity of Life
of a Man After the Death of the Physical Body.
(SAMUEL, THE PROPHET)
(March 21ˢᵗ, 1916 | Received by James Padgett)

I AM HERE. *Samuel.*

I desire to continue my message on the subject of the continuous life of a man after the death of the body, as shown by the manifestations of nature.

As I was saying, the apparent death and resuscitation of things of the vegetable kingdom do not furnish any argument that man will continue to live after the death of the physical body.

Now, I know it is difficult to understand what there can be in the manifestations of nature to prove such persistent life, and that the people for whose benefit I am writing this will not be willing to use evidence of things of a spiritual nature to prove this continuous life. Hence, I will confine myself to material matters.

Well, in the first place, there is no such thing as the death of anything in all the material universe of God! Every primal element has life in it, even though that life may not be apparent to the consciousness of men. But it is a fact. Every atom or electron (as the scientists term these particles of matter) that is reduced to its infinitesimal proportions is pregnant with life. And the very apparent decay of material substances is nothing more nor less than the results of the operation of the life that they contain that is working out the changes of form or expression.

If the scientists will investigate and analyze the constituents of particles of all matter, notwithstanding that they appear to be devoid of the life principle, they will find that life is contained in these particles in some of its expressions, and that there is nothing in the material things of nature that is completely inert. There is no such thing as inertia; it only appears to exist. And while it may not be apparent to the natural eye that everything in the material has life within itself, and that there is force and motion as a result therefrom, yet such is the fact.

This life principle permeates everything. It applies to, and forms a part of, everything that has the appearance of natural existence. The grain of sand on the seashore or the dust of the decayed tree has life within it, and this life is no more nonexistent or absent from these material things than are the elements that compose this visible form of matter ever lost, or without existence. It is true that these elements change their forms and their compositions; yet they never cease to exist or become nothing. "Nothing" means a void, and, in God's Creation, there is no void. Everything is of substance, and there are no vacancies unfilled.

Hence, as life is the foundation principle of existence, and life exists everywhere, with there being no void in nature, life permeates everything, whether visible to the mortal eye or senses or not.

When that which is material decays or disintegrates, it does not do so as the result of the absence of life, but as the result of the operation of this principle of life upon the material in such a way as to cause the separation of its elements and their change into new forms and appearances.

I know it is said that the workings of the elements—that is, fire and water and air and chemicals, known and unknown—cause the disintegration or even the disappearance of material things, but this is not strictly true. For these elements do not affect these things themselves, as a primary result of their working, but what they affect is the life within these materials. And as that life lessens or changes the materials of which that life is a part, causing them to disintegrate or dissolve into thin air, as is sometimes said, never does any part of the material substance, no matter how minute it may come to be, die—that is, in the sense of losing life.

Life is a thing of such delicate nature, and is so susceptible to a division or reduction to a smallness almost to infinity, that no substance can become so small that life is not a part of it and the vital principle of its existence.

As is known, the solid rock may be reduced not only to dust but also to a liquid, and then to a vapor and then to a gas, and then to that which is not sensitive to the consciousness of men. Yet, the life principle exists in all these forms of that material rock. And that which ultimates into apparent nothingness contains life, just as does the original rock, or any of its subsequent forms, in the process of reduction to seeming extinction.

The materialist accepts these phenomena as true. And blindly and with full assurance, he announces that nothing in creation is ever lost or annihilated. This being true, why is not the conclusion logical that the apparently inanimate rock, or the animal without reasoning powers, or the man with the reasonable faculties is never annihilated or lost or, in other words, never dies the death that results in nothingness?

But they say that, while this may be true, yet, the materials which form these various aspects of existence do not necessarily, or probably, come together again and reform the identical being that once appeared as an existing thing, and then dissolved into the elements that composed the thing. And, hence, while the elements may continue to live forever in some form, yet, that form in which they once existed will not again appear. I know that this is a reasonable conclusion, and one in accord with the demonstrations of science. And it is applicable to the merely physical man, just as to any other manifestations of the material things of nature.

But even these materialists admit that, in the case of man, there is something in his formation and essential being that is more than, or in addition to, the merely physical portions of him. And while they may say that this something is wholly of a material nature, yet, they admit that it is of material that is different and distinct from the material that forms the visible physical body.

I do not speak of the soul or spiritual part of man, but of the intellect and of the five senses and of the reasoning powers, all of which, of course, includes the memory. That part of man that embraces these things, the materialist must admit, is distinct and different from the mere body. And even though it were here to be conceded that they are material, yet, no man has ever seen them or felt them, or in any way perceived their existence, as he has that which he knows to be of the material. He has seen and heard and known the effects of the existence of these invisible material qualities, as he may call them, but he has never demonstrated that they died when the physical body died. The furthest that he can go in this direction is that they disappeared and became lost to his consciousness. But that they disintegrated or dissolved or were reduced to a gaseous substance, or were lost in thin air in which he has seen the visible physical body disappear, he cannot affirm. The limit of his knowledge is that, with the death of the physical body, this other material part of man, as he terms it, disappears and never again reappears to his physical senses.

As I say, while he has never observed, and has no knowledge of, any disintegration of these invisible material parts of man into any primary elements or atoms or electrons, as he applies such terminology to the physical body, hence, he is not justified in concluding that any such results to this invisible material follow the death and dissolving of the flesh and blood and bones of man. To so conclude is more of a speculation than to hold that the invisible material did not dissolve into forms more invisible, if such an expression can be used.

As I have said, life is in all things, visible and invisible, and there is no vacuum in nature. While man is living, it is demonstrated that life is in this invisible part of man, and more abundantly than in the merely visible body. And as life continues in the elements of this latter body after death, why cannot we declare that life continues in the invisible part of man after death? Nothing is ever lost or annihilated, and, hence, these parts of man cannot be annihilated; and, existing, they must contain life.

Has the materialist ever been able to demonstrate, to his own satisfaction, even, that this invisible part of man, which he says is material, ceases to live? He cannot say that the elements of the physical body, no matter what form they may assume, cease to live. But, on the contrary, he affirmatively asserts that they are never annihilated and continue to exist; and, as life is necessary to existence, these elements must continue to have life.

So, according to their own arguments and demonstrations and ultimate claims, the death of the physical body does not destroy the elements which compose that body, but only the form in which these elements were combined. Then, from this, the most that they can claim as to the invisible material part of man is that, while the material which composed this invisible part is not dead or annihilated, yet, its formation may be disintegrated or changed; hence, the identity of the man, as to this portion of him, no longer exists. But this conclusion does not follow as a logical sequence. The materialist has nothing upon which to base this conclusion, except that he has seen and knows that, when the visible body dies, it disintegrates and ultimately disappears.

He has never seen the disintegration of this invisible part of man, though he has seen its manifestations decay and even be destroyed. But the cause of this is shown to be some decadence or disorganization of some part of the visible body through which the invisible manifested.

These materialists have knowledge of the facts that men have been deprived of their arms or legs or other parts of the body, and, yet, the invisible parts remained perfect, performing their functions. It is also true that men have received injury to their physical organs of sight or hearing, and, as a consequence, the invisible organs of sight or hearing did not function. But that fact constitutes no proof that they were dead or had ceased to preserve the form they had before the physical organs were impaired. For when the defects of the physical organs were removed, and these organs again came into condition to do their functioning, the invisible faculties of sight and hearing manifested their existence again, just as they had existed before the physical organs were impaired. And, so, many similar instances might be referred to, to show that death or destruction of any or many parts of the visible body does not destroy or disseminate the invisible material part of man into its elements.

And, besides, let the materialists consider the great difference in the powers and objects of the creation of these visible and invisible parts of man, and they will realize that the purely physical is wholly subordinated, and is used merely to enable the invisible parts to manifest themselves and show that the real man is the invisible part; and that man can lose part of his physical vestment and, yet, exist and perform his functions and exercise his powers.

I have thus tried to show that, while no argument can be drawn from any analogy between the vegetable things of nature—dying and coming to life again—and man's dying, yet, neither can any argument be drawn from the fact that the visible body of man dies and goes into its elements, never to be resuscitated again as the same body, to show that the invisible body of man dies and is dissolved into its elements, and that man ceases to be the individual that he was before the death of the physical body.

I may not have made my message as plain and convincing as I would desire. But, in a discussion of this kind, it is difficult to transmit the various shades of thought through the medium of a mortal. I thank you for your courtesy and will stop now.

So, with my love and the Blessings of the Father, I will say good night.

Your brother in Christ,

SAMUEL

*What is the Real Body That Is Resurrected at the Time
of the Physical Death?
(PAUL, THE APOSTLE)*
(October 4th, 1916 | Received by James Padgett)

I AM HERE. *Paul.*

I come tonight to write you upon a subject that may be of interest to you and is important to all mankind. If you are in condition to receive my message, I will write.

Well, the subject is: "What Is the Real Body That Is Resurrected at the Time of the Physical Death?"

Of course, there will be but one resurrection, and that takes place at the time the mortal becomes an inhabitant of the spirit world. There will never be what is called a general resurrection of the dead, for the mortal can die only once. I mean in a physical sense. And, in order to live in the spirit realms, it is necessary that the mortal have a spirit body that preserves the identity of his individuality. And having this body, and never having been without it after the soul is incarnated in the earthly body, the mortal does not need an additional body being added to the one that the soul already has.

When a man ceases to be a mortal, the physical body that dies disintegrates into its elements and never again do these elements form the same body that becomes decayed. Hence, it is impossible for that body to be resurrected. The only body that is ever resurrected is the body that encloses the soul of the mortal at the time he gives up the earth life.

I know that many believe that, when the man dies, his conscious existence ceases, and he becomes, as it were, dead in body, soul and spirit; and that although the physical body decays and returns to dust or ashes, yet, in some mysterious and unexplainable manner, the soul and spirit continue to exist as an unthinking, sleeping entity, not subject to sensation or activity. And the soul so remains until the great day of judgment, or of Christ's coming, when, in response to the summons, it arouses itself, answers the summons, and again becomes clothed in the body which it possessed while in the human form. In their belief, it may not be the exact or identical body which once existed, but the new body will be one of flesh and blood, and of such a nature as to be the same body in substance that was dead and buried and decayed.

But this is not true. For the very laws of nature with which men are acquainted prove the impossibility of such an occurrence. And many arguments have been formulated and declared to prove that such a resurrection cannot be—that it will be wholly impossible for the elements that constituted the old body to again assemble in the same form, and give to the soul the body that it discarded when it experienced its freedom from the bands of flesh.

But the advocates of this untrue theory respond by saying that God is All-Powerful, and, in some way not understood by men, will resurrect this old body and clothe the soul therein so that the identity of the individual will appear. It must be remembered that God works and produces beings and entities in accordance with laws that He has established, and not by any special, sporadic act, irrespective of, and, as said, in contravention of, these laws.

Man understands, to some extent, the working of these laws in what he calls nature, or the normal. And some spirits understand not only what man understands but also the workings of these laws that may be called above nature or supernormal. And the laws work the same, and without change or interference, in the one case as in the other.

As it would be impossible to clothe a mortal having one body of flesh with another body of flesh, so, in the spirit world, it would be impossible to clothe the spirit who has a spirit body with any additional body, whether of flesh or other substance. This spirit body is a thing of real substance, and not susceptible to being enveloped in any other body.

Well, I see that you are not in condition to write. I will postpone the remainder of the message until later.

I have not written to you for some time, and am glad for the opportunity to again write.

(If you can manage to come more often, perhaps you will also find me in a better condition more often, which should result hopefully in an increase and improvement in the quantity and quality of your communications.)

I understand what you mean and will act on your suggestion, as I think it a very wise and desirable one. I will come more often and write.

So, with all my love, I will say good night.

Your brother in Christ,

PAUL.

Paul Continues His Message on the Spirit Body's Resurrection.
(PAUL, THE APOSTLE)
(October 5th, 1916 | Received by James Padgett)

I AM HERE. *Paul.*

I will furnish my message tonight if you are so inclined. Well, we will try.

As I was saying, the body that is resurrected at death is not the physical body but the spirit body; and never after the first resurrection is there another. I am now dealing with the resurrection other than that of the soul, or the resurrection from the death of which I have before written.[*]

The body that is once laid in the grave will never be resurrected, and neither will any of its elements enter into any other body for the purpose of a resurrection. The body of flesh is created for one purpose only; and, when that purpose has been accomplished, never will that body, or any derivative

---

[*] The message that Paul is referring to here is contained in "The True Resurrection" chapter in volume I of *Angelic Revelations of Divine Truth*, and is entitled: "The True Resurrection That Jesus Taught, Without Which Our Faith as Christians Is in Vain."—Ed.

from it, be used for any resurrection. This body of flesh is of matter. And, like all matter, it is used only for the life on earth, and cannot be used for any function, or for clothing any spirit, in the spirit world; and neither can it be translated into the spirit realms.

All material bodies must die. And never will there come a time when men can leave the earth and enter the spirit life in these material bodies.

I know that it has been written that certain of the prophets of old were translated into the spirit heavens, clothed in their fleshly bodies, but this is not true. For it is impossible that such a thing could be, as the same laws apply to the physical body of the saint as to that of the sinner. Both are of the earth, earthly, and must be left behind when the spirits of men enter the heavens of spirits.

So, when men believe and preach the general resurrection of the material body, or the special resurrection of the same, they are in error and do not believe or preach the Truth.

Flesh and blood, or flesh without blood, cannot inherit the Kingdom. And no belief or teachings can make that true which is untrue.

I do not desire to write more on this subject because many men who are acquainted with these laws know, and will know and understand, the impossibility of the material entering the realm of the spiritual.

So, thanking you for your kindness, I will say good night.
Your brother in Christ,
PAUL.

Chapter 12.

The Truths of the Spirit World.

I. The Spheres of Progression.

MESSAGES INCLUDED IN THIS CHAPTER.

Jesus Explains That Many of the Ancient Spirits Are Not in the Celestial Heavens but Are in the Sixth Sphere, Possessing Merely Intellectual and Moral Development. (JESUS) 301

George Washington, the First President of the United States, Confirms That Some Ancient Spirits Wrote Through Mr. Padgett. He Relates That Many Came from the Celestial Heavens and the Lower Spirit Heavens. (GEORGE WASHINGTON) 303

A Celestial Spirit Describes Certain Experiences of Newly Arrived Spirits in the Spirit World, and of Their Eventual Progress. (JOHN B. COMEYS) 305

Mrs. Padgett Describes Her Home in the Third Sphere, and Discusses the Importance of Seeking for the Divine Love. (HELEN PADGETT)...307

Ann Rollins Corroborates Mrs. Padgett's Experience and Tells of the Happiness of Spirits in the Celestial Spheres. (ANN ROLLINS).........311

Ann Rollins Gives Her Description of Some of the Spirit Spheres. She Also Criticizes a Book That Mr. Padgett Was Reading. (ANN ROLLINS)...314

Ann Rollins Describes Her Home in the Second Celestial Sphere. (ANN ROLLINS)...316

Ann Rollins Describes Her Experiences in the Second Celestial Sphere. She States That She Can Never Die Again, and That She Has Passed Beyond the "Second Death." (ANN ROLLINS) 317

Samuel Conveys a Description of the Celestial Heavens. (SAMUEL, THE PROPHET) 320

12.

I. The Spheres of Progression.

Jesus Explains That Many of the Ancient Spirits Are Not in the Celestial Heavens but Are in the Sixth Sphere, Possessing Merely Intellectual and Moral Development.
(JESUS)
(June 2nd, 1915 | Received by James Padgett)

I AM HERE. *Jesus.*

The spheres in which Saleeba [*] lived are the ones that your grandmother described as being the homes of merely intellectual spirits. In these different spheres are many subspheres. And the different races of mankind naturally congregate with those spirits of their own race so that, while this Egyptian may have lived in these different spheres, it does not follow that she lived in the same subspheres with the spirits of other races. In all probability she did not. She is a very ancient spirit, but her age as compared with eternity—that which has passed as well as that to follow—is a grain of sand on the seashore compared to all the rest of the sand. She is old as men consider age, but, as we look upon it, she is of the now and not very old.

She will tell you of the spheres in which she lived, but they will not be any different from, or any greater than, the ones your grandmother described. She has not progressed above the Sixth, and cannot until she receives the Divine Love and Essence of the Father.

So, as she describes these spheres to you, keep in mind the fact that she has never gotten beyond the Sixth, as described by your grandmother.

She may have passed through what seems to her many more spheres than the ones described by your grandmother, but all the various stages through which she has passed constitute no more than the six lower spheres. She never was in the Seventh, or passed through it.

So, let your mind be settled on this point: No spirit who is without this Love has ever gotten beyond the Sixth Sphere.

The ancient Bible patriarchs and prophets—such as Moses, Abraham, Elijah, and the others—never got beyond the Sixth Sphere until my coming, when they first received the Divine Love. And the fact that they are ancient spirits does not necessarily imply that they are in a very high sphere now.

---

[*] Saleeba is an ancient spirit and a former princess of Egypt who first learned of the Divine Love through her communications with Mr. Padgett.—Ed.

Your grandmother, for instance, is in a much higher sphere than all of the ancients who have never received the Divine Love.

So, the fact that a spirit is ancient does not, of itself, mean that it is of a very high order of spirit. Many a spirit who passed over comparatively recently is as high in the Sixth Sphere as are these ancient ones. And many a spirit who came to the spirit world within a short time—your wife, for instance—is in a higher sphere than many of these ancient ones who have been in the spirit life for centuries. Yes, centuries upon centuries, and for the reason that these ancients have only the mental development which can carry them into the Sixth Sphere only, while your wife has the soul development which has already carried her to the Celestial Spheres.

So, do not think that because a spirit who comes to you may be an ancient spirit, it may be in a high sphere or can instruct you in those things which will lead you to the Father's Kingdom, for it is not true.

The Egyptian who came to you is now seeking this Love, and she will receive It and progress higher as she develops her soul. But she will never get higher than the Sixth Sphere until her soul development fits her for the higher spheres. The mere fact that she has the mental development which enabled her to progress to the Sixth Sphere will not help her in any degree to progress above it.

As her soul develops, she will leave the Sixth Sphere and inhabit a sphere of soul education which is in unison with her development. And it may be the Third one. But this sphere will enable her to make more rapid progress than if she should remain in the Sixth, because of the reasons that your grandmother portrayed in her message.

So, do not be impressed with the thought that, because spirits are ancient, they can help you or instruct you in those things which pertain to your soul development. Of course, their mental qualities are developed to a high degree, and they can tell you many interesting things about the time in which they lived, and of their experiences in the spirit world. But these things, while interesting, do not help you to attain to the Divine Kingdom. As regards this soul knowledge, they may be mere babes, and totally devoid of all the things necessary for the soul developing and obtaining the Divine Love.

I have many things yet to write about and, as we write, you will see that I am the true Jesus, and that my knowledge of the Father's Kingdom is the greatest possessed by any spirit, be he ancient or modern

I wish that I could write to you every night, but, under present earthly conditions, I cannot because it might interfere with your life on earth. But, as I have told you, very soon you will be in the condition where I will have your services all to myself and my work.

I will not write more tonight, but will only say: Believe, and you will see the Glories of the Father and your own salvation and happiness!

Your friend and brother,

JESUS.

George Washington, the First President of the United States,
Confirms That Some Ancient Spirits Wrote Through Mr. Padgett. He
Relates That Many Came from the Celestial Heavens and the Lower
Spirit Heavens.
(GEORGE WASHINGTON)
(August 12th, 1915 | Received by James Padgett)

I AM HERE. *George Washington.* (Celestial spirit.)

I am the same who wrote to you a few nights ago.

Well, you are my brother and I am pleased that you call me your brother. In this world of spirits, we have no titles or distinctions because of any fame or positions we may have had on earth.

I came to tell you that I have watched with interest the many communications that you have received from the various kinds and orders of spirits, and I am somewhat surprised that you could receive these several messages with such accuracy. In earth life, I never supposed that such a thing could be. And, since I became a spirit, I have never seen such demonstrations of the powers that exist on the part of spirits to communicate, and mortals to receive, the messages that come to you. I know that such communications have been made by spirits to mortals very many times, but what I mean by "surprising" is the great variety of spirits who come to you. They come from the Celestial Spheres as well as from the earth planes. And what they write is not only new to mankind but also many of their declarations of Truth are new to many of us spirits.

Very seldom do we have the opportunity in the Celestial Spheres to communicate with any of these ancient spirits who live high up in the Celestial Heavens. And, when I see them come and communicate to you so frequently, I wonder at it all!

I know, of course, that such spirits occasionally do come into the earth plane and try to influence both mortals and spirits to do good. But I want to tell you that their influence is usually exerted through intermediary spirits and not directly by these higher spirits in person, as they do through you.

The messages that you have received from these spirits who lived on earth thousands of years ago were really written by them during their control of your brain and hand.

I am trying my best to help you in your work, and will continue to do so. The work that you have been selected to do is the most important one that the spirit world is now engaged in. I mean the world that recognizes Jesus as its Prince and Master.

Some spirits come because they see the way open to communicate to mortals, and they naturally desire to make known the fact that they live and are happy in their spheres.[*] But their happiness is not the real happiness which the true believers and followers of the Master enjoy. So, when they come to you during your work, you may have the opportunity to tell them of this higher experience which the redeemed of the Father enjoy. Many spirits who are in these lower spheres would be in the Celestial Heavens if they only knew the Way.

We try frequently to show them the Way to Truth and the higher life, but we find it a difficult task. They think that we are merely spirits like themselves, having our opinions just as they have theirs, and that we are mistaken in our opinions. Hence, we can tell them nothing which will show them Truths that they do not know, or which will give them greater happiness than they have now.

When they notice the contrast in our appearance—that is, that we are so much more beautiful and bright than they are—they simply think that such beauty and brightness is a result of some natural cause, and that we differ from them merely as one race of men differs from another. They do not seem to think that there is anything about the contrast in our appearance that is caused by any higher spiritual condition than what they already have. And this is the great stumbling block in the way of their becoming interested in the conditions which we have, and which would otherwise motivate them to investigate and learn the true cause for the same. Hence, I wish to say that you may do them some good in this regard, for you are a third person who can call their attention to the great contrast and tell them the cause as you understand it. What you say would probably make some impression upon them, causing them to make inquiries. And, once they commenced this, our opportunity would then come to lead them into the Light of the great Truth of the Divine Love of the Father.

Well, I have digressed from what I intended to write, but it is just as well, for all the Truths of God are important to both mortals and spirits. I am very happy in my home in the Celestial Spheres of the Father, and I am trying to progress to those even higher. So, let me assure you of the Truths of what you have had written to you by your band and others of God's redeemed spirits.

I thank you for this opportunity, and I will come again sometime.

Your own true brother in Christ,

GEORGE WASHINGTON.

---

[*] These spirits have only the natural love developed to a pure state, but do not have the Divine Love. In a pure state, this natural love gives these spirits a wonderful glory and beauty. But compared to those spirits who possess the Divine Love, they are like a dim candle light in comparison to the brightness and glory of the midday sun.—Ed.

A Celestial Spirit Describes Certain Experiences of Newly Arrived Spirits in the Spirit World, and of Their Eventual Progress.
(JOHN B. COMEYS)
(December 22nd, 1915 | Received by James Padgett)

I AM HERE. *John B. Comeys.*

I desire to write you a short time to inform you of certain Truths which you should know pertaining to the spirit life, and to tell you what mortals may expect and be assured of realizing who lead the lives of good and pure men.

I am in the Celestial Spheres, but I shall not speak of these spheres—but only of the Spiritual Spheres where men may live after they become disembodied spirits and experience a happiness which they have no conception of on earth.

When a spirit first enters the spirit world, it receives a welcome from some one or more spirits whose duties are to receive such spirit, and to show the place where it is suited to live or exist.

Such spirit is then permitted to meet its friends and relatives and to commune with them for a short or long time, and receive whatever consolation such friends or relatives may be able to give it. And, in many cases, the gladness and happiness of these spirit friends causes the spirit to believe that it is in heaven, or at least in a place of great happiness.

But, after this first interview, by reason of the Law of Attraction, the spirit must go to the place where its condition of soul, or its condition of moral growth or intellectual development, fits it for, and there remain until such condition is made better, enabling it to rise to a higher place.

No spirit ever retrogrades after it once gets into the place where it is suited to live in, although it may stand still for a long number of years and never make any progress. But this is a Truth not known to a great many mortals, or spirits either: that the condition of the mortal at the time he becomes a spirit fixes his condition and place of living when he first enters the spirit world. As I have said, after he is put in such place by the Law of Attraction, and when once that place is found and occupied, the spirit never goes to a lower place. It will either stay in that place for a long time, or it will start to progress. But it will ultimately progress in all cases.

(Where do evil spirits go?)

Well, the evil spirits find these places of habitation in the earth planes, which are many and of varied kinds, having many different appearances suited to the conditions of the spirits who will occupy them.

A spirit who is in the lowest of these earth planes is said to be in the lowest hells, as all spirits who are in these planes where they suffer and encounter darkness believe and say that they are in hell. But this is merely a name used for convenience, for the hells are merely places forming a part of the one, great Universe of God.

These hells, as you may imagine, are very numerous, for the conditions

305

of spirits vary greatly. And each spirit has a place in which to live that is fitted to its condition.

As the spirit becomes freed from some of these conditions which, as to them, caused the Law of Attraction to work, he progresses to a higher and better place, and finds that his surroundings are not so dark and painful. And, as this progression continues, such spirit will ultimately find himself in the places of light and comparative happiness where, to a large extent, the evil recollections have left him. The good deeds which he did on earth then come to him and cause a happiness that makes him realize that he was not all bad, and that God has been good to him in relieving him from the sins and evil thoughts which bound him to the place from which he has progressed.

But, after all this, he has not gotten into any of the spheres which are above the earth planes, and he may have to remain in these planes for a great many years before he enters the Second Sphere, which is next in gradation to the earth plane. This latter plane is the most populous of all the spheres, for it has spirits coming to it in great numbers, and in greater numbers than are progressing from it to higher spheres. Hence, it has a greater variety of subplanes than has any of the other spheres, and is filled with a greater variety and kind of spirits than are any of these higher spheres.

When a spirit has remained in the earth planes a sufficient length of time to put him in condition to go to the next higher sphere, he makes his progress and is never prevented from doing so. I do not mean to say that the spirit is compelled to remain in the earth planes any particular number of years before progressing, for this is not true. On the contrary, the number of years that he remains there is determined by his condition of progress. Thus, some spirits may go through these planes in less than a year, and others may remain there many years.

In the Second Sphere appearances are brighter, and many opportunities are afforded the spirit to seek for and obtain happiness that he did not have before. And many spirits find great happiness in pursuing their intellectual studies and things of this kind, and in obtaining a knowledge of the laws of the spirit world governing what you might call the material nature of this world, and also of the earth world.

This sphere is not so well suited for the growth of the soul faculties. Those spirits whose desires and aspirations are for the development of their soul qualities do not stay in this world or sphere very long, for they do not find that the necessary provisions for such development exist. As a consequence, they progress to the Third Sphere where they find wonderful opportunities and surroundings which enable them to progress in these matters of the soul.

Well, I see that you are tired, and I will postpone any further writing on these matters to another time.

So, good night.

JOHN B. COMEYS.

Mrs. Padgett Describes Her Home in the Third Sphere, and Discusses the Importance of Seeking for the Divine Love.
(HELEN PADGETT)
(November 30th, 1914 | Received by James Padgett)

I AM HERE. *Helen.*

I am very happy, for I have so much love of God in my heart that I cannot think of anything that tends to make me unhappy.

(Do you have a nice home?)

Yes, my home is very beautiful and I am perfectly delighted with it. It is made of white marble and is surrounded by lawns and flowers and trees of various kinds. The grass is so very green and the flowers are so beautiful and variegated. The trees are always in foliage and have such beautiful limbs and leaves. I am most pleased with my home—I mean the building. There are many beautiful pictures on the walls, and the walls are all frescoed and hung with fine coverings. And the floors are inlaid with beautiful mosaics. I have all the splendid furniture that I could possibly wish for, and my library is full of books of all kinds—especially those that tell of God and His Love for man. You would be in your element if you could be with me.

I have music such as you never heard on earth, and instruments of various kinds which I am learning to play. And I sing with all my heart and soul as the days go by. I have beds on which I lie down, but I never sleep. We do not need sleep here; we only rest. For sometimes we get tired from our work, and are greatly refreshed by lying on the beds and couches which are so comfortable that we do not realize that we are tired after lying down a little while.

(Do you still like to sing?)

Yes, I do. And, when I sing, I think of you and wish that you could hear me as you did when I was with you in the body. I like "The Song That Reached My Heart." It seems to bring me more in rapport with you than any of the others, although "Sing Me to Sleep" is one that I enjoy to sing very much.

(Do you have food to eat?)

Yes, we eat fruit and nuts but do not do so because we are hungry, but more because we enjoy the flavors so much. And we drink water, pure and sweet, as it makes us feel so refreshed when we are a little tired. Our fruit is not of the earthly kind. It is so much more delightful that I am unable to describe it to you. And the nuts are different also. The water is purer than what you have and is more refreshing.

(Do you have any musical instruments to play like pianos or violins?)

No, our instruments are not like those on earth. They are not stringed instruments, but are played by our thoughts of goodness and love. We do not use fingers or lungs, but merely thoughts; and, if they are pure and loving, our music is very beautiful and not discordant.

(Are you free to leave me any time you wish?)

When you are asleep or doing something in the line of your work, then you do not need me and I am free to leave you. You must not think that I am not free to leave you when I am with you, for I am. I come to you of my own free will, but love compels; and, in that particular, I am not free and don't want to be. Your love is the greatest thing to me in all the world, except God's Love. And without it I would be very unhappy. You do not know how very necessary your loving me is to my happiness, and you must never cease to love me; for, if you do, I will not enjoy my home or the spirit world so much.

(You know that I have always loved you.)

Yes, I know. But I sometimes fear that you may forget to think of me as I want you to.

(Is your home a permanent structure?)

Yes, it is permanent. And the house and trees and flowers are more real to me than were ever the houses and trees and flowers on earth. They are not shadowy, as you may think, but are so very substantial that they never decay or grow old.

(Have you reserved a nice home for me?)

Yes, I have one selected for you now, and will make it so beautiful that you will wonder how it was possible for me to do so. There will be so much love in it that there will be no room for anything that is not in harmony with my love, and you will realize that your own Helen loves you with all the love that a soul can have for its mate.

(Will we always be together?)

Yes, we will be together in every way, and separated only while we are doing some of God's Work. You will be with me in all my thoughts, and I will be with you in your thoughts. Love will keep us through all eternity.

(Will we also have our parents and children to love?)

Yes, we will love our parents and children just as much as on earth, but they will not need our love so much because they will have their own soulmates to love them. We will visit them and be visited by them, and enjoy their society even more than on earth. They will love us very much, but the love that makes two souls one will exist only for the soulmates. God's Love will not interfere with that—I mean our love for God. It is of a kind that is different from our love for each other, and is of a more spiritual and holy nature.

I am so very much pleased to see that you are getting more of His Love in your heart each day, and soon you will do the work that the Master has laid out for you to do.

(Are you also praying to progress?)

Yes, I am going to try to progress into the higher planes, and hope to do so as rapidly as is possible. But you may rest assured that, no matter what plane I may be in, my love for you will not lessen, and I will not cease to be with you as I now am. The life in the higher spheres without you would not be complete, for you are necessary to my complete happiness.

God has decreed that two soulmates are intended to make one complete whole. This must be in order for soulmates to be wholly happy and to fulfill the laws of God's Love, and live together forever as one.

(I have been told that I can begin to progress while still living on earth.)

Yes, I know, because I have asked your grandmother and she has told me. You can progress on earth just as rapidly as I can here if you will let God's Love come into your heart as fully and as abundantly as I do. And you can if you will only pray to the Father. He does not require the child of His Care to be in the spirit world in order to develop his soul. You have the same soul now that you will have when you come here. And if you let God fill it with His Love while you are on earth, why should it not progress as much as it does here? God does not intend to wait until you come over here that He may give you the full enjoyment of His Holy Spirit. It all depends upon you. If you truly and sincerely seek His Love, you will get It on earth just as easily as you can get It after you have shuffled off the body. The Love of God coming into the soul of a man does not depend upon whether he is in the flesh or in the spirit. All souls must answer for the sins done in the body, but it is not necessary that such penalties be paid in the spirit world. You can pay the penalty while on earth. As you sow, so shall you reap, but the reaping is not necessarily here.

If you seek earnestly for God's Grace and Love, you can obtain them on earth; and I am informed that, when they are obtained on earth, the greater will be the progress of the spirit when it comes over. So, let me pray you to seek these blessings while you are in your present life, and not wait for them to be given to you after you have entered the spirit world.

Your grandmother says that she had that experience. When she came here, she entered the Third Sphere without going through a period of expiation or purification in the lower spheres. She is a wonderfully bright and pure spirit, and is very close to God, and has so much of His Love in her soul that her countenance really seems to be an illuminated face. She is in a condition of almost perfect love and peace, though she says that she is striving for a higher plane and a closer At-onement with her Heavenly Father. She is the one who can help you in your spiritual progress more than all others, except Jesus who is the grandest and most glorious spirit in all the heavens.

Let your thoughts be of a pure and holy kind and you will soon realize that God's Love is in your soul to a degree that will make you feel that He is your own near and dear Father. Do not doubt His Love or that He can come to you through the Holy Spirit, for that is His Messenger of Love. And It will never refuse to come into a man's heart and soul when the desire exists to have It come by earnest, sincere prayer or Its inflowing.

Be true to yourself, as I have told you, and you will soon be in God's Love and Favor. Do not let worries or disappointments keep you from seeking His Love and believing that He is waiting to enfold you in His Arms of Mercy and Love, for He is not only waiting but also wants you to call on Him. Do not let the thought that He is afar up in the heavens cause

309

you to think that He is not always near you, anxiously waiting your call.

HE IS NOT WILLING THAT ONE OF HIS CHILDREN SHOULD PERISH. WHEN THEY GO ASTRAY, HIS GREAT HEART OF LOVE YEARNS FOR THEM TO RETURN AND PARTAKE OF HIS BOUNTIES AND BLESSINGS. YOU MUST TRY WITH ALL YOUR HEART TO REALIZE THIS TRUTH, FOR IT IS A TRUTH. AND IT IS THE GREATEST TRUTH TAUGHT TO US BY JESUS WHO IS THE GREATEST OF ALL TEACHERS. MAKE YOUR DAILY LIFE ONE OF PRAYER AND ASPIRATIONS, AND YOU WILL SEE THAT WHAT I HAVE TOLD YOU IS NOT ONLY TRUE BUT THAT YOU CAN ALSO MAKE IT A PART OF YOURSELF. YOU HAVE ONLY TO LET YOUR DESIRES TURN TOWARDS GOD AND HE WILL MEET YOU MORE THAN HALF WAY, FOR HE NEVER SLEEPS OR CLOSES HIS EAR TO THE SUPPLICATIONS OF HIS CHILDREN. AND THOSE WHO HAVE SOUGHT HIM WITH AN EARNEST AND REPENTANT WISH AND LONGING DESIRE OF THE SOUL KNOW THAT HE HAS ALWAYS RESPONDED TO THEIR CALL.

You are now in the Way to obtain these blessings and I pray that you may continue, for you cannot find true happiness in any other way. THIS IS WHAT JESUS MEANT WHEN HE SAID, "I AM THE WAY, THE TRUTH, AND THE LIFE." HE KNEW THAT THERE WAS ONLY ONE WAY TO OBTAIN THE FATHER'S LOVE, AND THAT IS THROUGH THE NEW BIRTH, WHICH IS MERELY THE FLOWING OF THE LOVE OF GOD INTO THE SOUL OF MAN TO THE EXTENT OF ERADICATING ALL DESIRES AND TASTES FOR THINGS WHICH ARE NOT IN HARMONY WITH GOD'S LAWS AND LOVE.

You must give your thoughts more to this vital consideration of the Economy of God's Being.

It is not a question of what church you belong to, or what particular faith you may have, or who your preacher may be, or what duties you owe to the church or to the ceremony of baptism according to the church's dogmas, but whether you have sought God in spirit and in truth and have received His Favor and Love.

This is an individual matter, and no man can be saved by the sufferings or progress of another. Each soul is a complete unit when joined with its mate, and the spiritual condition of each soul towards God determines what its place and happiness will be in the spirit world. So, do not let the thought that it is necessary to believe in a special church dogma, or any ceremony, keep you from seeking the New Birth. This is the fundamental principle that operates in the At-onement of man with God, and all other doctrines are merely secondary and need to be believed only as they may lead to a belief in this foundation.

I am writing at the dictation of your grandmother,[*] for she knows. I, of

_____

[*] In another message, Jesus says, "Mr. Padgett's grandmother is well qualified to write on Divine Truths."—Ed.

course, would not be able to write in this way purely of my own thoughts and experience.

She says that you must try to get in condition so that the Master may write. That which he shall say will show to mankind the everlasting Truths of God's Kingdom and Laws. She is a mere tyro in the knowledge and ability to explain God's Truths that Jesus will teach you. So, try to become more spiritual so that you may learn the wonderful teachings of God's Love and Truth that he will give to you.

You must stop writing now, as you are tired and so am I.

So, love your own true Helen, and pray to God for His Love and your spiritual enlightenment.

HELEN.

Ann Rollins Corroborates Mrs. Padgett's Experience and Tells of the Happiness of Spirits in the Celestial Spheres.
(ANN ROLLINS)
(March 10th, 1915 | Received by James Padgett)

I AM HERE. *Your grandmother.*

Well, I am exceedingly happy and am glad that you are feeling so much improved.

You had quite a long letter from Helen and, I hope, a very satisfactory one. When she tries, she can write a very good letter.

I am, as you know, in the same sphere* with her and your mother. We are all very much together, though we live in different homes. Helen, of course, is not as far advanced as I am, and neither is your mother; but, nevertheless, we are very congenial and love one another very much. Soon, though, I will leave them for a higher sphere, and then they will miss me, I know, for they keep telling me so and say that they will follow soon after. And I believe that they will, for they are wonderful spirits in love and faith; and these two possessions, as you know, are the "open sesame" to higher things and spheres.

Well, my son, as Helen told you of her home, I want to tell you a little bit about the condition of the spirits in this sphere. No spirit who has not received this Great Love of the Father is here; or, better, all spirits who are here have received and possess this Love. Mere intellectual acquirements are not sufficient to fit a spirit for this sphere. And if a spirit ever realized that the gate is shut to him, it is because he has not this Love. Also, the great happiness that exists here could not be enjoyed by the mere mind, for the mind is limited in its capacity for happiness. Only the soul can enjoy this

---

* At the time of this message, Mr. Padgett's grandmother was in a higher plane of the Celestial Sphere referred to.—Ed.

great happiness.

I SOMETIMES THINK THAT IF MORTALS COULD BE PERMITTED TO REALIZE WHAT THIS HAPPINESS IS FOR ONE MOMENT ONLY, THEY WOULD NEVER LET THEIR LIVES SLIP BY WITHOUT MAKING THE GREATEST EFFORTS TO TRY TO FIT THEMSELVES FOR THIS GREAT LIFE IN THE CELESTIAL SPHERES.

Our time here is occupied in helping one another to a greater realization of the Truths of our Father, and in helping spirits who live on lower planes than we do. I do not now come to the earth plane to help other spirits or mortals very often. But, of course, in your case, I am so bound by my affections and desires that I am with you quite often, and more so with that darling little daughter of yours. For, as I have told you, I am her guardian angel and, so long as she lives, I will be with her to help and guide.

We are engaged in the study of things that pertain more to the spiritual things of this life than to studying the things of the other worlds of the universe. To us, these things are what might be called the material things. And while a knowledge of them would be very interesting, yet, our thoughts are turned to the more important Truths of God.

(Do you all have separate homes with libraries?)

Yes, we all have our libraries and homes, as Helen has told you of. But, of course, there is a great difference in these homes, depending upon the amount of Love which the spirit has in his soul. I am now living in a home that is so beautiful that I could not describe it to you in the short time that I will write tonight. But soon I will in detail, and then you can realize what a home it is.

(In a book I am now reading, allegedly dictated by spirits, some of the information given is different from yours.)

Well, do not believe everything in the book you have been reading because it is said to be written by spirits. Even if it is so written, the information given depends upon the condition and knowledge and belief of these spirits. Some may tell the exact truth as they conceive it to be, and yet it may not be the Truth.

(I wonder why this book makes no mention of the Master's teachings of the Divine Love.)

Well, the explanation is that the spirits whose communications you read have never learned the Truth taught by the Master. They only know what they have learned from what they have read, or from what spirits who have not this great knowledge have told them. Any spirit who says that Jesus is not the great spirit and teacher, and the only one of the great teachers who has ever lived on earth who shows the only and true Way to the Father's Kingdom, has never learned this Way or come under the influence of the Master. So far as that is concerned, do not pay any attention to what they say or let their communications influence you, for these communications will not help you spiritually.

There are certain great assembly places in the spirit world where the higher spirits meet and discuss the various plans that they think will benefit mankind, and also the lower spirits. And I believe the Master has attended these meetings and given his advice and encouragement. For you must remember that he is a teacher, not only of the Way to God's Kingdom but also of the acquiring of those things that will help and benefit mortals and spirits who have not received this Great Love.

Part of his mission is to make man and spirits happy, even though they may never become inhabitants of the Celestial Spheres. God loves all His creatures. And the Master, as His greatest instrument of love and beneficence, is doing all that he can to make these men and spirits happy; and, as some of these communications say, he has helped in many of these assemblies to do good for all. But, while this is so, yet, he is also the Father's greatest instrument in showing men the Way to the higher life.

(Concerning others of the world's great religious teachers of the past, why would some of them not have come to accept the Master's teachings by now?)

Well, that is a question that seems hard to answer. But if these other great teachers will not believe the Master's message as to the only Way to the Kingdom, they alone know why and will have to bear the consequences.

All spirits are not able to see these great Truths any more than mortals are. And the mere fact that they have so much greater opportunities to learn these Truths does not seem to persuade them to accept the same.

The higher spheres in which these ancient seers and wise men live are not the Celestial Heavens, but spheres higher up in the spirit world. And no matter how high they may get in these spheres, they will never partake of that Divine Essence or Nature of the Father, which we have told you of, unless they seek for and obtain the Divine Love to qualify them to enter the Celestial Heavens. They will always be nothing more than spirits possessed of the natural love which they had on earth, but, of course, more refined and free from sin. Yet, it is merely natural love and nothing more.

(Have you met any of the Master's disciples?)

Yes, I have met Paul and Peter and John and James and several others of lesser development.

(Are they all living in the Celestial Spheres?)

Yes, they are all in the Celestial Spheres and very happy; yet they go to the lower spheres to do the work set before them.

(One spirit I have read about, who makes no mention of the Divine Love, claims to have visited the home of John, the Apostle.)

No spirit who has not received this New Birth is ever permitted to enter the Celestial Spheres; and, hence, the spirit that you speak of has never seen the home of John, and never will until redeemed by the Love of the Father.

(What about mortals who claim they have visited the highest heavens through soul travel?)

I do not think these mortals who claim that they have left their bodies and entered the Celestial Spheres ever did so, and I have grave doubts that they ever entered the Spiritual Spheres above the Third.

This is a subject that I will write you more fully about some other time. I must stop now, and you must not write more tonight.

So, with all my love, I am

Your own loving,

GRANDMOTHER.

Ann Rollins Gives Her Description of Some of the Spirit Spheres. She Also Criticizes a Book That Mr. Padgett Was Reading.
(ANN ROLLINS)
(December 22nd, 1915 | Received by James Padgett)

I AM HERE. *Grandmother.*

I come because I see that you have been much interested in the description of the various spheres of the spirit world as contained in the book that you have just been reading.

Well, my son, I have read the book as you did, and I must say that I have grave doubts that any mortal ever had the experience of the doctor, as is related in that book. Of course, I will not positively say that he did not leave his body and visit some of the spheres of the spirit world, and attempt to give a description of what he saw. But I do not think it was possible for him to visit any sphere which is higher than his soul development would enable him to enter. And, as I am informed, not being a man with the soul development that would fit him for the higher soul spheres, I do not understand how he could possibly have entered a sphere higher than the Sixth; and I doubt that he entered that. For, from all the information that I have received, I have never heard of any mortal entering a sphere higher than the Third, which Paul says that he visited.

At any rate, the descriptions of the higher spheres as contained in the book—and I mean by this the spheres above the Third—are not correct in many particulars. For, as I have told you before, the Fifth and Seventh Spheres are not intellectual spheres in the preeminent sense. And there are not the great colleges and institutions of learning in them that the book refers to. Neither are the inhabitants engaged in any special study of the laws of nature with the mere intellect. For, in these spheres, the great studies and aspiration of the spirits are given to the development of the soul by obtaining the Divine Love. And to help in the work are teachers who devote themselves to instructing these spirits in those things which will lead to this soul development.

The mind of mere intellect is not given much attention, but is subordinated to the soul development. For, with this development, and as a part of it, comes a wonderful development of the faculties of what you might call the mind, but which we call, and which really are, the soul perceptions. I know it is hard for you to understand. But what we call the

314

soul perceptions may be compared to the mental faculties, as you commonly speak of them. In fact, the latter forms no part of the former, but are entirely distinct and of a different order and composition from these mental faculties. These soul perceptions, as such, cannot be cultivated or made to increase in their powers or qualities by mere study. But they and their progress are entirely dependent upon, and not separated from, the development of the soul in Love. I mean the Divine Love of the Father. In other words, unless there be a development of the soul by this Divine Love, there will be no development of the soul perceptions.

It is difficult to explain this to you, but you may possibly get some idea from what I have said.

The Sixth Sphere, as I have said before, is the great intellectual sphere, and in this are wonderful colleges and institutions of learning. Many spirits who were great men intellectually on earth are teachers in these institutions.

But you must not think that, because certain spheres are preeminently intellectual, there are not teachers of the higher Truth (pertaining to the soul and to the Divine Love) working in these spheres, for there are. And many great spirits of the Celestial Spheres are engaged in this teaching. But this I must say: that the work is more difficult, and the effort to convince these spirits of highly developed intellectuality and knowledge is more strenuous, than in any of the lower spheres. These bright-minded spirits seem to think that the mind is the great thing to be cultivated and looked after. And while they worship God in a way, yet, it is merely with the faculties of their minds. They do not think that there is any truth in the teachings of the New Birth and the Divine Love of the Father in contradistinction to the love which they possess, which is only the natural love.

I have been in these spheres and have worked in them, and what I tell you I know from actual experience.

(The doctor claims that there are no actual homes as such in the Seventh Sphere, and that its inhabitants appear to be naked or nearly so.)

Well, he is mistaken. For, in the Seventh Sphere, the spirits have homes just as they do in the lower spheres; only they are much more beautiful and bring more happiness and gladness because of the great number of additional things that are provided by the Father to increase the happiness of His children.

As to our clothing in that sphere, we are clothed in what you would say a modest and comfortable way. Our clothing is not so flimsy as to permit our forms to be seen, as if we had no clothing at all. This idea must have arisen from the fact that the inhabitants of that sphere have no thought of immodesty or what might result from the suggestions that a naked or half-clothed body might give to mortals, or even some of the lower spirits. But such an idea does not enter into the question of the nature of the clothes that we shall wear.

Our thoughts are all pure and free from mortal taint, and the character of our thoughts has no influence upon the character of our clothing. We wear clothes to cover our bodies because we think it proper to do so, and because we make our clothes by our own thoughts and will; and they are of the most glorious and shining appearances that you can imagine.

But, as all things in nature have a covering, so, in the spirit world, the spirits all have coverings. And this is even so in the Celestial Sphere in which I live. I have never seen such a thing as a naked or nearly naked spirit in these higher spheres.

Of course, the spirit of Dr.____ may have entered some of these higher spheres, as I have said. But his information, as the author of the book that was communicated to his mortal friend, was not correctly transmitted. For many things which he says are not true.

I would like to write more tonight, but it is late and you are tired.

With all my love, I will say good night.

Your own loving grandmother,

ANN ROLLINS.

Ann Rollins Describes Her Home in the Second Celestial Sphere.
(ANN ROLLINS)
(April 27th, 1915 | Received by James Padgett)

I AM HERE. *Your grandmother.*

Well, my darling son, I am so happy to be with you and tell you that I am now in the Second Celestial Sphere where everything is so beautiful, and happiness exists to a degree that I cannot portray to you. I am in my own home and I can scarcely describe what it is, for you have no words which are adequate to give you an idea of what I may mean in attempting to describe the glories of this sphere.

My home is of a material that you have no faint counterpart of on earth, and it is furnished with everything that is suited to make me happy and more thankful to the Father for His Love and Kindness.

I am living all alone, but I have many visitors; and Love is the ruling sentiment among all its inhabitants. No spirit who is not filled with this Divine Love of which I have so often told you can possibly live in this sphere. The spirit who has all the most wonderful intellectual acquirements and is without this Love cannot enter this sphere. Nor can the mere natural love of mortals or of spirits fit the spirit for inhabitancy here. Only the Divine Love of the Father can make a spirit so at-one with all the surroundings and atmosphere of Love that exists here.

When I left the First Celestial Sphere, I was taken in charge by a most beautiful and glorified spirit, and carried from my home in the First Celestial Sphere up to the entrance of the Second Celestial Sphere where many other beautiful spirits were waiting to give me welcome. And I never thought that such a welcome could be extended to a spirit who is progressing. But I was received with all the love and affection and evidence of joy that the spirits of this sphere have for a spirit who has progressed from the lower one. Oh, I tell you that my happiness was certainly beyond any conception of what I had in the home which I had just left!

I thought that the beauty and grandeur of the First Celestial Sphere could not possibly be surpassed, but when I tell you that comparison cannot be made between the beauty of the two places, it is the best that I can do.

My home was all ready for me, and I was carried to it by a whole host of spirits and told that it was for me, and that God had prepared it for my happiness and joy. It certainly is beyond description, and it would be useless for me to try to describe it.

The spirits here are so much more beautiful than those of any other sphere. They are more ethereal and their garments are all shining and white, and not one little speck reminds one of the earth or of the grosser spheres of the spirit world.

And the music here is entirely Divine and of such a great variety—all telling of the great Love of God, and sung in His praise and adoration. I have not yet seen all the beauties of this sphere, and I may later give you a more complete description of it.

(Have you found any spirits there whom you were acquainted with on earth?)

Yes, I met some spirits whom I knew on earth, but not many. I have also met some of the truly Christian men and women who lived and loved and worshiped God, and who passed over long before I did.

My own dear mother and father have progressed to this sphere, and they were ready to receive me. And how glad they were to welcome me and take me to their arms of love!

Well, I must not write more tonight, as you are not in condition for extended writing.

So, with all my love, which is so much greater than when I last wrote you, I am

Your own true and loving grandmother,

ANN ROLLINS.

Ann Rollins Describes Her Experiences in the Second Celestial Sphere.
She States That She Can Never Die Again, and That She Has Passed Beyond the "Second Death."
(ANN ROLLINS)
(April 27th, 1915 | Received by James Padgett)

I AM HERE. *Your grandmother.*

I want to tell you tonight of my experience in my new home among the redeemed spirits who have entered this Kingdom.

I am living in the Second Celestial Sphere, as I told you, and am surrounded by everything that makes me happy and in unison with the Father. I am also in close attachment with the Master, although he lives in a much higher sphere in the Celestial Heavens, and which, he tells me, is close to the Fountainhead of God's Love.

I have with me a great number of spirits who have received the Great Love of the Father in great abundance, and who are so good and beautiful that they are as of the Father. And here I must tell you that all angels in His Kingdom, which is ruled over by Jesus, are the spirits of mortals who once lived on earth, and not what the Old Testament refers to as angels. I am informed that there are beings who never had the experience of living in the flesh. I have never seen any of these angels, and I don't know where they live; but Jesus says they are a distinct class of God's Creation, and are separated from the heavens that he rules in. I have often wished to see some of these angels, but it does not appear that they ever come to our Celestial Heavens.

So, when you hear us speak of angels, we mean only those who were mortals, and who have been redeemed by the Love of the Father, and who are living in the higher spheres of our own Celestial Heavens.

Of course, I don't know whether these other angels will ever know anything about our Heavens or not. But, if they ever should, I doubt that they will ever realize the full meaning of a soul redeemed, because only those who have gone through the experience of living in the flesh, having had all the sorrows of mortals and the redemption from their condition of sin and error by the Love of the Father, can ever fully understand what redemption means.

So, I believe that no angel without this experience can ever enjoy the happiness that we, who have become inhabitants of Christ's Kingdom, enjoy. I may be mistaken in this, but this is my belief.

All ministering angels are spirits who once inhabited the physical body. Only such, it seems to me, can have that sympathy and love which fits them to understand and be able to sympathize with the sufferings of humanity. Why, if you will think for a moment, you will remember that even Jesus was not fitted to perform his great mission, and to declare the Love of the Father, until he had entered into the physical body so that he could understand fully all the frailties and sufferings and longings of mortals.

At any rate, no angel that comes to mortals to minister is other than the spirit of one who has passed through these suffering and sins of the mortal.

Well, as I have said, I am surrounded by many of these beautiful redeemed spirits, and they are all happy beyond conception by you who live on earth.

I am in a state of perfect happiness myself, and want for nothing that is necessary to make me realize that God is my Father of Love and Mercy. Yet, I desire the progression that will take me to the higher spheres—not on account of any discontent on my part, but because I am told that there are homes awaiting me and my companions in these higher spheres that are so much more beautiful than those which we now have. And, besides, the Law of Progression is constantly working here, and never are we permitted to cease our longing for the higher life and the greater abundance of the Divine Love that our Father promises us will be ours if we desire and seek for It. But you must never forget that, while we strive to progress, we are never dissatisfied with what our Father has provided for us, and what we possess.

My home here is a part of the Celestial Kingdom, and we who live in this sphere are all immortal in the sense that that word has been explained to you. We are greater in our attributes and qualities than were the first parents at the time of their creation. We can never die again, and have passed beyond the "second death," as it is written. For our Love is now so abundant that we are all partakers of the Father's Divinity to such an extent that It can never be taken from us—no, not in all eternity.

And, yet, with all this knowledge and consolation that it brings to us, we still have our love for those living on earth who have not yet acquired this Great Gift of the Father. And our work in trying to help mortals is a joy to us and never anything but a labor of love.

I will not tell you how much our interest centers in the work that the Master is doing for the salvation of mankind at this time, but will only say that his love for man and his desire for their redemption are greater than they were when he was on earth. And all his followers—all who are in the Celestial Heavens as well as those who are in the spirit spheres—are working in unison with him to accomplish this great work to its fullest extent.

Many mortals are inspired by him and by his spirit followers to assist in this work, and to make known to mankind the Truths of his teachings and the wonderful Love of the Father which passeth all understanding.

So, while the dogmas and teachings of many of the churches are not in accord with the Truth, yet, the teachings of the spiritual Truths of Christ's mission, and of the Gifts of the Father, are now being bestowed upon mankind. And they are the causes of many a soul being turned to God's Love and thereby securing their own salvation.

False beliefs and false doctrines, as taught in most of the churches, do much harm, retard the soul's progress, and keep many souls from the Light while on earth as well as in the spirit world. Yet, with all these false teachings are mingled some Truths of the soul's qualities for progress, and of the Way in which it may find the entrance of God's Love into the soul and into His Kingdom.

I know that many men die with these false beliefs and retain them for a more or less longer time after they become spirits. Yet, the fact that they have the faith in God's Love and in Jesus' teachings as a part of their beliefs will help them to grasp the real Truth, and to progress more rapidly after they have gotten rid of these false beliefs.

So, while you must pity the followers of most of these orthodox churches because they are living in the security, as they think, of these false ideas, yet, you would not be justified in attempting to do anything to abolish these churches in toto, because there is nothing to supply their places. The Truths which they teach would be destroyed, and there would be nothing left to serve the soul's interests.

BUT I TELL YOU THAT THE TIME IS COMING WHEN THE CHURCHES WILL TEACH THE REAL TRUTHS OF GOD'S LOVE AND OF JESUS' MISSION, AND THE WAY TO MAN'S SALVATION. THEN, HUMANITY WILL BE HAPPIER, AND THE KINGDOM OF HEAVEN WILL EXIST ON EARTH AS IT DOES IN OUR CELESTIAL HEAVENS. THE TIME IS NOW RIPE FOR THESE CHURCHES TO RECEIVE THESE TRUTHS, AND MEN'S LONGINGS FOR LIGHT AND HAPPINESS WILL DEMAND THAT THE TRUE GOSPEL BE PREACHED, AND IT WILL BE.

So, my dear son, you see the necessity for providing the means by which these Truths may be conveyed to mortals. The Bible is losing its hold on many—not only the students but the common people as well—and the Truths which were intended that that book should contain must be brought to the knowledge and consciousness of men and women.

For many years, the powers of the spirit world have been making efforts to have these Truths communicated to men, but with very indifferent success. Now, I believe that I can see before me, as a vision, that many good men and women will develop their psychic powers to such an extent that they can be used as mediums of communication. And they will be so honest and earnest in their work that men will believe the communications and learn the real Truths that the Master is striving to teach.

I must stop now, as I have written a long time and you must rest awhile before you continue to write.

Your loving grandmother,

ANN ROLLINS.

Samuel Conveys a Description of the Celestial Heavens.
(SAMUEL, THE PROPHET)
(August 17th, 1915 | Received by James Padgett)

I AM HERE. *Samuel, the prophet.*

I am the prophet who came to you before and wrote. Tonight, I want to tell you of the wonderful things which God has prepared for His redeemed children in the Celestial Spheres, where only those who have received the New Birth can enter.

In these spheres are homes made of the most beautiful materials that can be imagined, and which are of a real and permanent character, and not subject to decay or deterioration of any kind. They are not made with hands, but by the soul's development and the Love which each spirit possesses.

These homes are furnished with everything that is suited to make the inhabitants happy and contented, and not one element of inharmony has any abiding place therein. Every home has its library and the most beautiful furniture and paintings and wall coverings, and also rooms that are devoted to the various uses that a spirit may need them for. The music is sublime beyond conception, and there are all kinds of musical instruments which the spirits know how to play. And, as you may not suppose, every spirit has the ability to sing. There are no voices that are out of tune with the surrounding and with other voices. Every spirit has music in his soul, and every spirit has the vocal qualities to express that music.

Couches for repose are provided, and running fountains and beautiful flowers of every hue and variety, and lawns the most beautiful and green. Trees are in abundance, and are planted in the most artistic manner so that they are in harmony with the surrounding landscape.

And the Light that comes to our homes is of such a kind that I cannot describe It. I can only say that with It and in It are the most soothing and wonderful influences that spirits can conceive of.

All these things and many more are provided by our Loving Father for the happiness of His children. But above all is this: the wonderful state of happiness and peace and joy.

ALL THESE THINGS ARE FREELY GIVEN TO US, AND, WITH THEM, THE KNOWLEDGE THAT WE ARE A PART OF THE FATHER'S DIVINE BEING, AND HAVE, BEYOND THE POSSIBILITY OF LOSING IT, THE IMMORTALITY WHICH JESUS BROUGHT TO LIGHT WHEN HE CAME TO EARTH.

I HAVE BEEN IN THESE HEAVENS MANY YEARS AND KNOW WHEREOF I SPEAK. AND WHEN I TELL YOU OF THESE THINGS, I DO SO THAT YOU AND ALL MANKIND MAY KNOW THAT THESE DELIGHTS MAY BE YOURS AND THEIRS IF YOU WILL ONLY LET THE DIVINE LOVE OF THE FATHER ENTER YOUR SOULS AND TAKE COMPLETE POSSESSION OF THEM.

(What kind of social life do you have?)

Well, as to our social enjoyments, we are so loving, one to the other, that nothing arises, as on earth, to cause the slightest jar in our wonderful harmony. We visit one another and give our experiences of the Love life that we lead. We also have music and interchange thoughts about our continuous progress and our work in the spirit world. Every spirit in our sphere may visit every other spirit and know that the door is always open and a warm welcome awaiting him.

I cannot tell you of all these wonders because there are no words that will convey our meanings. Your capacity to understand is limited by your mental boundaries, and, hence, I am at a disadvantage. But this I can tell you: that, someday, if you get the Divine Love in your soul in sufficient abundance, you will see and understand for yourselves what God has in store for you. It was truly said that "NO EYE HAS SEEN, OR MIND CONCEIVED, THE WONDERFUL THINGS THAT AWAIT THE TRUE CHILD OF THE FATHER."

No, there are no streets or gold or walls of jasper, or any of these material things that John made use of in his Apocalypse to describe the City of God. They were merely used as symbols, but they did not express the wonders of our homes.

I will not write more tonight, but will come again sometime and tell you of things that are of more importance than a description of our homes. With all my love, I am

Your brother in Christ,
SAMUEL.

II. Individual Progression.

MESSAGES INCLUDED IN THIS CHAPTER.

Mrs. Padgett Tells of Her Experience in Leaving Her Physical Body and Going to the Spirit World. (HELEN PADGETT)................................325

A Mother Tells of Her Experience After Passing Over. She Died While Giving Birth to Her Baby. (GRACE STANHOPE) 327

Dr. Leslie R. Stone's Father States That He Is Making Earnest Effort to Reach His Wife's Home, and to Be With Her Through Prayer to the Father for His Love. (WILLIAM STONE)..328

Dr. Leslie R. Stone's Sister, Kate, Explains What Her Work Is in the Spirit World, and Informs Her Brother That His Efforts to Help the Spirits Turn to the Father for His Love Are Having Positive Results. (KATE STONE)..329

A Spirit Describes His Experience After Writing Through Mr. Padgett. He States That He Obtained the Divine Love and Made His Progress into the Third Sphere. (A. G. RIDDLE) 330

G.R. Enlarges Upon His Spiritual Progress and Acquired Knowledge. (A. G. RIDDLE)..333

Mrs. Padgett Relates Her Experience in Trying to Show a Spirit the Way to God's Love. (HELEN PADGETT)..336

Mr. Padgett Receives a Message from a Spirit Who Believed in the Creeds, but Who Awakened to the Truth After He Met Jesus. (SAMUEL B SOUTHARD) 337

A Spirit Gives His Experience, and How His Old Beliefs in the Creeds Retarded His Progress. He Affirms That Mr. Padgett Was Selected by Jesus to Receive the Messages. (G. H. _____)..338

Help Is Given to a Clergyman of the Orthodox Church. (W _____)...340

An Orthodox Minister Relates His Experiences After He Passed into the Spirit World. (F _____)..342

Saleeba, an Ancient Spirit of the Sixth Sphere, Requests Mr. Padgett's Assistance Concerning How to Obtain God's Divine Love.

(SALEEBA) *346*

Saleeba Describes Her Progress in Obtaining the Divine Love. (SALEEBA) *349*

Saleeba Declares That She Is Progressing and Soon Will Be Above the Third Sphere. She Also States That She Now Knows That Jesus Is the True Leader of All the Spirits Who Have the Divine Love. (SALEEBA) *350*

Saleeba Tells of Her Happiness and of Her Intention to Share What She Has Found with Her People. (SALEEBA) *351*

Saleeba Continues to Share Her Happiness with Mr. Padgett. (SALEEBA) *352*

Solomon Tells of His Position in the Celestial Spheres. (SOLOMON OF THE OLD TESTAMENT) *352*

Mrs. Padgett Explains That the Soul's Development Determines the Appearance of a Spirit, Not the Racial Characteristics of the Earth Life. (HELEN PADGETT) *353*

Samuel, the Prophet, Discusses His Experience in the Spirit Heavens and His Progress to the Celestial Kingdom. (SAMUEL OF THE OLD TESATMENT) *354*

Aaron, the Brother of Moses, Gives His Experience, and What He Now Knows About Immortality Since Jesus Came and Taught How It Can Be Obtained. (AARON) *356*

Sarah Declares That She Is Now a Christian. (SARAH, THE WIFE OF ABRAHAM) *358*

Hugh Latimer Explains That the Manner of a Man's Death Does Not Determine Which Sphere He Is to Enter in the Spirit World; Only the Manner of His Living and the Development of His Soul Qualities Determine This. (HUGH LATIMER) *359*

George Whitefield Relates That He Changed His Erroneous Beliefs That He Taught on Earth, and That He Is Now in the Celestial Heavens. (GEORGE WHITEFIELD) *360*

II. Individual Progression.

*Mrs. Padgett Tells of Her Experience in Leaving Her Physical Body
and Going to the Spirit World.*
(HELEN PADGETT)
(December 9th, 1914 | Received by James Padgett)

I AM HERE. *Helen.*

I am so very happy, as you are loving me very much tonight. I can see that your thoughts are with me so much more than of late, so let me continue to feel that you love me so much.

When I realized that the time had come for me to go, I did not fear to do so, but calmly waited and thought that all my sufferings would soon end. When my spirit left the body, I commenced to feel as if I were rising out of it, and that I was going upward to the place that I had so often heard my father speak about. But I had scarcely awakened to the fact that my spirit had left the body when your mother had me in her arms and was trying to tell me that I had nothing to fear or cause me to feel that I was not with those who loved me. She was so beautiful that I hardly realized that it was she. And, when I commenced to see that I was no longer in my body, I asked her not to leave me but to take me with her to where she lived. She told me that I could not go there but that God had prepared a place for me to go to, and that she would accompany me and show me the truth of my future existence. I went with her and she took me to a place that was very beautiful and filled with spirits who had recently passed over. She did not leave me for a long time, and, when she did, your father came to me and said, "I am Ned's father, and I want to help you to realize that you are now in the spirit world. You must not let the thoughts of the earth keep you from getting in a condition to learn that all of us are only waiting for the Love of God to help us to higher and better things."

Your grandmother soon came to me and told me who she was. She was so beautiful and bright that I scarcely could look at her, for her face was all aglow with what seemed to me to be a heavenly light; and her voice was so sweet and musical that I thought she must be one of God's angels that I had read about in the Bible. She told me of the things that God had prepared for me, and that He wanted me to love Him and feel that He loved me.

But, after awhile, I commenced to think that I must be deceived in my sight and hearing, and was still on earth and needed only my body again to know that I was still a mortal. Some time elapsed before I really became conscious that I was a spirit and was not on earth. For when I tried to talk to you, as I did, you would not listen to me and turned away from me as if you did not see or hear me. After a short time, your mother and father came to me again and tried to persuade me that I must not continue in my belief that I was still of the earth, but must believe that I was in spirit life and needed only the things of the spirit to make me more contented.

So, you see, I was so very fortunate in having your dear parents and grandmother welcome me when I passed over. If they had not received me, I do not know to what condition of fear and distraction I might have been subjected. No spirit can learn the truth of the change unless helped by others in some way.

So, you see, when you come over, I will be there to receive you and love you so much that you will never have to go through the period of doubt that I did. Your father is also waiting to receive you. And, in fact, all your spirit band have agreed that, when you come, you will have nothing to fear for want of help and love.

I first saw my parents after I commenced to believe that I was in the spirit world. And, when I saw them, they did not know me, but thought that I was still in the body and that they were still on earth, as they had not yet awakened to the fact that they were in the spirit world. They were very unhappy, and it took considerable talking to make them believe that they were spirits and not mortals. My father was more easily convinced than was my mother, for he commenced to recall sooner that, when death comes, the spirit must go to God Who gave it. My mother would not believe so soon, for she continued to think that she was with her acquaintances of earth, and that they were not treating her very courteously; for, when she spoke to them, they would not answer. But, thank God, they both now realize that they are in the spirit world, and that they must learn to love God if they would be happy.

When I commenced to leave the body, there was no pain or suffering— only a feeling that I was rising out of it. No darkness appeared to me, and I saw my body lying there as if it were asleep. I did not try to hold it, but thought that it was merely taking a rest, and that, as soon as it felt refreshed, I would enter it again and continue to lie as before. I did not wait for it to awaken, but continued to arise until, as I told you, your mother clasped me in her arms. She was my own dear mother as well as yours.

I did not know that I was dying, but felt that something unusual was happening; and I was not afraid. As I always dreaded death in life, as you know, the strange thing to me was that I did not look upon death as dying. It was only a pleasant dreamy feeling, and I only thought that I was going to become absent from my body until it was refreshed. My thoughts were not of death at all. I had been suffering pain, but I thought that I was getting well, and that the feeling of relief that came over me was the result of my getting better.

As my spirit arose, I thought only of my condition and how soon I would be able to return home and see my friends. No other thoughts came to me—not even my love for God, or the fact that I was not in condition to meet my Maker as regards my soul, as I had been taught. There was absolutely no fear of what might happen to me, or that I would soon be called upon to account for the sins I had committed. Just before my spirit left my body, I was unconscious. But, just as soon as the separation commenced, I became fully conscious and knew everything that took place, and did not feel at all as if I were in danger or needed the help of anyone.

I did not stay with my body at all when I commenced to leave it, but continued to rise, as I have told you, until your mother met me. So, you see, death, which I so much feared, was not such a dreadful thing to experience.

(Did you see our son at that time?)

Yes, when my son came to where my body lay, I returned to it and saw it taken away and afterwards buried. But I still did not understand what it all meant. Only when your grandmother told me that I would no more inhabit it did I commence to realize that I had left it forever. But, even then, I had some feeling that she was mistaken, and that, in some way, I would return to it again and continue to live on earth.

(But did you not meet other spirits?)

Yes, when I had been in the spirit world a short time, I saw other spirit forms and, even then, I was not in a condition of mind to fully understand that they were spirits and not mortals. The resemblance is very real to one who has never had his spiritual eyes opened. And even though the spirit forms all appear much more beautiful and bright, yet, to me, they all seemed to be human forms; and I thought that I was not in condition to fully see just what they were. You must let me stop now, for I am tired.

Your own true and loving,

HELEN.

A Mother Tells of Her Experience After Passing Over. She Died While Giving Birth to Her Baby.
(GRACE STANHOPE)
(December 21st, 1917 | Received by James Padgett)

I AM HERE. *Grace Stanhope.*

Come to the bridal chamber, death! Come to the young mother when she feels her newborn's breath for the first time. So death came to me when I was but a young bride and lived in expectation of a new, loving being that would be a part of my flesh—yet I died when my baby came. As life came to it, death came to me; and we missed each other at the very moment that I heard its first cry.

When I came to life in the spirit world, I was bitter and thought God to be so heartless and cruel to take me from my baby. I was so unhappy and wanted to die over again.

I would like to tell you of my misery and gloom and hatred of my very God Whom I had believed in and thought that I loved, but I cannot now. But this I must say: that my unhappiness was for a short time only. For bright spirits came to me and comforted me, and assured me that I was not separated from my baby but could go to my baby and watch over him and give him my mother's love. And so I did, and am now doing; for my baby is now a man, and still I am with him! And I know that I have been a greater blessing to him as his spirit mother than I would have been had I remained his mortal mother.

I write this to comfort mothers who have to leave their babies as they come into the earth life, and to assure them that, though they disappear from the visions of their loved ones, yet, they can always be with them—close, and in deep rapport with them in love.

Death comes as an enemy, but, when recognized, only a friend appears. Mothers, thank God for such a death and the great consolation it brings to the departing, and to those left behind.

Good-bye,

GRACE STANHOPE.

Dr. Leslie R. Stone's Father States That He Is Making Earnest Effort to Reach His Wife's Home, and to Be With Her Through Prayer to the Father for His Love.
(WILLIAM STONE)
(November 23rd, 1915 | Received by James Padgett)

I AM HERE. *William Stone.*

I am the father of that boy, and I want to say to him that I am happy, too, as well as his mother, but not as happy as she is. I am not in her high sphere, but am striving to get there and enjoy her home. Leslie, my son, I am also happy that you are trying to follow the steps of the Master in your love for the Father and in your soul aspirations.

Believe in this Truth and you will not be disappointed. When the great day of reunion comes, you will find more love waiting for you than you ever thought possible for a spirit to receive. So, trust in God and follow the teachings of the Master. I know the importance of this as one who was ignorant of these teachings on earth, and who has learned them only since coming to the spirit world.

I bless that dear mother of yours. If it had not been for her teachings after she came over, I would probably be an easy-going spirit, as I was a man, enjoying the happiness which my good nature and love of things generally gave me. But when she came and told me how much she loved me, and I saw she had a Love which I did not have but had to get in order to be with her, I sought for the kind of Love she had. And, with her help and that of the Holy Spirit, I obtained this Love. I am now very happy, for it is this Love alone which may make it possible for me to be with her where she is.

But I am not yet with her, as her soul condition is above mine. Consequently, I am not yet able to share her home. She is so beautiful and good that I am not content to live away from her. And I am trying with all my soul's desires to be together with her through prayer to the Father for this Divine Love—the one possession that can make me worthy of her.

So, Leslie, believe what we say! Trust in God and you will be happy.

Your loving father,

WILLIAM STONE.

Dr. Leslie R. Stone's Sister, Kate, Explains What Her Work Is in the Spirit World, and Informs Her Brother That His Efforts to Help the Spirits Turn to the Father for His Love Are Having Positive Results.
(KATE STONE)
(June 19,1917 | Received by James Padgett)

I AM HERE. *Kate Stone.*

Tell my brother that what he heard a few nights ago in reference to me is true, and that I am engaged with my whole heart and soul in the work of helping the dark and suffering spirits. When I succeed in turning some towards the light and the Father's Love, a happiness comes to me that I cannot describe. The fact of being an instrument in the redemption of one lost soul affords a greater happiness than any mortal can dream of. And, when I tell my brother that I have succeeded in showing the Way to many of these spirits, he may perhaps realize what my happiness is in a small way.

To me, the work is one of the greatest that we spirits can possibly engage in, and I never get tired or disheartened. And even though I sometimes fail to convince a spirit as to the Way to Light and relief from his suffering, yet, I never feel disappointed; for I know that sooner or later that spirit will perceive the meaning of my words and they will have their effect.

But not only can I see the result of my own work but also that of you three mortals,* for you all help these dark spirits by your talks with them. And my brother must not think that, just because he cannot write and thus be certain that the spirts are listening to him, he cannot perform this task; for I must tell him that he can and does. When he talks to them, they give him their attention and believe him. And many take his advice and seek the Father's Love through the only Way It can be obtained: through earnest prayer. He will know someday what the results of his efforts are. And, when he does, he will thank the Father that he was given this gift. Tell him to continue. Even though he cannot hear their responses, I will come at times to inform him of this result: A soul in darkness and torment has been rescued by a mortal who knows the Truth. A crown of one star, representing salvation of a soul, is a glorious possession. But a crown of many stars bestowed, for the saving of many souls, is a treasure beyond description!

This crown will be his. But while it will not be one to be worn, yet, it will be a crown set in the joyous countenances of spirits relieved of their sufferings and radiant in the Glory of the Father's Love.

I will stop now, as Helen says you are tired and must not write more tonight. With my love, I will say good night to you and Leslie.

Your sister in Christ,

KATE.

A Spirit Describes His Experience After Writing Through Mr. Padgett. He States That He Obtained the Divine Love and Made His Progress
into the Third Sphere.
(A. G. RIDDLE)
(January 20th, 1915 | Received by James Padgett)

I AM HERE. *Your old friend A. G. Riddle*

Yes, it is I, and I am glad to be able to write to you again. I told your wife that I desired to write and tell you of my progress in spiritual matters, and, as you are kind enough to give me the opportunity, I will try to tell you how my eyes were opened to the things of the spirit and my heart to the Love of God.

Well, as you know, when I first commenced to write to you, I did not exactly believe in a God or Jesus or his teachings, except as they related to the moral condition of men. When you first commenced to talk to me about these spiritual things, I thought that you were merely telling me the things that you had learned in your church or Sunday school, and that they were only intended for men who were only suited to receive what the preachers might tell them. So, you see, I was not in a very receptive condition of mind to enable me to believe that what you told me had any foundation in fact or in truth. Jesus, to me, was just the same as any other man who had received large conceptions of the truth. But he was only a mere man in the sense that, what he attempted to teach, he had learned by study and meditation, or through some worldly source that I did not know of. At any rate, I believed that his teachings were not the result of inspiration, or derived from a source any different from what mankind received of other information as to things of nature or of spirit. Well, as you continued to tell me that I was mistaken, and that there is a Source other than the mere mind or conscience of man from which all Good flows, I began to think about the matter. And when I looked around me and saw that your mother and wife, who claimed that they had received this Love of God which you insisted was waiting for me to obtain, were so beautiful and happy, while I and my folks were not very beautiful and not at all happy, I began to inquire as to the cause. And when you told me that their—I mean your mother's

330

and wife's—condition was due to this Love of God, I asked them to tell me about the nature of this Love and the Way in which they obtained It. And your mother, bless her soul, took great pains to instruct me in these things.

When I learned that prayer was the only Way to this Love, and saw you praying for me with all your heart and in great earnestness, I commenced to pray also; but I must confess that my prayers were not accompanied with much faith. But I continued to pray. And every night when you prayed for me, along with the many others who were praying with you, I tried to exercise all the faith possible and prayed for more faith. This continued for some time until, one day, your grandmother, who is a most wonderful spirit in goodness and beauty, came to me and said that she was your grandmother and was very much interested in me on your account, as well as my own. She commenced to unfold to me the great efficacy of prayer, and assured me that, if I would only try to believe and pray to God to help me believe, He would answer my prayers; and I would soon find that, with my earnest efforts, faith would come to me; and with faith would come this Love into my heart; and with this Love would come happiness and joy.

So, I listened to her and tried to believe that what she told me must be true, and that she was interested in me and desired only my happiness. I continued to pray, as I said, and, one day, after I had received some considerable faith, I met Jesus. He told me of the wonderful things that his Father had prepared for me if I would only believe and ask Him to give them to me. Jesus was so very beautiful and loving that I could not resist the influence which came over me. My faith then increased and I prayed with all my heart and soul.

At last, Light came to me and, with it, such an inflowing of Love as I never dreamed could exist, either in the earth or in the spirit world. But It came to me, and I felt as if I were a new spirit. Such happiness came as I never experienced before. And then that dear mother of yours came and rejoiced with me—and also your beautiful wife who had tried so hard to induce me to seek for this Love.

Oh, Padgett, I tell you that, in all the wide Universe of God, there is nothing to compare to this Love of the Father! Let me say that, in all my life, when only my intellect ruled me, there was nothing to compare with that which came to me with this inflowing of the Love.

I am now in the Third Sphere with many beautiful and happy spirits. Your mother and wife are higher up, and are so beautiful and good that, when I am in their company, I feel that I will become a much happier man if I will try to follow them. Your father has progressed too, and so has Professor Salyards.

Well, my soul is one now that is filled with this Love. My mind is elevated in its thoughts and not inclined to think of those things that are merely intellectual. I TELL YOU THAT, WHILE KNOWLEDGE OF ALL OF GOD'S LAWS AND NATURE'S APPARENT MYSTERIES IS DESIRABLE, YET, A KNOWLEDGE OF THIS LOVE OF GOD IS FAR AND ABOVE COMPARE—AND NOT ONLY MORE NECESSARY

BUT ALSO MORE DESIRABLE. I would not give up the feelings that come to me from the possession of this Love for all the sensations of delight that might arise from the discovery of the most stupendous and important law of the workings of nature.

Let this Love come first, and then the other acquirements will only help to show the spirit that God is a God of Wisdom and Power, as well as of Love. But as you have read, "LOVE IS THE FULFILLING OF THE LAW"; NOTHING ELSE IS. AND THE MAN WHO HAS ALL THE KNOWLEDGE AND WISDOM WITHOUT THIS LOVE IS POOR INDEED.

Jesus is the most wonderful of all the spirits in both Love and the knowledge of the Father's Attributes. He is the greatest, and knows that the Father's Plans to save and redeem mankind are such as he teaches. So, you must listen to him and believe.

I am going to try to learn more of his teachings and, when I do, you shall know what I learn. Jesus appears to me as being the one altogether lovely—he has no competitor. And no one who sees him, if he has any of this Love in his soul, can fail to know that he is the true Jesus of the Bible, and the only perfect son of his Father. I realized this only after this Love came to me. It seems that spirits who have not this Love do not realize who Jesus is, or how wonderful and glorious he is. This may seem strange to you, but it is a fact. Only when the spirit has an awakening of his soul's love for God does Jesus appear as the great brother and teacher of this Great Love of the Father.

You must not let the things of the material life lead you to think that you must wait until you come to the spirit world to get this Great Love. For I tell you that the man whose soul is opened to the inflowing of this Love while on earth is a much more fortunate man than he who waits until his earthly life ends. If I had only become conscious of this Love when on earth, I would have been saved many hours of suffering and unhappiness after I became a spirit. My own experience is so true to what so many undergo, and will undergo, that, if I could proclaim to every man on earth the necessity of becoming possessed of this Love while on earth, I would do so with all my might and strength.

I can tell you of my experience in passing over, but I do not think it best to do so tonight, as it would take too long and require more strength than you have tonight. Sometime soon I will do so in detail.

I am so glad that I have been redeemed by this Great Love and the teachings of Jesus, and received the help of your spirit relatives and the help of your prayers, that I cannot express the extent of my gladness. NOTHING IN ALL HEAVEN OR EARTH CAN COMPARE WITH THE FEELINGS OF JOY THAT COME TO A SOUL WHEN IT REALIZES THAT IT IS AT-ONE WITH THE FATHER IN LOVE AND POWER!

(I have been praying that some of my other friends, now spirits, will also seek this Love.)

Yes, they know and are with you every night as you pray. They don't seem to quite understand, though, that you can help them in any way. But still, in a manner, they feel some peculiar sensation as you pray and the others pray with you. Do not stop praying for them.

I tell you that you are a wonderfully blessed man in having such a loving Christian mother and grandmother to pray with and watch over you all of your life. If all men had Christian parents to teach and show them the Way to this Love of God, as they grew from childhood to manhood, many a time of suffering and unhappiness would be avoided, and many a spirit would come into this life with many less sins to atone for.

Your old friend,

A. G. RIDDLE

G.R. Enlarges Upon His Spiritual Progress and Acquired Knowledge.
(A. G. RIDDLE)
(February 20th, 1915 | Received by James Padgett)

I AM HERE. *Your friend, A. G. Riddle*

I am very happy tonight, and I am glad that you are so much better. You had rather a hard time of it, and this reminded me somewhat of the suffering that I used to undergo when I was on earth and in Washington. Well, you are cured of the indigestion, and your digestive organs will soon be in perfect working order.

(How was this accomplished?)

By the faith that you had in your prayers and the work of the Master! You were actually cured by your faith. The work done was only a means used to impress upon you the fact that God had answered your prayers. I do not see how you could have had such faith as you had at the time, but it is a fact that you had it; and, as a consequence, the cure was effective.

When you prayed, as you did, I was so very much impressed with your faith that I expected to see your prayers answered as they were. Jesus helped you to pray and also helped your faith. He also did the work that you observed through the power which he possesses. It is a revelation to me, I must confess, and caused me to believe more than ever in prayer and faith.

I am now so very happy in my new sphere that I cannot explain to you what that happiness means. I cannot express myself in language sufficiently strong and descriptive that you may comprehend. But this I will say: that my happiness now transcends all conception of what happiness might be when, as a mortal, I sometimes thought of the afterlife and the happiness which might be in store for me when I passed over.

I am in the Third Sphere, but am not contented to remain there; for your mother has told me on many occasions of the far greater happiness existing in the higher spheres. I am now striving and praying for this greater happiness, and I will never be content until I get it. Your wife is in a much

333

higher sphere, and is so very beautiful and so exceedingly happy that I know that such happiness must exist where she lives.

I am also happy because I have my soulmate with me so very often. Her love is so great and pure that it leads me on to higher things and enables me to seek the Great Love of the Father with so much earnestness, which I now believe is waiting for me if I only will strive to obtain It, and have the faith which all who have obtained a very large degree of this Divine Love tell me of.

Your grandmother is so wonderfully beautiful and filled with this Love that her very presence inspires me to believe and seek for the happiness of these higher spheres.

Well, as you want me to tell of some of the laws of the spirit world, I will say that the one great law is that God is Love, and that He is willing to bestow that Love on anyone, spirit or mortal, who asks Him for It.

I am not only very happy but also find that my mind is expanding to a great extent by reason of that Love which I possess. No man or spirit can possibly be filled with this Love and not have the wisdom that necessarily comes with the Love. I am not so much interested in purely mental phenomena, as I was before I received this Love and believed in a Father of Love and Truth; but I am able, nevertheless, to understand many things to a far greater degree than I could when I had merely the mental pursuits in mind. I am not yet fully conversant with the Laws of Communication, as I told you I would learn and instruct you in, but I know enough to be able to say that every spirit is trying to communicate with his friends on earth. And why they are not able to is because the mortals are not in that condition of physical rapport that will enable them to receive the communications of the spirit. I do not yet know why one mortal is so susceptible to these influences as to be readily understood, and another mortal is not. Some spirits say that the law controlling this matter is not understood by spirits who have been here for a great many years, and who have given considerable study on the subject.

But this I do know: that when the rapport exists, the communications can be made with the exercise of the powers.

But I don't know of any manifestation as satisfactory to both spirit and mortal as the writing, such as you are now doing, for we now have the opportunity for communicating and interchanging thoughts to such a greater extent. I am perfectly delighted at the possibilities given me of writing to you in this way. So, you must believe that I am writing to you and that all the others of your band are doing the same thing.

Your wife has more power in this regard than any of us, and she does not hesitate writing to you whenever you call for her. She is a wonderful spirit in her grasp of spiritual things and in her love for the Father. So, you must not let any doubt come into your mind when she writes to you and tells you of so many wonderful things, and of her love for you. She seems to love you with a love that has no limit or possibility of growing less.

I am now going to tell you of my progress in this Love and happiness.

When I last wrote to you, I told you that I had commenced to have faith in the Father and had received some portion of His Love. Well, since then, I have been praying and asking God to give me more faith and Love. And, as I prayed, my faith increased; and, as my faith increased, more of this Love came into my soul; and, with It, an increased happiness. So, I would not stop striving until I realized that my soul was commencing to get such an inflow of this Love that it seemed that all things which tended to retard this inflowing were leaving me, and only Love and Goodness were taking possession of me. I am now very far advanced over what I was when you first commenced to talk to me of this Love, and I shall remember and thank you for what you did for me through all eternity. I was also fortunate to have had your mother and wife with me very often, trying to show me the way to this Truth of the New Birth. And, then, when your grandmother came to me, it seemed as if I could not resist the influence to seek and try to find It.

Lastly, when I had received enough of this spiritual awakening to realize who Jesus was, I gave him my close attention. And as he continued to show me the Way to the Father, I commenced to grasp the Truth and believe that my salvation depended on my receiving this Great Love and becoming a finer and better man. I tell you that Jesus is the most wonderful of all spirits that I have seen or heard about. He is so filled with love and goodness that there seems no doubt in my mind that he is the son of the Father in the special sense of the term. I mean that he is so much nearer the Father, and has so many of His Attributes, that he is the greatest son in the sense of being more at-one with the Father. We are all sons of the Father, but there is such a difference in our spiritual conditions. The contrast between Jesus and us is so great that we can readily believe that he is the greatest true son, and that his great love and knowledge of the Qualities of the Father is greater than any Celestial spirit. I do not mean in the sense that he was created in a different physical way from other men—an immaculate conception or birth from the womb of a virgin. I do not believe this dogma, and the Master says that it is not true. For he is truly the son of a man and woman, as you or I am, so far as his physical being is concerned.

Now, I am also convinced that mankind cannot be saved from their sins unless they follow the Way showed them by the Master. No man can save himself, and I wish to emphasize the fact strongly that man is dependent upon God for his salvation from the sins and errors of the natural man. I do not mean that men have not a work to do themselves, for they have. God is willing to save them if they ask for it and acknowledge that, without His Help, they cannot be saved. But unless they do ask and believe, He will not interfere with their conditions. So, you see, I am not only a believer in God and Jesus but also in the doctrine that men cannot save themselves.

I thought that man was sufficient unto himself when I was on earth, but now I know that he is not. Man may be comparatively happy and free from what is called sin—that is, a violation of God's Laws—but that happiness is not the same, nor is man's condition the same, as when he gets this

Divine Love from the Father.

I will not speak longer of this subject tonight, but will reiterate that, when on earth, I thought that I might possibly become divine by my own exertions. Yet, now, as a spirit, I know that man is not divine and cannot become so in all eternity unless he receives this Divine Essence which comes to him by the New Birth. Divinity is of God, Alone, and only He can bestow It on man. Man, not having this Divinity, cannot create It by his own efforts. So, believe what I say and strive to get It, and you will then succeed and become as the redeemed in the Celestial Spheres.

With all my love and blessings,

A. G. RIDDLE

Mrs. Padgett Relates Her Experience in Trying to Show a Spirit the Way to God's Love.
(HELEN PADGETT)
(March 17th, 1915 | Received by James Padgett)

I AM HERE. *Helen.*

I want to tell you of my experience in trying to show a spirit the Way to God's Love, which I had a short time ago.

Well, I talked to this spirit of this Love, and told her that the only Way to happiness and to the Celestial Kingdom was through prayer and faith, and that all spirits who were inhabitants of those spheres had received this Great Love of the Father only through prayer and faith; and if she wanted to become an inhabitant of these heavens, she must seek for this Love in that Way. She said that she was told, when on earth, that if she only observed the rules and regulations of the church, and devoted herself to doing church work and looking after the interest of the church so that it might be sustained and fostered, she would go to heaven just as soon as she had left the earth life; and that that would be all that would be required of her, and that no other seeking or striving after God's Love would be necessary to enable her to get into the heavens where God is and all His angels. I told her that she must now realize that such performance of what she considered to be her duty had not been sufficient to carry her into these heavens, and that she must realize that something more was necessary. But she still persisted that her belief in what she had been taught in the church could not be changed, and that very soon she would become an inhabitant of these higher spheres. So, I left her because I saw that it was useless to try to convince her that she was laboring under an absolutely false belief.

So, I find that in this spirit plane there are many spirits in darkness and bigotry, which prevents them from seeing the Truth and progressing to the higher spheres. I do not think that mortals, when they become spirits, have any better opportunity, for some time at least, to realize and accept these Truths than they had when on earth. And the men or women who teach these things have a great sin to answer for; for Jesus said, "Cursed is he who believes and teaches these false doctrines." And I think he must have laid especial emphasis on false teaching as it affected not only the teacher but also many others who had faith in, and accepted, these teachings as true.

I am so glad that I, when on earth, was never fully convinced of these church dogmas, as I consequently found it so much easier when I came to the spirit world to believe the Truths as they are. Of course, I was exceptionally blessed in having your mother and grandmother, who are so well-versed in these things, to show me the Way. And, then, when Jesus came to me and corroborated what they said, I could not help but believe.

SO, YOU SEE THE IMPORTANCE OF LEARNING THESE TRUTHS WHILE ON EARTH. FOR THE GREATER OUR COMPREHENSION OF THEM AS MORTALS, THE MORE EASY WILL BE OUR PROGRESSION TO THE HIGHER THINGS OF THE SPIRITUAL LIFE.

Well, I thought I would tell you of this little incident, as it shows you a great and necessary Truth, and one which all men should know.

So, with my love, I am

Your own true and loving,

HELEN.

Mr. Padgett Receives a Message from a Spirit Who Believed in the Creeds, but Who Awakened to the Truth After He Met Jesus.
(SAMUEL B SOUTHARD)
(August 30th, 1915 | Received by James Padgett)

I AM HERE. *Samuel B. Southard*

I am here—the spirit of one who, when on earth, was a believer in the divinity of Jesus and in his being one of the three parts of the "Godhead", co-equal with the Father and with the Holy Spirit.

I died in this belief and, as a consequence, when I came to the spirit world, I was disappointed and also surprised to find that Jesus is not God, but a spirit made like the rest of the inhabitants of that world, though infinitely more beautiful and possessed of a very much larger degree of the Divine Nature of the Father.

I did not believe that this was true until a long time after I entered the spirit world, for my old beliefs clung to me. And while I did not find myself in heaven, singing psalms and playing on harps, as the Bible taught, yet, I was not very unhappy and was not in much darkness, and I settled down to the belief that the state in which I found myself was the one that I should probably remain in until the great day of judgment and the general resurrection of those who had died.

But, after a while, I met spirits who said they were from a higher sphere. They told me that there is no such thing as a fixed state in the spiritual world, and that the day of judgement is every day that I existed as a spirit; and that, if I chose to do so, I could progress out of my condition into higher spheres where I would find more happiness and light.

Of course, I did not readily belief this, for my old beliefs stayed with me, and I continued in my condition of hesitancy for a long time until at last I had the good fortune to come face to face with the Master. And then I knew that my beliefs were wrong and erroneous. I had no conception of such a beautiful and bright and loving spirit.

He told me that he was not God, and that he was only a son of the Father; and that I was a son, also, and could obtain the Divine Love, just as he had obtained It, if I would only pray to the Father and have the necessary faith.

Since then, I have been praying. And my old beliefs about Jesus being God, and the great day of judgment and the resurrection of the dead at the last day, have left me. And I am now a free spirit possessing the Love of the Father to a considerable extent.

I am not so exalted and bright, and have not the soul development that your band has, but I am progressing and know that the Divine Love of the Father is what we all, spirits and mortals, need to make us one with the Father and partakers of His Divine Nature and of immortality.

I am a stranger to you, and you must excuse my intruding. But I so desired to write as I have that, when I saw the way open, I could not resist the temptation to write.

I am S.B.Southard. I lived in the city of New York and died many years ago.

I am in the Fifth Sphere and am progressing.

So, thanking you, I will say good night and God bless you.

Your brother in Christ,

S. B. SOUTHARD.

A Spirit Gives His Experience, and How His Old Beliefs in the Creeds Retarded His Progress. He Affirms That Mr. Padgett Was Selected by Jesus to Receive the Messages.

(G. H. _____)

(date unknown | Received by James Padgett)

I AM HERE. *G.H. _____.*

I am here and want to   write a little tonight with the permission of your band and yourself. You will remember me when I tell you that I am an old friend of yours and a brother in the profession.

You knew me as G.H. _____, and I knew you as my young lawyer friend.

I am living in the Third Sphere and am comparatively happy, and I am trying to progress to the higher spheres. But, somehow, the old beliefs that I imbibed when on earth seem to retard my progress. As you know, I was a Methodist and believed in the Methodist doctrines, and yet was not so spiritual as I should have been. I have learned, or, rather, unlearned and learned many things since I have been here; and, as a consequence, I am in a better condition to appreciate the truth than when on earth.

(To what do you refer?)

Well, I know now that the blood of Jesus, as such, does not wash away sin, and also that he is not the savior of men because of any vicarious atonement. These were great stumbling blocks to me when I came into the spirit world, and my disappointment growing out of these beliefs was very great. It almost caused me to believe that there never was any Jesus or any God. But thanks to some of my spirit friends who knew the truth, I was prevented from becoming an unbeliever in the Truths of salvation and, so, was saved from what might have been a great stagnation of my soul and its progress.

(Has Mr. Riddle told you of his own progress?)

Yes, and I am somewhat surprised at Riddle's progress. For I must tell you that he is in a higher sphere than I am, and is more filled with this Love of the Father. He has told me somewhat of his experience, and how you first started him to right thinking; and then how your band—I mean your grandmother and the rest of your kinfolk—came to him and helped him to see the light and the necessity of seeking and obtaining God's Love. He is now a very bright spirit and has much faith. So, you see, a man may have his doubts on earth and yet succeed in progressing more rapidly than one who, though he believes in God and the Bible, stands still because of his erroneous beliefs.

(How is it that you came to write to me tonight?)

Well, I must say that I have been with you a number of times when the spirits were writing to you, and I was very much surprised at first that such a thing should be. And I saw that you were doing the dark spirits a great deal of good in the way in which you helped them out of their darkness and sufferings.[*] When I was on earth, I did not suppose that there would ever come a time when you would be in this kind of work. In fact, I did not know that there was such a work to be performed by anyone.

(Have you seen Jesus writing to me?)

Yes, I have seen Jesus writing to you a number of times, and only tonight did he do so.

My views as to him have changed very much since I was on earth. As you may have thought, I then believed him to be God, or one of three that constituted God, and that he was a way up in the heavens, sitting on the right hand of the Father and controlling the heavens and the earth. But, since I have been in the spirit world, my beliefs have changed. And now I

---

[*] Mr. Padgett directed them how to visualize and then receive the assistance of brighter and more highly developed spirits.—Ed.

know that Jesus is not God, but only His highest, best son, and a spirit such as I am. At times he has talked to me and told me of many erroneous beliefs contained in the Bible and in the dogmas of the churches. He is a wonderful spirit—the brightest in all the spirit world—and the one that is closer to the Father than any of the others, ancient or modern.

He is so very filled with the Divine Love of his Father that we adore him as our Master. But we do not worship him as God. I have been surprised at the great interest he has in you, and the abundance of love that he has for you. But I know that I need not have been surprised, for he has selected you to write his messages to the world.

What a fortunate man you are! I don't understand sometimes how such a thing can be, but he says that the world must have all the Truths of the Father. And he selected you because he saw that you could carry out his desires better than any other mortal; and, so, you are favored.

Well, I must stop, as I have written a very long letter, and some others wish to write also. So, my dear brother, I will say good night.

Your old friend,

G.H. _____.

Help Is Given to a Clergyman of the Orthodox Church.
(W_____)
(date unknown | Received by James Padgett)

I AM HERE. *W_____.*

Let me write a little. I need your help and believe that you can help me, as I have been told that you have helped others before me.

I am a spirit who has spent many long years in darkness and despair. I was a very bad man, but I never knew it until I came to the spirit world and saw clearly just what kind of character was mine. No man really knows his own condition until he has shuffled off the mortal coil and becomes a transparent spirit. Then, every inmost thought is apparent, and he becomes, as it were, a mirror of his own true self.

My life was not what the world would call an evil one, and I tried to live, as I thought, correctly in the sight of God and man. But it was all outward appearances only. I mean that I was deceiving myself. My soul was not involved, but merely my intellectual persuasions as to what was right and wrong. The Beatitudes were not mine and soul religion was not mine. I was a strict church member and conformed to all the conventions and dogmas of the church, so far as their outward appearances are concerned. But, at the same time, I did not have a true soul worship of God. I thought that, by observing the dogmas and creeds of my church, I was doing God's Will, and that nothing further was necessary. I was baptized and confirmed by the proper dignitaries of the church, and was told that I was a child of God and could be certain of salvation. And when I grew to manhood and became, as you may be surprised to know, a clergyman, I found a deep consolation in administering the services of the church, and receiving and confirming applicants into membership.

But, alas, this did not bring me true communion and At-onement with the Father, for I had not the Love of the Father in my soul. My intellect was all Christian, but my soul was not in unison with the Father's Love. How often I thought what a great and satisfying thing it was to be within God's Fold. I mean His church which had been established by Jesus and had come down to us in apostolic succession. But what a mistake! Apostolic succession is of itself a meaningless church government, and no such succession can confer upon any priest or clergyman the power to bestow upon the souls of men the Love or Mercy of the Father. This I have learned to my sorrow since I became a spirit.

So, I say, let those who think that any priest or bishop can bestow this Love of the Father, or can make the soul of man the recipient of this Love, awaken to the fact that no such power exists in these church ministers. Only, as I now believe, can God Himself do this Great Work.

So, when I came into this spirit life and found that I was not in my Father's Kingdom, as I had believed I would be, I was sorely disappointed. And, in my disappointment, I commenced to think that the whole of the Bible teachings were merely fairytales, and that God was not; or, if He existed, He had deceived His church by having it believe that the members of such church were the specially redeemed children of the Father. I have been in this state of doubt for a long time, and only recently have I commenced to see the Truth; and I have learned that the Way to God's Love is not through the churches as such, but only through the true and earnest aspirations of the soul. Also, that no mediator is necessary, but that God is waiting and willing to bestow this Love upon whomsoever may truly ask for It.

No priest or bishop can relieve a soul from sin, or forgive the sinner; and no man can reach the Father's Love or Favor except through this direct, individual supplication to the Father. The priest may show the Way if he knows how, but so few know for the reason that they not only teach but also believe that all a man has to do is to conform to the church's demands, and that, when he does so, God is ready to receive him into His Kingdom.

But let all such men know that, if they depend alone on such conformity to duty, they will be as disappointed as I was when they come into the world of spirits where only Truth can prevail, and where all that is hidden on earth is uncovered here.

Now, I am not to be understood as decrying the churches or the good which they do; for, notwithstanding the dogmas and creeds, many of their members have received this true soul union with the Father. And many preachers have declared Truths in their sermons which have been the means of leading their hearers to a true understanding of the Father's Love. What I intend to convey is that the churches, in their dogmas and creeds, emphasize too much the necessity of conforming to these dogmas and

341

creeds, and neglect to show men the true Way to the Kingdom.

THE ONLY PRAYERS THAT REACH THE FATHER'S HEART ARE THOSE WHICH CARRY THE TRUE ASPIRATIONS OF THE SUPPLICANT TO THE THRONE OF GRACE. MAN MAY REPEAT THE WRITTEN PRAYERS FOR A WHOLE LIFETIME, BUT IF THE PRAYERS DO NOT EXPRESS THE ASPIRATIONS AND DESIRES OF THE APPLICANT, THEY HAVE NO MORE EFFECT THAN WOULD THE REPEATING OF THE MULTIPLICATION TABLE.

If men will consider for a moment, they will see that this must be true. Only the soul of man can receive this Great Love of the Father. And when these written prayers are repeated without the longings of the soul entering into these repetitions, the soul is not open to the inflowing of this Love; and, hence, man can receive no possible benefit.

So, I say, let men learn to know that religion is a matter purely between God and each individual soul, and no church or priest or bishop, because of any claimed warrant existing in it or them, can save a man's soul from the sins of life, or make such soul one with the Father. All that such priest or bishop can do is to show the Way, if he understands it; and when he does that, he has performed a greater service to mankind than he may realize.

I now see the falsity of my depending on the performance of my duty to my church merely as a duty. I performed my duties, but I starved my soul—not intentionally, but because I thought that the performance of duty was all that was necessary. Someday, I hope that men will learn that there is only one Way to God, and that through their earnest, personal prayers, with faith.

Well, I have written enough.

I was a clergyman of a church in a western town. My name was W_____ and I passed over in 1871. I am now learning the Way.

I came to you for help because I saw that you are surrounded by bright and beautiful spirits who must have this Love in their souls to a great degree, and I thought that, if I could meet them and have them tell me of what this Love means from their personal experience, I might be benefited.

(Let them introduce themselves to you.)

Well, I have acknowledged the introduction, and I certainly feel myself fortunate in meeting them. They are so beautiful and lovely. I thank you very much and, sometime, with the permission of all of you, I will come again and write. So, with my best love, I will say good night.

W_____.

An Orthodox Minister Relates His Experiences After He Passed into the Spirit World.

(F_____)

(July 1st, 1917 | Received by James Padgett)

I AM HERE. *F_____.*

Let me say only a few words, as I am anxious to write and tell you that I was with you tonight on your last visit to the home of my son, (Mr. Fontain), and was hoping that the opportunity would present itself for me to write. But, as you know, I was disappointed, and I know that my daughter was also; for she expected that, in the event that you should call at her brother's home, she would be able to get a communication from me.

As I could not write there, I thought I would accompany you home in the hope that I might write, as I am now doing. For I heard you say that you had received a letter from your wife every night, and that, if that should happen tonight, I might have the chance to write.

Well, I want my daughter to know that I approve of her searching for the truth, which she may find in Spiritualism if properly sought for. And notwithstanding that some of my family do not believe in it and treat it with indifference or disbelief, yet, in it many truths may be found. It is a truth itself, and it is waiting for mortals to investigate and learn that it is true. In it are those truths that will lead them to much greater happiness than they now have on earth, and infinitely more than they can possibly find should they come to the spirit world without a knowledge of these truths.

My family knows that I was a strict orthodox and believed in the teachings of the Bible as the church to which I belonged taught, and which I, myself, taught. I died firmly established in that belief, and I came into the spirit world wholly impregnated with this belief, expecting to meet Jesus and to be admitted to the Presence of God. And, according to my beliefs, I was justified in having such expectation. But, alas, how different was my experience when I left the mortal world, and how my expectations were shattered in a moment, as it were!

As my spirit left my body, I was fully conscious of the change that was taking place, and knew that I was dying, but was perfectly calm and without a particle of fear. I suffered no pain or dread of what I should meet, but, rather, felt a happy expectation in the thought that my troubles of the earth life were past forever, and that soon I would be at rest, finding my home among the chosen children of God, and having Jesus welcome me and take me in his arms of love. All the expectations that I possessed before my passing were with me, and much accentuated, and no doubt of my realizing the same entered my mind for a moment to disturb my hopes. I also expected to meet my loved ones who had gone before, and to enjoy the happiness of their presence and purified condition of soul.

Well, I soon found myself a spirit, dissevered from my body, possessed of joy and, as mortals say, lighter than air. Figuratively speaking, I seemed to be walking on air, with nothing to interfere with my ascension to the bright realm where I expected to find my beloved ones and the Christ of my beliefs and love.

I hardly realized my separation from my body before some of my loved ones met me and welcomed me with love and cheer. They told me that they were so happy that I had come over, and that I must not be afraid or doubt that I was then an inhabitant of the spirit world. I can scarcely tell you how happy I was, how the memories of the cares and burdens of my earth life left me, and how I seemed to be in an atmosphere of love and heavenly joy. The meeting with them was more than I had anticipated, and I thought how it had not entered into my mind on earth to conceive of the beauty and grandeur of the spirit home[*] which Jesus had said he was in heaven preparing for all those who believed in him. Nor did I at first reflect upon the great sacrifice and atonement that Jesus had come to earth to make for me, and which he did make.

But, soon, I remembered that my great expectation was to see Jesus and to feel the influence of his love; and, also, to get into the heaven where the Father was, and to join with the mighty hosts in singing hallelujahs and songs of thanksgiving. And I then asked my angel loved ones where Jesus was, and when I should enter into the Presence of the Father to receive His Benediction of approval as a faithful and obedient child.

And, then, in a loving way and in a manner to make my disappointment less intense, they told me that Jesus was in the Celestial Spheres, and that they had never seen the Father; that He was a way up in the spheres where no spirit had yet entered; and that no spirit had ever seen His "face" or heard His "voice," no matter how exalted and developed that spirit might be. They told me that I was mistaken in my beliefs, and that it was only by the development of my soul in Love that I could possibly ascend to the Celestial Spheres where the Master was; that belief in the blood washing or in the vicarious atonement would not fit my soul for the Celestial Spheres; that only the Divine Love in my soul and the freedom from my erroneous beliefs would enable me to become a possessor of the mansions that Jesus was preparing for those who became in At-onement with the Father; that what they told me was the truth, and that sometime Jesus would tell me the same thing. And while I could not go to his home, yet, they told me that he frequently came to the earth plane and endeavored to help and comfort spirits who had not the soul Love that enabled them to become children of the higher spheres.

Well, you can imagine my astonishment and disappointment, and how the nakedness of my beliefs appeared to me. As I thought of the long life that I had given to the cultivation and establishment of these beliefs and expectations in my own mind, and that I had no other knowledge or hope of salvation, I became doubtful of everything that was told to me. My God became no God, and Jesus, as my savior, became no longer my savior, but a man who had deceived me during all the long years of my life. I became resentful and hardened, and refused to believe in anything, for I thought that I was honest with myself and honest with God while on earth. The Bible had been certified to me as God's true revelation, with the certain and only plan of man's salvation, and I had devoutly believed in this plan and endeavored to live the life that entitled me to salvation. When I thought of

---

[*] This is a temporary place before the spirit goes to the plane where its soul condition determines it shall first reside.—Ed.

these things, the realization of my deception made me rebellious, and I almost hated spirits and God.

I was permitted to indulge in these thoughts for a while without interruption. And then my friends told me that these thoughts were very harmful and would prevent me from learning the true Way to salvation and happiness, and that the longer I indulged in my feelings of resentment and thoughts of having been deceived, the greater would be my stagnation in my progress, and the darker would become my surroundings.

They told me very soon that all things in the spirit world were controlled by the unchangeable Laws of God, that these laws required that I should go to the place that my soul's condition fitted me for, and that they would have to leave me for the time being. They said further that all the beliefs in all the world will not determine the place in which a newly arrived spirit will have to find its home, unless those beliefs be true, and that the beliefs that I had, and on which I depended for my salvation, were not true.

Well, I found my place and, with it, darkness in which I remained for a long time, refusing to believe what was told to me as to the true Way to Light and happiness. And, just here, I want to say that it is not an easy thing to lay aside or get rid of the beliefs of a lifetime on earth, even though the surroundings and disappointments of the spirit show that such beliefs must be false; and that belief—a merely intellectual belief—is a very important factor in determining the temporary destiny of the soul.

I have written a long time and I will not relate in detail how I learned the Truth, found the Light, and was started on my progress to the higher spheres; or how Jesus came to me, showered on me his love, and told me of the things that would be mine if I would only follow his advice.

He said that the great stumbling block to the progress of a spirit in its search for the Truth and the mansions in the higher spheres is this erroneous and damning belief in his vicarious atonement, etc., which so many spirits who come to the spirit world bring with them.

I am now very happy, and I am in the Fifth Sphere where there is beauty and happiness beyond all conception. And if the opportunity were mine tonight, I would endeavor to give you some faint idea of my home and its surroundings, and of the beautiful spirits who are my associates.

(Is there any message you'd like to give your daughter?)

Someday, I know this home will be hers, for she will not have the burdens of the beliefs that I had to overcome. And, just here, I must say that, as she knows how very dear she is to me and how much I must love her in having so much of this great Love of the Father in my soul, she must also know that I would not deceive her for all the world. And, knowing this, she must take my advice and seek for this Great Love of God which made such a happy spirit of her father. Let these old orthodox beliefs as to the plan of salvation leave her, and let her pray directly to the Father for His Love, and she will receive all that is necessary for a great earthly happiness and for a joy unspeakable in the spirit world.

I am with her very often in her earthly troubles, and I try to help and console her; and, sometimes, I do succeed a little. She must remember that these trials are only for a moment, and then will leave her forever, and that the love and influence which her father is throwing around her will never leave her. In that moment which mortals dread the most—I mean of death—her father and other loved ones will be with her and take her in their arms of love. And she will never have a fear or dread as to where she is, for love will be so great that her soul will respond in such a way that all else will be forgotten. So, tell my daughter to try not to let her troubles and cares worry her so she will neglect the presence of the consolation which we try to bring to her.

Well, I have written as much as I feel I am justified in doing, as your time is needed for others as well. But your wife, who is so good, says that I must not fear that I have consumed too much time, for she is always interested in making known to mortals those things that will make them happy on earth and certain of heaven.

I should like to say something to my wife, but I see that she is not in condition to receive my message; for she is suffering as I suffered, unconsciously, in the dogmatic beliefs of her church. Oh, if I could only come to her in my appearance of earth and tell her of the errors of her beliefs, and of the Truths that have made me a free and a true child of the Father, I would do so with the rapidity of light and with the hope that all my love for her would give me! I never loved her on earth as I do now. And when she comes to the spirit world, she will not come as a stranger; for a greater love than she has ever conceived of will meet her, and she will know the lover.

Tell my daughter to read what I have written to her mother. And even though her mother will not believe, yet, some of the things that I have said will find a lodgment in her memory. They will come with her to the spirit world and help her in her disappointment in not having her expectations realized.

And what I have said to you, my daughter, I say to my sons; and I urge them to think of these things that are so vital to them as mortals, as well as when they become spirits.

Sometime, with your permission, I will come again and write to my folks. So, thanking you, and with my love to all my dear ones, I will say good night.

Your brother in Christ,

F_____.

Saleeba, an Ancient Spirit of the Sixth Sphere, Requests Mr. Padgett's Assistance Concerning How to Obtain God's Divine Love.
(SALEEBA)
(June 2nd, 1915 | Received by James Padgett)

Let me write just a little, as I need help. I saw how you helped the last

346

spirit[*] who wrote. It was wonderful to me what a change came to her as you told her of God's Love. And when she went with that beautiful spirit who spoke so lovingly to her, I thought that there was hope for me too.

So, I know you will help me, as I need it so much; and you seem willing to help us all.

I am a woman who lived a great many years ago in a land that is far distant from your home, and at a time that runs back into the centuries. I was an Egyptian princess and lived in the time when your Jesus, that I heard you speak of, was not known to the world. I was taught the philosophy of the ancient Egyptians, and Osiris and Isis were our god and goddess. We worshiped them, but not in love or soul adoration but in fear and dread. They were not the Loving Father, that you say your God is, but dreaded deities of power and wrath who called for our obedience through fear of punishment and the tortures of the hells. They were supposed to rule in these hells and torment the spirits of mortals who disobeyed them.

So, you see, our souls were not developed with love, but our minds were controlled with fear; and we offered our sacrifices to appease the terrible threatening of their wrath.

I was naturally a loving woman and, in my life, outside of my religious beliefs, I was compassionate and sympathetic. Those who were subject to me in our intercourse of government loved me, and were grateful and obedient subjects. But when it became a question as to our worship and religious duties, I sacrificed many of them to satisfy the wrath and demands of our gods. These sacrifices were made openly at first, but so great and deleterious to the good of the nation did they become in their political aspect that, later, our sacrifices were made in private; but they were made nevertheless.

Our beliefs were as real and as earnest as are the beliefs of you Christians in your God of Love and Mercy. And we did the will of our gods with as much belief that we were doing our duty as you have when seeking to do the Will of your Father.

But, as I now see, what a difference in the motives, and what a difference in the results! Our motives were to appease our angry gods, and thereby prevent their wrath from falling upon us who continued to live; and your motives are to get, and be filled with, the Love and Mercy of a Father of Love, and to have your souls filled with that which will enable you to live in His Presence and become supremely happy.

In the long years that I have lived in the spirit world, I have learned all this intellectually, and many other things that show me the cruelty and degradation of the beliefs that I obtained when I was a mortal, and which resulted in the physical deaths of many of my subjects, and also the death of their souls. Love, to us, was not a divine thing. Obedience and placating

---

[*] Mr. Padgett had just received a message from a spirit who was in darkness and suffering, and who wanted Mr. Padgett to instruct her as to what she should do to progress out of her dark and sad condition.—Ed.

the anger of the gods were the divine things to us.

And, now, while I have heard of this Love of your Father, and have seen the results of this Love upon their appearances, and the apparent happiness of the worshipers of your God, yet, I have never understood this Great Love except in an intellectual way. My soul has never felt the influence of this Love, and I have never before thought it necessary for me to seek the secret of obtaining the benefit of this Love. But I now see that there is something more to It than the mere knowledge of Its existence, which the mind tells me must exist. And, so, in my journeys to earth and hearing of your meetings with the spirits who are seeking this Love—or, rather, a way out of their darkness and sufferings—and having seen the effect of some of their efforts, I came to you to learn the Way, if possible, by which I may obtain the soul experience which I have heard you and the beautiful spirits who come to you speak of.

Of course, my ancient belief still has some influence over me, even though I have found that Osiris and Isis are myths. Yet, that negative knowledge has not supplied me with the means by which I can get this Love you speak of. While I know that the angry gods do not exist, still, there is a void in my soul which I realize has never been filled. So, if you can help me to the Way that will lead to my finding this soul-filling Love that you speak of, I will be greatly obliged if you will do so, and will follow that Way.

In the years since my coming into the spirit world, I have lived in a number of spheres, each one a progressive one in succession. But in none of these spheres which I have lived in have I found that the inhabitants are possessed of this soul Love that I am anxious to obtain. In the higher spheres in which I have lived, and in the highest, there is a wonderful development of the mental qualities. And the knowledge possessed by these spirit inhabitants is beyond all conception of mortals. Sin does not exist in these highest spheres, and happiness is very great; and the spirits are very beautiful and bright. But, in my comparison of the beauty and brightness of these spirits with those who claim this soul development of Love, I notice a great difference.

We have our loves and our harmonies, and peace reigns supreme. Yet, I am not satisfied, and so with many others who live where I do. But the cause of this dissatisfaction is not revealed to us. And, as I say, only in my visits to the earth plane and hearing of this Love have I become convinced that the great secret of our dissatisfaction may be found among those spirits who claim to have this wonderful Love.

So, I come to you and ask you to show me the Way to learn of It.
(Have you conversed with any bright spirits in the earth plane?)
Well, I have visited the earth plane many times since I have been a spirit and, occasionally, have conversed with the spirits who claim to have this Love. And they have told me of this Love to some degree, but I never thought much about It until lately. I was happy in my condition, and I have told you of it, and did not think it worthwhile to inquire into the fact of what

348

this Love meant. But, somehow, lately, the desire to learn of It has taken possession of me; and, hence, I come to you because I see others coming to you who say they need help.

I did not go to the others you speak of because I thought that I might get more help by coming to you first. The spirits who are seeking your help say that they can obtain an advantage in some way in coming to you first. I don't know why, but they believe it. And when I saw the effect of their coming to you, I thought it might be so; and, hence, I came.

(What is your name and when did you live on earth?)

I was the daughter of one of the early pharaohs, and my name was Princess Saleeba. I do not know how to compute the centuries, but I lived before the pyramids were built. So, you see, I have been in the spirit world a long time.

(Can you tell me something about the various spheres you have lived in?)

Not now, but sometime I will come again and write to you more in detail and give you a description of the spheres through which I have progressed.

(I would like to suggest that you seek out my mother, Ann Padgett. She will teach you the Way to acquire this Love.)

I have called for your mother and she is so very beautiful. She must have a great amount of this Love. She says that she will show me the Way to obtain It, and will love me herself, and will take me to the greatest spirit in all the spirit world in whom I can see this Love developed to Its greatest perfection. And I am going with her.

So, remember my promise to come again, for I will come.

So, with many thanks and my kindest regards, I will say good night.

SALEEBA[*].

Saleeba Describes Her Progress in Obtaining the Divine Love.
(SALEEBA)
(October 26th, 1915 | Received by James Padgett)

I AM HERE. *Saleeba.*

I am in a much happier condition than when I wrote before, and I want to tell you that the Love of God in my soul is the cause of my being happier. Your sweet wife was with me a great deal, telling me of this Love and showing me the Way to seek for It; and I believed her and followed her advice. And, as a result, I found a great deal of that Love. It is so very great a creator of happiness—and I want more of It!

I am living in the Third Sphere because I find so much more of that soul Love there than in the Sixth. And what I want now is that Love! So,

---

[*] Saleeba was a bright spirit from the highest plane of the Sixth Sphere.—Ed.

you see, I cannot live where this Love is not so abundant. When I get more of It, I shall go to the Sixth and tell the spirits there what a great happiness I have found, and try to persuade them to seek It also. And I believe that many will.

I am so glad that I broke into your writing when I did, for, if I had not, I would not have learned the Way to this Love and happiness. I shall always look upon you as my friend and brother, and will do anything in my power to help you.

I have not found any of my race in these soul spheres as yet, but there may be some of them there. But if I can possibly accomplish it, there will be some of them in my sphere very soon.

I have forgotten a great many things in connection with my earth life; but I remember my parents and some of my associates, and some portions of my religious beliefs. And, sometime, I will tell you of these things.

I will also tell you of my experiences in passing through these spheres in my progress to the Sixth where I had to stop progressing. It is strange that I did not find this out until recently, but it is a fact.

No spirit who lives in the Sixth Sphere is as beautiful as the spirits of the Third Sphere who have the soul development. And the merely intellectual spirit can never become as beautiful as those having the soul Love.

Well, I must stop, as I only wanted to let you know that I had not forgotten you.

I will come again soon and tell you what I promised.

So, I will say good night.

Your friend and sister,

SALEEBA.

Saleeba Declares That She Is Progressing and Soon Will Be Above the Third Sphere. She Also States That She Now Knows That Jesus Is the True Leader of All the Spirits Who Have the Divine Love.
(SALEEBA)
(July 5th, 1915 | Received by James Padgett)

I AM HERE. *Saleeba.*

Well, I am with you again. I want to tell you that I am so very happy, as I have progressed so much since I wrote you a short time ago.

I am still in the Third Sphere, but I am in a higher plane and with spirits who have the soul development to a very great degree. And, in their love, I am just so happy that I cannot express to you its extent.

Oh, what a wonderful thing the Divine Love is! And when I consider the long years that I lived as a spirit without knowing anything about this Love, I can scarcely express my regret at the unfortunate position in which

I lived. I know now that Jesus is the true leader of all the spirits who have this great soul development, and that he can show the Way to the Father's Kingdom as no other spirit can. And, besides, when I come in contact with him, I realize that he has so much of this Love himself that what he says must be true.

I will soon progress to a higher sphere, they tell me, and will get Love in more abundance; and then, in a little while, I shall go to my own people and tell them of the wonders and glories of my new-found home. What a blessed, happy time I anticipate among these spirits who are now in such ignorance of the only thing that brings this great happiness.

I am not in condition now to tell you of my residence or life on earth, as I promised, but sometime I will keep my promise.

You must think kind thoughts of me, and let your love come to me so that I may feel its benefit. For I must tell you that the loving thoughts of a mortal who knows what this Divine Love is have a wonderful influence on spirits and their advancement in the spirit spheres.

I will not write more tonight.

So, with my love and kindest thoughts, I am

Your sister in Christ,
SALEEBA.

Saleeba Tells of Her Happiness and of Her Intention to Share What She Has Found with Her People.

(SALEEBA)
(October 8th, 1915 | Received by James Padgett)

I AM HERE. *Saleeba.*

I want to say only a few words that you may know how happy I am, and how much my soul is filled with this Divine Love of which you first told me. Oh, my friend, it is difficult to keep from shouting the fact that I am a redeemed child of the Father, and one who knows that His Love is mine, and that I shall live through all eternity enjoying the happiness which His Love and Mercy have given me!

I intended to keep my promise and tell you of my life on earth many thousands of years ago, and so I will sometime. But now I am so happy in this great possession that I cannot think of those earthly things in such a way as to relate to you my experience as a mortal. Wait a little while and I will try to describe to you all the things of my earth life that may be of interest to you.

I will go very soon now to my people and tell them what I have found, and urge them to seek for It. And I trust that they will follow my advice. There are many of them that are good and pure spirits, with a natural love in such a state that they are very happy and contented. Yet, when I realize the great difference in the happiness that is theirs and that which may be theirs, I cannot refrain from going to them and telling them of it.

I know that you are glad that I am happy and are interested in my progress, and, hence, I love to come and let you know what my condition is.

I will not write more tonight. So, believe that I love you as a sister and pray for you, and ask the Father to make you happy and fill your soul with His Love and bless you.

Good night.

Your sister in Christ,
SALEEBA.

Saleeba Continues to Share Her Happiness with Mr. Padgett.
(SALEEBA)
(October 16th, 1915 | Received by James Padgett)

I AM HERE. *Saleeba.*

Yes, I only wanted to say that I am very happy, and feel that I must tell you because you first caused me to seek this Love and to find the Way to my soul's development.

I know that you are not so much interested in me as in some others who write to you, but I further know that no one feels more grateful to you than I do. So, you see, as I progress, I must come and tell you of my happiness.

(I want you to share your happiness with me.)

Yes, that is what I want, and you seem to understand just what is necessary; and I am glad that I can come to you. So, my dear brother, think of me sometimes, and pray to the Father to give me more of His Divine Love that makes me at-one with Him.

I will not write more, but will say good night.

Your sister in Christ,
SALEEBA.

Solomon Tells of His Position in the Celestial Spheres.
(SOLOMON OF THE OLD TESTAMENT)
(June 27th, 1915 | Received by James Padgett)

I AM HERE. *Solomon of the Old Testament.*

(Why is it that you come to write to me tonight?)

Well, I was visiting the earth plane and happened to see the last two spirits visit you. I thought that I would do so also.

I know Paul and John and converse with them sometimes, but I do not live in as high a sphere as do they. Wisdom, which I was said to have had

352

in a preeminent degree, is not the equal of Love in elevating a spirit in the Father's Kingdom. And John and Paul are possessed of more of this Love than am I. Yet, I have great hope that someday I will get this great soul-filling Love to a degree that will enable me to live with them and the others of the followers of the Master. I mean his disciples.

I became a follower of the Master many years ago, and know that he is the only way to the Father. By that, I mean the Way which his teachings show is the only Way. I may seem a little surprising to you that I, said to have been such a wise and good man, am not as exalted as are the disciples. Well, while I lived and died many years before the disciples, and one would suppose that I made more rapid progress than they, yet, such is not the fact, because my progress prior to the coming of Jesus was purely intellectual; and, after his coming, it was a long time before I started on my soul's progression. So, you must remember that a spirit who is called an ancient spirit does not necessarily mean that it is very highly exalted in the spheres. Prior to Jesus' coming to earth, a spirit could only make intellectual and soul progress in the natural love, and then not higher than the Sixth Sphere of the Spiritual Spheres. But after his coming, and with the rebestowal by God of immortality and the Divine Love on mankind, the ancients had the opportunity to make the soul progression which was intended, and which would enable them to ascend to the higher Celestial Spheres.

I would like to write more, but you are tired. So, I will say good night.

SOLOMON, THE WISE.

Mrs. Padgett Explains That the Soul's Development Determines the Appearance of a Spirit, Not the Racial Characteristics of the Earth Life.
(HELEN PADGETT)
(June 28th, 1915 | Received by James Padgett)

I AM HERE. *Helen.*

Well, sweetheart, you are tired and must not write much tonight for it will make you feel bad. So, after I tell you a few things, stop writing.

Well, I see you want to know if the spirits who wrote to you last night— I mean the disciples and Solomon—really wrote to you. I am glad to say that they did. They were whom they represented themselves to be, and you must believe.

After John wrote, I had a conversation with him. He told me that you are on the way to the Kingdom. He is so loving and so beautiful and seems so filled with Love that I really could not help but love him. But, yet, he is not so glorious as the Master. None are, for he is the one altogether lovely. But John is a wonderful spirit. He is interested in your work and will no doubt write to you at times.

(Did you speak with Paul as well?)

I did not talk to Paul, as he left just as soon as he stopped writing, but I will sometime when he comes to you, as he says he will.

(And how about Solomon?)

Neither did I talk to Solomon because he departed as soon as he had finished. You may think him a wonderful spirit in appearance because of the great number of years since he lived on earth. But the years make no difference in appearance. He looks as young as do your own band, though more beautiful and loving. He is not a spirit who has any of his racial appearance. But, as I have said, appearance is determined by the soul development, no matter what race one may have belonged to on earth.

When a spirit who was a negro on earth gets this soul development, he goes into that sphere which his development fits him for. And no distinction is made between spirits on account of what their race may have been on earth. When a spirit who was a negro on earth acquires this soul development, the color that distinguished him on earth leaves him, and he has the appearance which his soul development gives him. He is no longer a negro but a redeemed spirit, and has the color of one.

So, you see, the color of a mortal on earth does not determine his color in the higher spheres.

In the earth plane, the earth color clings to the spirit, and sometimes it is intensified. In fact, a purely white man may become very dark in that plane, and the negroes may become darker. As I have said, the condition of the soul determines the appearance.

So, the heaven of all races may be the same, provided that the individuals of those races obtain this Divine Love to the same degree.

How blinded we are on earth to the fact that all humans are God's children, and all loved by Him just alike, no matter what their color or nationality may be!

Well, you must stop now.

So, with all my love, I am,

Your own true and loving,

HELEN.

Samuel, the Prophet, Discusses His Experience in the Spirit Heavens and His Progress to the Celestial Kingdom.
(SAMUEL OF THE OLD TESATMENT)
(August 5th, 1915 | Received by James Padgett)

I AM HERE. *Samuel of the Old Testament.*

I want to tell you that I am in a condition to tell you of my existence here in the spirit world, and what I know about the Truths of the doctrines of Jesus as I have learned them since I became possessed of the Divine Love which he brought to earth and to the world of spirits.

I have lived a great many years in this spirit life—more than you may think from the account of my earth life as contained in the Old Testament. For that book does not state correctly the time when I lived as a mortal. Many thousand years have gone by since I lived and performed my work as prophet and teacher on the earth. And, in all these long years, I have learned many things about the spiritual world, and its conditions and laws.

In the first place, I am not a spirit who was given over to the evils that men are usually possessed of when they become spirits because, when I lived on earth, I was very close to the Father in His Thoughts and Love. I mean the love which He gave to man at that time. This love, while not the Divine Love, was a love that was sufficient to make men happy when they possessed it free from sin and error, and when they tried to do the Will of the Father as they understood that Will. Many men thought that they understood this Will when, in reality, they only knew that which the laws of Moses taught them to be right in the sight of God. But some men were given a deeper insight into the Mind and Love of the Father to bless and make men happy in their natural love, and, consequently, were closer to Him and better understood His Will and what was pleasing to Him.

Since my becoming a spirit, I have learned many Truths which I did not understand on earth, and which are necessary to know in order to be able to enjoy this love in its fulness.

I never possessed this Divine Love, though, until after Jesus came to earth and showed men and spirits what this Love meant, and how necessary it was to obtain It in order to become a part of God's Divinity.

I do not now see that I was any more in favor of God (as I then possessed only this natural love) than were many others who had the privilege of receiving the inspirations from His angels which came to them at times, and which made them able to tell the inhabitants of earth what was the Purpose of God to have them do.

I was only a man in the sense that I was only possessed of this natural love and, hence, could get no higher in the spiritual world than this natural love would enable me to attain.

I am now in a heaven which this Divine Love has opened up to me, and which enables me to enjoy the great happiness which that Love causes all to have who possess It.

When I lived in the spirit world before obtaining this Divine Love, I was only possessed of that happiness which comes from the natural love, and I knew nothing of the happiness which I now possess. So, you see, the spirit which has not this Divine Love can go no higher in the spiritual spheres than it is fitted to occupy by reason of this natural love. And the principal source of happiness is this natural love and the development of the mental faculties. On earth, it is possible for a man to obtain this happiness and live in the heaven of the perfect natural man, as I did prior to my obtaining this Divine Love.

I WAS A SPIRIT IN THE HIGHEST OF THE SPIRITUAL SPHERES AND WAS VERY HAPPY, AS I THOUGHT. BUT WHEN I OBTAINED

THIS DIVINE LOVE, I REALIZED THAT THE HAPPINESS OF MY FORMER CONDITION WAS AS NOTHING COMPARED TO THAT OF MY PRESENT CONDITION; AND I THEREFORE WANT TO TELL ALL MANKIND THAT THEY MUST SEEK FOR THIS HIGHER LOVE IF THEY WISH TO OBTAIN A BLISS THAT IS SUPREME.

I know that this rambling talk may not seem very instructive. But I merely wish to emphasize the fact that I lived a mere man in the spirit form before I obtained the Divine Love, and that only with the coming of that Love in my soul did I partake of the Divinity of the Father.

(What has become of some of the other great religious teachers of the past?)

They are still in the Spiritual Heavens* because they have not yet embraced the Christ doctrine of Divine Love. They are living and teaching the doctrine that they taught on earth, only much improved.

(But why have they not sought and found this Love in all these years?)

I don't know except that they have been satisfied with what they taught and the happiness that they live in. It may seem strange to you that they have not found this Love in all these years, but it is a fact; and they are not seeking for It. I feel that they have neglected a great opportunity and have lost very much by letting all these years go by without having sought the Great Truth.

The different teachers of the various religions which have come to earth are occupying planes in the Spiritual Heavens all to themselves. They, the Jews, still think that theirs is the only true religion and that they are the chosen people of God, and that all others are mistaken in their doctrines.

Well, I must stop. So, thanking you for your kindness, I will say good night.

SAMUEL.

Aaron, the Brother of Moses, Gives His Experience, and What He Now Knows About Immortality Since Jesus Came and Taught How It Can Be Obtained.
(AARON)
(October 23rd, 1915 | Received by James Padgett)

I AM HERE. *Aaron.*

I am the spirit of Aaron, the prophet of the Old Testament and the brother of Moses, as it is written.

I merely want to say that as you read the message, "Immortality," from the spirit of Henry Ward Beecher, I read also; and that is a wonderful description of what immortality is, and how it first was given to mankind after the fall of the first parents.

I know the Truth of what he wrote, for I experienced the want of this

356

Divine Love for many thousand years before the coming of Jesus and the rebestowal of this Divine Love, which is the only thing in all God's Universe that can bring immortality to man. So, let this great Truth be preached to all the world, and let man know that he can never become immortal until he gets this Divine Love. It is so difficult for man, and for those who come forward as the teachers of men in spiritual things, to understand this Truth, and to comprehend that only this Love will save them from their sins and make them a part of the Divinity of the Father and certain of immortality.

I lived in a time when we had not the privilege of getting this Love and, as a consequence, immortality. We had to find our happiness in our natural love, and that meant a love towards God as well as towards our fellowman. But while this love enabled us to experience much happiness, yet, it did not give that Divine Essence or Nature which now makes our happiness supreme and also at-one with the Father.

I had many experiences in teaching the Hebrew children that there was only one God. But, at that time, my conception of God was not what it is now. I then thought more of Him as a God of "wrath" and "jealousy" than as a God of Love and Mercy.

In my contest with the magicians of the Egyptian pharaohs, I was afforded the help of the spirit world. Unusual powers were given me such as I had never had before nor ever afterwards. But this was for the purpose of causing the king to let the people of God, as we called ourselves, depart from Egypt. When this was accomplished, I never again possessed those powers or had any occasion to.

But those powers were merely the influences that came from the spirit world. God, Himself, did not speak to me or to Moses, as it is written. Merely His spirits or angels told us what we must do, and they gave us the power to do it.

This power is still existing and, should the occasion arise again, it will be given to the instrumentality that may be selected to do the Will of the Father. Even as to Jesus, who had the greatest power conferred upon him of any mortal that ever lived, this power was given him by the angels of God in obedience to the Commands of the Father.

I cannot explain to you now in what way these Commands were given by God, for you would not understand me if I should make the attempt. But suffice it to say that the higher angels have such soul perceptions that they can receive and understand these instructions of the Father. All this, I know, is strange to you, but it is true. And because you do not understand, you must not doubt that there is such a close relationship between God and His Celestial spirits in that they know what the Will of the Father is.

I am in a Celestial Sphere and am very high up, but not so high as the apostles are. But I am high enough to know to be true what I write to you of my own knowledge.

I will not write more tonight, but will come again sometime and instruct you in the laws obtaining in our Celestial Spheres.

So, with all my love, I will say that I am
Your brother in Christ,
AARON, the prophet of old.

Sarah Declares That She Is Now a Christian.
(SARAH, THE WIFE OF ABRAHAM)
(October 23rd, 1915 | Received by James Padgett)

I AM HERE. *Sarah, the wife of Abraham.*

I want to tell you that I am now a Christian and live in the Celestial Spheres.

(It says in the Bible that you ordered Hagar sent into the desert to die.)

Yes, but there are many things in the Bible that are not true. When it says that I sent Hagar into the desert, or caused her to be sent into the desert, to starve and die—that story was a slander on me, and did me great injustice, because I was not such a wicked woman.

Abraham did not send her there either. She went of her own accord because she had done that which condemned her in her own conscience.

(What had she done?)

Well, she had taken my husband and had a child by him. I know the Bible says that that was commanded by God, or that I prevailed upon Abraham to have a child by her, but neither account is true.

(Are you now happy in the Celestial Spheres?)

Yes, I am happy, and so is Abraham and our son Isaac, and his son Jacob; but they were without this Divine Love for a great many years, as It only came to us when the Master came to earth.

I know that you think it strange that I should come to you and write. But as I was with Aaron in the earth plane, and was attracted to you by the light which fills the space around you, I followed Aaron and came to you; and, after he wrote, I wrote also.

(Are there many spirits present right now?)

Yes, I see a great number of beautiful spirits around you, and some of the apostles who are so very beautiful and bright. They seem to be so much interested in you, and they say that you have been selected to do the work of the Master on earth in the way of revealing the Truths which he shall write to you. I don't quite understand it all. But if the Master says that this is what shall be done, you will do it.

I must stop now. But please believe that I am Sarah, as I have told you. I will leave you now and say good night.
Your sister in Christ,
SARAH, the wife of Abraham.

I AM HERE. *Hugh Latimer.*

I was the martyr who was burned at the stake because of my belief in God, and in salvation by faith and works as taught in the Scriptures.

My name was Hugh Latimer.

I merely come to tell you that I am now a happy spirit and an inhabitant of the Father's Kingdom. I live in the Celestial Heavens and am a follower of the Master, as I was on earth.

(Do you worship Jesus as God?)

No, I do not now worship him as God. I believed that false doctrine when on earth. But now I know that there is only one God to be worshiped, and that Jesus is His most exalted son. I was surprised, I must confess, when I entered the spirit world and did not enter heaven and see God on His "throne" and Jesus sitting on His "right hand." But it was not long before I understood the Truth. For Jesus came to me himself and explained that he was not God, and that I must not worship him as such. But we who love God, as followers of Christ, adore the Master as our great teacher and elder brother.

When I first entered the spirit world, I found myself in the Second Sphere among spirits of brightness and love. And, after a little while, I entered the Third Sphere where Love is more abundant. Then, as my soul became filled with this Love, and my errors of belief left me, I progressed from sphere to sphere until I arrived where I am now living; and I thank God for His Love and Mercy.

I do not think the fact that I died a martyr to my beliefs had any effect in enabling me to reach a higher sphere than I would otherwise have entered. Not the manner of my death determined my place in the spirit world, but the development of my soul qualities did. If I had a belief in what I thought were truths, but which were not really truths, and that belief, proclaimed and persisted in, had caused my being put to death, you can readily see that the mere fact that I died for the sake of that belief would not have helped my soul development in the real Truth in any way. And, so, the mere fact that I died a martyr for what I believed to be true did not help me in obtaining a place in the spirit world that I would not have obtained had I died a natural death with the same beliefs. THE MANNER OF A MAN'S DEATH DOES NOT DETERMINE ANYTHING. BUT THE MANNER OF HIS LIVING AND THE DEVELOPMENT OF HIS SOUL QUALITIES ARE WHAT DETERMINE WHERE HE SHALL

LIVE IN THE SPIRIT WORLD.

Of course, the death of the martyr will sometimes awaken soul qualities or conceptions that might not otherwise have been awakened, and thereby increase the martyr's love for the Father. In this way, such a death may help him in his progress to higher things. But, as I say, the soul development fixes the first home of the spirit. I mean the development at the time of passing over.

My dear brother, I must stop now. But I will come again sometime to write to you.

Yours in love,

HUGH LATIMER.

George Whitefield Relates That He Changed His Erroneous Beliefs That He Taught on Earth, and That He Is Now in the Celestial Heavens.
(GEORGE WHITEFIELD)
(August 8th, 1915 | Received by James Padgett)

I AM HERE. *George Whitefield.*

I was a preacher of England and a contemporary of John Wesley. I am in the Celestial Spheres where are only those who have received the New Birth that has been written about by other and more ancient spirits.

I merely want to say that I am still a follower of Jesus, but a little different in my knowledge of what he was and is. I do not now look upon him as God, or a part of God, but as His true son, and the greatest of all the spirits in the spirit world. There are none to be compared to him in beauty or spirituality or in his knowledge of God's Truths.

I USED TO PREACH TO THOUSANDS ABOUT HIS VICARIOUS ATONEMENT AND HIS BLOOD SACRIFICE, BUT NOW I SEE HIS MISSION IN A DIFFERENT LIGHT. IT IS NOT HIS DEATH ON THE CROSS THAT SAVES MEN FROM THEIR SINS, NOR HIS SACRIFICE THAT APPEASES THE "WRATH" OF AN "ANGRY" GOD, BUT HIS LIFE AND TEACHINGS OF THE DIVINE LOVE BESTOWED ON MANKIND AND THE WAY TO OBTAIN THAT LOVE ARE WHAT SAVE MEN FROM THEIR SINS. THERE WAS NO ANGRY GOD—ONLY A LOVING AND MERCIFUL GOD. AND WHEN MEN THINK THAT UNLESS THEY TURN FROM THEIR SINS THEY WILL BE FOREVER BURNED IN A FIERY HELL, THEY ARE THE DUPES OF PREACHERS SUCH AS I WAS, AND WILL NEVER GET THE LOVE OF THE FATHER BY SUCH TEACHINGS. GOD IS LOVE, AND MEN MUST KNOW IT. HIS LOVE IS FOR ALL OF EVERY RACE AND CLIME.

I see now what a great mistake I made in my conception of God and of

Christ's mission on earth, how much harm I did to mortals in my preaching, and how I slandered the Father of Love. But I was honest in my beliefs and taught as I thought the truth to be. Yet, that does not alter the fact that many a mortal was retarded for a long time in his spiritual progress after he became a spirit because of these false beliefs which, in order to progress, he had to give up and start anew in his efforts to find the Truths of God.

As I worked hard and preached eloquently to make mortals believe these injurious doctrines while on earth, so I am now working hard and preaching eloquently to make spirits who come over with these beliefs unlearn them and see the Truth as it is.

I am in sympathy with the movement which the Master is now making to spread the Truth of these spiritual things on earth, and I am ready to follow him in all his efforts to bring about the salvation of men, not only from sin but also from erroneous beliefs.

So, I come to you tonight to express my sympathy and interest in the cause.

Let your work proceed, and do your best to make known to men the great Truths which the Master shall teach. We will all join in the work and do everything in our power to speed the great cause of men's redemption from sin and ignorance.

Man must have the soul development by obtaining the Divine Love, because you cannot inspire a man to preach grand and sublime spiritual Truths unless he has the capacity in his own soul to feel and understand the Truths.

I will not write longer tonight.

I am your true friend,

GEORGE WHITEFIELD.

III. The Hells.

MESSAGES INCLUDED IN THIS CHAPTER.

Nero, the Roman Emperor, Gives His Experience in the Hells and His Progress to the Celestial Heavens. (NERO, THE ROMAN EMPEROR)...365

A Spirit Describes His Experience in One of the Hells. (G.H.B.) 368

Mrs. Padgett Confirms That the Spirits Who Had Written Actually Did So. (HELEN PADGETT) 371

Emanuel Swedenborg Writes on the Hells. He Also Refers to Mr. Padgett's Work in Receiving the Messages. (EMANUEL SWEDENBORG)...372

King Herod Writes on the Hells, and Also Corroborates Swedenborg's Statement That the Hells Are Actual Places Where Suffering Is Experienced. (KING HEROD) 374

Mrs. Padgett Confirms That Herod Wrote on the Hells. (HELEN PADGETT)...375

John, the Apostle, Confirms That Swedenborg and Herod Gave True Descriptions of the Hells. (JOHN, THE APOSTLE).............................376

Caligula, the Roman Emperor and Murderer of Christians, Suffered All the Horrors of Hell, but Has Paid His Penalties and Is Now a Follower of Jesus and an Inhabitant of the Celestial Heavens. (CALIGULA, THE ROMAN EMPEROR)..377

Julius Caesar Writes That Earthly Position Does Not Determine One's Spiritual Abode. (JULIUS CAESAR)..379

Mrs. Padgett Confirms That Julius Caesar Wrote. (HELEN PADGETT)...380

Julius Caesar Relates That He Is Seeking for the Divine Love, and That Light Is Breaking into His Soul. (JULIUS CAESAR).....................380

Julius Caesar Returns to Give His Experience After Receiving Help from a Divine Spirit. (JULIUS CAESAR) 383

Mrs. Padgett Confirms That Julius Caesar Wrote Again. (HELEN

PADGETT) 385

Elias Discusses the Hope That All Mortals Have in a Future Destiny of Freedom from Care and Unhappiness. (ELIAS, THE PROPHET) 385

John Expresses His Regret That a Preacher Could Not Inform His Congregation Correctly as to Hell. (JOHN, THE APOSTLE) 387

Mrs. Padgett Explains That Man Himself Must Make the Effort to Overcome the Influence of Evil Spirits. (HELEN PADGETT) 388

Following a Personal Interchange with Mr. Padgett, Jesus Then Explains the Necessary Conditions Required So That the Higher Spirits Can Help Those in Lower Spheres. (JESUS) 389

Mrs. Padgett Confirms the Importance of Her Husband's Work Among the Dark Spirits. (HELEN PADGETT) 392

III. The Hells.

Nero, the Roman Emperor, Gives His Experience in the Hells and His
Progress to the Celestial Heavens.
(NERO, THE ROMAN EMPEROR)
(January 16th, 1917 | Received by James Padgett)

I AM HERE. *Nero, a former Roman emperor.*

I am here, the spirit of one who lived the life of a wicked man of earth. I was a persecutor of the Christians, and a blasphemer of God and everything that was pure and holy. And when I had lived the life to its end, and had shuffled off the mortal coil and became a spirit, I also became a dweller in the lowest hells where all is darkness and torment, and where the abode of devils[*] and everything that tends to make the spirit unhappy exists and is at variance with the Loving God.

I introduce myself in this way in order to demonstrate to you the wonderful power of the Divine Love. For I am now an inhabitant of the Celestial Spheres, and know that this Love is not only real but is also capable of making the vilest sinner a partaker and owner of the Divine Essence of the Father.

My sufferings were beyond all description, and I was the most desecrated of mortals. And I was almost worshiped by the devils of hell because of the great injury I had done to the followers of Jesus who, in my time, were possessed of this Love, and a faith which even the terrors of the wild beasts of the arena, or the torches of my own evil design, could not cause them to renounce. It was at the time of this great religion of the New Birth that the Master had taught them, and that the disciples were still teaching, when I put so many of them to death.

The devils loved me for the very evil that I had done.

But, strange to say, the spirits of those who I had sent into the spirit world before their time were not revengeful to me, and did not come to me with their imprecations or cursings. Then, when I had been in the spirit world a sufficient time to realize my surroundings and the nature of these evils, these spirits of the martyrs, which I had made, came to me in sympathy and pity, and, in fact, tried many times to help me out of my great sufferings and darkness. I did not understand all this unexpected kindness and evidence of love, and, for a long time, I would not believe that these spirits were sincere. And, so, I suffered for year after year, and century after century, and became convinced that my condition was fixed, that for me there was no hope, that the God that I had heard of was not my God, and that devils were the only companions that I was destined to have through

---

[*] "Devils" means former mortals, now spirits, who are undeveloped and who have yet to have progressed to higher spheres of light and happiness.—Ed.

all eternity.

And, so, I endured, wishing to die, but I could not. Oh, I tell you it was horrible and beyond all conception of mortals! The law was working and I was paying the penalty, and there seemed no end to the penalty.

I could find no consolation among those who surrounded me. The pleasures that I first enjoyed became mere things of mockery and derision to me, and my darkness and torment became the greater. How often I called upon God, if there was a God, to strike me dead! But the only answer to my call was the laughter of the grinning devils who told me to shout louder, as God might be asleep and may be deaf!

What to do, I knew not, and, so, I became isolated as best I could from these terrible associates. Many years of my living were spent in the darkness of lonesomeness, with never a ray of hope or the whisper of one word to tell me that there might be a fairer destiny for me. And, so, time went by and I waited in my misery for some kind power to come and annihilate me. But I waited in vain.

During all this time, the recollections of my earthly deeds were like hot irons scorching my soul and burning my body, as I thought, and the end came not.

Well, I suffered the tortures of the damned, and it seemed to me that I was paying the penalties for all the wicked kings and rulers and persecutors of earth. Many times, the shrieks of the Christian children and the groans of the men and women, as they were being torn asunder from limb to limb, or burned as living torches which I had made of them, came to me and increased my torment. I lived the life of centuries of torment in a few moments, as it seemed to me, and not one cooling drop of water was mine. It may seem impossible that I should have continued to live in this ever increasing suffering, but I did because I was compelled to. The law did its work and there was no one to say: "Enough!"

I might write a volume on this suffering of mine; yet you would not comprehend its meaning. And, so, I will pass it by.

In my loneliness and suffering, there came to me, on an occasion, a beautiful spirit, full of light and love, and all the beauty of early womanhood, as I thought. And with eyes of pity and longing, she said:

You are not alone. Only open your eyes and you will see the star of hope, which is the sign of the Father's Love and Desire to help you. I am a child of that Father and the possessor of His Great enveloping Love. And I love you, even though you took my young life from me when you threw me to the wild beasts to satisfy your desire to gratify your thirst for innocent blood, and to see the suffering and hear the groans of your victims. Yet, I love you not because I am a human with a kindly nature and forgiving disposition, but because I have in me this Divine Love of the Father which tells me that I am your sister, and that you are a child of His Love, just as I was the object of His Love.

You have suffered. And, while you suffered, His Great Love went out to you in sympathy and desire to help you. But you, yourself, prevented It from coming to you and leading you to light and surcease from sufferings. And, now, I come to you, your young and innocent victim, who had never done you any greater harm on earth than to pray for you and ask the Heavenly Father to take away the great wickedness from your heart that caused so many of my people to suffer persecutions and death. We all prayed for you and never asked our Father to curse you, or to do anything to you to make you suffer. And we have prayed for you often since we came to the spirit world; and we are now praying for you, and this because we love you and want you to be happy. Look into my eyes and you will see that love is there, and that what I tell you is true. And, now, can you not love us a little and open up your soul to our sympathy, and let your feelings of gloom and despondency leave you for a moment, and realize that, in this world of spirits, there are some who love you?

Well, to say that I was surprised does not express my feelings. As I looked into the love-lit eyes of that beautiful spirit, I felt the great sins of my earth life overwhelm me. And, in my anguish, I cried, "God be merciful to me, the greatest of sinners!" And, for the first time in all my life in the hells, tears came to my eyes, and my heart seemed to have a sense of living; and there came to me feelings of remorse and regret for all the evils that I had done.

It would take too long to tell what followed this breaking up of my soul, all shriveled and dead. Suffice it to say that, from time to time, I commenced to have hope come to me that I could get out of my awful condition of darkness. It took a long time but, at last, I got into the light. And this Love which the beautiful spirit first told me of gradually came into my soul, until, at last, I reached the condition of bliss in which I now am.

And during all the time of my progress, this radiant, loving spirit came to me very often with her words of love and encouragement. She prayed for me and never left me when I became, as I did at times, doubtful and discouraged. As my awakening continued, the Love came into my soul. And as she told me of the heavenly things that would be mine as I progressed and reached the soul spheres, where beautiful homes and pure, bright spirits are, I became more and more bound by my love to her. After a while, I got into the Third Sphere, and realized that what she had told me was true. Only I had not been able to comprehend the greatness of the Truth.

She then commenced to tell me of the happiness of the beautiful spirits of the two sexes that I so often saw together. She explained that they were soulmates, and that their love was the greatest of all the loves except the Divine Love, and that every spirit in all the spheres had its soulmate and, at the proper time, would find it.

My love for this loving spirit had then become so intense that, in the very depths of my soul, I wished and prayed that my soulmate might be such a one as she. And, at last, I became so filled with my love for her that I told her that the only thing in all the heavens that I needed to make my happiness full was she as my soulmate, but that I realized that that desire was hopeless, as I had destroyed her life, and, of course, she could not be my soulmate. And, oh, how I suffered when I realized that she could not be mine, but was another's!

As I told her of these longings and hopeless feelings of my soul, she came close to me and looked into my eyes with such burning love, and threw her arms around me and said:

I am your soulmate, and knew that fact a short time after you came to the spirit world and entered your hells of darkness. And, during all the long years, I prayed and prayed for the time to come when I could go to you with my love and awaken in your dead soul the response to my great love. And when the time came that I could go, I was so thankful to the Father that I almost flew to you—with some dread of disappointment, I confess—to tell you that you were not neglected or unthought of, but that there was some love in the spirit world that was going to you. Of course, I could not tell you of my soulmate love, for you would not then have understood. But, as your soul awakened and the Love of the Father came to you, I became happier and happier, and have waited anxiously for this moment when I could tell you that this love that had been consciously mine for so long is all yours!

Well, I will draw the veil here, but you can imagine what my happiness was. As I progressed from sphere to sphere, my happiness and love for her increased and increased.

Thus, I have told you the story of the life of the wickedest man in the spirit world that God ever permitted to live and gratify his feelings of hatred and revenge.

And I, who have passed through this experience and realized all that it means, say that the Divine Love of the Father is able to, and does, save the vilest sinner, and transforms the worst of all devils into a Celestial angel of His highest Spheres.

I have written long and you are tired.

I thank you and will say good night, and subscribe myself,

Your brother in Christ,

NERO, the Roman emperor, and,

at one time, a persecutor

of God's true children.

A Spirit Describes His Experience in One of the Hells.
(G.H.B.)
(January 5th, 1916 | Received by James Padgett)

I AM HERE. *G.H.B.*

I am a spirit who cannot tell you of the joys of heaven, but I can describe the horrors of hell. For just as these other spirits described to you their homes of beauty and happiness, I can describe my home of ugliness and torment.

Do you wish me to do so?

(Yes, please do.)

Well, know then that, when I lived on earth, I was a man of very considerable intellectual powers and acquirements, and also of an intense animal nature—so much so that it overcame my judgment and what moral qualities I had; and I became, at last, a slave to my appetites, which were varied, especially my appetite for drink.

I had many friends of position, social and otherwise, and I was considered a brilliant newspaper writer, and had access to the inner political circles that were then in control of the government.

My weakness, or rather the effect of the strength of my animal nature, was known to many of my friends. And, in many ways, they tried to help me and rescue me from my evil and destructive course of living; and, it was not for any great length of time before I would again relapse into my deplorable habits and become the controlled victim of my destroying appetites.

Of course, human friendship and sympathy had their limits, and my friends finally gave me up as lost and past redemption. And I surely and quickly sunk lower and lower in my moral condition and, at last, died a drunkard, unwept and unsung except for the evil that I had done. It was undoubtedly a relief to my friends and acquaintances, when I passed over, to be forever relieved of the shadow of my presence and the ghost of what I had been.

But such was my end. And, when I came to the spirit world, I found that I still was deserted by friends who had become spirits before me, except not by some who liked the flowing bowl as I did on earth, and who were inhabitants of the unattractive place that I found myself in when my habitation became fixed.

When on earth, I never thought much of the future life, except to convince myself that there was no hell, and, if there was a God, that He was not bothered about me, a mere man of many millions.

But, oh, the fatal mistake, and the unexpected realization of the fact that there is a hell! Whether there is a God I don't know, for I have never seen Him or felt His Influence. But since I came to you tonight and heard the messages of those two spirits who described their wonderful homes and their condition of happiness, and ascribed them all to the Kindness and Care of God, I have commenced to think that there may be a God and that my mistake was greater than I have heretofore realized. But this is a digression from what I started out to write.

That there is a hell I know to my sorrow and sufferings, for I have been the occupant of one for, oh, these many years! And it is always the same place of horrors and darkness, except, sometimes, it is lighted by the flame of lurid light that comes from the anger and sufferings of some unfortunate like myself.

369

In this hell of mine, and there are many like it, instead of beautiful homes, as the other spirits described, we have dirty, rotten hovels, all crooked and decayed, with all the foul smells of a charnel house ten-times intensified. And instead of beautiful lawns and green meadows, and leafy woods filled with musical birds making the echoes ring with their songs, we have stagnant pools filled with all kinds of repulsive reptiles and vermin, and smells of inexpressible, nauseating stinks.

I tell you that these are all real, and not creatures of the imagination or the outflowing of bitter recollections. And, as for love, it has never shown its humanizing face in all the years that I have been here—only cursings and hatred and bitter scathings and imprecations, and grinning spirits with their witch-like cacklings. There is no rest, no hope, no kind words or ministering hand to wipe away the scalding tears which so often flow in mighty volumes. No, hell is real and hell is here!

We do not have any fire and brimstone, or grinning devils with pitchforks and hoofs and horns, as the churches teach. But what is the need or necessity for such accompaniments? They would not add to the horrors or to our torments. I tell you, my friend, that I have only faintly described our homes in these infernal regions, and I cannot picture them as they are.

But the horror and pity of it all is that hope does not come to us with one faint smile to encourage us that there may be an ending to all these torments at some time. And, in our hopeless despair, we realize that our doom is fixed for all eternity.

As the rich man in hell said, "If I could only send Lazarus to tell my poor, erring brothers on earth of what awaits them, how gladly I would do so and save their souls from the eternal torment."

Well, I have written you a long letter, and I am tired because it is the first time that I have attempted to write for many long years. I find some difficulty in gathering my thoughts so as to be able to write in an intelligent and collected manner. So, I must stop.

(My dear friend and brother, don't despair, for I will attempt to help you out of your condition of darkness and suffering if you will allow me to do so.)

Well, I will say that you are the best friend that I have had since I became an outcast while on earth, and that I will do whatever you may advise. But you must not expect me to have much hope—not doubting your desire to help me, by merely your ability.

(Well, first you must open your heart and mind to receiving help from the Celestial spirits—spirits who were once sinful mortals like yourself before they became fully redeemed children of God by receiving His Divine Love through prayer. In addition, while you reach out to them in this way, I too will ask that they come to you with their great love and solicitude to provide you with the help you need. And as we thus both call upon them, simply look about you. Very soon, they will appear to your vision.)

Well, I have looked as you advised, and I see some spirits who are so

370

beautiful and bright that I can scarcely look at them. Never before have I seen such spirits, or imagined that such could exist. They must be gods, or why all the great happiness and beauty and love which they have? Tell me, what does it all mean? Is it a star of hope that has come to me from afar, and bids me trust that these hells shall not be my home forever? Oh, tell me, I pray you, are they the spirits of real mortals who lived and died as I did?

Such love I have never seen! They look at me with such encouragement and almost human eyes of love, and they beckon me to come with them. I have asked if Mr. Riddle is there, and one spirit comes to me and says yes, and that he is glad to have me come with him, as he knew me on earth and is acquainted with my sad life. And now I remember him, for he was a friend who lived in the same city as I did.

He says, "Come G_____, and I will try to show you the Way to light and relief from your sufferings." And I am going; and, as I go, a beautiful, glorious spirit comes to me and lays her hand on my head and says, "God bless you, my brother, and may His Divine Mercy be yours." And she tells me that they all love me and will help me.

Oh, tell me, what does it all mean? Am I dreaming? Are you real and are they real, or am I in one of the deliriums that I used to have on earth? Oh, they are so beautiful and heavenly! But they say no—that they are real spirits and once lived on earth, and were sinful mortals like myself.

How can I ever thank you? I am overcome and cannot write more, but I will come again. So, my dear friend, good night, for I am going.

G.H.B.[*]

Mrs. Padgett Confirms That the Spirits Who Had Written Actually Did So.
(HELEN PADGETT)
(January 5th, 1916 | Received by James Padgett)

I AM HERE. *Helen.*

Well, my dear, you have had a variety of writings tonight, and I have been greatly impressed with the last message that you received; for the writer was a very intelligent spirit and seemed to be without hope in his soul. He was a very dark spirit and did not seem to have any love in his soul, and was the picture of despair and grief. He firmly believed that his position in hell was fixed for all eternity, and, hence, the hopeless despair in which he was.

I am so glad that he came to you and described these hells, for he was

---

[*] This spirit stated that he had died in 1899. In a later message, he said that he had obtained the Divine Love in his soul and had reached the Third Sphere.—Ed.

capable. No one can describe them as well as he who has lived in them for many years and suffered and experienced all their torments.

He seems to be very grateful, and I think that hope has come to him. He has gone with Mr. Riddle who is much interested in him. We will all try to help him to progress. So, you must pray for him now—we all will.

It is late, and I will not write more.

Your own true and loving,

HELEN.

Emanuel Swedenborg Writes on the Hells. He Also Refers to Mr. Padgett's Work in Receiving the Messages.
(EMANUEL SWEDENBORG)
(December 17th, 1915 | Received by James Padgett)

I AM HERE. *Swedenborg.*

Let me write a few lines, as I desire to write to you some truths about what you and your friend were discussing; namely, are there any such hells as are described in the messages contained in the book (Dr. Peeble's *Immortality*) that you have been reading tonight.

Well, you must know that, in the spirit planes, hell is a place as well as a condition, and that, as a place, it has all the accompaniments that make it a reality to the spirits who inhabit it. Of course, the conditions of the spirits who are in these hells are determined by their recollections, worked upon by their consciences. But, notwithstanding that these recollections are the things that cause their sufferings, yet, the appearances of the locations in which they live are due to something more than these mere recollections. For, as you have been informed, all these spirits are in darkness, the degree of which is determined by their recollections. I mean that when the spirit has recollections of deeds done or not done, which are not so bad as the recollections of another, the former spirit is in a place where there is less darkness than the latter.

These places have their own fixed condition of darkness and of gloom, and many other attachments which increase the sufferings that spirits have to endure.

Of course, there are no fires and brimstone lakes, and devils with pitchforks adding to the sufferings of the spirits. But, yet, there are certain conditions and appearances which are outside of the spirits themselves, and which cause their recollections to become more acute and to work in a manner to produce a greater degree of suffering.

These hells may be places of caverns and rocks and barren wastes and dark holes, and other such things as have been written about. And mortals must know that evil spirits do not live in pleasant places, and that they suffer from this and from the punishments which their recollections bring to them.

While the hells of the orthodox are greatly exaggerated in their descriptions, yet, there is some truth in the ideas which these descriptions convey as to the fact that the hells are places in which there is darkness and many accompanying appearances that add to the tortures of the spirits of evil.

I tell you this because I see you want to know the truth, and for the further reason that you do not believe that there are such distinctive places as the hells, and that the darkness which the spirits speak to you of in their communications is produced, in your opinion, by the conditions of the minds and souls of the spirits who write.

But such opinion is not altogether correct, and it is best for men to know that the mere recollections do not include all of what the hells are.

You say you have your hells on earth sometimes, and that is true to a limited extent. Many men suffer very much from their consciences and remorse. But when they come into the spirit world, if they have not gotten out of the condition which these recollections and remorse place them in, they will find that there is that place or location waiting for them which will add to their sufferings that arise from the recollections of evil deeds committed while on earth.

The evil spirits live in communities, for the Law of Attraction operates in these dark and lower planes just as it does in the higher spheres; and it causes spirits of like or similar conditions to congregate together and find consolation (or what they may think at times to be consolation) in one another's company.

These hells are on the planes nearest the earth. And these spirits are not confined all the time to any particular hell. They have the privilege of moving at will along this plane. But, wherever they go, they find that they are in these hells, and they cannot escape from them unless they accept the help from spirits who can instruct them in what they must do.

When they come to you to write, they are not very far from these hells, because the plane in which they live is a part of the plane in which the inhabitants of earth live.

Of course, I don't mean to say that that portion of the earth plane that surrounds your earth is composed entirely of these hells, for that is not true. The earth sphere has considerable light in it and some happiness. And you must further remember that there are many planes in this earth plane.

While their habitations are in these hells, those spirits have the privilege of leaving these particular localities and wandering for a short time in and over other parts of this earth plane, but this is only for a short time. They have to return to the places where they have been placed, and which this Law of Attraction, that I speak of, draws them to.

There are thousands of millions of evil spirits, and there is never a time when some of them—thousands of them—are not surrounding and trying to use their bad influences on mortals. We do not know why this is permitted, but only know that it is so. And here, again, the great Law of Attraction operates, for many mortals are in similar conditions of development and evil thoughts of what these evil spirits are in. And, naturally, these evil spirits are drawn to them and do come to them. And, frequently, it happens that, while visiting these mortals of similar conditions to their own, they attempt to influence mortals who are in a better state of moral and spiritual condition, and sometimes succeed in doing them harm.

But the great fact is that these evil spirits have a place of living where they have to remain until, by the operation of the Law of Compensation, they are relieved from some of their evil tendencies and desires and are permitted to progress.

My principal reason in writing to you is to have you know that there are hells of places as well as of conditions, and that these places and their appearances add to the suffering of the spirits by reason of what they contain.

As I have written a long time, I will stop and say that I am a Christian and an inhabitant of the Celestial Spheres, and one of the spirit band that is helping you in the great work of the Master. So, in leaving you, I will subscribe myself,

Your brother in Christ,

SWEDENBORG, the seer.

King Herod Writes on the Hells, and Also Corroborates Swedenborg's Statement That the Hells Are Actual Places Where Suffering Is Experienced.
(KING HEROD)
(December 18th, 1915 | Received by James Padgett)

I AM HERE. *Herod.*

Let me write just a line before you close, as I am anxious to tell you of a matter that may be of importance to you in reference to the descriptions of the hells which you received last night from Swedenborg.

He says that the hells are places as well as conditions, and that they have certain appearances and surroundings as a part of them that make the sufferings of the evil spirits increase. Well, this is true. And, in addition, I wish to say that not only are these appearances and surroundings real and existing to the consciousness of the spirit, but they are also real as a fact, independent of the consciousness. If there were no spirits in these hells, these appearances and surroundings would exist just the same.

So, you see, a great many mortals whom I have heard express their opinions to the effect that hell is a mere condition of the recollections of the spirit, and nothing more, are altogether wrong in such opinions. They will find that the consolation from such opinions, if there be any, will not be found whenever they may become inhabitants of these hells.

I have passed through all of them and know whereof I write. For there is no teacher so efficient and convincing as the teacher called experience.

If I had only my recollections and remorse as the cause of my sufferings I know that they would have been much lighter and not so excruciating as they were. No, mortals will not find any consolation in such a hope, for there is no foundation for such hope. And the poor, deceived mortal who bases his ideas of hell on such a hope will be sadly disappointed. When you consider for a moment, you will see that there is nothing unreasonable in the facts that I have stated.

You and all others who believe in the happiness of the higher Spiritual Spheres, not to mention the Celestial Spheres, believe that the happiness of the spirits who inhabit these spheres is increased and made more real by the beautiful surroundings and the fruits and living water that so many spirits have described as being a part of that higher existence. Then, why is it not as reasonable to suppose that there are surroundings and appearances in the hells that will make the condition of the spirits, whose evil lives have caused them to become inhabitants of these hells, one of even more unhappiness, and create more suffering and misery? This supposition is one that no reasonable argument can prove to be incorrect.

I merely wanted to add what I have said to what Swedenborg wrote, for I know that conviction must come where statements are based upon actual experience, and where knowledge is derived from sufferings which come from the actual existence of things that are sometimes alleged not to exist.

I will not write more now, but, in closing, will say that I have long since left these hells, and am now an inhabitant of higher spheres and a follower of the blessed Master.

When on earth, I was known as Herod, the King of Judea, and the poor, miserable, mistaken man who thought that by slaying the babes of Bethlehem he would maintain his power as ruler.

So, good night, and God bless you.

HEROD.

Mrs. Padgett Confirms That Herod Wrote on the Hells.
(HELEN PADGETT)
(December 18th, 1915 | Received by James Padgett)

I AM HERE. *Helen.*

Well, sweetheart, you have had a letter tonight from a spirit who ought to know what he is writing about, as he was a most wicked man, and, as I have been told, suffered the torments of the lowest hells.

But as to you, personally, I want to say that it will make no difference to you what the nature of the hells is, or whether there be any or not. You will never see them, unless, when you come over, you have a desire to visit them for the purpose of doing good to some poor unfortunate. And I thank God for this assurance and knowledge.

I will not write more tonight. With all   my love, I am

Your own true and loving,

HELEN.

John, the Apostle, Confirms That Swedenborg and Herod Gave True Descriptions of the Hells.
(JOHN, THE APOSTLE)
(December 19th, 1915 | Received by James Padgett)

I AM HERE. *John.*

I merely want to say that I have listened to the message that you read, and to the remarks of your friend and yourself, and I believe that you have a true conception of the truth as to these hells.

Swedenborg gave you a correct description of their conditions as they actually exist, and Herod told you, with the certainty of experience, what he found to be true. And I, John, who have visited them in the efforts to allay the sufferings of the spirits who inhabit them, tell you that they exist as places, with all the darkness and surroundings that cause the sufferings of the unfortunate spirits to increase. I desire to make this statement so that this question of what hell really is may be settled for all time, so far as you are concerned.

I know that many mortals console themselves with the belief that, because of certain natural laws, there cannot possibly be any hells such as the orthodox teach, and that, therefore, there cannot be any hells at all. But this conclusion, drawn from the premise, is not correct. The mere fact that a man or spirit cannot burn eternally and never be consumed does not justify the inference that such spirit cannot be punished by surroundings which have a fixed locality.

No, man must not rest in the belief of there being no such hells as Swendenborg has described, because, if they do, they will be woefully mistaken and surprised, should they live such lives on earth as will cause them to be placed in these hells.

I merely wanted to say this much tonight, as I don't want you to receive any communication which is not in accord with the Truth.

It is of such vital importance that you receive nothing but the Truth that we who are interested in this work have determined that nothing but the Truth shall come to you. And whenever error or misstatements creep in, we will carefully correct the same.

Your brother in Christ,

JOHN.

Caligula, the Roman Emperor and Murderer of Christians, Suffered All the Horrors of Hell, but Has Paid His Penalties and Is Now a Follower of Jesus and an Inhabitant of the Celestial Heavens.
(CALIGULA, THE ROMAN EMPEROR)
(October 11th, 1915 | Received by James Padgett)

I AM HERE. *Caligula.*

I was the Roman emperor and the murderer of the Christians, and have since that time, and for my sins, suffered all the horrors of a hell which I can't describe. Suffice it to say that the hell of the Bible, or of those who interpret the Bible, is not equal in its torments and horrors to the hell that I passed through. I tell you this that you may know that every man will have to pay the penalties for the evil deeds he does when on earth. And as my deeds were so extremely evil, my penalties were correspondingly great.

But, thank God, I have paid my penalties and am now enjoying the happiness of the Christian heaven, for I am now a follower of that Jesus whose followers I persecuted.

Strange as it may seem to you, the cause of my conversion to Christianity was one of the very Christians whom I murdered. She was a beautiful spirit when I first saw her in the spirit world. And when she came to me and told me of the great Love of the Father, and the kindness and humility of the Master, I was then in much darkness, though I had suffered for many long years,   and my thoughts were commencing to turn to things that ultimately helped me to get out of my darkness and find relief from my sufferings.

But this Christian spirit came to me with such love and forgiveness in her speech that I was greatly affected by what she said and by her appearance. And I listened to her as she told me of the wonderful Love of the Father, and the great desire of the Master that I should seek for that Love and the happiness which It brings to spirits who obtain It.

She had many interviews with me and, at last, she told me that her happiness depended, to some extent, on my getting this Divine Love in my soul, and progressing with her to the sphere of Light and Love. She said that I was her soulmate and that my love was necessary for her happiness, and that I could not give her that love until I had become the possessor of the Divine Love to some extent. So, you can imagine what an effect this declaration had on me!

I saw that she was beautiful and pure and loving, and that I was not a fit soulmate for her, and that I must try to make myself a suited soulmate in order that I could be with her. And, in addition, when she told me of her love for me, and that we were necessary to each other's happiness, I had a most wonderful longing to be with her and enjoy her love. The desire soon took possession of me, and I commenced to inquire as to the Way by which I might get this great Love, or start to get It. She told me then of the love of the Master, and how he could teach me the Way, and what power he had to help spirits like myself to get out of the darkness and torture into light and happiness.

And, so, I continued in my longings and desires until, at last, my spirit seemed to have a power to rise out of the darkness and to meet other spirits who were not as dark and forbidding as I was.

She often came to me and taught me to pray. And I did pray and ask for forgiveness, and for just a little of that Divine Love of which she had told me.

At last, as I was praying and hoping for this Love and for deliverance, the Master came to me. And such a wonderful loving spirit he was—the most beautiful and loving—and, yet, the most humble that I had ever seen or ever have seen. He commenced to tell me of this wonderful Love of the Father, and how It was working for me to fill my soul and make me a child of God and at-one with Him. And he told me that the only things necessary were for me to pray to the Father and have faith, and in all earnestness repent of my great sins. He explained that, if I did so, the Love would come to me, and as It came into my soul, all the sins and recollections of my sins would leave me so that I would be able to progress to a higher sphere where Light and Love were.

I could not resist his influence, and I did not want to. For my soulmate was with me in her love, with pleading eyes and anxious looks, and I commenced to have this faith, and to pray with all the earnestness of my soul. And, at last, light came to me and Love came flowing into my soul. What a happy spirit I became, and I thanked God for His Mercy! My soulmate rejoiced with me, and we were so happy in our loves and in the Great Love of the Father.

From thence I have been progressing ever since. Now I am in the Celestial Spheres where Love is the ruling principle, and where only those who possess this Divine Love can live. And, here, Jesus is our prince and elder brother.

Caligula, the emperor, is now a humble follower of the "despised" Nazarene, and happy in his humility and in his following of such a loving savior.

My soulmate is with me. And whenever I look upon her and think that I was the cause of her sufferings and death upon earth, my whole soul goes out to her in great streams of love, and she knows it. That is a part of my great repentance. So, you see, even though a man may be the vilest of sinners on earth, yet, the Father's Mercy is so great that His Love is never turned away, or is His Mercy ever withheld.

I tell you that Love—the Father's Love—is the greatest thing in all the universe! And like unto It is the pure, holy love of the soulmate who has in her soul the great Love of the Father.

I must not write more tonight. But, as I was passing, I saw the brilliant light that is with you, and I embraced the opportunity to write.

(May I ask what was the name of your soulmate on earth?)

Yes, it was Celestia and what an appropriate name! My friend, you must also thank God for His Goodness to you; for I have seen your soulmate, and she is a most beautiful spirit.

So, with the love of a brother in Christ, I am

Your friend,

CALIGULA, the Roman emperor
that was, and the Christian that is!

Julius Caesar Writes That Earthly Position Does Not Determine One's Spiritual Abode.
(JULIUS CAESAR)
(September 16th, 1915 | Received by James Padgett)

I AM HERE. *Caesar.*

I am the spirit of one who, when on earth, was called Caesar.
(Which Caesar are you?)
Well, there was only one real Caesar. All others by that name were merely imitations. I was Julius Caesar and was the emperor of Rome, and the conqueror of the Gauls and of the Egyptians.

I am now in a condition of darkness, and also suffering from my deeds on earth, which were very wicked and numerous.

I am not an emperor now, but am a spirit who is the condition of one who has no one to do him reverence. Not the meanest of my former slaves deign to bow the knee or salute me as their superior. And why? Because, in the spirit world, a man is as his soul development makes him, and mine has been very much retarded by my want of belief and faith, as I now see.

I merely want to tell you this that you may know that no position on earth can determine the position of the person when he comes into the spirit world. I mean that the position of the man on earth does not in the slightest degree influence the position of this same man in the spirit world. Many of my slaves are higher in their development and in their spirituality than I am.

(But you may develop yourself as well.)
Well, that may be but I am in the condition that I say I am.
(There is a spirit I know who could help you.)
I don't know of any such spirit if there be any.
(Well, I dare say that there are some bright spirits around you right now who would like to help you. Look about you. And, when you see them, ask for Professor Salyards.)
I see some bright spirits and have asked for Professor Salyards, and find him to be a most beautiful and bright spirit. I am inclined to listen to what he may say. He says that he was well-acquainted with my history on earth, as he had read many books dealing with my life and exploits; and he is glad to meet me and show me the Way to a higher and happier condition

379

of existence. I rather like him, and believe that I will go with him and listen to him.

(You must also try to do what he suggests.)

Well, I will try.

So, I will say good night and good luck. I am your friend now, since you have shown such interest in me.

JULIUS CAESAR.

Mrs. Padgett Confirms That Julius Caesar Wrote.
(HELEN PADGETT)
(September 16th, 1915 | Received by James Padgett)

I AM HERE. *Helen.*

Well, I came to tell you that you must not write more tonight, as you are not in a very good condition. You may not think so, but it is a fact, and it is best for you to stop.

(Who was that last spirit who wrote?)

It was Caesar, as I am told. He is not a very bright spirit, but maybe your old professor may help him.

(When will I be hearing from the Celestials again?)

Well, they are not quite ready yet to resume their writing. It seems there are some of these ancients who want to write, and who have some object in writing to you which conflicts with the plan that these messages of the Master intends to be established and worked out.

I must stop now and will say good night.

Your own true and loving,

HELEN.

Julius Caesar Relates That He Is Seeking for the Divine Love, and That Light Is Breaking into His Soul.
(JULIUS CAESAR)
(December 13th, 1916 | Received by James Padgett)

I AM HERE. *Caesar.*

Well, I merely want to say that, since I last wrote to you, I have followed your advice and have listened to the advice of the high spirits to whom you sent me, and I have been praying as they instructed me. I am now in a much better condition than I was, and the view that I now have of life in the spirit world is very different.

I am still in some darkness, but light is breaking into my soul and consciousness. I am commencing to realize that my fate, as I have for so many years conceived it to be, is not fate at all, and that my conception of what my fixed state was is all wrong. It was the "child," if I may so call it, of my condition of mind and beliefs, that came to me when I came to the spirit world and realized that the fact of my having been what the world called a great man on earth did not fit me for any greatness in the spirit world. I was then so disappointed and shocked by finding myself a naked spirit of qualities that brought me into darkness and suffering that I tried to avoid the association of all other spirits. I nursed my disappointment in isolation and with the belief that, for me, there could be no change in my condition, or any possible progress out of the awful lonesomeness and weariness of my soul.

And, now, when I know how different the truth is, I feel that all these long years of my spirit life have been wasted; and I bewail the fate that held me so long in that condition of stagnation and pride and resentment and utter hopelessness.

I am now so thankful that I came to you when I did and told you of my condition. And when I realize that my coming to you was more a matter of curiosity to be satisfied—that I could communicate with the mortal world—than because of any hope of receiving any help or benefit that could possibly come to me, I thank my curiosity.

When you told me the things that you did, I thought that you were an idle dreamer, and the recipient of some of the harmless vices that existed among the men of my earthly days who used to declaim upon the glories of the spirit world. I had no faith in them, and I had none in you. And it was only when I realized that you were so earnest in what you were declaring to me, and when I came in contact with the higher spirits that you called to my assistance, and saw that they had in them something that I had not—and which I had never seen in any other spirit—did I commence to think that what you had told me might have some foundation of truth.

I also thought that I could not make my condition any worse by listening to these spirits, and learning what they had to tell me as to what they declared was the truth of spirit progress. And the more I listened, the more interested I became. After a while, I was convinced that there might be some truth in what they so earnestly asserted to be true; and, as an experiment, I concluded to follow their advice and seek for this wonderful Love that they told me would not only relieve me from my darkness and suffering but would also make a new spirit of me in body and soul.

And, oh, the wonderful surprise and experience that came to me! For I am no longer the gloomy, despondent and isolated emperor, but a mere spirit who recognizes that death is the great leveller, and that rank and position and greatness of earth do not in one iota determine the status of the spirit for position of exaltation. I am now a plain spirit in my consciousness, having only those qualities which the condition of my soul gives me. And I realize that I must pursue the same course and suffer the same purgation as must other spirits in the same condition of soul, be they princes or peasants.

Well, as I said, I am so thankful that this knowledge has come to me. For now I am rid of pride and ideas of superiority, and all those things that had caused me to believe that the Almighty had treated me unjustly in not recognizing my earthly qualities and giving me a position which, as I believed, my greatness entitled me to. I resented all this, and, in my resentment, I became a spirit who fed on my imaginary injuries. I thought that I would be sufficient unto myself, and that I would not seek the favor of such a God. So, you see what can be the effect of arrogance and pride and a self-glorious estimate of one small mind upon the possibility of a spirit's happiness and progress.

But now these things have left me, and I realize that I am a nothing, except that I am a child of God and the object of His Love, as your spirit friends have told me and are telling me. And in my humility—and I am humble, for I want to tell you that my fall was great and the consciousness of my littleness extreme—I know that I need the Help of the Father in order to become a spirit of Light in the least degree. And I am praying and longing and seeking, oh, so earnestly for this Love!

Caesar, the once mighty, is now Caesar the most humble and weak, but the most hopeful. I realize the greatness of God's Mercy and the great possibility of Its making me one of these glorious angels that come to you so often with their messages of Truth and salvation to mankind.

I was considered on earth a man of brilliant mind and wonderful intellect, and what of this I had I still possess. And now that the Way has been shown me, I am exercising these qualities to the best of my ability to help me in my search for Truth and Light.

I thought that I would write this tonight, for I know that you are interested in my advancement; and, besides, it does me much good to tell you. I am praying and longing, and these spirits are praying with me. But, as yet, I have not very much of this Love in my soul, but enough to know— I say know—that It is real and that It makes the hard, unbelieving soul open up to the inflowing of Its Divine Essence in greater abundance. The Father is Good, and I am trusting Him; and, with all the possibilities of my soul, I am longing for its filling with this Love, and the getting rid of all these century-old doubts and hardness of heart and unbeliefs.

I know the Way, and now I will never relapse into the state of mind that was mine for so many centuries. And I can say that Caesar has seen the beacon light of hope, and the great sun of knowledge, that these things which the loving spirits tell me are true.

I must stop now, but, as I progress, I should like to come to you and describe my progress.

I will say good night, and subscribe myself,

Your friend and well-wisher,

JULIUS CAESAR.

382

Julius Caesar Returns to Give His Experience After Receiving Help from a Divine Spirit.
(JULIUS CAESAR)
(May 1st, 1917 | Received by James Padgett)

I AM HERE. *Caesar.*

(Is this the same Julius Caesar who has written to me before?)

Yes, I am the spirit of that Roman who thought himself of so much importance, and then realized that he was a very insignificant spirit in his place in the spirit world.

Well, I am glad to be able to write to you again, and especially so because I can tell you that I have progressed out of my hells and torments since I last wrote you, and, I am now in the Third Sphere where there is so much love and happiness.* Now, this may seem a little surprising to you, but it need not. For you will remember that, when I last wrote to you, I informed you that I would then go with the beautiful spirit that came to me at your suggestion, and listen to his words of wisdom, as I now know them to be, and seriously consider what he might say to me. Well, I went with him. He was so loving and patient, and seemed to have such great knowledge of the Truths of God, that I not only listened to him once but many times, and made great effort to follow his advice.

I commenced to pray to the Father for the inflowing of that great Divine Love of which the good spirit told me, and continued to pray until I felt Its inflowing; and the effect on my soul was wonderful. For, as the love came to me, I found that the darkness left me, and also my sufferings. And with this Love came knowledge of these Truths of which I had been told—I mean a convincing faith that these things were true. When I commenced to have this experience, I continued to pray the harder. All the longings of my soul and mind and of every part of me that could have a feeling or aspiration went from me, and I continued to pray without ceasing.

As you may know, when on earth, I was a very positive and striving person, and I did not lose these characteristics when I became a spirit, notwithstanding that I remained so many centuries in a state of stagnation and helplessness. For, during all this time, I knew of no goal to which I could aspire, and of no peace that was better than the one in which I spent the long dreary years of my spirit life.

But as soon as I found that there was a future condition of light and happiness, I entered with all the energies of my soul to seek for that happiness. And as I was told that my progress depended so very largely

---

* Julius Caesar died in 44 BC. The first message James Padgett received from him communicating that he was in hell, was in 1915. Therefore at that time, the Roman general would have been in hell for 1,958 years. The date of this message indicates that it took only 19.5 months since starting to pray for God's Divine Love to ascend out of the hells to the third spirit sphere.

upon my own efforts, I permitted nothing to interfere with my strivings for the obtaining of this Divine Love; and, thanks to the Loving Father, I at last found relief from my torments and the fulness of Love that brought me to bliss and the companionship of beautiful and loving spirits.

But I must not neglect to say that, in all this effort on my part, I had the help and prayers of many loving spirits who seemed so anxious that I should get this Love and become in harmony with the Father and His Will. And now I am no longer the resentful and wicked Caesar, but a very humble and grateful child. For I am still but a child in the knowledge of the great Truths of which I have heard so much, and in that Love.

Even now, it is all so wonderful to me that I can hardly comprehend just what it all means. But this I know: that whereas I was for many long centuries a suffering, unloving and unloved spirit, seeking only solitude and nursing my resentment, I am now a bright, loving and beloved spirit, seeking and never tiring of the association of these bright spirits with whom I am now making my home. And, beside these, higher and more grand spirits come to me and encourage me to strive and pray, and tell me of the wonders that are before me and which can be mine.

I am of the last, but these spirits tell me that I may become of the first; and I feel that there is no power in all the hells that can, and no power in all the heavens that will, prevent me from progressing and obtaining a home in the Celestial Heavens.

I desire to say also that I have come to you many times when the spirits were writing you the wonderful messages of Truth, and I learned many Truths from them that I have tried to make mine, and which have helped me so much and revealed to me some of the Plans provided by the Father for the salvation of men and spirits.

You cannot conceive of the great number of spirits who are with you when these messages are being delivered, and how anxious many of them are to learn the Truth and receive the help that these Truths give to them. Many have found the light and happiness through the knowledge that is conveyed to them, and, further, through the help that these beautiful, loving spirits give them. For it seems that, whenever these spirits that are in darkness indicate a desire to learn the Truth, these high spirits are always ready and anxious to teach and help and comfort the dark ones.

I cannot explain to you how all this has not only astonished me but has also caused me to regret that I let so many wasted years go by without having sought the help of these spirits. For many a time they would come to me with their proffers of help and advice, but I would shun them and turn from them, not believing that they could help me. What a great mistake, and how I paid the penalty of neglecting this Way to salvation!

And I wish to say further that, as a fact, if I had not come to you, through curiosity, more than anything else, I would not now be in the condition that I am. For it was only after you talked to me and told me of the Way in which I could obtain relief, and brought me in rapport with these spirits and advised me to listen to them, did I think of the possibility of my being rescued or being able to find any relief from my then unhappy condition. And, so, I must express to you my gratitude for your kindness and, as you then told me, love for me.

Well, I am a different Caesar now.

I will not write more, but, as I told you before, I shall come sometime and write you a letter of some of my experiences on earth, and in the spirit world during the earlier years of my life as a spirit.

So, hoping that you will pray for me and give me your kind thoughts, I will say good night.

Your true friend,

CAESAR.

Mrs. Padgett Confirms That Julius Caesar Wrote Again.
(HELEN PADGETT)
(May 1st, 1917 | Received by James Padgett)

I AM HERE. *Helen.*

Yes, dear, it was Caesar who wrote, and he is so happy and thankful that he can hardly contain himself in his desires to write to you. He is an earnest spirit now, and, as he said, is striving with all the energy of his soul to obtain the Love in more abundance; and I can see that he will progress very rapidly.

Well, dear, every few nights, you experience the result of the work, and the redemption of some poor soul who has failed to seek for this Love that only can make a dark and suffering spirit a bright and happy one in a short time. There is nothing like this Love. It is all by Itself and so easy to obtain, and always waiting for the longing and aspiring soul, either in spirit or as a mortal on earth. Your own true and loving,

HELEN.

Elias Discusses the Hope That All Mortals Have in a Future Destiny of Freedom from Care and Unhappiness.
(ELIAS, THE PROPHET)
(December 3rd, 1916 | Received by James Padgett)

I AM HERE. *Elias, the prophet of old.*

I desire tonight to write a few lines upon a matter that I have been thinking might be of some interest to you, and that is: "The Hope That All Mortals Have in a Future Destiny of Freedom from Care and Unhappiness."

I know that a large majority of mortals (who believe in the Christian doctrines) believe that, for a very considerable number of mankind, there is awaiting an eternity of continuous torture and torment in the hells, and that, in order to avoid such a destiny or future state, men, while on earth, must believe in certain doctrines and conform themselves to such beliefs; for, after death, there can be no possible opportunity for being saved from such a fate.

Of course, these beliefs are the results of the teachings of those who claim to have the ability to interpret the Bible, mixed with a little of divine inspiration and mysterious power and wisdom that is conferred upon those who have the careers of ministers of the Gospel. And because of long years of training, or of inheritance from those who for long years believed in these teachings, men naturally exercise very little independent thought, and accept the declarations of these ministers as being almost the divine expressions of God, Himself.

In their workings, such doctrines have caused much harm to the mortal and much unhappiness to the spirits of men in the spirit world, because beliefs accompany the latter in their existence as spirits; and these beliefs keep them from learning the Truth for a long time after they become spirits.

It is a great pity that men can be bound by such false and damnable beliefs, and that generation after generation continue to become servants to the teachings of misguided instructors. And I wish to say that all these beliefs are untrue and have no foundation in fact. The sooner mankind knows this, the better it will be for their happiness on earth and their welfare in the world to come.

It is true that there are hells and punishment, and that the   majority of men will have to go into such hells and suffer such punishment when they become spirits. But the element of eternal or everlasting does not enter into the duration of such state or condition. For there is no punishment inflicted on the spirits of men for the purpose of causing them to pay a penalty that can never be satisfied through all eternity. This punishment is only for the purpose of purification. And when it is accomplished for the particular spirit who has suffered the same, the hell ceases to exist and the punishment ceases to have any necessity for its existence. Ultimately, the condition of every man will be that of a purified spirit, free from sin and defilement and the necessity for hell or punishment.

I know that what I have written has been written before in various forms, but I felt that I must say just this much, and in the way that I have done.

I am glad that you are feeling better tonight. And I want to assure you that, if you will pray to the Father, you will continue to grow in your spiritual development and, as a consequence, feel better in every particular.

With my love, I will say good night.

Your brother in Christ,

ELIAS.

John Expresses His Regret That a Preacher Could Not Inform His Congregation Correctly as to Hell.
(JOHN, THE APOSTLE)
(November 19th, 1916 | Received by James Padgett)

I AM HERE. *John.*

I was with you tonight and heard the sermon on hell, and was so sorry that the preacher could not tell his people more of the truths as to what hell is, and what the punishment of those who will be so unfortunate as to go to that place will be. It is pitiable that these leaders of the people are so blinded and without knowledge as to what the truth is in regard to this subject, as well as to many others that they so erroneously declare to their congregations. Of course, their knowledge is based upon what they consider to be the truths of the Bible, and, in many respects, what they say is justified by the teachings of that book. But their teachings are erroneous in many cases because of the wrong construction that they place upon many of the declarations of the Bible. In either case, they are teaching, as the truth, those things that are not true, and the harm accomplished is just as baneful as if their beliefs and teachings were the result of what they realized to be untrue. Untruth is untruth, no matter whether it arises from honest conviction or known error; and the harm done is the same in each instance. The preacher, I have no doubt, believes what he declared to be the truth. And some things he said were true. Yet, the fact that he believed these doctrines to be true will not palliate in any way his responsibility so far as the effects of these errors on his hearers are concerned. For their sufferings and darkness, which will certainly follow their beliefs in these erroneous teachings, will be no less because the preacher was honest in his declarations of what he supposed to be the truth. The source of error does not in any way modify or affect the results that flow from its acceptance and following. And while the preacher in this case is not a willful deceiver, yet, when he comes to the spirit world and learns the Truth, he will have the regrets and the sufferings which always flow from the spreading of falsehood and deception.

Error works its own punishment. But it may be of some consolation to know, and it will be to those who preach and to those who accept falsehood as truth, that such punishment will not be everlasting, that God is not a God of "wrath" or of "vindictiveness," and that His Justice never demands more than is necessary for the removing of error and the establishment of His Truths.

Why, His Justice would not be justice if He permitted error to continue, and prevented recovery of the Truths on the part of man or spirits just for the purpose of having those who had been disobedient suffer and be separated from Him for all eternity!

I merely wanted to say this much on the sermon. Sometime, I will come and write you a full explanation of what hell is, its purpose and work, and how long it continues.

Let all of you continue to pray to the Father for this Love, and have faith, and the time will soon come that faith will become as real and existing as the sun which you so much enjoyed today.

So, my brother, with all my love and blessings, I will say good night.

Your brother in Christ,

JOHN.

Mrs. Padgett Explains That Man Himself Must Make the Effort to Overcome the Influence of Evil Spirits.
(HELEN PADGETT)
(December 4th, 1917 | Received by James Padgett)

I AM HERE. *Helen.*

While, in many instances, the evil spirits influence mortals in their thoughts and actions, yet, this is not always the case, and it will not do for mortals to think so. They are not the mere pliant tools or subjects of these evil spirits, but are persons with free will, controlled by their own appetites. And for them to believe that all their evil acts are the results of the influence of these evil spirits would place them in a very subservient and deplorable condition and, at the same time, retard the development of themselves by their own thoughts and acts. No, the evil spirits are always working evil, but all the thoughts and desires that mortals have are not the results of the influence of these spirits.

Man must realize that the cause of his own evil thoughts and deeds is in himself, though increased by the influence of these spirits, and that he must master these thoughts in order to be able to drive them from him and overcome them by thoughts of a different and higher nature. It will not do for men to think that they are wicked only because of the influence of the evil spirits, for to think so would retard their development and, at the same time, take from them a realization of their own responsibility. On the other hand, the source of good thoughts is within themselves. And if they will only seek for this source, they will be able to progress in their moral condition. For while the good spirits can and do help them, yet, men must primarily help themselves from the good that is within them.

I would like to write you fully on this matter, and will sometime, but you are not in condition tonight and I will not try. But remember this: that whatever of evil is displayed or gives evidence of souls being possessed by it, yet, within themselves is the power to overcome and cause its eradication. I mean that men must make the effort and realize that they are masters of good and evil. We can help you if you will let us—it depends on you. And no other can take the praise or blame of the results of your thoughts or actions. Yet, you must also realize this: that when the evil ones form a rapport with you, and in a way obsess you, it will become the more

388

difficult for you to exercise your own will. Hence, men should pray to be given help from the higher Source to overcome the influences of these evil ones. The character of your company will determine to a considerable extent the kind of thoughts you may have and the deeds you may do. But good or bad be your associates, you alone will be responsible for the results of your thoughts and acts.

I must not write more. Good night.

HELEN.

Following a Personal Interchange with Mr. Padgett, Jesus Then Explains the Necessary Conditions Required So That the Higher Spirits Can Help Those in Lower Spheres.
(JESUS)
(May 8th, 1917 | Received by James Padgett)

I AM HERE. *Jesus.*

I see that your work has prevented you from receiving my message tonight. While I am sorry, I do not complain, for you must do your work and get in condition the more rapidly thereby to start the effort to accumulate in order to get in the position you desire, and which is so necessary to our work. You are better tonight, spiritually, and our rapport is very complete. I could easily write my message, but you are physically tired and I do not think it wise to attempt to write. So, I will postpone doing so until tomorrow night when I hope there will be nothing to interfere.

(Do you feel that I will be in better condition to receive perhaps a longer as well as clearer message tomorrow night?)

Yes, that is the correct idea. And I will endeavor to make the message as full and lucid as possible. I know how you feel in reference to the matter, and that you desire to receive the message in the best possible shape; and I know that you will do so. You must not think that I am not willing to wait whenever you have your professional work to attend to, or that I will not be with you even though we cannot write; for I am with you very often, trying to help, as I have said. So, you must keep up your courage and trust me, and have faith in my promises.

I will not write more now, and will say that you have my love and blessings.

(Will I be able to actually see you in some way before too long?)

Well, as to that, I know that you will be able to see me in the not distant future, as you say, for I am desirous that you do so. You have the power of clairvoyance, but it is not desirable that it be developed in you at this time, as we wish all your power to become centered in receiving the messages. But, some night, when you are praying and I am with you, the power will be given to you, and you will see me as I am while praying with you. I feel

389

that this may strengthen your faith and draw you closer to me, and I myself want you to actually see me as I am. [*]

Well, let us say good night and stop.

(Master, can you understand how I have rather expected to receive messages from you of a very high but yet more impersonal nature than those which you have actually written?)

Yes, I understand. But if I should come and write to you (as you may think) in the dignified way that an elevated spirit should write, you would not feel the nearness to me that I so much want you to feel. And, besides, you might not just understand what I intended to communicate. It is impossible for you to accommodate yourself to my condition, and, hence, I have to accommodate myself to yours. I want you to get as close to me as possible, and, in order that that may be, I have to become verily human, as you are. Otherwise, the rapport could not exist between us, and I would seem to you like some far-off nebulous being that you could not understand or feel the influences of. No, I am very human when I come to you.

But this I will say, in order that you may get a somewhat better idea of our relationship: that as you progress more in your soul development and in the possession of the Father's Love, you will be less human—I mean in your condition of soul, which is that in you that furnishes the rapport between us—and I will meet you on the plane that you may occupy. So, you see what a determining factor your condition of soul is in our rapport. If you consider this for a moment, you will more clearly comprehend why it is that the dark spirits can find a closer rapport with you, that enables you to help them, than they can find in the higher spirits. We try to make a rapport with them, but their souls do not respond. It is only after you have talked to them and directed their attention to us—which causes, as it were, an opening up of their souls to us—that we can come in that rapport with them that enables us to gain their attention and create an interest in them in what we may say to them.

This may seem surprising to you, as you believe that we who are more elevated must have great power with and over these dark spirits; and this is so for certain purposes. We do often restrain them from doing things that they should not do. But this, as you must understand, means that we arbitraily force them to do or not do certain things by our powers, just as your laws, or the enforcement of them, restrain those who desire to violate the laws from doing so on earth.

But when we come to the work of attempting to turn their thoughts to those things that affect their soul condition, this thing of constraint or force will not effectuate the work. We then must deal with the exercise of their free will; and, in such cases, only persuasion or love influence can possibly do the work of helping them out of their dark and tainted condition of soul. We must invite and persuade the soul to awaken; we cannot force it. And,

---

[*] Mr. Padgett told Dr. Stone later that Jesus did reveal himself, and that he saw him clairvoyantly while he was praying for more of the Divine Love.—Ed.

to do so, we must form that relationship with these dark spirits that will cause them to voluntarily open up their souls to our influences.

The great obstacle to our work among spirits of this kind is that they will not listen to us or come in conversation with us, and we cannot compel and accomplish our purposes. No man or spirit can ever be made by force to open up his soul to the higher thoughts and essentials of the soul's progress. Of course, when we once get in that rapport with them that enables us to enlist their attention, and they listen to what we say, we can then cause them to have an awakening by informing them of the sufferings and torments that will be theirs if they continue in their same condition. And by a kind of mental force, you may say, we compel them to think of these things that are holding them in their condition of darkness. But this does not occur unless we can first secure their attention and, to some extent, their confidence.

So, you may realize from this, to some degree, the importance of the work that you are doing among the dark spirits. Being in the condition of darkness and want of soul development, they cannot see any such development that you may have. To them, you are merely a mortal, as they themselves were a short time ago in many cases. And finding that they can communicate with you, they come to you just as one man would to another for the purpose of conversation. And outside of the phenomenon of spirit and mortal conversing, you do not seem any different to them from what men seemed to be to them when they were on earth. They are all very human and, to them, you conversation is very natural. Hence, they listen to you with the same feelings of confidence, or, rather, not of distrust, that they would have with another. And your opinions or ideas are just the same to them as they might expect if they were in the flesh, or if you were a spirit like themselves.

While these dark spirits may see the bright and beautiful spirits under certain circumstances, as they sometimes tell you they do, yet, they see only the appearance of the spirit body. They cannot see the condition of the spiritual development in these bright spirits, FOR IT IS A LAW THAT THE SPIRIT PERCEPTIONS CANNOT VISION CONDITIONS OF THE SOULS OF OTHERS OF A HIGHER DEGREE OF DEVELOPMENT THAN THEY THEMSELVES HAVE; AND THIS APPLIES TO ALL SPIRITS, NO MATTER WHAT SPHERE THEY MAY OCCUPY. HENCE, YOU WILL UNDERSTAND THAT, AS WE PROGRESS IN OUR SOUL SPHERES, THE HIGHER WE ASCEND, THE MORE CLEAR AND COMPREHENSIBLE OUR SOUL PERCEPTIONS BECOME OF THE FATHER AND HIS DIVINE QUALITIES.

So, I say, so far as the real perceptions of these dark spirits are concerned, they cannot comprehend the real spiritual development of the higher spirits whom they often see. The interior condition of these higher spirits is just as hidden from the dark spirits as is the interior condition of one man from another. Only when like meets like can there be a perception—that is, not a real visual perception, but a spiritual perception of each other.

But the higher spirits can see the interior conditions of those who are in spheres lower than they, and they can determine just what the soul development of these lower ones is.

Also, you must understand that the appearance of the spirit body indicates and portrays, to a large extent, the condition of the soul; and, from this, one spirit may judge the actual development of another. I mean those may so judge who have progressed above the dark planes.

Well, I have written more than I intended. But, as you were desirous to have some conception of what I have written, I concluded that I would attempt to explain these matters to you. I know from my explanation, though, that you cannot fully understand what I have been trying to make known to you.

But we must stop now.

So, with my love, I will say good night.

Your brother and friend,

JESUS.

Mrs. Padgett Confirms the Importance of Her Husband's Work
Among the Dark Spirits.
(HELEN PADGETT)
(May 8th, 1917 | Received by James Padgett)

I AM HERE. *Helen.*

Well, dear, you had a message from the Master tonight that you did not expect. It will enlighten you considerably on the subject that we have written to you about several times but could not satisfactorily explain, as we did not just understand ourselves. But I think that now you can get some idea why you are so important in this work among the dark spirits.

I will not write more now.

Your own true and loving,

HELEN.

PART II.

CONTEMPORARY MISCONCEPTIONS.

Chapter 13.

Corrections Made in Orthodox Christian Doctrine.

<u>MESSAGES INCLUDED IN THIS SECTION.</u>

Jesus Declares That Those Who Worship Him, as They Do in the Churches, Commit Blasphemy. (JESUS)...399

A Spirit from the Fifth Sphere Emphasizes That Mr. Padgett Must Believe in Jesus as a Savior, but Not Through the Vicarious Atonement. (JOHN B. CARROLL)..399

Luke Defines Religion as the Relationship and Harmony of Men's Souls with the Soul of God. He Also Discusses the Difference in the Teachings of Various Churches in Terms of Their Effect Upon Spiritual Development. (LUKE, THE APOSTLE) 400

John, the Apostle, Comments on the Beliefs of a Preacher. (JOHN, THE APOSTLE)...403

Ann Rollins Declares That the Blood of Jesus Does Not Save from Sin. (ANN ROLLINS)...403

Jesus Denies That He Is God, or That His Blood Washes Away Man's Sins. (JESUS)...404

What Should a Man Do Who Is Not Satisfied with Any of the Churches? (JOHN, THE APOSTLE)..406

Paul Expresses His Desire to Write What He Knows to Be the Truth, and to Also Correct Errors in His Epistles as Contained in the Bible. (PAUL, THE APOSTLE)...407

Jerome Cautions That the Truths of God Must Not Be Sought for in His Writings, or Those of the Disciples as Contained in the Bible, Because of the Many Errors in Both Sources. (JEROME, THE WRITER AND COMMENTATOR ON THE BIBLE)...408

Augustine Declares That Many of the Teachings of the Bible Cannot be Relied Upon. (AUGUSTINE)..409

John Explains That Not the Blood but the Divine Love Is What Saves and Redeems. He Cautions That "Revelation" of the Bible Is Not to Be Relied Upon as True in Many Particulars. (JOHN, THE APOSTLE). 411

Jesus Affirms That His Disciples Never Wrote All the False Doctrines in the Bible Attributed to Him. (JESUS) 412

John Again Denies the Vicarious Atonement. He Also Explains That Spirit Communion Was More Prevalent in His Day than Now, and That if Men Would Have Faith Like the Apostles of Jesus, Healing and So-Called "Miracles" Would Exist Today. (JOHN, THE APOSTLE) 413

Martin Luther, One-Time Monk and Reformer, Recommends a Test to Employ in Trying the Spirits. (MARTIN LUTHER) 415

Mrs. Padgett Explains That the Epistles in the Bible Are Not the Same That the Original Apostles Wrote. She Adds That the Divine Love Mentioned in the Bible Is Not Properly Explained, as Contradistinguished from the Natural Love. (HELEN PADGETT) 417

Saul Gives Advice to His People, the Jews. (SAUL OF THE OLD TESTAMENT) 418

Luther Declares That the Observance of the Ceremonies Which the Lutheran Church Still Uses in Its Worship Is Not Approved of by God or by Jesus. (MARTIN LUTHER) 419

Luther Again Denies the Vicarious Atonement. He Also States That the Bible Is Full of Contradictions and Errors. (MARTIN LUTHER) 420

Luther Denies the Efficacy of the Eucharist to Save Man. He Explains That Jesus Is Living and Teaching and Demonstrating the Divine Love in His Soul, and How Man Can Obtain It, and That This Is the True Way to Salvation. (MARTIN LUTHER) 422

A Former Preacher Discusses His Beliefs and Denies the "Trinity." (ROBERT COLYER) 423

Jesus Reaffirms That His Blood Does Not Save Men from Their Sins. (JESUS) 424

Paul Denies the Efficacy of the Vicarious Atonement. He Emphasizes That God Was Never a God of "Wrath" but Always of Love. (PAUL, THE APOSTLE) 425

John Declares That Men or Prophets Cannot Tell What Will Happen Centuries Ahead; This Can Only Be Known by the Father. (JOHN, THE APOSTLE)..427

John Cautions That Man Must Continue to Search for and Find the Truth. (JOHN, THE APOSTLE) 428

Cornelius, the Centurion, Declares That It is of the Greatest Importance That the Truths of the Way to Salvation Be Revealed to Mankind. (CORNELIUS) 430

Jesus Proclaims That Divine Truths Must Be Declared to All Mankind. (JESUS) 431

13.

Corrections Made in Orthodox Christian Doctrine.

Jesus Declares That Those Who Worship Him, as They Do in the Churches, Commit Blasphemy.
(JESUS)
(May 6th, 1917 | Received by James Padgett)

I AM HERE. *Jesus.*

I was with you at the church this morning, and I impressed you with my feelings in reference to what the preacher said as to my sacrifice and blood. But instead of calling upon his people to show their gratitude for the sacrifice and the cross, he should have taught them that the sacrifice and the blood do not save them from their sins. In that particular, there is nothing that calls for their gratitude. And to worship me as they do, and as he teaches them to do, is blasphemy, and a more heinous sin than ingratitude.

I was successful in impressing you with my feelings of dissatisfaction, and was glad that I could, for it shows that our rapport is becoming closer. After awhile, you will be able to receive my thoughts and inspirations as well as my writings.

You must pray and have faith, and, if you do, you will more often have the experiences that you did last night, which only means a quicker soul development.

Trust me and you will not be disappointed.

I will not write more now.

So, with my love and the Father's Blessings, I will say good night.
Your brother and friend,
JESUS.

A Spirit from the Fifth Sphere Emphasizes That Mr. Padgett Must Believe in Jesus as a Savior, but Not Through the Vicarious Atonement.
(JOHN B. CARROLL)
(October 8th, 1915 | Received by James Padgett)

I AM HERE. *John B. Carroll.*

Go to the Lord. Your strength will be renewed and your soul will receive a wonderful inflowing of the Divine Love so that you will be able to throw aside all worries and earthly cares and be in condition to receive the great Truths that are awaiting you. For you have the greatest spirit in all God's Universe as your helper and friend.

This I tell you because you need to be sustained, and will be as long as you live the life of a mortal.

I am not one who is known in the annals of the church or in the lives of the "saints" for I never was a saint on earth and neither am I here—but only a lowly follower of the Master who, to me, is the most wonderful of all God's creatures.

So, you must believe that he is your friend and savior, for he is. And you need not believe in his blood, or his vicarious atonement, or his self-sacrifice either. Only believe in the Divine Love and in the further fact that Jesus is the wayshower to all who may seek this great salvation.

I must not write more, for I am not one of the high Celestial spirits, as I live in the Fifth Sphere only. But, nevertheless, I have a very great deal of that Love, and a happiness which I cannot tell you of.

So, with all my love, I will say good night.

Your friend,
JOHN B. CARROLL,
a one-time resident of Baltimore, Md.

Luke Defines Religion as the Relationship and Harmony of Men's Souls with the Soul of God. He Also Discusses the Difference in the Teachings of Various Churches in Terms of Their Effect Upon Spiritual Development.
(LUKE, THE APOSTLE)
(April 25th, 1918 | Received by James Padgett)

I AM HERE. *Luke.*

Let me write a line. I was with you tonight at the church and listened to what the preacher said in reference to religions and their point of contact. I was somewhat surprised at his declarations as to the analogy which he drew between the believers in the various so-called "Christian" religions.

As you know, while there is implanted a longing in the souls of men for that which tends to elevate and spiritualize them, even though this longing may not be consciously present with a large number of them, yet, the beliefs as to the ways in which this longing may be made manifest and develop the spiritual nature of the soul are very different among those professing these various religions; and these ways are not equally efficacious in causing their spiritual development.

RELIGION IS A MATTER OF SOUL AND NOT OF INTELLECT.

400

THE GREATER THE DEVELOPMENT OF THE SOUL IN THE RIGHT DIRECTION, THE HIGHER WILL BE THE SPIRITUAL STATE OR CONDITION OF THE SOUL. MERE INTELLECTUAL BELIEF, NO MATTER HOW INTENSE AND UNDOUBTING, WILL NOT TEND TO BRING ABOUT THIS SPIRITUAL DEVELOPMENT. FOR RELIGION IS REALLY NOTHING BUT THE RELATIONSHIP AND HARMONY OF MEN'S SOULS WITH THE SOUL OF GOD.

THE MIND WILL NOT BE SUFFICIENT TO CREATE THIS STATE BECAUSE THE MIND OF MAN CANNOT POSSIBLY BRING THE SOUL OF THE CREATOR AND THAT OF THE CREATURE INTO HARMONY. MIND, IN ITS EXERCISE, MAY TEND TO AWAKEN THE SOUL TO THIS POSSIBILITY OF RELATIONSHIP, BUT ONLY THE WORKINGS OF THE SOUL CAN EFFECTUATE THE COMPLETE UNITY OF THE CREATOR AND THE CREATED. ONLY SOUL CAN SPEAK TO SOUL. AND MIND IS ONLY A HELPER, PROVIDED THE SOUL IS ALIVE IN ITS LONGINGS.

So, it is apparent that that form of belief which is wholly of the intellect can have no common meeting place with that belief which is the result of the development of the soul. Hence, to say that men of all the various religions are in an equal relationship to the Father, just because they are what are called Christians, is erroneous and misleading.

As regards the condition of man as the perfect man, these several religions may tend to bring about this state of perfection if the moral precepts which they teach are observed and practiced by men. But as regards man as the divine angel—that is, as a spirit having the Essence of the Divine in itself—only that religion which teaches the true Way to acquire this divinity can lead men to the At-onement with the Father in His Very Nature. In this respect, there can be only one true religion, and only one Way in which that religion can be practiced and possessed. And to say that all religions have a common point of approach is misleading and deceiving.

Among these various religions, I know that there are individuals who have found the Way to the method of becoming transformed into the Divine Nature of the Father, and, this, notwithstanding that the teachings and creeds of the several churches do not show the Way to this soul development into the spiritual of the divine. But, in these churches, there is wanting in their dogmas and doctrines that which will help men to this true religion.

Because it may be found in the churches that there are some who have this divine spirituality to a degree, there is still no justification in saying that there is any common place of meeting in these several religions.

Of course, the moral precepts may be and are taught by all the Christian churches, and, when observed, will ultimately lead all men to the condition of the perfect natural man. But only to this extent can it be said that they may have a common ground of religion arising from the belief in the moral teachings.

And the church which declares and teaches these moral teachings as its religion, with great exactness and more enlarged comprehension, is the church in which this "natural" religion, as I may call it, exists. And the more dissimilar these churches are in these teachings, the farther apart is their approach.

If a preacher of one church knows, with the conviction that arises from his sincere and honest investigation of the moral laws, that some other church is not teaching or insisting on the observation of these great moral truths on the part of its members, then he has no right to conclude and say this latter church is the possessor of religion as much as the church is in which these moral truths are taught and followed by its adherents.

It is a mistake for a preacher to say that, because there may be good and spiritual men in all churches, therefore, one church is as good and religious in its teachings as another church. Truth is of such a nature that it cannot be compromised. And the man or preacher who would compromise the Truth is not fulfilling his duty to God or man.

The church which teaches that there is nothing greater than morality, and that man can become no more transcendent than the perfect man, is devoid of the Truth. This church would not be accepted as a teacher of the full Truth, as would the church which knows and teaches the Way by which man may become a divine angel.

That the preachers of the various churches should accept all churches as equal and the possessors of the true religion (whenever these moral lessons are alike taught by these churches and have a common point of approach) is not to be wondered at, because these preachers do not know the higher religion and are not able to teach the Way to the same. And when it is understood that a moral truth is a truth, no matter where it may appear and by whom it is taught, there is some justification in declaring that all churches which teach the moral truths are on a plane of equality, and that one is entitled to as much respect and freedom from criticism as another. AND, FURTHER, AS THE GREAT TRUTH OF THE REBESTOWAL OF THE POTENTIALITY OF RECEIVING THE DIVINE LOVE, AND THE EFFECT ON MEN'S SOULS, WAS NEVER KNOWN AND TAUGHT UNTIL THE COMING OF THE MASTER, IT IS NOT SURPRISING THAT NONE OF THE CHURCHES CAN OR DO TEACH THIS GREAT SPIRITUAL TRUTH, AND THE ONLY TRUE RELIGION ARISING THEREFROM. THE KNOWLEDGE OF THIS TRUTH PERISHED FROM THE EARTH A SHORT TIME AFTER THE PASSING OF THE MASTER. AND, HENCE, NO CHURCH CAN TEACH THIS RELIGION OF THE SOUL THAT TRANSFORMS THE MORTAL INTO THE DIVINE.

THE RELIGION OF THE PERFECT MAN MAY EXIST IN VARYING DEGREES IN ALL THE CHRISTIAN CHURCHES. BUT THE RELIGION OF THE DIVINE ANGEL EXISTS IN NONE, ALTHOUGH SOME INDIVIDUALS OF THESE CHURCHES, TO SOME EXTENT, HAVE RECEIVED THE GREAT TRUTH IN THEIR

SOULS—THE DIVINE LOVE—EVEN THOUGH THEY HAVE NO INTELLECTUAL KNOWLEDGE OF THE SAME.

I thought it advisable to make these few remarks on the declaration of the preacher, as showing that his broad assertion of the equality of the religions mentioned, (which, to him, are all-embracing) may have a common meeting point with every religion.

When he learns the Truth, he will realize the errors of his human and brotherly declarations.

I will not write more. Good night and God bless you.

Your brother in Christ,

LUKE.

John, the Apostle, Comments on the Beliefs of a Preacher.
(JOHN, THE APOSTLE)
(August 29th, 1915 | Received by James Padgett)

I AM HERE. *John.*

The preacher said that there is no other salvation than through the blood of Jesus. How in error he is, and how he will find the Truth on his awakening in the spirit life! Let not your heart be troubled or your faith in the Master be shaken by anything that he or any other man may say.

I was at the meeting. And what the preacher said was all right, except when he implied that you must believe that only the blood saves from sin. He did not say that in so many words, but that was what he intended that his sermon should convey.

(Who are you?)

I am John. And I never said that the blood of Jesus saves from sin, and neither did Jesus or any of his apostles.

Let not the preacher's conversation cause you to doubt for a moment what we have written to you.

So, I will stop now and will only say further that we are all with you and want you to believe firmly in what we may write.

(But there are so many who believe in salvation through the blood of Jesus.)

Yes, I am sorry to say that is their belief, and what a great mistake they make. And how great the awakening will be for them when they shall learn the Truth!

So, believe and trust! JOHN.

Ann Rollins Declares That the Blood of Jesus Does Not Save from Sin.
(ANN ROLLINS)
(September 5th, 1915 | Received by James Padgett)

403

I AM HERE. *Your own dear grandmother.*

I came to tell you that I know now that the blood of Jesus does not save from sin. You will remember how, when on earth, I believed this doctrine of error—how I used to talk about the precious blood of Jesus being able to save from all sin, and used to sing with all my heart and belief in the old hymn: "There Is a Fountain Filled with Blood," and so forth. Well, I know now that that belief is all wrong, and that Jesus is so anxious to have men learn that it is a great error and stumbling block to the soul's progression.

Of course, I know that a vast majority of those now living will never believe that this saying of the Bible is erroneous until they come to the spirit world. But if they only could be taught to throw aside this belief and rely entirely on the Divine Love for their salvation while on earth, how much easier their progress would be when they come over!

So, you see that while many say that a belief does not amount to much, yet, I tell you that it causes more unhappiness and retards the progress of spirits to a greater extent than any other one thing.

I know that only the Divine Love of the Father saves from sin and makes mortals at-one with Him. So, in your work for the Master, you will have to make great efforts to cause people to give up this belief in the blood, and to turn to the Truth of the New Birth. Many of the orthodox will oppose your efforts and refuse to believe what you may tell them to be the Truth. But many will believe and seek this New Birth, and each will find the peace and happiness of a soul whose sins have been forgiven.

I must not write more tonight.

I will come again soon and tell you more of the result of your work among the unfortunate spirits who seek your help.

So, my dear son, I will say good night.

Your loving grandmother,

ANN ROLLINS.

Jesus Denies That He Is God, or That His Blood
Washes Away Man's Sins.
(JESUS)
(September 12th, 1915 | Received by James Padgett)

I AM HERE. *Jesus.*

I was with you tonight and saw that the Holy Spirit was filling your heart with the Divine Love of the Father, and that you realized Its presence. And you felt that, even though the people worshiped me in their ignorance, yet, they have this Love of the Father to a great degree.

I do not approve of their frequent reference to my blood as saving them from their sins, and keeping them in the Grace and Favor of the Father; for, as I have told you, my blood has nothing to do with the salvation of any

404

soul. Only the Divine Love of the Father saves a soul from sin and makes it one with the Father in His Love and Divinity.

But, nevertheless, these people have this Love in their hearts. And while they look upon me as God with their intellects, yet, their souls are turning to God. And, consequently, they receive the Blessings of the Father's Love, and are receiving the development of their souls to a large extent.

I am glad you attend these meetings,[*] for in them is a wonderful presence of the Holy Spirit and the Love of the Father. And while you may not be in sympathy with their doctrines as to Who and What saves them from sin and unrighteousness, yet, the influence of the Holy Spirit is so great that it helps your soul development.

I tried to influence the speakers to tell just what the conditions of their souls were, and what experience they had in receiving and enjoying this Divine Love. Many of them experience, and have as a part of their religious possession, just what they said they had.

It will be beneficial to you to attend this church, and to get the benefit of the presence of the Holy Spirit which is with them in their worship.

I was with you and tried to make you feel my presence, and I did; and you felt a little exaltation of your soul qualities and enjoyed the services, especially the singing and the prayers.

So, while you must not be influenced by their doctrines as to my being God or to be worshiped, yet, if you will ignore this and only consider that their real worship is of God, and that their souls are in unison with Him, you will find that these services will do you much good.

I am with you very much and am trying to get you relieved from the worries which come to you. I am also trying to help you get in that spiritual condition which is necessary in order for you to take and continue my formal messages.

(I feel that I am now receiving more of the Father's Love.)

Yes, you are, and I am glad that it is so. I want you to become a man so possessed of this Love, and of faith so strong, that nothing that you may encounter will swerve you from your convictions and from your work. I see that you are anxious to continue this work, and you will soon be able to do so.

(It will be hard to persuade people that many of the Bible's assertions are incorrect, as they pertain to you.)

Yes, I know that the Bible iterates and reiterates the statement that I am God, and that my blood saves from sin, and that I am a propitiation for mankind. But, nevertheless, the Bible is all wrong, and these false doctrines must be corrected and men taught the pure Plan of salvation.

I will be with you very often until we have commenced our work in the way that we desire to carry it forward. Let not anything that you may read in the Bible cause you to have a conception that may not agree with what I

---

[*] The Church of the Holiness, Washington, D.C.—Ed.

shall write. Let your mind be blank of these Truths and wait until I shall disclose them to you, and then believe me.

John never wrote these statements as contained in his epistles and gospel, and he will write to you denying that he did. The Bible contains many Truths and many of my sayings, but, also, many statements that were never made by me or by the apostles. And my mission now is to correct all these errors. So, you see, we have much work ahead of us, and we must commence it as soon as possible.

I am with you tonight to comfort and encourage you and help you to overcome your worries. And if you will only pray to the Father and believe, you will be successful in both particulars.

I will not write more tonight, as others are here to write, and I desire that they shall do so.

Your brother and friend,
JESUS.

What Should a Man Do Who Is Not Satisfied with Any of the Churches?
(JOHN, THE APOSTLE)
(October 19th, 1916 | Received by James Padgett)

I AM HERE. *John.*

I was with you tonight and heard the preacher answer the question, and some of his answers were very satisfactory. But there was one that did not exactly satisfy the true longings of the man who is in search of Truth.

I mean the one who asks what should a man do who is not satisfied with any of the churches.

Well, if he can find no church that provides Truths that satisfy that man's inquiring soul, then that man can never feel that he should go to any church for information as to those things which he has no knowledge of, or which he has grave doubts about.

The churches, of course, can give no information of Truths that the churches themselves do not know. And if the truths that these churches teach fall short of what the man is seeking for, then these churches cannot possibly be satisfactory to him. While the churches differ in their creeds and government, and perhaps in some particular construction or interpretation of the Bible, yet, they, the orthodox churches, are all founded upon the teachings of the Bible; and they cannot teach greater or other Truths than that book contains. Hence, if a man is seeking for Truths that are not in the Bible, his inquiries cannot be answered by those whose knowledge is confined to the Bible teachings. And the non-orthodox churches cannot give forth the Truths of the Spiritual Kingdom of God because they reject the Bible to a large degree, and they depend very largely upon ethical and moral doctrines, and the results of the works of mere

406

conscience, in determining the right and wrong of things. The spiritual things are not known or taught by these churches, and, consequently, the inquiring mind cannot get from them the information or help that it is calling for.

In such a condition and want of knowledge of Truth on the part of the churches, I know that such a man is without the privilege of having his cravings for the Truth of spiritual things satisfied. As a consequence, he must seek further to get the information which he may consider so necessary. And when he comes to so seek, he will find no place where such knowledge may be found.

The mere intellectual acquirements of students and philosophers will not supply what the man is seeking, and he is without any possibility of obtaining what he seeks for.

And, so, the preacher's suggestion that he and two others form a church of their own would have some force were it not for the fact that any church that might be so formed would have no greater possession of the Truth than the churches that he has failed to find any satisfaction in.

There are many men on earth today in the condition of the man spoken of. And many who refuse to seek in the churches for the Truth are without any recourse to other means or places of teachers from whom they can learn the things that they are searching for.

THE SPIRITS HAVE KNOWN OF THIS CONDITION OF MEN FOR THESE MANY CENTURIES, AND HAVE BEEN TRYING TO SUPPLY A WAY, OR CREATE A MEDIUM, THROUGH WHICH THE GREAT SPIRITUAL TRUTHS OF GOD COULD BE MADE KNOWN TO MEN. AND, FOR THAT VERY PURPOSE, WE ARE NOW USING YOU TO RECEIVE OUR MESSAGES OF TRUTH, AND TO MAKE THEM KNOWN TO MANKIND, AND PROVIDE A CHURCH, MAY I SAY, WHERE THE SEEKING MAN MAY FIND ANSWERS TO HIS INQUIRIES.

We shall complete our delivery of these Truths through you. Then the man who cannot find a church where his searchings can be satisfied will find a reservoir of Truth opened up to him that will not require any preacher or church to explain it.

As you proceed in your experience with the churches and teachers of the "old truths," as they call them, you will more fully realize the necessity for our work and your work.

I will not write more tonight, but will come soon and deliver a formal message. With my love and blessings, I will say good night.

JOHN.

Paul Expresses His Desire to Write What He Knows to Be the Truth, and to Also Correct Errors in His Epistles as Contained in the Bible.
(PAUL, THE APOSTLE)
(August 30th, 1915 | Received by James Padgett)

I AM HERE. *Paul.*

I desire to tell you that I am very anxious to disclose to you what are the true teachings of Jesus, and what errors my epistles possess as contained in the Bible.

I know now that it may seem strange to you that errors should have gotten into my epistles, but there are several reasons for their entrance. First, the epistles, as they now appear, are not what I wrote. I mean many changes have been made in my writings. Secondly, when I wrote the epistles, I did not know as much of the Truths of God as I do now. And, thirdly, I was not such a believer in the teachings of Jesus as I am now.

These are sufficient reasons why my epistles should not be accepted as containing all the Truths, or, rather, that all they contain are Truths.

There are apparent contradictions in these writings. And if what is said were true, there would be no real contradictions.

I fully realize this great defect in my epistles, and I have tried hard to impress those who attempt to explain my sayings as to the real Truth of what they attempt to explain, but with indifferent success.

Now I want to correct what is untrue or not in accord with the teachings of the Master. And the only way in which it can be done is writing through you. Of course, I realize that you have a great work to do for the Master, and that most of your time and energy will be taken up by doing this work of the Master, and that every other communication must be subordinated to those of Jesus. Yet, I believe that you will find time to take my messages at times.

Tonight, I will not attempt to write any message of these Truths. I will only say that I am much interested in your work, and will try to help you all I can. So, I must stop.

(Has salvation for man been provided through the blood of Jesus having been shed on the cross?)

NO, NO BLOOD SAVES FROM SIN; ONLY THE DIVINE LOVE OF THE FATHER DOES THIS! With much love, I am,

Your friend,
PAUL.

Jerome Cautions That the Truths of God Must Not Be Sought for in His Writings, or Those of the Disciples as Contained in the Bible, Because of the Many Errors in Both Sources.
(JEROME, THE WRITER AND COMMENTATOR ON THE BIBLE)
(August 17th, 1915 | Received by James Padgett)

I AM HERE. *Jerome.*

I came to tell you that I am an inhabitant of that Kingdom which

Samuel has so inadequately described, and that is the Kingdom of Jesus and, of course, of the Father.

You may not know anything about me, but I was canonized many centuries ago by the church because it thought that I had done the church so much good by my writings and discourses on religious things. But I must confess now that, when I wrote, I expressed many things as truths which I now see were not true; and I would like to be able to correct all these errors in my writings, but I cannot.

So, I will tell you in a few words that the Truths of the Master, which are the Truths of God, must not be sought for in my writings, or even in those of his disciples as contained in the Bible, because of the many errors that exist therein. This is not because the disciples and those to whom they conveyed these Truths did not write them correctly, but because the Bible, as now written, is not the same in many important particulars as to what the disciples actually wrote. AND, HENCE, JESUS, KNOWING THIS, IS SO ANXIOUS THAT THE WORLD SHALL RECEIVE THESE GREAT TRUTHS AGAIN THROUGH HIS WRITTEN MESSAGES.

I am trying my best to help the cause which he is advocating, and am behind you with spirits who are trying with all their spirit powers to direct you aright and enable you to receive the Truths.

I am in a Celestial Sphere very high up in the heavens. I cannot otherwise describe its location. These spheres are not numbered after the first few because they interblend so that there are no lines of demarcation. But I am not so high up as are the disciples and many others who are followers of the Master. The ancient spirits, such as Moses and Abraham and Isaac and Jacob, are in higher spheres. But they are not so exalted as are Jesus' apostles and disciples, and, as I am informed, many spirits who came to the spirit world since Jesus came.

I will not write more tonight, but will thank you and say good night.
Your brother in Christ,
JEROME, the writer and commentator on the Bible.

Augustine Declares That Many of the Teachings of the Bible Cannot be Relied Upon.
(AUGUSTINE)
(August 7th, 1915 | Received by James Padgett)

I AM HERE. *Augustine.*

I merely want to say that I am the "St." Augustine who lived after the death of Jesus and was well acquainted with his teachings, as they were preserved by the church. At that time, I never knew exactly what became of the manuscripts that were in existence when I lived. But the ones that are supposed to furnish the origin of many of the Biblical writings were not the ones that I was acquainted with. Those that I used were all written in

Greek and were written by the disciples of Jesus, and by those of his followers to whom the disciples had communicated the teachings of the Master. And they were the genuine ones, and were written from the actual communications of the disciples.

Of course, the teachings of Jesus were never recorded at the time of his teachings, but were merely the recollections possessed by the disciples of what they thought he really said. Consequently, as you may realize, they were imperfect and could not be relied on implicitly.

I know that great controversies have arisen in the church as to what portions of these writings should be accepted as genuine. Many needless disputes have caused the officials of that church to differ as to what were really the writings of the disciples and what were not. When on earth, I joined in these disputes, and maintained that certain of these writings were genuine and certain were not. But I was as likely to be mistaken as any of the others.

But even the ones that I thought were genuine were more or less flavored by the spiritual knowledge and beliefs of those who wrote them. So, I tell you that you cannot depend on these writings as a whole to learn what the Master actually did teach.

HE IS NOW IN CONDITION TO GIVE YOU THE GENUINE TRUTHS. AND WHENEVER WHAT HE MAY SAY CONFLICTS WITH WHAT IS CONTAINED IN THE BIBLE, YOU MUST CONSIDER WHAT HE NOW WRITES AS THE TRUTH AND DISCARD THE BIBLE ACCOUNT AS UNRELIABLE.

I tell you this because I am interested in having the world learn the Truths which he came on earth to declare.

I am a spirit of the Celestial Spheres and am a follower of the Master, and am trying to help in having these Truths come to the world again.

So, if you will pardon my intrusion, I will repeat: Pay attention to what Jesus may say now, and do not let the Bible statements, which do not agree with what he may write you, disturb you or cause you to doubt what you may receive.

Sometime, I shall come and give you my ideas of some of the spiritual Truths, and how necessary it is that men should know them.

I certainly believe in the New Birth, and I want to say most emphatically that it is one of the most important Truths of the spiritual world. It has not heretofore been very often understood, and its exact meaning is somewhat in doubt by even the best students of the Bible.

I will not write more tonight, but will say that you are my brother in the good work of showing the Truths to mankind that are so important to their future happiness and salvation.

So, with a Love that is in Christ, I am
Your brother,
AUGUSTINE.

John Explains That Not the Blood but the Divine Love Is What Saves and Redeems. He Cautions That "Revelation" of the Bible Is Not to Be Relied Upon as True in Many Particulars.
(JOHN, THE APOSTLE)
(September 7th, 1915 | Received by James Padgett)

I AM HERE. *John of the "Revelation."*

I saw you studying the Bible, or, rather, those portions of the book which treated of the salvation of mankind through the blood of Jesus, and that you made extracts from the revelation which declared that the blood of Jesus washes away sins of mankind and redeems them.

Well, I want to say that while I wrote Revelation, or, rather, dictated it to another to write, I never wrote the words declaring the salvation of mankind through the blood of Jesus, which declared that the blood of Jesus washed away sins of mankind and redeemed them; for I did not believe any such doctrine and had never been taught such a belief by Jesus.

MUCH OF THE MATTER CONTAINED IN THE REVELATION I NEVER WROTE. BUT MEN OR SCRIBES, WHO PROFESSED TO COPY THE DESCRIPTIONS OF MY VISION, ADDED TO IT FOR THE PURPOSE OF INCORPORATING THEREIN THE VIEWS OF THE CHRISTIANS OF THAT EARLY DAY, SO THAT THEIR VIEWS MIGHT BE EMPHASIZED AND WOULD BE IN UNION WITH SIMILAR VIEWS THAT HAD BEEN ADDED TO THE GOSPELS AND EPISTLES IN THE COPIES WHICH THESE SAME PERSONS, OR THEIR PREDECESSORS IN THESE VIEWS, HAD MADE.

Revelation is merely an account of a vision which I had when in a trance, and was undoubtedly intended to illustrate or predict those things which would be visited upon the believers and the nonbelievers in the Truths of God as taught by Jesus and his apostles.

At the present day, I cannot see that this book can serve any good purpose in making men acquainted with the Truths of God, or with the relationship of man to God. Many of the things contained therein are not true as Truths, but were used merely to illustrate a Truth. There are no streets of gold or pearly gates, or dragons or beasts or white horses, or other material things which are depicted in that book. And it is valuable only so far as imagery may show some spiritual Truth to mankind.

And, besides, it has been so embellished and added to that many of its figures or images do not illustrate any truth, or anything else, but merely serve to give the book the character and appearance of a book of mysteries.

So, I advise you, in attempting to search for the Truths that the Bible contains, do not waste your time in trying to discover the meanings for the various dark sayings and mysterious descriptions which this book contains.

THERE ARE ENOUGH TRUTHS IN THE BIBLE, THOUGH MIXED WITH MANY ERRORS, TO LEAD MEN TO THE LIGHT

411

AND TO SALVATION. LOVE IS THE GREAT PRINCIPLE, AND THE FACT THAT GOD IS WAITING TO BESTOW THAT LOVE ON MANKIND IF THEY WILL ONLY SEEK FOR IT, AS IT IS THE PRINCIPLE WHICH IS SUFFICIENT TO LEAD MEN TO THE CELESTIAL HOMES AND HAPPINESS.

I am not an advocate of all the isms which men draw or formulate from the Bible; but, on the contrary, I deplore and condemn the misconstructions of the Truths which it contains, and which men may understand if they will search for them in humbleness and in the spirit of a little child.

BUT WHATEVER ERRORS MAY BE WRITTEN IN THE BIBLE WILL BE SHOWN BY THE MESSAGES WHICH JESUS SHALL WRITE TO YOU. AND AFTER THEY ARE TRANSMITTED AND MADE KNOWN TO MANKIND, THERE WILL BE NO OCCASION FOR MEN TO ACCEPT OR BELIEVE THESE ERRORS.

So, I tell you that, while the Bible, even as now written, is a grand old book, yet, it is not the true mouthpiece of God in very many particulars, and is a stumbling block to man's acquiring a correct knowledge of the Truth.

These Truths will not conflict with the reasoning of the normal man who is not prejudiced by views which are erroneous, either in the scientific or the religious world.

A man who believes what is not true is just as much an infidel, whether that belief relates to the sciences or to religion. A belief in the false is a want of belief in the true; and, hence, as to the true, he is not a believer.

I will not write more tonight.

So, I will say good night and God bless you and your work.

Your brother in Christ,

JOHN OF REVELATION.

Jesus Affirms That His Disciples Never Wrote All the False Doctrines in the Bible Attributed to Him.
(JESUS)
(September 5th, 1915 | Received by James Padgett)

I AM HERE. *Jesus.*

I was with you tonight, and heard what you said about the Bible and its writers. And I desire to say that many things in it were not written by my disciples, or those to whom my disciples had delivered the sayings that I made use of while on earth.

The text as contained in the present Bible is not a true copy of what I said, or what was in the manuscripts of those who originally wrote; and I am trying to correct the many errors that the Bible contains.

THE SAYINGS IN THE EPISTLES AND IN THE GOSPELS AND IN REVELATION TO THE EFFECT THAT MY BLOOD SAVES FROM

SIN ARE ERRONEOUS, AND MY DISCIPLES NEVER WROTE THAT FALSE DOCTRINE. FOR I REPEAT HERE, WHAT I HAVE BEFORE WRITTEN YOU, THAT MY BLOOD HAS NOTHING TO DO WITH THE REDEMPTION OF MANKIND FORM SIN; NOR HAS MY BLOOD ANY EFFECT IN RECONCILING MEN TO GOD OR MAKING THEM ONE WITH HIM. THE ONLY THING THAT WORKS THIS GREAT RESULT IS THE NEW BIRTH, AS I HAVE EXPLAINED IT TO YOU.

So, do not let these sayings of the Bible disturb your belief in what I say now, or in what I may say hereafter.

(In John's "Revelation" there are words declaring the salvation of mankind through your blood sacrifice.)

Well, the Revelation of John is not true; it is a mere allegory, and not just as he wrote it. For it contains many things that are absurd and not in accord with the Truths as I shall write them to you. He has written you already on Revelation, and has told you what he did not write, as he has been annoyed by this book of the Bible and its interpretations by the preachers and others. It is nothing but a revelation of a vision which he thought he saw while in a trance. So, let not these things disturb you.

I see that you are getting more of the Divine Love in your soul, and your spiritual eyes will be opened; and, before long, your soul perceptions will see and understand many of the vital Truths of God.

I will not write more tonight. With all my love, your brother and friend,
JESUS.

John Again Denies the Vicarious Atonement. He Also Explains That Spirit Communion Was More Prevalent in His Day than Now, and That if Men Would Have Faith Like the Apostles of Jesus, Healing and So-Called "Miracles" Would Exist Today.
(JOHN, THE APOSTLE)
(September 12th, 1915 | Received by James Padgett)

I AM HERE. *John.*

I do not write "St. John" because I am not called by that name in the spirit heavens. I have written to you often enough now that you will identify me when I merely write "John."

Well, I heard what the Master said, and I can only add thereto that I never wrote the things which declare that I preached that the blood of Jesus saves from sin, or that Jesus was a propitiation for the sins of mankind. Neither in my gospel nor in my epistles nor in Revelation did I write such a doctrine. As I have told you before, many things contained in these books were written by others to carry out certain plans and ideas of the writers. I never said that Jesus was God and that he was begotten by the Holy Ghost,

413

or that he is equal with God, or that he saved a man from sin by reason of any personal qualities which he may have had.

So, let your mind eliminate these false doctrines and receive the Truths from the Master with a perfectly unbiased mind, free from all preconceived ideas.

(What did you mean when you advised mortals to try the spirits who communicated?)

I meant that many spirits would try to communicate with man and attempt to teach false doctrines as to Jesus and his mission, and that the only spirits who were capable of conveying the Truth, and were worthy of belief, were those who should acknowledge that Jesus was the son of God in the way that it has been explained to you—not that Jesus or Jesus Christ was God. Only those spirits who acknowledge Jesus as the son of God and have received the New Birth, and know something about the Kingdom of Christ, or of the Gift of the Divine Love of the Father and the Way to obtain It, as taught by Jesus, should be acknowledged. All the spirits who have not this knowledge, and, consequently, would not acknowledge Jesus as the son of God, are not to be trusted as being true followers of Jesus.

This is nothing mysterious or contrary to the laws governing the conduct or beliefs of men. If a spirit, or man either, knows nothing about a certain subject, he certainly cannot teach others its qualities or merits. And, hence, I was applying an ordinary law of nature to the way in which spirits should be tried. For I must tell you, and it is a Truth, and was a Truth at the time I wrote my gospel and epistles, just as it is a Truth now, and always will remain a Truth, that every spirit who acknowledges that Jesus is the son of God is a redeemed spirit and has received a portion of the Divine Love, and is progressing in the Kingdom which Jesus is now forming. And when I gave those instructions to my "children," as I called them, I intended that their communications should be only with those spirits or men who had received this New Birth.

I know that all the spirits who have received this Divine Love in sufficient abundance are good spirits, free from sin and error and having the power or inclination to influence mortals not to sin or to do anything which is contrary to the Will of the Father, while all the other spirits may or may not exercise the influence of evil upon mortals.

Hence, try the spirits. And if they do not acknowledge Jesus as the son of God, let them alone. Do not receive their communications or teachings, because they are not believers in Christ and the New Birth.

Among my children, or believers in the Christian religion, were many persons who had the power or gift of communicating with the spirits of the departed, and they did so communicate. Such communications were made known to the rest of the congregation and believed by them. And, hence, my injunction against communion with those spirits who were not believers in Christ.

You must not think that this is the only age in which spirits communicate with mortals. For I must tell you that, in my time, it was much

414

more common than now. And when worshiping in our congregations, and when in our gatherings, and often in private, we had these communications.

This was an important part of the services of our meetings, and one that kept us in constant harmony with the soul power of those who lived in the spirit form, and from whom we received powers of healing and of doing good in many other ways.

In those days, healing the sick and doing kindred things were a very important part of our work as Christians. We believed what Jesus had told us on earth, and we increased our faith and performed many works which the people, who did not believe as we did, thought were miracles.

To us, the healing of the sick and the doing of these other things were just as natural as eating and sleeping. I tell you that our faith then was a certainty. We possessed the Substance that Paul speaks of, and we expected to do these things, just as we expected to breathe and be able to do material good to our brothers.

But, after a few centuries, when men came into the church for other purposes than to receive the New Birth and do the Will of the Father, faith, such as I speak of, died; and the power to do these things was taken away from men, and the church became a congregation of men having the mere lip worship.

And all through the centuries from then until now, this power has not been with men, except that here and there some true believer, with a faith such as we had, has appeared and done wonderful things.

So, I say, let not what the Bible may say about Jesus being God, and having those other qualities with reference to the salvation of men, disturb you in your beliefs in what the Master may write you.

I will not write more tonight, but will say good night.

Your brother in Christ,

JOHN.

Martin Luther, One-Time Monk and Reformer, Recommends a Test to Employ in Trying the Spirits.
(MARTIN LUTHER)
(September 12th, 1915 | Received by James Padgett)

I AM HERE. *Luther.*

I came to tell you that you are not much benefited by the book (Pastor Russell's Atonement) you have been reading tonight, because it ignores the very foundation of the Plan of man's redemption—that is, the Divine Love which the Father bestowed on mankind at the coming of Jesus. The blood atonement is all wrong and misleading, and has done much harm to the Truths of God and to mankind.

I will admit that there are many truths stated in the book, and many that will do much good to humanity to understand and believe. But because of the great error in the vital point of the declaration as to the Plan of man's salvation, these truths which the book contains may not do the good that they otherwise might.

Of course, you, who understands the true Plan of salvation, may make the true discrimination between those declarations which declare the Truth and those declarations which do not. But, on the whole, I do not see that the teachings of the book will do you much good.

(John recommends that mortals try the spirits who communicate.)

Well, I know that the passage in John refers to the spirits of men who once lived on earth, and who communicated to the members of the early church in their places of worship and elsewhere. John has explained this to you, and I have been informed by others of the apostles that what he said is true.

The author of that book has certain theories, and, of course, he is construing all the teachings of the Bible in such a way as to sustain his theories. But he is wrong, and he will discover this when he comes to the spirit world.

He teaches that the soul as well as the body of man goes into the grave to await the great day of judgment, and that there is no such place as the spirit world, inhabited by the spirits of departed mortals. And, to maintain this position, he quotes from some of the old books of the Bible. But these books were not written by men who were inspired by God to declare the Truths. And the quoted expressions are merely the result of the purely human minds of the authors who did not know what they wrote to be a fact. But because of the conditions in which they were in, they concluded that such assertions must be true. Let not the writings of these old writers, or of the present day writers either, cause you to hesitate to believe what the Master may write as being true.

I merely wanted to say this, as I saw that you are interested in this book, and I wanted to warn you against letting it influence you in any way.

(Do you acknowledge that Jesus came to earth in the flesh?)

Yes, I say that Jesus Christ did come in the flesh, and I know it, for he is a spirit here and once lived on earth. But that fact does not prove that any spirit who acknowledges that is a true follower of him or a redeemed spirit of the Father.

There are many spirits in the spirit world who believe that Jesus, the spirit whom they sometimes meet, once lived as a mortal, and, if asked, would say that he lived in the flesh. But they are not believers in the Divine Love of the Father, or have had the benefit of His Great Plan of salvation, of have acknowledged Jesus as the savior from sin and error.

So, the test set forth in the Bible may have been considered a true test in the days of the early church, yet it is not now a very safe one for the reason that I have mentioned.

IF A TEST IS NECESSARY, I THINK A BETTER ONE WOULD BE: TRY THE SPIRITS, AND EVERYONE WHO DOES NOT ACKNOWLEDGE THAT JESUS IS THE BEST BELOVED SON OF

GOD, AND BROUGHT TO THE KNOWLEDGE OF MANKIND THE REBESTOWAL OF THE DIVINE LOVE, AND DECLARED TO MEN THE WAY IN WHICH THAT LOVE MAY BE OBTAINED, IS NOT A SPIRIT THAT SHOULD BE COMMUNICATED WITH FOR THE PURPOSE OF LEARNING SPIRITUAL TRUTHS.

THIS TEST IS BETTER BECAUSE NO SPIRIT WHO HAS NOT RECEIVED THIS DIVINE LOVE, OR THE NEW BIRTH, WILL ACKNOWLEDGE THE EXISTENCE OF THESE THINGS, BECAUSE IT HAS NO KNOWLEDGE UPON WHICH TO MAKE THE ACKNOWLEDGEMENT.

I must not write more tonight, but I hope the little that I have said may help you and others who have doubts as to what the meaning of that part of the Bible is which refers to the trying of the spirits.

I am very anxious to write to you again as to some of the higher Truths pertaining to the spirit world, and, soon, I hope that I may have the opportunity.

I will say good night.

Your brother in Christ,
MARTIN LUTHER.

Mrs. Padgett Explains That the Epistles in the Bible Are Not the Same That the Original Apostles Wrote. She Adds That the Divine Love Mentioned in the Bible Is Not Properly Explained, as Contradistinguished from the Natural Love.
(HELEN PADGETT)
(October 29th, 1918 | Received by James Padgett)

I AM HERE. *Helen.*

Well, dear, I see that you have been reading portions of the Bible tonight, and that you have not found in the same any mention of the Divine Love in the sense that It has been explained to you, or any evidence that the writers had any knowledge of the Love in the way of being born again. Of course, they used the expression, but the meaning that they gave to it is altogether different from the one that Jesus gave the other night.

Now, you have been told that he taught the apostles this true meaning and that they understood it to a more or less extent, and especially John. And as a Truth that is the very foundation of the Truth of salvation, it may be surprising to you that, if John wrote the epistles[*] which are ascribed to him, he did not speak of, or attempt to explain, the meaning of this New Existence. The apostles do not mention the New Birth in the light of the

---

[*] See also: "What Is the Fact in Reference to the Authenticity of the Bible," by Luke, in volume I of *Angelic Revelations of Divine Truth.*— Ed.

explanation that has been given to you, and you may very reasonably infer that these epistles were not written by any of the apostles to whom they are accredited, but by some writers who had some knowledge of the moral truths of Jesus' teachings, and of the great one that they should love their brethren as themselves. You will find very little in any portion of the Bible that will show you that the great Truth of the New Birth was understood by the writers thereof. All that you will find is that love between man and God, and man and man, with all that flows from it, such as patience and kindness and charity, etc., is the fulfilling of the Christian doctrines. No distinction is made between the natural love of man—the love God bestowed upon him at his creation—and the Great Divine Love which man never possessed until the coming of the Master.

It may seem strange that this knowledge that the apostles and many others had when on earth, in the time of the Master, should have been lost to the world. But it is a fact. And, as a consequence, for all these long years, the teachings of Jesus as to this great Truth have failed to work out his mission.

Well, I could write for a long time about this matter, but is not necessary as you already know of these things.

Good night.

Your own true and loving,
HELEN.

Saul Gives Advice to His People, the Jews.
(SAUL OF THE OLD TESTAMENT)
(June 1st, 1917 | Received by James Padgett)

I AM HERE. *Saul of the Old Testament.*

I will say only a word, as it is late and your wife says that I must not write much.

Well, I have not written for a long time, and I desire very much to write you a message regarding some important spiritual Truths that I know will be of interest to you; and, if you will give me the opportunity, I will come soon and do so.

I am interested in the Jews, and I desire to tell them of some Truths that may open up their minds to the Way to the Celestial Kingdom, and may cause them to cease to believe that their old orthodox beliefs in their father, Abraham, and the God of the Old Testament, are all that is necessary to bring them into the Presence of the True God.

I realize that it will be difficult to write anything that will convince them of the errors of their beliefs; yet I will try, and will pray to the Father to open up their understanding.

418

The happenings in the countries where war[*] is now raging will have their effect upon the Jews as well as upon the Christians and pagans. And, in their awakening consciousness, I desire that they may have the benefit of the Truth. So, if you will give me the opportunity, I will come soon and write.

I would like to say a few things more, but it is best that I do not tonight, and I will stop.

So, with my love and the Blessings of God, I will say good night.

Your brother in Christ,

SAUL.

Luther Declares That the Observance of the Ceremonies Which the Lutheran Church Still Uses in Its Worship Is Not Approved of by God or by Jesus.
(MARTIN LUTHER)
(June 29th, 1916 | Received by James Padgett)

I AM HERE. *Martin Luther.*

I desire to write a short message tonight on the subject: "The Observance of the Ceremonies Which My Church Still Uses in Its Worship Is Not Approved of by God or by Jesus." I will not detain you very long and will try to express myself as succinctly as possible.

Well, as you may not know, the church of which I am the founder believes and teaches the necessity of infant baptism and the observance of the "Lord's Supper" as necessary parts of its church doctrine, and that they are of such very great importance that, without them, it is difficult to become an accepted member of the invisible church of Christ.

NOTHING IS FURTHER FROM THE TRUTH THAN THIS DOCTRINE OF THE BAPTISM OF INFANTS, FOR IT HAS NO VIRTUE TO SAVE ONE FROM HIS SINS OR TO MAKE HIM IN AT-ONEMENT WITH THE FATHER. AND THE MERE FACT THAT WATER IS SPRINKLED ON AN INFANT'S HEAD, AND SOME BLESSING PRONOUNCED BY THE PREACHER, DOES NOT IN ANY WAY BRING THAT INFANT IN UNISON WITH THE FATHER. BAPTISM IS OF MAN'S CREATION, AND IT MEANS NOTHING MORE TO GOD THAN AN OUTWARD CEREMONY THAT AFFECTS THE INFANT MERELY AS REGARDS ITS CONNECTION WITH THE ESTABLISHED EARTHLY CHURCH. IT IS NOT POSSIBLE FOR THIS BAPTISM TO HAVE ANY EFFECT UPON THE SOUL OF THE INFANT. AND NEITHER DOES IT OPEN UP THE SOUL FACULTIES TO THE INFLOWING OF THE DIVINE LOVE.

---

[*] World War I.

GOD CARES NOT FOR THESE CEREMONIES, AND RATHER LOOKS UPON THEM WITH DISAPPROVAL. FOR THEIR TENDENCY IS TO MAKE MEN AND WOMEN NEGLECTFUL OF THE GREAT TRUTH THAT WILL BRING THEM IN HARMONY WITH GOD'S LAWS OF LOVE AND REDEMPTION.

AND THE SAME THING MAY BE SAID OF ANY AND ALL KINDS OF BAPTISM, WHETHER THE SUBJECT THEREOF BE AN INFANT OR A GROWN MAN OR WOMAN.

AS TO THE SACRAMENT OF THE "LORD'S SUPPER", IT HAS NO PART IN GOD'S PLAN FOR THE REDEMPTION OF MANKIND, AND IS MERELY A REMINDER OF THE ASSOCIATION OF JESUS WITH HIS DISCIPLES. IT CANNOT AFFECT THE CONDITION OR DEVELOPMENT OF THE SOUL; AND, AS NOW UNDERSTOOD AND PRACTICED, THIS SACRAMENT IS OF NO IMPORTANCE. FOR JESUS DOES NOT WANT TO BE REMEMBERED IN THE WAY OF RECALLING TO HIM THE TRAGEDY ON THE CROSS, WHICH WAS ONLY THE RESULT OF THE MALICE AND ENVY OF SOME OF THE JEWS. AND THE BLOOD SPILT IS NOT AN ELEMENT THAT ENTERS INTO THE PLAN OF THE SALVATION OF MEN. AND, BESIDES, WITH THIS SACRAMENT, THERE IS ALWAYS MORE OR LESS WORSHIPING OF JESUS AS GOD, WHICH HE, JESUS, ABHORS AND LOOKS UPON AS BLASPHEMY.

SO, YOU SEE, THE CELEBRATION OF THE LAST SUPPER IS A THING WHICH IS NOT ACCEPTABLE TO GOD OR TO JESUS. HE DOES NOT WANT MEN TO BELIEVE THAT THEY CAN BE SAVED BY ANY SACRIFICE OF HIM, OR BY ANY BLOOD WHICH HE MAY HAVE SHED AS A RESULT OF HIS CRUCIFIXION.

Of course, you will remember that the question of what the wine and bread of the sacrament really were was one that engendered much controversy, and even hatred and ill-feeling on the part of those who were assisting me in the great Reformation. If I had known then what I do now, no such question would have been debated or believed in by me and taught for many years. The blood of Jesus was no more than any other man's blood. And the commemoration of the "Last Supper" that Jesus gave his disciples before his death is a useless ceremony, and brings no help to those who indulge in this sacrament.

I see that you are tired and sleepy and I will not write more now. So, with my love and wishes for an increase of the Divine Love in you, I am
Your brother in Christ,
LUTHER.

Luther Again Denies the Vicarious Atonement. He Also States That the Bible Is Full of Contradictions and Errors.
(MARTIN LUTHER)
(September 5th, 1915 | Received by James Padgett)

420

I AM HERE. *Martin Luther.*

I came again because I want to tell you that I was with you this afternoon when you were reading the comments on the origin and different versions of the Bible. Among them was a reference to my version. And I want to say that, while my version was a pretty correct translation, yet, the manuscripts and other versions upon which I based my translation were not the real writings of those who profess to have written them. I mean that those manuscripts were not true copies of the original epistles and books written by those whose names they bear. Many interpretations and more constructions were given to the texts of the originals than you or any other mortal are aware of.

The Bible as now written, and as I translated it, is full of contradictions and errors and makes the Truth hard to ascertain. Take, for instance, that one subject of the blood redemption.

NO GREATER ERROR WAS EVER WRITTEN THAN THAT THE BLOOD OF JESUS SAVES FROM SIN, OR THAT HIS BLOOD WASHES AWAY SIN! IT SEEMS TO ME NOW SO ABSURD THAT I WONDER AND AM ASTONISHED THAT I COULD EVER HAVE BELIEVED IN SUCH AN ABSURDITY.

I KNOW NOW THAT THERE IS NO EFFICACY IN JESUS' BLOOD TO ACCOMPLISH ANY SUCH RESULTS. AND THE PITY IS THAT MANY MEN NOW BELIEVE THIS AND, AS A CONSEQUENCE, NEGLECT THE ONE VITAL AND IMPORTANT REQUIREMENT NECESSARY TO SALVATION; THAT IS, THE NEW BIRTH. THIS, AND THIS ONLY, SAVES MEN FROM THEIR SINS AND FITS THEM TO ENTER THE KINGDOM OF GOD, WHICH IS THE KINGDOM OF JESUS. FOR HE IS THE PRINCE OF THAT KINGDOM AND THE RULER THEREOF.

(The Bible records Jesus as saying that his blood was to be shed for many.)

JESUS NEVER SAID ANY SUCH THING, FOR HE HAS TOLD ME SO. THIS SAYING THAT HIS BLOOD WAS SHED FOR MANY IS NOT TRUE. HE NEVER SAID IT. NEITHER DID HE SAY THAT THEY SHOULD DRINK THE WINE, BEING HIS BLOOD, IN REMEMBRANCE OF HIM, FOR THE WINE IS NOT HIS BLOOD. AND NEITHER DOES IT REPRESENT ANYTHING THAT HAS TO DO WITH HIM OR HIS MISSION ON EARTH, OR HIS PRESENT WORK IN THE SPIRIT WORLD. HOW UNFORTUNATE THAT THIS SAYING IS MADE TO REPRESENT SOMETHING THAT HE DID NOT SAY!

So, in order to understand the real Truths of God, and man's relationship to Him and His Plan of salvation, you must believe what the Master shall write to you, and what his apostles may write. For now they understand what his true mission was, what he attempted and intended to teach when on earth, and what he is teaching now.

I will also write sometimes and give you the result of my instructions and knowledge, as I received them since being here.

I will not write more tonight.

Your brother in Christ,

MARTIN LUTHER.

Luther Denies the Efficacy of the Eucharist to Save Man. He Explains That Jesus Is Living and Teaching and Demonstrating the Divine Love in His Soul, and How Man Can Obtain It, and That This Is the True Way to Salvation.
(MARTIN LUTHER)
(January 31ˢᵗ, 1917 | Received by James Padgett)

I AM HERE. *Martin Luther.*

I have come merely to remind you that I am waiting to continue my discourse to my people. I am very anxious to do this and, as soon as you get in condition, I hope that you will give me the opportunity.

(When would you like to resume?)

Well, we will arrange that. All that we desire is for you to get in condition. We are with you a great deal and try to assist you in every way possible.

(Can you tell me whether or not Jesus was born with the actual Substance of God comprising his being, as the Bible declares?)

Well, you have asked me a question that I should like to have more time in which to answer than I have now. But, in short, Jesus was not of the Substance of God in the sense that the Catholic church, following the Nicene Creed, claimed. He took on a part of the Divine Substance as the Divine Love filled his soul. And so can you or any other man do this to the extent that you may receive this Love. But to say that Jesus was, in his very being, of the Substance of the Father to that degree that made him equal to God is erroneous, and should not be taught or believed in. He was born or created in the likeness of God in the way that has been explained to you, and in no other. He was a man and not God, or any part of Him. And if he had not received the Divine Love into his soul, he would never have been of the Substance of the Father. But being of a very spiritual nature and, in fact, so much so that he was without sin, this Love commenced to come into his soul very early—from his very birth, as you may say. And, at the time of his anointing, he was so filled with It that you may say that he was of the Substance possessed of the Divine Nature. He was no more divine, though, naturally, as I may say, than was any other mortal born of the flesh. I should like to write you a long message on this subject, and will sometime when convenient.

(Can you also enlighten me concerning the church's claims about the

422

Eucharist?)

WELL, ALL THE SPECULATION THAT HAS EVER EXISTED AS TO THE EUCHARIST, RELATING TO THE CHANGE IN THE QUALITIES OF THE BREAD AND WINE, IS UNTRUE. JESUS IS NOT IN THESE ELEMENTS IN ANY PARTICULAR OR VIEW THAT MAY BE TAKEN. HIS FLESH AND BLOOD WENT THE WAY OF ALL FLESH AND BLOOD OF MORTALS, AND NO MORE FORMS A PART OF THE BREAD AND WINE THAN DOES YOUR FLESH AND BLOOD.

THIS "SACRAMENT," AS IT IS CALLED, IS VERY ABHORRENT TO THE MASTER; AND, WHEN IT IS CELEBRATED, I MUST TELL YOU THAT HE IS NOT PRESENT, NEITHER IN FLESH AND BLOOD NOR IN HIS SPIRITUAL PRESENCE. HE DISLIKES ANY KIND OF WORSHIP WHICH PLACES HIM, AS ITS OBJECT, IN THE POSITION OF GOD, OR AS THE SON OF GOD WHO PAID A GREAT DEBT BY HIS SACRIFICE AND DEATH. HE WANTS GOD, ALONE, TO BE WORSHIPED, AND HIMSELF TO BE THOUGHT OF ONLY AS THE ONE WHO BROUGHT IMMORTALITY AND LIFE TO LIGHT BY HIS TEACHINGS, AND BY THE LIVING DEMONSTRATION OF THE TRUTH OF THE EXISTENCE OF THE DIVINE LOVE IN HIMSELF.

HE DOES NOT APPROVE OF THE TEACHINGS OF MEN THAT HIS DEATH AND HIS BLOOD WERE THE MEANS OF MAN BEING SAVED FROM THEIR SINS AND BECOMING RECONCILED TO GOD. HE SAYS IT WAS HIS LIVING, AND TEACHINGS, AND DEMONSTRATIONS OF THE LOVE OF GOD EXISTING IN HIS OWN SOUL THAT SHOWED THE ONLY TRUE WAY TO SALVATION.

But, I must not write more now. So, with my love, I will say good night.

Your brother in Christ,

MARTIN LUTHER.

A Former Preacher Discusses His Beliefs and Denies the "Trinity."
(ROBERT COLYER)
(August 5th, 1915 | Received by James Padgett)

I AM HERE. *Robert Colyer.*

I was a preacher. I am now a preacher and my doctrines are those of Christ, stripped of the creeds and dogmas of the churches.

I was not an orthodox preacher, but was one who believed in God and in Jesus as the best and most spiritual man that ever lived on earth, and who taught the Truths of his Father.

I am of the same belief still, and, since being in the spirit world, I have learned many things to confirm my belief. THE ORTHODOX

DOCTRINE AS TO JESUS BEING GOD, OR "ONE OF THREE GODS," IS A PERNICIOUS ONE AND AGAINST ALL REASON AND TRUTH. HE IS JUST WHO HE SAID HE WAS—THE SON OF GOD AND THE SON OF MAN. HE IS THE FIRST IN A SPIRITUAL SENSE, AND THE LATTER IN THE MATERIAL OR NATURAL SENSE.

AS HE HAS TOLD ME, HE NEVER CLAIMED TO BE GOD, AND HIS DISCIPLES NEVER UNDERSTOOD THAT HE WAS SUCH. THE FREEDOM OF MEN'S MINDS FROM THIS DOCTRINE OF HIS BEING GOD WILL DO MORE TO BRING MEN TO THE TRUTH, AND TO BELIEVE IN RELIGIOUS TRUTHS, THAN CAN BE CONCEIVED OF. WHEN HIS TRUE MISSION ON EARTH SHALL BECOME UNDERSTOOD, MEN WILL TURN TO THE TRUE WORSHIP OF GOD AND TO A BELIEF IN THE TEACHINGS OF THE MASTER. AND THIS WILL RESULT IN MANY A ONE BEING SAVED FROM THEIR SINS, AND IN HAPPINESS AND HARMONY AND BROTHERLY LOVE BEING MORE FIRMLY ESTABLISHED ON EARTH.

I am a believer in the Divine Love and the New Birth, and am an inhabitant of the Seventh Sphere where I am trying to progress to the Celestial Spheres.

I will not write more tonight, as you are tired, but will come again sometime. So, with all my love as a brother in Christ, I am,

ROBERT COLYER.

Jesus Reaffirms That His Blood Does Not Save Men from Their Sins.
(JESUS)
(September 19th, 1915 | Received by James Padgett)

I AM HERE. *Jesus.*

I heard the discussion between you and the other man about my blood saving from sin, and I felt that you were not benefited by what was said because his faith is based on ignorance of the true Plan of salvation and my mission on earth.

But he is so firmly fixed in his belief that no argument that you might make would convince him that anything but my death and "atonement" could save from sin. So, I do not think it would do any good to attempt to argue with any of these people in reference to the matter of my blood as the means of salvation.

They have received the Divine Love to a considerable degree, and the Holy Spirit is with them in their worship and is in their hearts. But It does not come to them by reason of their belief in my "atonement," but because they pray to the Father for Its coming and making them a new being so far as their soul development is concerned. They do not know that only the flowing of this Divine Love into their hearts in answer to prayer is what

424

gives them this New Birth.

They think that my blood has something, or, rather, that it is the great and only cause of this New Birth, and they will continue to think so. I would not let this matter deter you from attending their meeting because, as I have said, the Holy Spirit is present with them. Of course, they will learn differently when they come to the spirit world and see that I am not God.

(The orthodox believe that messages such as yours could only come from the devil.)

Yes, I know that is what all the orthodox believe, but that does not make it a fact; for no devil ever comes and teaches the things that I have written to you.

I will not write more now.

So, with the assurance that I am with you very often, and that I will guide you in the ways of Truth, I will stop.

Your brother and friend,

JESUS.

Paul Denies the Efficacy of the Vicarious Atonement. He Emphasizes That God Was Never a God of "Wrath" but Always of Love.
(PAUL, THE APOSTLE)
(August 20th, 1915 | Received by James Padgett)

I AM HERE. *Paul.*

I merely want to write about the Truth of the New Birth, because I speak, or, rather, it is written that the blood of Jesus saves men from condemnation and sin and death.

This is not true, and I never wrote such declarations of what purports to be true. Jesus did not save men by his death or sacrifice; and, as I am informed now, and learned when on earth, he never claimed that his blood or sacrifice saved men. And I hardly see how that could be so, because the blood does not have any efficacy to affect the condition or spiritual development of men, and his death cannot help men to become redeemed from any condition of evil or defilement that they might be in. Hence, there can be no possible connection between his blood or sacrifice and the condition of men, whether good or bad.

I know it is claimed that the blood of Jesus tended to appease the "wrath" of God towards men, as did his death, but this presupposes that God had a wrath against men and that only blood and death could satisfy it. What a barbarous assumption!

God was never a God of "wrath," but always of Love. And men can come to Him in reconciliation through Love only, and not through any sacrifice. Jesus never taught this doctrine of sacrifice, and does not now, but repudiates it and says that it is a doctrine that is doing his cause and the salvation of mankind a great harm.

425

IF MEN WILL ONLY THINK FOR A MOMENT, THEY WILL SEE THAT THE ONLY RELATION BETWEEN GOD AND MAN IS THAT WHICH ARISES FROM THE SOUL'S CONDITION. GOD, AS I SAID, IS LOVE. AND FOR MAN TO BE AT-ONE WITH HIM, MAN MUST BECOME LOVE. I MEAN THAT HIS SOUL MUST BE FILLED OR PERMEATED WITH THIS LOVE TO SUCH AN EXTENT THAT IT WILL BECOME IMPOSSIBLE FOR ANYTHING THAT IS NOT OF LOVE TO BE OR REMAIN A PART OF HIS SOUL.

I do not mean that it is necessary for men to obtain this Divine Love in order to live and enjoy a happiness which is far above the happiness that they have on earth, for that would not be true. God has given a natural love to man which, when enjoyed in all its intended purity, is sufficient of itself to make men comparatively happy. But this love does not make man a part of God's Oneness, or enable him to partake of the Divine Essence of the Father. And this oneness is absolutely necessary for men to become reconciled to God, as Jesus taught.

So, while the large majority of men may never become reconciled in the sense that I have mentioned, yet, they will be able to enjoy this inferior happiness in the spirit world, and to such a degree that no sin or evil will be permitted to mar it.

A small minority will become reconciled to God and enjoy the superior happiness which such reconciliation will bring to them. They will be like the Father in their nature and substance, having His Divine Essence and partaking of His Immortality.

BUT THIS RECONCILIATION CAN ONLY BE OBTAINED BY WHAT IS CALLED THE NEW BIRTH, WHICH COMES TO MEN NOT BY REASON OF ANY POWER OR EFFORT ON THEIR PART ONLY, BUT BY THE OPERATIONS OF THE WORKINGS OF THE HOLY GHOST—THE INSTRUMENT OF GOD IN BRINGING ABOUT THIS NEW BIRTH.

AND, YET, MAN HAS HIS PART TO PERFORM ALSO IN THIS GREAT RENEWAL OF HIS SPIRITUAL BEING. HE MUST OPEN HIS SOUL TO THE INFLOWING OF THIS DIVINE LOVE, AND MUST PRAY TO THE FATHER FOR THE INFLOWING OF THE HOLY GHOST. AND, WITH HIS PRAYERS, HE MUST BELIEVE THAT THE FATHER IS WAITING TO BESTOW THIS LOVE.

WITHOUT THE DESIRE ON THE PART OF MAN TO RECEIVE THIS DIVINE LOVE, WITH PRAYER AND FAITH, IT WILL NOT COME TO HIM. FOR GOD NEVER FORCES ANY HUMAN SOUL TO A NEW BIRTH AGAINST ITS WILL.

I TELL YOU THIS BECAUSE, IN MY OPINION, THIS IS THE ONE GREAT, IMPORTANT TRUTH OF THE MISSION OF JESUS ON EARTH, AND THE ONE THAT HUMAN BEINGS SHOULD UNDERSTAND AND TRY TO COMPLY WITH.

I know now, as I never knew on earth, the full meaning of this Truth; and I thank God all the time for His Goodness and Mercy.

Only those who receive this New Birth become divine angels. All other spirits remain mere spirits and subject to all the changes and conditions that belong to spirits. For there is nothing fixed as to those who may remain mere spirits, any more than there was in the case of the first man and woman. We know now that changes may take place in the conditions of these spirits during the working of God's Plans.

Many men, even when they know of the things that I have written, may be content to remain mere spirits and live their spiritual lives in the happiness which their natural love gives them. But it seems to me that all men will seek for the greater Love, and happiness and immortality, if they will only think a little, and understandingly.

I wanted to write this tonight, for I see that some of the teachings of my epistles may tend to lead men astray on this most important question as to what saves them from their sins and reconciles them to God.

I will not write more tonight, but will come at times and write to you in regard to the various spiritual Truths of this Kingdom.

I will say good night.

Your brother in Christ,

PAUL.

John Declares That Men or Prophets Cannot Tell What Will Happen Centuries Ahead; This Can Only Be Known by the Father.
(JOHN, THE APOSTLE)
(March 10th, 1918 | Received by James Padgett)

I AM HERE. *John.*

I see that you are in a much better condition tonight, and that your soul is more in harmony with the spirits of the higher spheres. We could write now, but your hand and arm are tired, and this is a matter that we always consider. We try not to cause you any unnecessary fatigue.

Other spirits are here tonight, hoping that they might write; but, under the circumstances, they will not. The Master is here also, and says that he will not attempt to write tonight, as he intended, but will soon come and deliver a message.

I am glad that you are feeling so much better spiritually and physically, and I feel that you will continue to do so. So, pray more to the Father and turn your thoughts to spiritual things, and you will find a wonderful happiness that even the worries of your daily life cannot take from you.

(During Old Testament times, is it true that there were some seers or prophets who could foretell what would occur centuries later?)

No, emphatically! And those who believe that there ever lived such mortals are greatly mistaken. The highest of us spirits cannot know or foretell the future in the sense in which the seers and prophets are supposed to have done in those centuries which the Old Testament authors wrote

427

about. No man, whether in the flesh or in the spirit, has the Omniscience of the Father. And to foretell what will happen centuries ahead is a Power that belongs only to the Father.

So, all the attempted application of prophecies, as contained in the Bible, to the happenings or future happenings of the present day are futile and without any justification. Man must depend upon the condition and acts of this day to determine what will happen in the short time that some expect the world to last.

What a position for them to take when we, who live so close to the Father, cannot possibly know!

All this, of course, refers to the material affairs of men in their lives on earth. As to spiritual things, we can tell what the future of each man, or nations of men, will be if certain conditions are observed or not observed.

(What are these conditions?)

Well, I will write to you on this subject when the opportunity presents itself.

I will not write more now.

With all my love and the Blessings of the Father, I will say good night.
Your brother in Christ,
JOHN.

John Cautions That Man Must Continue to Search for and Find the Truth.
(JOHN, THE APOSTLE)
(May 12th, 1916 | Received by James Padgett)

I AM HERE. *John.*

I desire to write tonight and, if you think it is not too late, we will do so.

Well, I will not make my message very lengthy, but will try to concise it in short sentences.

I want to tell you that when a man gets to know the Truths of the Father, he will become a very happy and wise man; for these Truths have only those principles in them that create happiness and wisdom.

I know that men believe many things on account of there being ancient or having the authority of their forefathers, or the authority of some great saint or writer who lived many centuries ago. But such a basis for truth, while worthy of consideration and examination, does not of itself, because of being old, afford any certainty that what is thus accepted contains the Truth.

Truth is a very old thing, and existed for many thousands of centuries before the times in which these ancient writers, as you call them, lived. And, in fact, those days of the writers, in comparison to what has gone before, are as yesterdays. Therefore, you will see that, just because the declarations of these writers are what you consider very ancient, they should not be received as having authority.

Truths of those days, and of the long ages prior thereto, and of the present time, are all the same, as Truth never changes or assumes new forms, no matter what the conditions of mortals may be as to intellectual or spiritual development. And these Truths may be revealed today, and are constantly being revealed as time progresses. And they should be accepted with as much credence and satisfaction as any Truths that were ever disclosed in ancient days.

In their spiritual natures or perceptions, men are just as susceptible now to the reception of these Truths as they were in the times of Abraham or Moses or at any time since.

THE MIND OF MAN WAS GIVEN TO HIM TO BE EXERCISED IN THE WAY OF INVESTIGATION AND SEARCH, AND NEVER WAS IT CONTEMPLATED THAT THE TIME WOULD COME IN HIS CREATION WHEN HE SHOULD ACCEPT ANYTHING AS THE ULTIMATES OF TRUTH AND CEASE HIS INQUIRIES. FOR TRUTHS ARE SO MANY AND GREAT AND DEEP THAT, SO FAR, IN THE MORTAL UNIVERSE, MAN HAS ACQUIRED ONLY A SMATTERING OF THESE TRUTHS. AND TO REST SUPINELY IN THIS ACQUIREMENT, UNDER THE BELIEF THAT THERE IS NOTHING MORE IN EXISTENCE THAT MAN MAY KNOW, VIOLATES AND SUBVERTS THE VERY OBJECT OF HIS CREATION. AND WHAT I HAVE SAID HERE APPLIES TO SPIRITUAL TRUTHS AS WELL AS TO MATERIAL ONES.

The churches, I know, declare and try to enforce the declaration that it is not possible to discover, or have revealed to men, the essential principles of spiritual Truths to a greater extent than has already been declared in the Bible and the churches' interpretation of the same; and, therefore, that it is contrary to God's Will that man should seek further for any additional Truths; and that men should accept, without question, the sayings of the Bible, and the dogmas and creeds of the churches which their claim is founded upon, and which they declare are the true principles of spiritual Truths. And, for many years, this has been the demand of the churches, and the members thereof have acquiesced without question or doubt.

Now, this has been one of the great causes why men have not progressed more, not only in their spiritual nature but also in what may be called their natural qualities. They have remained satisfied, and what was believed by them centuries ago is believed today. I say all this to show how stagnant the intellects of men have been and have remained for all these long ages, as they depend on search and investigation for growth. I further recite this to show the necessity for men to seek and criticize, and to accept or reject as the results of the search may demand.

In recent years, though, men have made greater progress, and the individual has come to the front. The old accepted fabrications of truths have been assaulted and shaken and denuded of their falsities to a considerable degree, and so it should be. Men must seek and criticize, and accept or reject as their own conscience and reasoning powers dictate; and therein will be freedom of the mind as well as of the will.

The soul, also, has been smothered in these dogmatic beliefs; and, as a consequence, its development has been slow. Knowledge of spiritual things has not come to men as it should have done, and as is necessary to teach them their destiny and the Truths which should control their lives on earth, and which will control their progress in the spirit world.

Well, as you are tired, I will postpone the balance of my discourse. When you feel tired, I think it best to discontinue the writing instead of attempting to force yourself into receiving it.

So, I will not write more. Believe that I am

Your brother in Christ,

JOHN.

Cornelius, the Centurion, Declares That It is of the Greatest Importance That the Truths of the Way to Salvation Be Revealed to Mankind.
(CORNELIUS)
(February 7th, 1917 | Received by James Padgett)

I AM HERE. *Cornelius.*

I want to write merely a few lines tonight. I am so very much interested in you and your work that I feel that I should give you some encouragement in the way of letting you know that there are many spirits present here tonight who love you very much, and who desire that you should receive their messages of Love and Truth.

As I have told you, I am in the Celestial Spheres and know what the Love of the Father is and what immortality means, as I am the possessor of the Love and the conscious owner of immortality. The world is now so anxious to know the Truths that pertain to God and to man's relationship to Him, and the messages that you are receiving give to the world what it so longs for.

I know that the Christian doctrines, as contained in the Bible and taught by many preachers and priests, are the only doctrines that the Christians have any knowledge of. Consequently, they are accepted by them as being the inspired revelations of God, and the truth of what He is, and what man must do in order to obtain salvation. And these people rest securely in these beliefs, and in the assurance that the Bible way is the only way to salvation. And, resting in these beliefs, the world does not see the necessity for obtaining the only thing that will place them in At-onement with God, and will make them inhabitants of His Heavens.

I merely write this to show you that it is of the greatest importance that the Truths of the Way to salvation be revealed to mankind.

I do not think that I have anything more to say tonight, and, so will leave you.

With all my love, I am

Your brother in Christ,

CORNELIUS.

Jesus Proclaims That Divine Truths Must Be Declared to All Mankind.
(JESUS)
(May 2ⁿᵈ 1920 | Received by James Padgett)

I AM HERE. *Jesus.*

Let me write, for I am anxious to tell you that you are in much better condition than you have been for a long time. And your thoughts of today, and especially tonight, have put you in a spiritual condition. If you continue in these thoughts and longings, you will soon enable us to make the rapport by which we can continue our messages with greater frequency, and with exact expression of what we desire to convey.

I have been with you a great deal today, and have tried to exercise an influence upon your soul and mind that will cause you to more fully realize the responsibility that rests upon you, and the importance of the work that you are to do. I was with you at church this morning and saw the impression made upon your mind by the preacher when he asked if anyone had anything to offer that would show him that he had not grasped all of the Truth as to the "spiritual things" (as he called them) that would cause men to aspire for and obtain a higher course of living. I also saw that you realized that your work, if carried to its conclusions, would answer that question. And, so, you must think of this question, and try with all the powers that have been given to you to learn these Truths so that they can be made known—not only to the preachers of the so-called "Christian" churches but also to all mankind. You already have Truths enough to show this minister that he is not preaching the true Christian spirituality that I came to the world to teach, and did teach; that he must not rest satisfied with his knowledge of spiritual things, but must seek for more Light and Truth; and, then, that he should make them a part of his own possessions and teach them to the world of men, and especially those to whom he has the opportunity of ministering.

I am much pleased that you are in so much better condition of soul. I want you to persist in your efforts to obtain more of the Love of the Father, and then you will be able to bring true enlightenment to the unthinking and unknowing world of the Truths that are so vital to their salvation.

I was also with you tonight and saw the impression made on you by the preacher when he set forth Samuel, as he then was, as an example to be followed by the true seekers after the important things that lead to spiritual

431

regeneration and perfect manhood. And I was glad that you could appreciate how far the character of Samuel fell short of what is necessary to make a man the divine angel, or even the perfect man. The preacher does not experience the Truth of the Divine Love in his soul and, in fact, has not even an intellectual knowledge of Its existence and operations. He believes that I am God, and that my blood washes away the sins of all men who believe in me; and, thus thinking, he is satisfied to rest upon the promise of the gospels, which he accepts as the true teachings of me.

Samuel is now here. He was with you at the church and realized how devoid he was, at the time spoken of by the preacher, of that thing which was necessary to his salvation. And he remembers his demand upon the people to behold him, and then to bring any charge of unrighteousness that they could against him and his conduct as a servant and prophet of Jehovah. This is a very pretty story and, to a certain extent, contains in it a teaching of the moral laws that work for good. But it is not more important than many other things contained in the Old Testament. Samuel will come sometime and write to you of his life on earth, and of his ministry as a servant of Jehovah.

Well, my dear brother, I will not write more tonight, but will soon come and write an important message which I know will not only benefit but also interest you.

(Might you write sometime upon what is God's Will for mankind?)

Well, I will write on this subject that you suggest. For this is an important thing for men to know, as so many think they are doing God's Will in their various courses of living and in their various forms of worship. His Will is one that corresponds with all the laws that affect man in every way, and men must know what this Will is.

I will come soon and write on this subject, and I hope that you may be successful in receiving my message as I intend to deliver it.

With my love and blessing, and the assurance that I will be with you in all times of need and will try to direct you in your thoughts, I will say good night.

Your friend and brother,
JESUS.

Chapter 14.

Corrections Made in Other Doctrinal Systems.

I. The New Jerusalem Church.

<u>MESSAGES INCLUDED IN THIS SECTION.</u>

Ingersoll, the Former Author and Agnostic, Comments on Swedenborg's Scientific and Theological Teachings. (ROBERT G. INGERSOLL)..435

Mr. Swedenborg Claims That He Did Not Know of the Divine Love, as Contradistinguished from the Natural Love That Was Bestowed on Man at His Creation. (EMANUEL SWEDENBORG)..................436

*Luke Affirms That Swedenborg Wrote, and Stresses the Importance of Errors Being Corrected in His Writings. (LUKE, THE APOSTLE)*437

Helen Affirms That Swedenborg Wrote. (HELEN PADGETT)............438

Martin Luther Comments on the Swedenborgian Pamphlet Entitled: "Incarnate God." (MARTIN LUTHER) 439

Chauncey Giles Changes His Beliefs About Jesus Being God. (CHAUNCEY GILES)..441

Helen Affirms That Luther Wrote on: "Incarnate God." (HELEN PADGETT)..442

Swedenborg Declares That He Does Not Want Mr. Padgett to Be a Failure in His Work, as He Was. (EMANUEL SWEDENBORG) 443

14.

I. The New Jerusalem Church.

Ingersoll, the Former Author and Agnostic, Comments on Swedenborg's Scientific and Theological Teachings.
(ROBERT G. INGERSOLL)
(March 29th, 1917 | Received by James Padgett)

I AM HERE. *Robert G. Ingersoll.*

I come first because I am more modest than the other spirits who are present, and will say a few words and then give place to the others.

I have been with you while you were reading the work of Swedenborg, and was much interested in the impression made upon your mind by what he said. And I found that your impressions were not very different from those that I had when I read his book while on earth, except this: that I had no belief in the spirit world, while you have.

Of course, you know from the knowledge that you have received, through the messages that have come to you, that many of his assertions are erroneous and the creatures of a mind that was fitted with a great knowledge of scientific things, as accepted in his day, and also of a desire on his part to reconcile his knowledge of science and of theological teachings with what he supposed had been imparted to him by spirits and angels. But the result was that they could not be reconciled, and the consequence was that he declared doctrines and teachings that were utterly at variance with spiritual Truths; and no one knows better than he does at this time of the falsity of many of his teachings.

Swedenborg had many opportunities for receiving and imparting the Truth, but his great learning in the sciences, and his beliefs in the old orthodox doctrines of the church in which he had been reared, led him to conclusions and declarations of truths, as he believed, that were contrary to both science and religion in its higher and true sense.

Well, you may wonder that I write on this subject. And to answer any question that may arise from your surprise, I only desire to say that, since I have received a knowledge of God's Plan for the salvation of mankind and some of His Divine Love, I have been investigating with all the energies of my soul the great Truths that exist, and which are never changed. And, in such investigation, I have talked with Swedenborg and have learned from him the sources of his wonderful declarations and doctrines, as set forth in his works. He is now in full knowledge of the Truth, and also of the errors of his own learned disquisitions, as his followers believe and pronounce them to be.

435

He can best explain to you the cause of his erroneous beliefs and what led him to attempt to explain the teachings that he received in the spirit world, and his experiences in writing in the mystical way that he did. I will not write more on the subject.

But, I, Ingersoll, who was truly and honestly an agnostic, can and do say that, in this spirit world, I had less darkness and less erroneous beliefs to get rid of than had Swedenborg. And while he had more of this Divine Love in his soul than had I—for I had none—yet, his mind was so warped by his intellectual conceptions of the truth that it was easier for me to find the true Way and progress in it, toward the Father's Love and the Celestial Heavens, than it was for him. This he has told me, and I have listened to him with much interest. And I have learned that the way to the narrow and bigoted orthodox believer is a harder road to travel than that of the agnostic who has not been defiled too much by sin and evil in his soul.

I am still progressing and praying and believing, and receiving the inflow of this wonderful Love. Oh, I tell you that this Love is the greatest thing in all the spirit world, as well as on earth, and the only thing that brings the soul in close union and harmony with the Father!

I will not write more now, but soon I will come and write my promised letter. So, my dear friend, with my love and gratitude, I will say good night.
Your brother in Christ,
ROBERT G. INGERSOLL.

Mr. Swedenborg Claims That He Did Not Know of the Divine Love,
as Contradistinguished from the Natural Love That Was
Bestowed on Man at His Creation.
(EMANUEL SWEDENBORG)
(April 8th, 1917 | Received by James Padgett)

I AM HERE. *Emanuel Swedenborg.*

I merely want to say that I have been reading my work as you read, and that I now realize how many statements of error and untruth I made in that work. The errors are so many that it will take a longer time than I have tonight in which to give you a bare outline of them. But I will soon come and write to you, and hope that you can give me an evening when I can write without limitations of time.

Since I have been in the spirit world, I have found that there are so many statements in my writings that were not truly conceived or interpreted while I was still a mortal (and when I was permitted in my spirit, or, as I then said, interiors, to enter the spirit world) that it is absolutely necessary that I should correct and describe these in accordance with what I now know of the Truth. This is especially necessary because I have a large number of mortals on earth who believe in my teachings and are trying to follow them in their lives and deeds. So, you will appreciate my anxiety to be permitted to write.

Tonight I will not write more.

(Were you not told of the Divine Love in your visits to the spirit world?)

Well, I am sorry to say that I did not know of the Divine Love which, by Its reception into the soul, made angels of men, and re-created them so that their souls became, in their very substance, divine. I did not know of this Love as contradistinguished from the love that was bestowed upon man at his creation, and which, in itself, has nothing of the Divine. No, I was ignorant of this and never learned it in the spirit world in my visits to that world, nor in my conversation with spirits.[*]

I know now that no matter how great is the ruling love of a man for falsity and evil when he enters the hells, he will have the opportunity to have that love changed, and that the loves of all who are in the hells will be changed ultimately into the love for good—in some instances into the Love of the Divine, and, in others, toward the purification of their natural loves, which will make them perfect men.

These are some of the things that I desire to write about, and there are many other former earthly beliefs of mine that were equally erroneous and in need of correction.

I am in the Celestial Spheres and, of course, am an angel of God and the possessor of His Divine Love that has caused my soul to become divine, and immortality to become a thing to me of understanding and possession.

I will stop now and, with my love and the Blessings of God and all the divine angels, I will say good night.

Your brother in Christ,
EMANUEL SWEDENBORG.

Luke Affirms That Swedenborg Wrote, and Stresses the Importance of Errors Being Corrected in His Writings.
(LUKE, THE APOSTLE)
(April 8th, 1917 | Received by James Padgett)

I AM HERE. *Luke.*

I come to tell you that you must not doubt that Swedenborg wrote to you. In answer to your questions, he actually wrote what you received. We are all desirous that he shall write to you on the subjects that he has expressed a desire to write upon, for many of the teachings and doctrines that are contained in his earthly writings are erroneous and must be corrected. They are being studied and believed in by many mortals, and this is leading them away from the Truth.

---

[*] Please refer to "Notes" at the end of this chapter.—Ed.

The one great error or untruth that must be corrected is his teaching that Jesus is God. This is blasphemous and abhorrent to all the angelic spirits, and more so to the Master than to any other. And, for the correction of this, Swedenborg must write.

Well, I will not write more tonight, except to say that another anniversary of the resurrection of the Master has come, as it is believed. Men are worshiping Jesus as God, and sending their praises and thanks to him as the great redeemer of the world by this death and resurrection,[*] while, as you know, his death had very little to do with that redemption, and his resurrection was not the true resurrection that he taught could be the experience and possession of all mankind.

It is pitiable and destructive to the Truth for men to believe and teach that the mere resurrection of the spirit from the body is the resurrection that Jesus came to teach and demonstrate! When we see the repetition of the observance of the anniversary of this rising of Jesus from his physical body each year, and again review all the false beliefs and teachings, we realize more and more the necessity for our Truths being made known to the world.

So, you must work harder and pray to the Father to increase your soul development so that our messages may be more rapidly received.

Remember what John said a few nights ago and believe, for the promises then made will soon be realized by you. I will come soon and write a message.

With my love and great desire that we become closer in our rapport and more expedient in our work, I will say good night.

Your brother in Christ,

LUKE.

Helen Affirms That Swedenborg Wrote.
(HELEN PADGETT)
(April 8th, 1917 | Received by James Padgett)

I AM HERE. *Helen.*

Well, dear, I come to say that Swedenborg actually wrote to you, as I realize that you had a doubt come into your mind as to whether he really wrote. He actually answered your questions in his own words, and not any thought contained in his answers came from your mind.

Luke also wrote and you must believe.

Good night and God bless you.

HELEN.

---

[*] See: "The True Resurrection" chapter in volume I of *Angelic Revelations of Divine Truth.*—Ed.

Martin Luther Comments on the Swedenborgian Pamphlet Entitled:
"Incarnate God."
(MARTIN LUTHER)
(February 28th, 1917 | Received by James Padgett)

I AM HERE. *Luther.*

I merely desire to say that, as you read the pamphlet, I read with you; and the description and explanation therein contained as to Who God is, is entirely erroneous and blasphemous.

While on earth, Jesus never claimed or taught that he was God, and this I say because he has so instructed us. He never has made any such claim since becoming a spirit, and the teachings of the New Church in this particular are all wrong and tend to lead men away from the true conception of Who God and Jesus both are.

Swedenborg has often conversed with me about his teachings, and he has declared that his explanations as to God are not in accord with the knowledge that he now has. The teachings as contained in his books upon this subject were the results very largely of his own speculations, and the results of his endeavors in trying to reconcile what he thought was an absurd conception of the Nature and Being of God with the true interpretation of the Bible. He could not accept the doctrine of the "Trinity," as explained and taught by the church; and, hence, being a believer in the inspiration of the Bible and its infallibility with respect to religious Truths, he sought some exegesis that might be consistent with the Bible and, at the same time, in consonance with his ideas of reason and common sense. But, as he now says, he added mysticism to mysticism, and irrational explanations to irrational explanations, and the result was that his teachings were more absurd and more difficult to understand than were the teachings of his church.

The doctrine of the "Trinity," as you have been told, is not true, and never had any authority in the teachings of Jesus or those of the apostles and Bible writers. It was merely the deduction of some of the old fathers of the church, arising from their speculations and desire to make of Jesus a god, though a lesser god than the Father, and, at the same time, one with the Father and a part of the "Godhead" that must be considered as being only one God. For it was taught by the Old Testament writers and prophets that there is only one God.

This doctrine, of course, was absurd and, hence, was one of the "mysteries" of God. But, nevertheless, it was taught as a truth and made incumbent upon man to believe, whether they could understand it or not, which, of course, they could not.

But the doctrine was not accepted by all the writers of the early days. For, as you know, there were bitter controversies among these expounders of (what they supposed to be) the Scriptures upon the question as to who Jesus was, and his relation to God. But, as the years went by, the doctrine of the "Trinity" became firmly established as a canon of belief in the church, and, in my time on earth, it was believed and not questioned by the church. And I believed it also, although I could not understand it.

Now, Swedenborg was a member of the church that bore my name and which I was credited with having founded. He believed in its doctrines, even as to the "Trinity," and in the actual transformation of the wine and bread into the blood and body of Jesus. And he continued in this belief up to the time of his wonderful visions of the spirit world and his experience in meeting the spirits and angels of that world, including Jesus, whom, in his writings, he claimed to be God, and with whom he had many conversations, and from whom he learned the spiritual Truths that he declared to the world.

As you have been told, in the working out of the plans of the Celestial angels under the leadership of Jesus, Swedenborg was selected as the instrumentality through whom the spiritual Truths should be revealed to mankind. And, in carrying out that plan, power was given to him to come in his spirit perceptions, or his inner sight, as he called it, into the spirit world, and there see the conditions of spirits and angels, and also of their environments, and learn the higher Truths from conversations with spirits and angels. And he did come in the manner indicated and communed, as he has claimed, except that he never talked with God, but only with Jesus who he misconceived to be God. And this cannot be wondered at, for Jesus was a spirit so transcendent in glory and love and wisdom that it was almost natural, as I may say, that the mortal in his new and unusual experience should conceive this glorious Jesus to be God, Himself. But it was not God, only Jesus, that this seer saw and listened to.

Having a conception of this kind, you can readily see that, when he came into his mortal self again, and many times this occurred, he firmly believed that Jesus, who had form and individuality in the spirit world similar to what he had when on earth, was actually God; and it therefore became easy for Swedenborg to reject the doctrine of the "Trinity." Jesus is God, manifested in the flesh, and God is Jesus, the "Divine Man."

Of course, you must understand that, in the exercise of this seership, he experienced the doubts and fears that, at times, what he saw and heard might not be things of actuality, and that, possibly, his imagination, or, as in these latter days, what is called the subconscious mind, was deceiving him. And being a man of extraordinary mentality and strong convictions, as well as established faith in the doctrines of the church to which he belonged, many of his interpretations of what he saw and heard, and his teachings therefrom, were limited and flavored by his existing mental condition and faith.

He has told me that, for many years before his experience as seer, he had to a more or less extent doubted the truth of the "Trinity," and accepted it only as a mystery. And because the church declared it to be a truth, and, after his experiences as such seer, believing in the statements of the Bible as the infallible words of God, and also believing that he had seen God in the person of Jesus, he sought an explanation of these Bible statements and a reconciliation of them with his belief that Jesus was God. And the result was his declared doctrine that Jesus is God.

And, so, in many other of his teachings, based upon his experience in the spirit world, he embraced many errors and misconceptions of the Truths to such an extent that, as you have been told, his mission, in its results, was a failure. The Truths that he had been selected to learn and declare to the world were never made known to mankind.

This failure was disappointing to the spirits who conceived this plan and in whom were lodged the spiritual Truths of God, and who were acting as God's instruments in their endeavor to make them known to humanity.

But it will be more satisfactory to you, and convincing to whomsoever may read the Truths that you are receiving from these same high spirits that selected him as their messenger, to have Swedenborg come himself and explain the working of his mission, and the causes and particulars of his failure in doing the great work that had been assigned him to do.

He says that he has one consolation regarding many who have founded churches and attempted to declare spiritual Truths upon which doctrines and creeds have been promulgated and believed in, and that is that his followers are so comparatively few in number; and, consequently, so many less mortals are being deceived by his teachings. And I can appreciate the consolation that he may have in this fact, for my teachings and beliefs that are false, as his are false, are believed in and followed by a very large number of mortals, to their injury.

Well, I am glad for the opportunity to write to you tonight. I am still waiting for the chance to finish my message to my people on the errors of continuing in my teachings, and the necessity for them to become undeceived and to learn the Truths that are now being declared to mankind.

I will not write further. So, good night.

Your brother in Christ,

LUTHER.

Chauncey Giles Changes His Beliefs About Jesus Being God.
(CHAUNCEY GILES)
(February 28th, 1917 | Received by James Padgett)

I AM HERE. *Chauncey Giles.*

Let me write you a line, for I am interested in what has been just written to you. When I lived on earth, I was a Swedenborgian, or New Churchman, and believed in the doctrines of that church. I especially believed in the cornerstone of its beliefs that Jesus was God and, as such, the only God to be worshiped and accepted as the incarnate God who came to earth and lived and taught among men the coming of God into the flesh.

Well, when on earth, I was a leader or preacher in that church; and,

441

during the course of my ministry, I not only taught but also wrote many pamphlets and some books upon this doctrine of God becoming man in the form of Jesus, and on many other doctrines that I now know to be untrue.

My authority for saying that this fundamental doctrine of the church is untrue is that I have seen and talked with Jesus in the spirit world, and I have learned that he is only the spirit of a mortal (but the highest and most glorious spirit in all the heavens), and that he is not God. I have never seen God nor know of any spirit who has seen Him with the spirit eyes, though Jesus and others of the highest spirits say that they have seen Him with their soul perceptions, which must be true because Jesus is so much like God in this that he cannot tell a lie.

But I know that there is a God, and my knowledge is based on certainty. But I cannot explain the basis of this certainty to you, as you could not comprehend my explanation. But God Lives and Rules and Loves, and is present with us and with you in some or many of His Attributes. And Jesus is not this God.

I wish that I could come to my people and tell them of the errors of their beliefs, and the Truths as they exist to the extent that is now known to me, but I have no hope of ever being able to do so. For one of the cardinal doctrines of the church is that, with the passing of Swedenborg, there passed the possibility of all communications between God, or his angels, and mortals as to spiritual Truths. And it is believed now that it is contrary to God's Will that mortals should attempt to penetrate the veil that separates the two worlds.

How such beliefs, as I taught, now cause me suffering and regret! For I see no way of remedying the wrong that I did, and of turning the thoughts of my followers into the paths that lead to Truth and the certainty of heaven.

As this is my first attempt to communicate, I am somewhat tired and must stop. But I thank you for the opportunity, and hope that I may have the privilege of writing again sometime.

Notwithstanding my erroneous beliefs, I have some of the Father's Divine Love in my soul that enables me to sign myself,

Your brother in Christ,

CHAUNCEY GILES.

Helen Affirms That Luther Wrote on: "Incarnate God."
(HELEN PADGETT)
(February 28th, 1917 | Received by James Padgett)

I AM HERE. *Helen.*

(Did Luther, the former monk and church reformer, just write to me?)
Yes, Luther wrote, and the other spirit I don't know. But I have no doubt that he is whom he represents himself to be. He seemed to be in much earnestness and was very anxious to write. And seeing that he was a good

442

spirit with a message, we let him write, and he felt better by having done so.

Swedenborg was here tonight and is very anxious to write, and soon he will, as he feels that he must write a message on the subject that you have been interested in recently.

I will not write more. So, with my love, I will say good night.

Your own true and loving,

HELEN.

Swedenborg Declares That He Does Not Want Mr. Padgett to Be a Failure in His Work, as He Was.
(EMANUEL SWEDENBORG)
(December 23rd, 1917 | Received by James Padgett)

I AM HERE. *Emanuel Swedenborg.*

I have heard the messages that you have just received, and I desire to impress upon you the necessity and importance of striving to follow the advice therein given; for if you fail now to do the work upon which you have entered, your regrets when you come to the spirit world will be so great that you will find it almost impossible to get rid of them, even if you progress to the soul spheres where the Love is all so abundant.

I know what I write, for that was my experience. And it seemed to me that everywhere I turned, as I sought to progress, I saw before me the word, "failure." And for many long years it was my ghost of a recollection. Failure, as you may know, is comparative, and men may fail in their ambitions and desires for fame and wealth and position. Yet, when they come to the spirit world, they realize that such failures mean comparatively little. In their progress in the Truth, they soon forget their failures and cast them behind. But when a mortal has conferred upon him a work which does not have for its object the accumulation of wealth or the attaining of fame or position, but the great and vital end of showing men the Way by which they can become reconciled to God, and partake of His very Nature in Love and obtain immortality; and also has given to him the privilege of receiving the great Truths of God in relation to the salvation of men, then I say that failure means a great catastrophe for him and a greater calamity for humanity, and that man is in a condition of mind and recollection beyond description!

Very few men have conferred upon them this great privilege and power and responsibility, and I was one of them. I was a failure not because I did not try to receive and deliver the truth, but because I prevented, by my preconceived ideas of what the truths should be, the real and pure Truth from coming to me and thence to humanity. In a way, I was unconscious of my failure; yet, when I came to the spirit world, and realized the failure that I had made, then everything was a failure to my conscience.

443

In your case, you have no such preconceived ideas to hamper you or prevent you from receiving the Truth. For you are used merely as an instrument for these Truths to be transcribed. They are delivered in the very language of the writers. And your failure, if such there shall be, will be entirely due to your indifference or want of effort to get in condition that will enable the messages to be written.

You must see your responsibility and your duty, and I may say your love, that should urge you to work. And you must not become a failure!

I am your friend and brother and co-worker in making known these Truths. I only write because, as a failure, I can speak from experience. So, my brother, turn your thoughts more to this work; and, if necessary, sacrifice every worldly consideration to carry forward your work and make perfect your efforts to fulfill the great mission with which you have been blessed. I will not write more now. May the Father Bless you with His Love.

Your brother in Christ,
EMANUEL SWEDENBORG.

II. Disciples of Christ – Churches of Christ.

MESSAGES INCLUDED IN THIS SECTION.

Alexander Campbell, One of the Founders of the Disciples of Christ and Churches of Christ, Confesses That He Did Not Understand the Plan of Man's Salvation When on Earth. (ALEXANDER CAMPBELL)..*447*

II.

Disciples of Christ—Churches of Christ.

Alexander Campbell, One of the Founders of the Disciples of Christ and Churches of Christ, Confesses That He Did Not Understand the Plan of Man's Salvation When on Earth.
(ALEXANDER CAMPBELL)
(October 28th, 1915 | Received by James Padgett)

I AM HERE. *Alexander Campbell.*

I am the founder of the Campbellites.
(Isn't that an incorrect spelling?)
Well, I have spelled it as it should be spelled. I know my followers are sometimes called Camellites, but that is not correct.

I merely want to say that I did not understand the Plan of man's salvation when on earth, and I taught erroneous doctrines as to this matter. I now see the great harm that I did. But, nevertheless, there was some good done also, for my people worshiped God as their Heavenly Father, and prayed to Him; and many of them received the ministrations of the Holy Ghost. So, I am grateful for what I taught, but also very sorry for the errors that I taught.

I am now in the Celestial Heavens and know that Jesus is a spirit and not God, and that his great work is still going on.

So, when I say that I am a follower of Jesus, I mean that I follow his teachings and try to imitate his life here as on earth. I am a stranger to you, but I felt that I must write to you and, so, took this opportunity.

So, thanking you, I am,
ALEXANDER CAMPBELL.

III. Seventh-Day Adventists.

MESSAGES INCLUDED IN THIS SECTION.

Helen Explains The Sabbath. She Also Cautions Mr. Padgett Not to Take the Seventh-Day Adventist Pamphlet He Was Reading Seriously. (HELEN PADGETT)..*451*

Helen Comments on the Book, "The Great Controversy," That Mr. Padgett Was Reading, and Declares That the Author Now Regrets Its Contents. (HELEN PADGETT) *452*

III.

Seventh-Day Adventists.

Helen Explains The Sabbath. She Also Cautions Mr. Padgett Not to Take the Seventh-Day Adventist Pamphlet He Was Reading Seriously.
(HELEN PADGETT)
(November 19th, 1915 | Received by James Padgett)

I AM HERE. *Helen.*

I signaled you, and merely wanted to say that I have been reading the pamphlet with you, and want to tell you that it is not true. It is all wrong and misleading and will never save a soul from sin. The writer is so filled with the idea that God Commanded the observance of the seventh day as the Sabbath that he, the writer, can see nothing in all the Bible that is of such great importance as the keeping of the Sabbath.

The Sabbath, as a religious institution, is not of more importance than any other day. And the man who believes that, by observing the Sabbath day, he can reach that condition of soul development which will fit him for an entrance into the Divine Kingdom will find himself much disappointed when he comes to the spirit world. The keeping of this day, as these people teach, or of any other day, will not develop their soul qualities or make them one with the Father, or even give them a great development of the natural love. For the doing of, or refraining to do, those things which the Commandment directs to be done or not done, which is the basis of their belief, will only benefit them if they will try to get into attunement with the soul requirements which are necessary in order to become partakers of the Divine Love.

So, do not let the thoughts or argument of this pamphlet influence you in any way as regards the essentials to a correct understanding of the Plans of God for the salvation of mankind.

As Jesus has told you, he will not come to earth with a shout, surrounded by his angels, and catch up into the heavens these Adventists, or any other human beings. But he will come, and is now coming, into the souls of men, through his teachings of the workings of the Holy Spirit, and in no other way.

Jesus is not the "God of wrath and judgment" that they teach, but merely the true son of his Father. And he comes to all men in love and sympathy, and with the great desire that men shall turn away from their evil thoughts and seek the Love and Mercy of the Father.

I felt that I wanted to write you this, as I realize what great errors are contained in that pamphlet; and men may be led to believe these errors.

451

While you may read such literature, do not let it cause you to turn your thoughts away from the pure and true teachings of the Master for one moment. For if you, or any other man, should base your salvation on what is taught in such writings, you will be deceived. And, when you come to the spirit world, you will be greatly disappointed in not finding what such writings may lead you to expect.

I must not write more now, as you are not in condition to write further.

Your own true and loving,

HELEN.

Helen Comments on the Book, "The Great Controversy," That Mr. Padgett Was Reading, and Declares That the Author Now Regrets Its Contents.
(HELEN PADGETT)
(January 14th, 1917 | Received by James Padgett)

I AM HERE. *Helen.*

Well, I see that you have been reading an Adventist book, The Great Controversy, that is full of error and untruth, and that will do you no good to read. The author of that book now knows that the "dead" are very much alive, that Spiritualism is a Truth, and that the spirits who communicate are not the "devils of Satan," as she calls them. Such reading is not worth the time that you waste in reading, and I do not see why you want to waste your time in such literature.

Mrs. White is now in the spirit world and realizes the great harm that her book has done and is now doing to humanity, and the great errors that so many of her followers believe in and try to follow as their guide in religious beliefs. She will come sometimes and write to you. For I must tell you that, when you borrowed the book and made some mention of its author, I tried to learn her whereabouts and succeeded. I wanted her to come to you and tell you of the utter falsity of what she had written. She has been here tonight and knows that you have been reading her book. She realizes that she must do something to correct, if possible, the untruthful teachings that the book contains. So, as I say, she will come to you very soon and write a message in reference to the same.

I see that you have been feeling better today, and have been comparatively free from your worries. I am so glad, for it makes a very great difference in your condition of mind and permits us to come in closer rapport with you as regards spiritual Truths.

Several spirits were here tonight expecting to write. But, when you commenced to read that book, they realized that they would not have the opportunity and left, very much disappointed. My advice is that you do not waste your time in the further reading of the book, as it will do you no good.

452

I love you with all my heart and soul, and want you to be happy and free from thoughts that may tend to draw your mind away from us and the work which you have to do. The only information that you will need, you will receive in the messages that will be written to you. And, so, you can readily see that there is no occasion for you to read books of the character of the one now before you.

I will come soon and write my promised letter, and I know that you will find more happiness in it than in a whole world full of books that speculate on the future life and the teachings of the Truths of spiritual things that these books do not know and should not speculate upon.

(And what will you say to me in your letter?)

Well, I will say what I have so often said: that I love you very devotedly. And all the other spirits who come to you love you also, and are with you very often with their influence, trying to help you in the development of your soul and in causing you increased happiness.

The Master was here and says that he will soon write his expected message. He is only waiting for you to get in good condition to receive it.

Your own true and loving,

HELEN.

IV. New Thought.

MESSAGES INCLUDED IN THIS SECTION.

Luke Comments on the Teachings of New Thought. He Explains Some of the Erroneous Beliefs   Associated with These Teachings. (LUKE, THE APOSTLE) 457

Jesus Adds to Luke's Comments on New Thought, and Stresses the Importance of Mankind Knowing the Truth of the New Birth. (JESUS) 460

Mrs. Padgett Comments on a Preacher's Sermon on New Thought. (HELEN PADGETT) 462

IV.

New Thought.

Luke Comments on the Teachings of New Thought.
He Explains Some of the Erroneous Beliefs   Associated with These Teachings.
(LUKE, THE APOSTLE)
(March 9th, 1919 | Received by James Padgett)

I AM HERE. *Luke.*

Let me write a few lines tonight, as you are in better condition, and I am able to make a rapport with you and deliver my message.

I was with you today at a meeting of the New Thought people, and saw the impression made upon you by the speaker in his efforts to show that God is within man, and that only the opening up of the soul or mind of man to the development of that God is all that is necessary to bring that man into a perfect At-onement with the Truths of God's Will. Well, I have to say that this speaker, when he comes to a realization of himself in the spirit world, will find that God is not in him or in anything that he may have possessed in his earth life, and that his development of the Kingdom within him, as he termed it, was a mere delusion and a snare to the progress of his soul in its career through the earth life, as well as through the heavens or spirit world.

He is mistaken when he announces that the Kingdom of Heaven is within him, or that he has within him that which can lead to the condition of the perfect man by its development in the sense that he spoke of. He is following a false way. And all the efforts that he may make will not lead him into the paths that end in the perfect man that partakes of the Father's Divinity.

He is also mistaken when he asserts that God is everywhere—in the flowers, in the thoughts of men, and in the heart—for God does not find His Habitation in any of these things. And men do not live and move and have their being in Him. He is a distinct and individual Entity, and is not spread over all His Universe, as the preacher proclaimed. He can only be found by the longings of the soul, followed by a development of that soul in His Love. No, God is in His Heavens, and man can reach Him only by the persistent longings of that soul for the inflowing of His Love. These things that the preacher declared were the Presence of God are only the Expressions of His Being. They do not declare His Presence in any other sense than as the evidence of His Existence in His Habitation, and from which these Expressions flow and make known His Presence to man as these things reflect It. I am sorry that this speaker has not more knowledge of the true God and of His Seat of Habitation, for then he would realize that these things upon which he places so much belief, as being the very God, Himself, are but the Expressions that flow from Him.

Man has within him that which has wonderful possibilities in itself. I mean the soul. And by the observance of the Way that transforms it into a divine angel, it may become divine itself; or, by the slow process of renunciation, it may only become merely the perfect man with his natural love in a pure state, which was the condition of the first parents. If men will listen to the call of their soul, they will realize this possibility and receive this divinity, and, with it, immortality. But, without this transformation, they never can become other or greater than the perfect man.

I know men teach that there is implanted within the souls of all men that which is capable of being developed into an existence like unto God, and that man needs only this development in order to become a god, and that there is nothing else necessary to make a human soul a part of the Soul of God. But men are mistaken in this teaching. At the stage of their highest development, they will find themselves to be nothing more than the perfect man. Man has within him only that with which he was created, and he can add not one thing of himself that will change him from this condition of his creation. By a right course of thinking and living, it is true that he can renounce those things that have tainted his soul and alienated it from the Father, and made it sinful and disobedient. But, when this is done, he is still only the perfect man and nothing of the Divine is in him. Jesus was the perfect man, and, as such, was an exemplar of what all men will ultimately become. And if Jesus had never become more than the perfect man, he would not now be an inhabitant of the Celestial Heavens and the beloved son of the Father. Yet, he became more than the perfect man. And it was only after he attained to this condition of excellence that he could say, "I and my Father are one." For it was then only that he possessed the Divine Love to that degree which made him at-one with the Father. Only he is at-one with the Father who realizes that he is possessed of the very Nature and Essence of the Father. And there is only one Way in which this can be obtained, and that is by the inflowing of the Divine Love into the soul. Jesus could not say to the multitude that they were at-one with him and with the Father, for they had only the natural love and had not experienced the transformation of their souls. And such sayings as this were addressed only to his disciples, or to those among his hearers that had received this Love.

The speaker spoke of the New Birth, but had no conception of what it meant. And like may other teachers, in and out of the churches, he believes that a mere condition of the purification of the natural love constitutes this New Birth, and that that is all Jesus meant when he taught the necessity of being born again. But there is only one Way in which this New Birth can be brought about, and that you already know.

As to the moral truths taught by the Master, such as are referred to in the Sermon on the Mount, if observed in the heart, undoubtedly they will bring about a regeneration of the soul that will lead men to the glory of the perfect man and make him at-one with the laws of his creation; and this condition is devoutly to be wished for and sought after by all men. And, when they attain to this condition, they will experience the Beatitudes that are mentioned in the sermon. But this is only the state of the perfect man, and nothing of the Divine enters into their condition.

"New Thought," as it is called, has something in it that is an improvement on orthodoxy. And men will be the better if they will embrace some of its teachings. The great stumbling block of the "Trinity," and of the vicarious atonement and the blood, would be removed from the worship of men. And, in the development of their souls for salvation, they would then rely on the moral truths, and would not rest supinely in the belief of the efficacy of the vicarious atonement. But some other things that it teaches are all wrong. And, when its followers come to the spirit world, they will find that there is a God to be worshiped, and that man has not within him that God to be developed by his own thoughts and deeds!

According to the orthodox teachings, I know that too little is thought of the natural goodness of man; that too much emphasis is placed on his innate depravity; that it is believed that nothing in man is worthy of the release from the sin and disobedience in which he is now living; and that he can do nothing of himself to bring about his purification and restoration to his original condition of the perfect man. But this is wrong, for man's redemption depends very largely upon his efforts. As the Master has said, "As a man thinketh in his heart, so is he." He is naturally good, and his present condition was brought about by his permitting his soul to be contaminated with sin. And, to become good again, he needs only to pursue that Way that will remove sin and its consequences from his soul. Man created sin, and he will have to remove sin; and the process will be slow. But, ultimately, it will be accomplished, and by the efforts of man himself. He will be helped in these efforts by spirits who are God's ministering angels. But upon him depends the removal of that which he created and imposed. And, here, let me say that, unless man wills it, he will forever remain in sin. God will not, contrary to man's desires, make him a pure and undefiled being. And man's belief, unaccompanied by striving and seeking, will not be sufficient to bring about this remedy.

The speaker is a good man, and has experienced the workings of his own will upon the conditions of his soul to a large degree. He knows that his own efforts have caused him to renounce many things that tended to defile him and cause doubt. And, in this condition, he realizes much happiness and thinks that he is sufficient of himself to attain to that which will bring him into a perfect unison with the God that he thinks is within him. But, in this, he is deceiving himself. For what he thinks is God is only an unusual condition of soul development in its natural love that gives him a happiness which causes him to believe that God must be in and a part of him.

As you have been told, the happiness of the purified soul is beyond all conception of humans. And the nearer a man approaches to that condition

459

of purification of his soul, the greater becomes his happiness. And with this may come the belief that God must in some way be in that happiness and form a part of it, when the fact is that this happiness is only that which was bestowed upon man in the beginning. As the soul becomes purer and relieved from the defilement of sin, man becomes what he was in the beginning, and has regained only that which by nature is his. He does not receive any part of the Divine, nor does the Father bestow upon him anything that was not his at the creation. And he must realize that, by the removal of sin, his soul becomes more and more in harmony with the Will of God, and less and less in harmony with his own perverted will.

Let New Thought progress until men may realize that they are at-one with themselves, their created selves. But let it not teach them that what they experience as a removal of sin from their own souls by their own efforts and thoughts is evidence of a development of any supposed God within them, for it is not true. It is merely evidence of the development of their own natural, created selves, freed from that which defiled and made them unnatural.

The speaker said that the Kingdom of Heaven is within all men, and needs only for men to realize that fact and to declare its truths; and that, then, they will become pure and like unto God, and find themselves in the Presence of God, and see Him face to face. Well, he all wrong in this, for the Kingdom of Heaven, or Celestial Kingdom, is not within men, though it may be. And neither is God in their souls and capable of being seen face to face. These men who teach purification of their natural love and a superior state resulting from that purification, and nothing more, will never see God. And they will always remain in the mere image in which they were created—a merely purified man made in the image of God, and nothing more. The Father will then be the same unseen Creator as He is now, and men will worship Him in faith only. For their soul perceptions, which are the only "eyes of the soul" that can see God, will not exist; and, to them, God will still remain the unseen and unknowable Being that exists today in the knowledge and belief of men.

Well, I have written enough for tonight. But I saw that you were somewhat interested in the teachings of the day, and thought it best that I should write to you as to the Truth of the subject of which he discoursed and evidently believed.

With my love to you, and the hope that our messages may now continue without interruption, I will say good night.

Your brother in Christ,

LUKE.

Jesus Adds to Luke's Comments on New Thought, and Stresses the Importance of Mankind Knowing the Truth of the New Birth.
(JESUS)
(June 15th, 1919 | Received by James Padgett)

I AM HERE. *Jesus.*

Let me write just a line, for I desire to tell you that I was with you tonight at the convention of the New Thought people, and saw the impression made upon you by the discourses; and I am pleased that what they said only confirmed your faith in our teachings. They are sincere in their efforts to obtain a knowledge of the Truth, but the difficulty is that, while they are free from many of the orthodox teachings of the church, yet, they have only the natural love and perceptions of the intellect, and, to some extent, of the awakened soul in its natural condition.

They know nothing of the Divine Love or the Way to the Kingdom, and are depending entirely upon the spiritual feelings that come to them with the consciousness of an awakened soul in its conflict with the things that prevent its purification and development into the perfect man.

These people are to be encouraged in their efforts and teachings, so far as they disclose the true, natural condition of man and the possibility of their becoming in harmony with the Will of the Father in their natural love. To that extent, they are progressing beyond the old orthodox ideas of what the real man is, and what is incumbent upon him in order to get into the condition of happiness that comes with a purification of his love, and a longing in harmony with the Laws of God governing that purification.

It is to be wished that these men will proceed in their teachings and thus give a knowledge to mankind of what man really is, and the possibilities that lie before him when he exercises the inherent powers that exist within. FOR, CONCERNING SIN AND INHARMONY, UNTIL THE GREAT TRUTHS OF THE NEW BIRTH AND THE TRANSFORMATION OF THE SOUL AND THE WONDERFUL KINGDOM OF THE CELESTIAL SPHERES ARE MADE KNOWN TO MEN THROUGH OUR TEACHINGS OF THESE THINGS, THESE GREATER TRUTHS WHICH LIE BEYOND THE KNOWLEDGE OF MEN AT THIS TIME WILL NOT BE THEIRS.

In their search for God, they are on the wrong track. They will never find Him if they pursue the search in the way indicated by their discourses. God is not within men, nor do they live and move and have their being in Him; nor is He everywhere, waiting to be developed by men as they grow better and purer. No, they are mistaken in their thought as to God and His Habitation. When they come into a knowledge of the Truth, they will learn God is not in man or in everything that surrounds him, but is separate from him and from the environments in which he lives and moves, and that He has His Locality in the Highest Heavens where He works out His Purposes, and makes Himself and the evidence of His Existence known to men by the Energies that control the universe in which men exist. He can only be "seen" by the soul perceptions of a soul that has been transformed into the divine angel. To men in every other particular, He is unseen and unknown, except as His Laws, and the effect of their operations, discloses His Being.

Well, I merely wanted to write this short message, and I am glad that

461

you can receive it. Good night.

Your brother and friend,

JESUS.

Mrs. Padgett Comments on a Preacher's Sermon on New Thought.
(HELEN PADGETT)
(May 11th, 1919 | Received by James Padgett)

I AM HERE. *Helen.*

Well, my dear, I see that you are happy tonight, and I am also; for I heard you read the messages and saw the effect that they had on your soul, and that they caused you to love both the Father and me more. You must not cease to love as you do tonight, for there is no other happiness that can supply the peace which this love brings to you.

I was with you tonight at the meeting and heard the preacher speak of the source of the greatest joy, and I was sorry that he did not know that Source. He talked of a happiness that came to him from a knowledge that he thought he had of God, and he was in earnest. But he did not realize the real joy or the Source thereof. His joy is that which comes from a great degree of the purification of his natural love, which must necessarily bring increased happiness to him. And I am glad that he talked in the way he did, but so sorry that he has not experienced the real Love that is the only Source of the greatest joy.

Well, sometime men will know what the Source means, and how different it is from the mere purification of the natural love; and, in addition, they will learn the Way to obtain this Divine Love and keep It as the greatest thing in all the universe.

The talk of the preacher is very beneficial to many of his hearers and causes much searching of their souls, and a better condition of living and an experience that makes them very happy. I would advise you to attend his meetings occasionally, for the influence is good. And sometime you may have the opportunity to tell him of the higher Truths.

There were a number of spirits present with you, desiring to hear and learn something that might render them happier and enlighten them as to the true Way. But some things that he said did not help much. He placed too much emphasis on the necessity of making life on earth the great object of their efforts and aspirations, and rather discountenanced the thought that there are heavens and conditions to be longed for and enjoyed in the spirit life. Yet, as I say, his preaching will do good; for the better it will be for them. And this will tend to make the earth life better and more in harmony with the laws of man's creation.

I am so glad that I can write you again and tell you of my love, and assure you of the Truths that have been already revealed to you.

Well, I will not write more tonight. We all love you. And, so, with my

462

love, I will say good night.

Your own true and loving,

HELEN.

V. Christian Science.

MESSAGES INCLUDED IN THIS SECTION.

Jesus Introduces the Subject of Christian Science, Declaring That Some of Its Doctrines Are in Violation of the Truth and Must Be Corrected. (JESUS) 467

Mary Baker Eddy, Founder of Christian Science, Confesses That Many of Her Doctrines Were Neither "Christian" Nor "Science." (MARY BAKER EDDY)...469

Ann R. Padgett, the Mother of Mr. Padgett, States That Mrs. Mary Baker Eddy Sees the Error in Her Teachings, and That She is Living in the Same Sphere with Her. (ANN R. PADGETT) 470

Mrs. Eddy Now Recognizes the Misleading Errors of Some of Her Teachings, and Is Relieved Whenever These Are Corrected Among Her Followers. (MARY BAKER EDDY)...471

Mrs. Padgett Confirms That Mrs. Eddy Wrote Through Mr. Padgett. (HELEN PADGETT)...472

Jesus Enlarges Upon Some of the Errors and Deficiencies of Christian Science. (JESUS)...472

V.

Christian Science.

Jesus Introduces the Subject of Christian Science, Declaring That Some of Its Doctrines Are in Violation of the Truth and Must Be Corrected.
(JESUS)
(May 11ᵗʰ, 1919 | Received by James Padgett)

I AM HERE. *Jesus.*

I had been present as you read the article on Christian Science, and was interested in your comments. And I am pleased to assure you that your annotations were correct and that, in the particulars that you criticized, the statements of the writer of the same were erroneous and not in accord with the spiritual laws of Truth and the understanding thereof. Sometime, I will come and write you a message at some length on the doctrines of Christian Science, for the reason that I think a correlation of the claims of this cult is very important.

The doctrines that it proclaims to the world contain many Truths and are beneficial to mankind, and are doing much good, both spiritually and physically. But some of the claims are so much in violation of the Truth that they must not be permitted to pass as truths uncontradicted.

The founder of this Science, or discovery, as her writings and followers claim, is here now, and deplores the fact that she left to the world so many false and misconceived concepts of the truth that so many persons believe and teach.

She is a spirit of much soul development, and is in possession of much of the Divine Love which she did not conceive the meaning of by her "carnal mind," as she called it. She was therefore not able to teach what this Divine Love is, and Its operations upon the souls of men, and the effect of Its presence in such souls.

She never conceived of any higher ideal for man than the perfect man—one who should become wholly delivered from sin and errors which all men have to a more or less extent. Also, her teachings that sin and error and disease are not things of reality, because God did not create them, are all wrong; for they have a reality that not only makes men unhappy and causes them suffering in the mortal life, but also prevents their progress towards her ideal of the perfect man in the spirit world. God, Only, is Good. And everything that He created is necessarily good, and cannot contain that which is evil or in conflict with His creations. But, as we have explained to you, while He created man perfect, knowing only good, yet, He bestowed upon him that great power of free will. And, after his disobedience, man exercised it in such a way that he violated the laws of his being, and sin and error resulted. This made man the creator of evil!

Mrs. Eddy will write you very soon on the subject of her Science, as she is very anxious to remedy the errors that she taught. And we have determined that it is advisable that she do so on account of both her followers and her own account. For her work here, and, so far as is possible, in the mortal world, is to "unteach," as it were, the errors that she taught.

I expected to write my message, or, rather, finish the message which I partly wrote a few nights ago. But you are not just in condition to receive it, and I prefer waiting until you feel better in this respect.

I am glad that you are so much interested in that message. When you receive it, I don't think that you will be disappointed; for, as you say, the subject is the one, fundamental Truth to be made known to mortals. I will deal with it in all its phases, and you must try to get in the best possible condition to receive it.

(At that time, for the best rapport possible, would it be helpful to have the presence of another mortal with me who might serve to attract additional spirit powers?)

Well, I do not think that that will be necessary. There will be such powers present that the presence of any mortal, and the favorable influences that he may attract, will not afford any assistance to you. You must know that I have greater power than all the other spirits have; and, when I come to you, the assistance of the powers of any other spirit is not needed.

If you will only get your soul in the best condition possible so that I can make the proper rapport, nothing else will be needed. I will not write more tonight. I love you very much and am with you quite frequently, throwing around you my love and influence, and trying to help you develop your soul condition and become in greater At-onement with the Father.

(Have you kept your promise to pray with me when I have requested this?)

Yes, I have kept my promises. When you call for me to come with you and pray, I come, and send up my earnest supplications in your behalf. And I know that the Father answers my prayers, not only because of the faith that I have but also because I can see the effect in your soul's condition.

(Sometimes, it is rather difficult for me to put away my conditioned belief that you are God, or a part of Him, as my church teaches.)

Well, you must not think that I am God or one of the "Godhead"; for, as I have told you, I am only His son, and the possessor of so much of His Divine Love that I get very close to Him and have communion. I have my home in the highest heaven where no other spirit of man has reached so far. But, notwithstanding, I am not of so exalted a condition, or in such a position, that I do not come to you in love and sympathy, and as your elder brother. In my exaltation, I am most humble. And I must tell you that humility is a certain and eternal accompaniment of great spiritual and soul development.

BUT BECAUSE I AM THE HIGHEST OF THE FATHER'S SONS, YOU MUST NOT DOUBT THAT I COME TO YOU AND DELIVER MY MESSAGES, AND PRAY FOR YOU AND THROW AROUND YOU MY LOVE AND INFLUENCE.

I HAVE EXPLAINED TO YOU THE GREAT REASON WHY I AM DOING THIS. THIS REASON IS ONE THAT INVOLVES THE SALVATION AND GOOD OF YOU AND ALL MANKIND. AND I WILL TELL YOU NOW THAT YOU ARE A CO-WORKER WITH ME, AND THAT YOU AND THE SPIRITS WHO WRITE TO YOU ARE ENGAGED IN THE GREATEST WORK THAT ANY SPIRIT OR MAN CAN DO. AND I WANT TO SAY FURTHER THAT YOU WILL ACCOMPLISH THE WORK, AND SUCCESSFULLY. AND, WHEN THE TIME COMES FOR YOU TO LAY DOWN THIS WORK AND COME TO THE SPIRIT WORLD, YOUR REWARD WILL BE BEYOND ALL CONCEPTION, AND YOUR HAPPINESS WILL BE COMPLETE.

I see that you have in your mind the thought as to what will be the future of your two friends[*] Well, they will perform their work, and it will be a great and important work that will bring them a reward similar to the one that is in store for you. And this reward is not the result of any special dispensation of the Father, but is the result of the work and the associations and experience that you all will have in doing and completing the tasks that are before you.

You, and they, too, are now doing a work which is laying up rewards in the spirit world for you when you come over—and not only there, for you are now experiencing some of the benefits that flow from your work. Continue in the efforts that you are making to show spirits and mortals the Way to the Father's Love and my Kingdom, and you will find a wonderful reflex happiness that will come to you while you are yet mortals.

If you men could realize the love and spiritual influences, and the number of highly developed spirits that are with you so often, and the efforts the latter make to help you and bring happiness to you, you would feel that you are truly Blessed of the Father.

Well, I must stop now. Remember what I have said, and believe that I am

Your brother and friend,

JESUS.

Mary Baker Eddy, Founder of Christian Science, Confesses That Many of Her Doctrines Were Neither "Christian" Nor "Science."
(MARY BAKER EDDY)
(December 17th, 1916 | Received by James Padgett)

---

[*] Mr. Eugene Morgan and Dr. Leslie R. Stone.—Ed.

I AM HERE. *Mary Baker Eddy.*

Let me write a few lines, as I am anxious to declare some facts which were not facts to my understanding and beliefs when on earth. And, oh, the pity of it all!

Today, I was present at the church where the preacher discussed and criticized my teachings, and me also, and I am compelled to admit that some of his criticisms were true and justified.

I am Mrs. Eddy, and the founder of the sect which bears the high sounding name of "Christian Science, " the doctrines of which are neither Christian nor science, as I now know from actual experience in the spirit world where many of my teachings are shown to be not in accord with Truth, and so misleading.

I now realize that my mind and soul were not in accord as regards the Truth, while I lived as a mortal, and that my mind was superior in causing me to have certain beliefs which I left to the world in the form of doctrines contained in my textbook and my other writings.

My soul possessed a considerable degree of the Divine Love, as that Love has been explained to you. And when I came to the spirit world, that Love was my salvation, notwithstanding the errors of many of my teachings as to mind and matter, and the non-reality of sin and evil.

I am too weak to write more. But I will come again soon, for I must declare the Truths. Good night.

MRS. EDDY.

Ann R. Padgett, the Mother of Mr. Padgett, States That Mrs. Mary Baker Eddy Sees the Error in Her Teachings, and That She is Living in the Same Sphere with Her.
(ANN R. PADGETT)
(December 5th, 1914 | Received by James Padgett)

I AM HERE. *Your mother.*

My boy, I am so glad to write to you again. It seems so long since I wrote to you. I love you so much and feel that I must tell you.

Go to the Universalist Church, as Helen told you. It is the best one now in existence, because it believes more in God's Love without having to worship Jesus. As you say, the Christian Scientists are good people, but their position on Spiritualism is all wrong. Mrs. Eddy now sees her error and wishes that she could undo it. She is in the same sphere with me, but she does not enjoy so much of God's Love as I do. I talk to her sometimes and she tells me that she is very sorry that she made the mistake of teaching that spirits could not communicate with mortals. She is a very bright spirit, but does not know all that she thought she knew when on earth.

(Might she write to me again?)

She may, I do not know, but I will ask her.

(Will you pray for me?)

Yes, I will pray for you, my dear boy, with all my heart.

So, good night.

YOUR MOTHER.

Mrs. Eddy Now Recognizes the Misleading Errors of Some of Her Teachings, and Is Relieved Whenever These Are Corrected Among Her Followers.
(MARY BAKER EDDY)
(June 13th, 1918 | Received by James Padgett)

I AM HERE. *Mary Baker Eddy.*

Let me write a line, for I have been interested in the conversation of the doctor[*] and want to express my thanks to him for his efforts to enlighten one of my followers as to the Truth. My obligation is based on the fact that I recognize the misleading errors of some of my teachings, and that I am responsible for the beliefs of many mortals that are not true, and have the effect of keeping them from the Truth. And, further, that whenever any of those who have embraced the beliefs that I taught are shown the Light and directed to the errors of my teachings, I am to that extent happier and relieved from the burdens which I carry with me that my teachings are keeping so many from the Truth. In all this, I refer to the great question of the Divine Love, and the Way in which mortals may obtain the same and become in harmony with the Father, and partake of His Divine Nature and Immortality.

I have examined these Truths since I came to the spirit world, and realize with a great conviction that the reflection of the Divine Love is not the possession of that mind which comes only with the possession of the Love of the Father.

I wish that I had time tonight to write you a longer letter on this subject, but your guide says that you are not in condition to receive a lengthy letter and I must stop.

Let me express the hope that you and your friend, whenever the opportunity occurs, will attempt to enlighten my followers as to the Truths which you know, and as to errors and the want of the true explanation of salvation in my books. With my love, I will say good night.

MRS. EDDY.

---

[*] Dr Leslie R. Stone.

471

Mrs. Padgett Confirms That Mrs. Eddy Wrote Through Mr. Padgett.
(HELEN PADGETT)
(June 13th, 1918 | Received by James Padgett)

I AM HERE. *Helen.*

Well, dear, I have been with you all evening and enjoyed your conversation. You may believe that the last communication was from Mrs. Eddy, for she actually wrote and was glad that she could do so. And because she carries the burden of which she wrote, we permitted her to write.

She realizes that, although she has a great amount of the Divine Love, yet, the knowledge that she believed and taught others to believe through the errors of her writings causes her much unhappiness in the way of possessing a great desire to undo or neutralize the effect of what she taught.

Love me and pray to the Father. Good night.

Your own true and loving,

HELEN.

Jesus Enlarges Upon Some of the Errors and Deficiencies of Christian Science.
(JESUS)
(July 9th, 1916 | Received by James Padgett)

I AM HERE. *Jesus.*

I come today to tell you that I am pleased with you in your efforts to find the Truth of what we have taught as to God, and of the relation of man to Him.

I have been with you in your reading of several days past, and have observed the effect upon you of the contrast between the beliefs and teachings of men, as you have read them, and the teachings of Truth that we have revealed to you in our messages.

While these writings that you have been reading have in them some things of truth, yet, there are many things that are wholly untrue and the mere results of speculation. Today, if you feel in condition, I will instruct you as to some of the errors and deficiencies of Christian Science, and the want of the true comprehension of its founder of the realities of being.

She writes and teaches that there is nothing real in sin and error and disease, that their apparent existence is wholly due to the mortal mind, and that they will no longer exist when this mind denies the existence of these things. Well, there is a large grain of truth in this assertion. But, in order to understand and apply this truth, more than a mere denial of their existence must be taught and believed by man.

It is true that God never created anything of evil or that which is not in harmony with His Nature and Essence, which are only Good, and that to ascribe the existence of these evils and discord to God is erroneous and blasphemous. But the fact remains that these things exist. And the mere denial of their existence does not remedy the harmful results that flow from such existence.

Man suffers from evil and error and disease, and has always so suffered since the fall from his state of perfection. And he always will suffer in consequence of there being these things of reality in his consciousness. But the mere calling them the result of "mortal mind" will not explain their existence or furnish a remedy by which they may be gotten rid of.

First arises the necessity of understanding how, and by what means, these things came into existence. Then it will become easier to understand the means and the way by which they may be eliminated from the life and apparent nature of mankind.

As I have already told you, these things, foreign to God's Creation, were created by man, alone, in the excessive and unlawful exercise of his will power in following out the suggestions and desires of his animal appetites, which unduly asserted themselves when man lost a part of his spirituality by his disobedience.

Their creation was the result of something more than what the founder of that Science calls the "mortal mind," for the mind is only a part of man's being. And while the faculties of the mind must be used in the operation of all the powers and qualities of man, yet, the mind is not the originator of all his desires and appetites and emotions. The emotional nature and affections are distinct from the mere mind, or the intellectual faculties, and, as regards sin and error, are generally the creators of the same, although the mind may and does foster and increase these things so created.

Then, man must understand that these excrescences to his perfect creation are real and existing, and result in his own damnation and alienation from the good. They are antagonistic to his original and natural condition of perfection, and they cannot be swept out of existence by the mere assertion that they are not real.

Again, man must understand that these excrescences are the creatures primarily of the inordinate exercise of the animal appetites and desires, and not of the exercise of the mind, and that they are to be eradicated by the same process in reverse order as was used in their creation.

Of course, it must not be lost sight of that the faculties of the mind must be brought into operation in using this process, just as they were used in the creation of these existences. And the great fact to be remembered in this process is that these things are real, and not things of the mere imagination, which is the equivalent of the founder's "mortal mind."

Now, when man grasps the meaning of what these things really are and how they came into being, as thus explained, then he will the more readily comprehend the way or the means by which they are to be destroyed and never again permitted to become a part of his being. For while they do not belong to his being by nature, yet, by reason of his being the creator of them, so far as his consciousness is concerned, they are, together with all the results flowing therefrom, a part of his being, and that part which keeps him in discord with the laws controlling his own existence. The purity of his true being is always besmirched by the impurities of his own artificial being, and always will be until he eliminates these impurities which, as to him and to his fellowman, are real, persistent existences.

The will, however, is the great force that must be used in the destruction of these excrescences. And as this will power is free and untrammeled in man, and follows the suggestions and desires of the appetites of man in its operations, both animal and spiritual, it therefore becomes apparent that these appetites and desires must first be controlled and directed in that direction that will cause the will to be exercised in such a manner as to lead the thoughts and deeds towards the realization of the desires and appetites that are in harmony with God's Laws.

As sin and evil are not the creatures of the spiritual desires, but wholly of the animal, then, to eradicate these things of evil and sin from man's being, the efforts of man must be directed towards the supplanting of the unlawful and inharmonious animal desires and appetites with appetites and desires arising from the same source that is in harmony with the laws creating this very source.

Man was created by God with animal appetites, just as he was created with spiritual aspirations; and the one is just as harmonious with the laws of his creation as the other. And the loss of the spiritual aspirations or the perversion of the animal appetites similarly causes man to become out of harmony with these laws. So, in order to become free from these foreign parts of his being, man must strive to re-create in himself (not by denial of their reality, but by the effort to supplant them) the animal appetites that are consistent and in harmony with those which were his when he was made the perfect man. In other words, he must possess only those of the Creation of God.

Of course, in this effort, he will have to use his mind, mortal or otherwise. But, in addition, he will also have to exercise the faculties of his emotional and affectionate nature, which are not of the mind but of the soul. Mere negation or belief will not be sufficient, but desires and cravings for these things which engender sin must be supplanted by desires and cravings for those things which are in harmony with his creation.

So, I repeat, the teachings that sin and error and disease are not real, and are no part of man's being as he now exists and lives, are erroneous. And, when not understood, these teachings are harmful and not sufficient to bring about the regeneration of man.

In one sense, it is true that sin and error and disease are not real. But that means that they have no existence so far as God's Creation of man is concerned, for He created only that which was good and in harmony with His Perfect Laws. But as man is a creator as well as a creature, and as these things are the creatures of man, alone, then, so far as the being of man is involved, they do have a reality which will persist until their creator, man, has destroyed them.

I am pleased that you gave me the opportunity to write today, and am also glad to find you in good condition.

Your friend and brother,

JESUS.

VI. Reincarnation and Theosophy

MESSAGES INCLUDED IN THIS SECTION.

Jesus Discusses the Nature of Mr. Padgett's Mediumship, and Makes Mention of the False Doctrine of Reincarnation. (JESUS)...................479

Goliath, the Famous Giant of the Philistines, Tells Mr. Padgett That He Was a Real Person Who Lived in the Days of the Old Testament. He Denies That There Is Any Reincarnation After the Death of the Mortal Body, and Disavows That He Was Killed by David, as Described in the Scriptures. (GOLIATH).......................................480

An Ancient Spirit Discusses Theosophy and Questions the Validity of Reincarnation. (LAMLESTIA)...482

Mrs. Padgett Affirms the Identities of Several Spirits Who Wrote. (HELEN PADGETT)..485

Saelish, a Spirit of Old, Declares That There Is No Such Thing as Reincarnation. (SAELISH) 486

VI.

Reincarnation and Theosophy.

*Jesus Discusses the Nature of Mr. Padgett's Mediumship, and Makes Mention of the False Doctrine of Reincarnation.**
(JESUS)
(June 13th, 1916 | Received by James Padgett)

I AM HERE. *Jesus.*

I intended to finish my discourse tonight, but it is now too late and I will have to postpone it.

(Is it true that some mediums have been completely taken over by spirits?)

Well, there are cases where such results follow, and it is not astonishing that it is so. For these mediums who surrender their own faculties and will and moral powers will find spirits take control of them. These spirits do not hesitate to use these mediums for any and all purposes that they may desire, and these desires are mostly injurious and detrimental to the mediums, both morally and spiritually.

In such cases of spirit control, the mediums absolutely submit their mental and will powers to the domination of these spirits. When once such spirits get control, they are never satisfied and care not for the conditions of the mediums; and, such being the case, the mediums suffer.

But the mediumship which you have is not of such a character as to permit any spirit who may write through you to obtain that control of your mental faculties as will enable them to exercise their wills and powers in a way that will prevent you from exercising yours as you desire. They do not become your masters, but are subordinate to your will and cannot use you for the purpose mentioned, unless you so incline. The exercise of your phase of mediumship will not do you harm, and you need not fear the results. In fact, it is necessary that your mental faculties should become vivified and enlarged in order for you to do the work. The greater development you have, the more you will be enabled to do our work in a more satisfactory manner.

I KNOW THE SUBSTANCE OF THE BOOK THAT YOU HAVE BEEN READING, AND THE FALSITY OF THESE SPECULATIONS THAT ASSERT THE DOCTRINE OF REINCARNATION. THERE IS NO SUCH THING AS THE SECOND EMBODIMENT OF THE SOUL INTO THE HUMAN FORM, AND NO RETURN TO EARTH FOR THE

---

* See: "Jesus Declares That the Doctrine of Reincarnation Is False and Utterly Without Foundation," in volume I of *Angelic Revelations of Divine Truth.*— Ed.

PURPOSE OF IMPROVEMENT OF THE SOUL'S CONDITION.

So, try to be in condition and we will continue the writing of my messages. With all my love and blessings, I am

Your brother and friend,

JESUS.

Goliath, the Famous Giant of the Philistines, Tells Mr. Padgett That He Was a Real Person Who Lived in the Days of the Old Testament. He Denies That There Is Any Reincarnation After the Death of the Mortal Body, and Disavows That He Was Killed by David, as Described in the Scriptures.

(GOLIATH)

(November 25th, 1916 | Received by James Padgett)

I AM HERE. *Goliath.*

I have been present for some time and have listened to your conversations on the various sects who are expecting a great teacher, and others who look for a reincarnation; and if it were not so serious to the welfare of mankind, it would be very humorous. But the matter is too serious to deal with in a humorous vein, and I will say a few words as to the utter falsity of both of these beliefs.

There will appear no such great teacher as is expected. Of course, many may appear on earth claiming to be such a teacher, and they may declare some moral truth that may be beneficial to mankind. But these teachings will not be such as these people may expect a great teacher to make known. And the result will be that if the world had to depend on such teachings, it would be very little, if any, better than it now is; for there is only one course of Truth. And in order for any great teacher to teach such Truths, he necessarily will have to have a knowledge of such Truths. And, here, I want to say that there is only one means of learning such Truths, and that is through the help of Jesus Christ and his followers, who know these Truths, and the Holy Spirit that speaks to all men if they will open their souls to Its silent voice of Truth and Love.

So, I say that these people who are expecting some earthly teacher to arise and come to them with a knowledge of Truth will be greatly disappointed. For it is impossible that any man will ever come in some mysterious and godlike way, and will be endowed with this knowledge. The souls of these people are longing for the Truth. And, not having a knowledge as to how it may come about, they are willing to conjure up in their minds some being that may possibly burst on the world and enlighten them in those Truths for which their souls are longing and wishing. No, in all time and eternity, they will never learn what they so anxiously desire from any great teacher of the kind that I have named and they expect.

As to the others who are equally misguided, and who believe that their salvation or future condition of happiness depends on reincarnation, I must say that they are now, and will be, disappointed, just as will be the first class that I mention. This doctrine of reincarnation is a false and misleading one, and will never enable any man or spirit to live the second time in the body as a mortal. It is so utterly absurd that it is astonishing that men can believe that such a thing can be! And, besides, if they will only think seriously for a moment, they will realize that there is no necessity for man to live again on earth; for the surroundings and things that prevent the progress of man to perfection are so detrimental to his progress that it would not assist him one particle, in acquiring such progress, to have to undergo a second incarnation.

When the spirit leaves the body, its possibility for progress then becomes greater than ever existed on earth, although some spirits for long ages do not take advantage of such possibilities; yet, they exist. And earth life can afford no equal means to them for making this progress towards what these people call "Nirvana." Someday, the Truths will become so plain and easily understood by mortals that these beliefs, of their own weight—and I mean weight that absurdity gives them—will cease to exist.

You may be somewhat surprised that I write on these subjects, but you must know that I am an angel of the Celestial Heavens and have a work to do. And, being present, I requested the privilege of writing; and, it being granted, I did so.

I know what Divine Love means and what progress means, as I came from the lowest hells and found no necessity for reincarnation. And you may be assured that if my condition of suffering and darkness could have been gotten rid of by reincarnation, I would have reincarnated centuries before I was relieved of my awful condition. I have met spirits who said they believed in the doctrine. But, strange to say, none of them had ever been able to reincarnate, though they persisted that they felt that other spirits had, who were just in that condition that permitted it, and that they would also reincarnate when they became in a condition that was suitable. But I have noticed that these spirits never got in that suitable condition, but simply progressed in the spirit world. And they now say that they were mistaken, and are thankful that there is no such thing as reincarnation.

I want to stop now. So, thanking you, I will say good night.

Your brother in Christ,

GOLIATH,

of whom men may think a mythical person, but who really lived and died, even though he may not have been killed by a slingshot of David, as the Bible relates, but who is yet a real living mortal who followed the ways of other mortals in sinning and dying, and who went through hell and is at last redeemed.

An Ancient Spirit Discusses Theosophy and Questions the Validity of Reincarnation.
(LAMLESTIA)
(December 17th, 1916 | Received by James Padgett)

I AM HERE. *Lamlestia.*

I was an inhabitant of India when that country was not known of to modern nations. I lived near the great Himalaya mountains on a plain that was then fertile and peopled by a vast number of inhabitants who worshiped the gods of whom the later Brahmans have written in their sacred books.

It may seem surprising to you that I should come and write to you. The explanation is that I became in rapport with you tonight at the meeting of the Theosophists. I saw that you were psychic and that I could communicate to you through the medium of the pen. There were many spirits present who, when mortals, lived in that far away country. They were, and now are, believers in the mysteries of the occult as claimed to be known now by those who profess to be leaders of the Theosophical movement. A number of their names were mentioned by the lecturer. And these spirits were attracted to the meeting by reason of the similarity of beliefs which the mortals present possessed, and they, the spirits, possessed.

I, also, was present because of that attraction. For, when on earth, I was a great believer in these doctrines, and especially those that teach reincarnation and karma. And I still believe in these things, although I have been a spirit for many centuries. Yet, these earth beliefs cling to me and hold me to the binding force of their truths, as I conceive these truths to be.

Many of those present, whose minds I could read as they thought, believe in these doctrines, but very few of them have any conception of what are the truths taught by such philosophy. Even the lecturer has a very slight comprehension of the scope and import of these teachings. Her attempt to explain the objects and workings of the principles of true Theosophy was a very inefficient effort; for, in order for her to be able to teach these doctrines, it is absolutely necessary that she have a knowledge of the same, which she does not have.

No, the knowledge that she has, and many others like her have, as to the fundamentals of this philosophy or religion, if it may be called such, is very superficial. And the fact that it is a system of mysteries, a few of which they have discerned an explanation of, causes them to conclude that their grasp of the scope of this philosophy is greater than it really is. And this affords them a kind of satisfaction that arises from the consciousness that they know some mysteries which the world does not know of.

She spoke about the great Masters in India who have a full knowledge of these mysteries, and, in certain conditions or circumstances, will be able to and will initiate the searcher into the esoteric meaning of these great truths. Well, these Masters know something of the mysticism, and of occult

482

powers and principles, but such knowledge is not sufficient to qualify them as teachers of the great truths of Theosophy, as I understood and now understand these truths.

We have in the spirit world, and have had for long centuries, communities of Theosophists who believe and teach to whomsoever will listen to these doctrines. And many of these spirits attempt to teach mortals these truths of the ages by impressions and thought transference, but with indifferent success. Hence, for most of those who think they would like to understand this philosophy, the great attraction is the mystery, which they believe must contain the truth because of its being a mystery.

In the search for the key to the opening up and solving of the doctrines, and the supposed mystery in which they are shrouded, progress and understanding has been very slow. And, as I said, we who have been engaged for centuries in this great effort have never had the existence of our supposed truths demonstrated to us. We are still plodding the weary way, supported by the faith that light will come to us at some time, and that that which has so long been enveloped in darkness will come into the pure light of understanding and comprehension.

But, as yet, very few of these mysteries have been solved. And neither have the truths been manifested that are supposed to be concealed therein.

To some of us, doubt has commenced to rear its head and cause disappointment. Such being the case with us, what can these mortals, who are groping in speculation and discord, expect to succeed in disclosing?

Tonight, I heard the lecturer declare that man is God, potentially, and that, when he develops into perfection, he will become God. Never was there a more delusive and untrue declaration of a supposed fact ever uttered! For we who have lived in this invisible world long enough to have had the realization come to us that we are gods all know that we are only and merely the spirits of men who lived on earth many years ago, even though we believed then that, in the far distant future and by our own exertions in renunciation, we would become gods. But,no, such is not the fact. And while we have renounced many of the sins and errors of our mortal lives, yet, we are still spirits with all the limitations of mind and soul that spirits are by nature bound.

And this I must say: that, in all the centuries of my spirit existence, never have I known a spirit, or the soul of a spirit, to reincarnate; and my disappointment in this has been grievous. Many spirits of our association have become perfect through renunciation; yet they have remained spirits and progressed to the highest heavens of our possibilities.[*]

Yet, strange as it may seem, in view of this experience, we still cling to our old beliefs in reincarnation to a more or less degree, thinking that there is something else to be done that we know not of in order for reincarnation to become the destiny of our souls.

Sometimes, I think that my beliefs in this particular must be wrong; for,

---

[*] The heaven of the Sixth Sphere.—Ed.

in comparing the condition of mortals—the most advanced in their mind and soul development—I realize that they are not in a small degree the equal of us in development. And then I wonder, and, wondering, cannot understand what good could be accomplished, or what improvement made in our condition for progressing, should we again enter mortal bodies.

As true Theosophy taught, as we conceived it, reincarnation was a supposed process of purification, and was necessary in order that the spirit could attain to a state of perfection and freedom from everything that defiles his soul, and prevents that soul from arriving at the blissful state of Nirvana—which means only that condition of soul when reincarnation is no longer necessary or possible. And when I know that many of our spirits—one-time believers in these doctrines—have arrived at that condition and entered a state of perfect happiness, I hesitate longer to believe. I only hold the faith because I fear that the experience mentioned may be the result of special circumstances.

But if I cease to believe these teachings, what shall I believe? No one can tell me that this reincarnation will not take place, and I fear to surrender the belief.

And I further believe that, in order for the working of karma to exist, as the doctrines hold, reincarnation is necessary, and that only in the mortal body could I do the reaping that my sowing demands. And, yet, I see and know that karma has been and is working in this spirit world to the extent that the reaping has all been accomplished, and the spirit made perfect, and this without any reincarnation. For, as I have said, never have I known or heard of the reincarnation of a spirit, or of anything that is connected with or represents the spirit.

Of late, I have been much in "cloudland" as to these beliefs and in my desire to find the light. I have visited the meetings of the Theosophists in all countries, and especially in India where the Masters, who are supposed to have the full knowledge and enlightenment, live. I have done so in hopes of finding the light, but all to no avail. My desires and longings cry for the light, but none can be found.

Tonight, I was attracted to the meeting where I saw you. And realizing that I could express to you my feelings and doubts, I made a rapport and came home with you for the purpose of doing what I have done. I know from your condition of mind that you do not believe in these doctrines of the Theosophists, and that your beliefs are of a different kind and are new to me, although I have heard of the doctrines that are the objects of your faith. There are spirits with whom I sometimes come in contact who attempt to tell me of another Way to a higher heaven than the one that I know of; but, as they are mere babes in comparison to my ancient existence, I do not listen to them. Hence, I am not acquainted with their teachings.

I must not write more tonight, and thank you for your kindness.

(If you are willing, and will permit me to do so in your behalf, I would be most happy to call upon one of the bright spirits who are present to come

to you and instruct you as to the True Way to supreme happiness, and to an eternity of joyful progression toward the very Fountainhead of God's Love and Light.)

Well, you seem to be very kind, and I thank you for your interest. Under the circumstances, I must accept your offer. And, I assure you, I will listen attentively to what may be said to me.

I have looked and there comes to me a beautiful spirit who says that she is your grandmother, and that she has heard your invitation and will be glad to show me the Way to Love and Light and Truth. She seems so bright and beautiful and loving that I must go with her. So, I will say good night and go.

Good night.

LAMLESTIA.

Mrs. Padgett Affirms the Identities of Several Spirits Who Wrote.
(HELEN PADGETT)
(December 17th, 1916 | Received by James Padgett)

I AM HERE. *Helen.*

Well, sweetheart, you are tired, and must not write more now.

I will say, though, that the spirits who wrote you tonight actually are the persons they represented themselves to be. I was with you at the various meetings, and these spirits were there and became in rapport with you.

The Indian was in truth an Indian, and was in the condition that he declared himself to be. He was a very bright spirit and lives in the highest Spiritual Heaven. He went with your grandmother.

Mrs. Eddy was very anxious to write. I am sorry that she could not finish, for the burden on her mind is great. She wants so much to write the Truth. I will have her come soon. She is in the Seventh Sphere and has much of the soul Love; yet she sees the possible injurious results of her teaching, and her work is before her. She says that the only way in which she can remedy the wrong is through the channel that she so bitterly denounced, and that she sees the difficulties are so much greater than it would be but for this grave mistake.

Pastor Russell is also anxious to write and he will soon come. I feel real sorry for him. His shock was so very great.

(Of late, your work seems to be taken up with telling me of unhappy spirits.)

Well, so it is. I must give my time to telling you of other spirits. But that is my work and yours, and we must not complain. They are all the Father's children.

So, my dear, take courage and believe, and all will be well.

(Was the Master with me this morning at church services?)

Yes, Jesus was with you at the morning service. He may write to you

485

about the same, but I am not certain. His love was with you, though, and he seems to want to be with you whenever he is not elsewhere.

He loves you and is caring for you.

Your own true and loving,

HELEN.

Saelish, a Spirit of Old, Declares That There Is No Such Thing as Reincarnation.
(SAELISH)
(November 3rd, 1915 | Received by James Padgett)

I AM HERE. *Saelish.*

When on earth, I was an inhabitant of the great empire of Assyria, of which Nineveh was the capital. I was not a king, but was one of a great king's magicians or wise men. When I lived, I was a man of great influence and power in that kingdom.

I came tonight to tell you a great Truth in connection with the soul. As you may infer, when I lived, we knew nothing of the one and only God. We worshiped many gods, great and little, and believed that these gods could help or harm us, just as we deserved their help or their injurious workings. And, so, in their treatment of us poor mortals, our many gods sometimes came in conflict so that, at times, we hardly knew whether our gods were our friends or our enemies.

Of course, the help that we sought for was all of a material nature, for never did we think of help in the way of preparing us for a future life. We supposed that was only for those of us who, by our great achievements in battle or in intellectual pursuits, would become gods ourselves upon death. The poor, ordinary mortals were only intended to live the mortal life—at least during the incarnation that they then had. And their expectations were that, perhaps in some future incarnation, they might have the opportunity and the favors of the unknown gods so that they might become gods themselves.

This was the substance of the beliefs and hopes of the Assyrians at that time. And many millions died in that belief and are now inhabitants of the several planes of certain spheres of the spirit world. None of them has ever returned for a new incarnation, thereby starting on their way to becoming gods. And this is for the reason (which is sufficient to satisfy them sooner or later when they become spirits) that those men who they supposed had become gods when they died were in the spirit world—spirits themselves—and were not gods at all!

SO, YOU SEE, WHEN ONCE IT LEAVES THE PHYSICAL BODY, THE SOUL NEVER RETURNS AGAIN TO ANY PHYSICAL BODY, BUT CONTINUES IN THE SPIRIT WORLD TO EXIST AS A SOUL WITH A BODY OF SPIRIT FORM AND SUBSTANCE; AND NO

SPIRIT HAS EVER EXPERIENCED THE SENSATION OF BECOMING REINCARNATED.

AND THIS IS THE TRUTH THAT I WISHED TO TELL YOU: THAT THE SOUL, WHEN ONCE IT LEAVES THE PHYSICAL BODY, NEVER AGAIN FINDS ITS HABITATION IN ANOTHER, OR THE SAME, PHYSICAL BODY, BUT FOREVER OCCUPIES THE SPIRIT BODY THEREAFTER, AND THAT IN THE SPIRIT WORLD ONLY.

WHEN A MORTAL DIES ON EARTH, SO FAR AS THE EARTHLY BODY BEING ITS HOME AGAIN IS CONCERNED, THIS BODY BECOMES A THING OF THE PAST. IT IS A MERE WAY STATION WHICH HAS BEEN LEFT BEHIND, AND IT WILL NEVER AGAIN APPEAR AS A STOPPING PLACE ON THE SPIRIT'S LINE OF PROGRESSION.

I thought it might do good for me to write this tonight, for it is the information from a spirit who lived on earth long years ago and believed in this doctrine of reincarnation, and who, during all the long years of its spirit life, has learned and experienced the truth that REINCARNATION IS A FABLE AND HAS NO REAL EXISTENCE.

No, the soul never retraces its steps or its methods of existence, for it never goes back from the spirit to mortal.

On the earth today, I know that there are thousands of mortals who believe in this doctrine of reincarnation, and many thousands more have died in that belief. Thus, many both live and die in that belief. And only when the truth comes to them do they realize that their belief was an erroneous one, and that they will never reach Nirvana by retracing their course of life through the physical body.

The soul never dies, but always lives. And whenever its position is such as to justify progression, it progresses.

I live in the Sixth Sphere, and am considered to be a very exalted spirit in my intellectual acquirements, and in my condition of freedom from sin and errors which belonged to me on earth, and which belong to every mortal. My happiness is very great and my home and surroundings are beautiful.

This sphere is a wonderful place, not only because of the surroundings and homes of the inhabitants but also because of the great mental and moral development of those who live in this sphere. No spirit who has not that development can live in this sphere, because of its unfitness.

Male and female spirits enjoy this wonderful development. Their intercourse in the intellectual things that exist in this sphere is free and frequent, and the interchange of thoughts brings much happiness and satisfaction.

We don't know of any spheres beyond the Sixth, although we have heard it rumored that there are other spheres. But we give little credence to these rumors because none of us—I mean the inhabitants of this sphere—has ever found a higher one, and many of us live in the highest planes of this sphere.

(Is there anything else you wish to tell me?)

No, I have nothing else to write tonight.

(Well, what if I were to tell you that there is a heaven above your own where there is happiness and wisdom far excelling that obtainable in the Sixth Sphere?)

Well, of course, I can't say that is not true, but I do say that you astonish me beyond all belief; for I cannot imagine that any spirit can make higher progress than we have made!

(The far greater happiness and wisdom that I am referring to comes only from God through prayer for His Divine Love. And it is very possible for you to obtain this Love and to become an inhabitant of God's highest Kingdom, the Celestial Kingdom, if you will but pursue that prayerful Way and seek the guidance of the Celestial spirits themselves.)

Well, what you tell me surprises me, and I would like to investigate and discover the truth of the matter. But I don't know how to commence such investigation, or where to start. Is it possible that you can show me the way in which I can commence this investigation?

(Well, the Celestial spirits always respond to a request for their presence and help if this comes from sincere longings of the heart. I would suggest, then, that you let your true heart's desire go out to them for their help. Then, look about you. If you truly seek them in the way that I suggest, they will appear to your vision. And, once they have appeared, they will provide you with all the help and direction you will need to begin your investigation.)

I have done as you suggested, and I do see some wonderfully beautiful spirits. They seem to be so very happy, too, and interested in you. One says she is your grandmother, and she seems to excel the others in her beauty and brightness.

She says that she is very willing to start me in my investigation, and that she herself will tell me the great secret of the great progression that you speak of. And she adds that, if I will accompany her, she will commence at once.

And, while I write, there comes another beautiful spirit who says that she formerly lived in the Sixth Sphere, and lived there many thousands of years before I lived on earth. She says that she was an Egyptian and that her name was Saleeba, and that she is now an inhabitant of the Third Sphere in order to prepare herself for the great progression that she will make to spheres high above the Sixth. And she tells me that, after I have conversed with your grandmother, she will be pleased to talk to me and tell me her experience.

I will be with her, you may rest assured.

All this is so wonderful to me that I hardly know what to think or do! But I will try to find the truth of it, if it can be found.

So, I have written you a long time, expecting to enlighten and not be enlightened myself. And, now, I am so anxious for that enlightenment! I will say that I am glad I came to you, and good night. SAELISH.

The statements made by Mr. Swedenborg in this paragraph have been, in the past, enigmatic to a number of members of our church. The question arose, "How could Mr. Swedenborg not have been aware of the Divine Love during his many years of visitation to the spirit world, when the expressed purpose of the Celestials was precisely to relate this to him so that he, in turn, could communicate this soul-saving knowledge to the world through his published writings?" Fortunately, two qualified mediums of our church subsequently received automatic writing messages of explanation and clarification from Jesus—one in February 1984, and another in February 1986. The following excerpts from the Master's February 1984 message, which resolves this perplexing question and issue, is now offered hereunder for the reader's enlarged understanding and appreciation of what in fact occurred with Mr. Swedenborg:

> I desire to write concerning Mr. Swedenborg and the concern of _____ as to this matter.
>
> Mr. Swedenborg thought that all love was of the Divine Nature of God, and did not know or teach the difference between the natural love—the love Mr. Swedenborg perceived to be of the Divine—and the Divine Love, which, when possessed by a man, makes that soul a new creature, endowed with the Essence and Substance of God's Eternal Soul. Mr. Swedenborg, therefore, did not know of the Divine Love in contradistinction to what he perceived to be the Divine Love—the natural love.
>
> Mr. Swedenborg was a man of great pride as to the thoughts and perceptions of his mind; and, along with the strong, false beliefs that he believed, this worked to prevent the real Truth from being made known to him.
>
> I know it may seem strange that, after many years of trying to teach him the Truth of the New Birth, we were not successful in relating this distinction between the two loves; yet it is true. The strong hold of false beliefs that a man may have affect his entire perception of God and His Nature, and of man in his nature as originally created. Often, men will see themselves, the natural love, and the nature of their souls as being of the Divine, which they are not. And such was the case with Mr. Swedenborg. He perceived the qualities of the natural love of his soul as being a part of the Divine Nature and Love of God. And, at the time of his trips into the spirit world and the subsequent teachings he taught, he had not any of this Divine Nature dwelling within him.
>
> Sometime, Mr. Swedenborg will come and write in detail

concerning his teachings and experiences, and how, while on earth, he had no true perception of the Truth of the Divine Love of God in contradistinction to the natural love of a man's soul.

Your friend, and Master of the Celestial Heavens,

JESUS.

Glossary
of Selected Capitalizations
And Lower Case Usages.

<u>CATEGORIES</u>	<u>CAPITALIZATIONS</u>		<u>LOWER CASE</u>

I. **GOD**

A. **Alternate**
Names

All-in-All	Maker	*(none)*
Almighty	Name	
Alone (God)	One	
Being (of God)	Origin (the)	
Creator	Oversoul	
Deity	Porter	
Divinity	Preserver	
Eternal One	Protector	
Father	Ruler	
Good Shepherd	Savior	
Great Soul	Soul	
Heavenly Father	Source (the)	
Jehovah	Spirit (of God)	
Judge		

B. **Attributes**

Activity	Control	*(none)*
Affection	Desires	
All-Good	Divine	
All-Holy	Divine Love	
All-Knowing	Divine Nature	
All-Loving	Divinity	
All-Merciful	Ear (Listening)	
All-Powerful	Emanations	
All-Wise	Energies	
Assistance	Entity	
Attribute(s)	Essence	
Beneficence	Eternal	
Benevolence	Existence	
Bidding	Expressions	
Blessings	Faculties	
Bounty	Forgiveness	
Care(ful)	Form	
Closeness	Glory	
Comfort	Goodness	
Compassion	Grace	
Confidence	Great	

491

CATEGORIES	CAPITALIZATIONS	LOWER CASE

B. Attributes
(Cont.)

CAPITALIZATIONS	
Guidance	*Personality*
Hand	*Potentialities*
Handiwork	*Power(s)*
Hearing	*Presence*
Heart	*Promise(s)*
Help	*Protection*
Holy Ghost	*Providence*
Holy Spirit	*Provisions*
Immortal(ity)	*Purity*
Immutable	*Purpose*
Influence	*Qualities*
Intentions	*Requirements*
Interest	*Seeing*
Kindness	*Self-Existing*
Knowledge	*Sight*
Life	*Solicitude*
Light	*Soul*
Listening Ear	*Spirit*
Love	*Substance*
Loving	*Sympathy*
Majesty	*Tender(ness)*
Mercy	*Thoughts*
Method	*Truth(s)*
Mind	*Unchangeable*
Nature	*Verities*
Omnipotence	*Watchful*
Omniscience	*Way*
Oneness	*Will*
Pardon	*Wisdom*
Personal	

C. Pronouns or Possessives

He
Himself
His
It (Divine Love, Holy Spirit, Gift, or Great Gift)
Its   (same)
Itself   (same)
Mine
My
Myself
What (is God)
Who
Whom
Whose

(None)

CATEGORIES	CAPITALIZATIONS	LOWER CASE

II. **PLACES OR LOCATIONS**

	CAPITALIZATIONS	LOWER CASE
A. **Heaven(s)**	*Celestial Heavens*	*heaven(s)*
	Divine Heavens	*(general usage)*
	Spiritual Heavens	
B. **Kingdom(s)**	*Celestial Kingdom*	*kingdom(s)*
	Father's Kingdom:	*(material, or*
	of Heaven	*general usage)*
	of the Divine Angel	
	of the Restored of Perfect	
	Natural Man	
	Spiritual Kingdom	
	Spiritual Paradise	
C. **Sphere(s)**	*Celestial Sphere(s)*	*sphere(s) (not*
	Divine Sphere(s)	*specifically*
	First to Seventh Spheres	*named)*
	First to Third Celestial Spheres	
	Spiritual Spheres	
D. **Realm(s)**	*Celestial Realm(s)*	
	Spiritual Realm(s) (all the heavens)	
E. **World(s)**	*Celestial World*	

III. **OPERATIONS OR LARGE-SCALE CREATIONS OF GOD**

	CAPITALIZATIONS	LOWER CASE
	Commandments	
	Creation(s) (of God)	*creation(s)*
	Decree	*(not of God's;*
	Fiat	*general usage)*
	Force(s)	
	Handiwork(s)	
	Plan (of salvation)	
	Principal (Christ Principal)	
	Ten Commandments	
	Universe	*universe*
	Universe of Creation	*(not of God's;*
	Word(s)	*general usage)*

493

CATEGORIES	CAPITALIZATIONS	LOWER CASE

IV.   *OPTIONAL TERMS*

A.   *Apostle(s)* — *John, the Apostle* — *apostle(s)*
(a specific name)(general usage)

B.   *Atonement* — *Divine or True (Atonement)* — *atonement*
(God's Plan of salvation; — *(general or in-*
Formal topic) — *formal usage)*

C.   *At-onement* — *The Great (At-onement)* — *at-onement*
(the New Birth; formal topic) — *(general or in-*
formal usage)

D.   *Resurrection* — *Resurrection: Transformation* — *resurrection:*
from the mortal into the im- — *(the immediate*
mortal through the receipt of — *raising of the*
God's Divine Love, which — *spirit body*
is the True Resurrection. — *after mortal*
death, which
is common to
all men)

E.   *Truth(s)* — *Divine Truth(s)* — *truth(s)*
Father's Truth(s) — *(moral,*
God's Truth(s) — *intellectual,*
great or higher Truth(s) — *material, or*
spiritual Truth(s) — *natural)*

V.   *MISCELLANEOUS TERMS*

Act of Creation (God's) — *angel*
Apocalyptic (writings) — *at-one*
"Atonement" (Erroneous — *baptism*
concept of Christian — *church*
orthodox understanding; — *communion*
formal topic)
Christ Principal — *conqueror*
Comforter (Holy Spirit) — *(pertaining*
Fatherhood (of God) — *to Jesus)*
Fold (God's) — *deliverer*
Fountain (of Love) — *(pertaining*
Fountainhead (Divine Love's — *to Jesus)*
Source: God) — *divine and*
eternal leader
(Jesus)

CATEGORIES	CAPITALIZATIONS	LOWER CASE

V. **MISCELLANEOUS TERMS**
    (Con't)

	CAPITALIZATIONS	LOWER CASE
	"Godhead" (Erroneous concept of Christian orthodox understanding) epistles	*immortal(ity) (pertaining to angel or mortal)*
	Great Gift or Gift (the Divine Love; the True Resurrection; the potentiality for the transformation of the human soul; immortality)	*prophet spirit (angel or deceased mortal; energy of the human soul)*
	Great Instrument (Divine Love)	*triumpher (Jesus)*
	Great Love (Divine Love)	
	Great Prize (Divine Love)	
	Great Soul Sphere (Celestial Sphere)	
	Great Substance (Divine Love)	
	Habitation (God's)	
	House (Father's)	
	Immortality (God's)spiritual	
	Instrument (Holy Spirit)	
	Kingdom of Christ (Celestial Kingdom)	
	Locality (God's)	
	"Lord of Lords" (Inappropriate term for Jesus; only God is Lord)	
	"Lord's Supper" (Inappropriate term for Jesus' last gathering with his disciples)	
	Master (Jesus)	
	Messenger (Holy Spirit)	
	Messiah (Jesus)	
	Name (of God)	
	New Birth (At-onement with God)	
	New Covenant (Rebestowed Privilege of obtaining the Divine Love)	
	New Heart (Transformation of a human soul into a divine soul)	
	New Heavens	
	New Jerusalem	
	New Kingdom (Celestial Kingdom)	
	New Revealment (of Truth)	
	New Revelation (of Truth)	

495

CATEGORIES	CAPITALIZATIONS	LOWER CASE

V.   ***MISCELLANEOUS TERMS***
       (Con't)

New Testament (of the Bible)
One Great Fact (God)
Pearl of Great Price (the Divine Love)
Pentecost (Descent of the Holy
Spirit to the apostles, conveying
The Divine Love into their souls)
Plan (the, or God's)
Prince of Peace (Jesus)
Scriptures
Seat of Habitation (God's Resistance)
Sermon on the Mount
Spiritualism
Spiritualist
Spirit Universe (God's)
Temple (of Jerusalem)
The Way, the Truth, and the Life
    (Jesus' message on, and
    Personal example of, the true
    Salvation of the human soul)
Third Heaven (Third Sphere)
Transcendent Love (the Divine Love)
Treasure (the Divine Love)
"Trinity" (Erroneous concept of
    Christian orthodox
    understanding)
True Resurrection
Way, the (Fervent, soulful prayer
    For God's Divine Love)
Word (of God)

Printed in Great Britain
by Amazon

30799718R00303